HE CIVILIZATION OF THE WESTERN WORLD

VOLUME I

THE ANCIENT WORLD

THE ANCIENT WORLD

BY

WALLACE EVERETT CALDWELL

PROFESSOR OF ANCIENT HISTORY
THE UNIVERSITY OF NORTH CAROLINA

FARRAR & RINEHART, INC.

PUBLISHERS   NEW YORK

FAMILIAE MEAE

PREFACE

IN writing this book my aim has been to present the important facts and factors in the rise of western civilization during ancient times. I have endeavored to give as brief a statement of the political history as is consistent with sound scholarship for each of the major periods of antiquity. This has been followed with a survey of political, economic, and social institutions and activities and a description of religious life and of cultural achievements. Emphasis has been placed upon general tendencies and major developments with sufficient detail to illustrate and clarify them. Although I have followed the usual division into periods for purposes of analysis, the continuity of the whole story of human advance and the interaction of peoples upon each other have received proper consideration. Wherever titles or technical words or expressions have first been used, an explanation is given.

A book of this scope owes much to the researches and writings of the great scholars of the past and present. I wish to express particular indebtedness to the late Professor Breasted, and to Professors Olmstead, Woolley, Glotz, Tarn, Homo, Rostovtseff, Ferguson, and Westermann.

To my teachers, the late Professors H. A. Sill, G. W. Botsford, and J. H. Robinson, and to Professor Jean Capart of Brussels, and to the many colleagues and friends with whom I have discussed the problems of antiquity, I am deeply indebted. My thanks are also due to those of my students, particularly Messrs. Shaw, Grimes, Keeney, and Suskin, who assisted me in the laborious work of checking, to Dean C. H. Oldfather of the University of Nebraska who read the manuscript in the first draft and gave me the benefit of his knowledge and experience, and to Dr. Henry David and Mr. M. I. Finkelstein, both of whom rendered valuable editorial assistance. Most of the line drawings have been prepared by Mrs. Caldwell.

I hope that teachers and students will find the book useful as an approach to the great subject of human achievement in antiquity and that the general reader may discover herein facts and interpretations of the past which will add to his understanding of the present.

W. E. C.

Chapel Hill, N. C.
April, 1937

INTRODUCTION

THE word history, originally Greek and meaning "inquiry," is used to designate both those things which have happened in the past and the recorded memory of the past. In the first sense, history may be said to include everything that has ever happened. All things which have a past have a history. When applied to mankind, history consists of all those deeds and thoughts and beliefs which have contributed to the story of human achievement. As record, however, history consists only of those things which inquirers called historians have been able to ascertain and relate. The record is constantly growing as scholars find and examine new evidences of human activities which enable them to add to historical knowledge. The first task of the historian, therefore, is to gather together all of the sources from which he may develop his story.

There are two main classes of sources: material remains and written records. Among material remains are such things as the skeletons and mummies of men themselves, buildings, walls, roads, and bridges; statues, reliefs, paintings, coins, and all the myriad kinds of artifacts like clothing, jewelry, pottery, and tools. They give definite information about the appearance and the dress of men in different lands and at different times and about their technical abilities and their artistic standards.

Written records include histories, poems, plays, novels, essays— all the literary forms which portray the life and thought of past epochs—as well as the existing great mass of documents, public and private. Treaties and diplomatic correspondence, constitutions, laws, and judicial decisions, the records of legislative bodies, decrees, and proclamations appear among public documents; letters, diaries, household accounts, estate records, and wills, among private documents. Public documents are of great value to the historian, since they furnish incontrovertible evidence of past events. Private papers give him an insight into the lives and thoughts of individuals. Literary records, while they provide pictures of the ideas and beliefs dominant in the many periods of the past, vary in their usefulness as historical sources according to the literary form and the reliability of the writer.

The types of sources which are available to historians vary with different periods. The only definite records of the earliest ages are the material remains of men, their artifacts, and their art. After the invention of writing there appeared lists of kings and magistrates, building and tombstone inscriptions, and finally records and literary works on stone, papyrus, clay tablets, and parchment. The enlargement of sources continues steadily, so that for modern times the historian must use newspapers and magazines, pamphlets, and public archives.

The historian's task is by no means finished when, after a careful scientific study of the sources, he has arrived at a knowledge of individual occurrences. From the facts at his disposal he must make selections of those which seem important. Then he must arrange them in a time sequence, distinguish between the more and the less important, explain causal relationships and make generalizations.

Selection depends upon the historian's theory of history. For many years history was considered primarily a record of political and military events. More recently, an interest in social and economic factors, in culture as expressed in literary works and in art, and in religion, has broadened the scope of history to embrace these fields, which are all properly included in a history of civilization. History in action has been a continuous process. We are where we are today because we stand on the shoulders of those who in their turn stood on the shoulders of the men of the past. The historian must therefore concentrate on those facts which are in the main stream of this process; the purely episodic or incidental, however interesting, must be passed by, except as illustrative material.

Causal relationships are most difficult to ascertain. The life of man is an exceedingly complex thing, so that events are usually caused not by one but by many influences, most of which go unrecorded. The historian, therefore, cannot assign definite causes to historic happenings with final certainty; he can only describe the circumstances which led to or surrounded an event and can only express his own judgment of the why and the wherefore. Needless to say, his explanations will be subjective, that is, they will depend upon his own attitude toward life, his philosophy of history, and his particular theory of causation.

Chronology, or time sequence, is the framework of history. Dates, if nothing else, serve as convenient pegs on which to hang facts which, when placed in their proper time relationships to other occurrences, provide an orderly sequence of events. Without dates the study of history would be well-nigh impossible. Ancient peoples, after the discovery of the year and the invention of the calendar, kept their records by the years of a king's reign, or by means of the names of chief magistrates, like the archons at Athens or the consuls at Rome. Sometimes they dated from extraordinary events of history or of nature. For example, the opening verse of the Book of Amos reads: "The words of Amos . . . in the days of Uzziah, king of Judah . . . two years before the earthquake." Modern chronology rests upon the work of a monk of the sixth century who divided time into B.C. (before Christ) and A.D. (the year of Our Lord). Though he made an error, as we shall see (p. 446), in determining the date of the birth of Christ, historians have fitted ancient chronological systems into his scheme and we continue to use it today. Astronomical events like eclipses, or the rising of stars, serve modern scholars as a check in determining the actual dates of certain occurrences and frequently provide the only clue for arriving at a fixed chronology. Even with these checks there is much dispute among scholars about many dates. Dates for the earliest periods before writing depend on geological or archaeological data and are highly conjectural and uncertain.

After the historian has assembled his selected facts and arranged them in order, he divides them into periods. Since history is dynamic, constantly changing, such divisions are largely conventional. Certain generations seem to show distinctive characteristics in the geographical centers and in the motivating forces of their activities. Consequently they are set apart and denominated ages, periods, epochs, or eras. Thus we have ancient, medieval, and modern history, and within these many subdivisions. There is much disagreement among historians, however, as to where one period ends and another begins, so much do they overlap and pass from one to the other. They are, however, convenient for purposes of study and have been used throughout this series.[1]

The historian of civilization must further give the meaning of the much used words "civilization" and "culture." The dictionary defines civilization as "a state of social culture characterized by relative

[1] This text is the first of a series of three which together constitute a history of western civilization. The succeeding two are *Medieval Civilization* by Loren C. Mac-Kinney, *Modern Europe* by Stringfellow Barr.

progress in the arts, science, and statecraft . . . an advanced state of material and social well-being. Culture, as applied to society, emphasizes the intellectual aspects of civilization." But both civilization and culture are used interchangeably and with much broader meaning. Anthropologists use "culture" to denote all the traits of a people—its practices, habits, tools, economic conditions, governmental organization, thoughts, and arts. We shall therefore use the word in that sense in dealing with the record of primitive men. When we reach the periods where civilization has attained the levels implied in the dictionary definition, we shall employ culture to denote religion, philosophy, and literary and artistic achievements.

The final question which the writer and the student of history must answer is, Why should we study history? There are many reasons. The study of the past helps us to explain and understand the present. It gives us a sense of the historic process, of the continuity of the life of man, and it shows us our place in that process. It is travel in time instead of in space and it has travel's broadening effect in helping us to understand other people and to appreciate the great achievements of men. Finally, history is the laboratory of the social studies. There we can see in operation the forces which govern society; we can study past attempts at political, social, economic, or religious reform, and measure our own programs by the experience of men. We learn to approach our problems with that humility and open-mindedness which is essential to real intelligence.

CONTENTS

CHAPTER   PAGE

PREFACE vii

INTRODUCTION ix

I. PRELITERARY HISTORY 3

II. THE EARLY ORIENT 20

III. EGYPT UNDER THE OLD AND MIDDLE KINGDOMS . . 38

IV. THE ORIENT DURING THE SECOND MILLENNIUM B.C. 60

V. THE CONFLICT OF EMPIRES (1500-500 B.C.) . . . 82

VI. THE RISE OF THE HELLENES 114

VII. ECONOMIC AND POLITICAL EVOLUTION 129

VIII. THE CITY-STATES 146

IX. THE CULTURAL RENAISSANCE 167

X. THE PERSIAN WARS 185

XI. THE GREATNESS AND FALL OF ATHENS (479-404 B.C.) 194

XII. ATHENS IN THE DAYS OF HER GLORY 211

XIII. ATHENIAN CULTURE 239

XIV. THE FOURTH CENTURY (404-338 B.C.) 261

XV. THE HELLENISTIC AGE 288

XVI. HELLENISTIC CIVILIZATION 306

XVII. THE RISE OF ROME 324

XVIII. THE EARLY REPUBLIC 344

XIX. THE ROMAN REVOLUTION (133-31 B.C.) . . . 393

CHAPTER | PAGE

XX. Roman Life during the Revolution . . . 425

XXI. The Age of Augustus (31 b.c.-14 a.d.) . . . 437

XXII. The Great Age of the Roman Empire (14-180 a.d.) 453

XXIII. The Institutions of the Early Empire . . . 464

XXIV. The Last Century of the Roman Empire (180-305 a.d.) 508

Chronological Tables 531

Bibliography 544

Index 566

ILLUSTRATIONS

PAGE

STONE AGE IMPLEMENTS 12

ART OF THE LATE PALAEOLITHIC AGE 18
Bison—Reindeer and Fish—Rhinoceros—Reindeer

SUMER AND AKKAD 19
Milking Scene—King Gudea of Lagash (*Photo
Giraudon*)—Seal of Gudea—Tablet of Lagash

TYPES OF WRITING 25

SUMER AND AKKAD 36
Fragment from the Stele of the Vultures—Hammurabi's Code—Victory Tablet of Naram Sin—Story
of the Creation and the Deluge

EGYPT—OLD KINGDOM 37
Step Pyramid—Pyramid of Snefru—Great Pyramid—
Sphinx

EGYPT—OLD KINGDOM (CAIRO) 54
Wooden Panel from the Tomb of Hesi—Khafre—
Rahotep—Nefert—Pepi I and His Son

MODEL OF BOATS FROM AN EGYPTIAN TOMB 55

PLAN OF THE PALACE OF CNOSSUS 72

PLAN OF THE PALACE OF TIRYNS 73

CRETE 74
Bulls in a Net—Cat Hunting Birds—Portrait from a
Fresco—Ladies in a Chariot

CRETAN ART 75
Octopus Vase—Wild Goat Suckling Its Young—Bull
Leaping

PAGE

DER EL BAHRI 82

EGYPTIAN EMPIRE 83
Game of Chess—Ikhnaton and His Family at Dinner—
An Egyptian Cartoon—An Animal Orchestra

EGYPTIAN EMPIRE 90
Market Scene—Sculptors at Work—Scene from the
Tomb of Nakht

EGYPTIAN EMPIRE 91
Ramses II—Nofretete—Hatshepsut—Nefreteri and the
Goddess Isis

IKHNATON SACRIFICING 94

ASSYRIAN AND PERSIAN ART 95
Assurnasirpal Besieging a City—Bull—Capital

ATHENIAN BLACK-FIGURED WARE 134
Chariot Race—François Vase—Foot Race

ATHENIAN RED-FIGURED WARE 135
School Scene—Heracles Slaying Geryon—Studio of
Vase Painter

TEMPLE PLANS 176

DORIC AND IONIC STYLES OF ARCHITECTURE 177

ARCHAIC GREEK SCULPTURE 177
Charioteer of Delphi—Statue of a Maiden—Wrestling
Bout

ATHENIAN SCULPTURE 178
Zeus—Hermes—Sacrificial Bulls

THE ACROPOLIS 240

THE PARTHENON 241

TYPES OF GREEK ARCHITECTURE 284
Erechtheum—House on Delos—Theater at Epidaurus
—Stadium

PAGE

ATHENIAN TOMBSTONES 285
Mourning Athena—Hegeso—An Athenian Youth—
Dexileos

THE ALEXANDER SARCOPHAGUS 310

HELLENISTIC ART 311
Old Shepherdess—Victory of Samothrace—The Dying
Gaul

ETRUSCAN ART 360
Bronze Caldron—Bronze Figures

ROMAN LIFE 361
Sale of Belts and Pillows (*Photo Alinari*)—Exhibition
of a Sample of Cloth (*Photo Alinari*)—Shipbuilding
(*Jahrb. d. D. Arch. Inst.*)—Blacksmith (*Museum
Aquileia*)

THE ALTAR OF THE AUGUSTAN PEACE 436
Earth Mother—Scene of Sacrifice

FOUR GREAT ROMANS 437
Pompey (*Photo Vilhelm Tryde*)—Cicero (*Photo Anderson*)—Caesar (*Photo Anderson*)—Augustus

ROMAN CONSTRUCTION 494
Pont du Gard—The Colosseum (*Photo Chauffourier*)
—Bath

ROME RECONSTRUCTED 495

POMPEII 504
House of Cornelius Rufus (*Restored*)—Temple of Isis—
House of Cornelius Rufus (*Ruins*)—Forum

EXAMPLES OF RELIGIOUS ART 505
The Good Shepherd—Household Shrine—Procession
in Honor of Isis (*Photo Moscioni*)

MAPS

THE CRADLE OF ANCIENT CIVILIZATION . . (*front end sheet*)

ANCIENT EGYPT 40

SYRIA 61

ORIENTAL EMPIRES 106

GREECE 116

GREEK AND PHOENICIAN COLONIZATION 133

ATTICA 157

THE ATHENIAN EMPIRE 203

ATHENS 240

ALEXANDER'S EMPIRE 292

ITALY 326

EARLY ROME 339

COLONIES AND MILITARY ROADS OF ITALY 360

THE MEDITERRANEAN WORLD IN 265 B.C. 365

HANNIBAL'S MARCH 370

ROME IN THE EAST 407

ROME UNDER THE EMPERORS 488

THE ROMAN EMPIRE . . . . . . (*back end sheet*)

THE ANCIENT WORLD

= I =

PRELITERARY HISTORY

ISTORY began to be enacted with the first appearance of men on earth. Yet long ages elapsed before men learned to keep written records of their deeds. Before the first written documents there were many men who wrought great deeds and made noteworthy discoveries and inventions but whose achievements have not been sung by poets nor recorded by historians. The centuries which have passed since the first introduction of writing are but a small fraction of the thousands of years of the history of mankind. The study of these unrecorded ages is called prehistory or, more accurately, preliterary history.

SOURCES The fundamental sources for our knowledge of preliterary periods are the material objects such as tools, weapons, pottery, the remains of dwellings, tombs, and monuments, and the skeletons of men and of animals, whose time-resisting properties have caused them to be preserved. Some historical ideas may be drawn from word-of-mouth traditions afterwards recorded, and from customs and institutions which persisted into later times. Finally we may use cautiously the information, furnished by anthropologists, about peoples, living today, who have not advanced beyond primitive stages.

From these sources there may be drawn, not an account of what happened, but rather a series of general pictures of how prehistoric man lived and toiled, along with some inferences about migrations or succeeding cultures.

CHRONOLOGY The chronology of the stages in the series is relative rather than absolute: scholars are able to establish the sequence of periods but not the actual dates. Dating by calendar years is totally impossible, and the establishment of time relations depends on the information of the geologists or upon the stratification of deposits. Geologists have divided the history of the earth's crust into epochs according to which they classify the rocks, and the beds of sand, gravel, or clay. Human remains can sometimes be dated in one of these epochs according to the place of the geologic deposit in which they were found. When a succession of peoples lives in the same place for a long period of time, there will be an accumulation of debris of bones, tools, pottery, and the like. Obviously the remains of first inhabitants will be on the bottom, with others in succession, and the latest on top. Careful study of the various layers or strata will therefore furnish relative dates for the cultures represented on the site. Comparison with other sites will establish these relationships and often provide evidence of migrations or of advances in civilization.

THE PRELITERARY AGES — The periods or cultures into which the preliterary age is divided are named after the material remains, or the geographical areas where these sources have been found. Since stone tools were the first records of primitive man to be found and studied, they formed the basis for the classification of the Palaeolithic or Old Stone Age, during which rough tools were produced by chipping, and the Neolithic or New Stone Age, distinguished by the development of the technique of polishing stone tools. More knowledge due to subsequent archaeological discoveries has led scholars to speak of an earlier Eolithic or "Dawn Stone" Age and to subdivide the other two ages into stages or cultures. There are six major stages of the Old Stone Age established according to variations in the making of tools. The New Stone Age, however, has been divided into cultures indicated, usually, by pottery remains or by types of dwellings.

THE OLD STONE AGE — Flint tools fashioned by early men have long been known to the people of Europe. At first they were regarded as instruments of magic and were called "thunder stones." Though a few scholars had early recognized their human origin, it was not until the nineteenth century that Boucher de Perthes, a Frenchman, succeeded in proving and securing general acceptance of this fact. Collection, study, and classification followed. The classes or stages were given names from so-called "type stations" which were the place in Europe where the first or greatest quantity of each class was found. Thus to the earlier part of the Palaeolithic Age, called Lower, belong Chellean, from Chelles, and Acheulean, from St. Acheul; to the Middle Palaeolithic, Mousterian from Le Moustier; to the later or Upper Palaeolithic, Aurignacian from Aurignac, Solutrean from Solutré, and Magdalenian from La Madeleine. There are other classes, as well, which are of use to specialists. The table which follows will help to make clear the sequences and time relations of these early peoples.[1]

THE DAWN
STONE AGE
    The beginnings of human history lie far back in the past and yet are comparatively recent in the geologic history of the earth. Earth's history has been divided by geologists into four great ages:

Primary, at least fifty million years ago;
Secondary, about ten million years ago;
Tertiary, between five million years ago; and the comparatively short Quaternary, which has occupied the last three hundred thousand years.

In the Tertiary or third period, the animal ancestors of our present mammals began to appear; among them were the primates, the precursors of the anthropoid apes and of man. To the last or Pliocene division of the Tertiary and to the first or Pleistocene division of the Quaternary belong the first evidences of the appearance of man. In gravels dating from the Pliocene and early Pleistocene there have been found quantities of flints roughly shaped like tools and showing possible signs of use. These are .called eoliths or "dawn stones." They do not seem to have been actually made or prepared for use, and controversy rages as to whether they were actually used at all. It seems probable that our ancestors in that early time employed as implements such objects as these, which they found shaped by nature and ready at hand, and that it was not until later that they learned to make tools for themselves.

THE LOWER PALAEOLITHIC AGE

GEOGRAPHIC
BACKGROUND
    The Palaeolithic Age of human history developed in the Pleistocene division of the Quaternary period. By that time Europe, Asia, and Africa had assumed their present forms, except that their elevation above sea level was greater than it is at present. The Aegean Sea had not yet covered the lower end of the Balkans; Italy and Spain were joined to Africa; England

---

[1] This table, which applies in a strict sense only to western Europe, is based upon Capitan, *La préhistoire,* 1931, pp. 24, 25.

ˡ

Geological Periods	Climate	Culture	Approximate Date of Beginning of Period
		Age of Metals	3,000 B.C. in Europe 5,000 B.C. in the East
Present or Holocene Division of the Quaternary	Modern	Neolithic	5,000 B.C. in Europe 10,000 B.C. in the East
	Post Glacial	Kitchen-Midden Azilian Tardenoisian	10,000 B.C.
		Magdalenian	16,000 B.C.
Pleistocene Division of the Quaternary	Fourth Glacial	Solutrean	25,000 B.C. Cro-Magnon
		Aurignacian	
	Third Inter-glacial	Mousterian	60,000 B.C. Neanderthal Man
	Third glacial		
	Second Inter-glacial	Acheulean	100,000 B.C.
	Second Glacial		
	First Inter-glacial	Chellean	200,000 B.C.
	First Glacial	Pre-Chellean	250,000 B.C. Piltdown Man Heidelberg Man
Pliocene Division of the Tertiary		Eolithic	China Man Ape Man of Java

was a part of the Continent. Over the vast expanse of the territory of these continents there wandered, under the impulses of climate and the search for food, herds of animals: reindeer and bison, huge mammoths and rhinoceroses, saber-toothed tigers, cave bears, wild horses, wolves, and many others. Some of these were doubtless followed in their migrations by companies of primitive hunters who depended on them for food.

It was an age of terrific climatic disturbances. From the north and from the mountains in Eurasia and North America huge glaciers descended and receded four times during the Pleistocene period, while to the south there were long periods of rainfall. These ice and pluvial stages are marked by moraines, or beds of gravel left by the glaciers, and by the terraces on the hillsides above the rivers of Europe and Africa. Great deposits of wind-blown sand, called *loess,* show the character of the interglacial periods. The remains of man and his possessions can thus be given an approximate geological dating according to their location in these deposits.

TOOLS   Man, who alone among creatures is a toolmaker, has left definite evidence of his presence on earth during the periods of glaciation in the form of artifacts which were certainly prepared for use. Implements of the first class, Chellean, are dated from just before the close of the first interglacial period. They are roughly chipped flint axes, usually called "fist hatchets," probably made by striking large nodules of flint with other pieces of stone. Shortly after the second ice age appeared axes of the Acheulean type, which were much finer in form and workmanship. It has been suggested that the use of wooden striking implements was responsible for the improvement. Acheulean implements are found in almost all parts of Europe and parts of Asia and in the desert above the Nile. In South Africa, where flint was lacking, volcanic stones were worked into the same general shapes.

THE FIRST MEN   We know very little about the men who used these early tools. In a gravel bed in Java dating from the late Pliocene or early Pleistocene, a Dutch doctor found a few bones of an ape man (*Pithecanthropus erectus*). From a Pleistocene sand bank near Heidelberg in Germany came a jawbone and from Piltdown, Sussex, in England, scattered fragments of primitive skeletons. Recently, fossils have been found in China which belong to the same epoch. These are all remains of creatures somewhat more manlike than the modern apes, but in many ways more primitive than modern man. *Pithecanthropus erectus* seems to have combined a small-brained, apelike head with an erect, relatively modern body. The men in China had similar heads, with slightly larger brains, more primitive in form but equal in volume to those of some of the smaller-brained races living today. On the other hand, the brain case of Piltdown man was very modern in form and size, except for very thick bones, but his jaw was extremely apelike. All of these men were without chins. A few flake implements were associated with the Piltdown remains. As yet, however, no skeletons have been found which can definitely be connected with the Chellean and Acheulean fist hatchets. The evidence indicates that the men who used these lived on the plateaus or terraces near the rivers; that they hunted and trapped such wild animals as the mammoth, the rhinoceros, the saber-toothed tiger, and the cave bear; and perhaps that they wandered widely over the continents along with the herds which they hunted.

THE MIDDLE PALAEOLITHIC AGE
As the increasing cold was giving warning of the third advance of the glaciers, a new implement period began, the Mousterian. Instead of making single axes out of nodules of flint, the men of this period broke the nodules into chips which in turn they shaped into a variety of tools. With careful flaking of small pieces they produced fine cutting edges for knives and scrapers. Other chips were rounded into disks or sharpened into points. Most of the Mousterian flints are found in caves or grottoes. Many specimens of a large flake industry have also been discovered in open places.

NEANDERTHAL MAN
With the Mousterian tools there have also been found remains of the men who used them. They received their race name from the discovery of a skeleton in a cave in the Neander Valley in Germany in 1856. Many other Neanderthal skeletons have since been found in Europe and in Syria, along with slightly different types of men in Africa. Though much higher in the scale of development than the "dawn" ape men, they had not attained the full development of human beings such as ourselves. Curved leg bones and short, straight spines indicate that they did not stand quite erect, and that they shambled in walking. Five feet five inches was the maximum height of the specimens found. Their heads were thick and heavy; a low sloping skull enclosed a large but undeveloped brain; large round eyes peered out over a broad nose and a

projecting chinless lower jaw. Yet they had taken the fundamental steps toward civilization. Whether the discovery was inherited from earlier generations or achieved by them, they certainly knew the use of fire; the quantities of animal bones found in their deposits prove that they were successful hunters; the wide variety of skillfully worked tools and the work places with heaps of prepared flints show a high degree of technical ability and imply specialization which in turn connotes social organization. The careful burial of some of the skeletons also suggests the beginnings of religion. These men of the Mousterian stage survived the third glacial period and the warm era which followed, but during the first part of the fourth advance of the ice they disappeared.

THE UPPER PALAEOLITHIC AGE

MEN AND TOOLS   The fourth ice age witnessed a complete change in the racial and cultural status of western Europe. Groups of men who came from Africa and the east occupied the land. New types of tools, made of flint, bone, and horn, are found in the deposits, and decorative art appeared in that region for the first time.

There are many skeletal remains from the period. The newcomers were fully developed human beings who stood erect, possessed chins, foreheads, and brains, like ourselves. Indeed one man, known as the "Old Man of Cro-Magnon" whose skeleton has been found, was over six feet tall with long legs, upright body, and a brain even larger than the brains of most modern men.

The tools of the Upper Palaeolithic are divided into three successive groups, Aurignacian, Solutrean, and Magdalenian. The Aurignacian class is marked not only by the wide variety of small tools of flint flakes—blades, scrapers, gravers, and points—but also by the presence of implements of bone and horn. Changing climate and perhaps the pressure of other peoples brought from the east an invasion of hunters of the wild horse. A whole series of beautiful and delicately flaked laurel-leaf flints, known as Solutrean, and the tremendous number of bones of the wild horse on which these people fed are the chief evidences of their presence.

During the last cold era which followed the fourth glaciation, the men of Solutré seem to have vanished, and the Magdalenian period began. The skeletons and tools show that this period was marked by the return of the men of Aurignacian times. Reindeer, bison, and woolly mammoths lived in the valleys of France and Spain, and Magdalenian men went forth to hunt them with weapons which show a new advance, javelins and harpoons of horn, ivory, and bone, which they propelled by cunningly carved spear throwers. Bone fish hooks enabled them to add fish to their diet. Other artifacts were made of the same materials, and the use of flint declined to a marked degree.

Animals and their by-products were fully utilized. The flesh was eaten and the marrow sucked from the bones, while fat furnished fuel for stone lamps. The skins, used for clothing, were sewn by means of bone needles and bodkins, and the teeth, as well as lucky stones and shells, served as decoration for the body. No evidence has survived of the implements which they, like their predecessors, made of wood, nor of the part which wild grains, vegetables, and fruits undoubtedly played in their diet.

During the winters these men lived in caves, grottoes, or rock shelters. In open weather they built for themselves huts, perhaps of the shape of those sketched in the caves. They certainly possessed some form of social grouping with division of labor within each group. There is evidence, too, of trade between the groups.

Though our knowledge of modern primitives and the discovery of the burial of the dead by the Mousterians enable us to postulate religion for earlier times, the existence of religion among the people of the Upper Palaeolithic Age is beyond question. Men felt themselves to be in the hands of a supernatural power or divinity upon which their lives depended. To this feeling doubtless the forces of nature, the emotions of group life, and the thrill of the hunt contributed. To gain the favor of this power they held weird ceremonies far in the recesses of the limestone caves. Probably they performed ritual dances led by a priest dressed in an animal skin, since on the wall of one cave is portrayed the figure of a priest thus attired.

Associated with their religious practices was a group of ceremonies and rituals, called magic, through which men attempted to control supernatural forces. The purpose of magic was the successful accomplishment of a desired end or the avoidance of threatening trouble. These people also practiced sympathetic magic, that is, the previous performance in ritual of a goal to be achieved. An example of this may be the dance with the skin-attired priest, which probably partook of the nature of a magical attempt to secure good hunting. The same magic contributed to the creation of an art which in technical skill and beauty of execution was not to be equaled again in western Europe for many thousands of years.

PALAEOLITHIC
ART
The deposits in the caves and shelters have yielded numerous tools of bone, horn, and ivory, delicately ornamented with carvings of varied designs. Some pieces were engraved with sketches of reindeer, mammoths, horses, fish, and other creatures. Some were carved to represent goats and birds as well as the larger animals. Special care was lavished on certain implements which seem to have been spear throwers. Sculpture appeared in the Aurignacian period in a number of figures of women with enlarged hips, possibly symbols of reproductive powers. Horses and bears carved in relief are found amid Solutrean remains, and against the wall of an inner room of a cave used in the Magdalenian period are two bison modeled in unbaked clay.

The great glories of this art, however, are the engravings and paintings on the cavern walls and ceilings, sometimes in narrow corridors and almost inaccessible corners. By taking advantage of freak shapes on the limestone-crystal walls and by the use of outlines and color, the artists produced the likenesses of animals. On clear spaces of the walls they engraved outlines with sharpened tools or, sketching with lampblack, manganese, or red or yellow ocher, they filled in the bodies with colors of the same materials. Most famous of their paintings are the bison in the cave of Altamira in Spain, and the mammoths, the rhinoceros, and the reindeer in the cave of Font-de-Gaume in France. Modern scholars questioned the accuracy of these early artists' portrayal of the woolly mammoths until one of these extinct animals, discovered frozen in the tundras of Siberia, proved the artists right and the scholars wrong. Strange designs that look like tents or huts are also found, and apparently the artists sometimes amused themselves by drawing the outlines of their hands.

These carvings on tools and these pictures, carved and painted in the caves with such fidelity by the uncertain light of stone lamps, were probably made to evoke magical assistance for the hunters. The excellence of this art indicates specialization, long training, and a high degree of technical ability. Though its products were not primarily objects of art or a picture gallery to be seen and admired, they nevertheless show a remarkable standard of aesthetic appreciation.

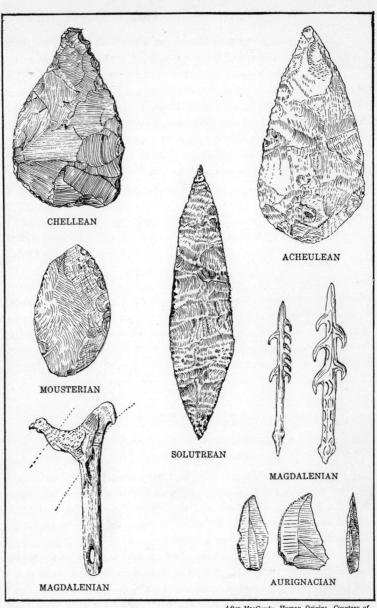

CHELLEAN

ACHEULEAN

MOUSTERIAN

SOLUTREAN

MAGDALENIAN

MAGDALENIAN

AURIGNACIAN

After MacCurdy, Human Origins. Courtesy of
D. Appleton-Century Company, publishers.

STONE AGE IMPLEMENTS

END OF UPPER PALAEOLITHIC These men of the Upper Palaeolithic Age in western Europe had thus reached the acme of Old Stone Age civilization. Mankind had taken long strides toward civilization. Men had learned the use of fire, not only for warmth and for cooking but for light in the dark caves; they had a wide variety of tools and weapons for hunting and fishing and probably for war and for the preparation of their food and clothing. For clothing they used the skins of animals, and there is some indication that they used bags of skin for storage purposes. In all probability they knew the food value of fruits, vegetables, and grains. Yet they were fatally limited by the fact that they depended entirely on nature herself for their sustenance, and natural causes brought their period to an end. The ice receded for the last time; the continents subsided to their present levels; the mammoth, the rhinoceros, and the cave bear disappeared; the bison declined in numbers, and the reindeer retreated to the north. Some men lingered on in the old region; others followed the reindeer north; a few eked out a wretched existence on shellfish. But the future belonged to those men who had begun to learn how to conquer and to use nature, who had discovered how to till the soil, to domesticate animals, and to practice a foresight that rendered them at least partly independent of the uncertainties of hunting animals and gathering such vegetable foods as the whims of nature chose to provide.

THE NEOLITHIC AGE

DISTINCTIVE FEATURES While the hunters of the Old Stone Age were still chasing the reindeer in the woods of western Europe, somewhere in the East men were making those notable advances in civilization which produced the Neolithic or New Stone Age. Where these men lived is a matter of dispute, and how they made their great discoveries can only be conjectured. The age takes its name from the fact that they learned to grind and polish tools made of flint and other hard stones. But other cultural features of the period are of far greater importance. Foremost among these were the domestication of animals, the development of agriculture, the making of pottery, and the invention of weaving. Life in village communities developed as a result of agriculture, which kept men in permanent association with the land; accumulation of wealth followed; religion and art kept pace; the working of metals was discovered; and increasing knowledge of natural processes led to the further control of nature and higher civilization.

The dates of these achievements are still conjectural and vary with different regions. The New Stone Age in the Orient may have begun as far back as 10,000 B.C., but neolithic peoples arrived in Europe about 5,000 B.C. The beginning of the Age of Metals correspondingly varies from 5000 to 3000 B.C.

Men gained mastery over certain of the animals. Dogs, perhaps in the last periods of the Old Stone Age, attached themselves to hunters and became faithful allies and servants; pigs, nature's scavengers, may have gathered around men's dwellings; sheep, goats, cattle, and horses were tended in their herds. From the domestication of these animals grew the pastoral nomadic or wandering type of civilization. Shepherds and goatherds ranged the hillsides from crest to valley with the seasons; the tenders of cattle and horses moved over the grasslands in search of fodder and water. Men, whether nomads or dwellers in villages, were thus freed from the chances of the hunt. They had ever at hand a supply of animals from which to obtain the meat and milk for their food, skins for their clothing, and fat as fuel for their lamps.

Along with this achievement went the amazing discovery of agriculture. Doubtless Old Stone Age folk knew that certain grains, fruits, and vegetables were good to eat, and they gathered and ate them where and when they found them. Perhaps it was the women who found that seeds scattered around their dwellings would grow and thus provide a safe and easy supply of these kinds of food. A garden culture where the women provided the vegetable or cereal food while the men still sought meat by hunting and fishing may well have preceded the development of a farm culture. Nomads, too, during their summer pasturage, learned to put seeds in the ground, supply the growing plants with water, and harvest the crops before they moved on in search of fresh grass or milder weather for their herds. The final stages in this advance came when some men learned the agricultural advantages of the river valleys, and, giving up the life of hunter or nomad for that of the farmer, settled permanently on the land.

The necessity for the storage or transportation of foodstuffs led to the development of receptacles. The first of these, of course, was the basket, made by the simple plaiting of grasses, reeds, or fibers, or the bag made of skin. A great step was taken with the discovery that baked clay keeps its form; thus was pottery invented. Improvement came later, when someone found that by covering the surface of the clay with sand a glaze was procured which made the pot waterproof. Each group in the Neolithic Age seems to have made types of pottery that were distinctive in form and in decoration. The virtual indestructibility of the fragments of these early pots has been of the greatest service to archaeologists. Groups of people can be definitely located, their wanderings traced, and the succession of peoples in single sites observed with certainty in the stratification of the potsherds in the dust heaps of the villages (p. 4). For these reasons, the various peoples are frequently named by modern scholars after their pottery, such as the Bell Beaker folk, the Red Ware folk, and the Painted Pottery folk. The plaiting of baskets also led to the invention of weaving, and garments of flax or wool began to take the place of animal skins as clothing.

In the manufacture of tools, flint was still used, and so great was the demand for it that in many regions it was mined. Grim evidence of this is the skeleton of a miner who was killed by the collapse of the shaft, with his deerhorn pick in his hands. Pits were sunk in the ground and shafts dug from them into the flint-bearing chalk. The flint so secured was made into tools by experts. In addition men learned to take hard stones, grind or polish them into axheads or knives, and then to haft them. Such tools made possible the cutting of wood and the working of the ground in a manner far beyond the reach of the men of the Palaeolithic Age. At the same time the invention of the bow and arrow made hunting easier and more effective and provided an implement of war.

SOCIAL ORGANIZATION
Study of primitive peoples in the modern world, correlated with knowledge of survivals in classical antiquity, has made possible a tentative picture of the structure of society in early times. The evidence indicates, however, that there was such wide variation in primacy of forms, types, and functions of social groups that no rigid system or generalization of development can be laid down. Among some there developed a matriarchal, more properly called matrilineal, type of organization where name, property, and membership in the group were inherited from the mother. Women managed the house, the garden patch, and the children; frequently they had social organizations of their own and held important priesthoods in religion. Though not in control, they sometimes exercised some role in government.

Of greater importance because of its influence on Hebrew and Roman society and law was the patriarchal type of organization. This seems to have developed particularly among nomads, where knowledge of grasslands, water supply, and routes of travel was most essential. It involved the control of the oldest man over the entire group, including not only his physical descendants but all the younger men and their wives and all family retainers and slaves. All relationship was traced in the male line, and property was inherited usually according to the rule of primogeniture, that is, the right of the oldest son to inherit the family estate.

The development of agriculture and of village communities produced modifications in both types of organization as power passed into the hands of those who possessed the largest tracts of land, as the essential duty of securing the good will of the gods conferred a status sometimes approaching divinity upon the priests, or as the needs of defense gave pre-eminence to the ablest warrior.

ECONOMIC LIFE Agriculture and stock-raising were the fundamental bases of economic life after the beginning of the New Stone Age. Yet the expansion in techniques and in the variety of tools and the great inventions of pottery and weaving led to the growth of industry. Flint mines and workshops and pottery kilns are visible proofs of specialization. There are many evidences, too, of trade in western Europe. Tools made of a peculiar honey-colored flint mined and worked at Grand Pressigny in Touraine are found in many parts of France; implements of obsidian and jade traveled far from their places of origin, and amber was carried from the shores of the Baltic to the Mediterranean Sea.

RELIGION Expanding aspects of life resulted in the widening of the religious experience. Throughout their efforts to solve their problems of living by natural means, men had felt themselves to be in the hands of a power or powers beyond their understanding. Their relationship to this supernatural power and their concept of it constituted the source of primitive religious thought and experience. It permeated every act of life. To secure the aid or avert the anger of dimly understood powers there developed rituals of prayer, sacrifice, dance, and feast, injunctions and taboos, and on a lower plane the paraphernalia of magic. The hunter of the Old Stone Age had employed such means to secure a bountiful supply of animals and to make certain of success in killing them (p. 10). The herdsmen sought the protection of the deities who looked after his animals. The farmer became vitally aware of the powers of sun and rain, of the differences between winter and summer, and of the long and anxious wait between seedtime when precious food was placed in the earth and harvest when new supplies might be gathered.

Explanations of these experiences are to be found in numerous myths of which those of Isis and Osiris in Egypt and Demeter and Persephone in Greece are examples. No ritual was too exacting, no sacrifice too great to secure the good will of those divine beings who gave grain to men. Then out of the planting and rebirth of the seed, out of the myth of the divinity who died and was reborn there came a strengthened hope of the resurrection and renewed life of man who died to be reborn again in a country where grain grew high, where fruit was always on the trees, and where soft breezes brought cooling draughts to bodies wearied with the toil of earth.

CULTURES IN EUROPE   The remains of villages, tombs, tools, and pottery of the New Stone Age have made possible the classification of the various peoples of the age into groups distinguished by their cultures. A number of such cultures have been found in western Europe. Belonging to the period of transition between the Old and the New Stone Age (ca. 12,000-10,000 B.C.) were three peoples, probable survivors of the Palaeolithic folk: the Tardenoisians, users of tiny chips of flint, the Azilians, painters of curious designs of lines and spots on flat pebbles, and the "kitchen-midden" peoples, who lived on the seacoast and secured their food in part from shellfish. The name for the third culture has been taken from the great heaps of shells and bones which they piled up and which are called from a Danish word, "kitchen middens."

The true neolithic men came into Europe from the east and the south approximately five thousand years B.C. Anthropologists divide these peoples into three racial groups: the Nordics, who occupied northern Europe, a tall, fair, long-headed race; the Alpines, who moved along the great plateau which stretches from Asia Minor through the Balkans and the Alps to the Pyrenees, a people distinguished for their round heads and their wavy brown hair; and the Mediterraneans, who came from the south as their name implies, a short, dark, long-headed group. In many regions the intermixture of these ethnic groups resulted in the formation of distinctive local cultures. Of the many cultures known, we shall consider but five, and these briefly.

The finest example of Nordic culture was the Scandinavian. These people are notable for their polished stone axes, some of which were so well made that a certain modern carpenter was able to cut and dress the timber and build a house with them in eighty-one days. The Danube Valley was occupied by a mixed group, the product of a fusion of long-headed men with Alpine round heads. The Danubians were peaceful farmers who worked the ground with simple tools made of pebbles, flat on one side and rounded on the other, and who pastured their animals on the slopes of the hills. They made poorly shaped black or gray pottery, decorated with bands or lines cut in the clay.

In the lake region of Switzerland appeared a group of Alpines called the Lake Dwellers, well known from the many relics of their life. Their culture started in the Neolithic Age and continued well down into historic times. In the shallow waters along the shores of the lakes they sank piles. On these they placed platforms, on which in turn they erected their houses. Log bridges and dugout canoes gave them access to the fields along the shores where they grew wheat, barley, flax, and vegetables, and herded their cattle and sheep. From wool and flax they wove garments. For knives and sickles they mounted little chips of flint in wood, and for hoes they ground pebbles after the Danubian fashion. Later they made fine implements and weapons of bronze.

The Mediterranean race occupied Italy and Spain and moved north through France into the British Isles. They mingled with Alpines and Nordics to form a variety of cultures. The distinctive feature of their remains is the small round hut, often half buried in the ground.

A people about whom little is known, called from their huge stone monuments the Megalithic folk, appeared in the late Neolithic and early Bronze Age. They seem to have traveled by sea and to have left their mark in Syria, on the island of Malta, in Brittany, and in England. They placed huge stones on end to form stately avenues, aisles, or circles. They erected stone tombs called dolmens and complicated structures of various kinds, all, certainly, for the purposes of religion. The most famous of their relics is Stonehenge in Salisbury Plain in England.

CONCLUSION   Thus in western Europe we have found evidences of the appearance of man and of his gradual advancement in the making of fire, in the manufacture of tools, in the domesti-

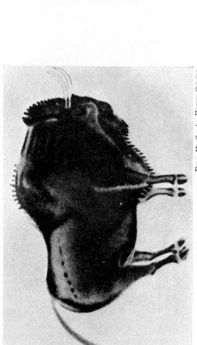

REINDEER AND FISH
ENGRAVED ON A ROUND BONE

REINDEER

From MacCurdy, Human Origins.

BISON

RHINOCEROS

ART OF THE LATE PALAEOLITHIC AGE

Bison from Altamiras, Rhinoceros and Reindeer
from the Cavern of Font de Gaume

A MILKING SCENE

KING GUDEA OF LAGASH

SEAL OF GUDEA

THE TABLET OF LAGASH

SUMER AND AKKAD

cation of animals, in the development of agriculture, and in the achievement of the other fundamentals of civilization. We have placed this study in that region because the information there has been gathered, classified, and studied more thoroughly than elsewhere. We have seen, however, that the men of the Upper Palaeolithic and of the Neolithic ages came from Africa and the east, where they had already taken their first steps upward in the path of civilization. New Stone Age cultures have been found and studied in the valleys of the Nile and of the Tigris and the Euphrates rivers, in the Aegean area, in the highlands of Asia Minor and Iran, and in Turkestan. Some place in this general area, where the domestication of plants and animals was probably first achieved, early men, with the introduction of metals, attained their final accomplishment in the making of tools. They found that certain stones could be melted with heat and cast or hammered into copper tools. Later some learned to add tin to the copper to make bronze, an alloy harder than copper. The discovery of metals brought a new age as copper and bronze gradually replaced stone as basic materials for tools. With metal tools men were able to build better houses and to reach greater heights in material civilization and in the arts. Swords, daggers, metal-pointed arrows and spears, and the body armor which these instruments made necessary led to great developments in the technique of warfare. With these achievements the Neolithic Age ended and the Age of Metals began.

═ II ═

THE EARLY ORIENT

HE foundations of our Western civilization were laid in the East. Although the cradle of civilization where men took the first steps into the New Stone Age is unknown, it is certain that in the great river valleys of Egypt, Mesopotamia, India, and China, great cultures developed at an early period. Of these only the first two belong to the history of the civilization that we are to trace. The cultures of India and of China, though interesting and worthy of study, did not enter the stream of European history until comparatively recent times and played no important part in the ancient history of Western life. In the valley of the Nile and in the area watered by the two rivers, the Tigris and the Euphrates, men passed through the Neolithic Age and discovered metals, invented writing, and created calendars. Industry, commerce, organized governments, imperial expansion, religious systems, science, literature, the mechanic arts and architecture appeared, to form great cultures from which our own descends.

THE LAND OF THE TWO RIVERS

In the land which today is called Iraq, whose modern capital is Bagdad, where anciently the Tigris and the Euphrates rivers emptied through separate mouths into the Persian Gulf, a marvelous structure of civilization was erected during the fifth, fourth, and third millennia B.C. It is commonly known by the terms Babylonia or Mesopotamia. Economic prosperity, founded upon the rich soil of the river valleys and upon the trade which followed the rivers, combined with a finely developed technique in the handling of metals to produce a rich material culture with which intellectual and artistic advance kept pace. The influence of the peoples of Mesopotamia spread to the west where it profoundly influenced the Hebrew and Greek cultures from which we have derived so much of our own civilization. Many of our familiar ideas, expressions, and practices, including parts of our systems of measurement, have come to us from the ancient Babylonians.

SOURCES   The recorded history of a people depends, as we have seen, upon the nature of the sources from which the historian draws his facts. The sources of our information about Babylonia are literary, archaeological, and epigraphic. The literary sources are late and of little value for the early period. Some knowledge may be gleaned from the Bible and from the writings of Herodotus and of other Greeks. About 280 B.C. a Chaldaean priest, Berossus, wrote a history of Babylonia, but only fragments and chronological lists have survived from his work. Traditions of early times and lists of kings with the years of their reigns, recorded by Babylonian scholars, have been found on tablets in the excavations. To this scant sum of knowledge archaeology has made and is making great contributions. In many places along the ancient rivers, archaeologists have found large mounds which excavation proved to be the ruins of ancient cities. Houses and walls were made in olden times of sun-baked clay. When they fell down or were melted down by rains, others were built on their debris, to collapse in their turn and to be succeeded by others. Thus these mounds rose above the level of the plain. When they are opened, the layout of the successive cities and the plans of the houses are revealed, and in the ruins are found the implements and the writings of the inhabitants.

The ancient Babylonians wrote on stone or on tablets of clay, which were dried in the sun or baked in kilns. Great numbers of these clay tablets have been found. They contain public and private records of all sorts, and such literary products as poems, prayers, stories, and scientific writings. Chiefly from these has modern knowledge of Babylonian culture been derived. Scholars have learned the names and deeds of many kings from the public records. Law codes and records of contracts and law suits disclose the busy life of the cities. Letters and works of literature and religion give keys to the thoughts and aspirations of the people.

GEOGRAPHY   For the understanding of any civilization, a knowledge of its geographic scene is essential, since geography conditions, if it does not actually determine, the course of history. The chief conditioning element in Mesopotamian history is the presence of the two rivers and their tributaries. The Euphrates, coming down in a westerly course out of the mountains of Armenia, is turned eastward by the plateau of Arabia and then flows in a general south-easterly direction. It soon reaches a level not much higher than that of the sea, and as a result its waters wander like those of the Missis-sippi in great loops and many turns. Innumerable sandbars, built up by the silt which it carries, obstruct navigation. Its total length is about fifteen hundred miles, of which one thousand is navigable by small boats.

The Tigris rises to the east, also in the mountains of Armenia, flows swiftly through the hill country of Assyria and only begins its wandering as it approaches its sister river. It is shorter than the Euphrates (eleven hundred miles with eight hundred navigable) but it carries a larger volume of water. It is straighter and hence better fitted to be a highway for commerce than the Euphrates.

At Bagdad the two rivers are but thirty-five miles apart. In the spring of the year, as the snow melts in the hills, the two rivers become swollen, overflow their banks, deposit silt in the land, and push their delta out into the Persian Gulf. Geographers estimate that the delta has been built up at the rate of a mile every seventy years. Today the ancient coast line lies far inland, and the rivers join before they reach the gulf.

Since the plain is broad and flat, the flood waters stay on the land; swamps are formed; and the land must be drained by canals. After the inundation there follows a long and rainless summer, during which the canals are used to irrigate the crops. The waters are so heav-ily laden with silt that the canals tend to fill up and have to be watched and cleaned with great care. Unity of irrigation control, though desir-able, was not essential in Babylonia, and separate systems of drainage and irrigation were developed for the support of many independent and flourishing communities. The valleys watered by the two rivers com-bine with the grasslands and valleys and coastal plains of Syria to form an area which has been happily termed the Fertile Crescent. The flat-ness of the land and the slow movement of the rivers, particularly of the Euphrates, made the task of cultivation for the early peoples an easy one, and the rewards were very great. The fertility of the land was celebrated in ancient times; its present poverty is due to the neglect of the canals during the later Middle Ages.

Trade naturally followed the rivers northward, then across the grasslands to the west, or southward to the Persian Gulf and by water to India. It brought enrichment to the cities of Babylonia, and many wars were fought for control of the routes of commerce. The people exported their surplus foodstuffs and manufactured goods and took in exchange metals, stones, and wood which were lacking in their region.

The land itself, in spite of its fertility, tends to monotony. It is broad and flat without hills to rest the eye or to kindle the imagination. The winter is short and rainy; the summer so long and hot as to discourage incentive and to sap energy. People who settled there rapidly lost their earlier vitality. The history of Mesopotamia is therefore largely the story of invaders who, attracted by the richness of the land, have come down from the hills or in from the grasslands, have overcome their decadent predecessors and absorbed their culture, have produced great kings, emperors, and lawgivers, and then have been content to settle into a placid enjoyment of their wealth until overwhelmed or enlivened by the next wave of intruders.

Invasion was easy and invaders were many. To the east and north were the plateaus of Iran and Armenia, filled with a vigorous hill folk ever ready to move swiftly down the valleys into the plain. To the west and south were the grasslands of the northern Arabian plateau. Here were sufficient rains to provide fodder for the herds of sheep and cattle which hardy groups of Semitic peoples have tended since early times. The increase of population or a sequence of bad seasons drove them either into the hill country of Syria in the west, or into Mesopotamia in the east. Hill folk and Semitic nomads have met, fought, and mingled, and thereby wrought the history and erected the structure of culture in the land of the Two Rivers.

EARLY
CIVILIZATIONS

The history of the region begins with the Neolithic Age. In Elam, a hill country southeast of the Tigris, a village of the New Stone Age has recently been found. Its houses were of sun-baked clay; its inhabitants used tools of flint and obsidian and made fine basketware pottery shaped on a turning stone which was perhaps the ancestor of the potter's wheel. They worked the ground with hoes made from pebbles and they raised cereals. They had domesticated cattle, sheep, and goats, and used the donkey as a beast of burden.

The earliest inhabitants of the river valleys were farmers who are known as the "Painted Pottery Folk." In small villages scattered along the rivers they built houses of matting plastered with mud and covered with flat or barrel roofs. They ground their grain in mills and kept cows, sheep, goats, and pigs. Pieces of flint or obsidian from the desert were shaped into hoes and knives. For weapons they had slings, bows and arrows, and pear-shaped maces. On their finely molded pottery they painted pictures of men, animals, and birds. This pottery, as well as that of their neighbors in Elam, seems to show relationship to a very early neolithic culture in Turkestan and Asia Minor. They may therefore have been a people from the northern highlands who moved down into the valley during a remote epoch.

THE SUMERIANS
About 5000 B.C. the Sumerians, users of metal and possessors of a high level of culture, entered the valleys. Who they were and whence they came are matters of controversy. Some scholars maintain that they came from central Asia, an offshoot of the Turkestan culture; others have seen in a culture recently discovered in India evidences which would connect them with land to the southeast of Babylonia. They were certainly mountain dwellers who had learned to fire bricks in kilns and to make tools of copper. They used the potter's wheel and that all-important invention, the wheeled vehicle. In the river country they overwhelmed the simple peasant folk and erected cities with strong walls and monumental buildings on mounds raised above the level of the inundation. Their material culture, their laws and literature, their religious ideas, and their writing formed the basis for future civilizations in the region.

CUNEIFORM WRITING
Certainly their most amazing achievement in Babylonia and one of their earliest, since it dates back before 4000 B.C., was the evolution of writing. The Sumerians began by using pictures to represent objects or ideas, drawing them on clay with blunt-ended reeds in such a way that the lines appear to be wedge-shaped—cuneiform. Later the pictures became formalized and came to represent sounds as well. Since the Sumerian language was agglutinative, that is, it was made up of syllables joined together to form phrases or sentences like the languages of the American Indians, these sounds were syllables, not words or letters; in fact, cuneiform never developed into an alphabetic system. Several hundred such signs were used, of which about eighty are common. Due to the flexibility of such a syllabic system, other peoples like the Semites, the Hittites, and the Persians, found little difficulty in adapting it to their languages, and even the Egyptian scribes learned to use it for diplomatic correspondence. It continued in use in Babylonia until the first century B.C. when it was finally superseded by the Phoenician alphabet.

HIEROGLYPHIC

HIERATIC

DEMOTIC

CUNEIFORM

CRETAN

PHOENICIAN

HEBRAIC

GREEK

ROMAN

TYPES OF WRITING

Drawn by Professor U.T. Holmes of the
University of North Carolina

Modern scholars learned to read it through the decipherment of an inscription of the Persian kings on the Behistun Rock in Persia. The honor of this modern accomplishment belongs to two men, a German scholar, Grotefend, who read the kings' names in 1802, and an English army officer, Sir Henry Rawlinson, who published a complete translation of the inscription in 1846.

THE CALENDAR Another great accomplishment of the Sumerians was the establishment of a calendar and the founding therewith of a system of chronology. They divided the year into twelve months based upon the phases of the moon, adding a month whenever necessary to bring the year into harmony with the seasons. Each city had its own names for the months and its own system of inserting extra months, until eventually the calendar of the city of Nippur was generally adopted and became official. Years were recorded by the names of some noteworthy event.

THE FLOOD After the time of the first Sumerian kings, who were said to have reigned thousands of years, came a great flood (probably before 4500 B.C.). A great Deluge Epic was written about this flood, which in all probability is the one referred to in the Biblical story of Noah. In the excavations at Ur and in a near-by village, Mr. Woolley, an English archaeologist, came upon a great deposit of clay some eight feet thick. Above it were Sumerian remains; below were artifacts of the early Sumerians and of the Painted Pottery folk—mute but definite evidence of this great catastrophe, which marked an epoch for the scribes and became the subject of legends. Apparently the older peasantry who lived in small villages were drowned while some of the more advanced Sumerians, living on higher and well-protected mounds, survived.

THE SUMERIAN CITIES After the deluge a number of cities such as ancient and holy Nippur, Kish, Eridu, Erech, Ur, Lagash, and Umma grew up or were rebuilt by the banks of the Euphrates or at the head of the Persian Gulf. This growth of city life was the result of geographic conditions. For protection against the annual inundation people gathered together on natural or artificial mounds above the water level; and since ramparts raised against the water served also as walls of defense, the communities became walled towns where rulers, priests, merchants, and peasants gathered to live and to which people on the outlying farm lands might flee for refuge from the waters or from foes.

The local god was titular ruler and chief resident of the city. His domains were the largest and the richest and his temple with its terraced tower, "ziggurat," was the finest structure in the city. The *patesi,* or king, was both chief executive and priest, as well as earthly representative of the local god. Often he himself was the recipient of divine honors. His chief task was the care of agriculture, the digging and dredging of canals, and the control of the land upon which the life of the people depended.

Though individuals owned tracts of land, since the institution of private ownership was certainly established by law, the necessity for strict regulation of the water supply gave such power to the king, the ruling class, and the priests that large estates tended to grow at the expense of the small farms. Under good management the land provided food bountifully for the people, and the cities prospered. Industry, trade, and the arts made great advances, and clay, stone, and metals (copper, silver, and gold) were worked with great skill. Architects who had mastered the use of the column, the vault, and the dome erected great buildings made of kiln-dried bricks and adorned with imported stones. Trade was carried on with India to the south, the hill country to the east, Armenia to the north, and Syria and Egypt to the west.

Mr. Woolley in his excavations found the tombs of the kings of Ur, which may be dated around 3400 B.C. and which give a vivid picture of those early times. When the king or the queen died, courtiers and servants with oxen and asses went into the tomb or into a pit beside it to die and to serve their sovereign in the next world. The tomb of one king contained no less than sixty-five bodies of men and women, with twenty-five more accompanying the burial of his queen. There is the charioteer with his animals still in harness and attached to the royal chariot, a harpist, entertainers, and the royal bodyguard. The jewelry, cups, swords, and other objects found in these tombs at Ur show that "the fourth millennium before Christ saw Sumerian art at its zenith." [1]

THE EMPIRES The flatness of the land, the absence of natural boundaries, the desirability of uniform control over irrigation, the community of language and culture among the cities, and the need of a strong defense against enemies without—all were power-

[1] Woolley, *The Sumerians,* p. 44.

ful arguments for unity. Opposed to such unity was local pride in the city and its gods, and the eternal jealousy of neighboring rivals. Wars constantly arose over canals or the possession of lands. Able kings in their chariots led forth citizen armies equipped with helmets, shields, body armor and short spears, and marching in phalanx (close) formation. They conquered other cities, reduced them to subjection and founded empires which lasted until a dynasty ended, a subject state led a successful revolt, or the ruler of another city became strong enough to establish an empire of his own. Sumerian history is filled with short-lived empires and constant civil wars.

Kish and Erech were the first cities to construct empires after the flood. Then about 3400 B.C. Mesannipadda founded the so-called First Dynasty at Ur. Under him and his successors the commerce and influence of Ur reached from the Mediterranean to the Far East. The tablets of the succeeding centuries contain the names of many cities and kings, the records of wars and of triumphs, of the digging of canals and the building of temples, of a busy and prosperous life on the farms and in the market places of the cities. Of the rulers the most interesting are Eannatum of Lagash (ca. 3050 B.C.),[2] who is famous for a relief known as the Stele of the Vultures, representing the king and his army (perhaps the finest piece of Sumerian relief sculpture); Ku Bau, a woman of Kish, who rose from keeping a brothel to ruling an empire, the first woman ruler of recorded history; and Urukagina, king of Lagash about 2700 B.C., who became a social reformer and endeavored to protect the poor against the greedy exactions of the officials, the priests, and the officers of the army. When in doing this he fatally weakened his military forces, Lugal Zaggisi, king of Umma, mindful of an ancient feud once arbitrated by the king of Kish, fell upon Lagash and destroyed it. The lament of an ancient priest over this "sinful" deed may still be read. From this victory, Lugal Zaggisi advanced until his power was established throughout the land of Sumer and even to the Mediterranean, only to succumb at last to the rising power of the Semites of Akkad.

THE SEMITES
The term "Semite" has been applied to widely scattered groups of peoples, who in historic times were found in Mesopotamia, the grasslands west of the Euphrates, in Syria, and in Arabia. Widely diverse in physical characteristics, they pos-

---

[2] The dates in this section correspond for the most part with the chronology of Eduard Meyer.

sessed a community of language, of ideas, of customs, and of apti-
tudes and temperament. The original Semites were probably a nomadic
folk wandering in the grasslands with their herds. Their social organization was patriarchal, that is, each group was under the control of
the oldest man, the "father" of the clan. Their material culture was
low, and their religion consisted of a belief in spirits. Their simple, direct language was capable of epigrammatic terseness and of expressing
word pictures glowing with imagery. These Semites showed marvelous
adaptability and facility in learning. When overpopulation, bad seasons, or restlessness drove tribes into settled communities, they speedily blended with and absorbed the older inhabitants and adopted their
ways of living. In agricultural regions they became skillful farmers; in
commercial centers some of them gained great success as merchants.
In western Arabia, in Syria, and in Mesopotamia, they built powerful
cities. Their leaders became great conquerors and organizers of empire,
and they have contributed to the world some of its greatest religious
teachers.

AKKAD   At a very early time groups of Semites moved down
the Euphrates from its middle stretches in the north-
ern part of the Fertile Crescent into the richer lands of the south. They
may even have preceded the Sumerians into the lands along the gulf
coast. There was always a strong Semitic element in the Sumerian
cities, derived either from the north or from the grasslands to the
west. The Semites were predominant in Akkad, the region north of
the Sumerians. The Akkadians adopted Sumerian practices in business
and in agriculture, Sumerian law and Sumerian culture, and fitted
the Sumerian writing to their own language. About 2650 B.C., Sargon,
king of Akkad, defeated Lugal Zaggisi of Umma and became ruler of
Sumer and Akkad, calling himself "King of the Four Regions of the
Earth." Sargon and his grandson Naram Sin led their professional
armies as far as Asia Minor in the west and the Zagros mountains in
the east. Roads were built to bind their empire together, and governors were assigned to districts to keep watch over local rulers. Naram
Sin left a record of his mountain conquests on a famous tablet.

GUDEA OF
LAGASH   This first Semitic attempt at empire lasted but a generation after Naram Sin. Then in a period of dynastic
weakness it was overthrown by a barbarous hill folk
called Guti, who succeeded as rulers of Sumer and Akkad. Though
the Guti continued the ancient customs of rule and organization, leav-

ing native princes in charge of the cities, and though some of their kings worshiped the Sumerian gods, the traditions and the remains of the century and a quarter of their rule indicate that they were barbarians who despoiled the land. The chief exception to this general condition of ruin is the city of Lagash, which prospered under the guidance of the local patesi, Gudea. Gudea revived the trade of Lagash with distant lands and was the patron of literature, architecture, and the arts. Tablets describe the temples which Gudea built, and eighteen of his statues, perhaps the best examples of Sumerian sculpture, have survived amid the ruins of his city. Later generations regarded him as divine.

THE THIRD DYNASTY OF UR Shortly after the overthrow of the Guti by the ruler of Erech, the kings of the Third Dynasty of Ur, Ur-Engur, Dungi, and their descendants (2298-2180 B.C.), led the most brilliant period of Sumerian history. All the land of Sumer and Akkad was brought under the rule of Ur. With the tribute which poured in from the empire, the kings repaired the canals in order to restore prosperity, and rebuilt the capital city. New walls, palaces, and temples were erected and a great ziggurat, tower temple, was built in honor of Nannar, moon god of Ur. A large part of this "Mountain of God" is still standing.

With the ending of this dynasty Sumerian history came to a close. The original Sumerian stock had become so blended with Semites that racial purity had been lost. Long centuries of residence in the low-lying river valleys had at the same time resulted in enervation and decay. Semites throve and grew ever stronger in a climate which took away the pristine strength of a mountain people. The long series of civil wars due to local pride had reduced all of the cities to such weakness that they fell an easy prey first to the Elamites (ca. 2180 B.C.) from the southeast, who ruled for a brief period, and then to the Amorites of Babylon. In vain Sumerian scribes wrote the history of the land to which they had given civilization in an endeavor to prove the right of the Sumerians to rule by the glory of their culture. Although later generations remembered their work, translated their books into Semitic languages, and worshiped their gods, and although the basic culture of ancient Mesopotamia remained Sumerian, the Sumerian's day was done.

HAMMURABI
(1947-1905 B.C.)

A fresh wave of Semites from the middle Euphrates began pushing in to the land of Akkad about 2200 B.C., and in 2049 B.c. established the Amorite dynasty in Babylon, thus bringing this famous city into history for the first time. A century later Hammurabi, ruler of Babylon, established his power over all the cities. He defeated the Elamites and the Semites around him, took and destroyed Ur, and made Babylon the political, economic, and religious center of the land of the Two Rivers. So effective and so permanent was his work that for nearly two thousand years Babylon remained an important and a holy city, and the region which had finally attained lasting unity came to be called Babylonia. After bringing all the cities under control, Hammurabi conquered the upper reaches of the Tigris and marched west into Syria and Asia Minor. Directed by the king's letters, which may still be read, his agents built temples, regulated the canals, kept order, and controlled affairs. For the better ordering of his empire, the king compiled a code of laws from Sumerian and Semitic records and traditions. The stone on which this code was engraved was recovered in 1901 and stands today in the Louvre; besides making Hammurabi's name familiar to the modern world, it affords a marvelous picture of life and culture in early Babylonia.

Since the empire and the law code of Hammurabi represent the culmination and, to a great extent, the crystallization of the centuries of Sumerian and Semitic development and blending, the period presents a suitable point at which to stop and examine the political, economic, and social conditions, the works of industry, art, and literature, and the religious life of the inhabitants of the land.

LIFE AND WORK IN BABYLONIA

GOVERNMENT

The center of all activities throughout the centuries from the coming of the Sumerians around 5000 B.C. to the achievement of unity by Hammurabi was the city with its surrounding farm land. This, as we have seen, was the natural product of this land of inundations and of wars. The Sumerians had given it vitality by establishing a god as the center of its devotion and as the source of its government. The king, earthly representative of the divinity was called *patesi*. If he was a conqueror, he added the title *lugal;* in Semitic, *sharru.* Since the patesi of conquered cities recognized the

sovereignty of the lugal and ruled in his name under the surveillance
of his messengers, the title of patesi sank with the growth of empire
to mean the ruler of a subject city. The king was assisted by a *nubanda*
or vizier and a host of subordinate officials. In earlier Sumerian times
the army was composed of citizens, but later, during and after the
first period of Semitic rule, the king relied on professional troops, who
were supported by lands assigned to them.

The law courts were originally administered by the priests in the
temples, but before the time of Hammurabi, civil courts had been
established in addition, and appeals to the king were allowed from the
decisions of both courts. The clay tablets of the time show that these
people were as fond of litigation as were the later Greeks and the
modern Americans. Sumerians and Semites alike had inherited traditional customs from primitive times. These had been interpreted in the
courts, and in each city there had developed bodies of judge-made law.
In many of the Sumerian cities these had been reduced to codes, notably
by Urukagina of Lagash and Dungi of Ur. Hammurabi drew the basic
structure of his great code from these earlier Sumerian drafts, especially from that of Dungi, although he made some modifications based
on Semitic tradition, for example, in the matter of punishments, where
the Semites were more drastic. The great contribution of his code lay
in the fact that since it was imperial it superseded all of the local codes
or bodies of tradition. One can hardly overestimate the value of a
written universal law in place of oral tradition and many local systems
in the safeguarding of the rights of the individual, in the abolition of
clan feuds and the rough justice of primitive times, and in the strength-
ening of the power of orderly government.

HAMMURABI'S CODE — Hammurabi's code covers a wide range of family,
property, and contract law, and of civil and criminal
procedure. The ancient principle of retaliation (*lex
talionis*) was the basis of the criminal law. If a builder built a house
and the house collapsed and killed the owner or the owner's son, the
builder or his son were killed in turn. At the same time, however, enlightened justice substituted payments for injuries in place of such
primitive concepts. The law made distinctions between the nobles, the
common people, and the slaves, with privileges and penalties appropriate to the classes. Under the law the family was the basis of society;
the code provided for marriage contracts, for breach of promise suits,
and for divorce. Concubinage was not only allowed but special provi-

sion was made for it in case of default of heirs by a wife. The story
of Abraham, Sarah, and Hagar, in Genesis, is a good illustration of
this phase of Babylonian family law. If a free man had relations with
a slave woman, she and her children became free at his death. In
general the rights of women were better safeguarded than under any
other laws before the time of the Roman Empire. The law protected
the lower classes and even the slaves. The latter might own property,
marry, and will their possessions to their children; freedom was easily
obtained, and only runaway slaves were branded.

ECONOMIC LIFE   Agriculture was the chief basis of economic life, and
the code indicates that it was highly developed. Land
was owned by the king and his officials, by the temples, and by small
freeholders. Toward the end of the Sumerian period most of the land
had passed into the possession of the state or the temples, with only
houses and gardens privately owned. The code, however, reflects a
return to private tenure in which ownership might be held by families
or by individuals.

Property was rented on shares or for a fixed rent; in the latter
case the law provided for moratoria in case of flood or drought. Taxes
were levied on the land. There was forced labor on the canals and
roads. Herds of cattle and sheep were raised, and the donkey was the
chief beast of burden. Barley, wheat, spelt, some sixty vegetables, and
fruits, among which the date was the favorite, were grown. Herodotus
paid tribute to the extraordinary fertility of the land in the fifth century B.C.

Of all the countries that we know there is none which is so fruitful
in grain. It makes no pretension indeed of growing the fig, the olive, the
vine or any other tree of the kind; but in grain it is so fruitful as to yield
commonly two-hundred-fold, and when the production is the greatest even
three-hundred-fold. The blade of the wheat-plant and barley-plant is often
four fingers in breadth. As for the millet and the sesame, I shall not say to
what height they grow, though within my own knowledge; for I am not
ignorant that what I have already written concerning the fruitfulness of
Babylonia must seem incredible to those who have never visited the country.[3]

Industry was organized on a craft basis by means of associations
of craftsmen and apprentices. The law regulated the system of appren-

[3] I, 193, tr. by Rawlinson.

ticeship, fixed waxes for workmen, and assigned liabilities for bad workmanship. Commerce was active between cities and along the trade routes which led to India, China, or the Mediterranean. The law provided for partnerships, associations, and agencies for the carrying on of this trade, and many tablets containing agreements signed and witnessed have been found. All contracts were written and sealed, and agents had to furnish an accurate account of all transactions. Heavy penalties were assigned to dishonest practices. The law recognized loans of grain and of silver and fixed the rates of interest at one third of the principal for the former and one fifth for the latter.

Although coinage had not been developed, exchange was carried on by fixed weights of silver: the talent, the mina, and the shekel. Not only wages and interest but the prices of many products received maximum and minimum limits from the legislator. Grains, olives, dates, bricks, porcelain, gems, tapestries, and rugs were exported; stone, wood, and metals were the chief imports.

EDUCATION AND
LITERATURE

Education kept pace with economic growth. In the schools, which were ordinarily connected with the temples, students learned to read and write the difficult cuneiform and studied mathematics. Long after the Semitic had replaced the Sumerian tongue as the language of daily speech, Sumerian was used somewhat like Latin as the language of culture and religion; schoolboys studied it and priests used it in the religious services. To aid the priests in their work, interlinear texts were prepared. The literary forms were varied. There were religious epics, wherein were found stories of the creation of the world, stories of how the gods taught men the arts and manners of life, legends of the early kings and heroes, of Gilgamesh and the flood, histories recording the proud deeds of kings, liturgies and prayers, and laws and letters. The study of the stars, later developed into Chaldean astrology, was begun. The priests divided time into years and lunar months, and the days into two sets of twelve hours. In arithmetic they used sixty as a measure, and from this comes the sixty-minute hour and the 360° circle.

ART

Art in Babylonia never attained the splendor of Egyptian work, nor did the later artistic products maintain the level of the objects found in the early royal tombs. Some progress was made in sculpture. A few statues of Sumerian rulers, particularly of Gudea of Lagash, have survived. The bodies are squat, heavy, and ill-proportioned, with almost no neck and with overlarge heads. The

ability of the artists in the carving of low relief is proved by the Stele
of the Vulture, that of Naram Sin, and that on which Hammurabi's
code was recorded.

The craftsmen excelled, however, in the engraving of gems and
of the cylinder seals with which the Babylonians signed their contracts.
Thousands of these seals have been found in the ruins of the cities.
Made of lapis lazuli, steatite, serpentine, and other hard stones, they
were skillfully carved with inscriptions and representations of gods,
men, and animals.

The artisans were able to handle copper, gold, and silver. Tin, and
therefore bronze, was unknown, though at times they mixed lead with
copper to secure greater durability. From copper they made tools,
weapons, dishes, and votive statuettes of men, women, and animals.
Gold and silver vases, earrings, necklaces, and other pieces of jewelry
have survived in small quantities. Metals were melted and cast in
molds of clay or stone. Although small pieces were cast solid, men
knew how to cast larger works hollow. Many objects received designs
in engraving and there are known examples, as well, of *repoussé* (hammered) work.

RELIGION   The gods were the divinities of the city-state. The god
              of a conquering city became the overlord of the gods
of the conquered. With the union of many cities, there developed a
pantheon of deities, Sumerian and Semitic, to each of whom the priests
assigned specific functions. Thus Anu of Erech became the god of the
sky; Enlil of Nippur, god of the earth and air; Ea of Eridu, god of
the waters who was the first to separate land and water and who
taught men the arts of civilization; Nannar of Ur, god of the moon.
Over them all ruled Marduk, son of Ea, and god of the imperial city,
Babylon. To each of the gods was assigned a female consort, and
finally these were associated with the Semitic mother goddess, Ishtar
or Astarte, who is mentioned in the Bible. In many cities the king's
wife or daughter was joined to the god in ritual marriage.

Worship centered in the temple and its tower. The temple area
was surrounded by a wall. Within it were rooms for worship and
others for the keeping of the temple records and treasures. In the center
rose the ziggurat, a series of terraces of brick, beautifully adorned. On
the topmost terrace stood the dwelling place of the god.

Religious beliefs and practices were directed to the securing of
prosperity and long life in this world. The gods, always bringers of

good, had created men out of clay for their own service. Properly
served, they brought happiness. But if angered by men's sins, the
greatest of which was neglect, they withdrew their presence and protection and exposed men to demons, agents of evil, who brought
sorrow and disease. Magic charms and, in the case of sickness, simple
drugs expelled these workers of evil, while prayer and sacrifice secured
again the favor of the gods.

> Each day pay thy homage to thy god;
> Sacrifice, prayer, worthy incense.
> Before thy god have a pure heart
> That which is pleasing to the deity.
> Supplication, prayer, and prostration,
> Thou shalt render every morning and he
>   shall grant thee treasures.
> And thou shalt abundantly prosper
>   thanks to thy god.
> In thy understanding consider the tablet.
> Fear brings forth good will:
> Sacrifice adds to life
> Prayer delivers from sin.[4]

The constant performance of temple rituals, huge sacrifices, and elaborate festivals preserved the blessing of the god for the king and his city.
Temple prostitution, to secure fertility of land and population, was
regularly practiced, and the behavior of the priestesses was carefully
regulated by law. But in the end death was the lot of all mankind.
The shades, if properly buried, found rest in a colorless nether world.
The Babylonians had no real belief or interest in a future life.

The great Babylonian contribution to ancient religion, however,
was in the field of divination. All accidental phenomena, winds, storms,
and the movement of the stars were carefully observed and interpreted,
and meanings were assigned to dreams. The action of oil dropped on
water gave the soothsayers information about the future; the liver and
the gall of freshly killed sheep, considered the center of the life of the
animal, were carefully studied and charted by the priests as a means
of revealing the will of gods to men. The priests acquired extraordinary
power and wealth. They were not only intercessors, liturgists, magicians, and seers, but also judges, scribes, teachers, bankers, and busi-

[4] Delaporte, *Mesopotamia,* p. 162.

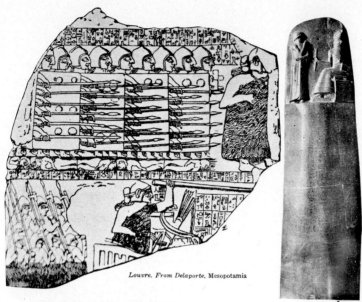

Louvre. From Delaporte, Mesopotamia

FRAGMENT FROM THE STELE OF
THE VULTURES

Louvre

HAMMURABI'S CODE

Louvre

VICTORY TABLET OF NARAM SIN

The Museum of the University of Pennsylvania.

STORY OF THE CREATION OF
THE WORLD AND THE DELUGE

SUMER AND AKKAD

THE GREAT PYRAMID

THE STEP PYRAMID

THE SPHINX

THE PYRAMID OF SNEFRU

EGYPT – OLD KINGDOM

nessmen. Only strong kings like Hammurabi could control them. The weight of their authority lay like a heavy stone in the path of progress.

THE DECLINE

The brilliant achievements of Babylonian culture were made in its first period. The lessons which had been learned were not forgotten and the people continued to be prosperous. During the second millennium, however, few new steps were taken on the highroad of civilization. The dynasty of Hammurabi lost part of its empire to people from the sea lands of the south and was itself overthrown when Hittite raiders descended from the north shortly after 1780 B.C. Before the nineteenth century B.C., the Kassites came down from the eastern mountains bringing the horse, and after the Hittite raid they became kings of Babylon. Cultured Babylonia lived on under the new rulers but played no important part in world affairs for a thousand years. The reasons for this decline are by no means clear. The engulfing of the Sumerians, who had been the chief source of culture of the land, was no doubt a chief factor. The lack of vigorous leaders among the descendants of Hammurabi or among the Kassite kings is another. Religious conservatism, guarded by the priests and more effective in a united empire than it was amid the jealous rivalries of independent cities, was an effective block to progress. The wealth of the land and the enervating effect of the climate on its inhabitants combined to make men content with what they had and did under the protection of the ancient gods. Not until the last pre-Christian millennium, when the Assyrians embarked on their career of conquest and culture, did the land of the Two Rivers step again into the forefront of history.

The early Babylonians had done their work well. They had achieved mastery over copper for the making of as wide a variety of tools as their work required. Their land responded most bountifully to their activities on the farms and to the irrigation systems. They had developed handicraft industry and their merchants carried their products far and wide. Organized life in cities and the final attainment of imperial unity established their prosperity on sound bases. Writing, the calendar, systems of weights and measurements, laws which regulated and protected all classes and all activities of the population, aided in the development of their wealth. Their intelligence produced great works of literature and fine objects of artistic merit. Religion provided them, so they thought, with the means of learning the will of the gods and of securing their favor. The lessons of civilization which they learned and transmitted to their contemporaries and successors have never been lost.

EGYPT UNDER THE OLD AND MIDDLE KINGDOMS

A THOUSAND miles west of Babylon in the valley of the Nile, the Egyptians were engaged in solving the problems of living and in producing great works of culture during the same centuries that witnessed the rise of the Sumerians and Semites along the banks of the Tigris and Euphrates rivers.

SOURCES There are striking similarities and important differences between the stories of Egypt and of Babylonia. The literary sources for the history of Egypt are much the same as for Babylonia: the Bible, Herodotus, and other Greeks, especially Diodorus. Manetho (ca. 290 B.C.), an Egyptian priest, wrote in Greek a history of his land which was used by later chroniclers but is now lost. The list of thirty dynasties, or families, into which he divided the kings of Egypt has been proved generally accurate by modern archaeological discoveries, and his dynastic divisions are still used in the writing of Egyptian history. For the most part, again, our information is derived from the surviving written records and the actual physical remains of Egyptian civilization. But these differ greatly in character from the archaeological discoveries in Babylonia.

The Egyptians built their temples and monuments of enduring stone, and many of them are still standing. Their tombs were "houses of eternity," likewise constructed of stone or cut as chambers in the rocky cliffs to the west of the Nile. On the walls of the temples the kings carved inscriptions and pictures to record their wars and achievements beside religious texts designed to secure the good will of the gods. In the endeavor to secure the perpetuation of the life of this world in the next, as we shall see (p. 53), the Egyptians placed all sorts of objects in the tombs, and carved or painted on their walls scenes of work and play accompanied by texts recounting the positions and the deeds of the occupant of the tomb along with the magic formulas necessary to continued existence.

Quantities of papyri (Egyptian "paper" made from strips of the papyrus reed) have been found preserved in the dry soil of Egypt and inscribed with religious texts, works of literature and science, letters, accounts, and many other kinds of private and public papers. Though the mass of records of daily life such as have been preserved in the Babylonian clay tablets is not nearly as great for early Egypt,[1] and though fewer ruins of dwelling places still exist, yet from the available sources of Egyptian history, monumental, written, and pictorial, historians have been able to present a fuller, and in many respects clearer, picture of the history and life of Egypt than of the Sumerians and the Semites in the land of the Two Rivers.

GEOGRAPHY "Egypt is the gift of the Nile"; so wrote the Greek Herodotus. All phases of Egyptian life depended on or rose out of the geographic features of the Nile Valley, and of these the most dominant is the river itself. The rivers which join to form the Nile rise in the lakes of central Africa and in the mountains of Abyssinia. As the united river leaves the region today called the Sudan, it winds its way tortuously northward in great loops, its path obstructed occasionally by masses of hard rock which create the six cataracts of the Nile. Below the first cataract and to the north lies the ancient land of Egypt, where the Nile flows through a desert some seven hundred and fifty miles long and twelve to thirty miles wide between the cliffs on either side. Augmented by the spring rains of Africa and the melting of the Abyssinian snows, the river swells, gathers black soil as it comes down through the hills, and then overflows its banks wherever it can. The deposits of silt which it leaves behind as the waters recede renew the rich land of Egypt. The arable soil of the upper valley ranges from nothing to ten miles in width and tends to vary in size with the rise of the Nile. Midway in the river's course in Egypt a secondary channel branches to the left, flows parallel with it for a distance, then turns west, creating a fertile oasis, called the Fayum. When the waters of the Nile meet the Mediterranean, they drop what is left of their burden of soil. Here through the centuries they have gradually constructed in

---

[1] This generalization will not hold good for the later Macedonian and Roman periods of Egyptian history for which we have a bountiful supply of such records (pp. 289, 325).

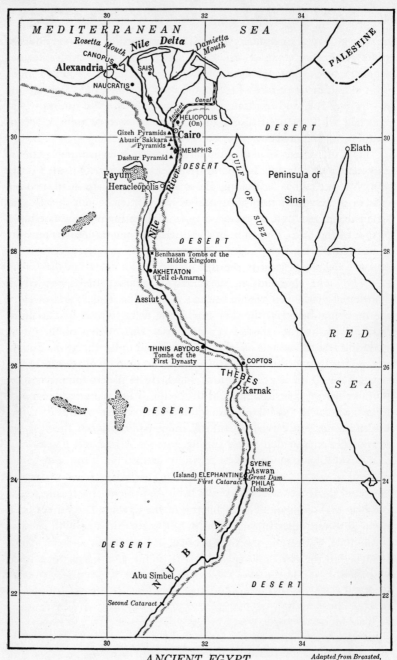

ANCIENT EGYPT

Adapted from Breasted,
Ancient Times. Courtesy of
Ginn and Company, publishers.

an ancient bay a triangular piece of land, measuring over one hundred miles from base to apex, called the delta. The total cultivable area from the first cataract to the sea is less than ten thousand square miles. The inundation begins in June and is over by December. For the rest of the year the land must be irrigated, and today, as in antiquity, the water is still lifted into canals and ditches by water wheels driven by animals, or by buckets carried by peasants.

The sun ranks second only to the Nile as a controlling factor in Egyptian life. The night is dark and cold, but when the sun rises in splendor and sheds its warm, life-giving rays, all the land rejoices. Sunrise and sunset are so glorious, the warmth of the sun so welcome, that one can readily understand why in ancient Egypt men worshiped it as the chief god. The air is dry and pure; in winter the temperature is balmy, and even the heat of summer is not oppressive. Egypt was and is a delightful land in which to live.

The same problems of centralization and particularism which Babylonia faced were met in ancient Egypt. The long, narrow valley of the upper Nile and the divisions of the delta formed by the many branches of the river tended to create local units, proud of their local gods and jealous of their neighbors. On the other hand, the river itself, as the chief route of travel, was a bond of unity. The ultimately recognized necessity of a single control over irrigation, lest some parts get too much, and others too little, of the water, strengthened the hands of those kings who ruled over the whole country. The periods of union under strong kings were periods of prosperity; the generations of disunity were ones of depression and decline.

A great advantage which Egypt possessed in comparison with Babylonia was its relative isolation. The deserts and the sea which surrounded it proved effective barriers to prevent those continuous troubles with invaders which Babylonian rulers faced. There were occasional difficulties with peoples to the south; the Libyans who lived in the narrow stretch of fertile land along the northern coast of Africa filtered into the delta and caused some trouble on its western border; and there were, as we shall see, a few invasions of people who came by sea or across the Syrian desert on the east. But for the greater portion of their history, the Egyptians lived tranquilly and developed their civilization unmolested. When properly watered, the rich soil rewarded them with a bountiful supply of food; the river provided an easy highway for trade and furnished their tables with fish; the marshes pro-

duced reeds for their dwellings and papyrus for their writing and
were the habitat of many varieties of edible birds; the animals who
lived on the edge of the desert gave them opportunities for hunting;
the stone of the cliffs—sandstone, limestone, granite, and the finer
alabaster and diorite—furnished materials for temples and statuary;
in the hills to the east and in Nubia on the south were deposits of
copper and gold. Only wood was lacking; except for the acacia, the
sycamore, and the palm, there were few trees in Egypt. The cedar and
other fine woods which the Egyptians delighted to use had to be
imported. The Egyptians were well content, and their political, economic, and social structures, their writing and their calendar, their
religion and their art—all show the influence of the land itself.

THE PREDYNAS-
TIC PERIOD

The long centuries which intervened between the first
appearance of man in Egypt during the pluvial ages
and the achievement of unity by the first dynasty are
included in the term "the predynastic period." The materials upon
which our knowledge is based are scarce, and most of those available
have only recently been discovered: a few Old Stone Age implements,
the remains of a few villages, and, most important, graves which contain bodies, pottery, implements of stone and metal, jewelry, and other
objects. Some information too may be gleaned from later customs and
from legends, but most of the actual records, unfortunately, lie buried
in the mud of the Nile.

Chellean and Acheulean axes lying on the sands of cliffs and
terraces bear witness to the presence of men in the region of the Nile
during the early ages. As the Sahara dried into desert, some of its
people undoubtedly sought refuge in the valley, where traces of them
have been found at a place called Badari and in the Fayum. The
Badarians, a short, slender race with small, narrow skulls, were already skilled in all of the neolithic arts. They lived in villages, worked
their farms, tended their animals, wove linen, made fine pottery and
excellent tools of pressure-flaked flint and polished stones; they even
knew slightly the use of copper. They adorned themselves with beads
of stone and shells and with combs of carved ivory, and they painted
their faces under the eyes with malachite, ground on slate palettes.

A second wave of invasion from north Africa was followed by the
intrusion of Semites from Asia into the delta. There is also some evidence of a movement of peoples down the Nile from the south. The

newcomers blended with the Badarians to form a single people with a language which contained both African and Semitic elements.

The Egyptians of the full predynastic period were like the Badarians, short and slender; their hair was dark and often curly, and the men wore short, pointed beards. They used the skins of animals as clothing, the chieftain signifying his power by a lion skin, but they also knew the values of flax and they made fine linen garments. They worked flint to make knives, securing by pressure a saw-tooth edge, which is at times so fine as to be almost invisible. For large tools and weapons they polished harder stones into axes, spearheads, and maces. With bows and arrows they hunted the animals of the desert and, with throw sticks, the birds of the marshlands. They made fine pottery, some of which they adorned with pictures of boats and men, of animals, birds, and fishes and which they learned finally to coat with a glaze. In the latter part of the period they achieved the making of stone jars and dishes. From green slate they made palettes, often in the shapes of animals and sometimes engraved with pictures, and on these they mixed the paints with which they decorated their faces. The earth, tilled with the hoe and with a primitive plow drawn by oxen, produced wheat, barley, and flax. Goats, sheep, and cattle were herded, and geese and ducks were kept as domestic fowl. Men lived in houses of wattle or of sun-dried brick. Their dead were buried in the desert in pit graves, sometimes lined with brick or wood, and occasionally in jars or coffins of clay, a few tools and supplies of food for the next world in jars comprising the furniture of the tomb.

The greatest achievements of this early period were made in the region of the delta, perhaps because the greatest mixing of peoples and ideas took place there, or perhaps because the people of that area were certainly in contact by land and by sea with Crete, with Syria, and with Mesopotamia, where civilization was likewise advancing. The men of the delta discovered or learned the use of the potter's wheel, advanced the working of metals, developed art, created a method of writing, and invented a calendar. The earliest records of Egyptian art are found on pots and on the walls of the predynastic tombs.

Writing, the product of art, began with pictures of objects and actions. Soon the pictures came to represent sounds, too. Although some signs, by a process of simplification of their values as sounds, were used to represent single letters, hieroglyphic writing never became truly alphabetic. The older usages continued, and the texts which have survived contain a mixture of signs which represent single consonants (there are no true vowels in hieroglyphics), of others which stand for groups of consonants, and of still others which are true pictures of objects. This picture writing was to a striking degree drawn from the life of the Nile Valley. Thus the lizard, because of its ubiquity, came to represent infinity. A boat with its sails up represented south or upstream, one with its sails down, north or downstream. On the monuments and in the tombs the pictures were often drawn with great care and fidelity. The Greeks, who misunderstood the character of Egyptian monumental writing, thought that it concealed the secrets of the priests and called it hieroglyphics or sacred carving.

For records, for literature, and for ordinary writing, the Egyptians were fortunate in possessing the papyrus plant in place of the cumbersome Babylonian clay tablet. This reed grew in the swampy regions which abounded in Egypt. Strips, taken from the stem of the plant, were used alone at first; then men learned to place them vertically and horizontally and press them together. The natural glue which the plant contained bound the strips fast so that the "paper" thus made had extraordinary lasting qualities. On it, as well as on the walls of temples and tombs, the Egyptians wrote in hieroglyphics. But for ordinary work, such picture writing was too slow and laborious. Accordingly, the scribes in later ages simplified the pictures into single lines and produced a running or cursive script which the Greeks called hieratic, i.e., priestly. Later a still further simplification produced the demotic or popular style.

For many centuries all knowledge of the Egyptian language was lost. Finally, in 1822, a Frenchman named Champollion, after a study of Coptic (the Egyptian language of the Christian period written with modified Greek characters) and with the aid of the Rosetta Stone, succeeded in reading the hieroglyphics. This famous stone holds an inscription with the same text written in hieroglyphics, demotic writing, and Greek. It was found near the Rosetta branch of the Nile by one of Napoleon's officers. Since the time of Champollion, great numbers of inscriptions and writings on papyrus have been copied and translated.

After writing, the greatest invention of these men of the delta was the calendar. Through observation of the skies and the recurrence of the inundation they arrived at the concept of the year. Some early astronomer, noting that Sothis, the Dog Star (our Sirius), rose just before the sun on the same day on which the inundation began, established a year of 365 days on the basis of that star. The year was arbitrarily divided into twelve months of thirty days each with five feast days at the end. This year was actually a few minutes less than six hours too short, and despite the fact that gradually the rising of Sothis failed to correspond at all with the inundations or with the seasons, the Egyptians nevertheless clung to it as the beginning of the official year. After each 1460 years, comprising a Sothic cycle, the agreement between the year and the star was again established. Modern scholars have calculated that the first Sothic cycle was begun, that is, the calendar was first established, in 4241 B.C.[2]

The primitive political unit of the New Stone Age in Egypt was a small village or group of villages, later called by the Greeks a *nome*. The chieftain of the nome, who controlled the land and the peasants thereon, was regarded as the embodiment of the local divinity. Each nome had a special divinity, male or female, usually in the form of an animal or bird which symbolized the power of fertility or the majesty of the sun, and another who watched over the dead in the western desert.

Wars between nomes resulted in conquests, and these in turn to the formation of two kingdoms, the delta, or northern, and the upper, or southern, kingdoms. About 3400 B.C.,[3] when the kings of the south succeeded in conquering the north, Egypt was united and the classic era of Egyptian history began.

THE DYNASTIES   The first period of the history of unified Egypt is known as the "Old Kingdom," comprising the reigns of the first six dynasties or families of kings listed by Manetho. Tradition recorded the name and deeds of a king called Menes, who achieved this unity and founded the first dynasty. Recent discoveries, however, have brought to light three men, the "Scorpion King," Narmer, and Aha, all of whom had a share in the conquest. The last two had the surname *Men*. It seems likely, therefore, that the Menes of tradition may be a composite memory of the deeds of all three, associated with the last king, Aha, who lived about 3400 B.C. Succeeding rulers of the first and second dynasties completed the work of unification from their capital at Thinis. With the kings of the third dynasty (2980-2900 B.C.),

---

[2] A good description of this calendar is in Shotwell, *History of History,* p. 46.
[3] The dates here follow Breasted, *A History of Egypt.*

who moved the capital to Memphis at the head of the delta, Egypt began to reap the fruits of unity.

These rulers, particularly Zoser and Snefru, perfected the organization of the administration, conquered land beyond the first cataract of the Nile and in the mining area of the peninsula of Sinai, and developed trade by sending vessels to Syria for cedar logs. Zoser's prime minister Imhotep, a renowned physician and architect, built the Step Pyramid (pp. 54 f.), and Snefru erected the first true pyramid. The highest point of power and prosperity during the Old Kingdom was attained in the period of the Pharaohs of the fourth dynasty (2900-2750 B.C.), Khufu, Khafre, and Menkure, for whose tombs the three great pyramids of Gizeh were erected.

The fifth dynasty (2750-2625 B.C.) witnessed the introduction of the worship of the sun god, Re, as chief god of Egypt and father of its kings, the earlier kings having been worshipers and earthly representatives of Horus, another deity of the sun. Henceforth the kings bore, in addition to their older names and titles, a Re name and the title "Son of Re." For this god an official priesthood was established and great temples were erected.

The rulers of the dynasty expanded their trade with Syria and with the upper Nile and opened up commerce by way of the Red Sea with Punt (probably Somaliland), whence came myrrh and incense. They were unable, however, to control the growing power of the nobles. The land of the nomes and even the office of viceroy became hereditary possessions of noble families to the detriment of the central authority. The sixth dynasty (2625-2475 B.C.) saw the process completed by the end of the long reign of Pepi II, who ruled for over ninety years. After his death Egypt was again broken up into a series of small states. With this political collapse came also the decline of culture and the fall of the Old Kingdom. Under six dynasties, occupying a thousand years, Egypt had passed from disunity to unity, to great power, and then to disunity once more.

GOVERNMENT   The rulers of the third and fourth dynasties developed a highly centralized and efficient organization for the management of their kingdom, a pyramid of officials with the king at the apex. All Egypt belonged to him. He embodied in his person all of the divinities of the nomes and of the two kingdoms. Thus he became in his own person the god Horus, the strong bull, the vulture, the cobra, the reed, and the bee. After the fifth dynasty, he was regarded also as the physical son of Re. As king of both upper Egypt and lower Egypt he had a dual personality which required him to wear two crowns and, in the case of many kings, to have two tombs.

Ceremoniously he was addressed by all of his names and titles; familiarly he was known as the "Good God"; in the administration he was called the "Great House," Peraa or Pharaoh. Not only was he regarded as a god, but he was also the chief priest of all Egypt, representing the land before the gods. Every ceremony, every sacrifice, was performed either by him or in his name. The prosperity of Egypt was thought to depend on him, and it was believed that he called forth the waters of the Nile. He was the owner of all the land; he issued the calendar and set the times for planting; he regulated the water supply; he controlled and operated the quarries and mines; the workshops were his; all the temples were built by him and the tombs of the nobles were built only with his permission; in the period of the inundation he called the people out to labor on his buildings or to fight in his army. That he might know his possessions, a census of the land was taken every two years, and later, every year. Justice was established by written law under which rich and poor were treated with no discrimination. The god Re, in the days of his earthly rule, it was believed, had been just to all men and had brought prosperity to the earth. The king, as his son and successor, must follow in his footsteps and maintain justice by the power of Maat, goddess of truth. For this early period of human development the ideals of government thus set before the king and his assistants were very high.

To assist the king in carrying out his many duties there was a large group of royal princes, nobles, and scribes, at the head of which was the viceroy, the chief assistant of the king in all of his undertakings. Under the fourth dynasty, the crown prince normally served in this capacity, directing a highly centralized bureaucracy concentrated within the "Great White Wall" at Memphis. Theoretically there was a dual administration, one for each of the two kingdoms, but actually the duality did not extend beyond the titles. A prince or noble, appointed by the king, governed each of the nomes, superintending irrigation, the keeping of order, and the collection of taxes, calling out men for service in the local militia or for forced labor on order of the king, and administering justice in accordance with the written law. On the walls of the tombs of these nobles are inscribed proud boasts of their justice and philanthropy, and of the prosperity which they brought to their districts.

At the bottom of the official scale were the scribes, men who had learned to read and write in the temple schools. Their primary duty was the keeping of records. The Egyptians were inveterate record keepers and the pictures indicate that everything was written down in triplicate. The scribe also assisted in the administration of the nome or the bureau. Men who showed ability in this capacity or who developed special talent might rise rapidly to higher office and, if they gained the favor of the king, could reach the very summit of the administration, as the story of Joseph illustrates.

This elaborate bureaucracy was supported by an equally elaborate financial system. Taxes or rents were laid on land, houses, cattle, trees, produce, objects of industry, and persons, and were paid either in produce or in service. The service accomplished the works of the king, buildings, pyramids, irrigation ditches, and work in the quarries and mines; and the produce was used to supply the king's servants and to feed his laborers and dependents. Officials and priests received as salaries the income from taxes of specified towns or lands. When the nobles became powerful enough to regard their official positions and their sources of income as family possessions and therefore hereditary, the king lost control. Whereupon, the bureaucracy, and with it the central power, collapsed.

LIFE AND WORK UNDER THE OLD KINGDOM

From the literature, the pictures and inscriptions in the tombs, and the objects which have survived, the life of the people and the methods and results of their labors may be reconstructed. We may learn of the dwellings, the family life, the work and the play of the king and his nobles, the profession and knowledge of the scribes, and the toil and the products of the lower classes.

THE KING The king dwelt in his royal palace, surrounded by the nobles, courtiers, scribes, and workmen. The capital city thus created was usually located near the royal pyramid and consequently moved with each succeeding reign. The king had always a queen of the blood royal, whose son alone might inherit the throne, and in addition a harem of concubines, who had no legal existence and whose children might claim no share in inheritance. All of the royal activities, dictated by custom even to walks and meals, were surrounded with elaborate formalities. Courtiers had to prostrate themselves before the king and address him by a long list of titles and prayers before they could perform their duties. Such regulations must have added greatly to the already onerous burdens of his official and religious life. It is little wonder then that the Egyptian tales often represent the monarchs as being affected with ennui in the midst of their pomp and power.

THE NOBLES

Indeed the life of the nobles must have been freer and happier. The noble, like the king, had one wife whose children were legitimate and with whom he is often represented in statuary and pictures; many nobles doubtless had harems of concubines as well. The nobles lived in houses of brick or of wood with roofs supported by columns made of palm trunks, or of bundles of papyrus or of lotus reeds. These commodious and airy dwellings were surrounded by trees, shrubs, and flowers; the garden pools were adorned with water lilies and contained fish. Tapestries and paintings gave bright color to the rooms of the houses, and the furniture was both elegant and comfortable. The appurtenances of life were equally refined. Men wore simple, short skirts or aprons of fine linen, while women attired themselves in tight-fitting garments which reached from the shoulders to the ankles; wigs were worn by both sexes, the beard of earlier times having been completely abandoned;[4] many cosmetics and ointments were used in the toilet, and jewels, cunningly worked, added decoration to the appearance. Foods and beverages were varied and abundant.

The responsibilities of the management of estates or of government office were lightened by many amusements. The king or the noble might play a favorite game, resembling chess, with his wife, or visit the harem, or disport himself with his children in the garden, or go boating on the "lily lake" in the marshes or on the river; he might hunt for birds with a throw stick, or catch fish with a two-pronged spear. Sometimes he rode abroad in a sedan chair carried on the shoulders of his servants and watched the artisans in their shops or the peasants working in the fields or guarding their herds. Acrobatic stunts, wrestling contests, and water sports delighted him. Magicians performed their tricks, or storytellers related tales of olden times for

---

[4] The gods and the kings in their statues are usually represented with square beards, reminiscent of earlier times.

his delectation. Of the many stories which have survived, one tells of the magician Dedi.

Now when he reached the residence, Prince Hardedef entered in to make report to the majesty of King Kheops. And Prince Hardedef said: "O king, my lord, I have brought Dedi." Said his majesty, "Go bring him to me." Then his majesty proceeded to the pillared halls of the palace and Dedi was brought in unto him. And his majesty said, "How is it, Dedi, that I have never seen thee before?" And Dedi said, "It is he who is summoned that cometh. The Sovereign summoned me, and lo I am come." And his majesty said, "Is it true what is said, that thou canst put on again a head that is cut off?" And Dedi said: "Yea, that I can, O king, my lord." And his majesty said: "Have brought to me a prisoner that is in the prison, that his punishment may be inflicted." And Dedi said: "But not on a man, O king, my lord! Lo, is not such a thing rather commanded to be done to the august cattle?"

And a goose was brought unto him, and its head was cut off; and the goose was placed on the western side of the hall, and its head on the eastern side of the hall. And Dedi said his say of magic, and thereupon the goose stood up and waddled, and its head likewise. Now when one part had reached the other, the goose stood up and cackled. And he had a duck brought unto him, and there was done unto it the like. And his majesty had an ox brought to him, and its head was made to tumble to the ground. And Dedi said his say of magic and the ox stood up behind him.[5]

The greatest glory of the noble was the service of the king, for which he received the ultimate reward of a tomb in the royal cemetery. On its walls he proudly recorded his titles and the favors which the "Good God" had bestowed on him even to the great privilege of being allowed to kiss the royal foot.

EDUCATION   Since education was a prime necessity for the ruling class and the sole means by which men might rise through service from the lower to the higher ranks of society, there developed in Egypt a group of learned men who made great advances in the realms of knowledge. In the teaching of reading and writing, moral training was also given the student through the copying of precepts, proverbs, and literary works.

Elementary knowledge of arithmetic and geometry was essential. The Egyptians could do ordinary sums and could solve problems involving one unknown quantity, but their work was complicated

[5] Erman, *Literature of the Ancient Egyptians,* pp. 42-43.

by the great difficulties they encountered in dealing with fractions. They could measure the area of land by means of triangles and calculate the number of bushels a granary would hold, or the weight of a piece of granite. Men of skill advanced far beyond these simple achievements. The architects learned much of surveying and of mechanics; the preparation of the calendar required the study of astronomy. In the midst of magic, the doctors developed from experience a remarkable knowledge of medicine and surgery. All knowledge or search for knowledge, however, was essentially practical, applied to the problems of daily life; even the ethical maxims were devoted primarily to the behavior necessary for worldly advancement.

TRADE AND INDUSTRY
Merchants carried goods up and down the Nile and engaged in active trade in the town markets where exchange was carried on both by barter and by means of established weights of gold and silver. The king sent merchants to Crete and into Syria whence came wood and probably goods of the Babylonians. We have accounts of exploratory expeditions of officials of the sixth dynasty into Nubia for ebony and ivory, and there are records of voyages down the Red Sea to Punt for incense and spices.

Artisans toiled in the great workshops attached to the palaces of the king and the nobles and to the temple of Ptah, god of artisans, at Memphis. In addition there must have been craftsmen in the towns who supplied the needs of the everyday life of the people. Many exceedingly fine products of their work have been found in the tomb deposits: jars and boxes of clay, some beautifully glazed and painted; stone dishes of almost porcelain thinness and great beauty of form; comfortable furniture of wood, the finest made of Lebanon cedar; garments and tapestries of linen; vessels and tools of gold, silver, and copper; jewelry inlaid with colored paste and precious stones; paper, rope, mats, and nets of papyrus; and boats of either papyrus or wood. In all phases of industry the artisans had attained a high level of technique, and the quality of their products proves an aesthetic appreciation and a demand for beauty in objects of daily use.

Of the social status and privileges of these merchants and craftsmen we have almost no information, since apparently in this period they did not have the great privilege of burial in tombs, and since the papyrus records of their affairs have perished. The middle class of merchants and businessmen in the towns were certainly prosperous, however, and there were probably many free artisans.

AGRICULTURE
The land, which belonged to the king, was granted by him to subjects. Large tracts were held by the temples and the nobles and, in the earlier period, by free farmers of lower estate. The increasing power of the priesthood and of the hereditary officeholders during the fifth and sixth dynasties led to the decline if not to the disappearance of the small farmers. The great bulk of the peasantry were at all times serfs on the landed estates, living in mud-brick houses clustered in little villages or in the towns. They scratched the ground with crude plows, broke clods with hoes, and used goats or cattle to tread in the seed. After the planting their important task was the handling of the water in the irrigation ditches. At the harvest the men cut off the heads of the grain, while the women and children gleaned. After the grain had been threshed on the treading floor, it was stored in barns, the scribes keeping accurate account. Herds of cows, goats, and sheep were tended and ducks and geese were fattened in the barnyard; birds were netted in the marshes and fish in the river. During the period of the inundation the peasants were called to labor on the works of the king, being then lodged in huge barracks and fed from the royal stores.

The Egyptians are represented on the walls of the tombs in all their multifarious activities as a happy, easygoing folk continually exchanging badinage with one another. Even though they complained of the taxgatherer and engaged in occasional strikes against unjust or dishonest officials, they were contented so long as they received a sufficient supply of food. The celebration of the festivals of the local deities provided them with their chief forms of pleasure.

RELIGION
All phases of the life of Egypt were permeated by religion. Though for the average man, the local deities remained the center of life, out of the multiplicity of these primitive local gods the priests erected a theocratic hierarchy. When, with the fifth dynasty, Re, the sun, became the great god of all Egypt, many of the local gods came to be regarded as identical with him. Thus Amon, the ram-headed god of Thebes, carried the sundisk between his horns, and Sobk, the crocodile god, wore it on his head. Other divinities were grouped around Re in enneads (nines). Ptah, god of Memphis, was the god of artisans, the maker of the universe "who existed from the beginning with all things in his thought," and Thoth, scribe of the gods, taught men to write. Osiris, who represented the Nile and its fruitful black soil, became the center of an immortality

cult. The story was told of how Osiris was killed by his brother Set; how Isis, his sister-wife mourned and wandered in search of his body until she found it; how his son Horus warred with Set and was victorious; how then Osiris was restored to life and established as the ruler of the dead in the Western world.

Belief in immortality seems to the modern student to have been the dominant feature of Egyptian religion, and preparation for the next world the consuming interest of life in this. In fact life in the valley of the Nile was so delightful that the Egyptian endeavored by every available means to continue it in the hereafter. Concepts of immortality were many and varied, and there were several names for the vital principle which survived death, the most familiar of which were the *ka* or spiritual double, and the *ba* or soul. The preservation of the body in the dry sands of the desert convinced the Egyptians that life continued in the body itself after death. To protect the body so that the ka might continue to live in it, they built massive tombs and developed the science of mummification. The god-king "slept in his pyramid" and the courtiers in their mastabas around him (p. 54). In case the body should be destroyed despite all precautions, the tomb was provided with statues and pictures in which the ka might continue its life. All sorts of objects were put into the tomb for the use of the dead, and offerings of food were made in the tomb from endowments established for the purpose. Then lest these offerings should fail and the ka starve, pictures of food offerings were carved and painted on the walls to serve the needs of the dead by magic means. Pictures of all sorts of activities were added to carry out the illusion of continuing in the tomb the life of the Nile.

The Egyptians believed that there was also a place somewhere in "the Western world," along the banks of the Celestial Nile or of the Nile of the underworld, where the dead gathered for eternity. This idea seems first to have been associated with the king who crossed the "lily lake" or mounted the ladder to the sky to become one with his father Re and to traverse the heavens and pass through the underworld with him. With the development of Osiris worship the idea grew of a land where the water of the Nile was always abundant, where grain grew taller than a man's head, where cool breezes always blew and life was eternally delightful. To reach and enter this land was not easy. First it was necessary to cross a desert filled with snakes, scorpions, and evil spirits. This done, the soul entered the judgment hall of the gods. With Thoth, the scribe, keeping record, the heart was weighed against the feather of truth; if found guilty, a fearful creature waited to devour it. Then before the throne of Osiris and by a formula which is today called the "negative confession," the dead man pronounced himself guiltless of murder, theft, deceit of any kind, or of mistreatment of the poor and needy. If the gods judged him "true of words," he became one with Osiris forever. In this eternal felicity, noble, scribe, and eventually even common men might hope to share.

ART AND
ARCHITECTURE
Our knowledge of the artistic skill of the Egyptians is derived for the most part from those examples which were dedicated to the service of the gods and of the dead. From the pictures in the tombs we have learned that they built beautiful houses, elegantly adorned; but of these houses and their decorations nothing remains. Stone jars and painted vases, a few pieces of furniture, jewelry, and amulets are living evidences of the skill of the craftsman and the aesthetic taste of the Egyptians. But for architecture, sculpture, and painting we must depend on the temples and the tombs, "houses of eternity."

The temples, built of stone, were in later periods and almost surely in the Old Kingdom, made in three divisions: an open forecourt surrounded by a colonnade and wall, a lofty pillared hall, and to the rear a series of small rooms. The central one of these was the holy of holies where was kept the cult statue of the god; the others were used to house the implements of service. Many forms of columns were employed to support the heavy stone ceilings: square pillars, fluted shafts, and stone replicas of the columns of lotus, papyrus, or palms which served the houses of the living. The total effect was massive, often heavy, but always awe-inspiring. The fifth-dynasty temples of Re, approached through a covered causeway from a chapel on the edge of the cultivated land, consisted of an arcade surrounding a huge obelisk, a massive pillar of stone surmounted by a pyramidion or small pyramid, the symbol of the sun.

The building of tombs required the greatest ingenuity of the Egyptian architects. The earliest kings were buried in underground tombs entered by sloping tunnels and later made up of many chambers. These were replaced by simpler underground tombs with superstructures of brick shaped like a bench and called today *mastabas*. Imhotep, architect of King Zoser, began the building of pyramids when he erected a mastaba of limestone and then superimposed on it five similar

WOODEN PANEL FROM THE TOMB OF HESI   KHAFRE

RAHOTEP   NEFERT   PEPI I AND HIS SON

EGYPT — OLD KINGDOM
Cairo

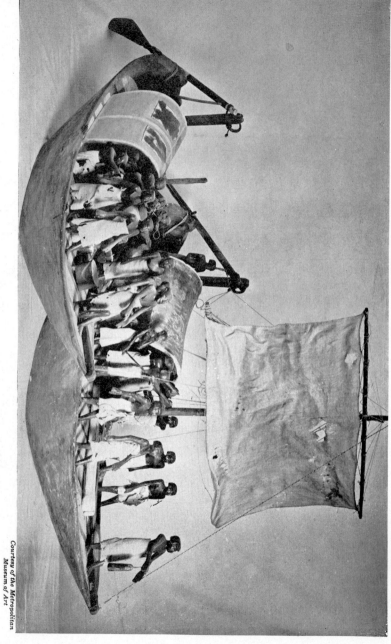

MODEL OF BOATS FROM AN EGYPTIAN TOMB

structures, thus creating the terraced monument known as the Step Pyramid. At the base he built a temple for the worship of the king and around the pyramid a series of small chapels noteworthy for the first known use of fluted columns. The whole area was surrounded by a massive stone wall. This first stone structure remains today one of the masterpieces of architecture. Snefru improved on the work of his predecessor by creating a structure of seven terraces and filling in the steps.

Pyramid building achieved its highest point in the great tombs of the fourth dynasty. The great pyramid of Khufu, 755 feet square at the base, 481 feet high, and containing 2,300,000 blocks of stone which average 2½ tons each, took, Herodotus says, 100,000 men twenty years to build. The blocks were cut in the quarries to the east of the Nile, carried on boats to the site, dragged up ramps to the structure, lifted into place, probably by wooden cranes, and fitted with marvelous precision. Passages and rooms, indications of great architectural ability, provided burial places for the king and queen within the pyramid. At the base stood a temple, access to which was given by a causeway leading from a smaller temple on the edge of the desert. This lower temple of Khafre remains, and beside it the famous Sphinx with a lion body and a human head, portrait of a king and symbolic of his power. The three pyramids of Gizeh, symbols of the sun god and tombs of the kings, are tributes to the power of the rulers and their ability at organization. Around the pyramids were arrayed in orderly fashion the limestone mastabas of the nobles of the successive reigns.

The statuary which has survived was dedicated not to the aesthetic enjoyment of the living but to the services of the dead. Wood, copper, limestone, and even such a hard material as diorite were carved or modeled into likenesses of men, their wives, and children that the ka might dwell in them. Some of the figures are seated, others standing with one foot advanced as in the act of walking. While there is a certain stiffness, due in part to the material and in part to convention, there is also high artistic value in the dynamic modeling and the life-like expression of many of these statues. The wooden statue known as the Sheik el Beled, the limestone group of Rahotep and Nefert, the diorite statue of Khafre, and the copper statues of the two Pepis deserve to be ranked among the great works of all time.

Pictorial art, likewise devoted to religious purposes, dealt with the practical problems of the service of the gods or the dead, and was dominated by convention rather than by aesthetic consideration. On wood and stone the artist carved in low relief and painted all the scenes of daily life. A noble sits before an offertory table, or stands, staff in hand, watching his workmen; although his face is in profile, his eyes are full face; his shoulders are forward, but his hips and legs are sideways. The artist, it is easy to see, either did not know or was not interested in perspective. Peasants, workmen, and animals follow, in general, the same conventions. Scenes which belong in the same plane are placed in successive rows upon the walls. No attention is paid to relative size, since in magic the small picture has as much value as the large. Modern concepts are thus rudely violated; yet the pictures have such an air of reality, such an amazing vitality, that one soon forgets the modern in enjoyment of the ancient.

CONCLUSION   The Egyptians had solved the problems not only of living, but of living gracefully and joyously and righteously. Like the contemporary Babylonians they had learned the processes of agriculture, industry and trade. They possessed a system of writing and the Sothic calendar. Highly centralized government and written law had brought prosperity and a fair amount of happiness to the people. The fundamentals of mathematics and science and the basic principles of stone architecture were Egyptian contributions from the Old Kingdom, while sculpture and painting had been brought to heights which later generations of Egyptians could scarcely equal. Enthralled with the pleasant life of the Nile Valley, the Egyptians had endeavored to look beyond the veil and to answer the eternal question of life after death. On imperishable materials they had left records of their achievements by means of which, when political stability was again secured, later generations were enabled once more to advance.

THE MIDDLE KINGDOM

After three centuries of disunion, the rulers of a city on the upper Nile, known to the world by its Greek name, Thebes, succeeded in reuniting Egypt under their sway and establishing the age called the Middle Kingdom. The period which followed the sixth dynasty was marked by confusion. Manetho records the kings of two dynasties (the seventh and eighth), who reigned without power at Memphis, and of two others (the ninth and tenth) at Heracleopolis, a little further south, who made boastful but unenforcable claims to power. Fragments of the writings of a sage named Ipuwer give a picture of revolutions and disorders, of foreign invasion and universal ruin. There were certainly inroads of Negroes into the south and probably of Semites and Libyans into the delta.

The work of rehabilitation was begun by princes of Thebes, the Intefs and Mentuhoteps of the eleventh dynasty. The most renowned memorial of their achievements is the mortuary temple of Mentuhotep III, a small pyramid surrounded by a series of colonnades, backed up against the cliffs to the west of Thebes. The work which they began was finished by the kings of the twelfth dynasty (2000-1788 B.C.), established with Thebes as its capital by Amenemhet I. These Pharaohs, the most famous of whom were Sesostris III and Amenemhet III, established order throughout the land and restored a unified system of irrigation control. They protected the border of the delta from the Libyans on the west and invaded Syria on the east. They dug a canal around the first cataract, conquered the land up to the second, and erected great fortresses in Nubia to the south. Trade with Syria, with Crete, and with the land of Punt was actively renewed, and a canal, precursor of the modern Suez Canal, was dug from the eastern branch of the delta to the Red Sea.

A large tract of wonderfully fertile land was opened to the Egyptians when a great embankment and a series of irrigation ditches were built to regulate the flow of water into the Fayum, the swampy oasis west of the Nile. The area thus reclaimed was held as crown property and became the favorite abode of the kings. A great palace, later known to the Greeks as the Labyrinth, was erected there with offices for the central bureaus, an office for each nome, and a shrine for each nome god.

GOVERNMENT The governmental structure of Egypt under these twelfth-dynasty kings differed from that of the Old Kingdom in the changed relations between the king and the nobles. The nobles, whose particularism had led to the confusion of the preceding centuries, had learned the necessity of unified control. The Pharaoh was therefore still recognized as the divine son of Re, and thought to be the source of all power and prosperity and to control the life-giving waters of the Nile. With the revenues from taxes, crown lands, mines, and trade, he supported a standing army and maintained an effective administration. Royal supervisors, "the Eyes of the King of Upper Egypt, the Ears of the King of Lower Egypt," traveled up and down the river to enforce his edicts. Trade on the Nile and commerce with foreign lands was directed by his agents, and the towns as centers of trade were governed by royal officials.

Hereditary nobles, however, governed the nomes. Though they were educated at the king's court and invested by him with their powers, they were miniature Pharaohs in their own districts. They controlled the land, maintained order, settled disputes, and collected taxes, a portion of which they paid to the king. They called out the militia only at the king's command, but the local services of forced labor were subject to their direct order. The peasants were required to quarry the stone which was carved into statues of the nobles, and to hollow their tomb chambers out of the western cliffs. Boastful accounts of their justice, mercy, and philanthropy were recorded on their tombstones.

LIFE, LITERA-
TURE, ART
Under the benevolent rule of the nobles, the lower classes prospered. Many peasants were free and owned or rented lands, sometimes in more than one nome. The maintenance of local courts, in addition to those of the king, increased the demand for scribes and enabled many of them not only to gain wealth and power but even to erect tombs for themselves and to proclaim the excellence of their calling. Artisans and merchants shared in the general prosperity occasioned by increased local demand for all kinds of goods and by the development of foreign commerce.

The happiness and prosperity of the period are reflected in its literary and artistic productions. It was the classical age of Egyptian literature, during which the tales of Sinuhe and of the Shipwrecked Sailor, the speeches of the Eloquent Peasant, the fable of the Two Brothers, and stories of magic were composed. Maxims, which show a shrewd sense of the practical in ethics, model letters, and schoolboy copybooks are found in Middle Kingdom papyri. The jewels and the small works of art which have survived from this period are the finest products of Egyptian handicraft. In sculpture, painting, and architecture, however, the period shows little advance. A certain tendency toward colossal statues, expressions of the "superhuman strength and imperturbable calm" of the kings, may be noted. The kings still erected pyramids, but of small size and inferior construction. The cliff tombs of the nobles, with colonnades cut in the living rock, are the most noteworthy architectural achievements.

RELIGION   The triumph of the Theban princes placed Amon, ram-headed god of Thebes, at the head of the Egyptian pantheon. He was identified with the ancient sun god and was known henceforth as Amon-Re. The priests of many of the nome gods sought recognition for their divinities by a similar identification. The small gods who had looked after the dead coalesced with Osiris, who became the national god of the dead, the "First of the Westerners," the god before whom all men must appear for judgment after death. All men shared in his domain; nobles, scribes, and even workmen and peasants might hope to find the joys of a future life. To assist them in attaining it, a collection of charms and instructions (known to modern scholars as the *Book of the Dead*) was made.

This halcyon age lasted for only a single dynasty. Under the weak kings of the thirteenth and fourteenth dynasties centrifugal tendencies again brought such disorder and confusion that Egypt fell an easy prey to invaders from Syria.

THE ORIENT DURING THE SECOND
MILLENNIUM B.C.

DURING the second millennium B.C. the range of historical activities, hitherto centered in the great river valleys, broadened out to include the western section of the Fertile Crescent called Syria, the plateau region of Asia Minor, and the islands and coasts of the Aegean Sea. In Syria groups of Semites developed small but prosperous states; northerners invading Asia Minor established there the great Hittite Empire; the peoples of the Aegean developed a brilliant civilization which they transmitted to other groups of northerners who penetrated the area and who, after learning the lessons of civilization, overthrew their Aegean teachers.

SYRIA

GEOGRAPHY   Between the great states of Babylonia and Egypt lay, like a bridge, the land called Syria, dominated by two parallel mountain ranges which run north and south. Toward the north the Lebanon Mountains, famous for their cedars, approach so closely to the sea that they leave but a narrow strip of land where flourished the ancient Phoenician cities of Tyre, Sidon, and Byblos. Between the lower end of the Lebanon range and Mt. Carmel is the great valley of Esdraelon, battlefield for the armies of the world from the days of Abraham to the World War.

South of Mt. Carmel the mountains recede from the coast, leaving a widening coastal plain and a piedmont land of low-lying hills with fertile soil well watered by mountain streams and seasonal rains. On the other side of the range is the trough where flows the Jordan. This famous river rises in the Anti-Lebanon Mountains, passes through the little Sea of Galilee and sinks far below sea level into the Dead Sea.

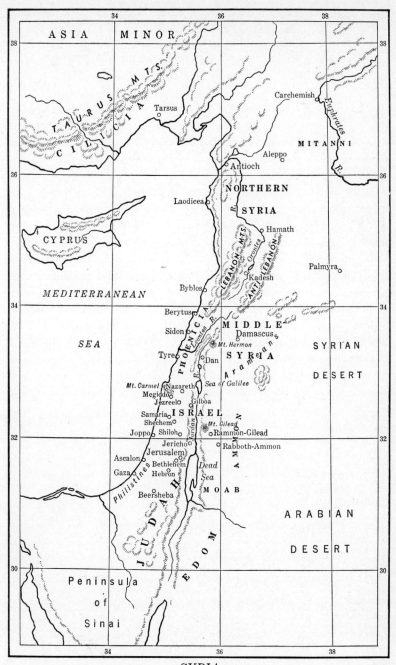

SYRIA

Beyond the eastern mountains lie grasslands whose inhabitants became famous in Biblical history, and north of them is a plain watered by the Abana River. In this plain at the head of the Mesopotamian caravan route lies Damascus, city of history and romance.

EARLY HISTORY   The history of Syria very nearly covers the span of human existence. Skeletons of the Neanderthal man have been found around Galilee. The Harajel culture on the slopes of Lebanon was a transition culture in the period between the Old and the New Stone Age. Massive stone structures give evidence of the presence of the Megalithic folk. Cave dwellings, hilltop shrines, and ruined villages bear the records of New Stone and Bronze Age peoples. When the earliest written records were made, the land was occupied by Semitic tribes akin in dialects to the Akkadians and Amorites of Babylonia. Southern Syria was occupied at a very early period, possibly before 3000 B.C., by the Canaanites. During the third millennium the Phoenicians entered the northern seacoast, and in the latter half of the second millennium the Aramaeans filtered into the region around Damascus, and the Hebrews came into the land of Canaan.

Throughout the third and the second millennia before the Christian era these regions were the prey of the Mesopotamian emperors on the one side and the Egyptian Pharaohs on the other, yet at the same time they formed the connecting link between the two great regions of culture. Sargon of Akkad (2600 B.C.) invaded northern Syria, crossed the Taurus range north into Cappadocia, and may even have reached Cyprus. Hammurabi's empire (1900 B.C.) certainly included the same part of Syria. The Biblical stories of Amraphel, who may possibly have been Hammurabi, and of the kings of Sodom and Gomorrah undoubtedly reflect memories of these early conquests.

So strong was the imprint of Babylonia upon the Syrian peoples that their scribes used the difficult cuneiform script and the Babylonian dialect even in their diplomatic correspondence with Egypt, and Syrian law and tradition show the influence of the eastern civilization. Even the local systems of weights and measures were Babylonian in origin.

At the same time Egyptian interest and influence were powerful in Syria, although there were apparently no attempts at conquest, nor any conflicts between the two great powers. The Pharaohs of the first dynasties traded with Byblos for cedar, and the Lebanon region played a part in the legend of Osiris. The story of the flight of

Sinuhe into Syria gives evidence that the name of Egypt was known and respected throughout the land during the Middle Kingdom. Shrines of Egyptian gods, Egyptian votive objects, inscriptions, and tombs in Syria bear witness to the presence of Egyptians there and to close relationship between the native rulers and the powerful monarchs of the south. Trade showing the influence of Egypt flowed actively along the routes which ran by the seacoast to the Phoenician cities, or through the hill country and then by way of Esdraelon or Shechem into Galilee and thence to Damascus. Along these routes there grew the powerfully fortified cities of the Canaanites, ruled by native princes.

THE
CANAANITES
Agriculture, in spite of the volume of trade, was the basic source of wealth to the land of Canaan. The story of Sinuhe ("there is barley there together with spelt; all kinds of fruits are upon its trees; and its wine is more plentiful than water"), the report of the Israelitish spies, and the "vine and fig tree" which recur in Biblical story all attest to the fertility of the land. Pottery and metal work, both native and copied from Egyptian and Babylonian wares, prospered. In high places the Canaanites worshiped agricultural divinities, called *Baalim,* often represented by huge stones. A central element in their religion was the worship of Ashtoreth, or Ishtar, the eastern mother goddess, and they freely adopted the gods of the Babylonians and the Egyptians.

THE
PHOENICIANS
North of Canaan along the seacoast was the land of the Phoenicians. Driven to the sea by the narrowness of their fields, they took readily to fishing and to commerce. Byblos and Sidon early became flourishing cities, and the inhabitants of one little village, crossing to a near-by island to gain security and to obtain better harbors, founded the great city of Tyre. Cedar and wool from the hill country behind them were their chief sources of wealth. The wool was woven and dyed purple with juice obtained from mollusks found along the seashore. They purchased and copied the goods of Babylon and Egypt and developed a rather high degree of skill in glass manufacture. In customs and in religion they did not differ much from their fellow Semites in Canaan. Throughout the early centuries the Phoenician cities were under the watchful eyes of the Egyptian Pharaoh; the great power and expansion to which they owe their fame came in a later age after the collapse of the power of the Nile.

THE AMORITES   In the fertile land east of the mountain ranges and along the banks of the middle Euphrates during the third and second millennia dwelt the Amorites, a third group of Semites closely akin to the Canaanites. Ever restless and troublesome, they were cursed as enemies by the Egyptians. Invading Mesopotamia, they established the great dynasty of Hammurabi in Babylon.

THE NORTH

The pressure which threw these Semitic peoples of Syria into confusion and drove them to invade Egypt found its origin far in the barbaric north where little-known events were preparing the future development of European history.

THE INDO-EUROPEANS   In the river valleys of eastern Europe during the New Stone Age lived a people known today as the Indo-Europeans. Like the Semites they were primarily nomads who wandered in the grasslands with herds of cattle and sheep. But they had domesticated the horse and had invented or adopted the wheeled cart, which made possible the development of an elementary agriculture in fertile river bottoms. Like the Semites of the south, too, their social organization was patriarchal, but their families were strictly monogamous. They worshiped a god of the sky and of the sun, the father of gods and men. Their greatest achievement, however, was their language. Their language moved, perhaps, even beyond the borders of the migration of the folk themselves. The result was that in the last millennium before Christ, a widespread group of peoples, not necessarily related racially, were all speaking dialects derived from the Indo-European tongue. Descended from it are the major European languages of today. It must be added, however, that in some regions local or more powerful tongues overcame the Indo-European and the only evidence of its original presence is to be found in the names of gods and men.

Of the movements of these people we have but scant knowledge. One or more groups apparently pushed into the Danube Valley, where they blended with older Danubians and Alpines. Thence some of this blend moved west to mingle with still other tribes and to become the Teutons and the Celts; others pushed south into Italy to form the Italic tribes. The ancestors of the Greeks crossed the Balkan range into the Greek peninsula in successive waves. Similar waves crossed from Thrace or over the Caucasus range into Asia Minor, where they formed combinations which produced the Hittites, the Phrygians, and other tribes. One group pushed down into the middle valley of the Euphrates, where the Egyptians later found a people called the Mitanni, who had conquered or displaced the Amorites and whose kings had Indo-European names.

Still other tribes which spoke Indo-European languages moved into the plateau of Iran and even reached India. The Kassites, who brought horses into Mesopotamia and conquered and ruled Babylon during the second millennium B.C., were the first of these in the plateau; the Medes and the Persians succeeded them, while the Sanskrit-speaking Aryans established themselves in India.

THE HITTITES   The Hittites entered Asia Minor during the third millennium B.C. and conquered and settled in the eastern half of the peninsula. This region is a great tableland, almost entirely surrounded by mountains. Through its center flows the Halys River, which rises in the mountains of Armenia, flows west, and then, with a wide-sweeping bend, turns northeast and cuts through the northern range to empty into the Black Sea. In the center of this bend, on a hill overlooking a tributary of the Halys, was located the Hittite capital called by them Hattusas but known today as Boghaz Keui. Information about the Hittites rests almost entirely upon archaeological evidence. Remains have been found of a primitive folk whose pottery shows close relationship to the earliest peoples of Turkestan, of Elam, and of Mesopotamia. Egyptian records furnished an account of the contacts between Egypt and the Hittites.

Archaeologists had become acquainted with the ruins of the capital and with a number of statues and reliefs which were carved in the rocks of the mountains when, in 1906, a German scholar unearthed in the remains of the capital a collection of clay tablets written in cuneiform. Some were in Semitic, which could be read; others were written in unknown tongues. In the midst of the World War a Czech scholar, Hrozny, announced his discovery that the Hittite language was akin to Greek and Latin and that he could read the tablets written in Hittite. Since then scholars have succeeded in deciphering the other tablets as well. When read, the documents were found to contain the archives of the great Hittite emperors.

The Hittites, on entering Asia Minor, established themselves as a ruling caste among the native tribes. They acquired sufficient strength so that about 1750 B.C. they were able to raid and to plunder Babylon itself. By 1400 B.C. they had built a great empire with all of Asia Minor in their grasp. Along the trade routes to the Bosporus and to the Aegean are graven reliefs, memorials of their power. The Trojans were their allies, and the tribes and cities of southern Asia Minor and of the Taurus region their subjects. Their might kept the rulers of Crete and Mycenae out of the Aegean littoral, and under their great king, Shubiluliuma, they were able to conquer northern Syria and to contend on equal terms with the power of Egypt.

The records, fragmentary though they are, are yet sufficient to prove that the Hittites were a people of great genius for organization. The king, symbolized by the winged sun disk, was absolute and sacred. A well-knit group of officials assisted him in the management of the realm. The empire was established on a federal basis by treaties between the Great King and his vassals, the kings, princes, or chieftains of subject states. A general assembly composed of these local rulers met regularly to give advice to the ruler, but the central authority kept full control over foreign affairs. Local government was in the hands of native rulers who, whether subjects or allies, were closely watched. A written code of laws, which in many ways resembled Hammurabi's code, established order and justice for all classes of people, even attempting to regulate prices and wages. The laws indicate that pasturage, rather than agriculture, was the basis of economic life. A system of roads and bridges connected the capital with the outlying sections and carried the goods of trade from Babylonia to the Aegean. Wealth came also from gold and silver mines and especially from the plentiful iron mines in the northern mountains.

The Hittites were probably the first people to mine and work iron.[1] A letter, probably from Hattusil to Ramses II, expressed regret that iron could not be sent to Egypt on request because the supply was exhausted. The letter added, however, that when more iron was received from the mines it would be forwarded. In the meantime the king was sending an iron sword as a present.

Around their capitals and around many of their cities the Hittites built massive walls of polygonal stones well fitted together and

---

[1] There is evidence of earlier use of iron by the Egyptians and Babylonians, but the metal was probably obtained from meteors. If the Hittites did not actually discover the process of smelting, they certainly practiced it and were responsible for a wide extension of the use of iron.

strengthened by towers at frequent intervals. In front of the palace gates stone lions stood on guard, and the walls were carved with figures in low relief. Near the palace is a remarkable shrine with a series of reliefs representing native princes who, attended by their local gods, were present at the union of the god of the Hittites and the mother goddess of Asia Minor. Many reliefs, presenting Hittites in characteristic dress with conical caps, short gowns, and pointed shoes, have been found in various places in Asia Minor, but the Hittite hieroglyphs frequently connected with them have not been deciphered.

The Hittites worshiped the sky god, whom they called Teshub, god of storms. For the sun, with whom they associated their king, they used the Egyptian symbol of the winged sun disk. In addition they worshiped the Anatolian mother goddess and her divine son who survived in later times as Cybele and Attis, respectively.

Although Hittite culture was a composite of the many elements which made up their empire, its basis was Babylonian, which had been introduced into Asia Minor in the long-past period of Sumerian supremacy. From that source came writing and the use of the clay tablet; from it also came law. Religion and art, however, were distinctive products of the people themselves. The great contribution of the Hittites to the civilization of the world was the mining and use of iron.

BABYLONIA AND ASSYRIA

The impact of the northern invaders was felt throughout the Oriental world. After a Hittite raid (ca. 1750 b.c.) brought to an end the dynasty of Hammurabi (p. 37), the Kassites, a people whose gods and kings bore Indo-European names, made themselves rulers of the great city and maintained themselves in power for 576 uneventful years. Their sole contributions to the history of the region were the extension of the use of the horse and the practice of numbering the years according to the reigns of each king. Their chief enemies were the Assyrians.

The origin of the Assyrians is obscure. A fiercely independent nation of peasants, they were probably Sumerian colonists, mingled with later Semitic invaders, who dwelt in the hill country of the upper Tigris. The list of Assyrian kings begins in 2250 b.c., after which there are records of their wars with the Amorite rulers of Babylon. Their opportunity for expansion to the west was blocked by the Mitanni, and an early bid for power about 1850 B.C. was effectively stopped by the Hittites. For centuries thereafter they carried on desultory wars with the hills people around them and with the kings of Babylon; then, in the last millennium B.C., when they had reduced to impotence the peoples of the Tigris-Euphrates, dawned the day of their greatness.

THE AEGEAN CIVILIZATION

DISCOVERY

Another great civilization to reach its climax and then fall before the might of the northern invaders was that which had developed during the early millennia in the Aegean area. Vicissitudes of time had wiped out all memory of it save for a few Greek legends until modern archaeologists restored it to its rightful place in history. The story of its recovery is a romance. Heinrich Schliemann, as a schoolboy in Germany, refused to accept the dictum of scholars that the Homeric story of the Trojan War was a myth. After accumulating a fortune he retired from business to devote his time and his wealth to the proof of his faith in Homer. In 1871 he began to dig into the hill of Hissarlik, the traditional site of Troy. There he found remains of nine settlements. In the second from the bottom he found ruins of a strong fortress and a deposit of fine jewelry. It was the sixth city, however, later excavated by Dörpfeld, which fitted the description of Troy in the *Iliad*.[2] Schliemann followed his success in the Troad by going to the mainland to search for Agamemnon's tomb and to excavate Mycenae where Agamemnon had lived. Again success attended him; on this ancient site he found the ruins of a great palace and the remains of rich burials.

Other archaeologists followed Schliemann in Greece and on the islands and built up the picture of the so-called Mycenaean civilization reflected in the Homeric poems. But there was no explanation for this civilization until further discoveries revealed its source in Crete. Encouraged by the successful excavations of legendary sites in Greece, an English archaeologist, Sir Arthur Evans, determined to excavate the site of Cnossus. There, according to the legend, Minos, the son of

---

[2] According to a recent report from the excavation which is being conducted by Professor Blegen of the University of Cincinnati, the seventh, not the sixth, city on the site appears to have been the Homeric Troy. The presence of large storage jars for grain, wine, and oil in the floors of the houses might be interpreted as suggesting that preparations had been made to withstand a siege, and there are many indications that the city was destroyed by fire. The sixth city appears to have been overthrown by an earthquake.

Zeus, had ruled and there Daedalus had built for him the labyrinth to house the Minotaur, a monster to which seven youths and seven maidens of Athens were yearly sacrificed. The Greek historians of the classical period called Minos the first founder of a thalassocracy (sea power) in the Aegean, and Plato and Aristotle referred to his laws. In 1899 Sir Arthur secured permission to dig the site of Cnossus. The first season's work (1900) opened up remains of a magnificent palace, and further excavations at Cnossus and elsewhere in Crete disclosed a civilization which rose from neolithic beginnings to magnificent heights, only to suffer decay and destruction. Of this culture the Mycenaean civilization was a relatively late and decadent product.

A series of terms have come into general use to describe the various phases of this culture, the whole complex being called Aegean civilization. Evans coined the word Minoan to apply to the Cretan phases; the contemporary culture of the islands is called Cycladic and that of the mainland, Helladic. Each phase has been divided according to pottery into Early, Middle, and Late periods, and these into still smaller subdivisions. Late Helladic is also called Mycenaean by a perpetuation of the older term. The chronology of these periods has been determined by the discovery of Egyptian remains in Crete and by the appearance of Cretan pottery in Egyptian tombs. Middle Minoan was contemporaneous with the Middle Kingdom in Egypt; Late Minoan corresponds with the first period of the Egyptian empire, and the Mycenaean period had begun by the reign of Amenhotep III in Egypt. The culture of the second city of Troy was in close relationship to Early Minoan; that of the sixth city, to Mycenaean.

RACE From the examination of skeletons scholars have concluded that in Crete the predominant element was long of head and short in stature, obviously of the type called Mediterranean and closely related to the Libyans of northern Africa. In the islands the same types have been found along with skulls of the round-head variety, indicating the presence of Alpine stock from the hinterland of Asia Minor. The mainland presents an additional mixture of Nordic peoples.

THE NEW
STONE AGE The archaeological record of civilization in the Aegean area begins with the New Stone Age. The inhabitants of Crete were farmers, herdsmen, and fishermen who lived in round or oval huts gathered together in villages. They made tools of obsidian and of polished hard stones, of

wood, bone, and horn. They wore garments probably of skin, though linen, perhaps from Egypt, had made its appearance. Their goats and sheep fed on the plains in winter, climbed and ranged over the mountain sides in summer. Acorns, nuts, fruits, and grains furnished the people with a supply of food which was augmented by the fish abounding in the Aegean. Fishing, perhaps, led to trade by sea, and daring sailors found their way to Egypt. The religion of this primitive folk centered around a mother goddess and curious, violin-shaped idols have been found in the islands.

AEGEAN
HISTORY

Of the actual events in Aegean history little is definitely known, and its course must be conjectured from archaeological discoveries. The introduction of copper, probably from Cyprus, and later of bronze made possible a great advance in civilization about the beginning of the third millennium B.C. Agriculture was further developed; industry flourished and trade expanded; the potter's wheel appeared and with it a brilliant technique in the decoration of pottery. Prosperous settlements grew up on the Greek mainland, on many of the islands, and on the hill of Hissarlik (Troy II, the second of Schliemann's nine settlements). In Crete, during the Middle Minoan period, flourishing cities appeared, and princes built fine palaces for themselves at Cnossus and at Phaestos.

In the fifteenth century B.C. (Late Minoan) Cnossus gained control over Crete and, possibly through a great fleet, over the whole Aegean basin. Many of the older settlements disappeared or were destroyed, notably Troy II and the village of Melos. A magnificent palace was erected at Cnossus as the center of this power. The city and palace were unfortified save for a small bastion, since the ruler of Cnossus held Crete under his control and dominated the sea with his fleet so firmly that he needed no wall for his defense. But during the second millennium the Greek mainland had been occupied by northern tribes, and toward the end of the fifteenth century B.C. these restless people began to assert themselves.

The power of Cnossus was declining when, around 1400 B.C., a band of marauders from the north fell upon the palace and sacked it. Marks of the fire are still everywhere evident in the ruins; the royal chessboard was dropped in the corridor; religious paraphernalia were abandoned in the shrine after a last desperate appeal to the gods; and unfinished vases were left standing in the workrooms. After the catastrophe, a miserable remnant of the people crept back to live in a corner of the once mighty structure, but they soon disappeared. Dust covered the place, and Minos became but a legend. The same fate befell Phaestos and the other settlements in Crete which had shared in Minoan culture.

THE PALACE   The palace was the great glory of the brilliant life of the Minoan age. It was a large and exceedingly complex structure of four stories so built on sloping ground that the main entrances and the great court, the center of palace life and official activities, were on the third floor. On the upper side of the huge central court were the throne room, the offices, and the storerooms equipped with huge jars—receptacles for the oil, wine, and grain collected as taxes. On the upper story were the reception rooms for social affairs. On the lower side, spreading downhill, were the domestic and industrial quarters. Here also was the royal family's two-story apartment with its private staircase and its bathroom with even a terra-cotta bathtub for the royal infants, a schoolroom, an olive press, workrooms, and chapels. A colonnaded staircase led from the central court to the lower levels. The whole structure was supplied with a system of sanitary drainage, which was still working when the excavators found it. Not far from the palace was a basilica, where Minos perhaps sat in judgment, and a theatral area or *choros* such as Homer says Daedalus built for "Ariadne of the flowing tresses," and in the valley below was a pavilion, where visitors stopped to wash their feet in a basin of ever-flowing water.

GOVERNMENT   At the head of the government of the Minoan empire AND SOCIETY   was the priest-king whose shrine was the palace and who survived in the memory of the Greeks as a lawgiver. A bureaucratic system collected taxes in kind and kept careful written records of the royal possessions. Of the details of this, and of local government nothing is known, although there were apparently royal representatives resident in the towns. A wealthy, landowning nobility surrounded the king; merchants and craftsmen lived in Cnossus and in the smaller towns; the peasants worked the land and tended their herds.

SOCIAL LIFE   From the decorations of the palace comes our chief information about the life of its denizens. The men wore kilts or tight-fitting "shorts" brilliantly colored. To these they added belts holding beautifully inlaid daggers, and they affected an abundance of jewelry, armlets, wristlets, anklets, and necklaces. On

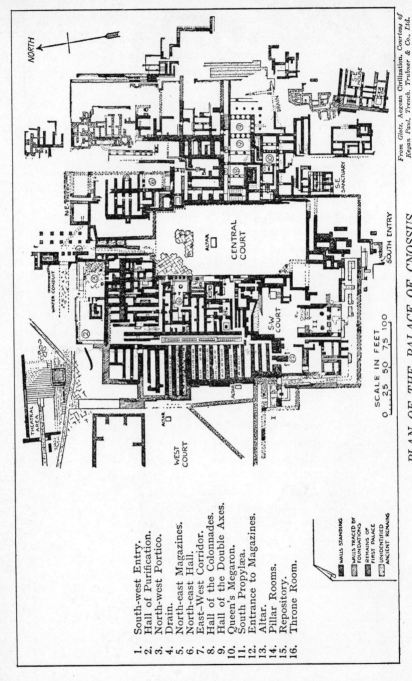

PLAN OF THE PALACE OF CNOSSUS

1. South-west Entry.
2. Hall of Purification.
3. North-west Portico.
4. Drain.
5. North-east Magazines.
6. North-east Hall.
7. East-West Corridor.
8. Hall of the Colonnades.
9. Hall of the Double Axes.
10. Queen's Megaron.
11. South Propylæa.
12. Entrance to Magazines.
13. Altar.
14. Pillar Rooms.
15. Repository.
16. Throne Room.

SCALE IN FEET
0 25 50 75 100

From Glotz, Aegean Civilization. Courtesy of
Kegan Paul, Trench, Trubner & Co., Ltd.

WALLS STANDING
WALLS TRACED BY
FOUNDATIONS
REMAINS OF
FIRST PALACE
UNIDENTIFIED
ANCIENT REMAINS

NORTH

THEATRAL
AREA

WEST
COURT

ALTAR

WATER CONDUIT

N.E. ENTRANCE

ALTAR

CENTRAL
COURT

S.W.
COURT

DRAIN

S.E.
HOUSE

S.E.
SANCTUARY

SOUTH ENTRY

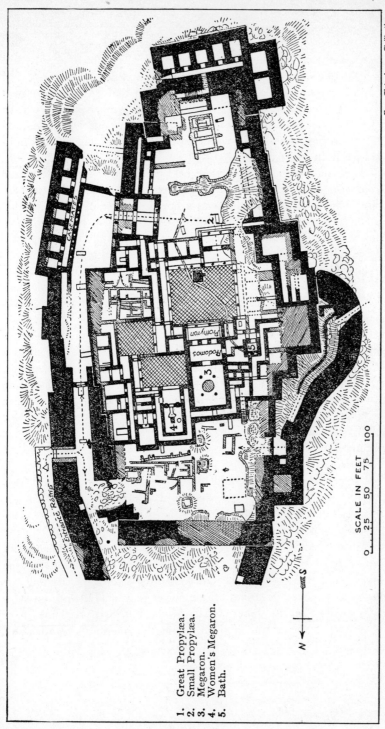

From Glotz, Aegean Civilization

PLAN OF THE PALACE OF TIRYNS

SCALE IN FEET
0   25   50   75   100

1. Great Propylaea.
2. Small Propylaea.
3. Megaron.
4. Women's Megaron.
5. Bath.

ceremonial occasions they wore a long robe. The women were garbed in cut and sewn garments of varied styles, flounced and scalloped and at times extremely décolleté. Colored designs and little gold plaques which frequently represented some religious symbol were sewn on their dresses and used for ornaments. The restraint which marked Oriental social relationships was apparently lacking, and women mingled freely in society.

Brilliant court assemblies were held, with music furnished by the seven-stringed lyre, the flute, and bagpipes. In the theatral area there were probably dances. Boxing was a favorite source of entertainment, but the greatest sport was bull-leaping. Athletes were trained to meet the charging bull, grasp his horns, and vault gracefully over his back.[3] Every indication points to a highly artificial but delightful culture.

THE COMMONERS The villagers worked their farms or, as of old, ranged the hills with their cattle. The common people who dwelt around the palaces and in the cities, however, apparently lived in comfort, doubtless following court customs and dress. Their houses were two and three stories high and sometimes contained as many as twenty rooms; doors and windows gave them a very modern appearance. For food the people had fish, meats, grains, beans, peas, goats' milk and its cheese, olive oil, and wine. Elaborate sets of cooking utensils of clay and copper have been found. From the town of Gournia comes the chief information about their industries, among which were weaving and dyeing, shoemaking, carpentry, ceramics, stonework, metallurgy, and the making of jewelry. In all these activities the small shop was the unit of work.

A surplus of wine, oil, and industrial products, on the one hand, and the lack of metals, ivory, and hard stones, on the other, made commerce essential, and the Cretans therefore became the first commercial people of the Mediterranean. Market places were built in the towns, and roads connected the various parts of the island. Cretan boats ranged the seas; their trade encompassed the islands of the Aegean and the coasts of the Greek mainland, even penetrating the Black Sea region. The strong Hittite power prevented them from gaining a foothold on the shores of Asia Minor, but their goods may have traveled over the Hittite highways into the interior. The island of

[3] Modern rodeo experts say that this feat is impossible. Pictures and models are our only evidences of its accomplishment. Evans, in *Palace of Minos*, III, discusses the problem.

Vaphio Gold Cup

BULLS IN A NET

Fresco from Hagia Triada

CAT HUNTING BIRDS

Candia

PORTRAIT FROM A FRESCO

Painting from Mycenae, Restored

LADIES IN A CHARIOT

CRETE

From Gournia. From Glotz,
Aegean Civilization.

OCTOPUS VASE

Faïence plaque from Cnossus
From Glotz, Aegean Civilisation.

WILD GOAT SUCKLING ITS YOUNG

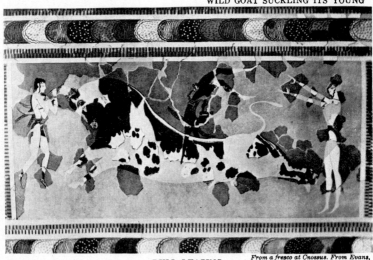

BULL LEAPING

From a fresco at Cnossus. From Evans,
Palace of Minos. Courtesy of
The Macmillan Company, publishers.

CRETAN ART

Cyprus, source of copper, was within their sphere of influence, and they carried on an active trade with Syria.

Their first contact with Egypt was established in the period of the Old Kingdom, and during the empire relations were constant. There were Egyptians resident in Cnossus; Egyptian influence was strong in art and architecture; and Egyptian records claim the subjection of the island and the payment of tribute. At the same time, pictures of Cretans and their vases, and objects of Cretan manufacture, have been found in Theban tombs. It is possible that the first great harbor works on the island of Pharos were built by these men for their trade with Egypt. In the west the name of Minos is associated with settlements in Sicily, and there is much archaeological evidence of Minoan activities in that island and in southern Italy.

For the furtherance of trade and government an elaborate system of weights and measures on a decimal basis was devised. Writing, too, was developed, pictographic at first but simplified into a linear script by the time of the great age, possibly alphabetic and surely not without influence on the Phoenician development of the alphabet. The records which have survived were cut on clay tablets, the use of which may have reached the Cretans by way of the Hittites. Unfortunately, since the Minoan script has not yet been deciphered, these tablets cannot be read; but they seem to belong to the palace archives. Of the literature of these people there is no evidence as yet.

WARFARE   The rank and file of the army was made up of relatively poor commoners, who wore no armor but carried slings or bows and sometimes spears supplied by the government. Cretan slingers and archers were famous throughout antiquity. The wealthier nobles rode to war in two-horse chariots and dismounted to fight behind huge man-covering shields, semicylindrical in form or shaped like the figure eight. Putties of leather protected the ankles of the warriors, and leather helmets, their heads; the size of the shields made other armor unnecessary. For weapons they used the straight sword of bronze, the lance, and probably the double ax.

ART   In life and in art these people were lovers of the beauty of nature. They preferred games, pageants, dances, and contests of strength and agility to the sterner pursuits of war, and these preferences are reflected in their works of art. Their favorite subjects were the human figure, the brilliant social gatherings of the court, animals, plants and flowers and trees, the octopus and the flying fish. No representations of war are to be found in the palace.

From the workshops of the Cretans came beautiful figurines of porcelain and ivory, and plaques of faïence work. In these miniature arts the workers showed great skill at representing the muscular structure of the human body and the posturing of animals. Goldsmiths and jewelers, exhibiting equal facility, engraved seal rings with pictures of animals, plants, men, and gods, and produced beautiful hammered work and inlay. The bull scenes from the Vaphio cups of hammered gold, the daggers inlaid with scenes of hunt and war (found on the Greek mainland but certainly of Cretan manufacture), and the gems of amethyst, chalcedon, onyx, lapis lazuli, and the like, are exquisite.

The finest of Cretan artistic achievements were their mural paintings. Though technique and conventions betray Egyptian influence, such pictures as the cupbearer, the dancer, the court scenes, the boy gathering flowers, and the cat hunting birds in the reeds show an eye for beauty in nature and a remarkable freedom and skill in reproduction.

The potters, in the forms and decoration of their jars, also produced work of aesthetic value, favoring, as subjects for ornamentation, flowers and the octopus. Vessels were made of stone and of metal; clay jars in imitation of metal forms have been found. The paintings and the vases of the end of the palace period, however, show the gradual appearance of formalism and the loss of the earlier zest and freedom.

RELIGION   Shrines, pictures, statuettes, engravings on gems and on rings, and votive objects are the chief sources of information about Minoan religion, and to these the legends and practices surviving into Greek times lend illumination. All of the evidence points to the fact that the chief divinity of the Minoans was a goddess, mother of gods, men, and animals, similar to, if not identical with, the Anatolian mother goddess. She is portrayed standing on a mountain top surrounded by animals, or sitting under a tree with a dove as her attendant, or coming from the underworld with snakes entwined around her. With her there often appears the Divine Youth, sometimes represented as a bull-man, or by the symbol of the double ax or the huge shield. Greek mythology indicates that he was believed to have died and to have returned again to life. The bull, represented by the story of the Minotaur, by many artistic portrayals of bulls and of men with bull's heads on their shoulders, and by the ever-present horns on the altars, played an important part in Minoan religion. In the shrines there appear many objects associated with divinity: trees, pillars, weapons—particularly the double ax—the horns of the sacrificial bull, shells from the sea, and terra-cotta plaques representing sacred animals. The divinities, possessing no temples, were worshiped in household shrines, in sacred groves, or in deep caverns. The most celebrated of the holy places was a cave on Mt. Ida, where many votive objects have been found and where later legend asserts that Minos went once every nine years to consult the gods about the well-being of his kingdom.

An important element in the religious ideas of the Cretans was a belief in immortality. The dead were buried sometimes in huge jars, sometimes in elaborate sarcophagi. The bodies of great men were placed in caves or in chamber tombs hollowed out of the hillsides. In the later period these tombs were rounded and covered with a cupola so that they looked like old-fashioned beehives and hence are called "beehive tombs." Offerings of food and drink were made to the dead, and in the graves were placed toys, weapons, vases, jewelry, and other objects of daily life.

DECLINE The concentration of power and wealth in the hands of the king at Cnossus seems to have resulted in general exhaustion and decadence, the drying up of the sources of inspiration in art, and a stultifying conservatism. There are indications that the peasants were sinking into serfdom and that craftsmen were forced into a paralyzing guild system. Conventionalism, checking initiative, appears on the vases and in the later pieces of art. When the Northerners sacked the palace about 1400 B.C., the whole structure of Minoan civilization in Crete collapsed. Its influence continued powerfully, however, on the Greek mainland, where leadership was assumed by a people whose civilization had been derived from Crete.

THE MYCENAEAN CIVILIZATION

The history of the Greek mainland during the Aegean Age is based on two sources: legendary accounts and archaeology, which by their diverse character and their failure to agree with each other have created many problems for the student. The historic Greeks had many legends about earlier non-Greek inhabitants whom they called Pelasgi,

Minyans, Leleges, and so on. These are followed by stories of invasions of Ionians and Achaeans, of Pelops, of Heracles and Theseus and Oedipus, of wars and raids, of the war with Troy and of the return of the warriors. While archaeology has proved the fundamental truth in the background of legend, it has not yet established the historicity of the Greek heroes.

THE INVASIONS   In an early period the first inhabitants of Greece had had Danubian affiliations with a strong infusion of the Mediterranean race. About 2000 B.C. bands of Indo-European raiders from the north appeared in Thessaly. They stayed there long enough to locate their sky god on Mt. Olympus and then moved south, probably in small warrior bands.

Of the movement south and the blend of the conquering invaders with the older peoples, the legend of Pelops may be a vague memory. It is fairly certain that the language of the newcomers prevailed. Place names which end in *-nthos,* like Corinthos (Corinth) and Tirynthos (Tiryns), and words with the stem-ending *-ss,* like *thalassa,* "the sea," [4] are examples of the survival of the older tongue.

Nothing certain can be told of the tribal relationships or of the sequence of tribal movements. The legends tell of Aeolians in the north, Ionians in central Greece and in the western Peloponnesus, and of Achaeans to the south. Archaeology, however, indicates the presence of at least two dynasties at Mycenae, neither of which can be definitely equated with the legends.

THE BLEND OF CULTURES   The newcomers speedily adopted Cretan civilization, which reached them about 1700 B.C., probably through the peaceful channel of commerce. In the resultant culture certain northern elements remained, at least for a time. Among these were gabled houses with central hearths, loose garments caught together by the fibula (safety pin), and the custom of wearing beards and mustaches. Minoan architects, however, probably helped them to build their palaces, to surround their citadels with walls, and to construct their roads and bridges. The walls of their buildings were adorned with frescoes in the Minoan style. Pottery, gold cups, jewelry, inlaid daggers—in short, the refinements of life—came from Crete or were made by local artists of Cretan blood or background. Before the end of the period the kings were constructing beehive tombs and the women were wearing garments Minoan in pattern.

[4] The word for "sea" seems to have been absent from Indo-European.

Political and social structures likewise felt the impact of civilization. In place of tribal leaders stood kings (the word *basileus,* meaning "king," is certainly non-Greek) bearing golden scepters and with god-given powers. Artisans were organized into guilds, and peasants were reduced to a semiservile status.

Similarly in religion there was a fusion of the two cultures, and the gods of the northerners were identified with the divinities of the countryside. The Great Mother extended her care to the newcomers. Zeus, sky god of the Indo-Europeans, dwelling on Olympus, became also Zeus, the Divine Youth, who was born in Crete and who died there. Athena, guardian of the citadel, apparently Aegean in origin, extended her control over the Achaean fortresses.

About 1400 B.C. the mainland communities entered upon the period of their greatest prosperity. They raided Cnossus and broke the power of Minos. Egyptian objects in Mycenae and Mycenaean wares in Egypt indicate the transfer of Egyptian interests occasioned by the shift in power.

ARCHAEOLOGI-
CAL REMAINS
Remains of the Mycenaean Age are found in many parts of the Greek world: a tomb at Orchomenus and a castle of Gla in Boeotia; the foundations of the royal palace on the Acropolis and Mycenaean graves recently discovered below the Areopagus at Athens; buildings and graves at Eleusis, at Corinth, and at many places in the Peloponnesus. Greatest in scope and best preserved are the structures at Tiryns and Mycenae (cities connected with the legend of the house of Atreus).

A massive fortress was erected on the hill of Tiryns at a point which controlled the head of the Argolic Gulf and the maritime terminus of the great commercial road to the Corinthian Gulf. The hill was surrounded by a tremendous wall pierced only by a well-guarded entrance and a small postern gate. Within the wall itself were galleries and chambers, perhaps for the storing of supplies against a siege, and, at the end of a well-built road which led through a series of formal gateways to a courtyard beyond, the royal palace. This structure was built on the northern plan, a vestibule and antechamber leading into a large room. The technical term for such a house is "megaron." A narrow passage at the side of the megaron led to the women's megaron to the rear. The walls of the buildings were beautifully decorated with a frieze of blue glaze and with wall paintings in the Minoan manner.

The establishment at Mycenae covered a larger area and was more elaborate. Mycenae was located in a commanding position at the head of the Argive plain, controlling both the plain and the highway which led north from Tiryns to Corinth. An early family of kings had possessed the site. They had attained great wealth and, with their families, were buried in pit graves amid a profusion of gold: gold masks on the faces of the king, gold jewelry, and gold plaques attached to the burial garments. Probably about 1400 B.C. a new dynasty took and rebuilt the citadel. A great wall was erected around the hill, and over the main entrance was placed a large triangular block bearing in relief a sacred column flanked by heraldic lions. Directly inside the gateway was the burial ground of the earlier rulers. Around this a circular wall was built, a row of seats within, thus enclosing an area, "a sacred circle," such as appears on the shield of Achilles in the *Iliad*. On the slopes of the hill were the houses of the nobles and retainers, and on its crest stood the palace, similar in plan and construction to that at Tiryns. To the rear of the palace a long staircase carefully covered by the wall gave access to a never-failing supply of water. A series of large beehive tombs were dug and erected in a near-by mound for the burial of the mighty kings of "golden Mycenae."

The sixth settlement on the hill of Hissarlik was contemporary with the citadels of Tiryns and Mycenae. The walls are still standing to a considerable height with three gates flanked by towers. Of the interior of the city little remains. The houses were constructed on the megaron plan, and all evidence indicates that the culture of the city approximated that of Mycenae except for certain local peculiarities, particularly in pottery where the Trojans exhibited a fondness for animal forms. The city occupied a favorable position near the entrance to the Hellespont and at the head of a trade route into the interior. Its power is indicated not only by the remains of its walls but by the legend which represents it as the center of a great alliance of the peoples of the Anatolian coast lands.

CULTURE   The civilization of the age was brilliant. Palaces were equipped with windows, bathrooms, and drains, and were beautifully adorned and furnished. The lords and ladies dressed elaborately and drank their wine from exquisitely made golden cups. Youths carried daggers of bronze, plated with gold and silver, inlaid with ivory. The great nobles wore plumed helmets of bronze, breast-plates, and greaves (leg armor), and carried large cylindrical shields, which they later replaced by small round bucklers. They rode to war and to the chase, of which they were very fond and which the ladies attended in two-wheeled chariots.

Legend and archaeology combine to furnish evidence of widespread trade. The story of the Argonauts may be a reflection of dangerous voyages into the Black Sea, and the adventures of Odysseus may suggest hazardous experiences in the west. They carried on an active trade eastward with the Hittites of Asia Minor, with Cyprus, Syria, and Egypt. In the west there was trade with southern Italy and Sicily, and their ships reached even to Sardinia and Spain. In the courts of the kings and nobles, bards sang of the deeds of great men and the wars which they waged: of Heracles, Perseus, and Theseus, who rid the land of many perils; of Oedipus and the Seven against Thebes; of Jason and Medea; and of many others.

The culmination of the age was the Trojan War, the historicity of which cannot be questioned, although the details are lost in the mists of poetry. Perhaps Helen did have

> The face which launched a thousand ships,
> And burnt the topless towers of Ilium.

Indeed, among all peoples in the Heroic Age the theft of a woman was a sufficient cause for war. Or perhaps the future possession of the littoral of Asia Minor was at stake. Already Mycenaean settlements had been planted there as the legend of Bellerophon indicates and as archaeological discoveries at Miletus and elsewhere prove. Perhaps the true cause of the war was Trojan interference with trade through the Hellespont. Certainly the Achaeans prevailed, and Troy fell and was destroyed. The traditional date, 1184 B.C., is fairly well substantiated by the remains.

DECLINE   Archaeological evidence proves the decline of Mycenaean culture in the twelfth century B.C. The decoration on pottery became geometric, and metal work degenerated. During the same century a fresh invasion of Dorians from the northwest into the Peloponnesus and of other tribes into Thessaly and Boeotia brought an end to the Mycenaean period and introduced a period of historical darkness in the Aegean. The repercussions of the disorder produced by this series of northern invasions, which first destroyed Cnossus and then brought Mycenaean culture to an end, reached even to Egypt, which during the centuries of Aegean prosperity had suffered calamity, recovered and regained great power, and then fallen into a long decline.

═ V ═

THE CONFLICT OF EMPIRES
(1500-500 B.C.)

EMPIRE, imperial expansion, and wars between empires are the pervasive features of the history of the Orient during the thousand years from 1500 to 500 B.C. In the first half of this period, the Egyptians, recovering from disaster, established an empire in Syria. The Hittites, descending from the Anatolian plateau, fought with the emperors of the Nile and won possession of half of that land. After a brief interlude, which gave an opportunity for self-development to the Phoenicians and the Hebrews, a second period of conquests followed as the Assyrians, the Chaldaeans, the Medes and the Persians, each in their turn, conquered and ruled over the eastern lands.

THE EGYPTIAN EMPIRE

THE HYKSOS — The period of the Egyptian Empire was prefaced by a great catastrophe. Under the pressure of the invasion of the Mitanni and the Hittites, the Semites of Syria moved upon the delta of the Nile. The invaders are known from the Egyptian records as the Hyksos, a name usually translated after Manetho as "Shepherd kings," though it seems to mean "rulers of countries," or "princes of the desert." Drawn for the most part probably from the well-civilized Canaanites with probably some Anatolian allies, they were no barbarian horde but intelligent if cruel conquerors whom Egypt, in her weakened condition, was unable to withstand. An additional reason for their success was their possession of horse-drawn chariots, which they had been taught by the northerners to use. Lower Egypt was laid waste, and upper Egypt gradually came under their control. On the borders of the delta, the Hyksos rulers established their capital, called Avaris, whence they ruled over possessions stretch-

DER EL BAHRI

GAME OF CHESS

*Tomb of Nebimut
Der el-Medina
Thebes*

AN EGYPTIAN CARTOON

British Museum

EGYPTIAN EMPIRE

IKHNATON AND HIS FAMILY
AT DINNER

*Tomb of Huy
Tell el-Amarna*

AN ANIMAL ORCHESTRA

Turin Museum

ing from the Euphrates to the first cataract of the Nile. They acquired Egyptian culture, worshiped Set, god of the delta, took Egyptian names, and set up their records in hieroglyphic inscriptions. Manetho listed them as the fifteenth and sixteenth dynasties. Their only lasting contribution to Egyptian life was the use of the horse.

To the Egyptian, however, they were never anything but hated foreigners and usurpers. After the princes of the south, the so-called seventeenth dynasty, had rebelled against them in vain, Ahmose of Thebes, the founder of the eighteenth dynasty, led the Egyptians to triumph. He drove the Hyksos from Egypt, besieged and took Avaris, and followed the enemy into southern Palestine. The age which followed, the eighteenth, nineteenth and twentieth dynasties, is known as the period of the Egyptian Empire or the New Kingdom.

EGYPTIAN
EMPERORS

As a result of the work of Ahmose (1580-1557 B.C.), a new day dawned for Egypt. Under the foreigners the hereditary nomarchs of the Middle Kingdom had been wiped out. When the Egyptian ruler of Thebes drove out the invader, he occupied the land by right of conquest as a personal royal possession. Egypt was now a military state ruled by an emperor who who wore the helmet of a general in place of the ancient double crown. He had an effective army that was well equipped with horses and chariots and quick to learn the profits to be gained by conquests. Succeeding kings raided Syria to the north and Nubia to the south to gain the glory, the booty, and the tribute of the empire.

The reign of Hatshepsut, first great woman of Egypt, provided an interlude in the series of wars. She sent an expedition down to the land of Punt via the Red Sea and recorded its success and the treasures with which it returned on the walls of her beautiful mortuary temple at Der el Bahri. Her husband and successor, Thutmose III, the greatest of Egyptian conquerors, made seventeen campaigns into Syria. Some were made by land, while for others he established bases on the Phoenician seacoast and carried men and supplies northward by water. All Syria to the Euphrates lay under his feet. The Kassites in Babylon and the Hittites in Asia Minor sent gifts, and the rulers of Crete seem to have made submission. On the walls of the temple at Karnak he had carved records of his conquests, pictures of the gold and silver vessels of the tribute, and even portrayals of the strange plants and animals he had come upon in Syria. Of the obelisks which he erected to celebrate his jubilee, four are still in existence, one each in Constantinople, Rome, London, and New York.

AMENHOTEP III   The successors of the great conqueror maintained the
(1411-1375 B.C.)   Syrian empire and added territory along the upper
                 Nile River as far as the fourth cataract. When Amen-
hotep III became king, the empire was at its greatest extent and power. Diplomatic correspondence on clay tablets known through the place of its discovery as the Tell el-Amarna letters, shows the prestige and wealth of the Pharaoh. The kings of Babylon and Mitanni sent princesses to the royal harem and requested gifts of gold "for gold is as common as dust in thy land."

To Nipkhuriria, King of Egypt:—Burraburiash, King of Karduniash, your brother. It is well with me; with you, your house, your wives, your sons, your land, your chief men, your horses, your chariots, may it be very well.

Since my father and your father with one another established friendly relations, they have sent to one another rich presents, and they have not refused one another any wish however great. Now my brother has sent me, as a present, (only) 2 minas of gold, but send me much gold, as much as your father, and if it is less, send half of what your father did. Why did you send me only 2 minas of gold? The work on the Temple is now great, and vigorously have I undertaken its accomplishment; send me therefore much gold. And you, whatever you desire from my land, write, that it may be brought you.

In the time of my father, Kurigalzu, the Canaanites as one man wrote to him: "Against the border of the land we will march and make an invasion. With you we will make an alliance." My father wrote them as follows: "Cease trying to ally yourself with me. If you cherish hostility against the King of Egypt, my brother, and ally yourself with another, take care lest I come and plunder you, for he is in alliance with me." My father, for your father's sake, did not listen to them. Now the Assyrians, my subjects, have I not written you in regard to them? Why have they (nevertheless) come into your land? If you love me, they should not carry on any business; let them accomplish nothing at all.

As a present for you, 3 minas of lapis lazuli and 5 span of horses for 5 wooden chariots I have sent you.[1]

Syrian princes educated at the Egyptian court aped the manners and customs of the conquering rulers. Custom houses were established,

[1] Hugo Winckler, *The Tell-el-Amarna Letters,* p. 15.

and goods from the Aegean, from Asia, even from the Far East, and from Punt and Nubia to the south, were brought to the markets of Thebes by strange-looking merchants. The ancient harbor of Alexandria, recently discovered submerged off the island of Pharos, was probably built at this time.

Wealth made possible great luxury in the houses of the nobles, in their dress and adornments, and in the palaces of the kings and the temples of the gods. Across the river from the capital, Amenhotep III caused a lake to be constructed in the desert for his royal wife and by it he built her a palace. On the edge of the desert he erected for himself a great mortuary temple guarded by two colossal statues. Of all this extravagant array, there remain only the statues, known to the world as the Colossi of Memnon.

The conquest had a pronounced effect on Egyptian thought, art, and religion. In this land where nothing decayed, the power of the past hardly needed the forces of a conservative religion to make itself felt. The methods of agriculture and of industry, the canons of sculpture and of architecture, the subjects and the methods of paintings in the tombs, the religious texts and formulas, and the concepts of the gods of Egypt—all had scarcely deviated from the principles laid down in Old Kingdom times. The powerful and wealthy priests of Amon, led by the high priest of the temple of Karnak, were actively opposed to all change, but contact through conquest and trade with foreign lands had brought not only new goods but new ideas. The numerous foreign merchants and slaves in Egypt and the Syrian and Babylonian princesses in the royal harem doubtless contributed to the ferment of change. The effect of these influences became patent when, under Amenhotep III, a new generation arose, imbued with hostility to tradition and a desire for a new realism in manners, art, and religion. The leader in this group was no less a person than Queen Tiy, the daughter of an Egyptian of ignoble birth whom the king had married for her beauty and charm. This movement for reform reached its fruition in the reign of her son.

IKHNATON
(1375-1358 B.C.)

Amenhotep IV, later called Ikhnaton, came to the throne in 1375 B.C. Around this strange person, his physique, his ideas and his career, there is a great deal of controversy. What sort of a person was he, and what were his plans? Were his reforms a product of developments in Egypt, supported by older ideas, were they influenced by Syrian beliefs, or were

they peculiarly his own? Did he endeavor to establish a true worldwide monotheism, or was he merely creating a new religion for
Egypt? On none of these questions is there any agreement. This much
seems certain that, apparently under the influence of his mother, Tiy,
and his wife, Nofretete, he determined to build a new Egypt. The
first object of his attack was the priesthood of Amon and the theology
which held Egypt in traditional paths. By royal decree he swept out
of existence the many gods of Egypt headed by Amon, and in their
place he set one god, lord and giver of light and life to the whole
world, under the symbol and name of the sun disk, Aton. In this he
doubtless had the support of the priests of the ancient sun god Re at
Heliopolis in the north, ever-jealous of Amon. Yet in his concepts,
expressed in his own composition, the glorious hymn to Aton, he went
far beyond them. The endowments of the temples were transferred to
Aton and his priests, the name of Amon was chiseled out of the inscriptions in the temples, and men were forbidden to worship the old
gods of the land. The king changed his own name to Ikhnaton, and
when opposition became too strong at Thebes, he transferred his capital to a new city, Akhetaton, modern Tell el-Amarna. There he
gathered the supporters of the new regime, both the sincere advocates
of reform and those who had been won over by gifts from the treasure
of the gods.

In the new capital the king completely abandoned the old restrictions on the royal office and appeared freely in public with his wife
and children. Realistic art was expressed in the decorations of the
houses; the discovery of a sculptor's workshop in the ruins of the city
has shown that sculpture departed from the old canons. Ikhnaton encouraged not only unconventional sketches but even caricatures of
himself. And in all the reliefs appears the sun disk Aton, its rays
reaching down to earth and extending the emblems of life, health,
and prosperity to the king and his followers.

Of the machinations of the dispossessed priesthood against him
we have no record. They were not powerful enough to overthrow him
or to block his reform while he lived, though they doubtless made
their influence felt among a people bewildered by the loss of time-
honored gods and by the demands of a cult which they could not
comprehend. But the king himself played into their hands by his
failure to recognize the needs of his kingdom and his empire.

While Ikhnaton was absorbed in the task of remaking Egyptian

religion, Egypt was falling into pieces around him. Uncontrolled officials began an orgy of corruption which resulted in disorder. In
northern Syria the Hittite kings, seeing their opportunity, began a
policy of expansion which they would never have dared in earlier
times. Syrian princes rebelled, and tribes from the grasslands called
Khabiri (possibly Hebrews) pushed into Syria. King Ribaddi of
Byblos and King Abdkhiba of Jerusalem sent letter after letter appealing to Ikhnaton for aid.

To my lord, the king:—Abd-khiba, your servant. At the feet of my
lord the king, seven and seven times I fall. What have I done against my
lord the king? Some one has slandered me before my lord the king (say-
ing): "Abd-khiba has revolted from his lord the king." Behold, neither
my father nor my mother appointed me in this place. The strong arm of
the king inaugurated me in my father's territory. Why should I commit
an offense against my lord the king? True as the king lives, because I said
to my lord the king's officer:—Why are you favorable to the Chabiri and
unfavorable to the (native) princes, for this reason they slander me before
my lord the king. Because I say:—The territory of my lord the king will
be ruined, for this reason they slander me before my lord the king. Let my
lord the king know that my lord the king had stationed a garrison, but
Jankhamu has taken (it). . . . Let the king care for his land, and [pay
some heed] to his land: the cities of my lord the king, belonging to Ili-
milki, have fallen away, and the whole territory of the king will be lost.
Let my lord the king therefore care for his land. I think I will go to the
court to my lord the king and see the tears of my lord the king, but the
enemies are powerful against me, and I am not able to go to court, to my
lord the king. May it seem good therefore to my lord the king to send a
garrison in order that I may go to court and see the tears of my lord the
king. As long as my lord the king lives,[2] when an officer goes forth, I
(always) say:—The land of the king is going to ruin. If you do not listen
to me, all the dependent princes will be lost, and my lord the king will
have no more dependent princes. Let the king therefore turn his attention
to the princes, and let my lord the king send troops. The king has no
longer any territory; the Khabiri have devastated all the king's territory.
If troops come in this year, the territory will remain my lord the king's, but
if no troops come, the territory of my lord the king is lost. To the scribe
of my lord the king:—Abd-khiba, your servant. Bring plainly (aloud)
before my lord the king (these) words: "The whole territory of my lord
the king is going to ruin." [3]

[2] This is an oath, meaning "by the life of the king."
[3] Hugo Winckler, *op. cit.,* p. 303.

Their letters still survive, but their loyalty was ineffective, the king would not concern himself with wars and empires while his religion was at stake. When he died, leaving no sons to carry on his uncompleted work, three daughters and their husbands endeavored to rule. It fell to the lot of the second of these royal consorts, a young prince called Tutenkhaton to surrender to the hostile forces. He left Akhetaton, returned to Thebes, restored the ancient glories of Amon and changed his name to Tutenkhamon. Upon his early death he was buried in a small but richly furnished tomb which was the source of unusual interest and wonderment at its recent discovery and excavation.

After another brief reign the eighteenth dynasty came to its end amid general confusion. The conservative forces had triumphed. Egypt was not ready for the far-reaching changes of the reformers. The people, who knew and loved only the old gods, would not take a new religion, however noble, at the king's command, and in the contest between the priests and the king, the former won. Though Egypt recovered much of the prestige and power it had lost in the last years of the eighteenth dynasty, its future was inevitable crystallization, stagnation, and decay under the leadership of a reactionary priesthood.

THE SECOND PERIOD

The kings who established the second period of the empire were faced with difficult tasks. The administration of Egypt had broken down; southern Syria was in confusion, and northern Syria was in the possession of Shubiluliuma, the Hittite emperor, who had wiped out the Mitannian allies of Egypt across the Euphrates.

After the collapse of the eighteenth dynasty a general of the army, Harmhab, reigned for a brief period and restored order in Egypt. He was followed by the kings of the nineteenth dynasty, the first of whom was Ramses I, who ruled but for a short time. His son, Seti I (1313-1292 B.C.), restored some of the earlier greatness of Egypt, defeating the Libyans in the western delta, checking the Hittites, and establishing firm control over southern Syria. Ramses II became king in 1292 B.C. and ruled until 1225 B.C. The length of his reign, the grandeur of his court, the success of his wars, and the extraordinary extent of his building activities made him a legendary figure for later generations. He fought the Hittites in a drawn battle at Kadesh on the Orontes where, outmaneuvered and ambushed by them, he saved the situation by his own intrepid courage and by the steadiness of the Egyptian troops. A poem, in which his glorious deeds were recounted, was carved on the walls of his temple in Egypt.

The treaty which he made in 1276 B.C. with the Hittite king, Hattusil, is of unusual interest because copies of it have survived on Egyptian monuments and in Hittite archives. It provided for peace between the two great powers, for military assistance against internal or external danger, and for the extradition of fugitives from either state.

In Egypt, Ramses II built or enlarged many temples, erected colossal statues of himself in many places and carved his own name on the statues of earlier kings. Under his rule Egypt seemed prosperous and secure.

THE INVASION   After his death another storm descended upon Egypt. Phrygians and other invading tribes came from the north into Asia Minor and swept the Hittites, already weakened by famine, out of the area. Of the great Hittite Empire, all that was left was a small Syrian kingdom with Carchemish as its capital. Tribes from the north, probably the Achaeans (p. 78), went down into Greece and threw the whole Aegean area into confusion. The first warning of trouble came to Egypt during the reign of Merneptah (1225-1215 B.C.), able son of Ramses II, who successfully defended Syria and the delta from "the peoples of the sea." The full deluge of northern tribes fell upon Egypt in the reign of Ramses III (1198-1167 B.C.), second king of the twentieth dynasty and the last of the great Egyptian rulers. With an army of mercenaries, hired from among the invading peoples themselves, he repelled a great invasion by land and naval battles in 1194 and 1192 B.C. Although he lost southern Syria to the Peleset (the Philistines of the Bible), he saved Egyptian civilization from destruction.

A long period of somnolence followed in Egypt. Ramses III was followed by a line of kings who bore the name of Ramses but whose helplessness was a subject of derision in Syria. The high priests of Amon at Thebes displaced them as the twenty-first dynasty. Later, Libyan and then Ethiopian rulers established themselves as Pharaohs. Eventually, in the seventh century, the conquering Assyrians took possession of the land.

CIVILIZATION UNDER THE EMPIRE

GOVERNMENT   The military character of the Egyptian Empire produced fundamental changes in the political and social
structure of the land. The hereditary nobility had been wiped out by
the Hyksos, and with them passed all semblance of the Middle Kingdom relationships. The Pharaohs owed their supreme position to the
military triumph of Ahmose; but they insisted as of old on their divine parentage and on their god-given right to rule. The walls of the
temples were inscribed with pictures and texts to prove their birth as
sons of the queen mother and the god Amon. From Amon they received the truth and law by which they ruled, and to him they gave
praise for their victories. The formal seclusion of the god-king of
olden days was now gone, for as general the Pharaoh appeared in
public, wearing the military helmet and surrounded by his officers
and his troops.

The administration was organized on a military basis, and the
officials from highest to lowest were officers of the king-general. At
the head of the army stood the southern vizier. He directed the administration, superintended the official cults, acted as viceroy when the
king was absent on campaigns, collected the tribute from the empire,
and controlled all foreigners in Egypt. His was the supreme court of
the land. Associated with him was the chief treasurer of the king.
These two made daily reports to each other. A northern vizier was
stationed at Heliopolis to watch over the lower kingdom. Under the
viziers officers of the king governed the nomes. These, however, had
lost their traditional character and had become arbitrary administrative
divisions, fifty-four in number. States of the empire outside of Egypt
were ruled by their native princes under the watchful eye of Egyptian
residents, assisted by garrisons placed in strategic centers. The sons
of these princes were taken to Egypt to be educated in the royal court
and to be trained in loyalty to their suzerain, who undoubtedly dictated their succession to power.

Written laws governed the land. All officials had judicial powers
in their own spheres, and local disputes were settled by courts composed of priests or elders. Appeals were allowed from all courts to the
supreme court of the southern vizier, who was required to sit with the
forty rolls of the law before him and to hear all cases as they were pre-

MARKET SCENE

Tomb of Fetekta
Sakkara

SCULPTORS AT WORK

Tomb of Rekhmire
Thebes

Thebes

SCENE FROM THE TOMB OF NAKHT

EGYPTIAN EMPIRE

RAMSES II

NOFRETETE

HATSHEPSUT

NEFRETERI, WIFE OF RAMSES II,
AND THE GODDESS ISIS

EGYPTIAN EMPIRE

sented. Delay was allowed only in case of land disputes where the records had to be brought from a distance.

For the settlement of such disputes, as well as for purposes of taxation, the royal scribes kept careful records of all property. Though in theory all the land belonged to the king, citizens held possession by grant or lease and could transfer it to others freely. The officials collected for the king about one-fifth of the produce of the land, made monthly reports of their collections, and on their own share of the income paid taxes in gold, silver, cattle, or linen.

SOCIAL LIFE   The wealth of Egypt in the imperial period resulted in a general well-being, not only reflected in social life but shared by all classes of the population. Great luxury characterized the activities of the official class. An insistent desire for display and for pleasure led Hatshepsut to create a garden, and Amenhotep III a lake, in the desert itself, and caused the great queen to cap her obelisks with gold which, she proudly declared, was measured for that purpose by the bushel. Imperial palaces and private houses were more spacious and luxurious than in older times. Elaborate gowns of fine linen, costly jewelry, jars and boxes of alabaster, and vessels of gold and silver constituted an abundant paraphernalia of wealth. The great men are depicted on the walls of their tombs, like the men of the Old Kingdom, hunting and fishing, enjoying their gardens, or directing their workmen. There are also pictures of fine parties with wine, music, and flowers. For the pleasure of such a party the harpist plays and sings:

Spend the day merrily, O priest! Put unguent and fine oil together to thy nostrils, and garlands and lotus flowers . . . on the body of thy sister whom thou favourest, as she sitteth beside thee. Set music and singing before thy face. Cast all evil behind thee, and bethink thee of joy, until that day cometh when one reacheth port in the land that loveth silence.[4]

Nor was this prosperity confined to the upper class alone. The scribes grew in number, in riches, and in pride. An interesting text found in the papyri illustrates their ability to calculate the weight of an obelisk, the number of bricks to be used in the building of a ramp, or the amount of food needed for a military expedition to Syria. Other documents contain instructions to students, model letters, and collec-

[4] Erman, *Literature of the Ancient Egyptians*, p. 252.

tions of maxims, and display the superiority which the scribes felt over artisans and farmers.[5]

The expansion of trade which came in the train of conquest brought prosperity to the merchants and artisans. From Nubia by the route of the Nile came gold and precious stones, ivory, hides, ostrich feathers and animals. Hatshepsut renewed the trade down the Red Sea with Punt, whence came incense, myrrh, ebony, and sweet-scented woods. A brisk trade with Syria in all sorts of objects accompanied the conquest of that land. The Egyptians sought particularly, however, for wood and its manufactured products, and for fish, cattle, and horses. Goods from Babylon, brought overland, were secured by the Egyptians in the Syrian cities. Some of this trade passed on the great road which ran from the delta across the desert and along the coast to Joppa, Tyre, Beirut, and Byblos, and inland to Damascus; most of it, however, went by sea from the delta to the Phoenician ports. Egyptians maintained an active interest in the rich centers of Aegean civilization at Cnossus and Mycenae. The Syrian commerce continued during the period of decline as Egyptians still sought for the cedar of Lebanon and the other products of the eastern land. The horse trade was so active during the period of the Hebrew kingdom that Solomon himself had a hand in it, greatly to his profit.

The ability of the Egyptian craftsmen to satisfy the demand of the upper classes for luxury and display is proved by the furniture, canes, jewelry, boxes, jars, and other objects found in the tomb of Tutenkhamon and in similar deposits. The gold coffin of Tutenkhamon in particular is exquisite in its artistry. Such pieces as these attest the existence of an enterprising and prosperous artisan class at the close of the eighteenth dynasty. It is interesting to note that a row of tombs recently excavated at Thebes indicates that some laborers could afford fine burials. During the period of decline, however, when Egypt was under priestly control, wealth, demand, and ability suffered together. Methods and designs became crystallized, crafts became hereditary, and caste restrictions prevailed.

Agriculture remained the basis of Egyptian life. The peasants, some free, others serf, lived and worked as they had in former times and as, with few changes, they do today. The later generations saw a steady increase in serfdom as classes in society became stratified by the priests.

[5] These texts are translated in Erman, *op. cit.*, pp. 185-242.

The second period of the empire saw the formation of a new and powerful group, the mercenary soldiers. As the Egyptians themselves wearied of war or retired to enjoy their booty, the kings hired foreigners to take their places. The army of Ramses III, as we have seen, consisted almost entirely of mercenaries drawn from the very same tribes with whom he was fighting. Later kings employed Hebrew and Greek soldiers, a practice of great importance particularly to the Greeks, who thus learned their first lessons of Egyptian civilization. Lands were assigned to these professional troops for their support, and they thus became a permanent class in the Egyptian world. Great numbers of aliens were brought as slaves or allowed to settle in the delta or in Thebes as merchants and artisans. Some even became attendants and officials of the king.

The priests slowly but surely became the dominant element in the population. The great conquerors, in return for the victories which they attributed to Amon, lavished their riches on his temples and made him rich gifts of land, cattle, and slaves.[6]

Under the weak Ramessids, the priests steadily added to their possessions until the wealth of Egypt was concentrated in their hands and the high priest of Amon became king of Egypt.

RELIGION   The religion of the period centered around Amon-Re, the ram-headed god of Thebes who had been identified with Re during the Middle Kingdom. It was he who gave Thutmose III his victories; he who came to the rescue of Ramses II at Kadesh; and he who enabled Ramses III to save Egyptian civilization from the peoples of the sea. "If Amon share my life" became a familiar expression among the people. The great temple at Karnak was built

---

[6] Thanks to inventories drawn up at the death of Ramses III which are preserved in the great Harris Papyrus in the British Museum, we know that "he [Amon] possessed 5,164 divine statues, 82,322 vassals, servants and slaves, 421,262 head of cattle, large and small, 433 gardens and orchards, 868,168 aroura of corn-land, which make about 2,393 square kilometers (about 691,334.23 acres), 83 vessels, 46 building-yards, 65 cities, boroughs, or villages, seven of which were in Asia. And this is not all. During the thirty-two years of the reign he had received as votive gifts or offerings 31,833 kilograms of gold, 997,805 kilograms of silver, 2,395,120 kilograms of copper, 3,722 pieces of cloth, 309,950 hectolitres of corn, 289,530 birds; thread, linen, oil, wine, incense, and vegetables in considerable quantities. All these substances represent payments in kind or dues over and above the ordinary revenues which were furnished by the landed estate. Amon was therefore a very substantial lord; the most substantial in Egypt after the king. He ruled over at least one-tenth, perhaps one-eighth, of the valley and like all mortmains, his showed a tendency to increase rather than to become restricted."—Capart, *Thebes*, p. 69.

for him on the spot where a small temple had stood in Middle Kingdom days. Thutmose I began the erection of this noble edifice, and
through the centuries to Roman times many succeeding kings added
to its glory. Its avenue of rams, its mighty pylons, its great courtyards,
colossal statues, and lofty obelisks are still a reminder of the ancient
greatness of Egypt. Most celebrated is its hypostyle (colonnaded) hall,
a forest of huge columns with a central nave and side aisles, one of
the finest examples anywhere of the use of clerestory [7] in architecture.
The whole temple area covered sixty-two acres of ground. Of the many
other buildings which have survived—the beautiful temple of Hatshepsut, the lofty colonnade at Luxor, the temple of Seti I at Abydos,
the huge structures of Ramses II at Thebes and at Abu Simbel, and
the fortress portico and temple of Ramses III at Medinet Habu—all
bear witness to the great achievements of the Egyptian architects in
the building of houses of eternity for their gods and for their kings.

The great Amon was too grand, too remote, for the ordinary
Egyptians. They worshiped the statue of a dead king, or relied upon
the divinity which dwelt in a single column in a temple, or lavished
such veneration on the animals sacred to the gods that the Greeks
later accused them of animal worship.

The worship of the great triad of Isis, Osiris, and Horus continued to be so powerful that Ikhnaton himself dared not trifle with
Osiris, before whom it was believed all men from the highest to the
lowest appeared for judgment after death. Priestly technique, however, destroyed the ancient ethical values of Osiris worship. By the
magic power of amulets and charms: clay copies of beetles (the famous
Egyptian scarabs) and eyes of Horus, both symbols of immortality;
by figurines called *shawabtiu* (or *ushebtiu*), "answerers," to serve the
dead in the future life; and by means of the formulas of the *Book of
the Dead,* all provided by the priests to those who could afford them,
the gods themselves were deceived and overcome and all men secured
the blessings of eternal life in the fields of Yaru.

Deceased kings, as of old, crossed the "lily lake" to dwell with
the sun god and to traverse the upper and underworlds with him.
But the manner of burial underwent a change with the abandonment
of pyramids. Thutmose I went back into an obscure valley behind the
western mountain at Thebes and there had a chamber-tomb dug into

[7] The two center rows of columns were made taller than those on the sides to
admit light. This type of architectural construction is called *clerestory.*

IKHNATON SACRIFICING

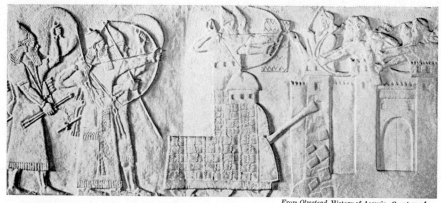

ASSURNASIRPAL BESIEGING A CITY

BULL

From the palace of Sargon

CAPITAL

From a Persian palace

ASSYRIAN AND PERSIAN ART

the cliff, where he vainly hoped it would remain concealed and inviolate. Then on the edge of the western desert he built a mortuary temple, where his worship was to be carried on. His example was followed by his successors. Today the valley where these tombs were dug is known as the "Valley of the Kings." The tombs were composed of long corridors with many chambers, were adorned with pictures, and were filled with funerary trappings. Most of them were violated and plundered in antiquity by grave robbers.

Queens and royal children were buried in another valley to the south. Along the foot of the cliff were clustered the tombs of the nobles, the scribes, and the lower classes. These were chamber tombs decorated like the mastabas of the Old Kingdom with scenes of daily life. The hopes to which these people held fast are expressed in the constantly recurring inscription,

"All ye, who pass by, who love life, and who hate death, stop and say a prayer for the ka of the dead. An offering which the king gives to Anubis, may he give a thousand loaves of bread, a thousand jugs of wine, a thousand pieces of cloth, a thousand of everything that is good to the ka of the dead who lie herein."

CONCLUSION   By the end of the second millennium B.C. the ancient Egyptians had almost completed their act on the stage of history. They had achieved greatness in government and law, in architecture and art, in science, literature, and religion. As a result of the expansion of the imperial period their civilization made a deep impression upon the peoples of Syria and the Minoans of Crete. What they had discovered or accomplished later generations cherished during the long period of decline. The Greeks, the Macedonians, and the Romans drew continually from the fount of Egyptian wisdom the fundamental principles of building and of sculpture, mathematics, especially geometry and mechanics, the beginnings of scientific thought, principles of government, law and land ownership, and, from the colorful and powerful worship of Isis and Osiris, their doctrines of immortality. Ancient Egypt, like Babylon, ceased to be active, but its achievements continued as a vital force in the stream of history.

THE RISE OF SYRIA (1100-800 B.C.)

The little states of Syria, long the plaything of the great emperors, found an opportunity for independence and prosperity in the simultaneous decline of Egypt, the collapse of the Hittite Empire, the weakness of Babylon, and the failure of an Assyrian bid for power. The Phoenicians and incoming Philistines on the seacoast, the Aramaeans and the Hebrews, who had barely completed their conquest of the interior, enjoyed the sunlight of freedom until the Assyrians and the Chaldaeans rose to overwhelm them.

THE
PHOENICIANS

First to reap the benefits of the situation were the Phoenicians, into whose hands the sea-borne trade of the Mediterranean had passed after the fall of the Cretan sea power. The goods which they secured from Egypt or Babylon, or which they produced in their own shops, they carried into the Aegean, throughout the Mediterranean, and through the Straits of Gibraltar to Cape Verde and the Azores Islands in the Atlantic. They sailed to the Cassiterides (perhaps the Scilly Islands) in the north in search of the tin of Cornwall, and established trading posts at strategic points, such as Utica, Hippo, and Carthage in Africa, and Gades (modern Cadiz) in Spain. They became so wealthy and powerful that their kings dared flout an envoy of the Pharaoh himself.[8]

The Phoenicians were famous in antiquity for the skill with which they loaded and navigated their broad-beamed boats. They learned to sail by the stars at night, and the North Star was known as the Phoenicians' star. One company of Phoenicians, under the aegis of a Saite Pharaoh of Egypt, circumnavigated Africa.

Though the extent of their influence over the rising civilization of the Greeks is a matter of controversy, they made their presence felt, and as traders the "black-browed Phoenicians" were well known to the Greeks of the Homeric poems. Eventually Greek merchants displaced them in the Aegean and challenged their power in the west (pp. 129, 134).

Tyre, secure from attack on its island and equipped with magnificent harbors, achieved great wealth and prominence. Its woolen goods, dyed with the famous purple, and its glassware were everywhere in demand, and its ships traversed the known seas. The temples of its gods, the palaces of its kings and merchant princes, its workshops and markets, and its throngs of people made it a fascinating city whose only drawback was the odor of the decaying mollusks from which came the dye. A vivid memory of the impression which

[8] The story of Wen Amon, Erman, *Literature of the Ancient Egyptians*, pp. 174-185.

its greatness made on the contemporary world is recorded in the twenty-seventh chapter of Ezekiel.

The Phoenicians' chief gift to the world was the diffusion of the alphabet. The problem of its origin has not yet been solved. Syrian inscriptions found in a temple in the mining region of Sinai, and dated variously between 1900 and 1300 B.C., seem to furnish a proto-type. An inscription found at Byblos, possibly as old as 1300 B.C. and certainly before 1000 B.C., is the earliest known example of the developed script. It seems probable that the Phoenicians, influenced by Egyptian hieratic writing, by earlier attempts at simplified writing in Syria, and possibly by the linear script of the Cretans, evolved a system of signs which represented individual consonants, vowel signs being a later contribution of the Greeks. By the ninth century the Phoenician alphabet had spread throughout Syria. Adopted and trans-formed by the Greeks during the tenth or ninth centuries B.C., it has descended to us.

The Phoenicians were the great middlemen of culture. Their civilization was blended under Egyptian and Babylonian influences, and what they learned from the older peoples they put to good use in their own work and in the products that they carried throughout the Mediterranean.

THE
ARAMAEANS

The peace of the rest of Syria was disturbed during the latter half of the second millennium B.C. by the invasions of the Aramaeans, the Philistines, and the Hebrews.

The Aramaeans entered the fertile region of Damascus from the Arabian grasslands during the latter half of the second millennium and slowly but completely absorbed or displaced its older inhabitants. The position of Damascus at the head of the caravan route across the desert to Babylon gave them control over the inland trade and they became the carriers of merchandise between Mesopotamia, Phoenicia, and Egypt. They enjoyed independence and prosperity, and their rulers appear as vigorous fighters in the historical books of the Old Testament until they fell in 732 B.C. before the might of the Assyrians. Nevertheless loss of freedom did not destroy their commercial pre-eminence. The Aramaic dialect, becoming the international language of the East, was universally spoken throughout the Levant in the time of Christ. Damascus, since despoiled by many conquerors, still lives with the longest continuous history of any community in the Western world.

THE
PHILISTINES

The wandering tribes which descended upon Egypt in the reign of Ramses III wrought great havoc in Syria. After their defeat in the delta, the Philistines, who had played a major part in the attack, fell back upon Canaan and settled there. They are said by tradition to have come from Caphtor, possibly Crete. Their civilization, as portrayed in the Egyptian records and in the Bible, indicates that they came from the Aegean area. The fondness for public shows and assemblies which they displayed is reminiscent of the Minoan frescoes. But their dress and armor were Anatolian rather than Cretan. It is possible therefore that they came from Caria rather than from Crete. Iron weapons and disciplined organization gave them a great advantage over the Canaanites. They became firmly entrenched on the coast and extended their power over the disunited and barbaric Hebrew tribes of the interior. Never more than a ruling caste, they sank rapidly into oblivion following a decisive defeat by David shortly after 1000 B.C.

THE COMING OF
THE HEBREWS

During the period of Philistine dominance the land of Canaan passed into the hands of the Israelitish tribes of the Hebrews. Because of their religious significance, the Hebrews have received a greater share of attention than their importance in other respects warrants.

Tradition ascribed their ancestry to a patriarch named Abraham who left Ur about the time of its destruction by Hammurabi, moved north into the region of the middle Euphrates, and thence south into Canaan. The circumstantial character of the story of Abraham, the application of Sumerian law in his family relations (p. 33), and the fact that Palestinian archaeology, still in its infancy, proves that the description of Canaan in the fourteenth chapter of Genesis is substantially correct, all seem to indicate a basis of truth in the legend. The stories of Isaac, Jacob or Israel, eponym and hero of the later Israelites, of Joseph and his brethren, of the settlement in Egypt, the Oppression, and the Exodus, are too familiar to require retelling. Internal evidence in the stories makes it certain that the narrative contains a thread of historical fact.

There can be no doubt that a group of Hebrews entered Egypt and settled in the eastern edge of the delta. There the great leader, Moses, whose personality and accomplishments are so vivid that he must be considered as an historical character, centered their devotion in a tribal deity of the desert, long worshiped in southern Arabia and called Jahweh (Jehovah), then led them out of Egypt, and in the desert taught them the worship of this god. After the death of Moses they began a series of raids into Canaan and eventually gained possession of the land.

The task of fitting these tales and the records of the conquest in Joshua and Judges into the framework of known history is exceedingly difficult, and there is little agreement among scholars. Some believe that the entrance into Egypt took place during the Hyksos period, and the Exodus about the time of the expulsion of the foreigners (1580 B.C.). Archaeological discoveries at Jericho might be taken to prove that the capture of that city, recorded in Joshua, took place about 1400 B.C. This solution of the problem would definitely identify the Israelites as the Khabiri of Ikhnaton's letters (p. 87). The most recent and best-founded opinion [9] is that the Khabiri were Hebraic tribes who endeavored to make an entrance into Canaan at an early period, that the great body of the Israelites entering Egypt, as was the recorded practice of many nomadic tribes during the empire, suffered oppression under Ramses II and escaped in the following reign.

The Book of Judges, containing a series of tribal hero stories with some contemporary poetry like the Song of Deborah, proves sufficiently that the conquest of Canaan was difficult and gradual, succeeding first in the extreme north and south with Jerusalem and the plain of Esdraelon remaining in the hands of the Canaanites. The nomadic tribes, though they clung to their patriarchal and tribal organization, blended with the older inhabitants, from whom they learned industrial arts and the methods and the religious ceremonies of an agricultural people. The Hebrews received a rude check when they reached the eastern foothills, where the Philistines (p. 98) stopped them, later conquered them, and forbade them the use of iron.

THE UNITED KINGDOM These difficulties forced unity among the tribes and served to keep alive the religion which had been established by Moses and nurtured by the patriarchal leaders or "judges." Finally Samuel, last of the great judges, yielded to the force of necessity and brought about the election of Saul of the tribe of Benjamin as king. This able warrior defeated the Philistines and took Esdraelon from the Canaanites. Soon, however, he broke with Samuel, and in the dissension which followed he was defeated and killed by the Philistines at Mt. Gilboa.

[9] See Lods, *Israel*, pages 181-189, for a complete discussion of the problem.

DAVID (CA.
1010-970 B.C.)
David, who took over the place and the work of Saul, laid the foundation of the greatness of the Hebrew kingdom. Jerusalem was taken and made the capital; the Philistines were defeated in the valley of Rephaim and completely crushed; the tribes crowding in from the east were soundly chastised; a centralized government was organized over the united land of Israel, and a commercial alliance was made with Hiram, king of Tyre.

SOLOMON (CA.
970-CA. 935 B.C.)
David's conquests and wealth were enjoyed by his successor, Solomon, son of David's favorite wife, Bath Sheba. Solomon established a typical Oriental court with a large harem headed by an Egyptian princess, organized his kingdom into twelve tribal divisions, and levied taxes and task work. In alliance with Tyre, he sent his ships across the Mediterranean to Spain and down the Red Sea to Punt. Solomon adorned with palaces the capital city which David had fortified, and with Phoenician aid he built a temple for Jahweh on the summit of the hill of Jerusalem. His commands and judgments gained for him such a reputation for wisdom that later ages attributed to him the wisdom literature in the Bible.

Under his son Rehoboam the kingdom fell apart. Among the ten tribes in the more fertile northern land, the blend with the Canaanites and the acceptance of their agricultural methods and gods had been more thorough. The greater part of the wealth of the kingdom lay there, and the people objected to the religious restrictions, the taxes, and the labor imposed on them from Jerusalem. The southern area, hilly and less fertile, was occupied for the most part by herdsmen, who were nearer in occupation and in spirit to the original teachings of Moses and who were prone to criticize the devotion of their northern tribesmen to Canaanitish gods. When Rehoboam refused to lighten the load on the north, the people, under the leadership of Jeroboam, rebelled and established a separate kingdom whose capital was later located at Samaria.

DEVELOPMENT
OF HEBREW
RELIGION
The Hebrews in the grasslands were nomads who worshiped the forces of nature, mountains, trees, springs, and rivers, believed in demons, and practiced magic. Moses established their allegiance to a tribal god, Jahweh. With Him they made a covenant of loyalty and obedience and in return they believed that He would fight for them

and take care of them. The intensity of this religion, its exclusive character, and the moral inspiration which the great lawgiver embodied in it gave it the power to withstand the strain of the Canaanitish influences and made possible its future development into greatness. The conviction that Jahweh had promised them Canaan and was fighting for them strengthened the Israelites throughout the period of conquest and the struggle with the Philistines, and helped to bring about their union under the monarchy.

As a result of the conquest, however, Jahweh suffered transformation. His people, originally shepherds and herdsmen, blended with the Canaanites and became farmers. Instead of accepting the local Baalim (agricultural gods), they substituted Jahweh for them, assigned to Him the altars in the high places and ascribed to Him the festivals, laws, and practices which fitted their new occupation. Though Jahweh thus conquered the gods of the Canaanites, His worship was henceforth a mixture of cults. Yet the moral force of His religion was too powerful to allow the acceptance of the baser elements of the agricultural cults, such as infanticide and religious prostitution.

The formation and prosperity of the monarchy seemed the fulfillment of promise and resulted in a great revival of Jahwism, in the writing down of the traditions which recorded His interest in His people, and in the formulation of a code of laws, the Covenant Code, authorship of which was ascribed to Moses. Nevertheless there was sin in Israel. Many of the people worshiped strange gods and followed forbidden practices. The kings even set up temples of the gods of their foreign wives. At the same time social and economic evils, hostile to the spirit of Jahweh's religion, began to appear as the rich and powerful grasped greedily for land, corrupted the courts, and dispossessed the poor. A series of great religious teachers, the prophets, appeared, to deal with these offenses. With inspired words they proclaimed the wrath of Jahweh and the inevitability of punishment. But in their search to know and teach Him, they came to conceive of Him not merely as a national but as a universal God with power over all nature and all nations and with moral attributes which led Him to demand righteousness and justice.

THE PROPHETS   The first of these prophets, Elijah, appeared during the reign of Ahab (ca. 876-853 B.C.), ablest ruler of Samaria. This warrior king secured an alliance with Tyre by marrying Jezebel; he rebuilt and adorned Samaria, fought successfully with the rulers of Judah and with Ben Hadad of Damascus, but he met his match in Elijah. This prophet from the grasslands, horrified at the worship of the Canaanite Baalim, and especially at Jezebel's having established temples to the Tyrian Melkarth and Ishtar, proclaimed the supremacy of Jahweh over the Israelites. Indeed his actions indicate that he went so far as to deny power and even existence to the foreign gods. Elisha, his successor, aided an usurper, Jehu (841 B.C.), to overthrow the dynasty. Amos (ca. 750 B.C.) broadened the concept of God by sounding the note of social and economic justice by predicting punishment for a nation whose leaders "sold the righteous for silver and the poor for a pair of shoes"; and Hosea taught the lesson of the forgiving love of God. These men were teachers in the northern kingdom of Israel. In 722 B.C. Samaria fell before the Assyrians; its people were carried into captivity, and colonists were settled in their places.

The later prophets arose in the southern kingdom of Judah. Micah, the first of these, advanced far beyond old tribal concepts when he denied the validity of sacrifice and preached "What doth the Lord require of thee but to do justice, to love mercy, and to walk humbly with thy God." The greatest of the prophets of the south were Isaiah and Jeremiah.

Isaiah played a dual part of statesman and religious teacher. He was adviser to Hezekiah (ca. 722-ca. 696 B.C.), the king who strengthened the walls of Jerusalem, constructed an aqueduct to secure water for the city (it is still in use), and successfully resisted the Assyrian king, Sennacherib. Isaiah's religious writings, containing some of the noblest lines ever written, proclaimed the supremacy of God over the whole universe and announced the ultimate coming of a divine kingdom through which justice and goodness shall be established in all lands.

Jeremiah was a member of a reform group usually called Deuteronomist. To stop the use of Canaanitish rites and symbols at local shrines of Jahweh, the reformers worked for the abolition of the shrines and the concentration of the worship of Jahweh in the temple at Jerusalem. When a scroll containing rules in conformity with their ideas, but purporting to be the work of Moses, was found in a recess of the temple by servants of King Josiah (ca. 637-609 B.C.) and was accepted by the king, the movement triumphed. Though Jeremiah came from a priestly family which lost its position as a result of the reform, he supported the movement and with burning zeal inveighed against the economic and social as well as the religious evils of his time. He taught the universal power of God over Gentiles as well as over Jews and the consequent unreality of the pagan divinities. To older ideas of national morality he added the great idea of individual responsibility. He saw the impending fall of Jerusalem, which he felt was the punishment for sin, and he wept over the nation even when it persecuted him.

In 597 b.c. Nebuchadrezzar of Babylon took Jerusalem. After a revolt, he returned again in 586 b.c., destroyed the city, and carried the people into captivity.

THE EXILE   The exile presented a supreme test to the religious leaders of the Jews. The people, who had been taught that God could be worshiped only at Jerusalem, asked, "How can we sing the Lord's songs in a strange land?" Ezekiel and the author of the second part of the Book of Isaiah gave definite and magnificent answers to this question. God is omnipresent and omnipotent, they said, and the creator and ruler of the universe, who may and must be worshiped at all times and in all places. To Ezekiel, however, the chief essential of worship was holiness, which implied obedience to the Law. This idea was put into effect by the Jews in Babylon, by those who had fled into Egypt, and by the people who returned when the Persians allowed the restoration of Jerusalem. Henceforth the Law was the center of Judaism.

Out of the hardships of those troublous times arose the problem of human suffering. To this the writer of the Book of Job gave the answer that the ways of God are inscrutable, man is but as clay in the hands of a potter, and his only refuge is trust in God. A code of morals of the highest order and based on the Law, a belief in one God, the creator and ruler of all mankind, and the precept of trusting submission to His will were the great achievements of the Hebrew teachers.

ASSYRIA

RISE OF   During the constant wars which the Assyrians (p. ASSYRIA   67) had waged for centuries against the Babylonians and the mountain peoples to the north and east, the fiercely independent peasants of this nation became welded into one of the most efficient fighting forces the world has ever seen, almost irresistible under proper leadership. The kings who ruled during the period from the ninth to the seventh centuries B.C. provided such leadership and built the Assyrian Empire.

Assurnasirpal II (885-860 B.C.) began the great rise to power. With an army well equipped with iron weapons and brilliantly organized into corps of infantry, chariotry, and engineers, with ferocity unparalleled in the annals of military history, he swept over northern Mesopotamia and Syria and into the near-by mountain lands. His notable achievements were recorded upon the buildings which adorned his capital. His successors continued his policies and gained control over Babylonia. The expansion of Assyrian power to the north was temporarily limited by the growth of the empire of the Haldians in the hills around Lake Van, but the Haldians, though they caused the Assyrians constant trouble, could not long withstand the superior forces that came against them.

TIGLATH
PILESER III
(746-727 B.C.)

In 746 B.C. an usurper, Tiglath Pileser III, seized the throne of Asshur, and under him the name of Assyria once more became formidable. He conquered Babylon, making himself its king, took Damascus in 732 B.C., forced Israel and Judah to pay tribute, and checked the Haldians in the north. An extensive reorganization of imperial administration was undertaken with the establishment of provinces, governors, garrisons, and the regular collection of tribute. To destroy local feeling, to unify his empire, and to discourage rebellions, he developed a system of deportation and colonization. Sargon II (722-705 B.C.) brought Assyria still further along the path of empire. Samaria had fallen in 722 B.C. and the ten tribes to the north deported; the last remnants of the Hittites were wiped out and Haldia destroyed. To glorify the gods Sargon built a new capital, Dur Sharrukin.

SENNACHERIB
(705-681 B.C.)

Sennacherib is the best known of the Assyrian rulers because of his part in Biblical history. Nineveh, which he made his capital, became synonymous with the Assyrian Empire. He took Sidon and brought Tyre to terms by diverting its trade to other cities. He made demonstrations against Egypt, whose Ethiopian kings were constantly stirring up trouble for him in Syria. He was recalled from his first attack on Jerusalem by a revolt in Babylon; the second invasion was ended by a plague which fell upon his army. But he manned boats on the Tigris with Phoenicians and sailed them down the river and through the inter-river canal into rebel Babylonia, where he proceeded to destroy Babylon itself.

DECLINE OF
ASSYRIA

Sennacherib's pious son, Esarhaddon, rebuilt Babylon and carried out the conquest of Egypt, establishing as governor of that land Necho of Sais, a native prince of the delta. The last Assyrian of note was Assurbanipal (669-626 B.C.), and to him we owe much of our knowledge of the period. This enlightened monarch collected a great library and set scribes to work copying ancient texts and digging into the forgotten lore of the land. Rebellions and wars called him away: his brother had to be suppressed in Babylon; Elam to the south was taken and denuded of population; Tyre was besieged and forced to surrender; Egypt, however, was lost to Psamtik I, who established the twenty-sixth dynasty of Egyptian Pharaohs. After the death of Assurbanipal, an invasion of Scythians from the north swept over and weakened the Assyrian Empire. Then a coalition of Chaldaeans who had occupied Babylon, of Persians who had moved down into empty Elam, of Medes from the plateau of Iran, supported by Egypt, easily prevailed over the Assyrians. Nineveh was taken in 612 B.C. and so completely destroyed that its very site was forgotten.

ASSYRIAN
CIVILIZATION

To the contemporary world the Assyrians were a nation of warriors "whose arrows were sharp and all their bows bent; the horses' hooves were like flint and their wheels like a whirlwind." The Book of the prophet Nahum is a vivid picture of the fear and the hatred they inspired among the peoples of Syria. But their importance in history is much greater than their reputation as fighters. To the art of war and to imperial administration they contributed organization. Their army, as we have seen, was divided into corps of infantry, chariotry, and engineers, with a well-directed service of supply. Their empire was divided into provinces with appointed governors, garrisons, and regularly collected tribute, and with client kingdoms along the frontier. To unify the empire and break down local feeling they ordered deportations and promoted colonization in conquered areas, and to secure better control and easier communication they built a well-planned system of military roads. Later conquerors followed their military example, and the empires of Persia, Macedon, and Rome borrowed much from the organizing genius of the Assyrians.

The purpose of the Assyrian rulers may have been plunder, but their achievements resulted in a period of comparative peace and unity in the Levant. Their imperial system, especially the practice of

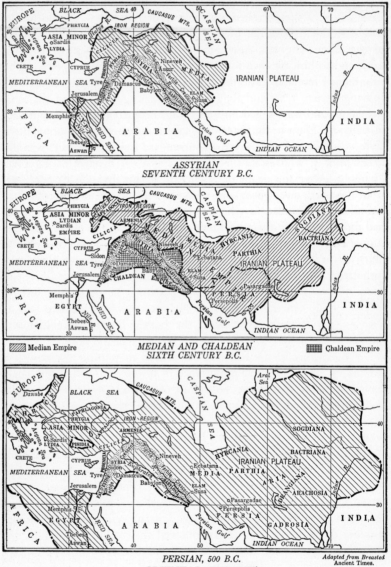

ASSYRIAN
SEVENTH CENTURY B.C.

Median Empire

MEDIAN AND CHALDEAN
SIXTH CENTURY B.C.

Chaldean Empire

PERSIAN, 500 B.C.

Adapted from Breasted
Ancient Times.

ORIENTAL EMPIRES

deportations, aided the spread and assimilation of civilization, and their roads promoted commerce. The result was the development of industry, widespread exchange of goods, the building of cities, and the growth of wealth and luxury. In commerce a great step forward was taken when the Assyrians stamped values on pieces of metal called Ishtars and thus created the precursors of the Lydian and Greek coins.

Assyrian triumph was reflected in the life and art of the people. The wealthy dressed in garments of wool, linen, or cotton, and lived luxuriously in beautiful houses. The palaces and temples built by the kings were fine works of architecture with monumental gateways, arches, colonnades, and towers. On their walls were carved in brilliant relief pictures and texts that recorded the deeds of the kings in warfare and hunting. Scribes studied and copied the ancient Babylonian texts and wrote on tablets and prisms accounts of the royal campaigns and other works of literature. Astronomers continued the study of the stars which had been begun long before by the Sumerians, and priests repeated and advanced the Babylonian methods of divination. Asshur, warlike sun god, was the patron of the kings and the creator of all other gods and men; but Ishtar, Marduk, and the rest of the Mesopotamian divinities were worshiped according to the ancient rites.

The sturdy peasantry, which formed the bulk of the population of Assyria, had been in the beginning the source of the country's strength in arms. But the power and wealth of empire created vital changes in the character of social organization and proved disastrous for the peasants. An officeholding nobility gained possession of the land; a middle class organized into professional and craft guilds developed in the cities; the peasants rose to these ranks, or sank into serfdom, or were killed in war. In later days there were large groups of rural serfs and city slaves, and the army was filled with mercenaries drawn chiefly from the subjects of the empire. Therewith the task of maintaining an extensive empire became too great for the strength of the Assyrians, and finally Assyria fell before the accumulated hatred of her neighbors.

THE CHALDAEANS

With the fall of Assyria, Egypt regained its independence under the twenty-sixth dynasty, and the Chaldaeans of Babylon fell heir to

Assyrian power in the Fertile Crescent. For centuries a new tribe of Semites called Chaldaeans had been sifting into Babylonia. They finally attained ascendancy there, and it was they who formed the backbone of the resistance to Assyria. After their king, Nabopolassar, and his allies had succeeded in capturing Nineveh in 612 B.C., a new Babylonian monarchy was established.

In 604 B.C. Nebuchadrezzar mounted the throne. His first care was the rebuilding of the capital with the great walls, the palaces, and the famous hanging gardens, so brilliantly described by Herodotus as a ziggurat-like series of terraces said to have been built to please his mountain-born Median queen. Nebuchadrezzar's chief enemy was Egypt, whose control of Syria he challenged. The armies of Egypt were defeated; Tyre was compelled to yield after a famous siege; Jerusalem was taken and destroyed and the Jews carried to Babylon in exile. For a brief period Babylon regained its olden glory.

Nabonidus, the last of the dynasty, was an antiquarian who set scholars to work collecting texts and studying the Sumerian language. So thoroughly did the Chaldaeans assimilate the ancient culture that the Greeks and Romans attributed to them the entire Babylonian astrology and systems of divination, and the Jews believed that Abraham came from "Ur of the Chaldees." Internal dissension eventually weakened the power of Nabonidus, and in 539 B.C. Babylon fell to Cyrus, the Persian. Jewish memories of this event are recorded in the famous story of Belshazzar's feast in the Book of Daniel.

SAITE EGYPT The twenty-sixth and last native dynasty to establish and maintain itself in Egypt was founded by Psamtik I of Sais. Made governor of the delta by Assurbanipal in 663 B.C., he gradually, with the aid of Greek and Syrian mercenaries, gained control of upper Egypt and by 640 B.C. had become independent of Assyria. He and his successors dreamed of restoring the former power of Egypt. His son, Necho (609-593 B.C.), defeated Josiah, king of Judah, and regained control of Syria to the Euphrates, only to lose it to the Chaldaeans. A brief inscription in Greek, cut tourist-fashion on the leg of a statue at Abu Simbel, is the surviving record of an attempt on the part of Psamtik II (593-588 B.C.) to reconquer Nubia. Under Amasis (569-525 B.C.) the dynasty attained its greatest prosperity. But the rulers of Egypt were looking to the past. Ancient ceremonies and rituals were restored; ancient texts were sought out,

copied, and studied; every possible attempt was made to bring back
to life the ideas and practices of earlier periods. But only in art was
there advance; the statuary in stone and bronze and the objects of industry, particularly in faïence, are freer and more graceful than those
of former times, though the tomb painters deliberately copied from
the walls of Old Kingdom mastabas. In the midst of this recrudes-
cence, Egypt was opened to the Greeks, who, coming as mercenary
soldiers, as merchants and as tourists, learned fundamental lessons
from the old civilization of the Nile. But later Egypt, without real
strength, was but a hollow shell of the past, and in 525 B.C. the dynasty
fell, as had the Chaldaeans, before the advancing power of the Persians.

CONCLUSION   The ancient Orient had run its course. Sumerians,
Semites, and Egyptians had solved well the problems
of material existence: of agriculture, of industry and trade, of law, of
architecture, and of art. The Assyrians had contributed military and
imperial organization, and the Phoenicians had carried the achievements of the East throughout the Mediterranean. The peoples of
Babylonia had developed the means of divination; the Egyptians had
created a religion of immortality; and the Hebrew prophets had
evolved their concept of monotheism. The accomplishments of these
peoples were not lost. In the East the Persians assumed the power and
absorbed the culture of the Babylonians. In the West the Greeks were
the heirs of Egypt and Babylon. But with all its achievements, the
Orient had failed to recognize the importance of the individual in
society. The god and his earthly representative, the king, were all-
important. Man, as the Hebrew prophets taught, was but as clay in
the hands of the potter. "As the flower of the field, so he flourisheth.
For the wind passeth over it and it is gone; and the place thereof
shall know it no more."

THE RISE OF NEW POWERS IN THE ORIENT

LYDIA   In Asia Minor, of the many new states arising in
place of the Hittite Empire, the most powerful and
important was Lydia. The Phrygians, whose invasion had contributed
to the downfall of the Hittites and whose wealth drawn from the
gold-bearing streams in the interior gave rise to the Greek story of
King Midas and the "Golden Touch," were crushed by an invasion

of Cimmerians in the eighth century B.C. The Lydians rose to take their place as the dominant people in Anatolia. Led by able kings, the Lydians secured control of the Greek cities on the coast and of the entire plateau west of the Halys River. They contested with the Medes for the possession of the land beyond the river in a war which was brought to a sudden end when, in the midst of a battle in 585 B.C., an eclipse of the sun terrified both armies. Thereafter the boundary was fixed at the Halys, and an alliance was formed which lasted until the Median dynasty was overthrown by Cyrus the Persian.

Gold from the streams, wool from the flocks on the hills, and the commerce which passed overland from Babylonia through Sardis to the Aegean gave Lydia extraordinary wealth. To the Lydians Herodotus attributes the first coinage of gold. The splendor of their armored chariots and infantry, the high level of Lydian culture, and the fabulous riches of King Croesus, which have made his name a byword, are reflected in the poetry of Sappho and in the charming stories of Herodotus. But the period of Lydian supremacy was short-lived.

MEDES AND PERSIANS

THE MEDES AND THE PERSIANS   The fall of Nineveh in 612 B.C. and of Babylon in 539 B.C. signalized the rise to power of new peoples appearing from the plateau of Iran. The Medes, Indo-European in origin, secured control of the plateau and under their great king, Cyaxares, took part in the attack on Nineveh and gained possession of the Assyrian lands north and east of the Tigris, while the closely related tribes of the Persians occupied Elam to the south. Expansion to the west into Asia Minor brought Cyaxares, as we have seen, into that conflict with the Lydians which, ending with the eclipse of the sun, forced the western boundary of his empire to stop at the Halys River.

In 550 B.C. a dynastic revolution took place when Cyrus, the Persian, killed and deposed his suzerain, Astyages, successor to Cyaxares. The transition to Persian rule, which made no perceptible change in the empire as a whole, brought new force and energy to the direction of affairs and led to renewed expansion, to the subjection of Lydia and the Anatolian Greeks, and to the capture of Babylon. As king of the Medes and Persians, Cyrus became one of the world's great conquerors.

CONQUEST OF
ASIA MINOR
The first region which Cyrus added to his empire was Asia Minor. Misreading the situation, Croesus of Lydia determined on the conquest of the territory east of the Halys River, as soon as he heard of the fall of his Median ally, Astyages. After a drawn battle with Cyrus, he retired to Sardis to gather adequate forces for the war. Cyrus made a sudden charge upon Sardis, caught Croesus unprepared, and took and burned the city in 546 B.C. The Lydian power thus came to an end and the Greek subjects of Lydia were speedily added to the Persian Empire (p. 147).

His western frontier secure, Cyrus made several campaigns to the east, and then in 539 B.C. he took Babylon from the Chaldaeans and became king of that ancient city. He allowed the Jews who were in captivity to return and rebuild Jerusalem. After some vicissitudes the few who took advantage of this permission succeeded in establishing in Palestine a small theocratic state under Persian suzerainty.

CAMBYSES
Cambyses followed his father as king when Cyrus died fighting in the northeast in 529 B.C. He invaded Egypt, overthrew the Saite dynasty, and crowned himself Pharaoh. After unsuccessful attempts to conquer lands to the south of Egypt, he became insane and died in 523 B.C. Confusion followed his death, until Darius of the Achaemenid family established himself as king of Persia in 521 B.C.

THE EMPIRE
OF DARIUS
Darius completed the organization of the Persian Empire. More than twenty large provinces, called satrapies, were established, each under either a relative of the king or a Persian noble of high rank. As checks on the power of the provincial governor or satrap, the king appointed a secretary and a commander of the garrison and inspectors who, as "the eyes and ears of the king," traveled from province to province. Within the satrapy great latitude was allowed in respect to local customs: the Jews were ruled by their priests, and the Greek cities by their tyrants; tribes retained their accustomed organization; and many petty kings were allowed to keep their titles. Darius himself was king of Babylon and Pharaoh of Egypt. The whole empire was bound together by a well-developed system of roads and by couriers who allowed "neither snow, nor rain, nor heat, nor the darkness of night to hinder them in the prompt completion of their allotted tasks."

In the center of Persian imperial government stood the king, "King of Kings," advised by seven councilors, surrounded and assisted by the Persian nobility, and guarded by the Ten Thousand Immortals, pick of the Persian army. The imperial structure was supported by tribute from the subject peoples paid in kind or in coinage. Darius issued gold coins called Darics after the king or "archers" because they bore the picture of a Persian archer. Some of the satraps also coined silver in the ratio of thirteen to one (silver to gold). All subject states were called upon to furnish for the royal army troops who fought in their native fashion. The seaboard peoples such as the Phoenicians and the Greeks supplied the navy.

THE PALACE
OF THE KING

At Persepolis Darius constructed a great palace which represented the combination of cultures under the Persians. The architects drew inspiration from Egypt, from Babylon, from Assyria, and from the Greeks, and combined their lessons to erect for the King of Kings a truly splendid abode, in which were collected the great treasures of the empire. The palace stood on a huge artificial terrace, to which access was given by a ramp and a royal stairway. Entrance to the terrace was guarded by a gateway faced with lions in the Assyrian fashion. The Hall of a Hundred Columns, reminiscent of some of the great Egyptian colonnades, provided an audience chamber. King Xerxes later added a hypostyle hall. Behind the great hall were gardens and the dwelling of the king. The building was plundered and burned by Alexander and is now being excavated and studied by scholars of the Oriental Institute of the University of Chicago.

COMMERCE

All the East from the Mediterranean to the Indus, from Egypt to the Black Sea, was united under the single control of the Persian emperor. The peace which prevailed, the uniformity of weights and measures, and the introduction of coinage fostered the development of trade along the great military roads which bound the empire together. Contact was established with India and overland with China; Darius sent an expedition to explore the water route from India to Egypt and another to survey the Mediterranean. In the interest of trade the canal from the Nile to the Red Sea was reopened. The land prospered and tribute poured in from its fifty million inhabitants to the great enrichment of the King of Kings.

ZOROASTER

The Persians were, in origin, a vigorous mountain folk who taught their sons "to ride, to shoot the bow, and to speak the truth," and whose highest glory was to serve the king. Their early religion was associated with fire worship, but under

Darius the worship of Ahura Mazda seems to have been established as the official religion. Zoroaster, the great Persian religious teacher, probably lived shortly before the time of Darius. The Avesta, the sacred book which developed from his teaching, was composed at a later period and it is uncertain what came from Zoroaster himself. From the older experiences of his people and from his own insight he developed a militant theology of monotheistic character called Zoroastrianism. Ahura Mazda, god of light, created the world and placed man upon it. He demanded of his followers obedience, morality, and truth. Other gods such as those adored by the Magi, priests of the old religion, by the Greeks, Jews, or Egyptians, were his agents or his enemies. Against the forces of darkness or evil, led by Ahriman, he and his worshipers waged a constant war. He promised a reward in paradise to those who died fighting for him, and to the world the ultimate triumph of truth over falsehood. The Persian king, earthly representative of the god, received from him a divine mission to practice justice, to overthrow injustice, to reward friends, to punish enemies, and to establish law over the lands in the light of Ahura Mazda. The Persian Empire thus became a state with a divine command to conquer the world in the name of religion.

The later activities of Darius and his successors were so completely involved with the history of the Greeks that they are best treated in connection with the story of the Hellenes.

═ VI ═

THE RISE OF THE HELLENES

REEK history is the central and vital element in the story of the ancient Mediterranean. As the Greeks learned the techniques which the Oriental peoples had achieved, they transformed with their own genius everything which they acquired. They developed literature, art, architecture, and the science of government to extraordinary heights. They created the ideas of liberty and democracy. They began the study of natural philosophy and laid the foundations of the sciences. Greatest of all, they discovered the individual. In answer to the Oriental concept of man as the creature and plaything of the gods, they offered the statement, "Of all the wonders on earth, none is more wonderful than man," and the dictum, "Man is the measure of all things." On the basis of the individual they developed the philosophy of the good life. There is hardly any field of human endeavor in the modern world which does not rest upon the achievements of the Greeks.

The Greeks called themselves Hellenes, and the lands in which they lived, Hellas. The central area of their culture was the basin of the Aegean Sea—Greece itself, the islands, and the Anatolian littoral. When they expanded and founded colonies around the shores of the Mediterranean and in the Black Sea region, the term "Hellas" was enlarged to include these new foundations. Wherever there were Greek communities there was Hellas.

SOURCES OF GREEK HISTORY

The ancient Greeks have left for us much more information about themselves than did the Orientals. The histories of Herodotus, Thucydides and Xenophon (pp. 252 f., 279) have survived with fragments from many other historical writers. Plutarch's *Lives* (p. 502) are sources of inestimable value. All the works of Greek literature which have come down to us contribute to the picture of Hellenic life. The ancient habit of recording laws, decrees, proclamations, treaties, and other kinds of permanent records on stone has resulted in the preservation of great numbers of inscriptions, which epigraphists have copied, studied, and published to amplify and verify the literary story. Archaeologists have excavated or are excavating the ancient sites—Olympia, the market place of Athens, Corinth, Delos, Delphi, Olynthus, and many others. Museums are full of the statuary, vases, and antiquities which have been found throughout the ancient world. Every season adds its quota to our information of what the Greeks did and how they lived.

GEOGRAPHY

THE SEA

Just as the Nile and the Tigris-Euphrates were the centers of the world of Oriental culture, so was the Aegean Sea the dominant feature in the history of the Greeks. During the Pleistocene period the southern spur of the great European mountain range sank, forming a trough between it and the Asiatic plateau of Asia Minor, and leaving to the west a confused mass of mountainous area, the Greek peninsula. The water rushed into the valleys, creating harbors and gulfs and straits which so penetrated the land that no point in it was far distant from the sea. Scattered mountain tops pushed up out of the waters and formed islands.

The islands furnished easy steppingstones; mountains and promontories afforded easily recognized landmarks. In the absence of tides, land breezes in the morning and sea breezes in the evening carried boats in and out of the harbors. The Etesian winds of summer blowing all day from the north to northeast carried boats south, while the counterbreezes of evening sent them slowly north again. Summer seas thus became as natural a route of travel for the mainland or island dwellers as was the Nile for the Egyptians. Skilled sailors could navigate in the dangerous westerlies of spring and fall, but the stormy winter winds kept them all at home. From the sea came also fish and salt for food, and mollusks to furnish the purple dye which the Tyrians had made famous.

GREECE

From Rostovtzeff, History of The Ancient World.
Courtesy of Oxford University Press, publishers.

THE MOUNTAINS   When we turn from the sea to the land, the most prominent feature becomes the mountains, which form four-fifths of the total area. Between masses of schist, limestone, and marble lie mountain valleys and small flat plains. On the mountains are scanty forests of pines, firs, beeches, and oaks, which furnish lumber for building and wood for charcoal. From the wildflowers which carpet their lower regions the bees draw material for their honey. The hillsides furnish pasturage for sheep and goats, who nibble the young shoots and prevent nature from replacing the trees cut down for the use of man. In antiquity there were small deposits of gold, silver, copper, and iron. The sculptor and builder found whole mountains of marble, and around the bases of the hills lay a Tertiary deposit of clay ready for the hand of the potter.

While few of the mountains are high, many of them are famed in literature. Above Olympus (about 10,000 feet) was the dwelling place of the gods. Below it lie Ossa and Pelion; Parnassus, sacred to Apollo, towers over the Boeotian plain. Pentelicus and Hymettus look down on Athens, and Helicon, the home of the Muses, overlooks Thebes.

There are few rivers worthy of the name in the Greek peninsula. None is navigable, and most are mountain torrents which ravage the plains in winter and push out alluvial deposits into the sea, leaving dry, stony beds in the summer. The mountains block the flow of waters in the interior. But the waters have dissolved the limestone and secured underground passages for themselves, whence many of them come forth again in perennial springs for the watering of land. The little flat plains are wonderfully fertile in the production of grains, vegetables, fruits, and, in the southern areas, olives. The islands, too, possess their small plains where similar products are raised. The two-field system (one-half of the farm land left fallow each year) commonly used in antiquity accentuated the natural lack of space. At best there never was enough food and this fact turned moderation into a primary virtue. Wars were fought for the control of little areas. Bad seasons or increasing population sent men abroad in search of new lands or drove them to industry or to the sea in search of a livelihood.

CLIMATE   The combination of mountains, valleys, seas, the protecting heights of the Balkan range to the north and the warming influence of the Sahara and the Mediterranean to the south serve to give the Aegean world a mild, equable climate. Although Athens is but a little south of the latitude of Washington, its range of temperature more nearly approximates that of Georgia, and parts of southern Greece are subtropical. From November to March it is rainy, with rare snowfalls. There are occasional showers in the spring and fall, but from June to September it is dry. Grains are planted in the fall and harvested in the late spring, a fact of decided importance in the ancient Greek calendar. The air is mild, but invigorating, fresh and free from fog or dewfall.

GEOGRAPHIC DIVISIONS
    Greece is divided into a number of areas with fairly definite geographic boundaries which received tribal or political significance in antiquity. In the extreme north of the peninsula was Macedon. Below it lay Thessaly in the east and Epirus in the west. A number of divisions follow to the south, the most important of which are Acarnania and Aetolia on the west, Phocis, containing Parnassus and Delphi, shrine of Apollo, in the center, and the Boeotian plain to the east. This rich plain furnished sites for many cities, of which Thebes was the greatest. Across a narrow strait lay the island of Euboea, site of Chalcis and Eretria, famous for its copper. As a spur from the mountains south of Thebes, Attica, with its poltical center at Athens, juts out into the Aegean.

The Saronic Gulf on the one side and the Gulf of Corinth on the other cut Greece into two parts connected only by the narrow Isthmus of Corinth. On the isthmus were two states, Megara and Corinth. The ancients called the southern area Peloponnesus, "island of Pelops." Its divisions are clearly marked by natural features. South of Corinth lay Argolis, center of Mycenaean culture, later dominated by Argos. In the mountainous center, west of Argos, was Arcadia, famous for its oaks. The northern edge of the mountains along the gulf was occupied by little Achaean cities. On the west was the rich plain of Elis wherein were held the renowned Olympic games. To the south lay two fertile river valleys: Laconia, site of Sparta on the Eurotas, and Messenia, with its capital Messene, separated by the lofty Taÿgetus range, source of iron.

In the Aegean the islands circle around the sacred little isle of Delos to form the Cyclades. Of these Paros, known for its fine marble, Naxos, and Melos were the most important.

The plateau of Asia Minor approaches the sea and is terminated by many islands, of which Lesbos, Chios, Samos, Cos, and Rhodes are the largest. On the mainland several rivers separate the heights, create rich valleys, and furnish routes of trade with the interior. Of these the wandering Maeander, near whose mouth was Miletus, is celebrated. Along the coast, in places suitable for agriculture and for trade, lay numerous cities, among them Ephesus and Smyrna. Across the southern end of the Aegean the island of Crete lies like a dike.

THE OUTER WORLD   The sea makes the Aegean area a well-defined unit. Travel beyond its borders was none too easy for ancient mariners. Since the voyage around Cape Malea or Cythera was dangerous, most sailors preferred to carry their goods, and even their boats, across the isthmus and sail down the Gulf of Corinth. Thence a series of islands, notably among them Ithaca, home of Odysseus, guided them north to Corcyra. A swift, daring trip across the stormy Adriatic landed them on Italian shores. If they wished to venture further, they would have to round the stormy corners of Sicily or run the dangers of Scylla and Charybdis in the Straits of Messana.

The swift current of the Hellespont made it difficult for the Hellenic sailor to travel northeast into the Propontis and the always-treacherous Euxine (Black) Sea. The summer trip to Egypt, however, whether one went direct from Crete before the Etesian winds, or coasted east and south, was easy; the return, more difficult. The river routes of Asia Minor and the sea-borne traffic of the Mediterranean brought the Aegean world into contact with the older civilizations of the East, and it was there that the Hellenes learned their first lessons in culture.

THE GREEK MIDDLE AGE

During the earlier millennia (p. 68) a great civilization had risen in the Aegean, had flourished, and had fallen. Though its influence on later Greek culture was great and enduring, its historic position in Greek history is difficult to determine for lack of contemporary written records. Almost certainly the peoples of the Mycenaean Age were Greeks and the familiar Greek legends represent later memories of this period. The first period of classical Greek history is the period of darkness called the Greek Middle Age. This came with the Dorian invasion and the migrations which accompanied and followed it; its first written sources were the Homeric poems.

About 1200 B.C. pressure from the north drove east and south the inhabitants of the northern area of Greece. Groups of clans pushed into Thessaly and Boeotia, while others crossed the Gulf of Corinth to settle Elis and the Achaean communities. The great flood, however, was the movement of the Dorians, who overwhelmed the rest of the Peloponnesus. Messenia, Laconia, and Argolis were occupied; Corinth and Megara were taken in a northward thrust which was stopped only at the borders of Attica, and the great centers of Mycenaean life fell before the invaders. Those who could, escaped and began a movement across the Aegean. Attica, overcrowded with refugees, sent out bands of Ionians, who occupied the islands to the east and settled in the central area of the Anatolian littoral. Groups from Thessaly and the north moved in a parallel line to the northern islands, to the Troad, and to the neighboring area called thereafter Aeolis. One band of Achaeans fled to settle in Cyprus. The conquering Dorians followed the fugitives and took Crete, the southern islands, and the lower part of Asia Minor. The central area received not only Ionians but many other groups as well and became the melting pot of the migrations

This movement east, the repercussions of which were felt throughout the Mediterranean, was made possible by the collapse of the Hittite power. Wandering bands, dislodged from Asia Minor, the islands, or the mainland, overran Syria and fell upon Egypt in the reign of Ramses III (p. 89). Others went west, one group to be the ancestors of the later Etruscans in Italy (p. 330).

THE HOMERIC QUESTION

The only sources of information for the period which followed the invasion are scanty archaeological remains, particularly of pottery, and the Homeric poems, the *Iliad* and the *Odyssey*. Around the Homeric poems has raged a controversy which began in antiquity. Who was Homer? When and where did he live? Was there ever a Homer, or were the poems composed by an evolutionary process or by the gathering together of scattered songs? What civilization do the poems describe? That of the Achaean stage of the Mycenaean period to which the story belongs, or that of Homer's own time during the Middle Age of Greece? These questions cannot be satisfactorily answered. Many competent scholars hold today that Homer lived in southern Aeolis about the year 850 B.C. and that he drew his stories from the songs which older bards had brought with them across the sea. From these he created the greatest epics ever composed.

The material civilization—the palaces with their decorations, the

great wall of Troy, the gold and silver work—belongs to the age of
the stories themselves. The political structure and the social and economic life which he describes seem to be the reflection of his own experience. Yet there is much confusion, and the lines of division may
not be clearly drawn. At times the Homeric heroes go into battle with
the huge man-covering shields of the earlier period; again, sometimes
in the same scene, they carry the small round shield and wear the
complete set of body armor which seems to date after the Dorian invasion. The men of the Mycenaean Age used bronze, but iron weapons
and tools which belong to the later period appear in the poems. In the
Odyssey appears the famous line, "The very sight of iron leads men
to strife." Though the Homeric kings claimed god-given supremacy,
their actual powers were far less than those of the rulers who built
the great beehive tombs of Mycenae. More prominent in trade than
the seafaring Phaeacians, who belong to the ancient memories, are the
"black-browed Phoenicians" who entered the Aegean as merchants
after the collapse of Crete and Mycenae. Homeric characters wear
loose garments in place of the carefully fitted dresses which appear in
the Mycenaean pictures. Finally Homeric heroes practice cremation of
the dead instead of the inhumation characteristic of the earlier period.

The poems likewise disclose a process of transition from a pastoral
to an agricultural life such as took place in the period after the migrations. The Homeric heroes are restless warriors who go forth on raids
to seize the cattle of neighboring peoples and who are mighty eaters
of beef. Yet the similes in the poems and the pictures on the shield
of Achilles portray settled farming communities wherein the slave of
a landless man is the sorriest of all humans. The picture of society
which may be drawn from the poems thus apparently belongs to the
age of the poet, who was himself a keen and sympathetic observer of
nature and of humanity.

HOMERIC
SOCIETY

The society and polity which Homer describes were
aristocratic. The great families possessed large estates
under patriarchal direction. With Priam in the palace
at Troy lived his fifty sons and their wives, his twelve daughters and
their husbands. On these estates the nobles did a full share both of
direction and of work. Odysseus boasted of his all-round abilities as
farmer and craftsman; Penelope spun and wove, and Nausicaa with
her attendants did the family washing. Guilds of heralds, prophets,
and bards inherited the traditions of earlier times and were welcome

guests in the great houses. Lesser men, as tenants, serfs, slaves, or hired laborers, tended the herds or worked on the great estates under the watchful eye of the lord of the manor. A few owned farms of their own in the poorer lands. To such a farm Laertes, father of Odysseus, retired in his old age.

INDUSTRY   In this system, where each estate sought for self-sufficiency, artisans skilled in many trades were in great demand. Hephaestus was their heavenly prototype, and they occupied an honorable position. Archaeological discoveries have brought to light the fine geometric pottery which they made, a direct inheritance from Mycenaean times. The metalworkers, whose skill was likewise an inheritance, learned probably from Asia Minor the use of iron which was soon to produce great changes in the economic and political world.

TRADE   Survivors of the old regime did not forget, and the newcomers speedily learned, the simple principles of navigation. Shipwrights were singled out for honor. Though most of the trade with the East was in the hands of the Phoenicians, there are many indications of Greek activity, and the stories of the *Odyssey* indicate adventurous exploration of the Mediterranean. Yet trade was hardly differentiated from piracy. "Are you a pirate or do you come as a peaceful merchant?" was the customary greeting to a voyager who had just landed.

GOVERNMENT   The king, who was leader in war, chief priest and judge, was simply the most powerful noble. His income was derived from his own estates and from the spoils of war. In the distribution of meat, after it had been dedicated to the gods at the sacrifices, he was entitled to a larger share than the others. He made great pretensions to god-given power, which he could not enforce. Around him in council gathered the heads of the patriarchal families. They advised him, quarreled with him, and challenged his authority. The monarchy was slowly being transformed into an aristocracy.

The common people, toward whom the aristocratic poet is contemptuous, formed an assembly, but it had little power. When Thersites rose to attack the king, Odysseus with the approval of the mass speedily put him in his place; and when the commoners voted to return home, the nobles vetoed their decision and compelled them to remain. In accordance with ancient traditions, local disputes were settled by the village elders; conditions required nothing more.

RELIGION Homeric religion was the product of an heroic age. The gods and goddesses were but nobles, supermen, and superwomen, who tricked and defeated the will of their king, Zeus, as did the nobles of the earth. The very humanness of these divinities, however, was to be an important factor in the later development of Greek religious thought. The virtues of the Homeric age were social rather than religious in their origin—they were family and military virtues rather than divine. The faithful devotion of Penelope and Andromache, the filial loyalty of Nausicaa and Telemachus tell the story of a noble family life. Courage, ability in arms, readiness with words in the council were the greatest glory of man, while cowardice was the worst disgrace. The choice of Achilles, a short, vigorous life and glory everlasting, was the expression of the age's ideal.

INTERSTATE RELATIONS The sacred ties of guest-friendship bound some family groups together and prevented combat between their members. Otherwise anarchy prevailed save when ameliorated by the laws of religion. The gods protected embassies and heralds, and frowned on treachery, the breaking of oaths, and the use of poisoned weapons. But in this period of piratical raids, war was the natural condition of relationship between groups. Only between organized states could interstate relations exist, and references in Homer and archaeological evidence combine to prove that during the Middle Age such states were developing.

THE POLIS

Out of the confusion which followed the Dorian invasion the Greeks emerged into a period of new growth. Settled life in cities came to be the order of the day; colonies were planted around the seas; industry and commerce, art and literature developed; philosophers first dared to question the nature of the universe; and political leaders began the establishment of democratic institutions. In short, it was during this age that the Hellenic world laid the foundation upon which the civilization of its greatest days was built.

GROWTH OF
THE CITY-STATE
The city-state or *polis* became during this period, and remained for centuries, the normal form of government and the characteristic institution of the Greek world. Except in a few backward regions such as Aetolia, the older tribal organization, the *ethnos,* disappeared entirely or passed into a feeble bond based upon common worship of an ancestral god. In its place came a number of new organizations, based upon locality.

The steps by which this change took place are highly conjectural. The word "polis" would seem to have been applied to the fortress where in Mycenaean times the king and his retainers lived under the protection of the war goddess Athena, guardian of the citadel. Since these fortresses were usually built on those sheer mounds of limestone which rise out of the plains of Greece and lend themselves readily to fortification, the term *acropolis* ("high city") was frequently applied to them, and subsequently to the mounds on which they were built.

With the collapse of Mycenaean culture and the decline in the power of the king, many of these settlements were completely abandoned. Where they did not thus disappear, the religious element predominated and the polis or acropolis became primarily the dwelling place of the goddess and the religious center of the community. Here the people in the neighboring villages gathered for religious purposes, and accordingly there developed a local political tie which displaced the older allegiance to the tribe or *ethnos.* Wherever, with the coming of the invaders, the older sites were abandoned, new centers of this religious character were developed. It is a striking fact that in most of the states the guardian divinity was a goddess, Athena, Hera, or Artemis, in continuation of the earlier Aegean religious tradition.

Under the protection of the ruling divinity the polis would become the seat of government and by it the nobles would build their palaces. Since the polis was fortified, it could be used in time of necessity as a place of refuge from danger. Close at hand a market place would develop around which merchants and artisans would establish their shops and residences. Under favoring circumstances a city in the modern sense of the term would appear. But this was not essential to the idea of the polis; in Sparta the people lived scattered in villages over the plain.

If one polis was predominant in strength because of the location of its citadel, its religious or commercial pre-eminence, or its numbers, it might reach out and absorb neighboring city-states whose citizens, without moving to the center, would transfer their allegiance to it. Such a *synoecism* or "joining together" took place in Attica where Athens became the polis for all the smaller communities. In Boeotia, by contrast, the small cities remained independent and were united only through the loose ties of a league. Size was no more a criterion of the city-state than was the physical development of a city.

The location of the citadel, which thus became the religious and political center of the community, was influenced primarily by considerations of defense, of water supply, and of relationship to the plain, rather than by commercial advantages. In fact, for a coastal community an inland location was an advantage as a safeguard against piracy. When commerce expanded, seaport towns grew as an adjunct to the city.

NATURE OF THE CITY-STATE   In the course of these developments the word "polis," which originally meant "citadel," came to be applied to the political entity of the city-state, that is, to the group of people who used the citadel as a common religious, political, and economic center. Special emphasis must be laid on this fact that the city-state was a group, an aggregate of citizens, not a piece of territory. Boundaries were at all times vague and meant but little in ancient polity. Nor did the natural features, such as mountains, so sought after by modern states, always form the limits of ancient cities; sometimes the limits crossed natural boundaries. Elsewhere, in some of the great plains, several small communities would nestle undivided by any natural feature but each strong in its allegiance to its own polis. As a result, pastoral or agricultural rights over hillsides or fields in the borderland between two states were constant causes of disputes.

Membership in the citizen body depended on birth, not on residence in the locality. It could not be obtained except by gift of the community. Conversely, it could not be taken away, even by the destruction of the city itself. Messene was destroyed by Sparta shortly before 700 B.C. In 370 B.C. it was rebuilt by Epaminondas, and descendants of the original inhabitants, who had never given up their idea of citizenship, returned.

The older ethnic groups were carried into the organization of the citizen body. In the Ionian states were four, in most of the Dorian three, subordinate tribal divisions called *phylae*. These in turn were separated into *phratries,* brotherhoods of families, who fought and worshiped together and kept the rolls of the citizens.

With this development of the polis came the principle which was to remain the fundamental element in all Greek political thought— the right of each city-state, no matter how small, to absolute freedom in the control of its local government and of its relations with other states. The city-state was the largest political unit comprehensible to the Greeks. From loyalty to the city-state and desire to serve and glorify it came the idea of democratic liberty as the Greeks understood it, and those great achievements in art and literature which are the glory of Greece. Unfortunately, from these same impulses arose those endless wars which finally wrought the ruin of Hellas and made it an easy prey for Macedon and Rome.

THE ARISTOCRACY

GROWTH OF ARISTOCRACY
The development of settled conditions in agriculture and the growth of political organization in the city-state combined to finish the process begun in the Homeric Age—the replacement of the Zeus-nurtured king by the aristocracy. It did not take place everywhere at the same time, for kingship survived in Argos until the Persian Wars and in Sparta in circumscribed form throughout the classic period. But in most of the states, aristocrats who based their power on the land and traced their ancestry to the heroes and the gods assumed control through their council. Their names indicate their position in this pre-eminently agricultural period: *Hippobotae,* "horse raisers," *Geomoroi,* "farmers," *Eupatridae,* "well-fathered." Dreading interference with their possessions, they took away the civil powers of the king and appointed members of their order to hear cases affecting landownership and later all cases involving the ancient customs. In some states they gave the military power of the king to one of their number. Only the religious power was left to the kingship, which then came habitually to be an elective office. In Corinth the royal family was strong enough to keep control in its own group, though the individual kingship disappeared.

THE COMMON PEOPLE
At the same time the common people were deprived of such rights as they had had in the earlier period. The assembly ceased to meet. The aristocrats, as divinely appointed guardians of the god-given laws, controlled the courts, and though opposition to them was dangerous lest it anger the gods they were nevertheless open to bribes or to influence. Against this

land-greedy and corrupt nobility the small farmers had little chance.
Many of them sank into tenantry, serfdom, and slavery. Serfdom had
certainly existed in Mycenaean times, but it increased and spread
under the aristocratic regime. Those peasants who escaped this fate
were forced into the poorer lands which had formerly lain waste and
up on the rocky hillsides, where they terraced and hoarded the soil,
planted vineyards or olive orchards, and grew a few vegetables. Others
became charcoal burners in the woods or tended herds of sheep or
goats on the hillsides. Cattle pasturage declined and the forest began
to disappear.

HESIOD
The chief source of information for this period is the
poet Hesiod (ca. 750 B.C.), author of two didactic
poems written in the epic dialect and meter: the *Theogony,* or "Descent of the Gods," to instruct men about their divine relations, and
the *Works and Days,* a book of advice to farmers. His father had fled
from poverty in Aeolis to Boeotia where he had occupied a piece of
wasteland. Hesiod himself had suffered at the hands of his brother
and a venal judge, and his picture of the times was gloomy. The glorious ages of Gold, Silver, Bronze, and of the Heroes had passed, he
lamented, and he was living in the Iron Age when everything was
bad and growing worse. "Might shall be right, and one shall sack the
other's city." In the beautiful parable of the hawk and the nightingale
he portrayed the unjust princes and warned them of the punishment
of farseeing Zeus.

He admonished the poor man that his only hope lay in constant,
unremitting toil and the avoidance of litigation. The reckless man
might unwisely turn to trade and trust himself to the sea, but if he
had any wisdom, the poet advised him, he would sail only during the
time of the Dog Star. The farmer was at least safe if he worked hard
and watched the calendar. To him Hesiod gave advice as to the methods, the seasons and days propitious for his tasks, the hiring of
hands, and even about the more serious business of matrimony.

AGRICULTURE
Agricultural methods and the poor quality of the soil
combined to make the situation difficult for the small
farmer. The crude plow barely broke the soil, and clods had to be
crushed laboriously with the hoe. In the absence of proper fertilizer,
a two-field system prevailed wherein fields were left fallow in alternate years. To eke out a living the farmer planted olive trees and vines
and sowed the land between the rows of these with grain and vege-

tables. With the decline of pasturage, meat disappeared from the Greek table save for the great festivals. Cereals, vegetables, and fish became the chief articles of diet. Olive oil served as butter and as fuel. The scarcity of produce made prices high and increased the power of the great landowners and the distress of the poor.

VII

ECONOMIC AND POLITICAL EVOLUTION

THE leadership in the movements which brought the Greeks out of this period of agricultural self-sufficiency into full participation in the economic life of the Mediterranean world was assumed by the islands and cities along the seacoast of Asia Minor, of which Mytilene on Lesbos, Chios, Samos, Phocaea, Ephesus, Priene, Miletus, and Halicarnassus were the most important. In these communities, where aristocratic landlords ruled over serfs, the traditions of older times were still strong. The people, vase paintings show, still dressed in the ancient fashions of Mycenae. It was for these people that Homer and his fellow poets sang of past glory in their lays. But the narrowness of their fields and the fact that the strong powers of Phrygia and Lydia in the hinterland made expansion impossible drove the nobles to seek other outlets for the exploitation of their wealth. These they found in the development of trade with the hinterland and with Syria. Phrygia and Lydia loom large in the literature which was produced in Ionia, and the Israelite records contain mention of the "people of Javan," the Ionians who, after their flight across the Aegean, had continued or renewed their mercantile contacts.

The demands of this trade produced a revolution in agriculture when the nobles diverted their fields from the growing of foodstuffs to the production of olive oil and wine for export. While this stupendous change contributed greatly to the riches and power of the ruling class, it wrought terrific hardship on the poor, many of whom found themselves at once released from serfdom and dispossessed of the land which was their only source of livelihood. Similar developments took place in some of the island cities, particularly in Chalcis on Euboea and in Corinth and Megara on the mainland. The first solution of the problem was found in a movement for colonial expansion.

COLONIAL EXPANSION

CAUSES Though the causes of this expansion, which took place during the eighth and seventh centuries B.C., were manifold, the basic reasons were agricultural and political. In good seasons the fields of the average state produced hardly enough food to suffice, while a bad year brought on famine conditions in spite of the fact that there was often a superfluity of oil and wine. Families were large, and even the family estates of the nobles were insufficient to support all their members. Where division of estates among heirs was practiced, the farms soon became too small, and when heirs had recourse to litigation, the most influential won. The result was an increasing group of landless, discontented, and therefore troublesome individuals. Political and social factions among the nobility added to the confusion. The Aegean world boiled over. Civil strife broke out in many states, and the defeated were often expelled to add to the list of homeless wanderers. Some went to Egypt, Babylon, and elsewhere, to serve as mercenary warriors; others went forth in bands in search of new lands, to find an *apoikia,* "a home away from home," where they might have land and be farmers.

The desire for commercial expansion and the quest for raw materials and markets for industrial products and the superabundant oil and wine later led to the planting of commercial settlements. Thus the Megarians who had first founded Chalcedon on the Bosporus as an agricultural settlement later established Byzantium on the opposite side of the straits because the site possessed greater commercial advantages. The Black Sea settlements of Miletus, the colonies of Corinth in the west, and the city of Naucratis in Egypt were commercial in origin. Adventurous spirits found an outlet for their exuberance in the new lands. Within the space of two centuries, the Greek world, which came to be called Hellas, had expanded to include most of the littoral of the Mediterranean and Black seas.

METHODS At first the colonial movement was sporadic. Small bands under chosen leaders struck out for themselves and found or seized sites suitable for agricultural colonies. Countless little cities, some of which are known today only by their names and coins, sprang up here and there. In time, order came out of chaos. A contemporary religious development had brought the Pythian Apollo of Delphi, god of wanderers, to the fore, and the later colonies went forth under the advice of his oracle and the leadership of his priests. The priests seem to have been extraordinarily well informed as to possible sites and conditions around the seas. When a city determined, for one reason or another, to send out a colony, it first applied to the oracle. On its advice, a site was chosen and a leader appointed as founder of the new city. Laws and plans were carefully drawn up in advance. If sufficient numbers were lacking, the city might invite colonists from other communities to join the band. When the place of settlement was reached, the founder first set aside the proper area for the worship of the gods according to the cults of the mother city, and then proceeded to divide the land among the people by the casting of lots. The laws were set in operation and the new state was safely launched. The founder, who was usually a member of a great noble family, was venerated as a hero.

THE NEW STATES The independence of the new city-state was a basic principle of the movement. It was entitled to all the privileges of any of the older cities of the Aegean. Its ties with the mother city were, with rare exceptions, close, and based on blood relationship and on community of religious ideas and institutions. Colonists frequently returned home for the great festivals, and in most cases could regain citizenship at home if they so desired. In times of crisis the colony appealed to the mother city for help, as did Syracuse to Corinth in the turmoil of the fourth century. On the other hand, Corcyra, likewise a colony of Corinth, maintained for the mother city an enduring enmity which resulted in many wars.

Relations between the colonists and the natives usually followed one of two common patterns. In some places the Greeks had to fight for possession, and there they either reduced the older inhabitants to serfdom or slavery, or drove them back from the coast. In rare instances they failed to make their possessions good or permanent. Where they were received peacefully, a quiet intermingling took place, but the culture became Greek. Wherever they went, they endeavored to identify local gods with their own and to find sites connected with their myths and legends. The Corinthian settlers of Syracuse were sure that the fountain Arethusa was but the reappearance of the river Alpheus, which came out of Arcadia, flowed by the site of Olympia, and passed through the Mediterranean to greet them in their new home.

COLONIZING
CITIES
Nearly all of the important Greek cities except Athens, Aegina, and Thebes took part in this colonial movement. The most prolific, however, were the Asiatic cities, notably Miletus, whose colonists pushed north and east into the Hellespontine and Euxine regions. Megara had a share in the same area and looked to the west as well; Chalcidians from Euboea went north to the promontories along the Macedonian coast and west to Italy. Corinth occupied Corcyra on the route to the west and was the proud mother of Syracuse. Spartans founded one colony at Tarentum; Rhodes made settlements in Sicily; and the Achaean cities in the northern Peloponnesus settled thickly in southern Italy. Many colonies throve so well that they added settlements of their own.

THE WEST
According to tradition, Chalcidian Cumae near the Bay of Naples was the earliest colony in the west. Later commercial development caused the settlement of the "New City," Neapolis, or Naples. Rhegium and Zancle, which dominated the straits between Italy and Sicily, Naxos, Catana, and Leontini were also colonies of the Chalcidians.

Southeastern Italy was occupied chiefly by Achaeans. Sybaris, rich in its valley and in its control of an overland route from the Ionic to the Tyrrhenian seas, became famous for its luxury. Croton was not so fortunate in site but throve, nonetheless, to become known as an athletic center and the home of the Pythagorean sect. In the famous rivalry between these two cities, Croton triumphed. On the other side of the peninsula, Poseidonia, modern Paestum, known today for the ruins of its temples, was Achaean. In addition to these, so many small colonies dotted the coast line of southern Italy that the Romans later called it Magna Graecia.

Corinthians under the leadership of a member of the royal family, Archias, first settled on the island of Ortygia and then took possession of the near-by shore to establish Syracuse. That city, because of its harbor and its fertile lands, soon became the leading city in the west. Gela and Acragas on the southeastern coast of Sicily were Rhodian colonies.

A hardy band of Phocaeans pushed further west to found Massilia (Marseilles) near the mouth of the Rhone where it could control the trade with the rich lands of Gaul, and scattered colonies were also founded on the coast of Spain.

The Greeks in the west, however, were checked by the presence

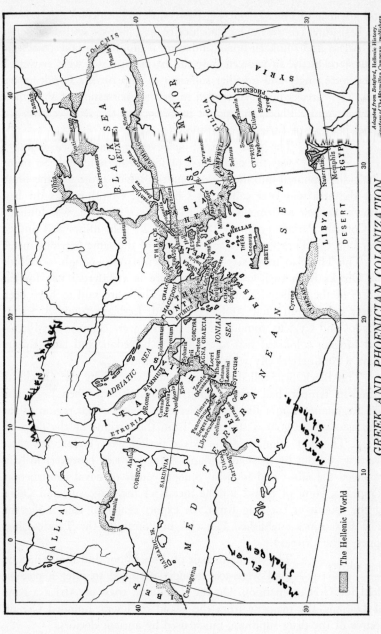

GREEK AND PHOENICIAN COLONIZATION

Adapted from Botsford, Hellenic History, courtesy of The Macmillan Company, publishers.

and advance of other colonizing powers, the Phoenicians (p. 96) and the Etruscans (p. 331). The Phoenicians had already settled in northern Africa and southern Spain and were beginning to take possession of western Sicily. In western Italy the Etruscan states were powerful. They were singly and together sufficient to stop further Greek expansion. The Greeks never succeeded in getting possession of the whole of Sicily, and a Phocaean attempt in Corsica in the sixth century B.C. failed because of Etruscan opposition (p. 332).

THE NORTH The most notable achievement in the Aegean Sea was the occupation of its northern littoral. So many Chalcidians poured into these promontories which project to the south that the area was later called the Chalcidice. Olynthus was the best known of their settlements. Potidaea, in the same area, was founded by Corinth. Parians occupied Thasos with its gold mines and pushed over into the Thracian mainland in quest of the same precious metal.

The Thracian tribes seem to have been strong enough to exclude the Greeks from their territory, but there is a different tale for the shores of the Hellespont and Propontis. There are said to have been ninety colonies in these stretches of land. Lesbians founded Sestus; Abydos and Cyzicus, famous for tunny fish, were colonies of Miletus; and Megara colonized first agricultural Chalcedon, and later Byzantium, a commercial city with a brilliant future.

The Black Sea, called Euxine, "well-favored," by the Greeks to soften its temper, had been entered in heroic times when Jason and the Argonauts sought the golden fleece in Colchis, that region of the Caucasus where gold is still taken from the streams by the fleece of sheep. The first colonies of the classic period were Ionian, but these were wiped out by the Cimmerians. After 650 B.C., however, Miletus renewed the effort and founded Sinope, center of naval construction, Trapezus, point of export for the metals of the Caucasus, and Olbia, at the mouth of the Bug River, an export center of fish and grain. The Byzantines established Heraclea in Pontus in the Tauric Chersonese (the Crimea).

THE SOUTH The southern coast of Asia Minor and the Syrian littoral were too strongly occupied to offer a possible field for Greek expansion. On the Tripolitan coast of Africa a band of Dorians, the majority from the island of Thera, founded Cyrene, source of the drug silphium, much used by ancient doctors.

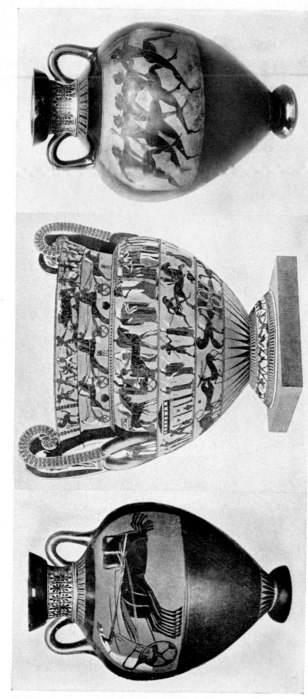

CHARIOT RACE

FRANÇOIS VASE

Florence

FOOT RACE

ATHENIAN BLACK-FIGURED WARE

SCHOOL SCENE

HERACLES SLAYING GERYON

STUDIO OF VASE PAINTER

Florence. From Walters, History of Ancient Pottery,

ATHENIAN RED-FIGURED WARE

Greek colonization in Egypt followed entirely different lines. The Saite monarch Psamtik II (p. 108), learning the military value of the bands of Ionian warriors who raided his shores, employed them as mercenaries. After his successful wars, he installed them on lands at Daphnae on the Pelusiac branch of the Nile. Psamtik's successors treated the Greeks so well that a national reaction took place against them, and finally Amasis (569-525 B.C.) moved them to the Canopic branch of the river and founded for their benefit Naucratis. It was a cosmopolitan sort of place. Nine cities had shops and sections there, each self-governing under a royal appointee for the whole city. It was obligatory for Greeks going to Egypt to reside there, and it became the chief center of communication between the old and the new civilizations.

RESULTS The colonial expansion spread the Greeks and their civilization around the shores of the Mediterranean and the Black Sea. Native tribes acquired a veneer of Greek culture from them and offered new opportunities to Greek merchants for the purchase of raw materials and the sale of industrial products. At the same time the mother cities underwent a transformation. The development of their political structure was materially affected by the study of institutions and laws required for the new settlements. Individual landownership in the colonies helped to break down family control of land in the older centers. The demand for home products, the opening of new markets, the increase of knowledge and new ideas about the world, and contact with alien peoples—all brought the Greeks into a consciousness of their own nationality. It was after the colonial movement that the Greeks began to use the words Hellas and Hellenes to include all Greeks wherever located in order to distinguish themselves from the barbarians.

ECONOMIC GROWTH

REVIVAL OF
INDUSTRY
The colonial movement was accompanied and followed by extraordinary advances in industry and commerce. Many forces contributed to the revival of industry: importations from Phoenicia, Lydia, and Egypt improved local taste and led to increased local demands; colonists sent back home for favored objects; new sources of raw materials were tapped; and specialized craftsmen took the place of "the old village black-

smith." Techniques which had survived from Mycenaean times were revived or expanded, and new methods were developed.

In the textile industry the Ionian cities assumed the leadership, and Milesian wool came into general demand. A bountiful supply of sheep in the interior furnished the raw material, while the purple dye secured from mollusks, which had been used by the Cretans, gave the woven materials color. Some flax was grown and linen was made, but Egypt remained the chief source of this material.

POTTERY   Pottery developed as a local industry whenever a sufficient abundance of clay was found. Ionian pottery and a type called by archaeologists proto-Corinthian, whose place of manufacture is not certain, were the earliest to be exported. In Ionian pottery Mycenaean survivals and Oriental influences dominated. The artists who made and decorated the vases discarded geometric influences and painted in black on a light slip [1] their figures of birds and human beings, interspersed with rosettes, scrolls, and linear decorations. Proto-Corinthian pottery was more under geometric influence, but at its best it produced fine miniature paintings in red or brown on a light-colored clay.

Corinth had a fine supply of clay and for a period was the center of an immense vase industry. Oriental, probably Phoenician, influence was very strong in the portrayal of strange hybrid forms of birds and animals. Figures of warriors and legendary scenes were portrayed with a fine degree of skill. Finally, in the last of the seventh and early part of the sixth centuries, Athenian ware, first black-figured on a red background, and later the finer red-figured on black,[2] displaced all others in the market, particularly in the west. More Athenian vases have been found in Etruria and in the Black Sea region than in the Aegean itself.

METALLURGY   The presence of local supplies of metals and an increased demand, the result of general prosperity, made possible specialization and important advances in the technique of the handling of these materials. Thus Chalcis became famous for

---

[1] Potter's clay in a liquid state used in the casting process and for the decoration of ceramic ware.

[2] The Athenians first painted figures with a black slip on the natural red background of the clay. Then they learned to fill in the background and to draw lines with the black slip leaving the figures unpainted and red. This made possible a finer development of drawings.

its bronze swords and armor made from the copper of Euboea, and in Lacedaemon the iron of Taÿgetus was used to produce armor and weapons, locks and keys. In the matter of technique, Rhoecus and Theodorus of Samos invented methods of hollow casting in bronze, and Glaucus of Chios discovered a process for smelting iron. These advances reacted to increase demand by reducing the cost of metal armor so that it became possible for the average man to purchase it.

The same influences made themselves felt in other lines of activity. In response to the demands of the growing and flourishing cities, the stoneworkers cut limestone and marble slabs from the quarries and used them for the construction of buildings and statues. The needs of commerce led to developments in shipbuilding, and naval warfare led to the invention of the trireme, for which Corinth claimed the credit. City life brought with it problems of engineering, particularly in the matter of water supply. A famous aqueduct was built in Athens, and the engineers of Samos dug a tunnel through a mountain to bring water to their city.

METHODS   With all the development and demand, however, industry remained on a small scale. The little family shop was the prevailing unit. There a man worked, assisted by his sons and possibly by an apprentice or two and by such slaves or hired men as he could afford. Chios was the first Greek state to use slaves for industrial work. Slaves from the Black Sea region or the European hinterland were used for the rougher work such as firing the potters' furnaces. But there were some Greeks who had fallen into slavery for debt or who had been sold as prisoners of war, and there were some Orientals who were highly skilled; these were employed on finer work. Within the shop a spirit of freedom and creative craftsmanship prevailed. The potters had models from which they worked, but of all the thousands of Greek vases in our museums no two have been found exactly alike.

Artisans in the same occupations tended to group themselves in the same quarter and to organize into guilds. They based the form of their association on the family organizations of the nobles. The bronze workers called themselves Chalcidae or "sons of bronze." They had their patron divinities and their religious activities and guarded the secrets and regulated the activities of their crafts.

Trade in the Aegean had never entirely disappeared during the Dark Ages. For a period it was dominated by the Phoenicians until the Ionian cities were strong enough to expell them and assume control. Meanwhile throughout Hellas the need of raw materials and food supply, together with the natural tendency to specialize in industrial products, led to the growth of an exchange economy. All of the forces which operate to develop trade were at work.

Outcasts became peddlers as they wandered from town to town, and fishermen became merchants. Border markets for local trade appeared at convenient points between neighboring communities. Meetings of religious leagues and the gathering of communities for games or festivals afforded opportunity for the display of products and thus became fairs. Demand was stimulated, and direct exchange took place between cities through middlemen. Aeginetan professional peddlers went with their mules throughout the Peloponnesus, and wagoners traveled along the sacred ways which led to the great shrines. Broadbeamed sailing vessels were built to carry cargoes, and penteconters (fifty-oared galleys) and triremes were built in turn to protect them. Anchors, an invention of the seventh century B.C., made sailing safer. Whereas in the time of Hesiod, seafaring was confined to the middle of summer, the skilled sailor of the sixth century B.C. set out in the spring to return in the fall. Safe routes came to be well known and followed. On long trips, men trusted themselves out of sight of land and sailed by the sun or at night by the Phoenicians' star. States found it essential to co-operate for the sake of commerce. Harbors were protected by moles; display houses and warehouses were constructed; foreigners were given permission to land and even to remain; seaport towns grew up when the city itself was inland. Men talked of a canal through the Isthmus of Corinth, but it was too great an undertaking. A plank road was constructed, however, over which smaller ships and goods were dragged on rollers.

In early times men passed beyond the crude basis of barter trade when they adopted such standards of exchange as cattle or sheep. The Oriental nations advanced to a still higher point when, as we have seen, they began to use established weights of the precious metals to represent value and when the Assyrians in their Ishtars produced the precursors of coined money. Coins, pieces of metal whose weight and fineness are guaranteed by the issuing power and accepted by the users, first appeared in the Greek world in the seventh century B.C.

The earliest attempts at metal coinage were copper or iron spits called "obols." Six of them made a handful; in Greek, a drachma. As these metals decreased in value, the obols became mere token coins, useless for large transactions or for trade between states, and the precious metals took over the field. To Asia Minor, either to the Lydians or to the Ionians, belonged the credit for the issuance of the first true money, when private individuals or the states stamped and guaranteed the weight and quality of pieces of electron, a natural alloy of gold and silver. The Lydians were the first to coin gold and to establish bimetallism on the basis of a ratio of thirteen and a third to one. Once introduced, coinage rapidly spread. Each city adopted its own standard coin, the drachma or didrachma of a definite weight and fineness, and its own design. The tunny fish stood for Cyzicus, the seal for Phocaea, the tortoise for Aegina, and the owl and the head of Athena for Athens. In general, only silver was coined by the Greeks, though Lydian and, later, Persian gold coins came into use. The varying standards produced much confusion and led to a profitable business in money changing. Most states, however, related their coins to one of two systems, the lighter Euboic and the heavier Aeginetan standards, both taken over from the Orient.

METHODS — Methods of trade were simple. A group of merchants would unite for a voyage, buy up a supply of local products, rent a ship, and set forth. On coming to a port town, they would land, lay out their goods for display, and carry on lively bargaining with local purchasers. With the money thus secured, they would in return usually purchase goods which they could sell at home. Similar transactions took place until the original cargo had been sold or the season was over. At home they sold the wares purchased abroad, paid off their debts, and divided the profits.

Such transactions between states brought up the question of rights of aliens in the courts. Because of the Greek conception of the family character of the state and its general exclusion of outsiders born without the family circle, full grant of rights was impossible. Recourse was therefore had to the ancient institution of *proxenia,* hereditary guest friendship. Where before individual families had guest friends, states now had them also. An Athenian family would become guest friends of Corinth. All Corinthians coming to Athens would apply to them for aid in the enforcement of contracts, for representation in the

Athenian courts, and for protection. The position was hereditary in the family and was highly regarded as an honor.

Thus during the eighth, seventh, and sixth centuries B.C. the economic character of the Hellenic world was being transformed. In the place of small communities ruled by landholding aristocrats there appeared large and prosperous cities with specialized industries and with a flourishing commerce facilitated by the invention of coinage and the establishment of interstate relationships. At the same time these varied commercial activities were spread throughout the Mediterranean and the Black Sea regions by the movement of colonial expansion. In spite of emigration to the colonies, population at home increased. In 600 B.C. Corinth had about 25,000 and Miletus about 30,000 inhabitants, most of whom were artisans or merchants.

POLITICAL CHANGES

OLIGARCHY   Under these multiple economic influences the states underwent startling political changes. The power of the landholding aristocracy suffered a severe blow when, in response to the needs of business, the laws were written down so that all men might know them. Therewith the laws passed from the domain of the gods and their earthly representatives to the realm of practical affairs and the control of ordinary men. Zaleucus in Locri and Draco in Athens (whose historicity some scholars have questioned) were famous recorders of the law. When the basis of wealth became money instead of land, many men rose from the ranks to riches and were able to demand and secure a share in the government. As a result oligarchies (rule of the few), in which wealth gained from any source rather than from landed estates became the chief requirement for the holding of office, succeeded to political power. The general policy of these oligarchies was the further development of industry and trade, and under such guidance the Ionian cities established their pre-eminence and sent out their commercial colonies.

The oligarchic rulers of Aegina, refraining from entrance into the colonial movement, fostered the manufacture of pottery (which a fine deposit of clay made possible) and the importation and working of metals to such an extent that Aeginetan bronze bowls and caldrons were everywhere in demand. As their trade expanded their coins and weights became a common standard. Aegina was the only western state to have a share in the founding of Egyptian Naucratis.

In similar fashion the great commercial expansion of Corinth was achieved under the guidance of its oligarchs, a small closely related group of nobles who were called by the name of the old royal family, the Bacchiads. These men, recognizing the trend of events and the value of the location of their city, directed their activities toward commerce. Port towns, built on both sides of the isthmus and connected by a tramway over which goods and even small boats were carried, and such colonies as Corcyra and Syracuse gave commercial pre-eminence in the western trade to Corinth.

TIMOCRACY When increased prosperity, cheaper metals, and improved methods of production brought armor within the reach of the average man, most states, following the example of Sparta, organized from among their well-to-do citizens the phalanx (solid body) of heavy-armed infantry. When the newly created infantry realized its power in the state, it was able to secure a share in the government, and the oligarchy yielded to the timocracy, the rule of those rich enough to equip themselves with heavy armor. This normally resulted in the formation of an assembly of the well to do, with powers of election and legislation, and in the creation of an administrative council drawn from the same body. In many of the states, however, the higher offices were still reserved for the wealthier classes, and the policies of the leaders, like those of the oligarchs, were directed toward expanding industry and commerce. These changes in government did not take place in all states or at one time or in any fixed order, but such was the tendency of the times.

TYRANNY In the course of the transition, many crises developed. Quarrels arose between factions of the aristocracy, between the aristocrats and the merchants, between the oligarchs and the artisans. Civil wars were fought with the utmost cruelty, and the survivors of the defeated faction were driven into exile. The poems of Alcaeus and Theognis are filled with the bitterness of spirit of the aristocrats against their successful moneyed rivals. The situation was aggravated by the fact that a shift from a barter to a monetary economy was particularly hard upon the debtor class, both farming and industrial. The laws of debt were rigid. The property, the family, and finally the person of the debtor served as forfeits for unpaid loans, with the result that many people were sold into slavery.

The disorders which frequently resulted from these intolerable conditions afforded opportunities in many states for able men to rise to power. Leaders of successful factions, prominent nobles with large bodies of retainers, leaders of the common folk, magistrates, or generals turned their official position or their prestige and power to good account in one state after another, and, seizing the citadel, they made themselves monarchs. Such unconstitutional kings were termed "tyrants" by the Greeks. In some cases they actually became kings, in others elections were held and the constitution continued to function under the supervision of the tyrant. In many states therefore the tyrant occupied much the same position that the political boss holds in a modern American city. The economic basis of the development of tyranny becomes apparent when it is realized that tyranny did not appear in states like Sparta and in Thessaly, which were unaffected by the commercial and industrial changes.

ACHIEVEMENTS OF THE TYRANTS Almost invariably the tyrant was a popular champion. The aristocrats were his chief enemies, and he therefore set himself to destroy their power, political, economic, and religious. The leaders of the aristocracy were sent into exile, and in some states their lands were divided up among the peasants. The political powers of the aristocratic council and of the great noble families therein were destroyed. Religion was transformed through the breaking down of some of the older cults and the establishment of new democratic festivals. The tyrant usually paid great attention to the industrial class, which prospered accordingly. His interest in trade expressed itself in the planting of commercial colonies and in the making of treaties with other states. He sought to glorify himself by becoming a patron of the arts, favoring poets especially, who clustered around him and sang his praises. He beautified his city with fountains, temples, and statuary. In short, the tyrant played an important role in the development of democracy, in industry, trade, and culture.

Nevertheless, the tyrants were always regarded by the Greeks as usurpers. Plots against them were frequent, and many became tyrants in the modern sense of the word. Few were able to establish a dynasty, and almost no tyrannies survived beyond three generations. When they were overthrown, their states became commercial oligarchies or incipient democracies.

The tyrannies in Corinth and in Sicyon afford noteworthy examples of the policies and the achievements of these rulers and of the prestige which they secured for themselves and for their states. Quarrels beginning between Corinth and Corcyra resulted in the first recorded naval battle in Greek history, which ruined for the moment Corinthian influence in the west and made it possible for Cypselus, a popular leader, to drive out the Bacchiads (p. 141) and become tyrant. There may be in his triumph some sign of the revolt of the pre-Dorians against the Dorian conquerors. He drove out the nobles, divided the land among the peasants, protected Corinthian commerce, and ruled peaceably for thirty years (657-627 B.C. are the traditional dates). He was succeeded by his son Periander, who was to become the outstanding tyrant of the period, and who completed the work of his father in Corinth. A new division of the state into eight territorial tribes was established. Men without occupation were forbidden to enter the city, and importation of slaves was stopped, with the result that the artisan class of Corinth was better off than the same class elsewhere. The introduction of a system of coinage and the construction of temples to Apollo and Aphrodite accompanied the other changes. At the festivals of Dionysus, Arion of Lesbos perfected the choral dithyramb out of which later grew the Athenian drama. At this time also the Isthmian games in honor of Poseidon were raised to a new position of importance.

Periander extended the power of Corinth by conquest and colonization and established his fame far beyond the bounds of his city-state. The western end of the Corinthian Gulf came under his control; Corcyra and its colony Epidamnus, on the Epirote coast, which dominated the entrance to the Adriatic and the trade route to the west, were conquered; in the east, he founded Potidaea, in the Chalcidice, to secure a source of naval supplies. He established close relations with Athens by a marriage alliance with a noble family. The tyrants of Ionia were his friends, and he corresponded with the kings of Lydia and the Saite rulers of Egypt. So great was his renown that he was asked to arbitrate a dispute between Athens and Mytilene and to arrange a treaty between Lydia and Miletus. Corinth under his rule had reached the height of its power.

SICYON
A little to the west of Corinth was the city of Sicyon. Rich in the production of grain and olives, it furnished supplies to the neighboring market of Corinth. Its pottery and metal goods supported a growing industrial class. Politically the city was dominated by a Dorian nobility with Argive affiliations. Then the

artisans and the peasants, many of whom were becoming serfs, found a leader in one Orthagoras, possibly a pre-Dorian and said to have been a cook, who became tyrant about 650 B.C., to be succeeded (ca. 600 B.C.) by Cleisthenes. Under him the nobles were crushed; the Argive elements in the local religious cults were suppressed; and Sicyon entered and took a leading part in a sacred war waged by Delphi to punish the little town of Crissa for offenses against Apollo. Temples were built and a brilliant school of sculptors established.

Cleisthenes, who had a lovely daughter, Agariste, invited young men of noble birth from all Hellas to spend a year at his court that he might pick her a husband. Among those who came were two Athenians, Hippocleides and Megacles, the Alcmaeonid. The former was the favorite, but at the final party of the year he danced so wildly that Cleisthenes was disgusted, and Megacles therefore won. From this marriage were to come the great Athenians, Cleisthenes, Pericles, and Alcibiades.

After the death of Cleisthenes, the tyranny ended. The nobles regained a moderate portion of their former power and Sicyon sank into the position of a second-rate city.

INTERSTATE RELATIONS The advancing power of the individual city-states was accompanied by the development of definite interstate relations. Peace under normal conditions took the place of the warlike status of earlier times; guest friendships were established; treaties were made and alliances formed; when directed against the Greeks, piracy was frowned upon; wars were formally proclaimed by heralds, and prisoners of war came to be held for ransom instead of being sold directly into slavery. Such practices as the use of poisoned arrows or the poisoning of wells were regarded as unethical. The large number of small states of almost equal power made war unprofitable, and the custom of arbitration developed; appeal was made by the warring states to the oracle of Apollo, to neutral communities, or to prominent individuals such as Periander, tyrant of Corinth, for the settlement of questions at issue.

AMPHICTYONIES Perhaps the greatest force for the development of interstate law, if not the actual origin thereof, was to be found in the religious leagues called *amphictyonies,* "dwellers around." The tribes or cities near an important shrine customarily united for the control of the property of the gods and for the direction of the festivals and of the fair which accompanied them. The Ionians thus met on the island of Delos, as described in the Homeric "Hymn to Apollo." The most famous of the religious leagues, however, was the amphictyony of Delphi. Originally composed of twelve tribes around the shrine of Demeter near Thermopylae, it later moved its chief center to Delphi, seat of the god Apollo, and expanded to take in Athens and the Dorian states of the Peloponnesus. Meetings were held in the fall and spring, and each member sent four representatives to discuss matters and two others to cast the vote. Their primary tasks were the supervision of the shrines and the property of the gods, the issuance of directions to the neighboring states for the repair of the roads leading to the shrine, and the protection of pilgrims from molestation and unjust tolls. If necessary, they declared a sacred war against violators of their rules. More famous, however, are their rules of war; though members were at liberty to war with one another, and the council only occasionally served as a board of arbitration, no member might destroy another or cut it off from running water in wartime or in peacetime alike.

Thus in the space of two centuries the Hellenic world advanced from the pastoral stage described by Homer into the ordered political and economic life of the city-states. Industry and commerce had taken their place beside agriculture, while cattle raising sank into the background. The king had yielded place to the aristocrats and they in turn to the tyrant or to the new men of wealth. In some states the first evidences of democratic institutions began to appear.

✓

VIII

THE CITY-STATES

THE ANATOLIAN CITIES

THAT leadership which the rich cities of the Anatolian littoral had assumed in the eighth century B.C. (p. 129) remained in their possession to the end of the sixth. The colonial movement eased the pressure of increasing numbers on the land, and the development of industry and commerce afforded the landless new opportunities for employment. The demand for oil and wine enriched the landholders. Wool from the interior, dye-giving mollusks from the sea, metals from the mountains and the Black Sea region, and a bountiful supply of clay furnished a variety of materials for the artisans. In return for these goods of the homeland in demand among the colonists came ample supplies of food. Goods carried by the overland route through Lydia to Babylonia or by the easy sea voyage to Syria and Egypt brought in return the luxuries and the influences of the Orient. Tourists, merchants, and mercenaries flocked to Egypt and to Babylon to return with new goods and new ideas gained by contact with the ancient cultures of the East. The wealth of Phrygia and Lydia made a deep impression upon literature, and Egyptian, Babylonian and Persian ideas contributed to the growth of philosophy. Oriental influences appear strong in the vase paintings, the architecture, and the sculpture of the Ionians. The trammels of the past were cast aside, and for a brief period these Anatolian cities were the torchbearers of civilization.

Strongest among the cities was Miletus, especially celebrated for woolen goods and pottery. Its colonies brought it dominance in the Black Sea trade, and alliances in the west, particularly with Sybaris, gave it a strong hold in Italy. Its position in Egypt and its treaties with Lydia made it the leader in Oriental activities, and its wise men caused it to be the leader in intellectual advances.

Ephesus, famed for its temple of Artemis, Mytilene with its poets and its lawgiver Pittacus, and later Samos under its tyrant Polycrates were in the second rank.

Internal weaknesses were to prove the ruin of the land. In almost every city there was civil strife between aristocrats and commoners, oligarchs and democrats. Tyrants seized the power and were overthrown; reprisals were fearful and hatreds undying. The poems of Alcaeus burn with an unquenchable hatred for political enemies. A fierce clinging to the idea of local independence made unity impossible, so that wars between the states too were frequent.

An eighth century B.C. invasion of Cimmerians was repelled; but before the organized forces of Lydia, the discordant cities were powerless. In the latter half of the seventh century the kings of Lydia conquered the smaller cities and made a treaty of alliance with Miletus. In the next century Croesus (ca. 560-546 B.C.), most celebrated of these rulers, sought to strengthen his position by securing cultural leadership as well as political domination. He invited the wise men of the Aegean to his court, made presents to the Greek shrines, and sought advice from Apollo of Delphi. The pre-eminence of his position in Greek story and the tales of his activities and wealth told by Herodotus are witnesses of the success of his program.

After the Persian conquest of Lydia (p. 111), the Greeks of Anatolia passed into the hands of the victors. Cyrus had made advances to the cities to secure their aid against his Lydian enemy, but they had remained loyal to Croesus. Accordingly after the capture of Sardis, the Persian king refused to grant them favorable terms. Only Miletus was permitted an alliance; the rest were reduced by armed forces, and placed under the rule of local tyrants and under the supervision of provincial governors in the interior.

POLYCRATES   The fall of the Ionian cities on the mainland offered an opportunity which Polycrates, tyrant of Samos, quickly turned to his own advantage. He built a great fleet, suppressed all piracy save his own, and brought many islands under his sway. He entered into close political relations with Amasis, king of Egypt, and then with the Persian enemies of the Egyptian king. Although Samian exiles with Spartan aid attempted to break his power, they failed. Polycrates enlarged and beautified the city of Samos. A tunnel was dug through the mountain to bring water to the city; a great temple was erected to the goddess Hera; and a mole was constructed to protect the harbor. Anacreon and many other poets and artists came to his court. Herodotus tells many stories about this man whose wealth, power, and arrogance made a deep impression on his contemporaries. He fell a victim finally to his own greed and to Persian treachery; when he crossed to the mainland to consult with the Persian governor about the division of a treasure, he was killed and his body crucified, and Samos was thereupon added to the Persian Empire.

The Persian conquest increased for a brief period the economic prosperity of the Anatolian cities. The roads which led into the interior were open to them as subjects of the empire. Their industrial and artistic products were sought in the new capitals of that empire. Their soldiers and sailors received occupation in the forces of the Persian kings. Greek leaders and wise men were welcomed at the court; Darius' personal physician was a Greek, Democedes of Croton; and the influence of Persian thought may be seen in the history of Greek philosophy. Yet the cities chafed under the yoke, and their effort at revolt resulted in a disaster to themselves which ended their period of leadership and helped to involve the rest of the Hellenic world in war with the Persian Empire.

SPARTA

During these centuries of Anatolian leadership, two states on the mainland, Sparta and Athens, were slowly developing those institutions and activities which at the end of the period brought them into the forefront of Hellenic affairs.

Of the early history of Sparta little is known and that is so confused by the clouds of legend that there is scarcely a fact not disputed by modern historians. The later Spartans assigned the origin of their institutions to a legendary ruler named Lycurgus. Since earlier writers knew nothing of him, and spoke of Apollo as the source of their laws, it is possible that the story of Lycurgus was a juristic fiction told to give additional sanction to the later institutions. Other evidence indicates that the Spartan system did not attain its final organization before the sixth century B.C.

LACEDAEMON The traveler from Argos crosses the Parnon range into the foothills of the Arcadian mountains and thence goes south until the road drops with comparative swiftness into a low-lying plain, between Mt. Parnon on the left and the Taÿgetus range on the right. Down the center winds the Eurotas, giving water to the rich bottom lands of "hollow Lacedaemon." As the valley approaches the sea, the mountains converge until finally the river cuts its way through a narrow gorge. Beyond lies a marshy plain with an inhospitable coast open to the wide stretches of the Mediterranean and flanked on either side by capes dangerous to round. Only the island of Cythera gives shelter to the mariner. The Parnon range cuts the valley off from the sea in the east. The inhabitants of Lacedaemon, as a result, were naturally farmers rather than merchants.

EARLY HISTORY   The stories of Helen and Menelaus combine with archaeological discoveries to show that there was a flourishing civilization in the valley in Mycenaean times. Achaean princes, subject to the kings of Mycenae, profited from the wealth of the land and played a prominent role in the legendary activities of the Heroic Age. In all probability the farms were even then tenanted by peasants in servile status, later known as helots. When the Dorians swept away the older culture, a few of the noble families of the Achaeans were absorbed by the invaders; the rest fled or, as serfs, joined their former subjects on the lands.

THE RISE OF   The Dorians took their stand at the head of the valley
SPARTA   in a commanding position, scattered, however, in four villages. A synoecism (p. 125) developed a common religious and political center at Sparta which became the city-state, but the men continued to live in their villages. When Amyclae was captured, a fifth village was added. The state then developed an organization of five divisions called *oboi,* based on the residence of the citizens, to take the place of the three Dorian tribes as the fundamental political and military units.

The conquered land in the valley was called civic land and was divided up among the citizens in inalienable and indivisible lots which descended regularly to the oldest son. A few nobles received larger shares than the rest. Hunger for land with increasing population in the restricted area drove the Spartans in the late eighth and early seventh centuries B.C. over the Taÿgetus range into Messenia. There they found a mixture of Achaeans and Dorians, who put up a vigorous resistance which centered around Mt. Ithome. After nineteen years of struggle, the Messenians were defeated. Some escaped and found refuge at Zancle in Sicily, henceforth known as Messana; the rest were reduced to serfdom. Their lands were divided up into lots and given to the Spartan families. Around the civic lands so acquired and distributed, the Spartans conquered or colonized a series of towns which possessed local independence and were known as the *perioecic* communities.

EARLY CULTURE In the early revival of culture, Sparta played a prominent part. The iron mines of the Taÿgetus range and a bountiful supply of clay led to a prosperous development of industry in the perioecic towns. In spite of the natural handicaps commercial relations were established with the outer world, and Sparta came into close touch with Sardis and with Samos. Many exquisite ivories, implying trade with Egypt and showing distinct Oriental influences in their carving, have been found by the excavators. The city built a fine council hall, a magnificent temple to Artemis Orthia, and a temple of wood covered with brass plates to "Athena of the Brazen House." Sculptors of reputation carved in wood and stone. Festivals attracted men from all over the Greek world. Terpander of Lesbos and Thaletas of Crete introduced the seven-stringed lyre and the choral dance. Alcman, said to have come from Sardis but more probably a native Spartan, wrote beautiful odes for the maidens to sing in their processions. Sparta was well on its way to cultural leadership in the west when its cultural advance was suddenly halted.

THE MESSENIAN REVOLT About 650 B.C. the Messenian serfs revolted under the leadership of their hero Aristodemus. Ithome, fortified again, held out for twenty years. At the crisis, Tyrtaeus, the last Spartan poet of merit, appeared. With vigorous war songs, he restored Spartan courage and, as their general, he led the Spartans to victory. When the war produced a political and economic crisis in Sparta, with a brilliant poem, "Eunomia," he allayed the incipient civil strife. A band of malcontents left to found Tarentum in Italy, and order was restored.

The Spartans had learned the lesson of the menace in their subject population. They therefore developed to its full extent a military and educational system in which art, poetry, and wealth had no place. Foreigners were jealously watched, and once a year all were ordered to leave the land. Henceforth Sparta was an army encamped in the midst of a hostile people.

THE HELOTS At the bottom of the social ladder were the helots, who were owned by the state and who could not be sold, transferred, or freed, except by its action. They were assigned to the lands of the Spartans and were ordered to pay a fixed quota each year to the owners thereof, the balance accruing to themselves. Improvements of the land were therefore to their advantage, and some became fairly prosperous. Some were called to attend the Spartans on their campaigns, and others served as light-armed troops in the army. In return for meritorious service, they might be freed by the state and even given an inferior form of citizenship.

For the most part, however, the helots had few real rights. The state watched them jealously; young men in training for the army were sent out to spy upon them; any helot who appeared dangerous might be slain forthwith, and in times of danger whole companies were led off and massacred. The treatment which they received tended to degrade them in mind and body. It is said that the Spartans compelled them to become drunk that the citizen youth might be impressed with the bestiality of drunkenness. They greatly outnumbered the Spartans, and the constant fear of revolt kept the Spartan army always on the alert and for a long period always near home.

THE PERIOECI   The *perioeci,* or "dwellers around," occupied a more favorable position. They were at least citizens of their own communities, where under Spartan supervision they governed themselves, although their foreign relations were entirely under Spartan control. They paid tribute to Sparta, served as heavy-armed troops in the army, and were employed to prevent helots from escaping. Most of the land in their communities belonged to Spartans, but they devoted themselves to industry, particularly to the manufacture of iron products and of woolen goods, the dye for which came from Cythera. Their locks and keys were renowned throughout the Greek world. Not subject to Spartan restrictions, many of them became wealthy. The Spartan expulsion of foreigners, which did not affect them, gave them a monopoly of the local market. As a result, they were for the most part loyal to Sparta, even in the days of her decadence.

THE SPARTANS   Ruling over these subject peoples were the citizens of Sparta who called themselves *Equals,* though actually divided into nobles and commons. Both classes, however, passed through the same system of training and were subject to the same rules.

The first requisite to citizenship was Spartan parentage on both sides. Immediately after birth, a child was presented to the elders, who decided whether or not it should be reared. If deformed or evidently a weakling, it was exposed on the slopes of the mountains. To the age of seven the boys remained under the control of the mothers and nurses, but thereafter they were brought up by the state. They were formed in companies, slept in barracks, where their only bed was a bundle of reeds gathered by themselves, and they were restricted to one garment. Their time was spent in continual drilling and exercising, each company being under the direction of a youth of over twenty. Given but scant meals, they were supposed to augment them by theft. If they were caught stealing, they were severely punished for being so clumsy as to be detected. Thus they were taught endurance under hardship, skill in foraging, and expertness in military tactics. At the festival of Artemis Orthia, an ancient religious rite of flogging was developed into a test of endurance, the prize going to the boy who endured the longest. For intellectual activity they were given passages to recite from Homer and the war songs of Tyrtaeus and other poets. The elder citizens regarded it as their especial task to supervise the boys, and they chastised them for the slightest infraction of the rules.

At the age of twenty, the young men were enrolled in mess clubs, which were lifelong associations. Membership in the clubs depended to some extent on residence. Votes were taken, and a single adverse vote threw the youth off the citizen rolls. If accepted, they lived and ate together in their clubs for ten years. They were supposed to marry, but were forbidden to see their wives save by stealth; and there were cases of Spartans with children who had never seen their wives by daylight.

At the age of thirty, the men received citizenship. Henceforth they might live at home and vote in the assembly. They were, however, required to eat the evening meal always at the public tables, where the chief dish was the famous black broth which none but a Spartan could eat. They were not allowed to engage in any industry, not even to the extent of supervising their family estates. They had to be eternally ready for the call to war, and hence could not leave the neighborhood of Sparta, save by order or special permission. Their days were spent in exercise or drill. Only on march were the rules relaxed, and it has been said that for the Spartans war was a relief from the horrors of peace. At the age of sixty, the men were released from the system and allowed to live at home and in peace. They spent their remaining years in supervising the youths.

The income of the Spartans depended entirely upon the payments in kind from the helots on their lands. Not only were all forms of economic activity forbidden to them but trade and industry were effectively checked by the monetary situation. Since the monetary system had developed before the appearance of gold and silver coinage, the law still restricted the Spartans to the use of the iron money of earlier times; in fact even possession of the precious metals was forbidden. After the appearance of gold and silver coins, the worthlessness of the Spartan iron coins reduced exchange practically to a barter basis.

From such income as the Spartan received, he was required to make a contribution to the expense of the public meals, failure to comply resulting in the loss of civic rights. Though the land passed regularly into the hands of the eldest son, it was regarded as a family possession; and if it were sufficiently large, contributions were provided for the younger sons as well. Marriages with Spartan heiresses or adoptions into heirless families provided for some. Otherwise they lost their standing as citizens. Because of these conditions there was a distinct tendency among the Spartans to restrict the size of their families. Not only failure to make their contribution but defeat in the vote in the clubs, infraction of the training rules, or cowardice in war resulted in the loss of citizenship. Thus there appeared in Sparta a class of Inferiors whose status was ill-defined and who added to the dangers surrounding the citizen body.

Shortly after the Second Messenian War (ca. 650 B.C.), the phalanx was developed in which the heavy-armed *hoplite* was used to the fullest advantage. The hoplite wore helmet, breastplate, and greaves, protected himself with a round shield, and carried sword and lance. Men marched in solid formation, shoulder to shoulder, and in files of varying depths, usually of eight men. Cohesion and weight gave this phalanx force. Through their training, the Spartans gained not only unity but a facility in maneuvers which made their phalanx superior to those of the Greek states who copied their organization but not their discipline.

The girls remained at home, but they passed through a series of physical exercises and competitions calculated to make them what the state desired them to be—fit mothers of soldiers. They, too, were taught the meaning of Spartan discipline. The Spartan mother's instruction to her son was "come back with your shield or on it." After a terrible defeat, those whose sons had been killed adorned themselves with garlands while the mothers of the survivors put on mourning.

The Spartan system produced a race of hardy and skillful warriors. For a period their athletic exercises made them leaders in the games, but when men from other states began to specialize, they lost this pre-eminence. Their courage in warfare and their simplicity in life won for them the admiration of later ages. Sparta needed no walls save its sons. On the other hand, Spartans were narrow in mind and character, venal and untrustworthy away from home, and knew no means of control save the force of arms.

The greatest danger to this oligarchic system was found in the decline of the Equals. Losses in war, the tendency to restrict the number of sons to one, the union of family possessions through marriage, and the rigidity of the rules produced a steady decrease in the population. In 500 B.C. the Spartans could put an army of eight thousand citizens in the field; two centuries later their numbers had dwindled to a few hundred.

GOVERNMENT If the Spartans were a small group of oligarchs dominating a large subject population, they themselves were no less dominated by a few of their own number. At the head of the state was a dual kingship, hereditary in two families, the origins of which are unknown. Originally, the kings enjoyed supreme power, which they gradually lost to magistrates and to the council. They were priests of Zeus and commanders of the army, although in later times even that command was weakened. Their death was a signal for universal mourning of a most extravagant type.

The chief civil magistrates were five citizens, called *ephors* or overseers, and elected annually to watch over the kings. They could fine the kings and on occasion compel them to abdicate, and two of their number always accompanied the kings on military campaigns. They supervised the training of the youths, the behavior of the citizens, the demeanor of the helots and the perioeci, whose death they could order without trial. They presided over council and assembly and were judges in civil cases.

The two kings, together with twenty-eight men over sixty years of age and chosen for life by acclamation from among the noble families, made up the *gerusia,* or council of elders. This body was the real power in the state. It prepared all measures for submission to the assembly, and could, if it desired, set aside the assembly's action. It also tried criminal cases affecting the citizens, assisted the magistrates in the direction of the training of the youth and the supervision of the behavior of the citizens.

The *Apella* or assembly was made up of all Spartan citizens over thirty in full possession of civic rights. A passive body without initiative, it acted only on measures submitted to it by the council and it elected the magistrates.

THE PELOPON- NESIAN LEAGUE
In the early sixth century B.C. the Spartans started once more on a career of conquest. Argos was their first enemy. This city, which had taken the territory and the place of Mycenae, had enjoyed a brief spell of power shortly after 700 B.C. through its king, Pheidon. He conquered the neighboring states, extended the Aeginetan system of weights and measures throughout the Peloponnesus but failed in an attempt to consolidate his power by securing presidency of the Olympic games. Under his weak successors the city rapidly declined. The Spartans defeated Argos and took from it Cynuria on the Aegean coast and Cythera. When after this success they tried to overcome the Arcadian cities of Tegea and Mantinea, they failed, and their failure resulted in a shift of policy.

In place of further conquest the Spartans began to effect a system of alliances which resulted in the creation of the Peloponnesian League, into which all of the states of the Peloponnesus save Argos and the little Achaean cities on the northern coast were brought. Corinth, prosperous under the rule of its merchants who secured control after the death of Periander (p. 143), and Megara, to which a favorable position on the isthmus and colonies in both the east and the west had brought wealth, and, for a brief period, Athens, were all included.

NORTHERN GREECE

Northern Greece, divided by the mountains into a series of little pockets, contained a number of tribes and states which played no role in the early history of ancient Greece. Epirus and the western areas were still in a state of barbarism in the sixth century B.C. The only important place in Epirus was Dodona, in which there was an oracle where Zeus gave advice to men through the rustling of oak leaves. Phocis gained its only renown from the presence of Delphi. The rich plain of Thessaly supported a number of horse-raising nobles who lived by the work of their serfs and who had no significance. Boeotia, however, was of greater importance. This fertile plain was occupied and was prosperous in the Mycenaean Age. During the time of the Dorian invasion, there was a fresh incursion of invaders, the Boeotians. Thereafter a number of small cities developed in the region, but no one was strong enough to compel them to unite, nor was there sufficient economic or military incentive.

Thebes, situated at the crossroads where the ways parted to go to Delphi, to the isthmus, and to Athens, became the largest community and the center of the league which held the cities loosely together. The southern cities of the plain protected themselves from Thebes by maintaining close connections with Athens. The region was agricultural, and the Boeotians were celebrated in ancient literature as stupid farmers. Nevertheless they produced Hesiod in the eighth century B.C., Corinna, a poetess whose works have not survived, and her contemporary, the great Pindar, at the end of the sixth.

The cities of Chalcis and Eretria on the island of Euboea are worthy of mention in passing. Their colonies in the west and in the northern Aegean and the renown of their metal products raised them in the eighth century to high rank. Shortly after 700 B.C. they waged a famous civil war over the Lelantine plain which lay between them, a war which involved most of the commercial states in the Aegean. However, they later lost their position in the west to Corinth, and in the east to Athens.

ATHENS

ATTICA   Attica juts out into the Aegean like a promontory. It is a mountainous land about one thousand square miles in area. About one-fourth is arable, and that is for the most part divided among the four plains—Marathon, Eleusis, the Mesogeia, and Athens. Its hills produced wood for charcoal; its plains, grains and olives; the slopes of Hymettus, flowers for honey; Pentelicus was a mountain of pure white marble; silver and lead were mined at Laurium; and the clay deposit for pottery was the finest in the Greek world.

THE SYNOECISM   Among the many small cities which the territory once contained, Athens was naturally pre-eminent. Its plain was the largest and richest and contained the best clay. It was protected by ridges through which there were openings to the other valleys, and it commanded Pentelicus and Laurium; moreover, the Acropolis was the strongest center of defense in the entire region. The wide, sweeping bay of Phalerum was well suited for the merchant of early times who pulled his boat up on the shore. Hard by, the little promontory of Peiraeus furnished landlocked harbors which needed little improvement to be adapted to the use of larger boats and war-ships when they appeared. It was almost inevitable that the land should be united under the leadership of Athens.

Though tradition ascribed this union or synoecism to Theseus, memories of later wars between the cities indicate that it was a gradual

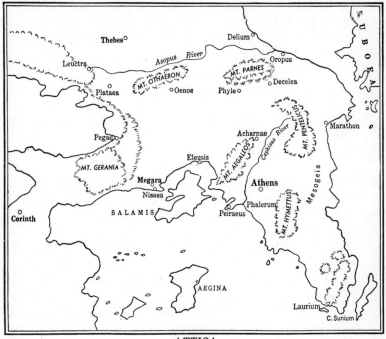

ATTICA

process not completed until the eighth century B.C., although local feeling survived into the sixth century B.C. At whatever time the process took place, it is evident that most of the people remained in their villages, while the nobles, moving to Athens for political and social reasons, tended to center their possessions in the plain around the city. At the same time, Athens recognized the local religious customs of the villages of Attica, raised some to the level of state festivals, and bound many others closely to the divinities of the city. In these ways, the whole area was knit closely into the city-state of Athens.

The people of Athens claimed that their ancestors had always lived in the land. This simply indicates that Attica never suffered violent invasion. It was first inhabited by men of the Aegean stock. During the early Mycenaean period, it received as immigrants a branch of the Achaean group called the "old Ionians." A palace rose on the Acropolis, which was fortified by walls of heavy stones, remains of which are still to be seen. In many places in Attica beehive tombs of the period are found. The Dorians did not enter the land, but during their invasion of the Peloponnesus it was a haven for those who fled from their homes. Thence men moved into the islands and across the Aegean Sea to the area later called Ionia.

THE DIPYLON AGE (CA. 1000 B.C.) The age that followed in Athens is best known from the fine funerary pottery, found near the Dipylon gate of the later walls, geometric in style and bearing pictures of men on horseback, in chariots, and going to sea in warships. During this period Athens was ruled by kings. They were assisted by treasurers whose name, *colacretai* ("butchers"), recalled the time when their income consisted largely of a share of the booty in war and of the sacrifices at festivals. Around the king in council gathered the heads of the noble families, and there was probably an assembly of the people.

Before their entrance into Attica, the Ionians had been divided into four tribes. This subdivision was kept, and the tribes became territorial divisons of the *polis* (city-state). Smaller organizations of a military, social, and religious nature were the *phratries* or brotherhoods, groups of families who claimed common descent and were accustomed to worship their common ancestors and fight together in war. Since such groups would naturally cling together in the settlement of the land, the phratries were also, in a measure, territorial. They kept lists of their members, recognized the legitimacy of children, preserved the citizen rolls, and took care of their mutual interests in court.

The landowning nobles, who called themselves Eupatridae, "well-fathered," were divided into family groups called *genē* with strong feelings of relationship. These were primarily religious organizations meeting for the worship of the family gods and ancestors, but they acquired much social power and control over family lands and customs. Between some of them occurred a great deal of rivalry. In the small valleys and on the hillsides dwelt the independent small-farming class or *georgoi.* The artisans, merchants and fishermen were grouped as *demiurgoi,* "public workers."

THE
ARISTOCRACY
With the unification and development of the city, the power of the king declined. First the nobles chose one of their number to be *polemarch,* commander of the army. Later another official called an *archon* was added to stand guard over property rights. The kingship was left with merely religious power, and it was changed into an office to which at first members of the royal family, the Medontidae, were elected for life, then for ten years, until finally, in 683 B.C., it was made an annual office to which all nobles were eligible. The archon thereupon became the chief civil magistrate.

With the development of commerce and the expansion of the state during the seventh century B.C., more judges were needed. Consequently six *thesmothetae,* "guardians of the established customs," were elected annually. These men were chosen and advised by the council of nobles. The council met in the market place for ordinary deliberations; but when it assembled as a murder court, it convened on the hill of the Areopagus near the shrine of the Furies. Hence it was called the Council of Areopagus. It exercised the same general supervision of the citizens as did the gerusia in Sparta.

The army was composed of the four tribal regiments commanded by the *phylobasileis* or tribe-kings who were nobles.

Military and financial exigencies during the seventh century B.C. led to a redivision of the people into census classes according to their wealth and according to the stage of development of timocratic government in Athens. Those whose estates were large enough to enable them to keep horses were called *hippeis,* "knights." They were probably all nobles, and served as officers in the state and army, furnishing such cavalry as the state possessed. The commoners whose farms were worked by oxen were called *zeugites,* "teamsters." They served in the infantry. The rest—laborers, renters, and artisans—were called *thetes.* At about the same time and for the same reasons, the state was divided into forty-eight local units called *naucraries,* whose purpose was the collection of funds to provide horsemen for the army and ships for the nascent fleet.

These political movements were the result of a gradual economic awakening which followed the economic revolution of the eighth and seventh centuries B.C. For a long time Athens had made but little progress. Land was limited and industry undeveloped or purely local. Aegina, Corinth, Megara, and Chalcis dominated the commercial field. The Athenian nobles, however, grasping for land and striving for wealth, followed the example of the Ionians in the production of oil and wine and sold their produce at famine prices. They entered into commercial activities, took Salamis from Megara, and founded Sigeium on the Hellespont to secure a share in the Black Sea trade. The last act led to a war with Mytilene on the island of Lesbos, which was settled in favor of the Athenians by the arbitral decision of Periander of Corinth.

The cost of the wars and the rise in prices attendant upon the growth of vines and olive trees in place of grain bore heavily on the lower classes. Many of the farmers of *zeugite* census labored under heavy mortgages or, failing to pay, lost their lands and were reduced to the status of *hectemoroi,* "sixth-parters," or tenants who paid the sixth part of their product as rent.[1] Members of the thetic class who failed to make their payments of rent or loans were sold into slavery for debt. The popular discontent which arose from these sufferings made Athens ripe for tyranny or reform.

CYLON   In the strife for power and wealth, factions arose among the nobles and feuds among the great families. One young noble, Cylon, married the daughter of Theagenes, tyrant of Megara, and with his assistance tried to become tyrant of Athens in 632 or 628 B.C. His failure was due chiefly to the opposition of the Alcmaeonid family, headed by Megacles. This nobleman, however, committed the error of putting some of his enemies to death in a sacrilegious manner, whereupon he and his family were accursed and exiled, and his descendants never fully escaped from the curse.

DRACO   Commercial development, legal confusion, and such feuds as that between the followers of Megacles and Cylon made a clearer conception of the laws necessary. Elsewhere, under the influence of Apollo of Delphi, laws were being written down during this period, and, in 621 B.C., Draco was elected thesmothete with powers and instructions to record the ancestral customs. Of his code but little has survived save a probably undeserved reputation for severity. This was due chiefly to the fact that the theft of food, which was scarce in Attica, received the death penalty. The Draconian laws

---

[1] It is not certain whether the *hectemoroi* paid a rent of one-sixth or of five-sixths.

of murder, however, were exceedingly enlightened, probably due to Apolline influence, and survived into later times. The various kinds of murder were defined and proper penalties were affixed; rites of purification were established for accidental or justifiable homicide, and the killer was protected from the vengeance of the dead man's kinfolk.

While the recording of the law secured a more balanced justice, it did not correct the fundamental economic evils which affected the period. Through debt or dispossession the peasants were steadily losing their lands and becoming serfs or slaves. The situation was aggravated for the debtor class by the scarcity of food, the introduction of coinage, and the high rates of interest. As a result, the army was ruined. Civil strife broke out, and in the confusion Mytilene took over the Hellespontine settlement, and Megara regained Salamis. The aristocrats turned back to a repressive agricultural policy and forbade anyone to mention Salamis.

SOLON
In the crisis, the first of the city's statesmen, Solon, poet, general, and lawgiver, came into prominence. With his poems he stirred the Athenians to victory over Megara. He, like Tyrtaeus, also wrote poems on the civil situation, and in 594 B.C. he was elected chief archon with plenary power. The reforms which he carried through were the first step toward Athenian greatness, and they deserve careful attention.

In his attempt to solve the economic problems, he canceled all debts secured by the land or by the person of the debtor. Those who had been enslaved for debt were freed; those who had been sold outside of Attica were redeemed by the state, and slavery for debt was henceforth forbidden. This much Solon did for the peasantry. Over the fields already in the hands of the nobles he had no power, and he refused to take the revolutionary steps necessary to redivide the land. On the other hand, he did much to aid the poor, especially by forbidding the exportation of foodstuffs, and by encouraging the production of olive oil, "nurturer of children." To develop Athenian industry he gave citizenship to aliens who would settle in Athens as skilled craftsmen. Tradition says that he provided that every man must teach his son a trade, or otherwise the son would be exempted from supporting his father in old age. He established a coinage system on the Euboic standard which freed Athens from Aeginetan influence and brought her into line with Corinth and Chalcis.

Solon's reforms also increased the power of the individual over the family by giving the property owner the right to will his land in default of direct heirs, and by providing that any citizen might go to the legal assistance of another, regardless of family or phratry.

In the constitutional field he was equally moderate, but he prepared the way for the later democracy. The census classes were clearly defined. To the first belonged the very rich whose estates produced five hundred measures of grain or oil. A few special privileges and duties were reserved to them. The second class, the three-hundred-bushel men, were called *hippeis,* "knights," and served in the cavalry. From these classes the higher officers were chosen. The two-hundred-bushel men, *zeugites,* chiefly small farmers, served as hoplites in the army and as members of a new council which he created. The landless and poor, still called *thetes,* gained the vital right of membership in the assembly and the court. The most important result of Solon's definition of the classes was the possibility that a prosperous man might rise to greater power, regardless of his origin.

The archons and thesmothetae were henceforth elected by the assembly, and after their term was ended they became members of the Council of the Areopagus. Although this body had lost its deliberative and administrative powers, great honor was paid to it, nevertheless, as the ancient murder court and as guardian of the laws and customs. A new *Boule* (council) of Four Hundred was established, one hundred from each tribe chosen by lot from the first three census classes, which supervised the administration and prepared measures for submission to the assembly. To the latter body, called the *Ecclesia,* all classes were admitted. It passed on measures submitted to it by the council and elected the magistrates. Solon added a new institution which was to be the cornerstone of the democracy, the *Heliaea* or Popular Supreme Court. To it all citizens over thirty were eligible. Its members might hear appeals from the magistrates and compel the officers to render an accounting of their administration.

PEISISTRATUS Although Solon's reforms tided over the crisis, they did not end the political and economic struggles. After he had left Athens, hated as a moderate by both sides, factional strife broke out afresh along social and, to some extent, local lines. The aristocratic landowners of the Plain, led by Lycurgus and Miltiades, found vigorous rivals in the merchants, artisans and fishermen of the Shore. That Alcmaeonid, Megacles, who had married Agariste of Sicyon, came to the head of this party, an indication of the future policy of that family. The small farmers, charcoal burners, and miners of the back country, the Hill, were organized and led by a young noble, Peisistratus, who had given evidence of great ability in a war with Megara. The rivalry was so keen that in some years no archons could be elected. Finally, in 560 B.C., Peisistratus won and made himself tyrant. A hostile combination drove him out; but a marriage alliance with Megacles gave him the support of the Shore and he returned. Once more expelled, he went north, gained control of silver mines in Thrace, and returned with mercenaries. Thereafter he ruled peacefully until 527 B.C., when he was succeeded by his son Hippias assisted by Hipparchus, the latter's brother.

WORK OF
THE TYRANTS

The tyrants carried on the work begun by Solon. Since most of the nobles were in exile, their lands were confiscated and distributed among the peasantry, who were assisted in the development of olive orchards. With this came prosperity to the farming class. Ionian artisans and artists were encouraged to settle in Athens and ply their trades. Coincident with the increase in the supply of olive oil was the production of the fine black-figured pottery, followed before the end of the tyranny by the beautiful red-figured ware. Many of the painters signed their names to their work, names which, in some cases, indicate the appearance of alien craftsmen.

A peristyle was built around the temple of Athena; a temple to Olympian Zeus was started on a grand scale. The great Panathenaean games held every four years and the Eleusinian mysteries were raised to national importance. The city festival in honor of the rural Dionysus was instituted, and Thespis won the first recorded prize in the drama. In the reign of Hippias, Anacreon and other poets visited Athens. Fine statues of maidens, *korai*, Ionian in style, were set up on the Acropolis. The tyrants settled additional colonies on the Hellespont, one under the leadership of Miltiades. Friendly relations were cultivated with the neighboring states, and Athens prospered. The tyrants did not interfere with the working of the Solonian constitution beyond seeing that their partisans were elected to the offices of state and maintaining a rigid control over finance.

In 514 B.C., a private quarrel led to a conspiracy and the murder of Hipparchus. The movement failed; the leaders, Harmodius and Aristogeiton, were killed, and Hippias was driven to violence to defend himself. The ultimate result, however, was his overthrow. The Alcmaeonids, backed by the Delphic oracle, whose temple they had magnificently rebuilt, and assisted by Sparta, which was urged on by this oracle, drove the tyrants out of Athens. Cleomenes, the Spartan king, doubtless hoped to add Athens to the Peloponnesian League.

The tyrants had contributed much to the development of Athens. By the confiscation and redivision of lands they had dealt a death blow to the power of the aristocracy and had established a vigorous and prosperous peasantry. Commerce and industry had been advanced and the cornerstone of the structure of Athenian arts and letters had been laid. The prosperity which their rule brought to the city caused many people to desire their restoration. Nevertheless the unconstitutional character of the tyrannical position, the collection of direct taxes inconsistent with the Greek idea of freedom, the use of mercenaries to overawe the citizens and to maintain their power, and the violence of the last years of Hippias—all combined to create in patriotic Athenians a hatred of tyranny which made restoration of the Peisistratids impossible. To such a pitch did this hatred develop that the tyrannicides, Harmodius and Aristogeiton, who had led the revolt, were celebrated as national heroes.

CLEISTHENES The nobles, led by Isagoras, regained control in Athens and, to make their political position safe, began to strike off the rolls all who did not belong to the ancient phratries but who had been made citizens by Solon and Peisistratus. Cleisthenes, the Alcmaeonid leader, defeated Isagoras in 508 B.C. in a victory notable in that it led to a reorganization of Athens and to the further development of the democracy.

The problems which Cleisthenes endeavored to solve were three-fold: first, he sought to bring to an end the local rivalries between the Hill, the Shore, and the Plain which had caused so much trouble during earlier generations; secondly, he wished to break the political power of the great families of the aristocracy which they exercised through their influence over the peasantry and to make secure the citizenship grants which had been attacked; and in the third place, he planned to prevent such party rivalries as had made possible the rise of Peisistratus and his own strife with Isagoras.

Cleisthenes took as the basic unit for the Athenian state the *demes,* or villages, which were scattered over Attica, and to correspond to them he divided the city of Athens itself into several wards. Each deme was given a local organization with a *demarch* at its head to conduct local government and to keep the roll of the citizens. In making this roll, all free residents of Attica were included, thus forever shattering the power of the great families and of the ancient genē over the citizen body. In typical Greek fashion, however, a man so enrolled remained a member of his deme, even though he might later move to another; and in the local assemblies of these demes the Athenians received fundamental training in self-government. The demes, one hundred in number, were combined artificially into thirty organizations called *trittyes* or thirds. These trittyes, approximately equal in population, were combined to form ten tribes, each containing sections of the parties of the Plain, the Hill, and the Shore. Thus local factionalism was made impossible thereafter, and the influence of the nobles over the people in their districts became of little avail. The tribes later served as the basis for military and financial levies. Each had a definite political and religious organization, the latter centering around one of the heroes of Athens.

The boule (council) was perforce reorganized. Each tribe chose by lot from the whole body of its citizens fifty men, roughly apportioned among the demes according to their size. The council was thus increased to five hundred. Since such a body was unwieldy in administrative affairs, the fifty men from each tribe were constituted as an executive committee for one-tenth of the year, the order of the tribes being determined by lot. These committeemen were termed *prytaneis* and the term of their service a *prytany*. They lived at state expense in the council house, and some of their number were required to be always on hand. With ordinary routine matters they dealt directly. More important measures they submitted to the whole council, and in anything that required general action they drew up a bill for submission to the assembly.

The army was reorganized into ten tribal regiments, and in 501 B.C. a board of ten generals under the supervision of the polemarch was established to command them. Any man who held land in Attica was eligible to the office of general.

To prevent further civil strife, Cleisthenes is said to have instituted the peculiar custom known as ostracism. Once a year a vote was taken. The issue had to be important enough to bring out six thousand votes, a number apparently considered as comprising a large majority of the voting population and much greater than the size of any ordinary assembly. The voters wrote the name of any man whom they considered dangerous to the state on a potsherd or *ostracon*. That man against whom the plurality of votes was cast was sent into honorable exile for ten years without confiscation of property. As a matter of fact, this powerful weapon was seldom employed except in the period after the battle of Marathon (p. 189).

The democracy was, however, not yet fully established. Many of the higher offices were still restricted to the upper classes; in others the poor could not afford to serve without pay. Conservative forces were strong in the Areopagus, which continued as a powerful body in the state. But the new arrangement of demes and tribes had brought to an end the strife of the sections; the institution of ostracism served as an effective check against party divisions which might prove dangerous to peace, and the general right of participation in deme affairs, in the assembly, and in the council laid the foundations of the later democracy.

Although civil strife had ended, Cleisthenes was forced to defend himself from outsiders, when Cleomenes led an army of the Peloponnesian League into Attica, and Thebes and Chalcis sought the opportunity to crush the rising power of Athens. But dissension sent the Peloponnesians back home, and the other cities were decisively defeated.

Cleisthenes had, in fact, completed the work of the century of reform. The power of the aristocracy had been broken; moreover, new political powers and the control over their leaders provided by the Popular Supreme Court and the institution of ostracism rendered the peasantry and the industrial and commercial classes in the city secure in their position. The bases of friction thus removed, popular discontent was brought to an end, and Athens was ready to forge ahead.

CONCLUSION   By the year 500 B.C., Sparta, strengthened by its army and by its league, and Athens, united and content save for a group of sympathizers with the exiled tyrannists, had emerged as powerful states ready to meet the coming struggle with Persia and to take over leadership in Hellenic affairs from the faltering hands of the Ionians.

═ IX ═

THE CULTURAL RENAISSANCE

THESE political and economic processes of the period 800-500 B.C. were accompanied and affected by a corresponding development in religion, art, literature, and thought—the Greek Renaissance. All of these cultural phases of life, developing or transforming to meet the growing needs of the people, felt the new influences, the rising power of the city-state, the greater importance of the lower and middle classes, and the increase of knowledge produced by the colonial movement and by trade and contact with Oriental civilizations.

RELIGION

It has been said that Greek religion existed to make men at home in the world. This religion penetrated every part of life and filled all that it touched with spiritual power. All nature was divine. Spirits lived in the trees and the flowers, in the springs, the streams and the sea. The sky, sun, moon, and stars, the light breezes of morning and evening, the winds and the thundercloud—all told men of their divine elements. In like manner, all of the daily acts of man—his work and his play—had their religious significance. The family, as its members gathered about the sacred hearth fire, while the ancestors hovered in spirit around, was conscious of its supernal protectors. At the larger political and social gatherings the gods were always present.

To these spirits, great and small, men turned for companionship in their joy and for comfort in their sorrow. The evil spirits which existed and brought fear to the hearts of men were given pleasant names or beautiful forms to avert their wrath. Fear was banished by beauty, and love for the gods and pleasure in their worship became the central theme of Greek religion.

Certain divinities were universal. These, connected with the larger aspects of nature and of life, were recognized as the great gods, the dwellers on Olympus. Zeus was in origin the sky god of the Indo-Europeans, wielder of the thunderbolt, sender of rain, king and father of gods and men. Hera, his wife, was the queenly embodiment of wife and mother. Athena, virgin goddess, was protectress of the king and of the citadel, leader in organized, intelligent warfare; and later, in Athens, she was to become the embodiment of wisdom. Poseidon, dwelling in the midst of the sea, was the god of the waters, sender of earthquakes and at the same time giver of horses to men. Demeter was the earth herself, giver of grain. Apollo, god of the sun and of light, leader and protector of wanderers, god of healing, prophecy and song, adviser of youth, became the personification of the Greek character with its intelligence and its sense of order. Artemis, the huntress, sister of Apollo, was goddess of the moon and of the woods, and watcher over the animals. Dionysus, a later addition to the family of the gods, was god of spring, of wine, of divine ecstasy. Aphrodite, said to have been born of the sea foam, was the goddess of the mystery of life and of reproduction; she later became the goddess of perfect physical beauty. Ares was the spirit of combat. Hephaestus, smith of the gods, was worshiped by artisans. Hades, brother of Zeus, was ruler of the underworld.

LOCAL GODS
Besides these great divinities were countless local deities worshiped at small shrines. In time many of them became identified with the great gods, and the name of the little god then survived as an adjective attached to the greater name. Thus at the shrine of Hyakinthos, Apollo absorbed the attributes of the pre-Hellenic divinity and was called Apollo Hyakinthos. At the same time, in appealing to a deity for aid of a special sort, men attached to his name an adjective befitting the request and, as it were, thus created a special divinity for a special task. To illustrate, Athena was worshiped in Athens as Athena Polias, guardian of the city, as Athena Ergane, patroness of artisans, as Athena Hygeia, giver of health, and as Athena Parthenos, goddess of wisdom. Technically, as a matter of cult practice, each Athena was a separate goddess worshiped only in that aspect; yet through all there flowed the realization of the unity of Athena herself.

This process of identification and separation led to a wide diversity in the characteristics of each divinity and to a very considerable overlapping of godlike functions from one place to another, a confusion increased by early combinations of northern and Minoan divinities. Thus the virgin huntress, Artemis, was blended with the old mother goddess of the Mediterranean to become the famous "Many-breasted Artemis of the Ephesians."

HEROES   Of lower order than the gods were the heroes, spirits of the great dead who continued to protect those interests which they had served in life. Groups worshiped as their ancestors the leaders of the epic period. Cities venerated their founders. Shrines called *heroa* were erected, rituals were developed, and sedulous court was paid to these demigods.

Beyond the gods lay something the Greeks called *Moira*, fate, a power to which the gods themselves were subject, a law created by them but by which they were bound. In close relationship to it was *Nemesis*, the personified jealousy of the gods, which pursued and destroyed the man who was too successful or who aimed too high.

DIVINATION   Like the Orientals, the Greeks sought to know the will of the gods and to peer into the future. From the East they learned divination by examining the liver or entrails of animals (p. 36). They watched the action of the sacrificial animals or that of the fire on the altar. They observed the flight of birds, regarded as the messengers of Zeus, and they believed in all sorts of accidental omens. In addition to these avenues of approach, men asked advice of the gods directly at one of the many oracles. The most famous of these were at Dodona and at Delphi. Zeus spoke to men at Dodona through the rustling of oak leaves, and at Delphi Apollo made known his will through the wild utterances of a priestess in ecstasy. Here the good sense of the Greeks recognized the right of the god to give deceptive advice which might lead men to fated ruin, or to give to presuming questions about the future those ambiguous answers which have given meaning to the modern phrase "oracular utterance."

In a future life the Greeks of the early period took but little interest. The shades of the dead dwelt in colorless form, flitting about in a place so dreary that Achilles would rather have been slave to a landless man than king of the dead.

MYTHOLOGY   To explain their religious experiences and their rituals the Greeks told many stories, products of a childlike but rich imagination, yet not essential to religious worship. From these our pictures of the gods are derived. The wide diversity of functions of individual gods, the essentially local character of the worship, and the absence of any authoritative pronouncement made dogmatism in matters of belief impossible. So long as local acts of worship were performed according to ancestral tradition, gods and men were satisfied. To secure such performances was the function of the priest. Because priesthoods were hereditary in great families of were elective, and because few men devoted themselves exclusively to the service of the gods, freedom of belief was preserved. Greek religion was not an individual matter but a concern of a group—family, genos, tribe, or city. Activity in the service of the group and its gods was the greatest virtue, and self-seeking arrogance the greatest vice.

RITUAL The sole essential to worship was an altar in the open air and a ritual prescribed by ancestral tradition. Prayer, hymns, choruses, processions, and sacrifices—all were employed to win the favor of the gods. In one form of sacrifice the aninals were butchered, the meat was cooked and passed out to the worshipers, while the entrails were placed on the altar and burned. Thus the god and his worshipers sat down to a common feast. In certain other sacrifices, particularly those to the earth divinities, the animals were burned entire for the propitiation of the gods.

GROWTH OF GREEK RELIGION There are many indications in myth and in religious language and customs that a large number of the Greek gods were once associated with animals or birds, or inanimate objects. With the development of mythology, however, they emerged from these crude beginnings and assumed the forms of men and women, a religious conception called *anthropomorphism*. This process was completed by Homer and Hesiod. In the *Iliad* and the *Odyssey,* poems of universal significance to all Hellenes, Zeus and his court appeared in human forms as supremely beautiful and powerful men and women with personalities of their own, and living human lives. The poet brought the gods very near to man and taught in marvelous guise "the humanity of God and the divinity of man," but by thus necessarily limiting them in time and place, he weakened them at the same time for their real service to mankind. In a later generation Hesiod endeavored to bring order into mythological confusion when in his *Theogony* he arranged the gods in a genealogical table. Then in his *Works and Days,* in which he laid emphasis upon the moral character of the gods, he warned the princes that Zeus would punish them for their corruption and injustice.

With the development of the city-states the gods were so woven into the political and social structure that they became the protectors and heavenly rulers of the communities. Devotion and service to them was implied in loyalty to the polis, and the performance of religious ceremonies to secure their favor was a matter of prime concern to the officials of the state.

APOLLO   During the period of colonization, Apollo of Delphi became a divinity of wide power and significance. Appeals came to his oracle from all parts of the Hellenic world and on all sorts of problems, and his answers were invariably in accordance with traditional usage and reasonable interpretation. His priests directed the course of colonization and settled disputes concerning territory between cities. States consulted his priests in the writing down of their laws, and the priests' influence is to be seen in the definition of the kinds of murder and the appropriate treatment. The priests developed rites of purification, some of which may have had Minoan origins, to salve the troubled conscience of the evildoer. Although this was a legalistic service, it was essentially a ritualistic legalism which did not reach far into the moral realm or subjugate human life to rules. Only through Apollo's fundamental pronouncements to men, "nothing to excess" and "know thyself," did his priests lay down principles which were later to be transformed into ethical systems. Arrogance and self-seeking were still, in the eyes of Apollo, the greatest crime against the gods.

New developments in religion took place as the result of the social and economic difficulties of the seventh and sixth centuries B.C., for when the old gods whose cults were under aristocratic control failed to answer the needs of the poor and the oppressed, emotional and individualistic religions arose to take their place.

DIONYSUS   In the forefront of these new rites was the worship of the god Dionysus, whose cult may have been an old peasant religion. He was a typical nature divinity who died and was brought back to life again. His worshipers roamed the mountain tops in wild revels, and sought union with the god in ecstasy. In the sixth century, one phase of his worship crystallized in the Orphic sect, which took its name from the mythical minstrel, Orpheus. The leaders of this group developed rituals, dogmas, and rules of life, and they believed in the transmigration of souls. To the initiate they promised release from the wheel of life, and eternal bliss as a reward for the sufferings of this world. This cult was especially favored by the tyrants; had it been universally successful, it would have meant the development of a priesthood and an authoritative dogma among the Greeks.

In Athens the tyrants began the development of the festivals of Dionysus at which dramatic contests were held in honor of the god. At Eleusis the addition of Dionysus to the ancient cult of Demeter and her daughter, Persephone, resulted in a religion of high emotional content. The ceremonies were open to all Hellenes. After a sacred procession and sacrifice and the initiation of newcomers, a "passion play," based on the myth of Hades' theft of Persephone, was presented in deepest secrecy. The *mystai,* or initiates, were assured of a blessed immortality, happier than the lot promised by the older beliefs.

GAMES

One of the most striking features of the Greek religious festivals was the idea of competition. There were contests of skill and speed in athletics, in poetry, music, choral dancing, and dramas. In some festivals men presented the products of their skill for awards. At one festival of Demeter, a prize was given to the mother of the best baby; at another, the man who could stand longest on one foot on a greased hide did honor to Dionysus, and in Megara there was even a contest in kissing.

Of all these contests the most famous were the athletic. Their origin may be found in funeral games held in honor of some deceased hero, but in any case they were a natural product of the outdoor life of the Greeks. Almost every state had its local games; but four attained the rank of national meets: the Olympic games held every four years at the shrine of Zeus at Olympia in Elis; the Pythian games, held every four years at Delphi, where Apollo was patron and where therefore the original contests were musical; the Isthmian, and the Nemean games, biennial affairs, both in the neighborhood of Corinth and performed in honor of Poseidon and Zeus, respectively. The Olympic games attained such prestige that later historians used the Olympiads as a system of dating.

The first Olympiad of record began in 776 B.C., though the legendary date for the origin of the games was much earlier. The fully developed program included elaborate religious ceremonies, athletic contests, and chariot races. Before multitudes assembled from all the Hellenic world the greatest runners contested barefooted in the dash for the length of the stadium (about two hundred yards), in the double course, in a race of about three miles, and in a race in armor; athletes threw the discus and the javelin, and strong men matched their strength in wrestling, boxing, and a combination of the two called *pankration*. The *pentathlon,* greatly esteemed, was a combination of the single and double course, discus and javelin throwing, and wrestling. Victory in the chariot race was especially sought after by men of wealth. There were contests for boys, mule races, and other events. To enter, contestants had to prove their Greek parentage to the governors and had to train at least one month at Olympia under their supervision. The prize was but a wreath of olive, but the victor found his real reward when he returned home a hero.

The earlier festival truce became a religious duty for all Hellenic cities. Heralds proclaimed the season to all; hostilities were laid aside; embassies to the games might pass through hostile territory in perfect safety under the protection of the god. The greatest disgrace, exclusion from the games, was visited as a punishment upon anyone who offended against the truce. At Olympia the leading men of every state foregathered. Views were exchanged, differences were harmonized, agreements were consummated and tablets recording them were set up in the shrine to ensure their fulfillment. Matters of interest to all Greeks were announced and discussed. Following close on the diplomat came the trader with his wares. Booths were set up and goods exchanged. The foundations for commerce between cities were laid here in the creation of demand for products.

An early king of Argos, Pheidon, saw in the games an opportunity for the unification of Greece under his influence and endeavored to secure domination over them. The rising power of Sparta drove him back, and never again was any man so presumptuous. Though Sparta had aspirations of the same sort, the little state of Elis guarded its prerogatives so carefully and fostered the public opinion of the Greeks so zealously that Sparta itself was not able to escape the penalty when it violated the sacred truce.

ARCHITECTURE

Anthropomorphism in religion and the development of the civic communities played most important roles in the development of architecture. Where caves and groves, courtyard altars and household shrines had sufficed in Minoan and Achaean times, the gods of the city-states needed houses in which to live. The builders thereof turned naturally to those fine dwellings which they knew. Some of the older divinities were housed in primitive round huts, made of wood covered with brass or of stone, but developed and elaborated. For the temples of the others men used as models those megara which had formerly been the dwellings of the kings. The simplest form consisted of a single room, in front of which was a porch supported either by square pillars terminating the side walls, with columns intervening, or by a row of columns called the *prostyle*. Later, rear porches and sometimes additional rooms were added and, in the interest of beauty, a series of columns called the *peristyle* was carried around the whole building. Within, the ceiling was supported by rows of columns, normally two in number.

While the plan of the building was essentially native and while many of its later features show its development locally and directly from wood into stone, there can be no doubt that the architects drew upon the traditions of the great builders of Aegean times and upon the experiences of the Orientals—Egyptian, Babylonian, and Hittite. Out of these, in varying proportions and in accordance with local demands and ideas, two distinct orders of architecture were developed: the one, Doric, chiefly in the Peloponnesus and in the west; the other, Ionic, in the east.

The chief features of the Doric order, in which Egyptian influence was predominant, were strength and simplicity. The column rested directly without base on the top step and was surmounted by a simple capital of two blocks, the first, curved, the second, flat. Above the architrave (the row of flat blocks connecting the columns), which was undecorated, was the frieze. This consisted of two alternating parts: the *triglyphs,* three projections, originally the sheathed ends of beams; and the *metopes,* square spaces between the triglyphs, filled with paintings or with stucco figures and later with relief sculpture in stone.

The Ionic order was more ornate, and it developed fittingly in the wealthy cities of Asia Minor under Babylonian, Hittite, or Egyptian influence. A base consisting of a series of convex and concave surfaces gave elaboration and height to the columns. The capital, originally probably a block of wood covered with metal in Oriental design, was transformed in stone into the *volute,* or scroll, which became characteristic of the Ionic order. The later Corinthian style was developed from the Ionic by the substitution of a more ornate and loftier capital produced by the carving of acanthus leaves in stone. The architrave was divided into two or three members called *fascias.* The frieze above was a plain band of stone which, when decorated by sculpture, presented a unified pictures across or along the building.

From the beginning the Greek architects sought after grace and proportion as the chief elements of beauty. With keen aesthetic sense they carved grooves, or flutes, in their columns, and gave to the columns themselves a gentle swelling curve called *entasis.* They experimented with the length and breadth of buildings and with the height and diameter of columns in search of the most artistic relationship. Many of the earlier buildings were too long or too broad, their columns too heavy or too thin. In the best period the peristyle established the proportions of the building, the side rows containing one more than twice as many columns as on the end. At the same time the shaft of the Doric column was in height five and one-half times its diameter, and the lighter Ionic had the ratio of eight or nine to one. Sometimes the architect secured a different but interesting effect by the use of human figures in place of columns.

The horizontal lines and the simple beauty of the Greek temple testify to the fact that it was erected not as a place of worship but as the civic home of a very human divinity.

The temples of the early period were products of experimentation. The oldest temple known from its remains was that of Hera at Olympia. Originally built of wood, probably in the seventh century B.C., its first columns as they decayed were replaced by stone according to the best technique of replacement at the time. As a result, those which have survived show diversity in proportion, in number of flutes and in forms of capitals. The temple of Apollo at Corinth and many of the structures which have survived in Sicily and southern Italy illustrate in their heaviness or their lack of proportion the failures of the early architects, but at the same time they reveal, in spite of their defects,

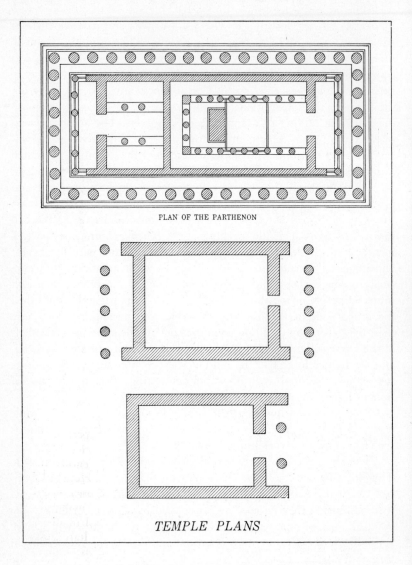

PLAN OF THE PARTHENON

TEMPLE PLANS

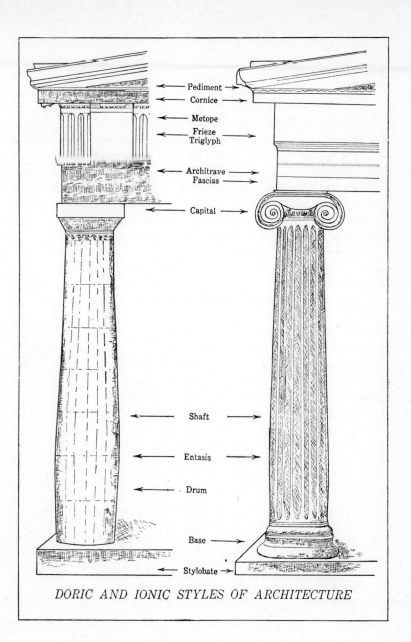

Pediment

Cornice

Metope

Frieze
Triglyph

Architrave
Fascias

Capital

Shaft

Entasis

Drum

Base

Stylobate

DORIC AND IONIC STYLES OF ARCHITECTURE

the ideals which animated the builders and which resulted in the perfection attained by their greater successors in the fifth century B.C.

SCULPTURE　　Sculpture, like architecture, was the product of Greek religion, of the need for cult statues of the divinities, and of the desire to decorate the temples with figures in relief. The games also inspired the idea of making statues of the victors, the athletes themselves serving as models. Although the first statues were of wood, the artists, probably under strong Egyptian influence, learned to use limestone, then marble, and finally, bronze. In Ionia, doubtless as the result of the predominance of the mother goddess in religion, great attention was paid to female figures, and to the arrangement of hair and draperies. On the mainland, however, where the athletic influence was strong, nude male figures predominated.

The early statues were stiff and ill-proportioned and followed the so-called Egyptian law of frontality (p. 55). The artists had to learn for themselves the proportions of the human body, the proper position of the eyes and the ears on the head, the relative length of legs and arms. In addition the artists had to acquire techniques in the working of the material necessary to give adequate representation of human hair and flesh, of the texture of draperies and the suggestion of the human figure underneath. In the relief sculptures on frieze or pediment, there arose problems of composition, of the relative height of figures, and of the representation of movement; but in the solution of all these difficulties the artists were inspired by an aesthetic ideal. Furthermore, their experiences in athletics and in religion gave the Hellenes a concept of the divinity of human beauty. Their efforts to represent this in stone give to the crude statues of the archaic era a freshness and a glory which transcend the sculptor's errors. The knowledge of anatomy and the mastery of technique which the early artists slowly acquired prepared the way for the finer works of later generations.

LITERATURE

The varied influences of the political and economic changes of this age were reflected in the literature and the thought as well as in the religion of the period. Epic poetry, in which the poet was but the teller of a story, was essentially the product of the heroic age. Though in later centuries men still turned to Homer for delight and inspiration, and though many lesser epics of which we possess but fragments

Museum at Delphi

CHARIOTEER OF DELPHI

Acropolis Museum

STATUE OF A MAIDEN

National Museum, Athens

WRESTLING BOUT

ARCHAIC GREEK SCULPTURE

ZEUS   *Athens*   HERMES   *Olympia*

SACRIFICIAL BULLS   *Parthenon frieze*

ATHENIAN SCULPTURE

were written in Ionia in the seventh century B.C., the epic no longer suited the temper of men, and so yielded place to new literary forms.

Hesiod's poems, though written in the epic meter, marked the first departure from the older style, since in his passion for justice for the oppressed of the land, he burst the bonds of tradition and expressed himself vigorously on current social and economic problems. But even the meter was unsuited to the new age of city-state life, of party strife, and of nascent individualism. New subjects and new emotions demanded new vehicles of expression. So in meters varied to suit the subject, poets sang the praises of their states or their party leaders and vilified their opponents. They praised victorious athletes, and wrote of love and wine and nature; or in sterner tone they rallied their countrymen to the defense of native land against present foes. Some composed choral hymns for youths and maidens to sing in concert in honor of the gods, or battle songs to rouse the warriors, who sang them with martial fervor.

Under the impetus of the times religious leaders asking new questions and making new demands upon the gods developed an emotional religion (p. 171). Thinkers, drinking deep of the ancient learning of the East, discovering themselves as individuals in a great universe, and beginning to ask questions of how and why, established Greek philosophy.

The leadership in all these intellectual movements came naturally from the Anatolian cities, where political and economic forces were most active and where the contact with Oriental culture was closest. Nevertheless these poets, religious leaders, and philosophers filled a pressing need in this age of ferment and found a ready welcome wherever they went. In many circles their presence was earnestly solicited. Speaking a language which all could understand, they became, like the great poets of the epic age, the common property of all Greeks and an added bond of union among them.

In the development of this early Greek literature the growth of writing and the importation of papyrus from Egypt were of paramount importance. The Greeks learned their alphabet from the Phoenicians and adapted to their own vowel sounds certain signs for sounds which they did not have. Varying alphabets developed in different parts of the Greek world, but the basic elements were the same. Finally, in 403 B.C., the Ionic alphabet was adopted by Athens and became the literary standard there. The earliest writing was on stone or clay. One of the oldest specimens of Greek writing known is that of some Greek mercenaries who went far up the Nile with Psamtik II and were the first of a long line of tourists to scratch their names on Egyptian monuments. Lists of officials, laws, and treaties were recorded on wooden tablets, on stone or, later, were cast in bronze. Trade with Egypt brought in papyrus, and written literature became possible.

The first personality to stand out vividly in the new literature was Archilochus, who developed the iambic satire. Born in Paros, he had there an unfortunate love affair. His verses are said to have driven the young lady and her family to commit suicide, whereupon he was forced to leave home and went as a colonist to Thasos. Thence he moved on to become a restless mercenary warrior. In describing himself as a soldier and a poet, he said, "I am the servant of the lord Enyalios, and I am skilled in the lovely gift of the Muses." He wrote religious poems, satirical fables, and a long series of personal poems varying in subject from wine to shipwreck. The literary importance of his work rests on the fact that he was the first Greek to use the poetic medium to express himself as an individual. In so doing he broke the bonds of the older meter and created new standards. His philosophy of life was typical of the age:

Endure, endure my soul, disquieted by griefs beyond remedy and setting thy breast against the foe, hold thy ground, taking thy stand firm and close amid the spears of the enemy. If thou conquerest, exult not openly, and if thou art conquered, lie not down in thy house and mourn. Rejoice in that which is meet for rejoicing and grieve not overmuch at calamities, but learn what condition prevails among men.[1]

Alcaeus of Mytilene in Lesbos is the best proponent of the era of adventure and political strife which ushered in the sixth century. A noble, a politician, a soldier, a traveler, a *bon vivant,* he is the product of Mytilene at the height of its greatest splendor. He took part in wars, was driven into exile by the democratic tyrant, and returned home from Egypt to a settled life. His songs were of war, of party strife, of love, of wine and of spring.

Sappho, contemporary of Alcaeus, was a product of the happy freedom and wealth of the social life of Mytilene. She stands supreme among the poetesses of love.

[1] W. E. Caldwell, *Hellenic Conceptions of Peace,* p. 53.

The fairest thing in all the world some say is a host of horsemen, and some a host of foot, and some again a navy of ships; but to me, 'tis the heart's beloved . . . one of whom I would rather the sweet sound of her footfall and the sight of the brightness of her beaming face than all the chariots and armored footmen of Lydia.[2]

Erotic poetry reached its culmination in this century in the work of Anacreon of Teos. His life was typical of the age. Driven from Teos by local disturbances, he settled at Abdera in Thrace, where he took part in wars with the native Thracians. After his poetry became famous, he spent many years in the court of that piratical despot and adventurer, Polycrates of Samos. From there he went to the court of Hippias at Athens. Amid scenes of splendor and glory he clung to the golden mean, envying neither pomp nor power nor wealth, but desiring tranquillity and happiness above all. Eros and Dionysus were his most loved divinities. In an epigram he described war as evil, for it took away the bravest of the city's youth and left the coward in his place. These odes, meant to be sung as solos to the accompaniment of the lyre, are known as lyric poems.

Other poets, such as Alcman at Sparta, wrote choral songs to be sung in procession by youths or maidens, or dithyrambs to be performed by the chorus at the festival of Dionysus.

Another form of verse was the elegiac couplet, consisting of alternate lines of six and five meters. Such poems were especially adapted for recital and were used as war songs or for political purposes. Among the poets who used this measure were Tyrtaeus, general in Sparta, who wrote a stirring war song to encourage his followers and another poem called "Eunomia"—"good laws well obeyed," to allay incipient civil strife; Solon, who used his verse to set his political ideas before the Athenians; and Theognis of Megara, a poet of the aristocracy who wrote verses as instructions to his younger friends. He bitterly attacked the democratic leaders and tyrants, the power of money over birth, and the tendency to marry out of class in the interests of wealth. The "good" were the aristocrats, and the "evil" were the baseborn.

The greatest of the lyric poets was Pindar (520?-441 B.C.), a Theban. So great was he that his contemporaries regarded him as a special favorite of Apollo, god of song, and reserved a seat for him in the

[2] Botsford and Sihler, *Hellenic Civilization*, p. 197.

temple at Delphi. Of his many poems on varied subjects, chance has preserved, aside from a few fragments, only his songs of praise of the victors in the national games. In these he praised not so much the individual as the city and its noble leaders. Throughout his poems runs the common theme of the greatness of nobility, of its duty and privilege of service to the state and to the gods, and of the glories of its achievements. His thought is colored by a deep religious feeling founded on Orphism. Though he lived in the next generation, his work and his ideas are the product and the culmination of the forces of the sixth century B.C.

PHILOSOPHY   The intelligence of men directed their eyes to natural causes, and they dared to examine the world in an endeavor to explain its origin, its form, and its purpose. Greek philosophy began in the sixth century B.C. with a bold attempt to reduce the universe itself to a simple principle. The most powerful element in the thinking of the time was the idea of descent, doubtless derived from Hesiod, who in his *Theogony* had attempted to explain the genealogy of the gods themselves in their descent from the first divinities. But though the Orphists clung to his ideas, contact with other lands and with other ideas had weakened, for many intelligent men, the structure of Hesiod's theology. Herodotus (II, 143) recounts the experience of Hecataeus of Miletus in Egypt. When, discoursing of his genealogy at Thebes, the Milesian declared that a god was his sixteenth ancestor, the priests of Amon showed him three hundred and forty-five statues of priests, each of whom they claimed was the son of the man before him, and denied that any man was ever born of a god. It is little wonder that after such an experience Hecataeus wrote, "The stories of the Greeks appear to me to be altogether foolish."

The first man to attempt a new explanation of the world was Thales (ca. 585 B.C.), general, statesman, and philosopher of Miletus, who declared that all things were descended from a first principle, water. The earth he described as a flat disk floating on water. He is said to have predicted the eclipse of 585 B.C. and, from his ability as a meteorologist, to have made a fortune out of a speculation in the olive crop. His search for a materialistic answer to the question of origins was continued by his successors, Anaximander and Anaximenes. Anaximander, who probably composed the first Greek book written in prose, denied the presence of any original matter save "the boundless" from which matter was separated by motion in the form of opposites, like hot and cold, wet and dry. In the pursuit of his studies about the world he made the first Greek map. Anaximenes, returning to Thales' concept, identified origin with air, from which all things are made by the processes of rarefaction and condensation. "In a word the Milesians had drawn the outlines of the theory of matter in the physicists' sense of the word, and these outlines still survive in a recognizable form in our text-books. That . . . is the central thing in the system, and that is why it is reckoned as the beginning of philosophy. It is the earliest answer to the question, 'What is reality?'" [3]

The philosophic studies begun by these men were continued in the last part of the sixth century B.C. by two Ionians, Xenophanes and Pythagoras, who fled in exile to the west. Xenophanes devoted his writings chiefly to religious and social problems. He declared the existence of one god, the earth, the beginning and end of all things.

> But mortals fancy gods are born and wear clothes, and have voice and form like themselves. Yet if oxen and lions had hands, and could paint with their hands, and fashion images, as men do, they would make the pictures and images of the gods in their own likeness; horses would make them like horses, oxen like oxen. [4]

He attacked the luxury of Ionian life and bitterly condemned those who praised and rewarded victorious athletes but ignored the wisemen. "For our wisdom is better than the strength of horses and men."

Pythagoras of Samos, after travels and study in Egypt, settled at Croton in Italy. Here he developed his famous explanation of the order of the universe in mathematics, the science of numbers. He laid emphasis upon chord and discord, harmony and its lack, and the proper balance of all things. His school developed under Orphist influence to become a religious sect, the members of which were essentially ascetic, living by rules laid down for every phase of life. His doctrines gave great impetus to the study of mathematics and made important contributions to medicine.

The beginnings of historical studies and of human geography were counterparts of Ionian philosophy. History, however, sprang out of the desire of the leaders of the day to prove their descent from the heroes of the traditional past. Hence the first historians were really genealogists, who endeavored from myth and tradition to discover the

[3] Burnet, *Greek Philosophy*, Part I, *Thales to Plato*, pp. 27-28.
[4] Bakewell, *Source Book of Ancient Philosophy*, p. 8.

ancestry of and to work out lines of descent for their contemporaries. Their conclusions were recorded in prose. Critical acumen caused them to rationalize or to explain the myths, although the influence of the past prevented any denial of their truth.

The leader of these early prose writers was Hecataeus of Miletus, who was also the first geographer. Anaximander had made a map, and on the basis of it, Hecataeus, who had traveled throughout the Mediterranean and Black seas, in Persia, and in Egypt, composed a description of the lands and peoples he had seen, together with some account of their past history.

Like the artists and the architects, philosophers and scientists during the sixth century B.C. inaugurated processes and methods, which through awakened interest continued to advance men's ability and knowledge until they reached fruition in the greatest works of the Greek intellect.

══ X ══

THE PERSIAN WARS

D URING the first years of the fifth century B.C. there took place the great war between the Greeks and the Persians, a contest memorable in itself and a prelude to nearly two centuries of struggle ending only in the later years of the fourth century B.C. when Alexander the Great destroyed the Persian Empire.

As the aftermath to the conquest of Lydia, Cyrus had added the Anatolian Greeks to his empire, placing them under the rule of local tyrants supervised by the satraps of the provinces. This conquest and the resultant development of trade led inevitably to relations with cities on the other side of the Aegean and with the Greek colonies scattered around the Mediterranean. There could be no doubt that the Greeks were intelligent and energetic, worthy subjects of conquest whose subjection would bring trade and tribute to Persia. Disunity and intrigue made the task appear easy: the Alcmaeonid party in Athens had appealed to Persia for aid against the Peloponnesians, and Hippias, deposed tyrant of Athens, and Demaratus, exiled king of Sparta, sought refuge and restoration from the Persians. Accordingly Darius (p. 111), undoubtedly planning conquest, sent a fleet guided by his physician, Democedes (who deserted at Croton) to make a survey of the Mediterranean.

EXPEDITION ACROSS THE DANUBE
As a first step Darius invaded Europe in 512 B.C. and marched north across the Danube to protect his rear against the Scythians of southwest Russia. Here he met with some success while his generals completed the conquest of Thrace. Ionian Greeks who took part in the expedition stood guard at the bridge of boats across the Danube.

THE IONIAN REVOLT
Shortly after Darius' return the Ionian revolt broke out. The plots of Aristagoras, tyrant of Miletus, precipitated the movement; and the cities of Asia Minor, constantly fretting under Persian rule, eagerly co-operated. Aristagoras

himself went across the Aegean in search of help. Sparta refused because Susa was too far away, but Athens and Eretria sent ships and men. The Greek army won an initial victory, captured Sardis and burned it. On their way home they were overtaken by the Persian forces and defeated, whereupon the Athenians withdrew. Persian success followed dissension in the Greek alliance. The Ionian fleet was defeated and destroyed off Lade, near Miletus, and one after another the cities were retaken until in 494 B.C. Miletus fell and was destroyed. Darius established democratic governments in place of the tyrants who had proved treacherous, and then proceeded with his original plans.

THE PERSIAN ADVANCE

In 492 B.C. Mardonius, son-in-law of the king, started a campaign against the Greeks with a combined land and naval expedition along the coast of Thrace. Thracian tribes defeated the army, and the Persian fleet, caught in a storm off Mt. Athos, was wrecked. This failure resulted in a change of plan: the king determined to strike directly across the Aegean. He sent envoys to demand earth and water, tokens of submission from the Greek cities. Many of the islands and mainland communities yielded, but the Athenians threw the envoys in a pit, and the Spartans dropped them into a well. These violations of the sanctity of ambassadors was a recognition of the inevitability of the struggle. In 490 B.C. Datis and Artaphernes, accompanied by the Athenian Hippias, led a force by sea against Athens. Naxos and Delos were captured en route, Eretria was taken and destroyed, and a portion of the army was landed at Marathon on the coast of Attica.

PREPARATIONS OF THE ATHENIANS

The situation in Athens was critical. The city had prospered under the Peisistratid tyranny, and the Areopagus had been filled with followers of the tyrants. A strong party could therefore be counted on to aid the Persians for the return of Hippias. The Alcmaeonid successors of Cleisthenes were under suspicion because of their earlier appeal to Persia for aid against the Spartans. Balancing these forces was the patriotic faction led by Aristides and Themistocles, the men who had been responsible for Athenian participation in the Ionian revolt. The failure and return of the army threw the balance against them. When the dramatic poet, Phrynichus, probably inspired and supported by Themistocles, produced a tragedy, *The Fall of Miletus,* the Athenian people fined him "for reminding them of their sorrows." The play secured its desired effect, however, and Themistocles was elected archon for 493-492 B.C. He used his year to good advantage by fortifying the natural harbor of Peiraeus and beginning the development of the Athenian navy.

Thus, when the Persians came in 490 B.C., the city was determined upon resistance, though its neighbors, Thebes and Chalcis, were openly hostile to Athens, and only Spartan intervention prevented Aegina from surrendering its important naval base to the Persians. Pheidippides ran to Sparta, one hundred and fifty miles in two days, to seek aid, but the Spartans were delayed by a religious festival and arrived too late to be of any assistance. Fortune favored the Athenians, however, by providing them with Miltiades. Since this commander, as tyrant of Chersonese, an Athenian colony on the Hellespont, had had experience with the Persian army in the Danube expedition, he was elected general, and the command was entrusted to him by vote of the other generals when Callimachus, the polemarch, cast the deciding ballot.

MARATHON

Information about this famous struggle at Marathon is scanty and confused. Apparently the Persian plan called for a division of forces. One portion of their army was to march upon Athens from Marathon while the other was to be landed at Phalerum. Traitors could then be relied on to open the gates. The Athenian army, aided by a small force from Plataea, occupied a strong position in the hills above the plain of Marathon and awaited developments. When the Persian fleet and army began to move, Miltiades waited until the enemy was well in front of him and then gave the order to charge. When his forces arrived within bowshot they advanced at the double quick; consequently the phalanx came to close quarters before the Persian arrows could do great damage. There the heavy-armed troops, fighting in close formation, proved their superiority over the lightly equipped Persians. The battle was hotly contested, but the Persians were beaten and driven back to their ships. During the night after the battle the Athenians marched back to Athens, so that when the Persian fleet appeared off Phalerum the next morning it was confronted by the waiting Athenian army. Not willing to risk another engagement, the Persians turned their ships around and sailed back across the Aegean. The Spartan forces, arriving too late to be of help, merely surveyed the scene of battle, complimented the Athenians, and returned to Sparta.

THE PLANS
OF XERXES

To the Persians Marathon was only a temporary check. Darius prepared again to invade Greece but he died in 485 B.C. It was not until 480 B.C. that his successor, Xerxes, completed his plans. Once more the Persians prepared with care and forethought for a combined land and naval attack along the lines of the first expedition. Supplies were gathered at convenient places across Thrace and Macedonia. A canal was cut behind Mt. Athos. All the subjects were called upon to send contingents, and a fine fleet of Phoenician, Carian, and Ionian Greek ships was gathered.

Herodotus' stories of the extraordinary size and diversity of the army which drank rivers dry and ate districts barren on the march are in a measure indicative of what the Greeks believed was coming against them. Small wonder that weaker states trembled and went over to the Persian side, while even Apollo of Delphi wavered. Athenians seeking advice from Apollo were driven from the temple with fearful imprecations of impending doom. They returned as suppliants on the advice of a Delphic priest and finally secured an answer which may have been inspired by Themistocles:

Pallas has not been able to soften the lord of Olympus,
Though she has often prayed him, and urged him with excellent counsel.
Yet once more I address thee in words than adamant firmer.
When the foe shall have taken whatever the limit of Cecrops
Holds within it, and all that divine Cithaeron shelters,
Then far-seeing Zeus grants this to the prayers of Athena,—
Safe shall the wooden wall continue for thee and thy children.
Wait not the tramp of the horse, nor the footman mightily moving
Over the land, but turn your back to the foe and retire ye.
Yet shall a day arrive when ye shall meet him in battle.
Holy Salamis, thou shalt destroy the offspring of women,
When men scatter the seed, or when they gather the harvest.[1]

TRIUMPH OF
THEMISTOCLES

In the ten-year interval since Marathon the Greeks had not been idle. The Athenians had cleaned house by exiling the tyrannist and the Alcmaeonid leaders. In 487 B.C. a law was passed which provided for the election of archons by lot. This democratic reform curtailed the office, and the leadership

[1] Herodotus VII, 141 (Rawlinson tr.).

of the state passed into the hands of the board of generals, one of whom was henceforth chosen as commander-in-chief. At the same time the opening of a new vein of silver in the state-owned mines at Laurium gave the city a surplus of wealth. The democratic leader, Aristides, proposed to divide it among the citizens in order to increase the numbers of the *zeugite* class and thus to strengthen the army. Themistocles, however, with a truer vision of the future, urged the building of a great fleet, ostensibly for the war which was being waged with Aegina, actually for the impending conflict with Persia. After a period of discussion recourse was had, in 483 B.C., to ostracism. In the test vote Themistocles won and Aristides was ostracized. Thus freed of his chief rival and opponent, Themistocles was able to secure his own election as general and execute his program. When the Persian forces appeared, Athens, under his leadership, was ready to meet them on the sea.

CAMPAIGN OF THERMOPYLAE

In 481 B.C. a conference was held at Corinth for the organization of an Hellenic league. The new league proved to be little more than an extension of the Peloponnesian League, but it put an end to such local wars as that between Athens and Aegina. On the motion of Themistocles, the command of both land and sea forces was entrusted to Sparta. The Spartans advised the abandonment of the north and the fortification of the isthmus, but Athenian pressure drove them unwillingly to a different plan: defense of the northern passes.

After a futile attempt to stop the Persians at Tempe, the Greek army took its stand at Thermopylae, the fleet at Artemisium protecting its rear. Sparta had sent an advance force of three hundred Spartans and twenty-one hundred helots under King Leonidas. These, with allies which brought their number up to six thousand, held the Persians at bay until a traitor showed the king a pass through the hills. Leonidas despatched his allies to the south, probably to stop the Persian forces as they came down from the hills. Then with his Spartans and a few Thespians and a Theban force of doubtful loyalty, he endeavored to hold his position rather than retreat before the enemy. It was a magnificent gesture, perhaps the finest product of the Spartan system. The allies failed to check the encircling movement and Leonidas was trapped. The Thebans deserted, and of the Thespians there is no further mention, but the Spartans fought to the last man. Simonides wrote their epitaph:

> Go, stranger, to the Spartans tell,
> That here, obedient to their laws, we fell.[2]

SALAMIS   The fleet had been successful in checking the Persian advance, but when the news of the fall of the pass came, the fleet fell back into the bay of Salamis, across from Athens. As the Persian army advanced, Thebes openly went over to the Persian side, and only a timely earthquake saved Delphi from plunder and destruction. Since the oracle had advised the Athenians to trust to the wooden walls, which Themistocles interpreted to mean the fleet, the population of Attica was removed to Salamis and Troezen. Athens fell and was sacked. Again dissension appeared in the Greek camp as the Spartans once more urged withdrawal to the isthmus. It required a combination of argument and trickery on the part of Themistocles (in which he was aided by Aristides who had been recalled from exile) to force a stand and thus bring about the battle. But when it came, the Greeks laid aside their differences to win. The clever planning of Themistocles trapped the Persians in the narrow strait between Salamis and Attica, and the victory was decisive. After the battle a vote was taken among the Greek captains as to who did the most to win the victory. Each captain received one vote (his own) for first place, but Themistocles was the unanimous choice for second place.

PLATAEA   After the battle, Xerxes, fearful for his communications, sent his fleet back across the Aegean while he himself returned the way he had come. He left Mardonius with a powerful army in Thessaly, however, to complete the conquest. The next winter Mardonius offered favorable terms to the Athenians if they would join him, but the memory of Marathon endured, and they refused. When the Spartans again proposed defense of the isthmus, the Athenians forced action from them with a threat to withdraw from Greece and establish a colony in the west. After the usual argument, during which Attica was again invaded, the Spartan army advanced into Boeotia under Pausanias, regent for the young son of Leonidas. The battle took place on hilly ground near Plataea, where the Persian cavalry proved ineffective, and the Spartan phalanx established its superiority. At the same time, the Persian fleet and a military contingent were destroyed by the Greeks at Mycale near Miletus. The Persian invasion had come to an end.

[2] Herodotus VII, 228.

THE WEST

While the Greeks in the Aegean were thus dealing with the Persian challenge, their colonies in the west, some of which had become large and flourishing cities, were likewise faced with an attack, by the Phoenician power of Carthage.

SYBARIS
During the seventh and sixth centuries B.C., the Greek cities in Sicily and southern Italy had shared in the development of trade, industry, and culture. For a period, Achaean Sybaris was the leading city in Italy. Its rich valley provided abundant resources and commercial relations with Miletus brought wealth from the East. A pass over the Apennines to the west and its colony Poseidonia, on the shore of the Tyrrhenian Sea, gave it control over the rich trade with the Greeks and the Etruscans of western Italy. Later moralists told many tales of the wealth and luxury of this city, where inventive cooks were given prizes and men slept on beds of rose leaves.

CROTON
Croton, immediately to the south, had a different history. Simpler and more vigorous in its life, it produced a series of famous athletes including the great Milo, who was six times victor in wrestling at the Olympic games. Pythagoras settled there, and his followers became prominent in the government of the city. In 510 B.C. a war broke out between Sybaris and Croton in which the Sybarites were defeated. Their city was taken and destroyed, and its site placed under a curse.

LOCRI
The little town of Locri is worthy of mention because it produced Zaleucus, the first Greek to write down the laws. The traditional date is 664 B.C. This code was even more severe than the later laws of Draco. A curious provision was added that any citizen who wished to propose a change in the laws must appear with a rope around his neck to be used if the people rejected his proposal. Locri thus became renowned for its conservatism in law.

OTHER CITIES
Though the Spartan colony of Tarentum possessed the best harbor in eastern Italy, its importance belonged to the future. The Straits of Messana were under the control of Rhegium, which at the end of the sixth century B.C. was governed by a tyrant, Anaxilaus. The town of Zancle on the Sicilian side was a subject of contention between Rhegium and Syracuse. After a series

of vicissitudes, it was finally occupied by fugitive Messenians, settled there by Anaxilaus, and its name changed to Messana.

CITIES OF SICILY — Of the Sicilian cities Acragas and Gela were for a period the most powerful. The former was ruled in the middle of the sixth century B.C. by a tyrant, Phalaris, who is said to have dealt with his enemies by putting them in a brazen bull underneath which a fire was built. Gela was governed by a series of tyrants who extended its power until in 492 B.C., Gelon, commander of the cavalry, made himself ruler. This able leader took advantage of local troubles in Syracuse in 485 B.C. to make himself king of that city also. From this date begins the greatness of Syracuse, which he enlarged in population by moving to it peoples from neighboring towns. Around the city he built a great wall. Then, in alliance with Theron of Acragas, he moved toward the conquest of the other cities of Sicily. This aggrandizement alarmed Anaxilaus and the Carthaginians, and conflict began when Theron seized Himera to the north.

CARTHAGE — The chief rivals of the Greeks in the western Mediterranean were the Phoenicians. Carthage had been founded by Elissa, princess of Tyre, about 825 B.C. Because of its harbor and fertile valley it had soon become the most important of the Phoenician cities in the west and had acquired leadership over the settlements in Africa, Sicily, and Spain. With communities around the shores of the western Mediterranean the Carthaginians made treaties securing for themselves exclusive rights to the sea-borne commerce. Affairs were directed by a council of oligarchs with two *suffetes* (judges) as the chief magistrates. In the classical period, command of the army was vested in hereditary generals of the family of Mago. Cambyses had been blocked in his intention to conquer the city when the Phoenician fleet refused to sail against their kinsmen. Tradition affirms, however, that the Carthaginian expedition to Sicily was inspired by Xerxes. Whether there is truth in this story or not, there was ample reason in Sicily for Carthaginian alarm at the advancing power of the Greek tyrants, which threatened its control over its own possessions in the northern and western sections of the island.

HIMERA — A large Carthaginian force despatched in response to appeals for aid from both Phoenicians and Greeks trapped Theron within the walls of Himera, and Gelon advanced to the aid of his ally. The Greeks claimed that the decisive battle was fought

on the same day as the conflict at Salamis. Gelon and Theron won
the day, and the Oriental menace in the West was checked. Gelon
was succeeded in Syracuse by his brother Hiero, who completed the
triumph of Syracuse by defeating a fleet of Etruscans off Cumae in
474 B.C. To his brilliant court came the poets Pindar, Simonides, Bacchylides, and Aeschylus, and the philosopher, Xenophanes. After his
death the tyranny was overthrown, and a period of confusion followed.

Acragas, too, profited from the victory at Himera, for the prisoners
of war became public and private slaves. With the wealth gained from
the spoils and the labor of these slaves, Theron adorned his city with
a series of magnificent temples, many of which are still standing.

CONCLUSION   In the east and in the west the Hellenic states had
                    successfully repelled the Oriental onslaught, although
to the Persians and the Carthaginians the defeats meant little more
than a check to further expansion. Continuing wealthy and powerful,
Carthage remained a constant menace to the western Greeks. Though
the Persian plans for conquest and control of the Aegean had failed,
and though this failure was soon followed by loss of the Greek cities
of Asia, still the power of the Persian kings suffered little and they
remained a force with which the Greeks had to reckon for another
century and a half.

For the Greeks, however, the victories had extraordinary significance. During the sixth century B.C. confidence in the justice of the
gods and in the moral order of the universe had waned, and an individualism which had found expression in religion and in philosophy
had become dominant. Then, in the test of war, the citizen armies of
the city-states, animated by a courage based on patriotic devotion, had
won a notable triumph against overwhelming odds. It seemed as if
the gods themselves had overthrown the arrogant might of Persia.
Individual doubt yielded to a sublime confidence in man's power as a
citizen, under the guidance of the gods of the state, to achieve all that
was humanly possible. Freed from the threat of Oriental oppression
and thus inspired by their victories, the Greeks were ready to advance
into the full flowering of their genius in the great age of Athens.

XI

THE GREATNESS AND FALL OF ATHENS
(479-404 B.C.)

THE years which followed the defeat of the Oriental invasions
formed one of the most brilliant periods in the history of mankind. The first generation, from 479-461 B.C., was an era of transition during which Athens, inspired by the memories of Marathon and
Salamis and strengthened by its great fleet, rapidly rose to leadership
in the maritime activities of Hellas. The Greek cities in Asia were
freed; the Persians and their Phoenician subjects were completely
driven out of the Aegean; and into the hands of the Athenians passed
the trade which had belonged either to Miletus before its fall in 494
B.C. or to the Phoenician merchants. The advance toward democracy in Athens begun by Solon and Cleisthenes was completed, and
the first steps were taken to rebuild and beautify the city. Art, literature, and philosophy continued the development of the earlier centuries. Then, under the guidance of Pericles (461-431 B.C.), Athens became the economic and cultural center of Hellas. Its wealth and its
artistic and intellectual achievements attracted to it the elite of the
Hellenic world. But its very pre-eminence aroused jealousy, and its
ambitions for expansion aroused fear in the hearts of the Corinthians
and the Spartans. The result of this jealousy and fear was the Peloponnesian War, which lasted from 431 to 404 B.C. and ended with the collapse of Athens.

THE PERIOD OF TRANSITION

Throughout the period of transition two problems were pressing
for solution: the one, the future of Hellenic unity; the other, the question of the political control of the agricultural and the urban elements
within the states.

GROWTH OF UNITY

The events of the Persian Wars had brought sharply to the fore the hope of a possible unification of the Hellenic world on a federal basis. The seventh and sixth centuries B.C. had seen the rise of great numbers of small city-states, each clinging fiercely to its right of absolute freedom. Not even the threat of Persia had been sufficient to force the Ionians to unite. However, the logic of events had been against them. On the mainland in the Peloponnesian League Sparta had risen to power over the small states of that area. Athens had united the land of Attica, had repelled her immediate neighbors, and, under the guidance of Themistocles, had prepared for eventual leadership at sea. The Ionian revolt had brought the states of Asia Minor together, at least temporarily. Finally, in 481 B.C., the Hellenic League had united the patriotic states of the peninsula under the command of Sparta and was soon to expand by taking in the states freed from Persian control. The victory itself had served to bring into sharp contrast Greek and barbarian, and to give impetus to the spiritual unity of Hellas.

Thus, though the principle of particularism remained to plague the statesmen and in the end to bring the cities to ruin, it seemed at the moment of victory as if the internecine wars of the Greeks might be ended and the eventual union of Hellas on a federal basis accomplished. Unfortunately, the past left other legacies which made this an idle dream, as the ever-increasing rivalry between Athens and Sparta wrecked all hopes of such an accomplishment.

NEW PARTIES

The economic and social movements of the preceding centuries, reflected in the political development, had created in most states two parties. The first, a conservative party, was made up of the old aristocratic families, who had opened their ranks to absorb the most successful of the commoners and, in union with them, clung to the ideals of aristocratic government. It was an aristocracy that prided itself on excellence, on achievement, and on intelligence. The land remained essentially its basis, and its strongest supporters were among the peasants, for whom the great names still had appeal. In Sparta the ruling class supported this oligarchic party. The leaders of this group in Athens were Aristides and Cimon, son of Miltiades. The lyric poet, Pindar (p. 181), and the Athenian dramatist, Aeschylus (p. 248), were its chief literary representatives. Added to the lofty position of these aristocrats was the patriotic memory of their heroic leadership in the war with Persia.

Commerce and industry, however, had resulted in the creation of an urban party of decidedly radical tendencies made up of men who looked to a domestic program of complete democracy and to a foreign policy of expansion. The time had not yet come when this group would develop its own leaders, but aristocrats were not lacking to follow in the path of the Athenian Cleisthenes and to set themselves at the head of the popular elements. Themistocles of Athens, himself a "new" man without the background of a great family, and Pausanias of Sparta planned for a new era. One concept dominated the minds of both parties and became an essential element of the new age —the idea that the basis of the state was law which knew not position, privilege, nor individuals.

SPARTAN
LEADERSHIP

The Spartans had proved their right to military leadership in the Hellenic League. But for the solution of the problems which that body faced Sparta was not fitted. The task of freeing the Asiatic Greeks and keeping Persia out of the Aegean was essentially a naval one. It required leaders who would be resourceful, adaptable, and tactful. Such men the Spartan system did not produce; its leaders knew no argument but force, and to their narrow viewpoint and natural arrogance was added a lack of interest in affairs outside of the Peloponnesus. Problems at home were pressing: the number of Spartans had begun to decline, the perioeci were at best of doubtful value, and the helots were a positive menace. The sending of large forces to the other side of the Aegean would be attended with serious dangers of revolt at home. Further, the conservative Spartans might well have feared what events proved: that individual Spartans were not to be trusted away from home when exposed to foreign wealth and foreign ideas. There was a considerable party favorably inclined to Athens who were willing to leave these tasks to that city, confident in its friendship and loyalty.

PAUSANIAS

As it happened, Spartan command failed lamentably. Pausanias, leading an allied fleet into Persian waters in 478 B.C., gained some success in Cyprus, then wheeled around and took Byzantium. But success went to his head. He had already been treating the allies with arrogant cruelty, and presently he entered into intrigues with Persia and set himself up to rule in almost Persian style, enjoying to the full his newly gained power and wealth. On the representation of the allies, he was recalled home, where he put his new ideas to work by planning a revolution, the freeing of the helots, and the modernizing of Sparta. After his plot became known, the ephors hesitated for a time to touch the hero of Plataea. When he fled to the shrine of Athena for protection, however, they walled him in and left him to die of starvation, releasing him only when he was on the point of death lest he pollute the shrine.

THE RISE
OF ATHENS

The naval leadership of the League then passed to Athens, which was pre-eminently fitted to undertake it. At the end of the war, Themistocles was the hero of the hour. Whirivri lie went ho was acclaimed, and states invited him to arbitrate their disputes. Under his leadership, Athens speedily regained all that the war had cost it and added to itself fresh laurels. Houses and temples were quickly, though for a time rudely, reconstructed. Despite the opposition of Sparta, a wall was built around the city, and the Peiraeus was fortified as a naval base. In the country the Areopagus supervised the reconstruction of the farms and the renewal and extension of olive orchards and vineyards. Trade connections were re-established with the Italian cities, with the Etruscans, and with the Black Sea region, and the friendship of the Ionian cities was cultivated.

Party struggles in Athens between the more. conservative forces, led by Aristides and Cimon and supported by the aristocratic families and by the farming class, and the growing industrial and commercial groups in the city, whose champion was Themistocles, resulted in victory for the former. Themistocles, whose pride and austerity had given offense, was ostracized. Later he was implicated in the plot of Pausanias, and when recalled to Athens for trial fled to Persia where, according to tradition, he ended his life by poison to escape compliance with an order to lead an attack against Hellas. His remains were later brought back to Athens, and Thucydides, the Athenian historian, recognizing the greatness of the man, pronounced a panegyric upon him.

The needs of Athens made it evident that the work which Themistocles had begun could not end. Though for a period the Areopagus was once more in power as a guiding force, and Athens was led by Aristides and Cimon, their policies were perforce but a continuation and completion of the program of Themistocles.

Cimon was a typical product of his time and class. Handsome, vigorous, aristocratic to the core, he had the ability to meet all men on a friendly footing and was personally very popular. As a naval commander, he was without rival, laying the foundations upon which the greatness of Athens rested in the next generation.

CONFEDERACY
OF DELOS
The first step in the rise of Athens came with the organization of the Confederacy of Delos, the brain child of Themistocles and the work of Aristides. A series of offensive and defensive alliances was concluded between Athens and the maritime states, according to which a fleet was to be provided to protect the Aegean from Persia. Those states that were able constructed ships; others paid contributions to the common treasury, out of which expenses were to be met. The old Ionian shrine of Apollo on the island of Delos was made the center of the Confederacy. The money was deposited in the temple in the care of its priests, and a congress of deputies met regularly under Athenian presidency. The commander of the fleet was to be an Athenian, and to this office Cimon was appointed. Under his leadership, the rest of the Asiatic Greek states were liberated, and in a battle fought near the mouth of the Eurymedon River in 468 B.C. the Persian fleet and army were routed.

The Aegean was freed for the time from the Persian menace. Some of the smaller states thereupon failed to make their payments, which seemed vexatious and unnecessary, but the fleet of the Confederacy compelled them to continue. In 468 B.C. Naxos, and shortly thereafter, Thasos endeavored to secede. Then force was used, and these cities were not only compelled to surrender but to enter into a treaty which involved political subjection to Athens. The first steps were thus taken in the transformation of the Confederacy into an Athenian empire.

THE HELOT
REVOLT
In 464 B.C., after an earthquake, the helots revolted in Sparta. Ithome was again fortified, and Sparta itself only just saved. In 462 B.C., after failing to put the revolt down, the Spartans appealed to their allies, and particularly to the Athenians, for assistance. Cimon favored their request, since the policy of his party had been established on the principle of Hellenic unity, and carried the day. But his victory proved fatal to him. The Athenian forces failed to do all that was expected of them, friction developed, and the Spartans finally requested them to return home and they subdued the helots without Athenian assistance. Cimon returned, only to be ostracized. In the meanwhile a new party had arisen in Athens. The younger generation was restless under the supervision of an Areopagus composed increasingly of mediocre men who were chosen by lot as archons. After the passing of Themistocles

and the death of Aristides, the radical group found a leader in Ephialtes, and, after his assassination, in Pericles. They first attacked and destroyed the power of the Areopagus and then accomplished the overthrow of Cimon. In 461 B.C., the Age of Pericles began.

THE AGE OF PERICLES

TRIUMPH OF
THE DEMOCRACY

The victory which Ephialtes and Pericles won over Cimon in 461 B.C. marked the completion of the work of Solon, Peisistratus, Cleisthenes, and Themistocles. Athens had been transformed from a small agricultural state into a flourishing commercial and industrial city possessing a powerful fleet and heading a maritime confederacy. As if in recognition of this transformation, the final steps were taken in democratizing the constitution. The powers of administrative supervision held by the conservative Council of the Areopagus were transferred to the democratic Council of the Five Hundred, and the judicial functions of the Areopagus were given to the Popular Supreme Court. To enable the Court to carry out its newly acquired tasks, it was established as a yearly panel and divided for the trial of cases into a number of juries. Finally, to permit all men, whatever their means, to serve the state, the principle of payment for public service was introduced. The shopkeepers or laborers in the city who served as oarsmen in the fleet thus won a share in the government of Athens along with the aristocrats and the farmers.

ATHENIAN
IMPERIALISM

The democratic party and its leader, Pericles, were firmly imperialistic, determined to secure for Athens leadership in the Hellenic world and control over Greek trade. As the first step in this program the Long Walls were constructed from Athens to Peiraeus, a distance of about four and a half miles. These parallel walls, five hundred and fifty feet apart, protected Athenian communications with the overseas sources of her grain supply. So long as the fleet controlled the sea, Athens could never be starved into surrender.

The problem of the supply of grain, it must be understood, was of supreme importance to the Hellenic cities. While in all of the states agriculture was the basis of economic life, it was so given over to the culture of the olive and the vine that few produced enough food to provide for their people. The chief sources of grain were the Black Sea region, Egypt, and the rich fields of Italy and Sicily. Athens was able to regulate the Black Sea trade through the colonies on the Thracian Chersonese and the presence of Byzantium on the straits of the Bosporus in the Confederacy of Delos. Control over trade with Egypt and the west would not only make the Athenians secure but would give them an effective strangle hold on the balance of the Aegean world. The only enemy they needed to fear was Sparta. Accordingly Pericles planned the development of a strong league on the Greek mainland, which might effectively challenge Sparta's Peloponnesian League, and the adoption of measures which would establish Athenian control over these sources of grain supply.

THE LAND
EMPIRE

To secure an outpost against Sparta, Pericles made an alliance with Argos, which at about this time had abolished its monarchy and established a democratic constitution. When Megara seceded from the Peloponnesian League and entered into alliance with Athens, the Athenians gained not only control over the isthmus but a foothold on the Corinthian Gulf. Thessaly was also brought into the alliance. Sparta countered by sending an army into Boeotia to strengthen the power of Thebes and to re-establish the Boeotian League, which had been destroyed by the defection of Thebes to the Persians. Though this army won a victory over the Athenians at Tanagra in 457 B.C., it failed to accomplish its purpose. When it returned to Sparta after the battle, the Athenians easily defeated the Thebans and drew Boeotia, Phocis, and Locris into the League.

THE WESTERN
TRADE

Athens fortified the position it had gained on the Corinthian Gulf by building walls across the isthmus connecting the seaports of Megara on either side. The Achaean cities on the southern shores of the gulf joined with Athens and the Messenian helots, who after their revolt had been allowed to leave the Peloponnesus and were settled at Naupactus (459 B.C.) near the mouth of the gulf on the northern shore under Athenian protection. The Gulf of Corinth thus passed into the control of Athens; Corinth was bottled up, and Athens dominated the western trade.

AEGINA

At the same time Aegina, most dangerous enemy of Athenian commerce because of its location in the Saronic Gulf, was overcome. The Aeginetans had vainly struggled against the loss of their commercial pre-eminence to the mainland city. An earlier war between the two had been brought to an end by the invasion of Xerxes. In 457 B.C. an Athenian force was landed on the island, and the following year the city surrendered, tore down its walls, and entered the Confederacy of Delos.

EGYPT   Not content with all of these undertakings, Pericles continued to prosecute the war against Persia with a vigorous campaign in Cyprus. A revolt which broke out in Egypt against Artaxerxes, son of Xerxes, gave him an opportunity to strike a deadly blow at the Persian king and to secure for Athens possession of the rich Egyptian trade. Accordingly a fleet was despatched to carry aid to the rebels. In this, however, Athens met with her first reverse. In 454 B.C. a Persian army put down the revolt and destroyed the Athenian fleet along with fifty ships which came too late as a reinforcement.

END OF THE   This blow to Athenian power and pride was serious.
PERSIAN WAR   When fear arose that the weakening of the Greek fleet might result in a renewed Persian attack on the Aegean, the treasury of the Confederacy was moved from Delos to Athens, and Cimon was brought back into power to handle the Persian menace. In 450 B.C. he negotiated a five years' truce with Sparta, and the following year he led an expedition against Persia. On the island of Cyprus, though Cimon died shortly before the battle, his forces won a victory over the Persians. Thus ended the Persian Wars. An Athenian, Callias, negotiated an oral agreement with Susa whereby each agreed to leave the other alone. The Persian kings, however, never formally recognized the loss of their Greek possessions in Asia Minor.

THE THIRTY   The failure of the Egyptian venture was followed by
YEARS' PEACE   disaster at home. The defeat of an Athenian force in 447 B.C. at Coronea in Boeotia resulted in the loss of Boeotia, Phocis, and Locris. The same year Megara and Chalcis revolted and a Spartan army invaded Attica. Pericles acted with great promptness; the Spartan king was persuaded, possibly by bribes, to withdraw; Megara was allowed to return to the Peloponnesian League; but the Chalcidian revolt was crushed. Athens had overtaxed her human resources, and the great dream of power had come to an end. In 445 B.C. a thirty years' peace was negotiated with Sparta on the basis of the *status quo*. Of her continental allies Athens kept only Plataea and Naupactus; Sparta was recognized as supreme on land; Athens, on sea. Neither was to interfere with the other, and all dis-

putes were to be settled by arbitration. Consolidation of the maritime empire, the possession of Athens under the treaty, was Pericles' next task.

THE ATHENIAN EMPIRE — The Confederacy of Delos had been organized originally as a union of free states for defense against Persia to which some members contributed ships and others money. The subjection of Naxos and Thasos by Athens when they revolted began the transformation of the League into an empire. The transfer of the treasury to Athens in 454 B.C., dictated by fear of Persia and proposed by Samos, strengthened Athenian control. Gradually in the following years the smaller states were reduced to a subject status, until only Chios, Lesbos, and Samos were left independent. In 440-439 B.C. Samos revolted and was also compelled to submit. The council of the League therefore ceased to meet, and henceforth the affairs of the empire were directed by the Athenian Assembly. Pallas Athena replaced the Ionian Apollo of Delos as the guardian divinity of the empire and the recipient of its treasures. The surplus of imperial funds was used in the beautifying of Athens for the glorification of the goddess.

ORGANIZATION OF THE EMPIRE — A new organization was developed after 445 B.C., partly through treaties with individual states and partly by Athenian legislative enactments. In the city-states secured by treaty, Athens supported democratic governments, while those cities which had revolted received charters prescribing their constitutions. In 442 B.C. a commission divided the empire into five districts for purposes of administration. The amount of tribute was fixed by Athenian officials every four years, but appeals from their decision might be carried to the Athenian juries. Cases at law involving capital punishment or loss of citizenship and suits involving large sums had to be taken to Athens to be tried before the Athenian law courts. The rights of independent coinage and the use of local weights and measures were likewise restricted.

CLERUCHIES — To hold the empire securely, military posts were placed in strategic towns, and groups of Athenian citizens were settled on confiscated lands in the empire. Such settlements were called *cleruchies;* the settlers retained their full rights in Athens and served, like the later Roman colonies (p. 348), as permanent garrisons to overawe and Atticize the subject states.

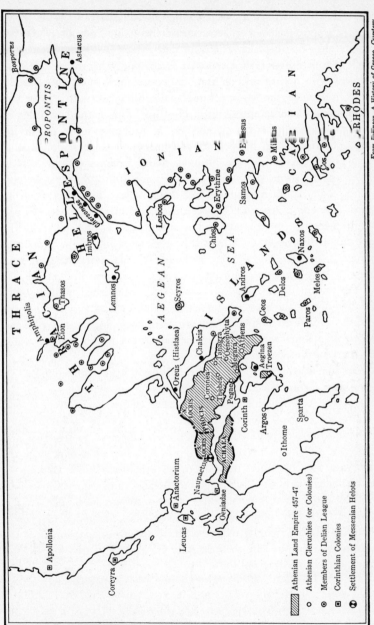

THE ATHENIAN EMPIRE

From Emerson, A History of Greece. Courtesy of Thomas Y. Crowell Company, publishers.

Athenian Land Empire 457-47
Athenian Cleruchies (or Colonies)
Members of Delian League
Corinthian Colonies
Settlement of Messenian Helots

THE BLACK SEA   After the reorganization of the empire had been completed, Pericles determined upon its extension into the Black Sea region in order to ensure and extend Athenian control of this chief source of food for the city. Accordingly he voyaged around its shores with a magnificent fleet, settled colonies there, brought the Greek cities into the empire, and made alliances with the native princes, particularly in the Crimea. He thus brought the rich trade of that region into Athenian hands and at the same time began the process of Hellenizing the peoples of southern Russia.

RESULTS OF IMPERIALISM   The empire brought many benefits to the Aegean world. Within it were peace, uniform coins, weights and measures, consistency in law, and freedom from piracy. Abroad, peace with Persia made possible trade with Egypt, with the Mesopotamian lands, and even with India. The control of the Black Sea area brought to Athens fish of that sea and of the Propontis, the metals, timbers, and other commodities of its shores, the grain of Russia and, by means of the route over the Urals, the products of central Asia and of China. Trade relations were established with the non-Dorian cities of the west, as far as Massilia. Athens, itself, center of commerce, obtained bountiful quantities of food and that wealth derived from tribute and from commercial profits which made possible the great culture of the age.

On the other hand, the imperial system was attended by evils. There was a complete lack of representation in the management of the empire. Athenian interference in local affairs of the Aegean and its complete control over the foreign relations of the cities offended the basic Greek idea of the right of each city-state to freedom and autonomy. Oligarchs everywhere opposed the empire, and even the democrats who benefited most were discontented. Public opinion in the Hellenic world ran high against Athens, and opposition to the Periclean program was not lacking even in Athens itself. The conservative party, led by Thucydides, son of Melesias, charged Pericles with treason to Hellas, tyranny over the allies, and mismanagement of the funds of the empire. In the test vote in 442 B.C. Pericles won and Thucydides was ostracized.

THE PELOPONNESIAN WAR

CAUSES

The Athenian empire was the fundamental element in the situation out of which came the struggle between Athens and Sparta known as the Peloponnesian War. Corinth, fearing the loss of trade, and well aware of the menace of Athenian control over the western sources of food, and Sparta, jealous of Athenian power, were ready to retaliate at the first sign of renewed Athenian aggression. A series of incidents brought the states to war.

In 435 B.C., Corcyra, at the mouth of the Adriatic, was at war with Corinth and offered alliance to the Athenians. The offer was cordially accepted, and Corinth was defeated. A second blow at the Peloponnesians was struck (probably in 432 B.C.) by the Athenian decree which excluded Megarians from all markets of the empire. This meant financial ruin and starvation to them, and it served as a warning to any other state which might block the path of the Athenians.

The Corinthians, fully aroused, appealed to Sparta to act in its traditional role as the defender of Hellenic liberty. To the Athenian offer of arbitration, made according to the treaty, the Spartans answered, "The honor of Sparta demands war." In the assembly of the Peloponnesian League which voted for war the keynote was sounded: "We are fighting for the liberty of Hellas." Arbitration as a means of preventing war had thus failed in the crucial test. The real cause of the war, the Athenian empire and all that it implied economically and politically in the Greek world, was not a problem that could be resolved by arbitration, and in 431 B.C. hostilities began.

THE CONTESTANTS

A land power and a sea power fought for control in Hellas. Athens, through its strong fleet, controlled the sea. Its treasury possessed an enormous reserve fund for carrying on a maritime war, and its Long Walls protected it by land so that siege would avail nothing. Sparta was superior on land, but it lacked both a fleet and the money wherewith to acquire one. Pericles' plan for the war was clear: when the Spartans invaded Attica, the Athenians were to withdraw within the city where, refusing to engage in combat on land, they could be fed by the fleet; in retaliation the Athenian fleet would harass the Peloponnesian coasts and fight with Corinth for control of the western trade.

THE PLAGUE   In the first year of the war the Spartan king, Archidamus, invaded Attica and destroyed crops and buildings while the Athenian fleet, as planned, menaced the Peloponnesus. But in the second year the Periclean strategy was wrecked by an unforeseen catastrophe. A plague, brought possibly by soldiers returning from the East, broke out in Athens. Because of the crowded conditions of the city and the general lack of sanitation, it spread rapidly and destroyed almost a third of the population. In the attendant confusion, the people suspended Pericles from office and fined him, then reversing their action, they re-elected him general. In the next year, however, he died of the disease. His place as leader of the people fell into the hands of members of the artisan class, Cleon, the tanner, and Hyperbolus, the lampmaker. Though a strong, predominantly agricultural party called for peace, the war continued.

THE ARCHIDAMIAN WAR   After the plague had subsided, the Spartans continued their yearly invasion of Attica, and in 427 B.C. they gained substantial success in the capture of the Athenian ally, Plataea. On the other hand, the Athenian cause also prospered. A revolt of Lesbos in 428-427 B.C. was rigorously suppressed. The fleet under Phormio won several brilliant victories around the mouth of the Corinthian Gulf, and an Athenian army secured control of its northern shore. Then in 425 B.C., by an unexpected victory, the Athenians gained possession of Pylos on the west coast of the Peloponnesus and took captive one hundred and ten Spartan soldiers. When Sparta offered terms of peace, Athens, led by Cleon, refused.

Confident of ultimate triumph in the war and over the opposition of the peace party, Cleon doubled the tribute upon the cities of the empire to secure funds for the prosecution of the struggle with Sparta. Though this financial measure increased the immediate resources of the city, nevertheless it wrought undoubted hardships on the allies and fanned the fires of hostility which later led to their revolt. Finally Brasidas, the sole outstanding Spartan of the war, found the Achilles' heel of the Athenian empire when he led his forces to the capture of Amphipolis in Thrace. Cleon went to meet him, and in the ensuing battle both were killed. Thereafter the peace parties prevailed in both cities, and in 421 B.C. the Peace of Nicias was made providing for the restoration of all lands and prisoners, and for an alliance between Athens and Sparta. This ten-year period, known as the Archidamian

War, had brought victory to neither side. Athens had lost prestige, and Sparta's Peloponnesian League was dissolved. Sparta could not even compel her erstwhile allies to carry out the terms of the peace. Into this unsatisfactory situation a new element was injected in the person of Alcibiades.

EXPEDITION
AGAINST
SYRACUSE

To the leadership of Athens came Alcibiades, the youthful nephew of Pericles. Brilliant and popular, but unstable, vain, and self-seeking, he proposed to restore Athenian supremacy by an alliance with Argos and by expansion overseas. The Argive alliance involved Athens in a disastrous conflict in the Peloponnesus between Argos and Sparta which ended with a Spartan victory at Mantinea and the restoration of the Peloponnesian League. Alcibiades' maritime scheme, however, called for the capture of Syracuse and the formation of a western branch of the empire. In 415 B.C. a great fleet started for the west with high hopes and with every chance of success. Scarcely had it reached its goal when Alcibiades was recalled to stand trial on a charge of impiety. The night before the expedition sailed, a band of roisterers had mutilated the busts of Hermes (*hermae*) which stood before the doorways of Athenian houses, and the sacrilege was alleged by his political enemies to have been committed by Alcibiades. Instead of returning, he fled to Sparta, where he disclosed the Athenian plans.

The Spartans sent aid to Syracuse and prepared to renew the war with vigor. The Athenian fleet was grossly mismanaged; one commander, Lamachus, a professional soldier, was killed; another, Nicias, a conservative who had opposed the expedition, proved utterly incompetent. Another fleet, sent as reinforcement in 413 B.C. under an able commander, Demosthenes, found Syracuse ready for an attack, and the offensive therefore failed. When Demosthenes proposed to return, Nicias refused to leave because of an eclipse of the moon. An engagement followed; the fleet was defeated, and blockaded in the harbor. The Athenians then attempted to retreat by land, but after fearful sufferings, they were forced to surrender to the Syracusans. Their generals were killed, and the men, imprisoned in stone quarries, suffered even greater agonies. Eventually the survivors were sold into slavery. The Athenian fleet and the flower of the Athenian army had been destroyed.

THE DECELEAN
WAR

The position of the Athenians was critical in the extreme. They had lost their fleet and a large army, and the city and empire were in grave danger. Sparta, on the advice of Alcibiades, seized and fortified the stronghold, Decelea, in Attica, so that the Athenian farmers were obliged to remain within the walls of Athens. At the same time, Sparta approached the Persians seeking financial aid and the assistance of a Phoenician fleet. At the price of the Greek cities in Asia Minor, which the Spartans surrendered to him, the Persian king promised his aid.

In the face of these difficulties, the Athenians rallied and determined to defend themselves with vigor. To hold the empire and yet obtain funds they abolished the tribute collections and levied a five per cent import and export duty throughout the empire. To secure effective administration they elected a board of ten men as a Committee of Public Safety to direct the affairs of the state. Political revolution followed when a coalition of the clubs of wealthy men, led by Peisander and Antiphon, terrorized the people into the acceptance of an oligarchic government in Athens. A Council of Four Hundred drawn from the clubs was established to manage the state, and a definitive constitution was drawn up. The oligarchs hoped to alienate Persia from Sparta through the intrigues of Alcibiades, who wanted to return to Athens and who therefore promised to help them. By securing Persian support the oligarchs expected to bring the war to an end.

Alcibiades failed to keep his promise, and Persia remained on the side of Sparta. The Four Hundred proved incompetent in the direction of the war. Splitting into factions, this council was then overthrown by the moderates, who had the support of the army.

Full democracy was restored in 410 b.c. after Alcibiades, who had been recalled by the Athenians, won a brilliant victory off Cyzicus. This battle renewed the courage of the Athenians, and they refused a Spartan offer of peace, though most of the subjects of the empire had revolted. Samos remained loyal, and from it as a base the Athenian army and navy carried on the war. Alcibiades was banished again when one of his subordinates, disobeying orders, was defeated at Notium in 407 b.c.

The following year, however, the fleet won the battle of Arginusae. In the last stages of this battle a storm arose and, to save the fleet, the Athenian commanders made no attempt to rescue the sailors whose ships were lost in the battle. This failure, in spite of their victory, caused their trial and execution in Athens.

AEGOSPOTAMI

After Arginusae the tide turned once more in favor of the Spartans. They had found an able commander in Lysander, an unscrupulous, ambitious, but competent man, who drew to his aid Cyrus, son of the Persian king and satrap of Sardis. With Persian money and a large fleet Lysander attacked the Hellespont, route of Athenian supplies. There, in 405 B.C., he made such a surprise attack on the Athenian fleet at Aegospotami while the men were seeking food on shore, that only the admiral, Conon, and a few ships escaped. It was the final disaster for Athens. The Spartans laid siege to the city, and in 404 B.C. Athens capitulated. The Long Walls were torn down to the music of flutes, as the Athenians gave up their fleet, their democracy, and their claims to empire. Amid great rejoicing over the fall of Athenian power the freedom of Hellas was proclaimed.

RESULTS OF
THE WAR

"The Peloponnesian War," said the historian Thucydides, "was a protracted struggle and attended by calamities such as Hellas had never known within a like period of time. Never were so many cities captured and depopulated—some by barbarians, others by Hellenes themselves fighting against one another. . . . Never were exile and slaughter more frequent, whether in war or in civil strife. . . . There were earthquakes unparalleled in their extent and fury, and eclipses of the sun more numerous than are known to have happened in any former age; there were also in some places droughts causing famines and, lastly, the plague, which did immense harm and destroyed numbers of people." [1]

Truly the war had wrought havoc in the Greek world. In many of the cities, factions engaged in party strife. Megara had been completely ruined by the Athenian policy of exclusion and by the annual raids during the first part of the war. The Ionian cities had fallen back into the power of Persia. The island states passed under the control of Sparta and, with the collapse of Athens, their market had been ruined.

To Sparta, the triumph was of little real value because of her lack of interest in trade or in mobile wealth. Thebes was the chief beneficiary. From their raids into the north of Attica the Thebans had grown wealthy. Moreover they purchased at a low price the goods

[1] I, 23. Botsford and Sihler, *Hellenic Civilization,* p. 28.

captured by their Spartan allies. They had also gained a military experience which was to stand them in good stead during the next century.

The freedom of Hellas won by the Spartans proved to be a delusion. In place of Athenian control Spartan military hegemony now interposed its iron hand. Lysander, eager to secure power and glory for himself as well as for Sparta, saw to it that Spartan influence was established among the former allies of Athens. The democratic leaders who were favorable to Athens were driven out, and boards of ten men were put in control of the states. To keep them in power, Lacedaemonian garrisons under helot commanders, called *harmosts,* were placed in some of the cities. The result was "plunder, oppression and murder." Spartan power was based on military force and it would endure, therefore, only so long as Sparta was supreme on land and on sea.

In Athens a board of thirty Athenian oligarchs was established as the ruling power. These "Thirty Tyrants," led by Critias and supported by Spartan troops, held Athens in complete subjection and entered upon a policy of terrorism and corruption until, in 403 B.C., the democracy was restored after a popular revolt. The great days of Athens were over. She had failed to unite the Greeks and in her failure had fallen miserably. Yet during the generations of her power she had lighted torches of democratic liberty and cultural ideals which still burn brightly.

☰ XII ☰

ATHENS IN THE DAYS OF HER GLORY

 SAY that Athens is the school of Hellas and that the individual Athenian in his own person seems to have the power of adapting himself to the most varied forms of action with the utmost versatility and grace," were the words of Pericles.[1]

In the generation from Marathon to Aegospotami, Athens occupied the stage of Greek history. Its democratic government, its economic activities, its buildings and works of art, its literary productions, and its scholars—all made it the focal point of Hellenic civilization. Artists, philosophers, scientists, and enterprising men of business from other parts of the Greek world flocked to it to share in its wealth and glories. Athenian democracy and Greek democracy, Athenian culture and Greek culture, came to be synonymous.

Historians have long debated over the explanation of its greatness. Was it mere chance that there appeared so many great men in one city in the same period? Was Athenian culture the product of a small leisure class supported by slave labor? Or was it rather an achievement in which every resident of Athens, citizen, alien, and slave, had a part and to which the Hellenic world contributed of its best? The answer to these questions must be sought in a survey of the institutions, the people, and the achievements of the city.

THE DEMOCRACY

"It is true that we are called a democracy, for the administration is in the hands of the many and not of the few. But while the law secures equal justice to all alike in their private disputes, the claim of excellence is also recognized; and when a citizen is in any way distin-

---

[1] This and the following quotations of the words of Pericles are from the famous funeral oration, Thucydides II, 35-46. Botsford and Sihler, *op. cit.,* pp. 239-246.

211

guished, he is preferred to the public service, not as a matter of privilege, but as the reward of merit. Neither is poverty a bar, but a man may benefit his country whatever be the obscurity of his condition. . . . An Athenian citizen does not neglect the state because he takes care of his own household; and even those of us who are engaged in business have a very fair idea of politics. We alone regard a man who takes no interest in public affairs, not as a harmless, but as a useless character; and if few of us are originators, we are all sound judges of a policy." With these words Pericles gave utterance to his ideal for Athenian democracy. The organization of the state at least made possible its attainment. Without any material change in structure, the political constitution of Athens had broadened and deepened since the reforms of Cleisthenes.

THE
POPULATION
Accurate information about the population of Attica and its distribution is lacking. The most recent estimates, based upon such scraps of information as are available, indicate a total in 431 B.C. of about 315,500, consisting of 172,000 citizens, 28,500 resident aliens, known as *metics,* and 115,000 slaves. According to the same compilation, 60,000 citizens, about one-third of the total, together with 25,000 aliens and 70,000 slaves, lived in the city and the port town. The urban area would thus have a population of 155,000. Of the approximate number of 43,000 male citizens, 25,000 were rich enough to buy armor, and about 18,000 belonged to the *thetes.*[2]

ATHENIAN
CITIZENSHIP
An Athenian citizen was the child of Athenian parents. In earlier periods, marriages of Athenian men with foreign women had been regarded as legal. But the greatness of Athens, the high value of citizenship in an imperial city, and the desire to keep Athenian blood pure caused Pericles to propose a law in 451 B.C. which declared the children of mixed marriages ineligible for citizenship. It is interesting to note that had this law been in effect earlier, Pericles himself would not have been an Athenian citizen, since his great-grandmother was Agariste of Sicyon. Tombstone inscriptions and later attempts at purification of the citizen lists indicate that this law was not strictly enforced.

[2] These are the estimates of A. W. Gomme of the University of Glasgow (*Population of Athens in the Fifth and Fourth Centuries B.C.,* Oxford, 1933), who frankly recognizes the uncertainty of the figures. In the opinion of the present writer the number of slaves is much too large.

THE CENSUS CLASSES   The Athenian constitution retained among its legacies from the past the four census classes of Solon's laws (p. 162): five hundred-bushelmen, *hippeis* (knights), *zeugites,* and *thetes,* an apparent though not actual contradiction of the democratic ideal. Only a few financial offices were still restricted to the upper classes, the five-hundred-bushelmen and the knights. The archonship, however, was opened to the third class, the *zeugites,* and the officials actually made no objection when the lot fell upon a citizen of their classification. The classes served as a convenient means whereby the state might exact financial and military services according to the ability of each man to render them. At the same time the measure of classification shifted from the bushel to the drachma. This made it possible, in the era of prosperity, for a member of the lowest class, the *thetes,* to rise to the highest if he prospered in business. In the major political activities of the citizens, in the deme, council, and assembly, the classes played no part.

THE DEME   The deme was the local unit of government. Its members held meetings, elected local officials, dealt with local business, kept the list of citizens, provided for the necessary nominations for state office, and gained in all this a fundamental training in self-government. Each deme had its local divinities and heroes, whom the demesmen worshiped in local festivals. So satisfying were these political and religious experiences that many a country demesman never felt the urge to go beyond them to participate in the larger affairs of the city. To all, the deme was the first object of affection. One of the most beautiful passages of the plays of Sophocles was written in praise of his own Colonus. Every Athenian was known by the name of the deme to which he belonged.

There is a danger here, however, of reading into the situation a modern concept of territorial division. The deme, though originally a piece of territory, was politically a group of people, not an area of ground. Membership was gained by inheritance, not by residence. If the demesman moved, he still belonged to his ancestral deme, and, in fact, paid a small fee to the deme in which he took up his residence for the privilege of living there.

THE TRIBES   The demes were united in the artificial and, for the most part, spiritless *trittyes* (thirds) and, through these, into the ten tribes. Each tribe took its name from a hero of Athens and celebrated a festival in his honor. Each had its assembly which chose its leaders and dealt with tribal affairs. Through the tribes war taxes were apportioned and levies made for the army. Men marched into war in the tribal regiment, and tribes set up tablets in honor of their heroic dead. Though these tribes were political creations and had none of the binding force of tradition possessed by kinship groups, their responsibilities to the state gave them such life and importance and solidarity that when an individual was injured men said a whole tenth of the state suffered with him.

THE BOULE (COUNCIL) OF 500   Fifty men from each tribe, apportioned among the demes according to their size, were chosen to serve in the Council of Five Hundred. The payment of a drachma a day, introduced by Pericles, made it possible for any citizen to serve the state as a councilor. Since no man could serve more than twice, it is fairly safe to assume that any man who had the slightest inclination to public service could at some time hold this office and obtain actual experience in governmental administration. Each tribal group of fifty served as an executive committee, or *prytaneis,* for the whole council, for a tenth of the year, a *prytany.*

The *prytaneis* lived in the council house during the prytany and some of their number had always to be on duty. One of them was chosen by lot to preside over the council and the assembly. The committee dealt with routine matters and with emergencies, reporting daily to the whole council whose agenda they prepared and which, in its daily meeting, received and acted upon these reports. In unimportant matters of state administration, the council could pass decrees binding upon the people for a year. In all matters of importance it discussed and prepared bills for submission to the people.

In itself a sort of executive committee for the Athenian citizen body, the council's duties were many and various. It examined the qualifications of the magistrates and of the new council to see that no persons unworthy or unqualified by law were chosen. It supervised the execution of the decrees of the people, the management of public property, the collection and expenditure of public moneys, the erection of public works, and the condition of the army and navy. After the downfall of the Areopagus, it assumed guardianship of the constitution and of that moral discipline which the ancient states always felt necessary. The councilors thus had manifold opportunities to learn the problems and the aims of statecraft.

THE ASSEMBLY   All male citizens over eighteen belonged to the *Ecclesia,* or assembly, the number present at any meeting depending upon the degree of public interest at the moment. The laws required that the assembly meet at least four times a prytany and whenever summoned by the council. At the first regular meeting of each prytany, it received the reports of the magistrates and provided for their recall and trial if these were deemed unsatisfactory. The same meeting dealt with questions of grain supply and defence. Under the presidency of one of the *prytaneis,* chosen by lot, the assembly debated freely and approved or rejected measures presented to it by the council. The magistrates, particularly the generals, addressed it, after them precedence being given according to age and service. But anyone could move to amend or initiate legislation. All new proposals were referred to the council for consideration and report; however, each individual was held responsible for his proposals. Even though the people passed his bill, if within the year it was thought to be unconstitutional or detrimental to the best interests of Athens, a "writ of illegality" was brought against him and his decree. If the court where the writ was presented gave adverse decision, the decree was set aside and the proposer punished. After a bill had been in effect a year the people as a whole assumed responsibility for it.

LAWS   Measures thus passed by the people were called *psephismata,* administrative decrees. The laws, *nomoi,* dealt with fundamental constitutional questions, and the council, the assembly, and the magistrates were all subject to them. For these laws a special procedure was adopted, probably during the period of the Peloponnesian War. In the first prytany of the year, the thesmothetae reviewed the existing laws before the people. If they found any which were obsolete or in need of change, they presented their recommendations. At the same time, any private citizen who desired to do so might propose amendments. After discussion in the fourth session of the prytany the people provided for the drafting and pay of a special jury, usually of five hundred and one citizens, called *nomothetae.* When this jury met, the laws under discussion were put on trial as if they were persons. Those who proposed changes were the prosecutors, while five advocates appointed by the people acted as defenders. The majority decision of the jury determined the law.

THE
MAGISTRATES
While the structure of the magistracies had not been changed since Cleisthenes, they had been considerably democratized by the development of sortition (choice by lot), the introduction of payment for public service, and the great increase in the number of those serving the state in official capacity.

THE ARCHONS
The nine archons and their secretary were chosen by lot, originally from five hundred candidates of the first three census classes nominated by the demes, and later from one hundred presented by the tribes but in such a way that there should be one from each tribe. Those chosen had to prove to the council that they had the requisite means for their census class, that their ancestors had been Athenians for three generations, that they worshiped the traditional "Household Zeus" and "Paternal Apollo," and that they had fulfilled their duties to the state and to their parents. During their year of office they received four obols a day and after it, ineligible for re-election, they became life members of the Council of the Areopagus.

The archons, formerly so powerful, had become merely religious officials and clerks for the law courts after the law of 487 B.C., which, by providing for the choice of archons by lot, had brought mediocre men into office and transferred direction of the state to the generals. The chief archon dealt with cases involving family matters and the protection of widows and orphans, and presided over the Great Dionysia. The king archon had jurisdiction over religious cases and conducted the Mysteries and other festivals; his wife was united in ritual marriage to the god Dionysus. The polemarch had the direction of all cases involving foreigners and of certain rites connected with war. The six thesmothetae guarded the laws, and prepared all other cases for trial by the courts.

THE GENERALS
Executive direction of the state was in the hands of ten generals, *strategoi,* who were elected by the assembly, at first one from each tribe, but eventually from the entire citizen body without reference to tribes. The only qualifications were Athenian citizenship and the possession of land in Attica. They were apparently unpaid save when on active military service in time of war. They could be re-elected, and it was this office that Pericles held over thirty years. While all ten were theoretically equal, except as the people assigned special duties to them, it was inevitable that the one among them who had the most forceful personality or the greatest

experience, or was the best orator, should gain ascendancy over the others and act as their spokesman. This is what occurred in the case of Pericles. The *strategoi* were commanders-in-chief of the army and navy, looked after the defenses of the city, and dealt with its foreign relations. They recommended measures to the council and asked it to call meetings of the assembly. Thus they were the executives of the state, and the directors of its public policy. Although accustomed to follow their recommendations, the people kept sharp watch over the generals at all times.

LESSER
OFFICIALS

Besides the officials just mentioned, there was a host of others of all kinds, regular and special, most of them paid for their services. A few of the financial officials were elected; the remainder were chosen by lot and usually in boards of ten. Only members of the first two census classes could hold financial offices. Some of the other positions were restricted to the *zeugite* class, but most of them were open to all the people. Nominations were usually made by the demes or by the tribes. There were receivers of revenue, treasurers, auditors, and supervisors of the grain supply, of the water supply, of the market place, of the roads, and of the religious functions. For special tasks, such as the supervision of the erection of public buildings like the Parthenon and the handling of emergencies that required unusual attention, temporary committees of ten were established by public enactment. Aristotle says that there were normally seven hundred citizens in the service of the state in these capacities, besides a large number engaged abroad in the affairs of the empire.

ATHENIAN
LAW COURTS

The stronghold of the democracy, perhaps the most distinctive feature of the Athenian government, was to be found in the jury system developed by Pericles out of Solon's Popular Supreme Court. Every year six thousand jurors, called *dicasts,* were selected by lot from all those over thirty years of age who wished to be enrolled. These jurors were divided by lot into sections of two hundred and one, three hundred and one, five hundred and one, and even one thousand and one, called *dicasteria,* the number depending upon the importance of the case. To them all cases which could not be settled by arbitrators were submitted. The jurors took an oath to judge the case before them in accordance with the laws and statutes of Athens, and received two (later, three) obols for each day of service.

The procedure in law suits was fairly simple. Civil cases were first submitted to a man over sixty who served as arbitrator. If his decision did not satisfy, an appeal was carried to a jury. Criminal cases went directly to the court. The plaintiff, who in public cases would be a magistrate or an advocate appointed by the people, entered a charge with the proper official, who was in ordinary cases at law one of the thesmothetae. After the defendant was notified, a preliminary hearing was held. Plaintiff and defendant then submitted briefs containing statements of the charge and denials thereof, citation of the laws involved, and evidence in the form of depositions. If the magistrate deemed the charge unsustained, the case was dismissed. If the magistrate sustained the charge, after appropriate oaths had been given by the litigants, the briefs were sealed in an urn. On the day appointed for trial, the case was assigned to a jury. The magistrate who presided opened the urn and read the statements. Conducting their own cases, the plaintiff and defendant then addressed the jury. Witnesses might be called on for evidence, and special pleaders might be drawn in. If the special pleader were a fine speaker and popular, the jury would probably applaud. Appeals were frequently made to past services, to patriotic feeling, to family sentiment, and to all the foibles and prejudices of the jury.

After the case was finished, the jurors cast their votes, and a majority decided the case. If a penalty was involved, a verdict of guilty was followed by a second action. Plaintiff and defendant submitted alternate verdicts, and in a second ballot the jury chose between them. Public penalties were enforced by the magistrates. The settlement of private claims was left to the individuals involved, which sometimes necessitated further legal action.

FINANCES — Though more orderly than in most of the other Greek states, the financial system of Athens was still decidedly irregular from the modern point of view. The aversion which all Greeks felt for direct taxation as unbefitting the character of freemen made it impossible for the state to collect any such regular source of income. But it owned a great many properties in the form of public buildings, olive orchards, pastures, and mines, from all of which rental was derived. The most important, the mines at Laurium, were leased to contractors who paid yearly a rather large and fixed amount, and possibly also a tax on the annual production. The treasury derived occasional income from the sale at auction of houses and movable property which came into the possession of the state by confiscation. Port and market dues, an import and export tax of two per cent ad valorem, sales taxes, court fees and fines, and a tax collected from all resident aliens resulted altogether in a substantial sum. The rich were called upon regularly in turn to perform liturgies, special tasks which required them to provide out of their own means for certain expenses of the fleet and of the religious festivals. In wartime the *eisphora,* a special war tax on capital, was levied on the tribes as needed and collected from the citizens according to the valuation of their property. The greatest source of income during this period was, of course, the tribute from the subject states of the empire.

Out of these funds the expenses of the government were met, the magistrates and the jurors paid, the army and the navy maintained, religious festivals held, public works erected, gifts of honor made, the orphans of citizens slain in war and invalid soldiers supported, and, at times, the poor assisted. The surplus was added to the treasuries of the gods as the people directed.

The Athenian recognized the importance of proper control of finance. The financial officials, always men of wealth, were elected, not chosen by lot, and often for long terms of office. Each year the council prepared a budget of the needs of the state; on its advice the assembly specified the distribution of moneys, and efforts were made to devise means of raising the necessary funds. It was understood that court fees and fines should be diverted to the payment of the jurors, and that the first charges upon the imperial revenues were the fleet and the maintenance of a war chest. The latter was entrusted to the temple of Athena as a reserve for emergencies. At the outbreak of the Peloponnesian War it amounted to six thousand talents. Yet the haphazard character of financial control and the general reliance upon irregular or external sources of income made it possible for Gladstone to say without exaggeration, "Athens perished because of its poor public finance." [3]

THE ARMY   The army was composed of the able-bodied citizens of Athens. The tribal military commander of each tribe kept for it the muster roll or list of all citizens from the ages of eighteen to sixty of *zeugite* census or above, arranged according to the years of their enrollment. Resident aliens (p. 225) were enrolled

[3] Quoted in Andreades, *History of Greek Public Finance,* p. 207.

on these lists through the deme in which they resided. The wealthy who belonged to the first two census classes and could not show physical disability were called out for the cavalry. They and their horses were carefully examined each year by the council. If accepted, each knight was given an allowance for the upkeep of his horse, and received special training in horsemanship and cavalry maneuvers. To be a member of the knights was a great honor. They formed a corporation with special privileges, and appeared in public processions, notably the Panathenaea. At the outbreak of the Peloponnesian War, there were about one thousand knights in the army.

All others were liable to military service in the infantry as hoplites, heavy-armed warriors. At the age of eighteen, when the youths were first enrolled, they took the oath of service and entered upon a two-year period of training. During the first year they were instructed in gymnastics and in the handling of weapons. At the end of the year, the state presented them with a spear and a shield, and they donned the hat and cloak which were their marks of distinction. For the second year they garrisoned the fortresses of Attica and were drilled in field tactics. They were not called out for active service but, with the older men, formed the line of home defense. From the age of twenty to fifty they were liable to service or call as the people might direct. At times of crisis, the entire army could be called out. In 431 B.C. this meant an effective force of twenty-five thousand men. The hoplite's equipment, which he furnished himself, consisted of shield, helmet, breastplate, greaves, sword, and spear. Only the orphans of men slain in battle received from the state their panoply, or full set of armor. Each warrior carried with him three days' provisions, and received a drachma a day for himself and one for his servant. The *thetes* were called upon for service as light-armed troops and as bowmen.

The troops were enrolled in tribal regiments, but according to necessity the commanding officers reorganized them into field battalions. Although no match for the highly trained Spartans, but with the tradition of Marathon behind it, the Athenian phalanx acquitted itself respectably. Contemporaries credited it with special aptitude in the siege and capture of fortified places.

THE NAVY The glory of Athens lay in the fleet, which it owed to Themistocles and Cimon. In 431 B.C. the fleet consisted of three hundred triremes, ships of the line, and a reserve of one hundred select ships for the defense of Peiraeus. At the beginning of each year the state picked certain men of the first census class as *trierarchs,* or commanders of triremes, warships propelled by oarsmen arranged in three banks. To each of the trierarchs the state furnished a ship, together with a supply of canvas and rigging. The trierarch purchased the remainder of the equipment necessary and engaged the crew. Usually ten hoplites were picked as marines. A number of skilled seamen and mariners were also chosen to direct the sailing of the ship. Finally, there were the oarsmen, sixty for the upper row and fifty-four for each of the two lower rows. These were recruited from the *thetes,* from the resident aliens, and from the citizens of the allied states. All were paid by the state, the upper row of oarsmen, usually all citizens, receiving somewhat more than the others. The trierarch might hire the captain or assume command himself, the latter usually being the case. It was a notable chance for a citizen of wealth to distinguish himself in the public service. A golden crown was offered as a prize to the trierarch whose ship was first ready to sail, and meritorious service in war was certain to receive proper recognition. On the other hand, it was recognized at the same time that the use of the *thetes* in the fleet formed the surest foundation and safeguard of the democracy, since it assured to that class political rights, just as service in the infantry had earlier given similar power to the heavy-armed warriors of the middle class (p. 159).

DEMOCRACY IN ATHENS
If the right of every citizen, whatever his rank or means, to participate in political decisions and in the direction of the state, and the obligation of every citizen to serve the state with money and in person according to his wealth and ability constitute a democracy, then Athens was democratic. The charge is often made, however, that the Athenian citizen body constituted a small, privileged group ruling over a large number of foreigners and slaves resident in Athens who could not acquire citizenship, and that Athens was therefore not a true democracy. From the modern point of view this contention is valid, but it is one which the ancient Greek would hardly have understood. Citizenship was a natural right acquired by inheritance and protected by ancestral divinities. Residence in a city, therefore, no more made one a citizen than the renting of a room today makes one a member of the family of the house.

The foreigners were citizens of their own communities who were residing in Athens by their own choice, and under no constraint to remain there. Since they could not worship the ancestral gods of the Athenians, they could not hope to participate in the activities which were under the protection of the gods unless the state, in return for services rendered, granted them those rights by an act equivalent to adoption.

Slavery was a recognized institution. In the Greek view, slaves were inferior subjects, and any thought of allowing them participation in politics was absurd. Athens, governed by its body of citizens, the *demos,* as the Athenians called it, was, by the standards of the ancient Greeks, a democracy.

THE PEOPLE OF ATHENS AND THEIR OCCUPATIONS

The Athenian citizen body, with its varied groups and classes— the fishermen of the seacoast, the merchants and artisans of the city, the farmers of the plains and valleys, and the herdsmen and woodsmen on the mountainsides—presented almost a cross section of the Greek peoples and brought to bear upon the life of the city a wide diversity of experiences and ideas. In addition, the large group of aliens and slaves, Greek, Oriental, and barbarian drawn from every corner of the ancient world, made its own contributions to Athenian civilization.

THE PEASANTRY In the villages scattered over the land lived a sturdy peasantry, in the Periclean Age fairly prosperous and contented. They made their living in various ways. On the hillsides they raised goats and cattle, or they cut and dressed wood, or made it into charcoal. They kept bees and found a ready market for honey. They terraced the hillsides and planted vineyards. In the valleys they tended olive orchards and raised grain between the rows of trees. They still employed primitive implements and the two-field system. Near the city, truck gardens of vegetables, fruits, and flowers provided excellent sources of livelihood.

The assemblies and offices in the demes and the local religious festivals, particularly those in honor of Dionysus, furnished the peasantry with sufficient opportunities for political and religious expression. Most of them were wealthy enough to belong to the *zeugite* class, and they formed the main body of hoplites in the army. Content with their village life, they seldom went to the city, save when political or military requirements demanded, or perhaps when the great festivals were held. Aristophanes, the comic poet, who knew and loved them, represents them as bewildered by the noise and confusion in the city, thoroughly unhappy until they found themselves back on their native hillsides. Naturally conservative, they were a steadying influence in the Athenian assembly on the rare occasions when they made their presence count.

THE
ARISTOCRACY
Most of the great aristocrats who had maintained ancestral estates in the plain lived on them in fine villas and operated their estates with the help of tenant farmers, hired laborers, or slaves. Others moved to the city and left their farms in charge of stewards. These estates would not be considered large in modern times since the largest of which we know was sixty-four acres. Agricultural slavery was apparently unprofitable and not practiced except on the larger estates, though the small farmer frequently hired slaves in the rush seasons.

Many of the aristocratic class, like Pericles and Nicias, rejoiced in the glory of Athens and were proud to serve her with their wealth and their abilities. Others despised the democracy, and fought the policies of Pericles in state and empire. These were temporarily demoralized by the ostracism of Thucydides, son of Melesias, but they vigorously renewed their activities during the Peloponnesian War, which they opposed. In the early days of the war their motto was "business as usual," and they built for themselves fine houses in the city, adorned with tapestries, carpets, and mural paintings. The Decelean War bore heavily upon them, however. Their country estates were ruined; twenty thousand slaves (most of whom were employed in industry) escaped, and the burdens of the trierarchy increased.

Blaming their troubles upon the democracy, they withdrew from active participation in politics to avoid contact with *hoi polloi* ("the masses"). In their social clubs, they discussed ideal oligarchic constitutions and planned the overthrow of the democracy. Their attempt to accomplish this, however, in setting up the Four Hundred and in writing the definitive constitution was a complete failure. The establishment of the Thirty later restored them to power for a brief and inglorious period.

For the most part their education turned them against the traditional religion. One club burlesqued the Mysteries and brought severe penalties upon its members. Another, or possibly the same, was probably responsible for the mutilation of the Hermae. Critias, a leader among them, went so far as to declare that religion was merely a device developed by clever men to control the rest. Others, such as Nicias, who refused to move during an eclipse of the moon, clung to a strict obedience to old customs and superstitions.

THE COMMON PEOPLE   The commoners earned their livelihood in all the variety of ways known to a big city. Some were farmers who lived in town and went out by day to work their near-by farms. Herdsmen led their sheep and goats out to pasturage and back into the city by night; the walls of the gates which are still standing were worn smooth by the wool of the herds. Many owned or rented houses in the city and in them plied their trades as blacksmiths, carpenters, potters, weavers, dyers, tanners, cobblers, retail dealers, or schoolteachers. Others worked as stonecutters or masons on private buildings and public works. Still others were day laborers, porters, and the like. Probably few engaged in the wholesale trade, which was left for the most part to the resident aliens. The more prosperous gained knightly or *zeugite* census rank. Many were employed by the state in all sorts of capacities. Older men particularly delighted in the excitement and the pay gained from service on the juries.

Pericles decreased the number of landless by settling some six thousand in the cleruchies throughout the empire. When the suffering of the poor became intense during the last period of the war, the state provided them with a dole of two obols a day and began a program of public works to provide them with employment. Ordinarily they made up the bulk of the assembly, and for years they followed Pericles implicitly. But under the stress of war they became restless and excitable, easily roused to high pitches of enthusiasm by Cleon or Cleophon, and as easily depressed by news of disaster. Their treatment of Pericles during the plague was an example of their fickleness. After the overthrow of Mytilene, they voted on the advice of Cleon to put all male citizens to death and sent a trireme to carry the order to the army. The next morning they reversed their decision and issued a new command for the execution of the leaders only. A second trireme set out amid great excitement and arrived only just in time to save the people.

In 416 B.C. the people again showed their bitterness when the little Dorian island of Melos, an important harbor on the route to Egypt, refused to submit to Athens on demand. When it was taken, all men of military age were put to death and the rest of the people sold into slavery. Similar action under stress was revealed by the treatment of the generals after Arginusae (p. 208). Yet, except for these incidents, they bore well the sufferings of the war and fought to the end with undaunted courage.

THE METICS   Business opportunities attracted numerous aliens to Athens, and the state, following the policy begun by Solon, was hospitable to them in most respects. They were not allowed to own land in Attica and they could not obtain citizenship, save by special grant, which indeed many received as a reward for meritorious service. They had to have an Athenian patron to represent them in the law courts and to pay a small tax for the privilege of living in Attica, where they were called *metoikoi* (metics, "dwellers with"). Apart from these restrictions, there was little to differentiate them from the citizen body. Many of them found prosperity in Athens and proved as loyal as the citizens. They were proud to serve with their money in the performance of liturgies or with their strength and lives in the army and the fleet. The wealthy metics were received freely in Athenian society, save for the restrictions on marriage between citizens and foreigners. The occupations of these aliens were as varied as the interests of the city. They engaged in foreign commerce in Peiraeus; handled money-changing tables, which eventually developed into banks; and participated in all industries, excelling in textile, pottery, and metal working. They worked side by side with citizens and slaves in the shops and quarries and on the public works. In contradiction to the traditional view, there is reason to believe that they by no means monopolized either wholesale trade or any of the industries to the exclusion of the citizens.

In addition to the metics there must have been many foreigners, merchants, teachers, and tourists who, coming to the city as transients, were not enrolled as resident foreigners but helped to swell the numbers of its population.

THE SLAVES   Slaves, who were being pressed into ever-increasing uses, constituted the lowest class of the population. Most of the work of the better class household was done by them under the supervision of the mistress. They did the cooking, the cleaning, the spinning, and the weaving. Old slaves accompanied the boys to school as *paidagogoi* ("leaders of the boys") and had general supervision over their behavior. Others acted as guards to the mistress or her daughters when they went out into the city. A trusted slave served as private secretary or steward to the master. Pericles, for example, turned over his entire family estate to a slave steward to manage.

Except on the lands of the rich, as it has been observed, there was little, if any, agricultural slavery. Agriculture was on too small and intensive a scale for it to pay.

In the city, however, slavery was everywhere present. In the potters' shops slaves tended the furnaces and elsewhere did much of the rough work normally done by unskilled labor. In most occupations skilled slaves who had learned their trades before slavery overtook them, or who were trained by their masters, worked side by side with their master and with free citizens and aliens. Some of them managed retail or manufacturing shops of their own or belonging to their masters and paid a share of the proceeds to their owner.

The state owned slaves who worked on the roads, in the dockyards, in the mint, and on public buildings. The Scythian archers who formed the police of Athens, the executioner and his staff, the inspectors of weights and measures, and many of the heralds and clerks were the property of the demos. The lowest class of slaves worked in the mines at Laurium.

Many men of wealth invested in slaves, whom they rented out by the day to the mine contractors, to the state, or to business. There was a recognized place in the market where those who wished to hire slaves for unskilled labor might find them. In this fashion, Athens took care of the problem of casual labor.[4]

The sources of slaves were many and varied. Piratical raids were made on the barbarians around the shores of the Mediterranean and the Black Sea; prisoners of war who could not find means of ransom were regularly sold into slavery; dealers gathered up unwanted children who had been exposed to die by their parents and raised them for service. In some states, parents were permitted to sell superfluous offspring, and men were still sold into slavery for debt. Of course, there were also some children born into slavery, although the breeding of slaves was rare because it was unprofitable. As a result of these varied sources, there was a wide diversity in skill, intelligence, and race among the servile population. Comparatively few were Greeks.

The lot of the slaves in Athens was not entirely bad. In the mines

---

[4] Gomme (*op. cit.*) estimates thirty-five thousand industrial slaves, one-third of his total, and the same number of domestics in the city, leaving another third for the domestic and agricultural slaves in the country.

they undoubtedly suffered hardships, but in the city the master's own interest and the law intervened to protect them. New household slaves were received with showers of confetti and came under the protection of the family divinities. The shop owner strove to protect his investment, and skilled slaves found the same opportunities for self-expression as the free laborer and without many of the latter's worries. Most slaves received a small share of the proceeds of their labor and, particularly those who worked for hire or managed shops, were able to amass enough to purchase their freedom and secure recognition as resident aliens. Slaves were protected from murder by law. If the master's treatment was outrageous, the servant might appeal to the magistrates for protection and receive it. Such license was permitted the slaves in the streets that the conservatives complained of it.

SLAVES AND CITIZENS — Slaves were never so numerous, so widely owned, or so generally used as to justify the modern idea that Athenian civilization consisted of a small leisure class resting upon slave labor while the bulk of the citizen population was supported by the state. The major portion of the work of Athens was done by its citizen body. Because of the restrictions on repetition of offices, state support was at best a meager and intermittent source of income and, except in wartime, was directed not at charitable relief but at making possible active participation by all citizens in public affairs. There is further ample evidence in the writings of the period that the later philosophic contempt for work was not shared by the people as a whole. Indolence was frowned upon, for the law still required every man to teach his son a trade. "To own to poverty," said Pericles, "with us is no disgrace; the true disgrace is in doing nothing to avoid it."

INDUSTRY — Industrial and commercial methods had not changed materially since the earlier period. Some wealthy men might own large establishments with as many as twenty or twenty-five workers, but, as in the earlier period, the personnel of the average shop comprised the owner, his family, an apprentice or two, and one or two slaves, perhaps, to do the rougher work. Specialization, however, had become the general practice. Not only was there a sharp line between crafts, but in most cases there were specialists within the craft who centered their activities on one phase of the work. Thus one shop would be devoted to the making of tunics and another to that of cloaks. Within the shop the different tasks were parceled out, though there was not so high a degree of specialization as in the modern factory. Many articles were made to order, and sometimes the purchaser even furnished the raw material. But the increasing demands of trade led naturally to a larger supply of goods on hand for sale to the consumer, to retailers, or for export.

Athenian pottery, found wherever Athenian trade went and especially in the Black Sea region and in Italy, where it was in great demand among the Etruscans, is the best surviving witness of an industry which flourished by production not to order but for export. Its fine quality and beautiful decoration likewise give evidence of the skill and aesthetic perceptions of the artisans of Athens.

COMMERCE   In trade as in industry, an increase in volume and a tendency toward specialization were the chief features which distinguished this period from the earlier ones. Peddlers still went about the countryside, and Megarians and Boeotians traveled by land to the near-by Athenian market. Some merchants followed the great roads to Delphi and Olympia to participate in the fairs which accompanied the festivals. Most of the traffic, however, followed the sea. Boats had been improved, and the knowledge of navigation and of routes had been increased. Consequently, the season for shipping had been extended somewhat and the traveling time shortened. But in stormy weather, as before, shipping was at a standstill. During the season, boats went to the Black Sea, to Syria, to Egypt, and to the west, carrying Athenian pottery and other manufactures, wine, and oil. From these regions they returned with slaves, grain, drugs, tapestries, linen, papyrus, and the myriad products of the lands which they visited.

The state zealously fostered this trade. The peace with Persia, Pericles' expedition to the Black Sea, the constant activities of Athenian agents in Egypt and in Italy, the work of the navy both in the suppression of piracy and in the opening of new markets, and a widespread network of commercial treaties both within and without the empire made Athens the focal center of Mediterranean trade. The wise policy of the state in firmly maintaining the value of Athenian coins, known as "owls," and securing their acceptance throughout the civilized world greatly facilitated the commercial transactions of the Athenians.

The major public interest was in the grain trade, vitally necessary to the Athenians and a major cause of Athens' wars. Not only did the state take measures to control or develop the sources of supply, but it passed regulatory laws. All grain ships over which Athens had control were compelled to stop at Peiraeus, and two-thirds of all the grain they carried had to be sold in Athens. The other third could be exported only after local needs were satisfied. On occasion officials took vigorous action to prevent the merchants from cornering the market or unduly elevating the price of grain. Trade in lumber, needed greatly for shipping and the navy, was subject to similar regulations.

The financial system developed to meet the needs of trade. Men of wealth invested their money in loans on shipping or in other commercial ventures at rates of interest depending upon the risk involved. Commercial banking carried on by the money-changers, however, was just beginning at the end of the period.

THE AGORA The *agora,* or market place, center of all economic activities, hummed with life. There the businessmen held their conferences; the money-changers set up their tables; the farmers sold their produce; the hucksters their vegetables, flowers, or fish; the artisans displayed their handicraft; the merchants their goods from home and abroad. The cries of the salesmen bewildered the countrymen who came into the city to make their purchases, while the Athenians and their friends were all busy at the congenial tasks of working, bargaining, and making money.

ATHENIAN PRIVATE LIFE

EDUCATION The training which men and women received and the part they played in life depended, of course, on their social and economic status. On the tenth day after the birth of a son in an Athenian family he received his name, and at the following celebration of the *Apaturia,* an ancestral festival of Zeus and Athena, his name was enrolled by the phratry if the family record was clear, and his citizenship was thus acknowledged and assured. Then until his seventh year he and his sisters remained under the care of his mother and nurse. Spartan women, it may be noted, were particularly sought after in Athens as nurses. Thenceforth, the lives of brother and sister followed different lines.

If the family means were scant, the boy received instruction in reading, writing, and arithmetic in some inexpensive little school which the family could afford. He learned his trade in his father's

shop or was apprenticed to another, and received the rest of his education in the streets of the village or the city.

Wealthier Athenians assigned the care of their sons to elderly
slaves, the paidagogoi who accompanied them to and from school and
who apparently watched over them during school hours. It was their
task to see that the young men behaved fittingly in school and at play,
learned to arrange their clothes properly and to walk in the streets
with easy rhythmic stride and proper demeanor, yielding place defer-
entially to their elders.

Schools for the most part were taught by poorly paid and generally
despised men of inferior class who eked out their living from tuition
fees. There were no public schools, but the state paid for the education
of the sons of citizens who had fallen in battle. After instruction was
given in the elementary subjects, poetry, singing, and the art of play-
ing on the lyre were taught. The poems of Homer and the other epic
writers, of Solon, of Theognis, and of Pindar were memorized to
teach high lessons of morals and patriotism from the deeds of the
heroes of the past and to inculcate into the youth by means of recital
that rhythmical speech which befitted a gentleman. The boy learned
also to accompany himself upon the lyre so that later he might enter-
tain guests with song and music as an Athenian gentleman should.
This whole division of education was called music.

In the afternoons, the boy went to the exercise grounds and there
engaged in a variety of athletic sports to develop his physique. He
learned how to swim, and in his playtime he enjoyed games of tag,
ball, blindman's buff, marbles, and the other immemorial games of
childhood. This continued until about his sixteenth year. Then, if
his father could afford it, the boy, in order to learn rhetoric, argument,
and "all the knowledge necessary for a statesman," went to one of
the new teachers called Sophists who were beginning to appear in the
city. On his eighteenth birthday, he was enrolled on the list of citizens
in his deme and became legally a man and a full citizen of Athens.
The state then called him to arms, and for two years he served as an
ephebos, learning the military art. His education, however, was not
yet at an end. For, in the discussions in the market places and in the
barber shop clubs, in the assembly and on the jury, in the dramatic
festivals, either as participant or as spectator, and at the evening banquets, he learned all that men were thinking in the world.

In the meantime, his sister had remained at home under the tutelage of her mother and her nurse, learning to spin and weave, to cook, to manage the household stores, and to direct the servants. Such housewifely accomplishments formed the main body of her education. She might and presumably did learn to read and write. While still quite young, she was usually married to a man much older than herself. The marriage was arranged by her parents, frequently through the medium of a professional matchmaker and with due regard to financial considerations. In spite of this, many marriages resulted, as the inscriptions show, in real tenderness and affection. Her dowry remained her possession and was restored to her in case of divorce. Social custom confined her to the women's quarters in the house, and she went abroad only when accompanied by a male member of her family or by a slave. At banquets, when her husband brought guests to the house, she did not appear. "Not to be talked about either for good or evil" was set forth by Pericles as the ideal of womanhood. The state assumed wardship of an heiress, and family property considerations dictated the idea that she should marry the nearest of kin among her male relatives outside of her immediate family.

In practice these customs did not result at all times in the rigid seclusion of women, a subject which has been given far too much emphasis by modern writers. Women played a prominent part in the Panathenaic festival. They were present at the festivals in honor of Dionysus and at the Eleusinian mysteries. They had, as well, their peculiar religious observances, to which women alone were admitted. They visited their feminine friends and were visited in turn. Their education and influence in the home and in public life depended largely upon their personalities. The wife and the sister of Cimon, for example, wielded powerful political influence. The noble women depicted by the dramatists had their prototypes in real women of the day. The writings of Plato and the comedies of Aristophanes indicate a widespread discussion of woman's place and position in Athenian society; in the *Ecclesiazusae* Aristophanes even goes so far as to represent the women as taking over the government. None of the restrictions noted above applied to women of the lower classes, who were driven by economic necessity to work on the farms, in the shops, in the booths of the market place and elsewhere as opportunity might arise.

The law of citizenship made the status of women of the metic class somewhat different. Public opinion allowed greater freedom to them, although in the ordinary course of affairs their behavior could not have been materially different. Tradition has ascribed to them, however, superior intellectual training.

ASPASIA   The most famous of the women of metic class was Aspasia, a Milesian woman, well educated and of remarkable personality, who came to Athens probably to set up a school of rhetoric. Her mental ability and personal charm rapidly drew around her the intellectual elite of her day. Socrates paid tribute to what he learned from her, and Pericles fell in love with her. Unhappily married, he divorced his wife at her request, found for her another husband, and then, in violation of the law, married Aspasia. Their children, however, were later legitimized by the Athenian people. Aspasia's influence on Pericles and on the group of men around him was extraordinary. To her house also came many of the women of Athens, and she apparently combined sage counsel on wifehood with an attempt to secure more education and greater freedom for Athenian women. Her activities and influence aroused great opposition among the conservatives of both sexes, and foul charges were made against her by the comic poets. Prosecuted on a charge of impiety, she was acquitted after an impassioned plea to the jury by Pericles himself.

HETAERAE   Women of the poorer class of citizens and many of the metic class formed a group called *hetaerae* ("companions") who made their living in the service of their goddess, Aphrodite. Some were flower, flute or dancing girls, in demand for entertainments. Others, ranging from ordinary courtesans to educated ladies who perhaps modeled themselves after Aspasia, were beautiful women who were successful in their ambition to become mistresses of men of wealth and position.

DWELLINGS   Built of sun-dried brick covered with stucco or lime and with a flat roof of clay tiles, the houses in which the residents of Athens lived were simple in the extreme. There was frequently a second story, usually the women's quarters. The floors were of hard-packed earth or of cement, and except, perhaps, for the houses of the very rich, the interiors were undecorated. The rooms opened off the inner court, which was the dominant feature of the house and the very center of family life. In it stood the altar of Zeus of the Household and the statue of Paternal Apollo. Of furniture there was not much—couches, used for reclining at meals as well as for resting, chairs, stools, light tables, and storage chests. Light was provided at night by torches or lamps. Braziers filled with coals and ashes furnished heat in cold weather. Implements were made of pottery, bronze, or iron. Rain water was collected in cisterns, and drinking water was carried into the house from springs.

CLOTHING   Clothing likewise was simple. A tunic for ordinary wear and a gown and sandals for public appearance wore the basic elements of dress for both sexes. The wealthier citizens wore colored gowns, and the ladies spent much time in the graceful arrangement of draperies for which they were renowned in their day and of which there is ample evidence in the sculptured monuments.

THE SOCIAL   The Athenians could never understand the solitary man who withdrew into his study to ponder. Houses DAY   they considered primarily as places for sleeping and eating, to be lived in only when the weather was inclement.

Athenian life was intensely social and out of doors. For the men, social life centered in the market place and in the exercise grounds; for the women, it centered in the courtyard. The citizen of wealth, after a light breakfast, would normally spend his morning marketing, supervising his financial interests, and greeting his friends and business acquaintances in the market place. About noon, a hearty lunch was served in the portico of the courtyard. The afternoon he would devote to exercise in one of the *palaestrae* (exercise grounds), or perhaps to some less strenuous sport like checkers, or to walks and conversation with his friends. In the late afternoon he bathed in one of the public bath houses.

THE   Dinner was served early. If there were no guests, it was eaten with the family, but if guests were present, SYMPOSIUM   as was frequently the case, the women and children retired. Invitations were informal, and an invited guest would often casually bring a friend along with him. After the serving of the food followed the symposium, the chief feature of the dinner. The bowl was brought in, a libation poured, and a ruler of drinking was chosen. His first duty was to supervise the mixing of water with the wine, usually in the proportions of two of water to one of wine. Then the cups were passed around and the drinking and the entertainment began. Flute or dancing girls or other professional entertainers might be brought in; the lyre might be passed around and each guest called upon to perform; or the leader might set some topic, light or serious, for general discussion. The conversation might even run along decidedly serious lines as is recorded in Plato's *Symposium*. When the entertainment was over or the discussion at an end, the slaves lighted their masters home, and the day was over. The disputants in Plato's dialogue continued their arguments so long that morning found all the guests save Socrates asleep around the table.

ATHENIAN CLUBS — The wealthy men belonged to social clubs in which their activities centered and which played an important part in political and legal affairs. Comparable social groupings were not lacking among the poorer citizens and the resident aliens. While we do not hear much of the guilds of commerce or industry which had been licensed by Solon, they undoubtedly existed. The shops themselves furnished social centers, not only for the people who worked in them but for idlers and shoppers. Socrates frequented the stoneworkers', the armorers', and the saddlers' shops, where he could always find an audience. Blacksmiths' forges and barber shops frequently served as clubs. The demesman from the country who came up to town made his headquarters at a favorite shop where he could find fellow demesmen. On feast days, all in the shop, even the slaves, partook of a sacred meal together for which the employer paid. Then there were numerous religious associations which brought together all classes of the peoples. The palaestrae, or gymnasiums, and baths were open to all citizens alike and the Cynosarges, one of the palaestrae, was open to aliens as well.

ATHENIAN RELIGION

Permeating all phases of Athenian life was the element of religion. The Athenian people were intensely religious, at least as far as cult was concerned. Every deme had its local divinities and its local hero in whose honor there were festivals, some of which became of state importance. The way in which these local religious cults had been reorganized by the state and bound to the central religious activities in Athens accounted in large part for the successful unification of Attica. The family upheld religious unity based on its gods and ancestors, to whom due reverence was paid at meal times, on leaving and returning home, and on festal occasions. The nobles perpetuated the religious features of their gentile [5] organizations (p. 158) after their

[5] The family organization which the Greeks called *genos*, pl. *genē*.

political significance was lost. The groups of workmen in the various crafts had their especial patrons among the gods and the demigods. There were also special festivals for the women. Young girls enjoyed the festival of Artemis Brauronia, in which chosen ones of their number played the part of bears. Later, as married women, they celebrated the *Thesmophoria* in honor of Demeter as founder of political life, patroness of marriage, and giver of children.

FESTIVALS The series of state festivals held at different times consumed from sixty to seventy days of the year. There were festivals in honor of Theseus and of the heroes of Marathon and Salamis; the *Epitaphia,* when sacrifices were offered to the ancestral heroes and the annual oration was delivered in honor of Athenian citizens who had died in service during the year; the *Synoecia* when the union of Attica was celebrated; the *Oschophoria* when boys carried grapes and chanted while others raced from a temple of Dionysus to that of Athena at Phalerum; the *Apaturia* where the phratries honored Zeus and Athena. The greatest of the festivals were in honor of Dionysus, Demeter, and Athena. In early spring came the *Anthesteria,* a Dionysiac festival in which the slaves took part. During the winter the rural *Dionysia* were celebrated in the country demes with buffoonery and dances. Out of them grew two city festivals, the *Lenaean,* or *Lesser, Dionysia* and the City, or *Greater, Dionysia.* The *Greater Dionysia* was attended not only by Athenians but by all residents of Attica, by delegations from the cities of the empire, and by a host of visitors. After a procession and a feast of wild rejoicing, there followed three days devoted to the performance of tragedies and comedies in competition. It was from this festival that there came the great dramatic productions which are a lasting memorial of the age. In the presence of the assembled multitude, the sons of those fallen in war, on their attainment of manhood, received from the state the panoply of arms. A charge of two obols was made for attendance at the dramatic festival, but, so that all might worship the god, the state furnished the poor with the price of the tickets.

THE ELEUSINIAN MYSTERIES The great festival in honor of Demeter was the celebration of the mysteries of Eleusis after the harvest. Participants had prepared by a purification during the winter. Then in the fall, ambassadors were sent forth to proclaim a sacred truce in an attempt to make the feast as Panhellenic as the great games. As usual, it began with a procession. Then, after the king archon had pronounced the sacred formula which excluded the unclean, notably those branded with infamy or stained with crime, the celebrants marched to the sea with their sacrificial white pigs, purifying themselves and their sacrifices in the salt waters. The following two days were consumed with the sacrifices, after which took place the procession to Eleusis, the secret rites of initiation, and probably the performance of a sacred drama dealing with the story of Demeter and Persephone. Out of the symbolism of seed planting and harvest—the loss of Persephone and her return—the *mystai* learned something of the meaning of life and achieved a hope of something better in the life to come.

THE
PANATHENAEA

The greatest of all the festivals, however, was the *Panathenaea*. Celebrated annually in honor of Athena, it was held with especial magnificence in the third year of every Olympiad, when it attained almost as much renown as the great national games. The series of contests included athletic sports for boys and men, torch races, and a regatta. The prize for the winner consisted of a jar decorated with a figure of Athena and a picture of the event, and containing oil from the olives of the sacred olive trees. The central feature of the festival was the great procession, when priests, cavalry, sacrificial animals, and all the people conducted to the old temple of Athena Polias the maidens bearing a *peplos,* or cloak, which they had woven and decorated appropriately. Phidias' famous frieze on the Parthenon was a picture of the Panathenaic procession.

ATHENIAN
TOLERANCE

It is to be noted that this religious activity was essentially a matter of cult performance, not of dogmatic belief. There were few professional priests. The chief archon and the king had supervision over many religious ceremonies, but the Eleusinian mysteries were in the hands of the Eumolpid family; the worship of Athena and Erechtheus was conducted by the Butadae. Other priests were elected for life or for a term. Most of them engaged in their usual occupations, save for the period of the festival. Their chief task was to see that the ceremonies were properly performed, not to direct the worshipers how to behave or what to believe. Only in the Mysteries was there a moral element. Men might believe and say what they chose, so long as they did not become dangerous to the state through blasphemy or interference with the cult. Even then the people were tolerant, save in times of emotional

stress. The philosopher Anaxagoras was regarded with suspicion because he said that the sun and the moon were not gods, but when he
was banished, it was for political reasons. The execution of Socrates
was likewise the result of politics rather than of intolerance.

The true center of the Athenian's religion was Athens itself, of
which the goddess Athena was the personification. "I would have you,"
said Pericles, "fix your eyes upon the greatness of Athens until you
become filled with the love of her." The city was replete with reminders
of the achievements of its citizens, statues of the great men of the past,
pictures of Marathon on the Painted Porch, inscriptions written on
tablets set up on the Acropolis. Above all, in the minds of men there
was a sure sense of the stability of law and of the wisdom sprung
with Athena from the head of Zeus. The devotion thus aroused, the
desire to serve Athens loyally and fully, was the basis of the inspiration
which produced those works of arts and letters which make the age
one of the high points of human history.

COMPETITION   Through all these activities, social, economic, and
religious, ran the element of competition—competi-
tion in business, within the shop and between men of the same craft,
in the market place and in the wider market wherever Athenian goods
traveled; at social affairs where the guests vied with each other as at
the famous wedding feast of Agariste; in athletics, in the palaestra or
at the games; in music; in choral dancing; in the writing and production of plays; in the Athenian law courts; and in politics. The
competitive spirit penetrated every phase of Athenian life, and noteworthy service in any respect was likely to receive recognition. For the
citizen it meant honor and office; for the metic it might mean the
reward of citizenship; for the slave freedom.

Since such competition necessarily contributed to the development
of technique, the artisan improved his craft; the merchant his skill in
business dealings; the mariner his knowledge of navigation. Dramatists
studied the technique of the drama; young men aspiring to be orators
or leaders of the people studied rhetoric under professional teachers;
and the battle of wits in the agora and palaestra produced that master
of dialectic—Socrates.

There was thus ample opportunity for every man to express himself freely and fully as an individual and as a member of a group, and
to gain therewith such recognition as he had earned in whatever capac-

ity or station of life he found himself. The use of the technique which the individual had mastered in competing for the glory of the group to which he belonged resulted in a condition of competitive co-operation, most favorable for the production of that creative spirit from which came the great achievements of the Athenians.

═ XIII ═

ATHENIAN CULTURE

I N fulfillment of their desire to beautify the city, to serve the gods, and to glorify the state, yet at the same time to gain individual pre-eminence, the Athenians of the great age made noteworthy contributions to three fields of culture—art, literature, and philosophy. The buildings and the statues which they erected, together with the works of their great painters, made Athens the artistic center of the Hellenic world. The drama was an Athenian creation. To the city came scientists, philosophers, and teachers. In Athens the art and the science of history were begun, and its own citizen, Socrates, established the study of ethics. In all these fields of artistic and intellectual endeavor great names appear and productions have survived which have served as models for later ages.

ART

ARCHITECTURE

One of the first tasks which faced the Athenians after the Persian Wars was the rebuilding of Athens into a city worthy of its wealth and the glory of its empire. The Persians had sacked the city, broken its statuary, destroyed its temples. The hastily constructed private houses, built when the Athenians returned to their homes, were simple and without ostentation. Not until the period of the Peloponnesian War did the wealthy begin to erect luxurious residences for themselves; hitherto the wealth and genius of Athens had been devoted rather to public buildings and temples. To understand what was done it is necessary to have a conception of the topography of Athens.

The center of Athenian devotion was the Acropolis, a rocky mound which rises 512 feet above the plain. Its slopes are so steep that

239

it can be approached only on the west side. The residence of the kings and the chief stronghold in Mycenaean times, it was later the site of many temples and statues. On its southern slope was a shrine of Asclepius, god of healing, and at its base were the theater of Dionysus and the Odeon, a music hall. The hill of the Areopagus, upon which the famous council met as a homicide court, lies close to it on the west.

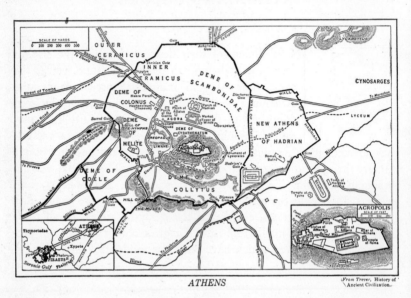

ATHENS

(From Trever, History of Ancient Civilization.)

Its name, traditionally derived from Ares, was more probably taken from the *Arai* or *Eumenides,* spirits of punishment, whose shrine was on its northern slope. A low valley, the market place of early times, separated the Areopagus on the west from the Pnyx where the assembly held its meetings. North of these hills was the agora, business center of classical Athens.[1] Beyond it lay the inner Ceramicus, the potters' quarter, which derived its name from the production of ceramics. The dwellings of the Athenians crowded around the Acropolis and spread out to the north and west.

The famous wall of Themistocles, about five miles in circumference, enclosed the city. On the south it ran close to the Acropolis. Outside the wall ran the Ilissus River, above whose banks rose the temple of Olympian Zeus, begun by the tyrants but destined not to be com-

---

[1] Now in the process of excavation by the American School for Classical Studies.

THE ACROPOLIS

THE PARTHENON

pleted until the time of the Roman emperor, Hadrian. Where the wall adjoined the potter's quarter stood a great double entrance, the Dipylon Gate. Beside it was a smaller opening through which flowed the Eridanus, a small stream which rose in the barren hill of Lycabettus to the northeast and traversed the city. In the outer Ceramicus, beyond the Dipylon Gate, was the Athenian cemetery, where many noble monuments have been found. Thence the roads led west to Eleusis and southwest to Peiraeus. The Academy, favorite grove and exercise ground of the Athenians, was slightly northwest of the gate. Other gates were located at convenient places in the wall, with the roads leading to various places in Attica.

Cimon began the task of rebuilding the city. He constructed a retaining wall around the Acropolis and laid the foundations for a temple to Athena. Pericles continued the work of Themistocles and of Cimon.

PEIRAEUS   Themistocles had fortified Peiraeus and made it the port of Athens in place of Phalerum. To reconstruct Peiraeus, Pericles hired an expert, Hippodamus of Miletus, who laid out the streets of the town at right angles, and built huge dockyards for ships and storage houses and display rooms for the local trade. Then Pericles connected Peiraeus with Athens by the Long Walls.

THE CITY   Porticoes and buildings of administration were erected in the agora, and on a slight hill above it there was built a beautiful Doric temple, still standing, dedicated probably to Hephaestus, though today it is wrongly called the Theseum. East of the theater at the foot of the Acropolis, Pericles built for the Panathenaic contests a round music hall, the Odeon. The roof of this was said to have been made of the masts and yards of the Persian ships taken after Salamis and to have been conical in imitation of Xerxes' tent. No remains of it have survived. The theater itself did not receive its stone seats and other improvements until the fourth century B.C. Until that time the spectators at the plays sat on wooden benches or on the grass.

THE ACROPOLIS   For the adornment of the Acropolis Pericles adopted a new and comprehensive plan. The Sacred Way starting at the Dipylon Gate and passing through the agora wound up the steep western approach to the ancient citadel. As it entered the Acropolis area it passed through a monumental gateway of marble, the Propylaea. On the western façade of this structure stood a Doric porch flanked by a small wing on the left, which was used as a picture gallery. The road passed through the porch, between rows of Ionic columns with steps on either side, and through a similar porch on the eastern side of the structure but facing the sacred area. The Propylaea formed a stately and superb entrance to the domain of Athena.

ATHENA NIKE The right wing of the Propylaea could not be built according to plan because the space belonged to Athena, the goddess of victory. On a bastion in this space, therefore, Pericles built a beautiful little temple, Ionic in style, with a frieze portraying events of the Persian Wars. Around the bastion there was later erected a balustrade with panels of "Victories," notably the well-known Victory Adjusting Her Sandal.

ATHENA PROMACHOS As the Sacred Way left the Propylaea, it passed Phidias' great bronze statue of Athena Promachos, and then with lesser shrines along its route, it curved around to the eastern entrance of the Parthenon, the greatest glory of Greek architecture.

THE PARTHENON In 447 B.C. a board was appointed to engage architects and supervise the erection of a temple to Athena Parthenos. Callicrates and Ictinus were chosen, with the sculptor Phidias and the painter Polygnotus as advisers. Built of Pentelic marble, the Parthenon was perfect in its proportions. Around the outside of the structure ran a peristyle of Doric columns thirty-four feet in height, eight on each end and seventeen on the sides, counting the corner columns twice. At each end within the peristyle was a prostyle of six columns. The entablature was Doric, and the pediment rose to a graceful angle so that the total height of the building from ground to ridgepole was sixty-five feet. To secure grace and life a slight convex curve was given to all prominent lines.

The interior was divided into two rooms. At the west end was a room forty-three feet long and sixty-three feet wide, its ceiling supported by four Ionic columns. This was originally called the Parthenon before the name was applied to the whole building. It faced the Propylaea and the business section of the city, and was used as the treasury of Athena. The main room, called the *naos* or shrine, was of the same width and one hundred Attic feet (about ninety-eight feet) in length. It was divided into two side aisles and a nave by two rows of short Doric columns. On these rested an architrave, and above it another row of columns supported the ceiling which was coffered. The interior was lighted only by the opening of the great doors. Within the naos stood the gold and ivory statue of Athena Parthenos by Phidias.

The building was adorned with sculptures carved under the directing genius of Phidias, their subjects taken from the legendary history of Attica. The metopes were single pictures of strife between Lapiths and Centaurs, Greeks and Amazons, Gods and Giants. The eastern pediment dealt with the birth of Athena from the head of Zeus, the western with the strife between Athena and Poseidon for the possession of the city. Around the temple walls inside the peristyle ran an Ionic frieze representing the Panathenaic procession.

The architects' plans and Phidias' designs of the sculptures were executed, not by slaves driven to their tasks, but by citizens, metics, and slaves working side by side—men who had learned their technique in the quarries and in stone masons' shops of Athens, and who, to the glory of Athena, polished the stones so that, when put together, they seemed to have been placed there by nature. Years after, Plutarch wrote, "There is a sort of bloom of newness upon those works preserving them from the touch of time as if they had some perennial spirit and undying vitality mingled in the composition of them." Even today the Parthenon, though shattered, is not a ruin but a glorious monument.

THE
ERECHTHEUM
During the Peloponnesian War the Athenians built the Erechtheum in fulfillment of a religious duty to the ancient divinities of Athens. The edifice was started about 421 b.c. and finished about 407 b.c. It was the joint shrine of Athena Polias, guardian of the citadel, and of the mythical king, Erechtheus. It was built on two levels; on the upper level to the east the shrine of Athena was faced by an Ionic porch; on the lower level a porch with six lofty Ionic columns was erected on the northern side because to the west, where the porch would normally have been, stood the sacred olive tree of Athena. A hole was left in the roof of this porch so that the sun might fall upon the fissure in the rock which, it was said, Poseidon had made with his trident.[2] On the southern upper

[2] In early times, according to the myth, Poseidon and Athena had contested for the possession of the city. Poseidon brought forth a spring on the Acropolis by striking the rock with his trident, but Athena won the victory by causing the sacred olive tree to grow. Marks resembling those of a trident in the rock are still plainly to be seen.

level and to the rear corner of the building was the beautiful Porch of the Maidens, the Caryatids. These maidens bore on their heads a chest which contained objects used on the festivals of Erechtheus. With consummate grace sculptured human beings thus served as columns. The final result was a building which ranks next to the Parthenon as one of the most perfect pieces of Greek architecture.

In addition to these temples, there were on the Acropolis record houses, small shrines, and many statues of famous men, along with stone tablets inscribed with laws, treaties, and honorary decrees.

SCULPTURE

In sculpture as in architecture, the artists of the fifth century B.C. approached closely to classic perfection in the portrayal of the human form and in the expression in marble of human ideals and aspirations. THE AGE OF During the period of the Persian Wars the Doric TRANSITION school of athletic sculpture was blending with the soft, voluptuous Ionian carving of draped statuary, so that artists were competent to handle both the figure and the drapery with equal skill. Prolonged study had given them sufficient knowledge of anatomy and proportion to enable them to avoid the errors of earlier times, and mastery of their material made possible a departure from the law of frontality and a presentation of subject with freedom and grace. Nevertheless, during the age of transition a certain stiffness remained in the carving. This stiffness, combined with failure in representing the hair and the emotional expression of the face, as well as a hardness of finish in the marble, caused the statues of the period to be described as "severe" in style. The pediments and metopes of the temple of Zeus at Olympia and of Aphaia on the island of Aegina illustrate the characteristics of the period. The statues of Harmodius and Aristogeiton at Athens, though powerful in execution and vigorous in pose, are nevertheless hard in muscular treatment and incompetent in the treatment of hair and facial expression.

The finest surviving product of the artists of the severe style is the bronze "Charioteer of Delphi." Originally part of a group of which only fragments survive and possibly the work of the Athenian Calamis, the youthful charioteer stands erect, strong, and dignified. The modeling of the hair shows greater ability and freedom, his face is serene, his garments drop from his shoulders in folds like the flutes on a column, and in this piece, "exquisite workmanship is combined with accurate observation of nature and great dignity of conception." [3]

THE GREAT AGE   Three fifth-century Greeks—Myron, Phidias, and Polyclitus—represent the fulfillment of the promise of the work of earlier sculptors. Myron, an Athenian, oldest of the three, became famous for his statues of animals and of athletes. The ancients claimed that his bronze cow was so lifelike that living cattle gathered around it. His Discobolus, discus thrower, has survived in Roman copies; the details of position are carefully studied; the expression of physical power in the athlete is superb, but his face is without any expression of the intensity of his action.

Phidias, younger contemporary of Myron, was renowned for the beauty and the idealism of his statues. He planned and supervised the execution of the sculptures of the Parthenon, and his Panathenaic frieze ranks supreme among works in relief. His two most famous works were gold and ivory statues of Athena Parthenos and of Zeus at Olympia. To these he was able to impart such religious feeling that he was said to have added something to traditional religion.

Polyclitus, the Argive, third of the masters, endeavored to reduce the treatment of the human body to a canon of measure and thereby to produce statues of ideally beautiful men and women. The Doryphorus, the Diadumenus, and the Amazon, which survive in marble copies of the original bronze, represent his achievements.

PAINTING

Of the art of painting, which developed by the side of sculpture, all of our information must be drawn from later descriptions of great works, or from vase decorations which imitated them. Painters of the archaic period had paid great attention to beauty of line, but their pictures were flat and severe in style and limited in the main to three colors, black, red, and white, with only occasional uses of yellow.

Both the need for decoration of the new buildings in Athens and the inspiration of the age led to great achievements. In Athens there were two native artists, Micon and Panaenus, the brother of Phidias, and to the city came Polygnotus of Thasos, who was the greatest painter of the period. These men covered the walls of the Painted Porch, of the Picture Gallery of the Propylaea, and of many other

[3] Fowler and Wheeler, *Handbook of Greek Archaeology*, p. 221.

buildings. Polygnotus used four colors by adding yellow to his palette and gained further values by mixing. He was able to represent emotion by skillful drawing and, avoiding flatness, he gained a sense of perspective (though not a real perspective) by arranging his figures on different levels on the walls. The figures, furthermore, were carefully posed and arranged in groups placed with symmetry and dramatic contrast. Polygnotus was a master at the representation of "transparent wind-blown drapery." His poses and drapery influenced contemporary sculpture, and the vase painters imitated his composition. Aristotle praised the ideal character of his portraits and the "moral uplift" of his paintings; in this Polygnotus was a fitting counterpart to the sculptor Phidias.

These artists, masters of technique, expressed in stone, in metal, or in color the same confidence in the ability of men, the same devotion to the gods, and the same search after perfect beauty which inspired the architects and the men of letters.

LITERATURE

THE DRAMA

Drama, like architecture, was the product of religion. In the first centuries of Athenian history it had been the custom for men dressed as satyrs, followers of the god Dionysus, to sing choruses in honor of the god at his festivals in the country. In 534 B.C. Peisistratus established the festivals in the city with competition between choruses. Thespis changed the choral performance into a play by introducing an actor who took various parts in turn and carried on a dialogue with the leader of the chorus. Aeschylus added a second actor and made the chorus subordinate to the dialogue. Sophocles completed this process of development by adding a third actor. The number of parts in the play, though always small, was not fixed, because each actor played several roles, but there could never be more than three on the stage at the same time.

THE CONTEST IN TRAGEDY Three poets were chosen by the chief archon to present plays at the Greater Dionysia. Each composed four plays and the music to accompany them. Originally the first three of these, a trilogy, dealt with a single theme; later, the poets were allowed to write on three different subjects. The fourth was always a "satyr" play in honor of Dionysus. To each poet the archon assigned a wealthy man as *choregos,* who paid the expenses for the hired actors and chorus. The last three days of the festival were devoted to the performances. Judges, selected with great care, awarded prizes to the best choregos, the best poet, and later to the best actor.

TRAGEDY   The origin of the word *tragedy* is unknown, though it may have come from a word meaning "goat song." Greek tragedy, springing from the worship of Dionysus and always performed at his festivals, partook of the nature of a religious ritual. This fact colored both its form and its choice of subjects. Essentially musical, it was always composed in poetry; and the chorus with which it began remained a fixed element in the performance even after it ceased to play an important part in the action. It must be remembered further that the plays were produced in competition and that the judges, already familiar with the story, doubtless based their opinions on the language, the rhythm of the poetry, and the interpretation of the action. The use of masks and heavy costumes made facial expressions and rapid or violent action impossible and accordingly influenced the work of both playwrights and actors by laying emphasis upon the speeches of the characters and the lyrics of the chorus.

The dramatists established, though they did not always respect, the three famous unities: interest, essential to any great drama; time, made advisable though not absolutely necessary by the fact that choral songs were the only interludes between episodes; and place, enforced by the impossibility of much scene shifting and the continual presence of the chorus.

The cults of the heroes vitally influenced the development of the drama, and most of the subjects were drawn from the great mass of legendary material of the heroic age. They dealt always with gods or with great personages, with grand themes of struggle and suffering. The dramatists used these traditional stories as vehicles for the discussion of the great ethical and social problems of their own day. Men saw portrayed in the plays the deepest feelings and passions of the human heart. The emotions of admiration, pity, terror, and sympathy which they awakened in the audience produced, said Aristotle, a catharsis, which may be defined as a purification of the emotions, though its exact meaning has long been the subject of discussion among literary critics.

AESCHYLUS
(525-456 B.C.)

Of the many tragic poets, three—Aeschylus, Sophocles, and Euripides—were regarded as supreme. Their most popular works were repeated in later times, and some of them have come down to us. Aeschylus belonged to the generation of the Persian Wars. A native of Eleusis, of an old Eupatrid family, educated, as befitted a noble, in athletics, in music, and in Homer, he was a follower of Cimon in his conservatism at home and Panhellenism abroad. He fought at Marathon and was prouder of this than of his contributions to the literary world. In his plays, seven of which are extant, he portrayed the spirit of his times.

In his trilogy dealing with the story of Prometheus, who had brought civilization to men against the orders of Zeus, employing majestic language he attacked the problem of eternal justice. Only *Prometheus Bound,* the second of the three plays, has survived. In it he seems to suggest as a solution for human struggles the concept that through the intelligent making and application of the laws of Heaven justice must and will prevail. In three plays which deal with the story of the fate of the house of Agamemnon the same idea appears in human guise. Agamemnon falls because of his crimes. Clytemnaestra cannot escape her fate, nor can Orestes avoid the consequence of his matricide. Not even the purificatory rites of Apollo can save him until, through Athena and the ordered channels of the law, release from suffering is obtained from the Court of the Areopagus. In the last of these three plays may be seen a protest against the radical assaults on the powers of the Areopagus. In the *Persians,* and its accompanying plays (now lost), the poet dealt sympathetically with the punishment of Xerxes for that overweening arrogance which led him to his assaults, not only on the Greeks, but on their gods.

Aeschylus was confident of the justice of the gods, of the soundness of a moral order founded on intelligence, and of the right of the intelligent noble to rule. He died in Gela in Sicily in 456 B.C., and his place in Athens was taken by Sophocles.

SOPHOCLES (CA.
496-406 B.C.)

Sophocles developed the technique of dramatic composition on which he is said to have written a treatise. One of his plays, the *Oedipus Tyrannus,* was designated by Aristotle as the perfect tragedy. Of the many plays which he composed, seven have survived. The greatest of these are three drawn from the Theban story of Oedipus, the *Oedipus Tyrannus,* the *Antigone,* and the *Oedipus at Colonus,* the last having been produced in 401 B.C. after his death. The plays are motivated by the same forces which produced the Parthenon, and although they exhibit less majesty than do the plays of Aeschylus, they have greater serenity and more perfect symmetry.

The poet, himself, of good family and of some wealth, was distinctly a product of Periclean Athens. As a boy, he led the chorus that celebrated the victory of Salamis. He grew to manhood in the days of Aristides and Cimon and, as befitted a true citizen, he served the state in official capacity. His political insight, his fine knowledge of human psychology, his nobility of character, and his supreme courage and confidence in the city and in the eternal justice of the gods must have been drawn from the life of the city around him and in which he participated. The noblest expression of the Periclean spirit is in a. chorus of the *Antigone:*

Wonders are many, and none is more wonderful than man; the power that crosses the white sea, driven by the stormy south wind, making a path under surges that threaten to engulf him; and Earth, the eldest of the gods, the immortal, the unwearied, doth he wear, turning the soil with the offspring of horses, as the ploughs go to and fro from year to year.

And the light-hearted race of birds, and the tribes of savage beasts, and the sea-brood of the deep, he snares in the meshes of his woven toils, he leads captive, man excellent in wit. And he masters by his art the beast whose lair is in the wilds, who roams the hills; he tames the horse of shaggy mane, he puts the yoke upon its neck, he tames the tireless mountain bull.

And speech and swift-winged thought and all the moods that mould a state hath he taught himself; and how to flee the arrows of the frost when 'tis hard lodging under the clear sky, and the arrows of the rushing rain; yea, he hath resource for all; without resource he meets nothing that must come; only against Death shall he call for aid in vain; but from baffling maladies he hath devised escapes.

Cunning beyond fancy's dream is the fertile skill which brings him now to evil, now to good. When he honors the laws of the land and that justice which he hath sworn by the gods to uphold, proudly stands his city; no city hath he who for his rashness dwells with sin. Never may he share my hearth, never think my thoughts, who doth these things! [4]

[4] Botsford and Sihler, *op. cit.,* p. 328.

EURIPIDES
(480-406 B.C.) The third of the great tragedians, Euripides, was the least successful in his competitions but the most popular in later generations. Eighteen of his tragedies and a satyr play, the *Bacchae,* have come down to us. Most of his plays were composed during the Peloponnesian War, and they therefore reveal the stress of wartime. Deeply interested in men and in their problems, he was ever the spokesman of the poor, the humble, and the oppressed. Though at first he championed the cause of Athens against Sparta, his later plays protest against war and portray its horrors.

O miserable mortals, why do ye get yourselves spears and deal out death upon each other? Stop and withdraw from these toils. Peaceful, 'mid the peaceful, guard your towns. Short is your span of life. Best then to pass through it as gently as may be, not worn by burdens.[5]

The Trojan Women, a picture of the sufferings of women in war, is thought to have been composed as a protest against the Athenian treatment of Melos. In the *Medea* he set forth in most poignant language the feelings of wronged womankind. He brought the gods down to earth and discussed their actions in the light of human reason. He criticized them for allowing evil on earth and for their failure to sustain the moral order. In the last analysis he reduced them to psychological forces. Then in his old age he wrote the *Bacchae,* a perfect Dionysiac satyr play. Some modern critics regard this merely as an attempt to display his dramatic artistry; others believe that he found in mystical religion the answer to the problems which had beset him. Professor Glover of Cambridge describes it as "the play of all his plays where men find most the note of freedom and escape—escape from the sea and its storms, the haven reached and toil ended." [6]

Euripides was an expert dramatic technician, a scholar who devoted his life to the writing of plays, not a citizen to whom playwriting was incidental. In his desire to express himself, he departed from classic standards, introducing befitting costumes and using varied meters for effect. These changes, along with his ideas, offended the conservatives of his day, and Aristophanes made mock of him. Yet Euripides was much admired; it was said that after the disaster in Sicily in 413 B.C. the Syracusans set free all Athenians who could recite for them verses from Euripides.

[5] *Suppliants,* 949-954.
[6] *From Pericles to Philip,* p. 139.

COMEDY

On the afternoons of the days of the dramatic contest, comedies were produced, likewise in competition. The first contest was held in 488 B.C. Comedy seems to have been the result of a combination between the vulgar buffoonery of the country festivals and of farces which had developed at Megara. Because of its origin and development, comedy was free from the strict requirements of tragedy and gave free rein to caricature and ridicule, which often descended to vulgarity. Even the gods were treated with a license which at times seems blasphemous. Its subjects, however, were drawn mostly from the passing scene, and it played much the same part that the cartoon and the newspaper column play today.

ARISTOPHANES
(CA. 450-
385 B.C.)

The greatest of the writers of comedy was Aristophanes. His major work was done during the Peloponnesian War, though he continued to write well into the fourth century B.C. He was a conservative democrat, hostile to the passions of the city mob, to the war, and to those whom he held responsible for it, as well as to the new learning and its exponents (p. 256). All that he disliked he held up to ridicule in his plays with a courage that at times verged upon daring. His imagination was vivid, his sense of the comic, inimitable, and his ability to puncture pretense by a cartoon of words is unequaled in literature. With ribald license, impossible in the modern theater, with daring boldness, and yet with deep feeling for the realities of life, he attacked the leaders of the Athenians, the whims and foibles of the people, and sham or corruption wherever he saw it.

He loved the simple farmers of the Attic countryside and admired the old gods and the old manners. He charged Pericles and Aspasia with causing the war, and the professional soldiers and self-seeking demagogues with continuing it. Cleon he held up to especial scorn. In a beautiful play, the *Peace,* he portrayed the rejoicing of the Greeks over the Peace of Nicias. Later, when war was renewed, he wrote the *Lysistrata,* an amusing and ribald representation of an attempt of the women to end the war, a play filled with an all-embracing spirit of Panhellenism. He made fun of the Athenian jurors in the *Wasps;* he played with the ideal states of the oligarchs in the *Birds,* in which the birds create a new state, called "Cloud-Cuckoo Land." He criticized Socrates and the new learning in the *Clouds.* His most celebrated play was the *Frogs,* a remarkable piece of literary criticism containing a savage attack upon Euripides. Some of his lyrics, notably in the *Frogs* and the *Birds,* are among the most beautiful in any language.

HISTORY

History as a branch of literature and a scientific study, distinct from the genealogical or geographical compositions of the earlier Ionians, and, like drama, a contribution of fifth-century Greece, began with the writings of Herodotus, the "Father of History," and Thucydides, the first "scientific historian."

HERODOTUS (CA. 484- CA. 425 B.C.) Born in Halicarnassus in Asia Minor, Herodotus was early involved in political troubles and set forth upon a series of travels which carried him to Egypt, Babylon, the Black Sea region, and Italy, but his second home was Athens from which he drew his inspiration. He wrote a history (the Greek word means "inquiry") of the Persian Wars that "time may not obliterate the great and marvelous deeds of the Hellenes and the Barbarians and especially that the causes for which they waged war with one another may not be forgotten." He envisaged the war as an episode in the conflict between East and West. Accordingly, he traced the background of these struggles in the sixth century B.C., proceeded to a description of the lands which were in the Persian Empire, and wrote an account of the war itself. While somewhat credulous, he was eminently fair-minded. He felt it his duty to inquire and then to report what he learned, whether he himself believed it or not. When opinions conflicted, he presented them all. He was an inimitable storyteller, and the greatest charm of his book is to be found in the many digressions when he turns aside to tell a story.

Though freed by the enlightenment of his generation from much of the supernaturalism of his predecessors, he believed firmly in the justice of the gods and paid due respect to the gods of other lands. But above all, he believed in the happiness of the individual as a citizen, an individual not so arrogant as to offend the deity and bring down vengeance upon himself, but mindful of the gods and of the limitations which they placed on all human achievements. His ideal of human happiness is best illustrated by the story he tells of Solon's visit to Croesus. When Croesus asked Solon whom he deemed to be the happiest of men, the sage replied, "Tellus of Athens . . . because he lived in a well-governed commonwealth and had sons who were virtuous and good; and he saw children born to them all and all surviving; in the next place, when he had lived as happily as the condition of human affairs will permit, he ended his life in a glorious manner; for coming to the assistance of the Athenians in a battle with their neighbors near Eleusis, he put the enemy to flight and died nobly. The Athenians buried him at the public charge in the place where he fell and honored him greatly." [7]

THUCYDIDES
(CA. 460-
CA. 395 B.C.)

Thucydides,[8] the Athenian, who recorded the history of the Peloponnesian War began to write, he said, at its very beginning because he felt it was going to be great and memorable above all wars. His own part in the struggle ended with his exile in 424 B.C. after a defeat in Thrace for which, as general, he was held responsible, and he was thus enabled to devote himself to the gathering of materials. In performing this task, he became the founder of scientific history. He visited and studied the scenes of events, talked with eyewitnesses, copied documents, and used all available evidence to reach conclusions and to be able to state what actually happened.

In the treatment of events and personalities, he showed, for the most part, an admirable balance, except perhaps in the case of Cleon, against whom he was prejudiced. Interested in the problem of causation and with a mind freed from superstition by his education, he brushed aside traditional views. Earthquakes and eclipses were to him not divine portents but natural phenomena. He disregarded oracles and omens of supernatural interference and found his causes in the actions of man and in the relation of events. He failed, however, to emphasize sufficiently those underlying social and economic elements in history upon which present-day historians lay such stress. His comments on the actions of people under strain of war are, nevertheless, full of wise observations.

In one respect he disregarded modern canons. Instead of merely reporting speeches, he wrote them out in full in his own words. He acknowledged this practice frankly: "As to the speeches which were made either before or during the war, it was hard for me and for others to recollect the exact words. I have therefore put into the mouth of each speaker the sentiments appropriate to the occasion, expressed as I thought he would express them, while at the same time I endeav-

[7] I, 30.
[8] Not to be confused with Thucydides, the conservative leader, p. 204.

ored, as nearly as I could, to give the general purport of what was actually said." [9] Many of these speeches presented Thucydides' analysis of a situation, with arguments pro and con. Notable in this respect was the dialogue between the Melians and the Athenians before the destruction of Melos.

History to Thucydides was primarily a useful subject. "Very likely the strict historical character of my narrative may be disappointing to the ear. [Ancient books were written to be read aloud.] But if he who desires to have before his eyes a true picture of the events which have happened, and of the like events which may be expected to happen hereafter in the order of human affairs, shall pronounce what I have written to be useful, then I shall be satisfied. My history is a possession forever, not a prize composition to be heard and forgotten." [10]

He was not only a master of scientific history but of a literary style that showed a keen sense of dramatic values. His descriptions of the plague in Athens and of the retreat from Syracuse are marvels of exposition. Some critics think that the book was composed as a prose tragedy under the spell of the great dramatists. Certainly his subject was worthy of such treatment.

His book comes to an abrupt end in 411 B.C.; why, no one knows. He outlived the greatness of Athens, but probably he did not live to finish his account of the downfall of the city which he had helped to render immortal.

SCIENCE AND PHILOSOPHY

Under the inspiration of the same stimuli which had led to the works of art and literature, great advances were made in medicine, in philosophy, and in education.

Greek men of medicine took the first steps in freeing their practice from the age-old domination of magic and in establishing it as a science. Greeks who wished to be cured of their diseases were accustomed to rely upon charms or to visit the shrines of Asclepius, god of healing. They passed a night in the shrine, slept and dreamed. In accordance with their dreams the priests prescribed for them, and it was inevitable that these priests should acquire by experience a consid-

[9] I, 22. Botsford and Sihler, *op. cit.,* p. 29.
[10] I, 23. Botsford and Sihler, *op. cit.,* p. 28.

erable knowledge of drugs and of the treatment of disease. There were doctors, too, such as Democedes of Croton, physician to Darius, who knew much about medicine and probably learned what Babylonia and Egypt had to teach them. Yet magic prevailed until the appearance of Hippocrates of Cos. On the island of Cos stood the most celebrated temple of Asclepius, and its priests were regarded as the most skillful in Hellas.

Hippocrates, by birth a member of the priestly class, studied in the temple of Asclepius and went to Egypt for further instruction. Thus equipped he became a great physician, the founder of scientific medicine and of medical ethics. He abandoned the superstitions of the shrines and laid down in his teachings and writings the principles of natural causes and natural cures of disease. He noted the effects of climates and seasons. While many of his theories have long since been discarded, by insisting that scientific observation and experience are the only sure bases for the practice of the art, he laid the sure foundations upon which modern medicine rests. The Hippocratic oath, administered to ancient students of medicine and still taken by graduates of many medical schools today, expresses the highest ideals of the medical profession. There exists today a great body of medical writings composed by him and his followers.

Throughout the fifth century B.C. the philosophers continued their attempts to answer the questions raised by Thales and his successors (p. 182). Heraclitus of Ephesus, who lived during the first half of the fifth century B.C., in his search for reality, was impressed by the fact of constant change—"Everything flows; nothing abides." The neverending strife between opposites he expressed by the statement, "War is the father of all things." Yet amid this flux and strife there is a balance, a regular alternation as of day and night, which implied to him justice and reason in the universe. Accordingly he postulated a worldsoul symbolized by fire, which he called *logos,* the Word, a mysterious power which few can understand but which rules the universe.

Parmenides and Zeno (fl. 475 B.C.) of Elea in Italy opposed the views of their contemporary, Heraclitus, with famous arguments to prove creation and motion impossible. Creation is impossible because "from nothing, nothing comes"; motion implies empty space, which being nothing cannot exist. Further, Zeno endeavored to prove mathematically that Achilles could not catch the tortoise, because whenever he reached the place the tortoise had been, it had moved on. Thus the only reality, the firm principle of the universe, is unchanging stability.

Other men sought a way out of the impasse created by this divergence of views between Heraclitus and the Eleatics. Empedocles of Acragas (495-435 B.C.) described a world made up of four elements—earth, air, fire, and water—combined and separated by opposing forces, love and hate, which thus produced substance and change, life and death. His idea of the four elements, accepted by Aristotle, remained the basic theory of the universe until modern times.

Leucippus and Democritus (ca. 460-350 B.C.), refusing to accept the limitation of substance to four elements, conceived the thought of a universe of limitless particles, which they called atoms, moving through empty space and united and separated by a physical force, called gravitation. This atomic theory, rejected by the contemporaries of its creators as mechanical and atheistic, became the cornerstone of modern science.

Anaxagoras of Clazomenae (ca. 500-ca. 428 B.C.), who came to Athens and was a friend of Pericles, accepted the concept of many elements which he called "seeds," but he substituted for gravitation, or for the strife of opposites, a divine intelligence, *nous,* which directs all things. In his study of the world he reached the conclusion that the sun was not a god, but a mass of molten metal, somewhat larger than the Peloponnesus. He was banished from Athens on the charge of atheism, but his exile was really the result of a political attack upon Pericles.

These men with their never-ending discussions of the material of which the world is made, of the problems of motion and change, and of the motivating power which controls it all, presented theories from which the great philosophers of later centuries drew and which therefore have materially affected philosophic thought down to our times.

THE SOPHISTS   While these philosophers were boldly endeavoring to understand the universe, other thinkers, directing their attention to the problem of man in society, advanced the work of education. These teachers, called Sophists, "men of wisdom," arose to meet new needs created by life in the city-state. Those who wished to serve the democracy or appear before the law courts needed not only training to enable them to speak in public but education to acquire political wisdom. Accordingly, a group of teachers arose who taught men how to speak and instructed them in the practical workings of government and society. In their work they established the studies of grammar and rhetoric and began those examinations into the practices of men in society which have resulted in our modern social sciences—political science, economics, and sociology. In education, their doctrine was essentially utilitarian. Before them was a definite goal and only those studies—among them, history—which contributed to that end were worth investigating. They denied the value of philosophic speculations on the universe.

The Sophists professed to make their students better; yet the training which they gave in argumentation laid them open to the charge of training in cleverness rather than in virtue. Their opponents claimed that they taught the youth "to prove that black was white and to make the worse appear the better cause." The democrats suspected them because most of their students were drawn from the wealthy class which affected to despise the many. The aristocratic Plato condemned them for their ideas and because they accepted pay for their teaching. In spite of these charges against them, however, as the Sophists traveled from city to city to give instructions, they were eagerly sought after by ambitious youths. Leaders among them were Protagoras (ca. 490-415 B.C.) of Abdera in Thrace and Gorgias (ca. 480-395 B.C.) of Leontini in Sicily, both of whom taught in Athens.

Because the ultimate aim of Sophist teaching was individual success, the inevitable content of their thought was the place of the individual in the world. Consideration of this question made them skeptical of the established traditions of the gods, of the state, and of the standards of human behavior. In their teaching of ethics, they laid emphasis on those things which are practical, possible, and contributory to success, rather than upon those which are just or right in an absolute sense. The standard which they set up was the good of the individual. "Man," said Protagoras, meaning each individual for himself, "is the measure of all things; of things that are, that they are; of things that are not, that they are not." [11] The acceptance of this concept meant the end of the Periclean ideal of man, the citizen, under the gods.

SOCRATES
(469-399 B.C.)

The greatest intellectual figure of fifth-century Athens was the philosopher Socrates. It is hard to penetrate through the jibes of Aristophanes, the memoirs of Xenophon (p. 279), and the dialogues of Plato (p. 282) to Socrates' own thought, for he wrote nothing himself. But of his

[11] Bakewell, *Sourcebook of Ancient Philosophy,* p. 67.

dominant position in the history of thought there can be little doubt.

Born in a family of restricted means, he was trained in his father's shop as a stonecutter, a trade which he later neglected in order to spend his time arguing in the shops and the market place of Athens and wherever loiterers gathered. From such myriad conversations with all ranks of people he gathered the major portion of his education, the fundamental element of which was recognition of the principle that the admission of ignorance is the foundation of true knowledge. When a friend came back from the temple of Apollo at Delphi with the words of the oracle proclaiming Socrates as the wisest of men, he took the words as an order from the god to search after the truth and impart it to his fellow men. In that search he was indefatigable. His method was dialectic, that is, question and answer, argument in the analysis of a statement to find out what was true. He put aside the disputes in which the earlier philosophers were engaged as to the nature of the universe, to turn to those questions which dealt with men's relations with each other. He tried to discover what is true, noble, just, and pious. He was therefore the founder of the study of ethics. He felt that the Sophists were superficial and were engaged in training men for success rather than for character.

He believed in the gods, as ever-present and all-knowing. He performed with true piety all the traditional forms, though he was not interested in the Mysteries, and he felt himself especially guided by a *daemon,* or guardian spirit. Socrates' early manhood occurred in the Age of Pericles, and he learned then to believe in the state and in the fulfillment of the individual therein. He served Athens loyally in the army and in the council. So fond of the city was he that he could scarcely be tempted out of it. He strove to train intelligent men who would serve it and direct its course along lines of reason. He taught the beauty of the family and the dignity of labor.

Intensely social, he was always the center of a throng of men. Youths trooped at his heels to learn from him and to watch him break down the arguments of a man who was overcertain of his opinion. Notable among his followers were the young Alcibiades, Critias, and many future leaders of the intellectual group at Athens. Naturally, he aroused many enemies, and in the popular mind he was confused with the Sophists. In his old age he was made the victim of the reaction which followed the Peloponnesian War, and was accused of denying the gods and of corrupting the youth of Athens. The defense which he made, as reported by Plato, is a masterly exposition of his whole career and purpose, one of the greatest of all documents. In the passion of the hour, the jury condemned him. He was offered a chance to escape the penalty. This but gave him an opportunity to explain his attitude toward the laws of the state. Then after a discussion of immortality, in which he believed, he drank the hemlock.

EPILOGUE   For a brief period not only did all the forces of the Greek world focus upon Athens, but goods, men, and ideas from all parts of the civilized world concentrated there, where they found a citizen body, varied versatile, and receptive. The result was the Age of Pericles.

In his character, Pericles was a symbol of the spirit of the age as he was its leader. His career is an epilogue of the achievements of his generation. His father, Xanthippus, came of an old, priestly family renowned for its services to the state. His mother was Agariste, descendant of Megacles, the Alcmaeonid, and Agariste of Sicyon, and the niece of the lawgiver, Cleisthenes. Pericles' education was the best which the time could provide, and the artists, literary men, and philosophers of Athens were his friends and constant companions. His influence was the inspiration of the architects and sculptors of the Parthenon. Turning his property over to a slave to manage, he entered the service of the state and became its directing genius.

A majestic speaker, he swayed the assembly, and so dominated the policies of Athens that its actions are spoken of as his own. At the end of the first year of the Peloponnesian War he delivered a funeral oration in honor of those who had fallen during the year. It was a panegyric on the Age and the supreme expression of the statesman's ideals for his city. He described the institutions and customs of the Athenians and proudly declared that "Athens is the school of Hellas." He recounted the glories of the empire and the achievements of the city. "For we have opened every land and every sea to our arms and have everywhere planted eternal memorials of our friendship and our enmity." He called all citizens to the service of the city. The glory of Athens was the glory of its citizens. He praised the city rather than the men who had fallen, because "in magnifying the city," he said, "I have magnified them and men like them whose virtues have made her glorious." Pericles died of the plague in the third year of the war.

The Peloponnesian War deprived Athens of its wealth and power, and weakened the allegiance of its citizens. Yet the city had sufficient vitality in the next generation to revive and to make new contributions to the culture of the world. But the bloom of the classic age had passed. In comparison with it, the story of the next century, the fourth B.C., is dreary and dull.

THE FOURTH CENTURY
(404-338 B.C.)

THE fourth century B.C. was an age of confusion, difficult to follow through its various ramifications as one state after another
endeavored to obtain advantage or to rise to power. The fall of
Athens left Sparta supreme in the Aegean world, and the first attempts of Athens and of the erstwhile allies of Sparta, Thebes and
Corinth, to rehabilitate or to strengthen themselves were suppressed
by Sparta with Persian aid. In a second effort Athens was successful
in securing again maritime leadership, only to find that Thebes, under
its great commander Epaminondas, had been able to crush Sparta and
establish itself as a great and leading power. Theban failure after the
death of Epaminondas left Greece disorganized and dismayed, an easy
prey for the able and wily king of Macedon with whose victory the
period closed.

THE PERIOD OF SPARTAN POWER

The opening events of the fourth century B.C. proved that the
Peloponnesian War, which was to accomplish so much, had actually
settled nothing. In 404 B.C. Athens seemed to be safely in Spartan
power under the rule of the Thirty Tyrants. Sparta had feared too
much the growing power of Thebes, as well as the condemnation of
all the Hellenes, to allow the city to be destroyed. But the Spartan
tyranny was soon overthrown, and, with Persian assistance, Athens
rose again, rebuilt its walls, and became once more an aspirant to
power, the rallying center for all democrats against oligarchic Sparta.

Other cities, in addition, were ready to challenge the leadership
of the Dorian state. Corinth had suffered greatly from the war and
had received none of the expected benefits. Thebes, however, had
profited from the misfortunes of Athens. Its population had been in-

creased by refugees and by fugitive slaves, many of whom were highly skilled. Its wealth had been magnified by the spoils of the victory, and its control over the other Boeotian cities, lost at the time of the Persian Wars, had been renewed. Like Corinth, however, Thebes was dissatisfied with the attitude of Sparta at the end of the war and with its share of the booty. Both cities were ready to cause trouble.

Persia at this time was wealthy and vigorous. The king and his satraps had learned the power of money in the Greek states; they were ready to use it to regain control over the Asiatic cities and to prevent any Hellenic power from becoming strong enough to resist a Persian return to the Aegean. The Persians had helped Sparta break the Athenian empire and now were equally willing to assist Athens to weaken Sparta if that city became aggressive.

Against this array of hostility the Spartans could oppose only military force and the self-interest of a few oligarchs. With no commercial activity and no interest in trade, Sparta could never furnish the Aegean world with the economic center which had given vitality to the Athenian empire. Its power would therefore last only as long as it was supreme on land and sea.

An additional element which served to hinder conditions of peace was the great number of men available for mercenary service. In earlier times, though Greeks had served for pay in the armies of Egypt and Babylon, or as hired bodyguards for tyrants, the defense of the cities had been entrusted to its citizens. The Persian king and his satraps had found it advantageous, in their wars of the fifth century, to hire Greeks; and Sparta had made use of Arcadians in the overseas campaigns of the Decelean War. Mercenary service developed so rapidly during the fourth century, however, that by the end of the period professional soldiers had almost displaced the citizens in the armies of the Greeks and Persians. Several reasons account for this fact. The ending of the Peloponnesian War had let loose a large number of men whose careers had been devoted entirely to fighting and who were eager for further service. Other men driven from their homes by the strife of the war period wandered with their families in search of employment. Their number was constantly augmented by the civil troubles of the fourth century, by economic distress in the cities, and by an overflow from the agricultural regions of Arcadia and Aetolia. In early times such men had gone out to found colonies. But the available land had now been occupied, so that mercenary service provided the only outlet. All states made use of them. In the Persian armies which offered resistance to Alexander the Great, for example, were many thousands of Greek mercenaries. The presence of men eager for hire, ready to serve any state which would pay them and to plunder friend or foe with equal alacrity, made it easier for the citizens of the states to vote for war without peril to themselves. This, too, contributed to the confusion of the century.

THE ANABASIS
OF THE
TEN THOUSAND

The history of the period is tangled with rivalries, intrigues, and wars. It opened with an episode of minor importance but of great significance and of even greater interest. The interest results from the fact that the event was recorded by Xenophon in his *Anabasis,* the first textbook in Greek for generations of students. Darius II, king of Persia who died in 404 B.C., was succeeded by his eldest son, Artaxerxes II. Cyrus, younger and favorite son, challenged his brother's right to the throne. As satrap in Sardis during the Peloponnesian War, Cyrus had come into close contact with the Greeks and knew their conditions and their abilities. To put himself on the throne he therefore hired a band of some thirteen thousand mercenaries, mostly veterans of the Peloponnesian War, under a Spartan commander. With these and a large number of Asiatic supporters he advanced into Mesopotamia in 401 B.C. In the decisive battle at Cunaxa, the Greeks were victorious, but at the moment of victory Cyrus was killed. Shortly thereafter the Greek commanders were treacherously slain by the Persians.

The army, though victorious, was disorganized by the loss of its leaders and in a desperate plight in the heart of the enemy's country. Never did Greek training better justify itself. The soldiers organized themselves into a city-state without a city, drew up laws, elected generals (among them the Athenian Xenophon), and scrupulously obeyed them. With Xenophon as the directing genius, this reorganized band, now numbering about ten thousand, marched north across the mountains to the Euxine Sea, and, after much discussion of their future course, entered the service of Sparta and disappeared from history. They had exposed the weakness of Persia and proved the political ability of the Hellenes. Henceforth the leaders of Greek thought clamored for a war against Persia to furnish occupation and lands for the restless element among the Greeks. Throughout the century many Greeks drifted into Persia and some even enlisted in the Persian armies.

LYSANDER

At the end of the war with Athens, Sparta had endeavored, as we have seen, to establish a Spartan empire by setting up the Thirty Tyrants in Athens and the decarchies in the maritime states, all supported by Lacedaemonian garrisons. The Asiatic cities had been surrendered to Persia. The guiding spirit in these actions was Lysander. Son of a Spartan father and helot mother, this man of genius planned to use the wealth and position he had attained to make himself king of Sparta. The Spartan magistrates, suspicious of his designs, removed him from office. At the same time the Thirty were overthrown by the Athenians, and many of the decarchies and garrisons were expelled from the allied states. Still Lysander did not give up hope. He intrigued in Sparta and endeavored to get the oracles of the gods to help him. Though he failed in these plans, he still retained great influence over the Spartan people.

THE WAR IN
ASIA MINOR

Then, because of its participation in the expedition of Cyrus, Sparta became involved in a war with Persia. When an appeal for help came from Ionia, the Spartans sent forces to free the cities from the Persian satraps. In 396 B.C. Agesilaus, king of Sparta, was sent to take command. Agesilaus, though lame, had become king through Lysander's influence and through him Lysander had hoped to regain his position. But again Lysander was disappointed, for the king was independent and vigorous. Lysander, finding his advice disregarded, withdrew and was shortly after killed in a skirmish with the Athenians. Agesilaus, however, had succeeded in liberating most of the Asiatic states by the time that events in Greece called him home.

THE CORIN-
THIAN WAR,
395-387 B.C.

The enemies of Sparta had found common cause and had united to wage war once again for the freedom of Hellas. Athens, Thebes, Corinth, Argos, and many of the islands formed a league, and in 395 B.C. the Corinthian War began. In 394 B.C. Conon, an Athenian, now admiral of the Persian fleet, won a victory off Cnidus which destroyed Spartan naval supremacy, and then, with Persian money, aided in the rebuilding of the Long Walls of Athens. Persia knew well how to prevent united action among the Greeks. Athens, once again able to lift its head and to hope for a renewal of wealth and empire, refused to follow the lead of Sparta and began the formation of a new league among the islanders.

THE KING'S
PEACE, 387-
386 B.C. In spite of the naval defeat, Agesilaus was able to maintain Spartan supremacy on land, and the allies could make little headway. When the tide turned against Sparta, that city appealed to Persia. It was not to the interest of the Great King to allow Sparta to be crushed and the Athenians to return to power. In addition, the Lacedaemonians were willing to pay his price for support—to allow him once more possession of the Asiatic cities. Once his financial aid was withdrawn from Athens and its allies, they could do nothing but accept his terms. A conference met at Sardis in 387-386 B.C. of which this proclamation, known as the King's Peace, was the outcome.

King Artaxerxes deems it right that the cities of Asia with the islands of Clazomenae and Cyprus should belong to himself. The remaining cities, small and great, he wishes to leave independent with the exception of Lemnos, Imbros, and Scyros, which three as formerly are to belong to Athens. Should any of the parties concerned not accept this peace, I, Artaxerxes, together with those who share my views, will wage war against him or them by land and sea, with ships and with money.[1]

To the familiar terms of Freedom and Autonomy, a new principle had been added—the armed enforcement of peace. With the exception of the shameful surrender of the Asiatic cities, the peace seemed eminently fair and just to all parties. Yet it brought untold confusion. By the terms of the treaty, which set all small states free, the Athenian maritime alliance was broken and the naval power of Athens was so shattered that pirates once more ruled the seas. The Boeotian League was likewise disbanded and the hopes of the Thebans were crushed. The wealth of Corinth had been destroyed by the war.

Only Sparta gained. The principles of military power for which it stood had been vindicated in fact if not in word. It was generally understood that Sparta was to enforce the peace with Persian backing. Its power in the Peloponnesus was not broken by the peace and there was none that might gainsay Sparta, none to protect the weaker states or even the peace itself against that city. Autonomy was easily translated to mean rule by the friends of Sparta. Decarchies were once again set up, and there followed a new series of revolutions. Exiles again wandered in armed mercenary bands and menaced life and property throughout the land. The orator, Isocrates, declared that more cities

[1] Xenophon, *Hellenica* V, 1, 31.

were taken during the period of the peace than before the treaty had been concluded.

Sparta itself broke the peace. To punish Mantinea for disaffection it crushed and destroyed that city. Then a Spartan commander on his way to the Chalcidice seized the citadel of Thebes. When he was tried at Sparta for this infraction of the peace, Agesilaus defended him on the ground that he had acted for the best interests of the state, and he escaped with a fine, while Sparta kept the citadel.

THE
OLYNTHIAN
LEAGUE

To the north a group of states were offering a new solution to the problem of peace and unity. Olynthus in the Chalcidice had become the center of a federal union. Citizens in each state of the league were given full rights of citizenship in every other state and were thus held together by a common interest. Even those who had been forced into the organization soon lost their local interests in the welfare of the whole league. The character of this federal union was unprecedented and important. Not interfering with local affairs and bringing no states into subjection, the league did not offend the traditional Greek spirit of local independence. Instead, it created a higher loyalty and provided a program for the enduring unification of the fiercely proud cities of the Aegean. Its growing power was naturally regarded as a menace by its neighbors and by the Spartans. Federalism had no place in a world ruled by Sparta. When the Olynthian union had been destroyed by Sparta in a short war (379 B.C.), Spartan power had reached its climax. Agesilaus had attained the goal of his desires.

SECOND
ATHENIAN
CONFEDERACY

Athenian resistance to Spartan supremacy, both natural and inevitable, was made once more possible by the formation of the Second Athenian Confederacy in 378-377 B.C. When the decarchies were overthrown after the fall of Lysander, the maritime states had naturally gravitated to Athens for commercial reasons. The first attempts at alliance were broken up by the King's Peace. In the Confederacy of 378-377 every care was taken to avoid any breach of the peace and to prevent any recurrence of the abuses which had changed the Confederacy of Delos into an empire (p. 202). No state was forced to enter, and each treaty provided for local freedom and autonomy. The assembly of the allies met without Athenian interference and only required the sanction of the Athenian assembly for action. No tribute was collected, but ships and money were to be contributed when needed. The purpose of the league was defense against Sparta.

LIBERATION
OF THEBES
(379-378 B.C.)
Thebes, meanwhile, had been freed from its Spartan garrison. A band of exiles led by Pelopidas had crept back into the city. Disguised as girls, they were brought to a dinner given for the Spartan officers, whom they promptly killed. The garrison thereupon withdrew. The clever Epaminondas and his friend Pelopidas guided Thebes along the path which led to power in the Hellenic world. As a first step the Boeotian League was reorganized. Then, in alliance with Athens, Thebes declared war against Sparta for the freedom of Hellas.

WAR WITH
SPARTA (378-
371 B.C.)
Though the allies outmatched Sparta in strength, they were unable to agree on concerted action. Thebes, as a matter of fact, left the conduct of the war to Athens and devoted itself to increasing its own power in Boeotia and Phocis. Athens, alarmed at these activities of its neighbor, endeavored to secure peace.

PEACE
CONFERENCE
OF 371 B.C.
To this end a congress was called to meet in Sparta in 371 B.C. All the major states of Hellas, and Persia, as well, were represented at the meeting. It was recognized in the discussion that the chief difficulty lay in the governmental differences between Athens and Sparta. In every small state in Greece, the democratic party looked to Athens for support, while the oligarchic looked at Sparta. Alliances followed the will of the party in power, and party strife led to appeals to Sparta and to Athens from both sides. Thus the two leading states became involved in war with each other. It was agreed that the only solution lay in open friendship between the two powers and in an agreement not to interfere in such local disputes. To achieve this the peace provided that all governors should be withdrawn, that each state should be left free to choose its own form of government and its own alliances, and that both naval and military forces should be disbanded. Furthermore, "if any state transgressed these stipulations, it lay at the option of any power whatsoever to aid the states so injured, while conversely, to bring such aid was not compulsory on any power against its will." [2] The last provision proved to be the weak link in the chain.

The success of the plan involved the end of the growing power of

[2] Xenophon, *Hellenica* VI, 3, 20. Dakyns tr.

Thebes. Athens and Sparta would allow no rival. Epaminondas, the Theban representative, was ordered by the congress to sign for Thebes only and to allow the other Boeotians to sign for themselves. This meant the disintegration of the Boeotian League. Rather than yield to what they regarded as virtual destruction, the Thebans withdrew from the conference, and their state was consequently excluded from the treaty. Sparta thereupon took up the burden of enforcing the peace against Thebes. One Spartan opposed this action before the assembly and made a remarkable suggestion. He proposed that the army should be recalled and disbanded according to the treaty; that contributions should then be placed at Delphi; then, if any violated the peace or the independence of the states, all others could be invited in and funds would be at hand. The sanction of heaven and the enforcement of the peace would thus be secured with the least annoyance to the states. "But the assembly on hearing these words agreed that this man was talking nonsense." [3]

LEUCTRA
371 B.C.

A Spartan army met the Thebans at Leuctra in Boeotia. Epaminondas, in command of the Theban forces, proved himself a military genius. He made his left wing unusually heavy and arranged his center and right *en échelon*. While the Spartans were rallying to stop the charge of the wing, he sent his center and right against them successively. The Spartan phalanx was crushed for the first time in Hellenic history, and Spartan prestige was irrevocably destroyed. With it went all the bright hopes of the peace conference.

THEBAN
HEGEMONY
(371-362 B.C.)

Leuctra was followed by a brief period of Theban hegemony. Epaminondas at once invaded the Peloponnesus and even entered Lacedaemon. Though he approached so near Sparta that the people could see his campfires, he did not venture to attack the city, for such an attack would mean a battle to the death. Instead he crossed over into Messenia and freed the helots there Messene was rebuilt and fortified, and descendants of its ancient citizens returned from Messana in Sicily and from Naupactus. Then he organized a league among the Arcadians to keep watch over Sparta and persuaded them to found a capital city called Megalopolis, "The Great City." At the same time he was endeavoring to conquer Thessaly, build a fleet, break the Athenian Confederacy, and secure control over the sea.

[3] Xenophon, *Hellenica* VI, 4, 2.

Since Epaminondas recognized that his army and navy were not strong enough to accomplish all he desired, with the assistance of Persia he tried to secure recognition of the Theban position. Conferences were held at Delphi, at Susa, and at Thebes, but without any result.

MANTINEA
362 B.C.

At first Athens made use of the fall of Sparta to increase its own powers by bringing into alliance with itself many of the smaller states which had been allies of Sparta. Then, alarmed by Theban policies, Athens rallied to the assistance of Sparta. A great army, including even a contingent from Syracuse, was gathered in the Peloponnesus. Epaminondas met it at Mantinea in 362 B.C. In this battle the Thebans were victorious, but Epaminondas was mortally wounded. With his death the period of Theban hegemony ended. Pelopidas had been killed in Thessaly, and with these two men gone Thebes was stripped of great leaders. The battle which was to have decided the fate of Hellas resulted, instead, in general chaos. A meeting was held and a peace was made "so that," in the words of the treaty which has survived in an inscription, "putting aside the war against each other, each should make his own city as great and prosperous as possible and shall remain useful to friends and strong." From this treaty Sparta remained aloof, because she steadfastly refused to recognize the loss of Messenia.

THE SOCIAL
WAR

In the meantime, the Second Athenian Confederacy, from which so much had been expected, had fallen on difficult times. The Athenians had departed from their lofty resolves. They had failed to protect the allies properly and had spent the money of the league for their own purposes. Some of the states had been reduced to subjection, and others had been plundered by the mercenary soldiers who were hired to defend them. In 357 B.C., several of the islands, led by Chios, Rhodes, and the city of Byzantium, and supported by Mausolus, king of Caria, revolted. Persia interfered; the Athenians were compelled to recognize the independence of the seceders, and within a year the Confederacy collapsed entirely. Thus because of the shortsighted, self-seeking policy of Athens, the last experiment in Hellenic unification during the days of Greek freedom had failed. All the powers had passed—Athenian, Spartan, Olynthian, Theban, and Athenian again. There was no power strong enough to lead, no city willing enough to follow. When peace and unity came to the Hellenic world, it was enforced from without.

THE WEST

DIONYSIUS
OF SYRACUSE

The history of the western Greeks during the fourth century B.C. was dominated by the achievements of Dionysius, tyrant of Syracuse. After the time of Gelon and Hiero (p. 193), the western Greeks had played but little active part in the development of Hellas. They had produced brilliant thinkers and teachers, but most of these had gravitated to Athens. Trade with the Etruscan cities of Italy, with Rome, and with Gaul, was brisk, and Syracuse became, perhaps, the richest of the Greek cities. The Athenian attempt to secure control over this trade had failed. After the defeat of the Athenians, the Syracusans under a democracy had aided Sparta in the war in the Aegean. But the Carthaginians, who were watching Syracusan progress with jealous eyes, interfered and declared war.

When the city's generals failed to cope with the Carthaginian armies, a young clerk, Dionysius, grasped his opportunity. By attacking the generals, he secured his own election, and then, by a series of brilliant strokes, made himself tyrant of Syracuse in 405 B.C., remaining in power until his death in 367 B.C. He fought several wars with Carthage with varying success but was never able to drive the Phoenicians out of Sicily. He succeeded, however, in bringing all western Hellas under his control and in extending his interest into the Adriatic. He kept an eye on the Aegean and sent troops to fight in the battle of Mantinea. By the practices of enslavement of the population of entire cities, of mass ransom, and of the seizure of booty he introduced to ancient warfare methods whereby the enemy paid for his wars—examples which his successors in Sicily and the Romans, as well, most readily followed. Noteworthy contributions were made by Dionysius to the art of warfare when he introduced warships with five banks of oars, and huge catapults for use as siege engines. With the walls and the fortresses which he built, Syracuse became the most strongly fortified city in the Mediterranean. Many famous stories are told of this tyrant, among them the familiar one of Damon and Pythias.

TIMOLEON

After the death of the great tyrant the contests between his weakling son and his son-in-law produced confusion among the Greeks and enabled Carthage to recover. In despair the Syracusans appealed to their mother city, Corinth, for aid in 344 B.C., and Corinth sent them Timoleon. This able man drove out the tyrants and defeated the Carthaginians. He restored democracies in all of the Greek states and organized a federation to keep peace in Sicily. His work accomplished, the Liberator gave up his power and spent the rest of his life in great honor as a private citizen of Syracuse.

THE RISE OF MACEDON

To the north, in a valley above modern Saloniki, lay Pella, capital of the kingdom of Macedon. The land of Macedon, which consisted of several river valleys separated by mountains, was inhabited by warlike tribes of land-holding nobles and peasants, shepherds, and hunters who spoke a Greek dialect. Though the Macedonian kings claimed descent from Heracles, the cultured Greeks to the south regarded them as barbarians. Their early history was filled with wars for supremacy carried on among the chieftains in the valleys. An Alexander who had gained control shortly after 500 B.C., after participating in the defeat of Macedon in the first Persian expedition, perforce went over to the side of Xerxes, though he posed as a friend and adviser to the patriotic Greeks. After the retreat of the Persians, he cultivated friendship with the Greeks and took part in Greek festivals. Perdiccas (ca. 455-413 B.C.), cunning and unscrupulous, was at the same time friend and enemy of the Athenians, who controlled his outlets to the sea and who purchased lumber from him for their ships. During the Peloponnesian War he veered from one side to the other with the shifting of the fortunes of war. Archelaus, who succeeded him in power, made Pella his capital, and by building cities and roads and inviting poets and artists to his kingdom, endeavored to introduce Greek culture in his court.

PHILIP II
(359-336 B.C.)

After a period of disorder in the first half of the fourth century, Philip II seized the throne in 359 B.C. Philip possessed a shrewd mind, remarkable foresight, and a genius for organization. Held as a hostage in Thebes during his youth, he learned military science from Epaminondas and gained a clear conception of the weaknesses of Greece and an understanding of how these might be used to his advantage. It was his ambition to raise himself with his people to a controlling place in the Hellenic world.

Philip's first task was the organization of his own kingdom. All opposition was ruthlessly crushed; the tribes were firmly welded together, and the Paeonians and Illyrians to the west were brought into subjection. The peasants were trained in the newest methods of warfare and were organized in the famous Macedonian phalanx, a solid body of infantry armed with long pikes which presented to the foe a bristling wall of spears. The cavalry, drawn from the nobility, traditional force of the Macedonian army and bound closely to the king as his "Companions," was developed into an offensive weapon of tremendous power and employed for flank attacks on opposing forces. With every man in the kingdom assigned to his place and supplies of money and munitions gathered, the entire nation was placed on a war basis.

The problem of foreign relations was solved with the same efficiency. Spies in Philip's employ were everywhere, and Philip took precautions in many of the cities to secure friends and to prevent a coalition of Greeks against him. Gold was disbursed freely among the venal; for some, the flattery of friendship sufficed; others were won over by promises of support in local politics or in petty wars; exhibitions of power won the fearful; and a few able leaders, notably the Athenian Isocrates (p. 280), followed Philip from the conviction that under his leadership Hellas might secure peace. Before the final conflict began, there was a strong Macedonian party in every city of Greece, and some cities had declared themselves Philip's friends.

THE SACRED WAR
Two conditions were needed to establish Philip's place in the sun of the Aegean world: (1) recognition of his position as a leading power by the Greeks so that he might dominate their councils; and (2) supremacy over the stretch of seacoast reaching from the Chalcidice to Byzantium so that he might control the rich gold mines of Thrace and secure a vantage point against the naval power of Athens. A heritage from the past gave him the first. An old quarrel between Thebes and Phocis led to strife when the Amphictyonic Council accused the Phocians of trespass at Delphi and, under the influence of Thebes, declared a sacred war. The Phocians retaliated by seizing the treasure of the temple and hiring a large force of mercenaries. Thebes appealed to Philip for aid (356 B.C.). At the moment he was busy in the north, but in 346 B.C. he marched south and devastated the land of Phocis. He was given the two Phocian votes in the Council of the Amphictyony and was elected president of the Pythian games. His place in Hellas was thus recognized and his prestige tremendously enhanced.

THE WAR
WITH ATHENS
(357-346 B.C.)

In the meantime Philip had devoted all of his means to the conquest of the Thracian seacoast. Clever trickery, bribes, and quick action brought him such gains that Athens declared war in 357 B.C. But the Athenians were not sufficiently aware of the menace to take aggressive action. One Athenian saw the purposes of Philip and realized the threat. In 351 B.C., Demosthenes, the orator, made a vigorous attack on Philip in a speech known as the First Philippic, and endeavored in vain to arouse the Athenians. In 349 B.C. the Macedonians fell upon Olynthus and its neighbors. Though Demosthenes pleaded with the Athenians in his Olynthiac orations, little help was sent, and the cities were taken. Many of them were destroyed, their inhabitants killed or sold into slavery. By this victory Philip accomplished the first step in his rise to power. In 346 B.C. Athens made a peace with him which recognized his conquests and left him free to punish the Phocians.

THE PHILIPPICS

Demosthenes, realizing the necessity for peace, took part in the embassy which made it. But on his return to Athens he made a series of orations against Philip. So brilliant and so fierce were these speeches that invective orations ever since that time have been called philippics. The fire of the orator's eloquence aroused the people to momentary enthusiasm, but the spirit of earlier ages was lacking. They voted for war and large expeditions, and then failed to contribute money or to enlist. The small fleets and armies of mercenaries which Athens dispatched against Philip were often left unpaid. Not until Philip had continued his advance and, by appearing in the Bosporus, had threatened the Athenian food supply from the Black Sea was decisive action taken. Then a strong fleet was sent and Philip was driven back from the walls of Byzantium.

CHAERONEA
338 B.C.

Athenian power alone blocked Philip's path to empire. On the pretext of a sacred war against the little town of Amphissa near Delphi he marched south into Greece. Demosthenes rallied his countrymen and secured alliances with Thebes and a number of smaller states. The battle was fought at Chaeronea in northern Boeotia, in 338 B.C., where the citizen levies of Athens and Thebes were no match for the trained army of the Macedonian king. The deciding stroke, however, was the cavalry charge led by Philip's son, the youthful Alexander.

THE HELLENIC
LEAGUE

After Chaeronea, Philip held a congress at Corinth and organized an Hellenic League of mainland and island states, from which Sparta, pitifully weak but stubbornly defiant, alone remained aloof. Peace and order were to be established and maintained among the Greek states. Each state was to be independent, self-governing, released from the fear of encroachment or interference by other cities, and free to sail the seas as it chose. All attempts at revolution, the overthrowing of constitutions, executions or banishments contrary to law, forcible return of exiles, confiscations of property, abolition of debts, or emancipation of slaves for revolutionary purposes were strictly forbidden. Philip thus endeavored, by the terms of the treaty and the threat of reprisal, to bring to an end the political and economic unrest which had caused so much trouble during the preceding period. An offensive and defensive alliance with Macedon provided the basis for a combination under Philip's command for a war against Persia which was to secure Hellenic unity and to provide room for the settlement of the poor and the exiles. Already the march of the Ten Thousand had proved such an objective possible; Agesilaus had tried to bring it about, and the orators, particularly Isocrates, had pleaded for it with fervor. But in 336 B.C., when all was ready, Philip was assassinated at the instigation, it was rumored, of his wife, Olympias. The accession of his son, Alexander, ushered in a new age.

SPARTA AND ATHENS IN THE FOURTH CENTURY B.C.

SPARTA

ATTEMPTS
AT REFORM

Though Sparta was in a position of power during half of the period, its domestic history is one of decline. The treasure which Lysander had gathered and the tribute received from subject states were of no value to the simple agricultural city. Individual Spartans returned home wealthy, in violation of the law, but they could profit little from their wealth. Most of the money of private citizens was deposited in Arcadia and was lost after Leuctra. On the other hand, under the stress of war and of service overseas, many Spartans were reduced to the rank of Inferiors. Lysander's plans for revolution failed, and a conspiracy organized by an Inferior, Cinadon, in 398 B.C., was discovered and blocked. Conservative action by the council ended all thought of giving citizenship to Inferiors, helots or perioeci.

DECLINE OF
THE SPARTANS

The freeing of Messenia ruined many Spartans, and the disasters at Leuctra and Mantinea resulted in a severe loss in man power. A decline in the birth rate and the accumulation of land by Spartan heiresses, of which Aristotle speaks, were additional causes of decline. At the end of the period the Spartans in service numbered only seven hundred. Yet Sparta proudly refused to make peace or to join Philip's Hellenic League. The fall of Sparta and the breakup of the Peloponnesian League were disasters of the greatest moment, for they not only destroyed the structure which had been the military backbone of Hellas but made the Macedonian conquest sure and comparatively easy.

ATHENS

POLITICAL
RECOVERY

On the contrary, the story of Athens during this period is one of political recovery and economic prosperity. In 404 B.C. Athens found itself ruined by the loss of markets and slaves and by the destruction of the olive orchards. Politically she was under the cruel authority of the Thirty Tyrants. But Athens had too much vitality to remain in this position long. A band of democrats, led by Thrasybulus, seized Peiraeus, defeated the Thirty, and restored the democracy. After the leading oligarch, Critias, had been killed, a general amnesty was proclaimed. But Socrates paid the penalty for the sins of some of his students. Henceforth oligarchy was unthinkable in Athens, and the democracy was strengthened by a series of reforms. A code of laws begun in 411 B.C. was completed. To prevent bribery and the use of undue influence, minor changes were made in the administration and in the court system. For the purpose of official records the Ionian alphabet was adopted, a measure of great importance for the modern study of Athenian inscriptions.

STATE AID
FOR THE POOR

Advancing concepts of democracy demanded that the state should provide for its poor, the numbers of whom had been greatly increased by the decline in employment during the economic crisis entailed by the Peloponnesian War and the loss of the empire. The general rise in prices which took place during the fourth century was a heavy burden to the poor. Yet as Athenian citizens, they were felt to be entitled to participation in the political and religious activities of the city and to share in its wealth. During the later years of the Peloponnesian War a dole of two obols had been distributed among the very poor, and in the fourth century B.C. pensions were provided for indigent cripples. To secure political rights for the laboring class, pay was introduced for attendance upon the assembly, at first one obol, later three. To give them a share in the religious festivals, Eubulus secured the passage of a law which provided that the surplus income of the state be paid into the so-called theoric fund, from which two obols a day were drawn to buy tickets to the dramatic festivals for the poor. It was with the greatest difficulty that Demosthenes persuaded the people to stop this practice and devote all the means of the state to the prosecution of the war against Philip.

FINANCE The increased costs of government inherent in these policies and the cost of the fourth-century wars bore heavily upon a treasury which had lost its chief source of income—the tribute from the empire. To enable the state to meet these expenses recourse was had with startling frequency to the emergency capital tax, the *eisphora* (p. 219). To render collections simpler, after 378 B.C. the people were enrolled in associations called *symmories,* each of which was responsible for its share of the total amount. After 362 B.C. the three hundred richest citizens were called upon to advance the sum levied as a new form of liturgy (p. 219), to be reimbursed by later collections from the symmories. The burden of the trierarchy had become so great that similar associations were formed, each to finance a trireme. Some wealthy individuals, however, still earned repute by assuming the expense of outfitting boats. In this period the political leader of the state period needed, above all, to be a financier.

PROFESSIONAL COMMANDERS Perhaps the most striking political change in Athens was in the conduct of foreign affairs. With the development of mercenary forces warfare by land and sea had become more technical. As a result, the office of general in Athens became purely political and administrative, while the generals of the army were professionals hired for the war. In Iphicrates, who once succeeded in destroying a Spartan troop, the Athenians possessed a military leader of great skill; they also were fortunate in having such brilliant admirals as Conon and Timotheus.

THE INFORMERS Both their experience with the oligarchy of the Thirty
Tyrants and the attitude of the conservative rich
made the demos suspicious of their leaders and of men of wealth.
After the restoration of the democracy, we hear, accordingly, of many
impeachments and trials and of professional informers who lived by
blackmail. There is, however, surprisingly little evidence of convictions
or of wealthy families ruined by unjust persecutions. Indeed, the
stability of the Athenian people in their choice of, and obedience to,
their leaders in this age was notable. Though, like Plato, many of the
conservatives withdrew from politics, the democracy was well served
by a number of able administrators, particularly by such men as
Thrasybulus, Eubulus, and Demosthenes.

ECONOMIC Economic prosperity soon returned to Athens. Farm-
REVIVAL ing, to be sure, never quite recovered its earlier pre-
eminence after the despoliation of the fields and
orchards during the Peloponnesian War. The statistics that are available indicate a distinct movement from the country demes to the city.
Men of wealth acquired larger estates on which they began to introduce a three-field system and scientific methods of agriculture.

Athenian commerce revived rapidly as the maritime states returned, out of economic necessity, to their former allegiance. Trade
with the peoples of the shores of the Black Sea flourished, especially
with the cities and tribes of southern Russia. The reason for this was,
of course, the importance of the region to the Athenian grain supply.
As in the Age of Pericles, treaties were made with the kings of the
region, and their good will was so zealously fostered that many sent
their sons to Athens for education and at times made presents of grain
to the citizens of Athens.

The development of banks assisted the growth of commerce. The
money-changers first began to accept deposits of money and valuables
without interest for safekeeping. Since their occupation involved the
care of large sums anyway, the money-changers were able to render
this service. The next step was the payment of sums on order to creditors of the depositor and the transfer of credits on their books from
one customer to another. Finally, they were able to arrange for the
transfer of credits between financial centers. The money deposited
with them they loaned on interest to the state or to businessmen for
commercial transactions. Careful bookkeeping (usually done by slaves)
and an impeccable reputation for probity were the prime essentials for

the successful banker. The best known of these men was Pasion, a former slave, about whom we are told by Demosthenes. He had unlimited credit throughout eastern Hellas, and for his services to the state he received Athenian citizenship. An increase in the quantity of money due to the opening of temple treasures by loan or confiscation, to the circulation of large amounts of Persian coins, and to the working of the Thracian mines by Philip led to an increase of prices which bore heavily on the working class. Industry had increased as trade increased, but there was a tendency for larger establishments to employ slave labor exclusively. As a result, though wages rose, they did not increase as much as did the cost of living. The industrial class, on the whole, was less prosperous than it had been in the Age of Pericles, and the state, as we have seen, was forced to come to the aid of the very poor.

LITERATURE

The varied political and social interests of the age were reflected in literature, poetry yielding place to prose as the predominant form of composition, and individualism, developing under the influence of sophistic education, replaced civic devotion as the inspiration of thought. Athenians of the better class, who could afford the new education, came to pride themselves on the culture and refinement thus produced and endeavored to appear as an aristocracy of intelligence. Many of them withdrew from active participation in Athenian politics and spent their time in discussions of philosophic problems after the manner of Socrates. Others, however, continued in the service of the people and wrote or spoke primarily for them. The full development of the democracy and of the law courts made a high degree of training essential for the man who would take an active part in the life of the city, and from men so trained sprang the full flower of Athenian oratory. Still others, under the spell of Thucydides, wrote histories. In spite of the loss of political pre-eminence, Athens remained the center of intellectual activity for the Hellenic world, and to its school as teachers and students came the leading Greeks of the century.

POETRY The fourth century B.C. witnessed the end of Athenian poetry. Tragedies were still composed, but of such little originality or value, compared with the great masters, that none has survived. Aristophanes lived into the period, but he left politics alone and wrote on social issues. He made fun of women and their pretensions to power, and in the play called *Wealth* (*Plutus*) he disclosed what would happen if the blind god of wealth were made to see and visited men according to their deserts. After his time manners and customs became the subjects of comedy.

PROSE — Written prose, made possible by an increased supply of papyrus from Egypt and by the development of methods for the publication and distribution of books and pamphlets, became the form of literature characteristic of the period. Minds trained in science and in correct habits of speech and composition found it a more exact means of expression.

XENOPHON
(CA. 430-
CA. 350 B.C.)

The first literary man of the new age was Xenophon, an Athenian and a pupil of Socrates, whose memoirs he later wrote. Quitting Athens after the re-establishment of the democracy, he took a leading part in the expedition of Cyrus (p. 263). The *Anabasis,* which he wrote as a record of this trip, is considered one of the outstanding works in the realm of military history. Unable to return to Athens thereafter because of a sentence of exile, he spent the greater part of his life in the Peloponnesus, where he occupied his time in the composition of many works. His writings show the varied interests which he acquired from his teacher—history, education, household management, public finance, politics, and military affairs. His large historical work, the *Hellenica,* a continuation of the books of Thucydides, carried Greek history down to 362 B.C. It is a simple, direct tale, more the work of a journalist than of an historian, for he had little understanding of causes or of results and no sense of the underlying forces of history. His work reveals the influence of the Spartan point of view; for example, in deference to the feelings of his Spartan friends, he left out all mention of the loss of Messene, whose independence Sparta never recognized. His style was clear and entertaining, and he was at his best in the portrayal of personalities. In his devotion to the ideal of the city-state as an institution for the increase of virtue among its members and his belief in education as the only true title to public service, he represented the best features of his class and time.

ORATORY — With the exception of Xenophon, the writers of the age tended to specialize in one of the three branches of prose writing—oratory, history, or philosophy. The first was the ultimate product of Greek democracy. The frequent necessity of appearance before the law courts and the opportunities for expression in the public assemblies and for addresses before the throngs gathered at the great festivals gave rise to the greatest school of rhetoricians the world has known. Leading orators addressed the Olympic visitors or swayed the multitude in the assembly. Professional speech writers wrote pleas for the litigants to deliver before the courts and, on occasion and to the delight of the jury, appeared themselves.

LYSIAS (CA. 440- CA. 380 B.C.) The first professional orator, Lysias, was the son of the Syracusan Cephalus, who had come to Athens and grown wealthy as a manufacturer of armor. After he lost his property at the time of the Thirty, Lysias supported himself by writing speeches for others to deliver. His rhetoric was unadorned; his language, that of everyday life. Contemporary with him was the Chalcidian Isaeus, a resident of Athens, who applied his intellect to speeches dealing with cases of private law. The orations which these men wrote are valuable sources of information about Athenian law and social practice.

ISOCRATES (436-338 B.C.) The most influential teacher of rhetoric was an Athenian, Isocrates. He had studied under the great Sophist leaders of the Peloponnesian War period and about 390 B.C. set himself up as a teacher of practical wisdom. He wrote speeches as pamphlets to be read by other men, but he delivered none himself. He devoted the genius of his mind to solving the problems of the Hellenic world. At first he offered a program of federation in the *Panegyricus,* a speech to be delivered at Olympia in 380 B.C., in which he advised the union of all Greece, nominally under the leadership of Athens and Sparta, for war against Persia. Actually the burden of the speech was the right of Athens to command and the unfitness of Sparta. It was not without it effect on the formation of the Second Athenian Confederacy. He reiterated this theme in a series of later pamphlets which culminated in the *Panathenaicus,* in 339 B.C., in which he reviewed the past glories of Athens. Because he despaired of finding a leader in Athens he appealed without success to a number of outstanding men through all Hellas. Finally, he called upon Philip to organize a friendly alliance of all Greeks, to call a council in which the Greeks might deliberate under his presidency, and to lead them against Persia. His letter undoubtedly influenced the deliberations of the Congress of Corinth, which followed the battle of Chaeronea.

In the composition of his speeches Isocrates sought after musical rhythm and the balanced period; he is said to have spent ten years on the composition of the *Panegyricus*. His rules of style became the basis for later generations of orators and writers. As a teacher, also, he gained great fame, for from his school went orators, historians, statesmen, and generals to carry his influence with them throughout the Hellenic world.

DEMOSTHENES
(384-322 B.C.)

Athenian oratory reached its culmination in the speeches of Demosthenes. Deprived of inherited wealth by dishonest guardians, he trained himself in his youth in order to appear in the law courts against them. At the same time he secured a means of livelihood as a writer of speeches. Many stories are told of his assiduity. Practicing long hours, he steeped himself in the style of Thucydides. As a result, he became the most popular speaker in the law courts. Thereafter he devoted himself to the public interest, and among his many political speeches the most famous were the Philippics. Following the battle of Chaeronea he was voted a golden crown for his services to Athens. Charges were brought against the proposer of his award, and Demosthenes defended his friend in a debate with his great opponent, Aeschines. This speech, "On the Crown," is considered, from the point of effective argument and organization, the greatest of all pieces of oratory.

Estimates vary as to the value of Demosthenes' service as a statesman. To many he appears as the last champion of Greek democracy fighting a valiant battle against overwhelming odds; others have regarded him as a weak opponent of the progressive force of history. Nevertheless, the unquestioned courage of his stand against Philip has nearly always aroused the historian's admiration for him.

Demosthenes' rival, Aeschines, the professional speech writer Hypereides, and the statesman Lycurgus are also worthy of mention as able writers and makers of speeches.

HISTORY

After Xenophon, and under the influence of Isocrates history turned to rhetoric and to the search for exact information. Ephorus of Cumae, in Asia Minor, wrote in rhetorical style a universal history. In the same manner Theopompus of Chios continued Thucydides' work and wrote an account of the career of Philip. On the other hand, a group of chroniclers, of whom the greatest was Androtion, examined the past of Athens in great detail, discovering and systematizing the facts in works called *Atthides*. Of all these writings but few fragments survive.

PHILOSOPHY

PLATO (CA.
428-347 B.C.)
In the intellectual history of Europe two men, Plato and Aristotle, almost certainly rule supreme. Plato, a follower of Socrates, devoted himself first to recording the words of his master in a series of dialogues and in the celebrated *Apology of Socrates*. Later he established a school in the Grove of Academus, where he and his students discussed and developed philosophic concepts. His educational practice in his school, based on the theory that all knowledge is innate in man, adhered to the question-and-answer method which, instead of lecturing, draws out information already known and develops the power of clear and rational thought. He recorded the discussions in dialogue form, with Socrates always as the chief speaker. He presented a wide discussion in the philosophic field rather than any fixed system. "The object of our discussion," said Socrates to Philebus, "is not that my words may triumph over yours, nor that yours may gain the victory over mine, but that between us, we may discover the most perfect truth."

In this search for truth, intellectual freedom was for Plato the first necessity. Whenever in later history the minds of men have revolted against the bonds of authority, they have returned in spirit to Plato. His own search led him to the theory of "ideas," that is, the reality of the universal concept or ideal of which actual objects are but shadows.

His most famous work was the *Republic,* in which Plato, beginning with a discussion of justice, worked out in detail his conception of the ideal state. The concept of the Republic was based on the idea that the city-state was the best institution to achieve the perfection of man. Plato's state of about five thousand citizens was small enough to allow all to participate in its activities, and to be self-sufficient politically, socially, and economically, at the same time maintaining "the moral character of the state" and the code of social ethics which Plato emphasized. Since the state was to be governed according to a system of social ethics, its members should be subordinated as individuals to occupy that place in society where they could best serve for the good of all. Accordingly the mass of the people should provide industry; the warrior class defense; and the intelligent, by virtue of their special training and comprehension of realities, should rule. He was actually endeavoring to combine the best features of the intellectual freedom of

Athens with a system of control, derived in part from an appreciative study of Spartan institutions, which would render impossible the excesses of Athenian democracy.

Plato's thought has been described as vague and indefinite, with no sound explanation of the origin or nature of evil. Yet its influence was so great that ever since his time idealism, in one form or another, has been the basis of one of the major philosophic schools, and in certain political and scientific thinkers of the present generation there may be seen a definite trend in its direction.

The dialogues are masterpieces of dramatic form. Each has its setting from which the discussion flows naturally toward the chosen topic. The language is poetry without meter or rhyme. It is the high-water mark of Attic prose.

ARISTOTLE
(384-322 B.C.)

Aristotle, too, stands like a Colossus in the intellectual world. He was born of a Chalcidian family in Stagira in Macedon in 384 B.C. His father was a doctor, and Aristotle grew up in a scientific tradition and atmosphere. For twenty years he studied under Plato in the Academy. Thence he was called to Pella to be the tutor of the youthful Alexander. In 335 or 334 B.C. he established his school in a garden called the Lyceum in Athens, where he strolled as he discussed philosophic problems with his students. Because of this custom of walking his followers became known as the Peripatetics (walkers-around). After the death of Alexander in 323 B.C. he fled from Athens to Chalcis, where he died the following year.

For his subject he took the whole domain of knowledge, and he wrote books dealing with every branch of knowledge. In his lectures and his books he laid the foundations of scientific method and established the principles and the divisions of knowledge. The first step in his method was the study of knowledge already acquired. For this he collected the books of his predecessors and organized the first Greek library, the inspiration and model for the great libraries of Alexandria and Pergamum. The second step was observation and study. He and his students observed the actions of plants, animals, and heavenly bodies. To understand politics he studied and wrote the constitutional history of one hundred and fifty-eight Greek states. Of these compositions, only the constitution of the Athenians is in existence. Recovered from papyri in Egypt fifty years ago, it is almost, though not entirely, complete. From facts gathered by these processes he arrived at general conclusions inductively, and then by deduction applied his results to individual cases. In so doing he made use of his greatest contribution to knowledge, the creation of formal logic. However he said, "We must not accept a general principle from logic only, but must prove its application to each part, for it is in facts that we must seek general principles and these must always accord with facts."

He divided philosophy, or knowledge, into three groups according to purpose and further subdivided these groups into subjects. Within these subjects he established the categories of genera and species. The departments of our modern universities go back historically to the Aristotelian classification.

In the realm of philosophic theory he accepted the reality of the Platonic ideal but denied its separate existence. He defined the universal as that which a number of individual objects have in common but which exists in the individual object only. Every object, he taught, is composed of the four elements, earth, air, fire, and water, and has four causes, material, formal, efficient, and the final, or purposive, cause. Motion on earth he held to be rectilinear, therefore broken and productive of change; in the heavens, to be circular and therefore unending and perfect. He believed that throughout the universe is God, the efficient and final cause of all, Himself immovable who causes all else to move.

In the realm of human behavior, Aristotle treated ethics as a social and political problem rather than as an individual one. The determining principle of virtue is the "Golden Mean," or balance, which is based on reason and discoverable by intelligence.

In his political writings Aristotle showed himself a firm believer in the Greek city-state, but he maintained with Plato the idea that, to secure the greatest good for all, the state should be carefully regulated by law based on intelligence. He classified governments into monarchy, aristocracy, and "commonwealth," and condemned the perversion of these into tyranny, oligarchy, and democracy or rule of the majority, since these sought chiefly the good of an individual or of a group, and not the good of the whole state. He dealt similarly with the creative arts, particularly poetry.

During his lifetime he composed many books on a wide variety of subjects. Some of these he was many years in writing, and a few, like the *Politics,* remained unfinished at his death. Fortunately they were preserved, to dominate the learning of the medieval universities and to form the background of modern education. Continuing his

HOUSE ON DELOS

ERECHTHEUM

STADIUM

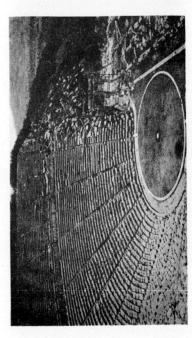

THEATER AT EPIDAURUS

TYPES OF GREEK ARCHITECTURE

MOURNING ATHENA

HEGESO

AN ATHENIAN YOUTH

DEXILEOS

ATHENIAN TOMBSTONES

Athens

work, his students collected libraries, made scientific investigations, and wrote treatises.

ART

ARCHITECTURE   The growing individualism and the democratic trend of the age reflected in oratory appeared no less clearly in the architecture and art of the period. In architecture, the luxuriant Corinthian capital is characteristic of the wealth and freedom from restraint which prevailed. Few noteworthy temples were constructed; cities began to build instead stadia and theaters of stone. The stone theater at Athens was completed about 340 B.C. by Lycurgus. A little later a majestic hall, the Telesterion, similar in style to the Egyptian hypostyle halls, was erected at Eleusis for the performance of the Mysteries. The most renowned structure, however, was the Mausoleum (ca. 350 B.C.), a tremendous creation to serve as a tomb for Mausolus, king of Caria, and his wife Artemisia. It was decorated with carvings by the sculptor Scopas.

SCULPTURE   Sculpture, too, showed a lessening of restraint. Scopas is renowned for the intensity of the emotion which his figures displayed. Praxiteles (fl. 360 B.C.), the greatest of all masters of the chisel, produced a series of beautiful portraits of divinities. His statue of Hermes, found among the ruins of Olympia, represents the youthful divinity in a moment of relaxation holding the infant Dionysus on his arm. On the face of the god transient human emotion is expressed rather than divine idealism. The marble has the texture of flesh; the god has become a supremely beautiful mortal. The same concept of divinity appears in the Aphrodite, which survives in a copy known as the Cnidian Aphrodite, and in the Satyr, immortalized by Hawthorne in "The Marble Faun." It is possible that the Aphrodite of Melos was produced under his influence. His statues are slenderer and more graceful than those of Polyclitus. Lysippus (fl. 335 B.C.) was a worker in bronze whose Apoxyomenos, Youth Scraping Himself with a Strigil, has survived in a marble copy.

PAINTING   Greek painting of the classic period reached its acme with the works of Zeuxis (fl. 425 B.C.), Parrhasius (fl. 375 B.C.), and Apelles (fl. 335 B.C.). These artists used the same four colors that Polygnotus used, but they advanced the technique of mixing and they also learned the use and value of shadow and gained in knowledge of perspective. They were cosmopolitans and temperamental.

Parrhasius signed himself "a friend of pleasure, but one who respects virtue, . . . the first of the Greeks in art." Zeuxis is said to have died from laughing at one of his own paintings. Pliny, the Elder, recounts this story of them.

The story runs that Parrhasius and Zeuxis entered into competition, Zeuxis exhibiting a picture of some grapes so true to nature that the birds flew up to the wall of the stage. Parrhasius then displayed a picture of a linen curtain realistic to such a degree that Zeuxis, elated by the verdict of the birds, cried out that now at last his rival must draw the curtain and show his picture. On discovering the mistake he surrendered the prize to Parrhasius, admitting candidly that he had deceived the birds, while Parrhasius had deluded himself, a painter.[4]

Apelles, the greatest of all classic painters, was a master of the use of light and dark and of illusion. According to Pliny he "painted for twenty talents, in the temple of Artemis at Ephesus, a portrait of Alexander holding a thunderbolt. The fingers seem to stand out and the thunderbolt to project from the picture. The reader should remember that all this was done with four colors. . . . Skilled judges of painting prefer among all his works his equestrian portrait of Antigonus and his Artemis amid a band of girls offering sacrifice, a painting thought to have excelled the lines of Homer that describe the same scene. Further, he painted the unpaintable, thunder, for example, lightning, and thunderbolts."[5] His most celebrated painting, Aphrodite Arising from the Sea, was praised for its flesh tones, the beauty of figure, the rendering of waves and sea foam. Of the wonders of this art we have a few memories surviving in mosaics and frescoes of later periods.

CONCLUSION   The classical history of Greece comes to an end with the battle of Chaeronea in 338 B.C. Alexander the Great, son of Philip II, created by his campaigns a new world in which there was no room for Athenian democracy or the free city-state. Greeks of genius made many more contributions to civilization in the later periods, but the mainspring of their endeavors had changed. The old order of things had passed, and the age of the city-state had come to an end. With eyes blinded by local patriotism the Greeks had refused to look beyond the borders of their own community save with

---

[4] Botsford and Sihler, *op. cit.*, p. 560.
[5] *Ibid.*, pp. 565, 566.

the greed of conquest or the fear of subjection. The city-state was too small a unit to control effectively the forces and movements resulting from economic expansion. Instead of combining politically, the cities wasted their substance and impoverished their people by continual wars. Their failure to work out any intelligent or even possible plan of peace and union made the Macedonian conquest easy, and unification came, not as a voluntary and progressive measure, but at the order of a conqueror and as a burden of oppression. Whatever its weaknesses, the city-state had taught the world lessons which it has never forgotten. The Hellenes had contributed the ideals of political and intellectual liberty, standards of perfection in literature and art, the inquiring mind and the instructive tongue, the example of men who first dared to look frankly at the universe and with open minds to question it and their place in it. In the same dialogue quoted above, the *Philebus,* Plato summed up the quest of the Greek spirit. "If we may not approach the Good with the aid of one idea, then let us overtake it with three—beauty, proportion, and truth."

═ XV ═

THE HELLENISTIC AGE

HE classic period of the Greek city-state ended on the battlefield of Chaeronea in 338 B.C. when Philip of Macedon secured ascendancy in the Hellenic world. During the next period, Greeks followed the armies of Alexander and his successors over the Eastern world, and the two streams of cultures, Oriental and Hellenic, mingled. Under the influence of this fusion, the civilizations of the Greeks, the Asiatics, and the Egyptians were transformed. The cultures which developed are termed Hellenistic, and the period which is characterized by them is called the Hellenistic Age. While Hellenistic culture had an important influence on Rome and survived as the basis of Eastern civilization under the Roman Empire, the Hellenistic period itself may be considered as ending with the Roman conquest of Egypt in 31 B.C.

SOURCES

HISTORIES   The age is of fundamental importance in world history, since it was the Hellenistic and not the Hellenic culture which influenced the Romans and which they transformed and transmitted to the Western world. Our knowledge of it, however, is very fragmentary. Alexander kept a daily journal of his campaigns and carried historians with him to record his achievements. Many of his generals wrote memoirs. Later historians wrote of his successors, the wars which they waged, and the kingdoms which they founded. All of these are lost save for scattered fragments. For Alexander's life we are dependent upon writers of the Roman Empire, a rhetorician, Curtius Rufus, who lived in the first century A.D., the biographer, Plutarch, and Arrian, an officer of Hadrian, who wrote the Anabasis of Alexander. For Alexander's successors there is the work of Diodorus,

288

the Sicilian, who composed his *Library of History* around the middle
of the first century B.C., and the brief summaries of late Roman writers
who made epitomes or abridgments of classic works. There is fuller
information about the Greek cities and leagues, because Polybius included, in his account of the Roman conquest, their history during the
period of Rome's entrance into the Mediterranean scene. Some pieces
of literature, particularly the work of the poets, and some records of
the achievements of the men of science have withstood the ravages of
time and are of use to the historian. Inscriptions and coins help to fill
the gaps.

THE PAPYRI — But the chief sources, only recently discovered, are
the Greek papyri in Egypt. In mummy wrappings
and in the dust heaps of the ancient villages of Egypt archaeologists
have found thousands of papyri, some written in demotic and others
in Greek for the Greek dwellers in the land of the Ptolemies. Lost
books of the classic period, such as poems of Bacchylides, of Alcaeus,
long sections of some plays of Menander, and Aristotle's *Constitution
of the Athenians,* have been recovered. Fragments of histories have
been found. Most numerous and important are papers which deal with
public and private life—official documents, laws, royal decrees, and
appointments, letters, and business and household accounts. These are
slowly unfolding the life of Egypt in the Greek and Roman periods.
Although they give information of the details of the life of the times,
they present as many new problems as they solve, and the story may
not yet be told with any certainty.

For centuries the Hellenistic Age was thought of as decadent in
literature and in art, unworthy of the attention of the historian. Consequently it was neglected in favor of the classic Greek and the classic
Roman. But in the middle of the nineteenth century the German historian Droysen drew attention to its real importance, coining for it the
word *Hellenistic.* Since then the discovery of papyri and inscriptions
have furnished such a wealth of new materials that with the researches
of scholars the age is slowly emerging from the obscurity in which it
was wrapped. It is now considered an age of advancement, of expansion, and of great importance and interest in the story of mankind.

ALEXANDER THE GREAT

THE YOUTH OF
ALEXANDER
The Hellenistic Age was ushered in by the campaigns of Alexander the Great. Of the youth of this brilliant son of Philip II and his Epirote wife, Olympias, many tales are told. Like his father, Alexander possessed shrewdness and an ability at cold calculation, and, like his mother, a vivid, glowing, romantic imagination. His tutor, the great Aristotle, trained his mind and imbued him with a wholesome regard for Greek culture. Homer was his boyhood god, and he longed for such a poet to sing his praises and for fame for himself equal to that of Achilles. He displayed his mettle as a warrior when, at the age of eighteen, he led the victorious cavalry charge at Chaeronea in 338 B.C. He was but twenty when his father's death put him into power and left him to expand and execute his father's plans. Philip had probably planned the conquest of only Asia Minor; Alexander enlarged the program until he reached distant India.

ALEXANDER'S
CONQUESTS
The joy of the Greeks at their seeming liberation by the death of Philip and by the accession of a boy of twenty was short-lived indeed. Alexander set his house in order in Macedon, and when Thebes, led on by a false rumor of his death, revolted, he swept down upon that city and ruthlessly destroyed it.

In the spring of 334 B.C. he began his campaign by the invasion of Asia Minor. A daring charge across the Granicus River gained him a victory over a Persian force composed chiefly of Greek mercenaries. The rest of the year was spent in freeing the Greek cities of Asia Minor and in securing control over the interior of Anatolia. The battle of Issus (333 B.C.) in Cilicia resulted in the destruction of the Persian forces and gained him entry into Syria. A series of sieges and assaults gave him possession of the coast cities, the siege of Tyre, which lasted ten months, being the most famous. The climax of this campaign was the conquest of Egypt, which fell without a blow. Alexander entered Memphis, then marched down the Nile and founded the great city of Alexandria, destined to supplant both Tyre and Athens as a commercial center. From Alexandria he took a dangerous trip into the Libyan Desert to the shrine of Zeus Amon in the oasis of Siwah. There the priests hailed him as the son of the god Amon and hence the legitimate ruler of Egypt.

THE CONQUEST
OF THE EAST
With the seacoast safely in his hands, Egypt under his control, and the rear of his army thus thoroughly protected, Alexander advanced to destroy the Persian Empire and to make himself King of Kings. In 331 B.C. he defeated the Persian host at Arbela on the royal road from Sardis to Susa. Darius fled and was later assassinated. Babylon, Susa, and Persepolis were taken, and the great wealth of the Persian rulers fell into Alexander's hands. As if in token of the ending of the history of Persia, the royal palace at Persepolis was burned in the course of Alexander's revels. Not yet satisfied, Alexander turned into the mountains and subdued the satrapies and monarchies as far as the Caspian Sea. Then he marched south into India, where he crossed the Indus and defeated the great king Porus. When his troops refused to go farther south with him, he turned back and followed the Indus to its mouth. Thence he dispatched a fleet to seek and study the water route to the Persian Gulf and the mouths of the rivers, while he himself led the army through the Gedrosian Desert to Susa and Babylon.

Safe in Babylon he began to regulate the organization of his vast dominions and to plan the conquest of Carthage and the West. But the hardships of his campaigns and a wound which he had received had weakened him. Moreover he had wasted his strength in revels, so that when in 323 B.C. he fell ill of fever, he died at the early age of thirty-three.

ALEXANDER'S EMPIRE

ALEXANDER GOD
Before his death Alexander had begun the organization of his conquests and revealed in part the conception which he held. The civilized world was to be united into one vast empire of which he, Alexander, was to be the divine ruler. In Egypt he was Pharaoh, son of Amon-Re; in Persia he was the successor to the god-given authority of the great kings. He demanded of the Greek city-states that they list him among the gods, possibly, as has been suggested, that he might control them without violation of the Greek tradition of political autonomy. From his followers he demanded the honors due a god, particularly prostration on entering his presence. To the Persians such obeisance presented no difficulties, but to the Macedonians and Greeks, independent in spirit, it was an intolerable burden. Several of Alexander's best friends and advisers fell athwart the conqueror's wishes and lost their lives as a result.

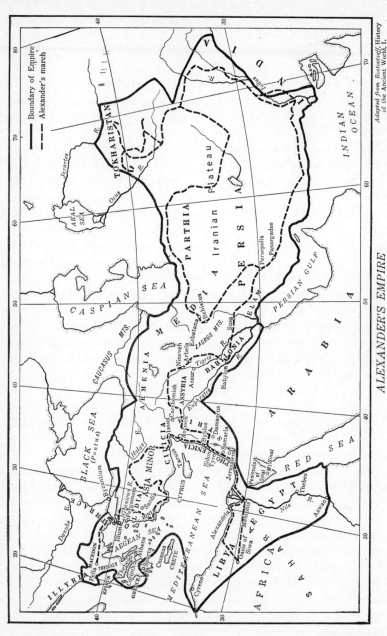

ALEXANDER'S EMPIRE

Adapted from Rostovtzeff, History of the Ancient World, I.

In this manner the concept of the god-king was introduced to the Hellenic world. How much Alexander's action owed to Egyptian and Oriental precedents, how much to Greek hero worship, and how much to contemporary philosophical ideas can hardly be determined. For some years the Anatolian Greeks had been paying divine honors as a compliment to such men as Lysander, and Alexander's claim may have seemed merely a further extension of such honors. The god-king idea, however, became a powerful force in both politics and religion in the Hellenistic world and the predominant unifying element in the Roman Empire.

UNITY OF EMPIRE

Unification of the empire was to be secured by the establishment of Greek culture as the official standard and by the combination of Macedonians, Greeks, and Persians into one race. Alexander himself had married Roxana, a Bactrian princess. Several of his generals followed his example, and ten thousand of his soldiers took Asiatic wives.

To establish Greek culture Alexander founded Greek cities in all sections of his empire from Egypt to India, the most famous of them being Alexandria in Egypt. This act served to provide an outlet for the surplus population of the motherland, but as civilizing forces, the cities were a failure. In charge of the satrapies Alexander appointed Persians, along with Greeks and Macedonians, reserving military command to the last-mentioned. This scheme also was unsuccessful, and the Persians were replaced by followers of the king. When thirty thousand Oriental youths were equipped and trained in the Macedonian fashion for the army, the Macedonian veterans mutinied. Special honors were given to placate them, and the use of Oriental troops was abandoned after Alexander's death.

Finally the confusion following Alexander's untimely death, and the subsequent division of his empire among his generals accomplished the ultimate ruin of his grandiose plans.

None of Alexander's measures had been able to produce complete unification, political, racial, or cultural. The amount of fusion which took place varied greatly between the major divisions of Egypt, Syria, and Mesopotamia. In Egypt and Syria, where there were large numbers of Greeks, Hellenic culture combined with Oriental ideas and customs, especially in religion. There was, moreover, some intermarriage among the peoples, particularly among the lower classes. But in Mesopotamia and its hinterland, Greek influence was slight, and although the later Parthian rulers (p. 300) assumed a veneer of Hellen-istic culture, the Greeks themselves were rapidly swallowed up in the vortex of other peoples.

THE WARS OF SUCCESSION

The fifty years which followed the death of Alexander were filled with the utmost confusion. There were intrigues and wars in which Olympias, mother of Alexander, Cleopatra, his sister, and other women had a share, along with the generals of the conqueror, and after them, their sons. At first attempts were made to preserve unity under regents for the posthumous son of Alexander and Roxana and for Alexander's half-witted brother, Philip Arrhidaeus. After the failure of these re-gencies, Antigonus, the One-eyed, made a brilliant attempt to secure control over the empire. In the course of his wars the famous siege of Rhodes by Antigonus' son, Demetrius, the City-taker, occurred. The other generals combined against Antigonus, and he was defeated and killed at the battle of Ipsus in 301 B.C. Seleucus, cavalry commander under Alexander, tried to unite Asia and Macedon, but he was killed by the son of Ptolemy almost at the moment of victory. When the wars had dragged to an end, the empire had fallen apart into three great kingdoms, Egypt under the Ptolemies, Asia under the successors of Seleucus, and Macedon under the descendants of Antigonus, as well as a number of smaller states kept alive by the rivalries of the great powers. Egypt and Asia contended for the control of Syria; Asia and Macedon were rivals in Asia Minor and Thrace; Macedon and Egypt endeavored to maintain control of the Aegean. This three-cornered struggle continued until Rome entered the field and became master of them all.

A SURVEY OF THE HELLENISTIC WORLD

ATHENS A survey of the Hellenistic states will reveal the ex-tent and the character of this world into which Rome was soon to enter. We may properly begin with Athens and the Greek motherland. From Philip after Chaeronea and from Alexander after the destruction of Thebes, Athens had received the signal favor of im-munity from interference. Alexander was even constrained into with-drawing his demand for the surrender of the anti-Macedonian leaders.

If this favor was due to his desire for the assistance of the Athenian fleet, it was rendered in vain.

Throughout Alexander's life, the city remained prosperous but quiescent. The pro-Macedonian Phocion, a man renowned for his probity, took the place of Demosthenes as a leader of policies. In charge of finances was Lycurgus, orator and financier of great ability. Under his direction the finances were well handled and public buildings, docks, and arsenals were maintained and improved. Against his rival, Aeschines, Demosthenes defended his anti-Macedonian policies ably in the great oration on the crown. When Harpalus, one of Alexander's treasurers who had embezzled and fled, came to Athens with funds to stir up a revolt, he was stopped and his funds were seized by the Athenian government. Demosthenes, accused of accepting bribes, was tried, found guilty, and heavily fined by the Council of the Areopagus. There is still doubt, however, of his guilt; he may have been the victim of political trickery. Nevertheless he fled into exile, where he remained until the death of Alexander brought him back to Athens.

A coalition of the Greek states was formed and a war for independence, known as the Lamian War (323-322 B.C.), was started against Antipater, regent in Macedon. At first the Athenian general Leosthenes was victorious, and Antipater was bottled up in Lamia. The death of Leosthenes, however, wrecked Athenian hopes. The Greeks were defeated at Crannon, and Antipater descended upon Athens. The anti-Macedonian leaders were put to death; Demosthenes took poison to avoid capture. The constitution was revised in favor of the well-to-do, and Athenian democracy was finished. A Macedonian garrison was stationed on the hill of Munychia. From 317 to 307 B.C. the city was ably controlled by the philosopher Demetrius of Phalerum. In 307 B.C. it passed into the hands of Demetrius, the City-taker, who was hailed by the Athenians as a liberator. For the succeeding generation Athens was the spoil of the wars of the generals until, after a last attempt at freedom, the Chremonidean War (266-262 B.C.), it passed into the power of Macedon. With that war the great political history of Athens came to an end.

SPARTA   Meanwhile Sparta had fallen upon evil days. The loss of man power in the battles of Leuctra and Mantinea, as well as the decline of military prestige, had been a serious matter to the state. When Epaminondas freed Messene, many Spartans were deprived of the means whereby they made their contributions to the public tables. The number of Spartans declined until there were but seven hundred in full possession of civic rights. Still Sparta refused to join the Hellenic League under Philip and Alexander.

After a brief and unsuccessful revolt in 331 B.C. Sparta sank into weakness, and the ancient system of training was neglected. Then in 244 B.C. Agis IV, the king (p. 310), came forth with a program of reforms to re-establish the ancient glory. The land was to be redivided; some of the perioeci were to be enfranchised; and the ancient Lycurgan discipline was to be enforced once more. The program failed when Agis was put to death in 241 B.C. for treason.

His son-in-law, Cleomenes, was more successful. By the use of vigorous methods and supported by mercenary troops, Cleomenes carried the reform movement through in 226 B.C. When he endeavored to restore Spartan power in the Peloponnesus, however, he found opposition in Aratus, general of the Achaean League, who, rather than yield, appealed to Macedon for help. In 222 B.C. Antigonus Doson defeated Cleomenes in the battle of Sellasia. The Spartan fled to Egypt, and the old regime was restored. In 207 B.C. revolution broke out again under the leadership of Nabis, who made himself tyrant, robbed the well to do, abolished debts, redistributed the land, and freed many of the helots. After his death his work was undone by the leaders of the Achaean League, and Spartan history ended in the utter ruin of the community.

THE AETOLIAN LEAGUE

The real power in Greece during the Hellenistic Age was in the hands of the Aetolian and Achaean leagues. The Aetolians had been a backward folk during the classical period of Greek history, organized in tribes and living in scattered villages in northwestern Greece. In the latter part of the fourth century B.C., however, they emerged with a well-developed federal union of city-states, among which there was potential exchange of citizenship. Each year two assemblies of the League were held in which all citizens of the member states might participate.

These assemblies, which voted on questions of peace and war and elected officials, possessed real power of control over the affairs of the

League. A council of one thousand was established, with its membership distributed among the cities in accordance with the number of troops furnished to the army. From this body an executive committee of thirty was chosen. At the head was a general, assisted by a hipparch, a secretary, and seven financial stewards. The cities were independent in local affairs, but the central government maintained full control over foreign affairs, wars, alliances, command of the army and direction of such matters as the uniformity of weights, measures, and coinage. As new cities were added, they were given full rights of citizenship with the old. This created a powerful and well-knit group. The League extended to the west, secured control over Delphi, gained great prestige by the defeat of a Gallic raid, and finally, in alliance with Macedon, controlled northern Greece from sea to sea.

THE ACHAEAN LEAGUE

The Achaean League was an ancient body composed of the little and insignificant states along the southern shore of the Gulf of Corinth. Its organization was similar to the Aetolian: an assembly of all citizens over thirty years of age met once a year; the cities were represented in a council according to their population; a general who could be re-elected to office only every other year was the chief executive; a board of ten advised the general. As in the Aetolian League, the central government controlled external relations and the uniformity of standards within the cities. To this the League added the idea of the guarantee of a stable government which would provide security for its wealthy citizens and prevent economic and political revolution.

The League became important when, in 251 B.C., Aratus led his city, Sicyon, to membership, and became the dominating force in the organization. He was elected to office every other year, with friends whom he could control as generals during the alternate years. Under his guidance the League expanded to take in Corinth, Arcadia, and eventually the whole northern Peloponnesus. Its conservative leaders were shocked and frightened by the social program of Agis and Cleomenes, and when, in addition, Cleomenes blocked Aratus' path to power, the latter laid aside his consistent policy of resistance to Macedon, invited Antigonus to end the Spartan menace, and surrendered control of the Peloponnesus to him.

MACEDON

Nowhere was there worse confusion in the years following Alexander's death than in Macedon, as one general after another endeavored to secure the throne of the victorious state. In the midst of the disorder there appeared a horde of Gauls similar to the band which had raided Rome a century before. They plundered Delphi and killed one of the holders of the Macedonian throne. In 277 B.C. Antigonus Gonatas, son of Demetrius and grandson of the great Antigonus, defeated them and by his victory secured control over Macedon. Henceforth until the Roman conquest he and his descendants were kings in Macedon. They secured and maintained control over Greece and in the Aegean defeated the Ptolemies in naval battles.

Macedon was a strong military monarchy of some four million sturdy peasants. The rulers were generals who were recognized as kings by consent of the army. Unlike Alexander and the rulers of Egypt and Asia, they made no pretense to divinity; indeed they would have been unsuccessful had they tried. The state was financed by income from the royal domains, the forests, the mines, and from duties and tribute. Ultimately, it allowed itself to become involved in the affairs of Rome and paid the penalty of defeat.

PERGAMUM

For a brief period Thrace and western Anatolia were controlled by Lysimachus, who was defeated and killed by Seleucus at Corupedium in 281 B.C. Seleucus in turn was assassinated, and Thrace then became the property of Macedon. Western Anatolia passed into the hands of Philetaerus, secretary of Lysimachus, who had gone over to Seleucus with the treasure of Lysimachus. Philetaerus was allowed to establish himself as a petty ruler in Pergamum, and by judicious use of the treasure he extended his power. His nephew and successor, Eumenes, defended himself successfully against the son of Seleucus. Attalus I, who followed, defeated a group of Gauls who had penetrated Asia Minor, and in memory of his victory erected the well-known statues of the Gauls.

The kings of Pergamum claimed divinity while posing as democratic rulers. Their government has been called an organized machine for the accumulation of wealth. Scientific agriculture was practiced on the royal domains, and the manufacture of textiles and the production of pitch from the highland forests prospered under royal direction. To break the monopoly of writing materials which Egyptian papyri enjoyed, the preparation of sheep skins into *pergamentum* (parchment) was developed into a large-scale business. The city of Pergamum, famous for the great altar of Zeus, was regulated by a public health law of a modern nature. A great library was collected and schools of literature and philosophy were developed.

RHODES — Rhodes was one Greek city which maintained its independence and prospered under the new regime. From early times there had been three little towns on the favorite island of the sun god, Helios. Shortly after 400 b.c. the three towns united to form one city at the head of the island, where nature provided two magnificent harbors. Alexander favored the city and made it a treasury depository. After his death, it declared neutrality in the wars of succession, and when Demetrius ordered it to unite with Antigonus, it refused. A siege was instituted by sea, but the swift ships of the Rhodians ran the blockade and took in supplies furnished by Egypt. Assaults by land were repulsed. When Demetrius constructed a huge nine-storied wheeled machine, the *Helepolis,* equipped with battering rams, catapults, and stands for archers and slingers, and moved by thirty-four hundred men, a Rhodian engineer turned the sewage of the city into its path. Demetrius gave up the siege after ten months, and thereafter all respected Rhodian neutrality. With the spoils from the Helepolis Rhodes erected a colossal statue of the sun god at the entrance to the harbor. This famous Colossus of Rhodes, one hundred and five feet high, had stood only a few years when it was destroyed by an earthquake.

Rhodes was the chief port of call for all ships sailing between the east and the west. In one year, a 2 per cent port tax on its transit business brought great wealth to the city. Its fleets became guardians of the sea and suppressors of piracy. When Byzantium in 220 b.c. endeavored to tax ships passing through the Bosporus, Rhodes, interfering to protect the freedom of the seas and its own commercial interests, punished the presumptuous city. Many cases were submitted to the neutral city for arbitration, which developed and enforced the Rhodian law of shipwreck dealing with salvage, taken over later in Roman law. Rhodes became famous for its school of philosophy, much visited by Romans, and for its sculptors, who produced colossal statues and the renowned Laocoön.

DELOS Another island community which gained advantage under the new regime was Delos. This island, sacred to Apollo and once the center of the Ionian amphictyony, then the meeting place and treasury of the Confederacy of Delos, had been consecrated by the Athenians, who removed all dwellings and made it into a sacred place. After it gained its freedom from Athens in 314 B.C. it speedily became an important city. Its central location among the Cyclades, its small but well-sheltered harbor, and the wealth of its temple, always a favorite depository for men of wealth, gave it great advantages. Beautiful houses were built on its hillsides and fine porticoes and halls in its market place. Merchants and artisans from the Greek lands and from the Orient flocked there in such numbers that there was a house famine during the middle of the third century B.C. It became the chief market for slaves. When the Romans abolished its 2 per cent export and import duty after 168 B.C. and made it a free port, Delos' trade and prosperity surpassed that of Rhodes.

Recently excavated by the French School at Athens, its buildings afford a fine example of a Hellenistic city, and its inscriptions, particularly the temple accounts, provide much information about the economic conditions—prices, rents, wages, and rates of interest—of the Hellenistic Age.

SELEUCID ASIA Asia, the largest of the succession kingdoms of the original Alexandrine Empire and occupying most of the area of the Persian Empire, passed definitely in 301 B.C. into the hands of Seleucus, cavalry commander under Alexander. He was the cornerstone of the resistance to Antigonus, was one of the victors at Ipsus, captured Demetrius in 285 B.C., and defeated Lysimachus in 281 B.C. Under his successors the large and widely scattered domains tended to break into pieces. Not only Pergamum but Bithynia, Pontus, and Cappadocia became independent kingdoms in Asia Minor. In the East a number of independent states were formed, and the plateau of Iran was held by the Parthians, whose kings claimed to be successors to the Persians. Southern Syria was the subject of contention between Egypt and Asia, with the latter finally victorious. In 222 B.C. Antiochus III, surnamed the Great, became king. He recovered much of the eastern territory, defeated the Ptolemies in a great battle at Raphia, and reestablished the power of Asia in Anatolia. Further advance brought him into unsuccessful conflict with Rome. From that time dated the collapse of the great Seleucid Empire.

THE KINGS　　　The Seleucid kings claimed power over thirty million people of many nationalities, scattered over a million square miles of territory. The unifying force in this great empire was the worship of the king. To the Orientals he was the vicar of the gods and successor to the kings of Persia. To the Greeks he was the descendant of Apollo, founder and patron of the Seleucid Empire. The Seleucids took such titles as *Theos* (God), *Soter* (Saviour), and *Epiphanes* (God Manifest). The empire was divided into many small satrapies in which civil, financial, and military powers were carefully separated. Local government of the natives was in the hands of officers of the king or of native rulers. The Greek communities were given constitutions and governed themselves. The administration was financed from a land tax, duties, and gifts, and from the large royal domains. Much of the land remained in the possession of the ancient temples and some in the hands of the Persian nobility. Most of the noble estates of the older regime, however, were handed over as possessions to the Greek city-states.

SELEUCID CULTURE　　　For the Seleucids, as for Alexander, civilization meant Hellenism. Hellenization was therefore a program of unity. Many cities were founded, Seleucus alone establishing some sixty—Seleucia, Antioch on the Orontes, Apamea, and Laodicea being the most famous. Seleucia, on the Tigris, took the place of Babylon as the great city of Mesopotamia. It is said to have had a population of six hundred thousand. Greatest of all was Antioch, capital of the empire, with a population of half a million Greeks, Syrians and Jews. The Persian road and postal system was maintained. The Royal Road ran from Sardis to Antioch, crossed the Euphrates by a bridge at Doura, where a flourishing town developed, and continued to Seleucia. A fleet was maintained on the Persian Gulf, and close connections were established with India where the great emperors, Chandragupta and Asoka, reigned.

In the attempt to spread Hellenic culture, Greek law was advanced, Greek gods were worshiped, philosophy and science studied, and theaters and stadia erected. At that time Greek curiosity led to a revival of interest in the old cuneiform literature and in Chaldean divination and astronomy. By the side of Apollo flourished the Great Mother, Ishtar, with her religious prostitutes. But the Greeks in the interior were being slowly absorbed by the native population. Loss of real contact with the motherland, whence sprang inspiration, broke down their Hellenism, and all attempts to Hellenize the Orientals failed. The effort of Antiochus IV to Hellenize the Jews led to open revolt and to the establishment of the independent Maccabean kingdom (p. 476). The Seleucid Empire was too vast, too unwieldy, and too diversified to be united successfully into a permanent structure. The Parthians in the east (p. 300) and the Romans in the west (p. 376) delivered the deathblows.

THE PTOLEMIES IN EGYPT   Our knowledge of the history, the administration, and the social life of Ptolemaic Egypt is richer than for any of the other Hellenistic states, because of the abundance of papyri and because of the literary and scientific pre-eminence of Alexandria. Egypt was the richest and most long-lived of all the succession kingdoms. Alexander appointed a Greek from Naucratis, Cleomenes, as financial administrator in 332 B.C. This able man organized the tax system of Egypt along Greek lines and in 330 B.C. gained great wealth for himself by cornering the grain market. He shut down on the export of Egyptian grain, bought up the crop, being careful to pay well for it, and then sold it abroad at famine prices.

In 323 B.C. Ptolemy was made satrap in Egypt. The year following the death of Alexander, Ptolemy murdered Cleomenes and seized his treasure. But in the wars of succession Ptolemy played a minor part. He had no ambition except to be recognized as a ruler of Egypt where, in 305 B.C., he assumed the title of king but rejected the offer of regency. He aided Rhodes against Antigonus, annexed Cyrene, endeavored unsuccessfully to hold southern Syria, but established himself in the Aegean by sending grain to the island states in a famine year. For this deed he received the title of *Soter,* "saviour." Ptolemy Philadelphus and his sister wife, Arsinoe (283-246 B.C.), followed their father in power.

Under these rulers and their successor, Ptolemy Euergetes, Egypt gained its greatest power since the days of Thutmose III and Ramses II. For a brief period the Ptolemies controlled Syria and the coast of Asia Minor; their fleet dominated the Aegean and the Hellespont; their money stirred up the Chremonidean War and enabled the Achaean League to hold Macedon at bay. However, Macedonian naval power proved too strong for them in the Aegean. On the mainland Aratus betrayed the Greeks to Macedon at Sellasia (p. 296), and Ptolemaic influence in Greece was completely destroyed. At the same time they lost in Asia when Antiochus III recovered Syria in the battle of Raphia in 217 B.C., a battle in which the fourth Ptolemy, Philopator, used native Egyptian troops. Egypt began to decline, and the kingdom became a protectorate of Rome with decadent Ptolemies ruling there until the dynasty passed in the blaze of the glory of the great Cleopatra.

The ruling Ptolemy was accepted by the native Egyptians as Pharaoh, divine son of Amon-Re. He bore in hieroglyphs the five names of the ancient kings, and from the time of Philopator went through the ancient ceremonies. Old temples were repaired or enlarged and new ones built upon whose walls inscriptions were cut and pictures carved of the Ptolemaic Pharaohs in ancient garb and style. The Ptolemy was acknowledged by the Greeks as a god-king, successor to the divinity of Alexander, whose tomb stood in Alexandria.

Under the king were the vizier, the directors of finance, the chief justice, and a host of secretaries organized into an elaborate bureaucracy. The ancient division of the land into nomes and into smaller subdivisions of districts and villages was maintained under Egyptian officials. By the side of the natives, however, were Greek military and police magistrates who overshadowed them and soon took their place. Finances were in Greek hands. Separate systems of courts for the Greeks and the Egyptians and mixed courts for cases which involved them both were established. The Ptolemies did not follow the policy of urbanization pursued by Alexander and the Seleucids. In fact, Alexandria was the only important Greek city. The Greeks and the Jews who thronged into Egypt were settled in the villages under separate corporate organizations of their own, which they managed under the watchful eye of the central administration.

The government was supported by produce, excise, sales, and poll taxes. In addition there were a number of state monopolies, particularly banking, and the manufacture of paper, perfumes, leather goods, and oils, all of which were farmed out under careful supervision. Foreign trade was likewise in the possession of the Ptolemy, and protective tariffs were levied on olive oil, wines, and woolens to protect the royal profits. Greek administrative ability put the governmental machine in order and kept it under such careful supervision that no more complete system of regimentation has ever been seen. The status of every individual, the condition of every piece of property was carefully defined and recorded. Local administration was directed to the full development of the economic wealth of the land, and Egyptian foreign policy was motivated by commercial ends—the promotion of trade with the Aegean, with Syracuse and the West, with Syria, and with distant India.

As of old, the land and all it produced were the property of the king, but granted by him to his subjects and classified according to its terms of grant—the royal domains, the sacred land of the temple, land in grant or gift to officials, nobles, and private citizens, and cleruch land, which was given to soldiers. The Greeks who became farmers seem to have controlled the land as their own; some were able to establish great estates, while the natives were, for the most part, serfs. Greek genius applied itself to farming, to manufacturing, and to exploiting the commercial wealth of ancient Egypt. While still clinging to the old lines of activity, it improved ancient methods, expanded the markets, and created extraordinary wealth.

ALEXANDRIA The center of Egyptian glory was the great city of Alexandria with its broad Canopic Way, lined with palaces, and its museum and library, its harbor and famous Pharos lighthouse. A large, self-governing Greek colony occupied one quarter, and a similar group of Jews another. The wealth, the literature, and the science of the world met in this city of Alexander.

THE WEST The history of the western Greeks followed the careers of three leaders—Agathocles, Pyrrhus, and Hiero. Out of the confusion which followed the ultimate failure of Timoleon's settlement of 338 B.C. (p. 271), an able tyrant, Agathocles (317-289 B.C.), rose to power in Syracuse. He regained control of Dionysius' empire in Italy and Sicily, fought with Carthage, and invaded Africa. In the last enterprise he was unsuccessful, and peace was made again on the basis of the division of Sicily between the powers. When Agathocles died, Syracuse once more collapsed.

In 281 B.C. Pyrrhus, king of Epirus, entered Italy on the invitation of Tarentum (p. 347) but with dreams of a great western empire. After his first battles with Rome he turned to the conquest of Sicily. Here he won some successes, but his methods and plans displeased the Sicilian Greeks and they failed to support him. He returned to Italy, was defeated at Beneventum, and returned to the East to become king of Macedon for a brief period.

Trouble with mercenaries, the Mamertines, in Messana, led to the choice of Hiero (269-215 B.C.) as king of Syracuse. This wise man handled the affairs of his city well during the long war which followed between Carthage and Rome. He entered into close relations with Egypt, organized his lands on the Ptolemaic model, and imported the papyrus plant which still grows wild in the marshes near modern Siracusa. His successor broke with Rome during the Hannibalic War, and Syracuse became the possession of Rome.

Alexander had carried Macedonian power and Greek civilization from the Aegean to the borders of India. The unity of his empire was dissipated by his successors in the wars which they waged with each other, but out of the final settlement emerged three great powers, Egypt, Asia, and Macedon, and the little kingdom of Pergamum. Athens and Sparta, leading states of the classical period, declined and in their place, as centers of political power, stood the Achaean and the Aetolian leagues. Rhodes, Delos, and Corinth succeeded to the commercial position once held by Athens, while the newly founded cities of Antioch and Alexandria became the commercial centers of the East.

HELLENISTIC CIVILIZATION

HELLENISMUS In this widespread Hellenistic world two currents of civilization, Greek and Oriental, met and mingled. Though they refused to blend and become one, nevertheless they acted upon each other like chemical reagents. The stronger element, however, was the Greek. For most Greeks the city-state, whether one of the older cities or one of the colonies in the Oriental world, remained the center of loyalty for the individual. At the same time the world was bound together by a sense of unity, the product of the expansion of Hellenism. Greek religion, Greek art, and the ever-present Greek artistic and dramatic festivals drew the Greeks together, while the bond was completed by the spread of a common language—not the literary Attic prose of Plato, but the *koine,* the spoken language of the common man. Philosophers talked of *homonoia,* a union of minds: "The educated man is a citizen of the world." After contact with other peoples they were ready to say that "Above all nations is humanity." The leagues and the great kingdoms were in a measure expressions of these concepts. "There are many cities, but they are all one Hellas." The wide use of arbitration in the settlement of disputes, the exchanges of citizenship, the granting of honorary citizenship or of the titles of friend and benefactor, the development of legal uniformity and of a recognized body of commercial law, the universal welcome to the Dionysiac artists who traveled around giving dramatic performances—all of these and more were at once the symptoms and the products of *Hellenismus.*

THE CITIES Though the independent city-state might be declining, the number and size of cities were increasing. Everywhere the Successors had founded new cities, some of which attained astounding size. Alexandria, Seleucia, and Antioch approached or even passed the half-million mark.

Rhodes, Delos, Ephesus, and Corinth grew into large and wealthy emporia. In these cities wealth ruled, for Greek democracy had gone with the passing of the greatness of Athens. Wealth, however, respected neither family, tradition, nor sex. The new alignment of society was rich and poor, not aristocrat and commoner, oligarch and democrat. Women of wealth who so desired were able to secure freer participation in public life; higher education was open to them; many secured election to public office and some were voted honorary citations.

Greek intelligence showed itself to good advantage in these cities. The newer settlements were carefully laid out with proper attention to water supply, sanitation, and drainage. They were equipped with fine buildings in the market places, splendid temples, theaters, and stadia. Market commissioners regulated weights, measures, and prices. Schools endowed by the rich or supported by the city offered opportunities for education. Many cities hired doctors to tend the sick, and state aid or private benefaction often brought relief to the very poor. Religious associations, social and athletic clubs, trade and industrial federations provided companionship and gave individuals dignity.

THE GOD-KINGS The power of the god-kings spread over all. Upon them prosperity depended. In times of disaster they might be counted upon to come to the rescue, and thus earn the title of Saviour or Benefactor. They might not be offended, nor their will crossed, even by the older cities of the Aegean. Ever present was the hope that one day a god-king might right the wrongs, put an end to the injustices of the world, and bring universal prosperity.

COMMERCE In the economic world expanding commerce and localities specializing in agricultural and industrial products were the most striking features. Throughout the Mediterranean, trade developed north and west along the routes from Alexandria and Antioch. Egypt, Asia, and Macedon contended in wars for the control of these routes. Rhodes, jealous of her interests, attempted to preserve the freedom of traffic and to suppress piracy. Syracuse and Messana prospered because of their trade contacts with Egypt. Trade in the western Mediterranean was still in the hands of Carthage, while Ptolemies and Seleucids both turned to the East. The Seleucids established a fleet in the Persian Gulf, sent envoys to India, and maintained a prosperous traffic with that fabulous country. The Ptolemies reopened the canal from the Nile to the Red Sea, renewed the caravan route from Coptos to the coast, established several ports on the Red Sea and controlled an active trade in its waters with southern Arabia. The commerce thence with India was firmly and jealously held by the Arab merchants until the last century B.C., when direct contact was definitely established between Egypt and India. Much of the trade from southern Arabia passed north by land in the hands of the Nabataeans through their famous "rose-red" city, Petra, and thence to Alexandria, Gaza, or Antioch. The Ptolemies exploited the coast of Africa as far as Cape Guardafui. Silk from China reached the Mediterranean by way of India until after the establishment of the Han dynasty when, about 126 B.C., direct contact was established by way of Bactria and the overland route. So much silk came into the Mediterranean that the city fathers of Messana found it necessary in 91 B.C. to pass a law prohibiting the women of that city from wearing transparent silk dresses.

From the Far East came silk, pepper, spices; from Africa, ivory and fine woods. Arabia produced frankincense and myrrh. Gold was supplied by India, Nubia, and Spain; silver by Macedon and Spain. Copper, as of old, came chiefly from Cyprus. Egypt and the Black Sea area were the granaries of the world. Wool from the highlands and the purple dye from the shellfish kept Tyre and the Anatolian cities prosperous.

INDUSTRY Industry expanded and became specialized with the development of trade. Though in all the cities there were, as always, countless small shops which supplied local needs, establishments of larger size grew more and more frequent in the great cities. The royal monopolies in Egypt and Pergamum were organized for mass production and distribution, and many private men of wealth owned and operated large workshops. At the same time, there was much regional specialization: Egypt supplied linen goods, paper, glassware, and vegetable oils; Pergamum produced textiles and parchment; though Athenian pottery had lost its pre-eminence, Athens still controlled the Mediterranean market with her excellent olive oil.

HELLENISTIC SLAVERY There were no fundamental changes in the types of slavery and in the employment of slaves during the Hellenistic Age. Increased wealth added to the number of slaves in domestic service, and the growth of great estates in Sicily and Italy led to the expansion of agricultural slavery in the West. But in Egypt and in Asia the native systems of serfdom were an effective bar to the extension of slavery there. Industrial slavery was introduced into the newer cities, but the large number of free poor and the low rate of wages made it unprofitable and led to a general decline in its ·use. The sources of slaves remained the same: in spite of the efforts of Alexander and his immediate successors, prisoners of war were still sold; victims were still enslaved by pirates; debtors and exposed children still appeared in the market. As the slave trade became international in scope, with Delos as its chief center, the creation of new markets in Italy and Sicily led, in the Roman period (p. 381), to a westward shift in the traffic.

HELLENISTIC
LAW

Both the political and the economic structure of the Hellenistic world contributed to the development of uniformity in law: the kings rendered decisions for the peoples under their control; the leagues fostered conformity among their members; and the great extension of commercial transactions made the formation of a recognized if unwritten body of contractual law an absolute necessity. The request of states for commissioners from without to adjudicate suits with even-handed justice created a rather large group of lawyers who made it their business to study legal systems. The informal method which these men used in their courts led substantially to an interstate system of equity and to a general understanding of obligations. This body of law was taken over by the Roman jurists as the *jus gentium* (p. 432).

MONEY

Money of gold and silver was plentiful after Alexander had turned loose the flood of Persian treasure, with a resultant rise in prices and decline in interest rates. The worldwide character of trade led to an enlargement of banks and an extension of banking transactions greater in volume, if not more complex in character, than those of the fourth century B.C. (p. 277). Through surviving papyri the records of the state-owned banks of Egypt disclose almost all financial practices—deposits, checks, drafts, loans, and letters of credit. Many private banks in the Greek cities had international connections and carried on a widely diversified business. Curiously enough, as this financial skill developed, public finance in the cities reached a low ebb. They spent far beyond their income and borrowed so continually from temples or from bankers, pledging their revenues and the property of their citizens, that most of them were on the verge of bankruptcy and were constantly calling on wealthy citizens and friends for aid.

RICH AND POOR The economic activity of the period brought prosperity to many and enabled some to build fortunes far beyond the dreams of earlier times. Yet untold suffering was the lot of the poor. Far from keeping up with prices, wages actually declined. The competition of slaves and of the many poor dragged free labor down to the subsistence level until wages became so low that it was cheaper to hire freemen than to own slaves. Hence industrial slavery declined, and particularly in Egypt. Though the wealthy man was generous in his gifts to the state, he was far from liberal in the wages which he paid. That the conditions of the poor did not escape notice is demonstrated by the fact that some states, particularly Rhodes and Samos, distributed grain to the indigent; others acted at times to lighten the load of debt, and the philosophers planned ideal states in which poverty should be abolished.

The disparity between the classes and the growing burden of debt and of poverty produced a constant threat of social revolution in many of the Greek cities. Such a revolution actually took place in Sparta, initiated by Agis and executed by Cleomenes and Nabis (p. 296). The leaders of the Achaean League probably opposed these men because of their fear that, if successful, the revolutionary movement would spread to their states rather than because of a fear of the rebirth of Spartan power.

CULTURE OF THE HELLENISTIC AGE

Royal patronage, private wealth, and civic pride contributed in this period to the development of a culture which a common language and the growth of travel made universal. As demand arose, scholars, scientists, literary men, and artists traveled about, forming groups, especially in Alexandria, Antioch, Rhodes, and Athens. The departures of this period from the standards of purity, idealism, and devotion to the gods, in contrast to the glorious period of the fifth and fourth centuries B.C., have caused admirers of the classics to regard the works of the Hellenistic Age as decadent. Such a question of progress or decline is a matter of taste; each must answer it for himself. Certainly, excellence in technique and a universal appeal to the educated of the day, and at times even to the ignorant classes, were to be found in the works of the Hellenistic leaders of arts, letters, and thought.

SARCOPHAGUS FOUND AT SIDON AND KNOWN
AS THE ALEXANDER SARCOPHAGUS

OLD SHEPHERDESS   *Rome*   VICTORY OF SAMOTHRACE *Louvre*

THE DYING GAUL   *Rome*

HELLENISTIC ART

ARCHITECTURE AND ART

**THE HELLEN-
ISTIC CITY**
Architecture and art in the Hellenistic Age were essentially secular in character. Allusion has already been made to the careful planning and construction of a Hellenistic city. Sites were carefully chosen for the market place, the theater, stadium, gymnasium, baths, and temples; and, in checkerboard plan, their streets were laid out with attention to these sites. On three sides of the market were *stoae,* long colonnades, usually in two aisles with rooms behind and sometimes with two stories. Theaters and stadia were equipped with stone seats. The temples of the age, of which the most famous was the temple of Apollo at Didyma near Miletus, were large and elaborately decorated, the ornamental Corinthian capital being preferred to the older Doric and Ionic. Though still simple in style—an inner court surrounded by rooms in one or two stories—private houses were much more lavish and elegant than were the houses of the classic period. Walls were adorned with pictures in stucco or painted on the plaster, and the pavement of the court contained elaborate and beautiful mosaics.

SCULPTURE
Sculpture demonstrated a complete mastery of technique and of subjects. Lysippus (ca. 330 B.C.), favorite sculptor of Alexander, bridges the period between the great artists of the fourth and of the third centuries B.C. Greatly idealized portraits were carved of the leaders of the age and of the great men of the past, and idealized figures represented the cities. The Fortune of Antioch, for example, is a beautiful statue of "a gracious and charming woman with a pensive face, seated on her mountain with the river-god Orontes at her feet; she was fully draped and wore a turreted crown . . . and held a palm leaf in her hand." [1] A long line of unveiled Aphrodites of great beauty followed the famous Aphrodite of Melos. Statues of shepherdesses, fishermen, boxers and wrestlers, and children were popular. The Rhodian school of sculptors sought for colossal effect; the tortuous Laocoön and Toro Farnese belong to the period of the decadence of this school. The sculptors of Pergamum displayed marvelous technical skill, a thorough knowledge of anatomy, and an extraordinary ability at realism in the famous statues of the Dying Gaul, and the Gaul and His Wife, remnants in copy of a great group carved to

[1] Tarn, *Hellenistic Civilization,* p. 261.

glorify the first victory of Attalus I over the Gauls. Most beautiful of all the Hellenistic works of art were the glorious Aphrodite of Melos, the graceful Apollo Belvedere, and the noble Victory of Samothrace.[2] In the latter Victory has just alighted on the galley's prow, bearing in her upraised right hand what is probably the victor's crown. The wind is sweeping through her draperies and as one looks up at her in the Louvre today she seems to be floating through space on her out-stretched wings.

PAINTING

The painters of the Hellenistic Age were masters in the handling of line and color, securing effect by means of realism and the expression of emotion. Where earlier painters had chiefly painted portraits, the Hellenistic artists either painted landscapes or gave their scenes backgrounds of natural scenery or of architecture. Scenes of daily life—sometimes brutal, often vulgar—and even pieces of still life were popular. The wealthy acquired collections of paintings and hired artists to adorn the walls of their houses with pictures. Of all this art, however, only a few echoes have survived in mosaics and in the later frescoes of Pompeii and Herculaneum.

INTELLECTUAL
LIFE

The intellectual life of the Hellenistic period was noteworthy for the production of books and the formation of libraries. Since the production of papyrus, under the royal direction of the Ptolemies, was plentiful, and slave copyists were numerous, books could be produced and sold at fairly low prices to a large reading public. Libraries were established not only in the great centers but in many of the smaller cities as well. The famous library at Alexandria is said to have amassed a total of seven hundred thousand rolls, and that at Pergamum, two hundred thousand. The great masters of the past were copied, read, and studied, and the output of the authors of the age itself was most varied and prolific. Drama, poetry, history, philology, science, mathematics, philosophy, and religion—in short, all branches of human knowledge and intellectual activity—were represented in the Hellenistic period.

DRAMA

The drama was never more universally popular. Every city apparently had its theater, and traveling groups of actors, the Dionysiac artists, went from place to place, putting on favorite plays of the great dramatists. Probably the texts which have survived are descended from these actors' collections. Tragedies

[2] The date of the last is doubtful. Possibly it was erected by Antigonus Gonatas to celebrate his victory over Ptolemy II at Cos (ca. 258 B.C.).

were written but, like those of the fourth century B.C., they were of such little consequence that they have completely disappeared. Comedy received a fresh impulse from the Athenian Menander (fl. 300 B.C.), fragments of whose plays have been recovered in the Egyptian papyri. In exquisite language, he composed comedies of manners, plays of society dealing with love intrigues, or dramas about exposed children who by chance become slaves in their own families, rescue their kindred from difficulties, and are at last recognized. These plays had great influence on the Romans, Plautus and Terence. In style and in content they are far different from the plays of Aristophanes. For the common folk mimes and plays were produced, many of them indecent, dealing with incidents of daily life. Of these a little sketch written by Theocritus and dealing with the adventures of two women in Alexandria at the Feast of Adonis has survived.

POETRY   The poets were masters of all kinds of verse. The Alexandrians, in particular, employed the older verse of Alcaeus and Sappho and experimented with a wide variety of exotic meters. Particularly popular was the short epic, or epyllion, which dealt usually with some local myth. Apollonius of Rhodes composed a long, rather dry epic poem on the subject of the Argonauts. The astronomer Aratus of Soli employed epic verse to describe the stars in a poem which became the model of Vergil's *Georgics*. These epics and epyllia were written chiefly by scholars and did little more than display the erudition of their scholarly composers, who vied with each other in producing short, witty epigrams or in writing love poems or epitaphs for their friends or for men of older times.

The idylls, another form of expression in vogue at the time, were short but graceful pictures of life. Masters of these poetic forms were Callimachus of Cyrene and Theocritus of Syracuse, both of whom lived and wrote in Alexandria under the second Ptolemy. The poems of Callimachus were excellent in form and wording but were lacking in heart and substance; Theocritus, on the other hand, loosed his very soul in a series of pastoral idylls portraying in verse the fishermen, shepherds and lovelorn girls of his native Sicily. His poems have furnished inspiration and served as models for many later-day poets.

PROSE   Prose flourished under the dual impulse of rhetoric and science. Books of history and geography, travel accounts and memoirs, pamphlets, letters and stories, philosophic and scientific treatises made their appearance, some appealing to the learned, others to the lay public. The writer of Ecclesiastes, who lived during this period, fittingly remarks, "Of the making of many books there is no end, and much learning is a weariness to the flesh." In most of these works rhetoric dominated. The manner in which a fact was stated was more important than the fact itself, and contact with reality was frequently sacrificed to literary style. On the other hand, books which were strictly scientific tended to be difficult, dry, and almost unreadable. It is nevertheless a great tragedy that almost all of these many productions have been destroyed by the vicissitudes of time.

HISTORY The most important branch of prose was history. Many of Alexander's followers, notably Ptolemy, wrote memoirs or histories of their own period. Writers produced literary histories covering the period of the conquests and the struggles which followed, or dealing with particular phases thereof. On the other hand, scientific historians presented careful studies of their own states, such as the *Atthis* of the Athenian Philochorus. Some scholars, after collecting and studying inscriptions, wrote on the antiquities of the cities.

The greatest names in scientific history are Timaeus of Tauromenium (died 264 B.C.) who wrote, after careful study, a monumental history of the western Greeks; Hieronymus of Cardia, assistant of the first three Antigonids, who covered the period of the Alexandrian Wars; and Polybius of Megalopolis (ca. 198-117 B.C.), who recorded the history of Rome, and of the Greek leagues during the period of the Punic Wars and the Roman conquest of the East. Such fragments as we have of the first two we owe to Diodorus the Sicilian, who drew chapters from them for his historical library.

Of the forty books of Polybius, only the first five and fragments of others have survived. His philosophy of history is set forth not only by the character of his writing, but by his digressions when he turned aside to criticize previous historians for their shortcomings and to expound his own views. He agreed with Thucydides that history was a useful subject written for the instruction of future generals and statesmen. However, his concept of the universality of history gave his work a broader base than was inherent in the Thucydidean devotion to a period. Though in his earlier pages he alluded to "Chance" as a dominant force, his ideas of causation grew to such an extent that not only did he come to realize the importance of geographic and climatic elements, the significance of men and of institutions, but also to declare that nothing happens without a natural cause. He distinguished, too, between motive, cause, and occasion. He was most specific in his statements of the obligations of the historian, the first object of whose search must be the truth, for "if you take truth from history, what is left is but an idle tale." To arrive at the truth, he said, the first requisite is a careful study and criticism of all sources; the second is knowledge based on travel and on the scrutiny of the sites of the events described; and the third is that practical experience of politics and warfare which alone makes possible the understanding and explanation of history. Polybius himself had been active in the affairs of the Achaean League until captivity in Rome interested him in his subject and inspired him to commence his great work. He criticized his predecessor, Timaeus, as a bookworm historian, "When history is written by the book-learned without technical knowledge, and without clearness of detail, the work loses all its value. For if you take from history its element of practical instruction, what is left has nothing to attract and nothing to teach." [3]

Polybius' style was dry, matter-of-fact, uninteresting, and his composition lacked the artistry of Herodotus and Thucydides. Yet the greatness of his subject, his concept of history, and his devotion to his work place him in the front rank of historians of all times.

SCIENCE

Hellenistic thinkers made extraordinary advances in philology (a science which they created), in botany, biology, and medicine, in geography, astronomy, and mathematics. Their work, studied and expanded by scholars during the Roman imperial period, became the basis of knowledge during the Middle Ages.

Alexandria was the center of scientific achievement. The first Ptolemy founded the museum as a home for scholars who were subsidized by the government. "Fatted fowls in a coop," an envious rival called them. In this city the great librarians established the canons of literary criticism; they collected and arranged the epic poems and started the never-ending discussion of the Homeric problem; they issued texts with critical commentaries of the great masters; they

---

[3] These quotations are taken from the selections translated in Botsford and Sihler, *op. cit.,* pp. 646 ff.

studied grammar, style, and word-usage—they founded, in short, the science of philology.

NATURAL SCIENCE

Beside the philologists stood a great group of natural scientists, not all of whom were Alexandrians. Biologists continued the work of Aristotle. In Athens Theophrastus (ca. 320 B.C.) studied botany, and Ptolemy Philadelphus built in Alexandria a great zoological garden filled with little-known animals among which was a polar bear. Physicians contributed to the knowledge of drugs. Herophilus of Chalcedon (fl. 300 B.C.) learned that the arteries carried blood, not air, on impulse from the heart, learned the significance of the pulse in disease, and discovered the nervous system. He performed major operations, practiced dissection, and is said to have practiced vivisection on criminals furnished him by Ptolemy I for the purpose. Other physicians made advances in treatment and without the use of drugs cured many by dieting, massage, exercise, and baths. Popular medicine was still dominated, however, by magical cures effected in the temples of the gods.

GEOGRAPHY

Alexander's march had rekindled the interest in geography which Hecataeus and Herodotus had started. His admiral Nearchus (fl. 325 B.C.) wrote a treatise on his voyage from India to Babylon. Subsequently many exciting tales and descriptions of India were brought back from the court of Chandragupta by Megasthenes (fl. 290 B.C.). Another contemporary of Alexander, Pythias of Marseilles, sailing north along the coast of Europe to Britain and Jutland, learned there of the existence of the Arctic Ocean. The greatest of the geographers was Eratosthenes of Cyrene (275-200 B.C.), who lived and worked in Alexandria. He was a man of amazing versatility in every branch of knowledge, but his geographic studies were astounding. He drew a map of the known world in which he utilized parallels of latitude and longitude. Deciding that the earth was round, he measured the noontime shadows at Alexandria and Syene and then computed its circumference at 252,000 stades, probably 24,662 miles (the true measure is 24,857)—a remarkable achievement.

ASTRONOMY

The astronomers based their work on the discoveries of the long line of Babylonian, Egyptian, and Greek scientists who had preceded them. Aristarchus of Samos (ca. 310-230 B.C.) learned from earlier scholars that the earth turned on its axis and declared that the sun was some three hundred times larger than the earth. From these facts he evolved the heliocentric theory of the solar system many centuries before Copernicus. Unfortunately, his contention that the earth and the planets moved in circles did not accord with known facts, and his theory was rejected. Hipparchus of Nicaea (fl. 140 B.C.) offered in its place a complicated series of cycles and epicycles to explain the motion of the heavenly bodies. Learning much from the Babylonians, he explained, if he did not discover, the precession of the equinoxes, calculated the length of the year, and made a catalogue of the stars. His erudition made it possible for him to correct errors in the latitude and longitude of Eratosthenes' map.

Last in the succession of geographers and astronomers before the Roman Empire was Poseidonius of Rhodes (135-51 B.C.). This famous scientist journeyed to Gades to study the tides, attributing their cause to the wind but their variations to the phases of the moon. He calculated the size and distance of the sun and the circumference of the earth. Furthermore, he argued that a man sailing west could reach India. On this statement Columbus later based his hopes of a western voyage to India.

MATHEMATICS
AND PHYSICS

Mathematics kept pace with and made possible many of these studies. Euclid (fl. 300 B.C.) collected geometric theorems and prepared the textbook of geometry which was used down to the twentieth century and which is the cornerstone of all modern handbooks of geometry. Apollonius of Perge (ca. 250 B.C.) wrote a book on conic sections and began the study of trigonometry which Hipparchus further developed.

In mathematics and mechanics Archimedes (ca. 287-212 B.C.) towers over all the Greeks. He advanced the study of geometry, calculated the value of π, and began the study of calculus. On his tombstone was engraved the figure of a sphere within a cylinder. His law of floating bodies, based on his discovery of specific gravity and still known as Archimedes' principle, he is said to have discovered by noticing the water he displaced in his bath and to have jumped out and run home naked, shouting "Eureka" ("I have found it"). He invented the double pulley and the water screw, both of which are still in use. He understood the principle of the lever. "Give me where to stand," he declared, "and I will move the earth." He held a Roman force at bay with grapnels and, tradition says, with burning glasses. By the irony of fate, he died at the hands of a Roman soldier.

After his death some progress was made in hydraulics; and clocks, mills, and organs worked by water were invented. One scholar produced a catapult operated by compressed air, and Hero of Alexandria (fl. 100 B.C.) discovered the expansive power of steam.

That these scientific achievements were not put to actual use was due to two circumstances. In the first place, they were made by men who regarded themselves as philosophers and who thought it beneath them to apply their discoveries practically. (Even the inventions of Archimedes were partly incidental to his theoretical studies.) In the second place, labor was so cheap and so plentiful that machinery was unnecessary, unprofitable, and undesirable. In the period of the Roman Empire an inventor presented to Vespasian a road-making machine. The emperor thanked and rewarded him but put the machine aside with the remark, "What would I do with my poor people?"

PHILOSOPHY

It was to the problems of these poor people and their betters in a complex world that philosophers and religious teachers, following in the train of Socrates, addressed themselves. Men were but little individuals in an overwhelming cosmos, composed of great kingdoms, huge cities, and decadent communities. When a bad harvest or a cornered market in Egypt might ruin a good man in Greece, the well-being of an individual was no longer dependent upon his own labors but upon the will of a mighty king or upon a capricious providence. The old moral sanctions of the family and the state had been destroyed by the collapse of the state and by the migration of many families. Men everywhere, rich and poor alike, felt the helplessness of the individual. On all sides men were asking the question: "What must I do to be saved?" To this problem philosophy and religion endeavored to give an answer.

THE PHILO-
SOPHIC SCHOOLS Under such conditions philosophy became ethics with enough cosmology to explain or justify the ethical position. On one thing all philosophers were in agreement: the aim of living is the good life, which may be termed happiness or virtue. On the definition of these terms, however, and on the method of attaining the good life there was much disagreement. Out of the attempts to solve this problem arose many new schools of philosophy, while the old schools naturally declined. Aristotle's Lyceum, for example, survived its founder but a brief period, while the Academy of Plato devoted itself to dialectic and became barren as method asserted

its authority over content. Among the new schools the Cyrenaics taught that happiness was sensual pleasure. They were the true founders of the dictum, "Today let us eat, drink, and be merry, for tomorrow we die." The Skeptics in Athens denied the possibility of knowledge and accomplished nothing beyond an attack on superstition; their most illustrious exponent was Carneades, whom we shall meet later in Rome. The three most important schools were the Epicurean, the Cynic, and the Stoic, and these dominated philosophic thought to the close of antiquity and beyond.

EPICUREANISM   Epicurus set up his school in Athens in 306 B.C. To him the world was a soulless mechanism. Atoms flying through space swerve and meet to create life; they fly apart to cause death. Men are but a part of these. Since men have always believed in gods, then gods may well be, but they live apart in perfect happiness, and have nothing to do with men. Consequently all human hopes and fears, all prayers, charms, and magic arts are but idle fancy. Man, once convinced of this and thus freed from the weight of superstition, may raise his head from the earth and see it and himself for what they are, simply mechanisms. The chief end of life is indeed happiness. But, Epicurus taught, happiness is not sensual pleasure. On the contrary, it is negative: the avoidance of pain, an escape into a gentle, quiet world of the intellect, typified by the garden in which Epicurus taught and which gave its name, the Garden, to the school. It appealed, and has appealed since, to the few of strong intellect. But it furnished no salvation for the masses.

CYNICISM   To the masses the Cynics ministered. Antisthenes, pupil of Socrates, founded in Athens in the Cynosarges gymnasium the school of which Diogenes, whose name has become a legend, was the most famous exponent. The Cynics taught that the end of life is virtue; virtue is knowledge; and knowledge concerns oneself alone. All the conventions of society, all the ties of state and family are as nothing to the free individual. The cares and worries about friends, fortunes, reputation, and even daily living must be laid aside. Whatever is, is right; therefore take what comes. When Alexander the Great offered a boon to Diogenes at the Isthmian games, the philosopher simply asked the king to step to one side because the latter was keeping the sunlight from shining upon himself. Until late in Roman imperial times, the Cynics traveled, usually in pairs, carrying a message of endurance to the poor and simple. Their disregard of the amenities of life offended the rich and the intellectual, few of whom became Cynics.

STOICISM   The Stoics, taking possession of the best elements in Cynicism, developed a philosophy which swept the Graeco-Roman world. Zeno, a Phoenician from Cyprus, began to teach the Stoic philosophy in the Painted Porch (Stoa Poikile) in Athens in 302 B.C. His followers, Cleanthes, Chrysippus, and Panaetius of Rhodes, clarified and systematized his teaching. Stoic philosophy received from its founder a religious tinge and a missionary fervor. The world of inert matter, it taught, is animated by a divine fire which is God; all living and moving things partake therefore of the divine. God has established for the world, according to his divine and perfect wisdom, a perfect universal law. Virtue and therefore happiness depend upon obedience to that law. But the flesh is material and blunts the vision. Life, as a result, becomes a struggle to overcome the flesh, an upward climb toward virtue by means of knowledge. The truly wise man, said the Stoics, will know the law and be sincerely happy. To him affairs of the body and the problems of daily life will be of no importance when compared with matters of the mind and soul. He will understand that whatever comes must be endured as a part of the divine plan, and he will know that the inner man which is the mind can only be injured by itself. But the Stoic went further than that. Since all men partake of the same divine element, he argued, it follows that all men are brothers, and all are parts of one divine and universal state. Each man has, therefore, his obligations to his fellow men, his duties to this ideal fatherland. Like an actor, he is given a part to play on that stage which is the earth, and whatever part it be, he must play it like a man. When it comes his turn to leave the stage, he must go willingly and cheerfully. The Stoic insistence on individual moral growth and on the performance of duties in the world make it a practical, livable philosophy of never-ending value. It was a noble creed, but its appeal was essentially intellectual: the Stoic was but trying to save himself by the powers of his own reason. It was only natural therefore that the great mass of the people should turn from Stoicism and its rival schools to religion where they might find salvation by faith in gods and by the performance of ancient rituals.

'

RELIGION

THE NEW GODS The old gods of Greece had been divinities of the city-state. Philosophy and criticism had weakened their position, and their mythology had nearly destroyed them; but their real failure was due to the collapse of the city-state on which they had depended. The individual in a great world needed a more personal religion than they could offer him. Some men cast religion aside, sought no gods but gold and silver, and worshiped material success. Others worshiped *Tyche,* Fortune, Lady Luck, and sought to win her favors with charms and amulets or to learn her will by attending oracles, practicing divination, or reading the stars. While the power of the old oracles of Dodona and Delphi was declining, new oracles were springing up on every hand. Charlatans peddled amulets and books of magic charms and secret names. Astrology came from Babylon to fasten itself on the Western mind with a grip which has not yet been entirely broken.

The worship of the god-king provided a center of devotion and a hope of economic salvation. At the same time there came into the Greek world a flood of Oriental divinities whose appeal and promise of help was more personal and satisfying. Greeks going east readily identified the divinities of the lands to which they came with those of Olympus and worshiped them, but the Orientals settling in the Aegean brought their gods with them. While the Oriental rejected the Greek divinities, the Greeks, in their search for religious satisfaction, accepted what the Orient might teach. In every Greek community there appeared many little religious associations in which, as in the modern fraternal order, men found under the protection of a friendly deity brotherhood and dignity in a bewildering and humbling world. Such an association was the Jewish synagogue. The part which the Jews played in this Hellenistic world, however, we leave for later consideration (p. 475).

MYSTERY RELIGIONS The so-called "mystery religions" had the most universal appeal of all. These, basing their dogma and ritual upon ancient myth, by their initiatory rites awakened in their converts a sense of sin and of purification; they established an insistent order of elaborate ceremonials and a code of ethics; and they promised to the faithful the rewards of a glorious immortality. While Demeter continued to be worshiped at Eleusis,

Dionysus ranged the earth with renewed vigor. The dramatic festivals were in his honor, and his artists were everywhere in demand. Moreover, the Orphist Neo-Pythagoreans had dramatized the legend of his earthly life, death, and resurrection, and furnished to his worshipers the magic words by which they might escape the ever-turning and recurring wheel of life and enter into the Elysian Fields of eternity. In Egypt, Ptolemy I created a god, Serapis, out of a combination of Osiris, Apis, and elements of Zeus and Dionysus, associated him with Isis and Anubis, and set him up as the god of the Greeks in Egypt. He was a god of healing, a kindly god who protected his followers and led them to the fields of Yaru.

THE MOTHER GODDESS
Among the throng of goddesses, the most beloved were the mother goddesses. In Anatolia men and women prostrated themselves before Cybele, or Ma, and her divine son, Attis, and men mutilated themselves in her orgiastic rites. The worship of Cyprian Aphrodite inspired Theocritus' lovely ode on the mythical death of Adonis. But loveliest and greatest and most widely worshiped of the goddesses was Isis. Faithful wife and mother, herself, she presided over marriage and childbirth, and to the weary and worn she extended a mother's arms. Human beings found in her the culmination of all their desires. "I am all that is, all that has been, and all that shall be," she said in her ritual. Under the spell that she cast over the Mediterranean world Rome, too, was destined to fall.

CONCLUSION
Greek history draws to an end with the close of the Hellenistic Age and the Roman conquest of the East. The Greeks of the classic period had achieved greatness in their city-states, had taught the world the lessons of democratic government and of the nobility and power of man both as a citizen and an individual. Though the later period had seen the city-states decline, and though many had fallen under the sway of god-kings, the leagues had proved the advantages of federalism, and men had risen above local feelings of city and of race to concepts of cosmopolitanism and the unifying force of a world culture. The standard forms and principles of art, architecture, and literature had been developed and lifted to extraordinary heights. Philosophic studies had resulted in great products of human thought, in the advancement of science, and in the study of ethics. Continuing failure to solve the problems of unity and at the same time to preserve those civic and religious institutions which were

the mainspring of culture was perhaps the chief contributing force to the downfall of the Greek city-states. Yet the story of Hellenic culture does not end with the Hellenistic Age. There were Greek architects, artists, scientists, and men of letters of great ability under the Roman Empire. Greek influence on the development of the Christian Church was strong, and a genuine revival of Hellenism took place in the Byzantine period. Mingling with the currents of civilization in the Western world from the time of the Romans to the modern age, the Hellenic stream is still a potent element in our own culture.

$$\equiv XVII \equiv$$

THE RISE OF ROME

HILE the Greeks in the Aegean, in southern Italy, and in Sicily were attaining the heights of classical culture, a community on the banks of the Tiber in Italy was developing in the fire of tribal warfare and intestine strife those institutions and traits of character which made it the conqueror and lawgiver of the Mediterranean world and the civilizer of Western Europe. Within the space of five centuries Rome was to rise from insignificance to such power that it became and remained for centuries the center of civilization.

SOURCES

LITERARY SOURCES

The sources for the history of Rome are similar in character to those for the history of the Greeks. For the period of growth we are dependent upon the Roman Livy, and upon such Greeks as Polybius, Diodorus the Sicilian, Dionysius of Halicarnassus, Plutarch, and Dio Cassius. Other books which dealt with Roman antiquities, such as those of Varro and of Verrius Flaccus, survive only in fragments. For the late republic the historical works of Sallust and of Caesar, the orations, letters, and essays of Cicero, and other literary products help in filling in the details. Tacitus, Suetonius, the late writers of the *Historia Augusta,* and Ammianus Marcellinus provide us with the history of Rome under the empire, a history illuminated by the essays, letters, plays, and poems of the writers of the great ages of Latin literature. Commentaries on the law, now known chiefly from the Digest of Justinian's Code (p. 471), along with references scattered throughout the writing of other Romans, provide information about Rome's most enduring contribution to the world.

ARCHAEOLOGY   Archaeology contributes its substantial studies. There are remains, though few, from the early period—the cemetery and the Black Stone in the Forum, fragments of walls erected during the republic, foundations of temples and houses. For the later ages the remains of temples, arenas, theaters, arches, houses, statues, mosaics, and pottery are found in great abundance, not only in Rome but throughout the empire. The Italian government is at present engaged in uncovering the ruins of the imperial city and in pushing forward the excavations at Pompeii, Herculaneum, Ostia, and the many other Italian cities from which have come vivid pictures of Italian life. For this later period the great quantities of Roman coins supply much information.

INSCRIPTIONS   Inscriptions, however, are the chief aid to the Roman historian. Scant for the early republican period, they gradually increase in number and in value until under the empire they bring knowledge of events, of organizations, and of social and religious activities from every corner of the Roman world. For the Roman as for the Hellenistic period the papyri of Egypt give information about the administration and life of that vitally important land.

GEOGRAPHY

THE MOUNTAINS   Just as Egypt, Babylon, and Greece were influenced by their respective environments, so Rome shows the effect of the geography of Italy. The long, narrow, boot-shaped Italian peninsula lies northwest to southeast, with the Alps on the north, and Sicily at the toe. Its dominant feature is the range of the Apennines, which rises to the northwest behind Genoa, curves, in crescent shape, the length of Italy, and terminates in the mountains of Sicily. Along its western slope were many volcanoes. Those which lay to the north were active until about 1200 B.C., but since that time they have become extinct. To the south, Vesuvius, Aetna, and Stromboli still maintain their fires. As a result, while the basic rocks of the mountains are granite, limestone, and sandstone, on the western side there lies a deposit of volcanic rocks.

THE PLAINS   The mountains divide Italy into four parts. To the north is the broad fertile valley of the Po, protected against the cold winds of Germany by the Alpine mass. Because of racial differences and geographic obstacles this area was not con-

ITALY

sidered a part of Italy by the Romans of the republic. Instead it was known as Cisalpine Gaul, from the Celts or Gauls who occupied it during the fifth century B.C. On the east the mountains reach their greatest height and approach so closely to the Adriatic that their slopes and sandy coasts are adapted only for the raising of cattle. Southern Italy and Sicily face the east. Their history was bound up from very early times with that of the Greeks on the other side of the Ionian Sea. The fourth area, the coastal plain to the west of the Apennine curve, is the heart of Italy. Here lie the most fertile lands, the richest and loveliest regions. The plain is cut by transverse hills into the three sections of Etruria, Latium, and Campania, watered by the three fine rivers, the Arno, the Tiber, and the Volturnus, respectively.

AGRICULTURE Italy was destined by nature to agriculture. In contrast with the many inlets which tempted the Greeks to the sea, in all of its two thousand miles of coast line there are but two real harbors in Italy, the Bay of Tarentum and the Bay of Naples. Raw materials for industry were scanty: some copper and iron in Tuscany and in the island of Elba, and some clay suitable for pottery provided barely enough supplies for local needs. On the other hand, the mild and equable climate has a sufficiently wide range from north to south and from the sea level to mountain valley to favor the production of a variety of foodstuffs. The soil in the western plains, enriched by volcanic ash, was exceedingly fertile, particularly in Campania. The richness and the extent of the arable land in Italy are particularly noteworthy in contrast to the small plains and the poor soil of Greece.

On the farmer, however, the land made very definite demands. Although the soil was rich, it was young and thin, easily eroded, and quickly exhausted. When the torrential waters of the spring rains were allowed to course over the fields, when the working of the land was neglected, or the hills were bared of their trees, the farms were soon destroyed. The hillsides above Rome are covered with a network of ditches dug in early times to prevent this erosion. Further, the river beds were not large enough to contain the full waters of the rainy season, and, unless the water was controlled, the lower lands were consequently subject to floods. The basic volcanic rock was porous and absorbed great quantities of water which, as the land approached sea level, came out again to form great marshes, breeders of mosquitoes and sources of fever. Epidemics were therefore a constant menace to the peoples living along the coastal plain.

Thus to secure the great rewards of the land hard work was necessary. The Italian gods of agriculture were jealous gods, and the farmer's religious calendar was full of ceremonies designed to secure their favor. In fine, the lessons which the Italians learned from their land were the need for discipline and the values of conservatism.

"Beyond the Alps lies Italy!" The sunny skies, the mild climate, the fertile soil of Italy have always attracted outsiders. Over the Alps, whose northern slopes are gradual and easy of ascent, across the narrow Adriatic and the sheltered Ionian seas, from Africa by way of Sicily and the calm shallow Tyrrhenian Sea, have come wave after wave of peoples, to remain in and to be absorbed by this pleasant land.

THE PEOPLES OF ITALY

EARLY INHABITANTS

Throughout the long centuries from the first appearance of man in Europe down to the beginning of recorded times, Italy was inhabited. Flint tools of the lower Palaeolithic Age have been found on the hills, but as yet no traces have appeared of the finer tools and art of the later Old Stone Age. In the Neolithic period, men of Mediterranean stock entered the land, some from Africa by way of Sicily, where possibly there existed a land bridge. Others came by way of Spain and Gaul and approached Italy from the north. They lived in small round huts clustered in villages, farmed in crude fashion, tended their herds of cattle and sheep, worshiped the Earth-Mother, and buried their dead in pit graves.

The Bronze Age brought fresh invasions into the south and the north. Into the south came men from across the Ionian Sea. Ancient legends record Minoan contacts with southern Italy and Sicily; archaeological remains of pottery, of implements, and of beehive tombs indicate that this area had begun its long history of contact with the Aegean (p. 75). After the Minoans came the Greeks; hence the region came to be known as Magna Graecia, the history of which we have studied (pp. 132, 191, 270).

THE TERRE-MARE FOLK

The northern invasion brought into the Po Valley peoples of the Indo-European language group who had developed a distinctive culture. In their former home in the Alpine lake country or in the upper Danube Valley they had learned to live over water in houses built on piles, but the swifter streams of the Po and its tributaries would not permit villages of the lake-dweller type. The people nevertheless demanded for themselves dwellings built on piles and protected by water. Accordingly they laid out an area trapezoidal in form and surrounded by a moat filled with water deflected from a near-by stream. The dirt taken from the moat was piled up on the inside and strengthened with stones to form a rampart. Within the area thus fortified were placed piles on which platforms and houses were erected. The settlement was most carefully laid out in checkerboard fashion; a bridge across the moat led into a broad, main street which ran the length of the platform. Parallel to it were side streets and, at right angles, cross streets, the largest one of which lay in the center of the village. In an area in the middle of the eastern side circumscribed by a special moat was the dwelling of the chieftain and the site of the performance of religious ceremonies. The plan was strikingly similar to that of the later camps of Caesar's legions.

The inhabitants of these pile dwellings were farmers and herdsmen. They brought with them into Italy the horse and the wheeled cart, and they made excellent bronze tools and fair pottery. Their dead were burned; the ashes were placed in urns; and the urns were ranged side by side in a near-by area enclosed by its own ditch and wall. During the nineteenth century B.C. farmers south of the Po found that certain mounds on their lands contained soil of remarkable fertility which they called *terra mara* in Italian, plural *terre mare*. The finding of objects of bronze and of pottery in these mounds led to investigation and the discovery of these pile villages. The people who lived in them have ever since been called the Terremare folk.

As the Terremare folk moved south, they abandoned the pile villages and placed their houses instead on hilltops which could readily be surrounded with a moat and wall. Apparently, however, memories of the ancient village plan survived in military science until historic times.

The Iron Age culture, which is known as Villanovan, was introduced either by trade with central Europe or by a fresh invasion from the north. Its distinctive feature is a biconical or a hut-shaped urn for the ashes of the dead. Otherwise it seems a continuation and development of the older culture.

Our first literary information, approximately the fifth century B.C., shows us that Italy was occupied at that time by a diversity of tribes produced by these invasions and the consequent blending of stocks. In the mountains back of Genoa dwelt the Ligurians, descended from or related to the Neolithic peoples. The Po Valley was occupied in the fifth century B.C. by Celts who had come over the mountains from southern Gaul. At the mouth of the Po dwelt an Illyrian tribe, the Veneti. The eastern coast of Italy was likewise occupied by Illyrians who had crossed the Adriatic. Sicily still contained Elymi, Sicans, and Sicels, probably all remnants of the Mediterranean stock. The heart of the peninsula was in the possession of tribal groups descended from the Indo-Europeans but blended in varying degrees with the older peoples. These tribes are divided by modern scholars into two dialect-groups, the Latins and their neighbors in the valley of the Tiber and the hills of Latium, and the Umbro-Sabellian group, with the Umbrians to the north of the Latins and the many tribes of the Sabellians to the east and south.

Lack of unity and the absence of the knowledge of civilized ways made these peoples easy prey for more highly skilled invaders. Into the southern area came the Greeks; into western Sicily, the Phoenicians from Carthage; and into the valley of the Arno, the Tyrseni from the East who were to give that land the names it still bears, Etruria or Tuscany, from their Latin name, Etruscan.

THE ETRUSCANS

ORIGIN
The Etruscans were the first civilized people with whom the north Italian tribes came into contact. They attained a high level of culture and spread their influence over all the western and northern areas. Many features of their culture survived in later history, and archaeologists have found many remains of their occupation. Yet their origin remains a mystery. The questions as to who they were and whence they came have long been disputed among scholars. Ancient tradition, recorded by Herodotus, related them to the Lydians and brought them by sea from Asia Minor. Certain elements of their civilization show affinities with Crete and with Babylon. Their language, though written in Greek letters, cannot be translated, since it is related to no known tongue. Some argue that they were a native

people of Neolithic origin who developed their peculiar culture in Italy, but others claim that they came overland from the East. Most scholars today believe that they were one of the Aegean tribes dislodged by the invasions which brought the Dorians into Greece, and some connect them with the Tursha who accompanied the Peleset against Egypt in the days of Ramses III (p. 120).

ETRUSCAN CONQUESTS

Probably the Etruscans came by sea in small bands during the eleventh century B.C. and settled along the coast north of the Tiber. They reduced the natives to subjection and, while they adopted some elements of language and religion from them, for the most part they maintained their own culture. Sometimes joining smaller communities together to form one unit, they combined their cities into a league of twelve units. In the seventh century B.C. they expanded south across Latium into Campania, where Capua and Pompeii were among their settlements, but further movement in that direction was checked by the Greeks (p. 134). In the sixth century B.C. they moved north into the Po Valley and settled such towns as Bologna, Parma, Verona, Placentia, and Cremona. In both Campania and the Po Valley this expansion, though it was not organized conquest, resulted in the formation of leagues of twelve. Apparently Etruscan families with their retainers struck out in search of new lands and, with superior knowledge and better weapons, they were able to conquer, control, and organize native communities.

ETRUSCAN CITIES

In the founding of their cities they followed a careful ritual. A furrow was dug by a plow drawn by a cow and heifer, creating a sacred moat and wall. The plow was carefully carried over the places where the gateways were to be placed. Walls with arched gateways were raised within the sacred boundary and constructed with polygonal or rectangular stones carefully fitted together. Within, an area was set apart for the gods; streets were carefully laid out; drains were dug; and houses were constructed. These houses belonged to what is called the "atrium" style, the feature of which was a large room whose ceiling sloped downward in the center to draw the rain into a cistern which lay below in the room. Around this room were arranged smaller rooms with sometimes a second story above them.

ETRUSCAN LIFE In early times these cities were ruled by kings and later by groups of luxury-loving aristocrats. Their wealth came from the products of the land and from the iron of Elba and the copper of Etruria. They traded with the Carthaginians in Africa, with the Greeks in Italy and Sicily and, during the sixth and fifth centuries B.C., with Athens itself. As we have already noticed, more Athenian vases have been found in Etruria than in any other part of the Mediterranean. From the Greeks the Etruscans learned the alphabet, the phalanx type of military organization, and the basic principles of their art and temple architecture, though they almost certainly brought knowledge of the arch with them from the East. In fine arts they did beautiful work in terra cotta and in bronze. Of the former, a fine statue of Apollo has survived, and of the latter, numerous examples of utensils and of statuary.

The Etruscan aristocrats clothed themselves in dress of the Ionian fashion, wore fine jewelry, and admired themselves in bronze mirrors. They rejoiced in banquets and in gladiatorial games. Their women, freer than those of Greece, played a prominent part in society. When the nobles died, they were buried in chamber tombs richly adorned with pictures of banquets, of battles, and of monsters that filled the underworld.

Central in their religion was the triad, Jupiter, Juno, and Minerva. Their books of sacred lore contained the rules of ritual according to which they founded cities, measured land, opened and closed assemblies, summoned and purified armies, and learned the will of the gods from lightning, thunder, the flight of birds, and the condition of the entrails of sacrificial animals. Like the arch, liver divination was a certain sign of early relations with Babylonia in their eastern home. These ritualistic performances were powerful assets in holding the subject peoples in check.

COLLAPSE OF ETRUSCAN POWER When the Etruscans were at the height of their power, western and northern Italy lay at their feet. They combined with the Carthaginians to halt the Greek advance (p. 134) and they drove a colony of Phocaeans out of Corsica. They failed, however, to produce an organization stable enough to secure unified action by their cities. Within many of the communities they were never more than a ruling class surrounded by retainers and supported by serfs. Defeats by Aristodemus of Cumae at Aricia in 505 B.C. and by Hiero I of Syracuse at

Cumae in 474 B.C. cost them Campania. During the fifth century B.C. the Celts drove them out of the Po Valley. Native reaction deprived them of many Latin communities. The Romans, after they had learned the basic lessons of civilization from the Etruscans, expelled them from Rome and finally overwhelmed and conquered them. The Etruscans continued, however, as a wealthy, distinguished, and respected people, much sought after as soothsayers, until the days of the Caesars. Their place as the unifiers and civilizers of Italy was taken by the leader of the Latin peoples who lived just across the Tiber.

THE LATINS   The low hills and plains to the south of the Tiber were occupied by a blend of peoples in which the Terremare element was predominant. The higher hills which surrounded Latium in the east and south were occupied by the Sabines, Aequians, and Volscians of the Umbro-Sabellian stock.

The Latins placed fortified towns (*oppida*) on the hilltops, and digging hillside drains to protect the soil, they settled down to farm the land intensively. They were united by the worship of Jupiter Latiaris and by a league centering in the temple of Diana of Aricia and commanded in time of war by a dictator. Many of their towns were seized by Etruscan nobles in the seventh and sixth century B.C. and so were brought into the current of Italian commercial life. Though their trade was in the hands of the Etruscans or Greeks, about the end of the sixth century B.C. they threw off the Etruscan yoke and began a more vigorous, independent development.

THE EARLY DAYS OF ROME

SOURCES   No other period of human history of equal importance is so completely lacking in contemporary or even in trustworthy sources as are the centuries from the founding of Rome to her rise to importance in Italy. The Romans did not become history-conscious until they found it necessary to explain themselves to the Greeks. The first Roman annals were written by Romans in Greek about 200 B.C. after Rome had risen to supremacy in the western Mediterranean. Other annalists, who wrote in Latin, followed during the next century. Of all of these, however, only fragments have survived. The earliest consecutive books which have come down are those written in Latin by Livy and in Greek by Dionysius and Diodorus, all of whom lived in the last century B.C., but who depended for the most part on the works of the annalists. The problem which confronts the modern historian is therefore the nature and the authenticity of the sources which these earlier writers used.

Sources of a public nature were available, such as local traditions and records of the kings, lists of magistrates, of triumphs, and of extraordinary events, kept by the priests throughout the history of the republic; documents such as laws and treaties which were recorded on lasting materials; and institutions and customs, political and religious, which survived into later times. Much of the written material was destroyed about 390 B.C., when Rome was burned by the Gauls. Archaeological evidence indicates, however, that a good deal survived the catastrophe and probably much was replaced from memory. Private family traditions of great deeds were preserved in the *laudationes funebres,* speeches delivered at family funeral ceremonies. By 200 B.C., Greek mythmakers had been at work drawing the Romans into the framework of the Heroic Age. Poets, such as Ennius, and annalists also embellished their work by transferring to Rome stories from the Greek epic and even tales from Herodotus. Out of such material, these men created the history of Rome. Livy himself acknowledged the weakness of the sources on which he depended.

It was the discussion of these problems by a Dane, Barthold Niebuhr, in Germany in 1815 which started the modern school of scientific historical studies. During the nineteenth century rigorous criticism denied the historicity of the traditional account. Recent archaeological discoveries in and around Rome, along with excavations in the Aegean which have given the color of authenticity to Greek legends, have led many modern scholars to accept as correct the basic elements of the tradition. There is no general agreement among scholars, however, as to the extent to which the stories can be trusted or used as sources.

THE LEGENDARY STORY   The traditions have definite value, indeed, because of the way in which they exemplify the ideals of the men who wrote them, and because of their great importance in later literature. According to legend, Aeneas, fleeing from Troy with his father, his infant son, and his household gods, came, after many vicissitudes, safely to Italy. There he married Lavinia, daughter of King Latinus, and founded Lavinium. His son Iulus built the great Latin city, Alba Longa, whence his successors for twelve generations ruled over the Latin people.

THE FOUNDING
OF ROME

After three hundred years of peace, the twins Romulus and Remus were born to the god Mars by Rhea Sylvia. Exposed, suckled by a she-wolf and raised by a shepherd, they left Alba Longa to build a city on the banks of the Tiber. Remus was killed in a quarrel, and Romulus became the sole founder of the city on the Palatine which he called after his own name, Rome. The official date of the founding was fixed by later antiquarians as April 21, 753 B.C.

To secure men for his city Romulus opened an asylum on the Capitoline Hill for fugitives from other cities and secured wives for them by the celebrated "Rape of the Sabine Women." Inviting the Sabines to a festival at Rome, he ordered his men to select each for himself a Sabine girl and at a signal to seize and carry her within the city walls. According to the legend this resulted in a war which ended, after the intervention of the women, in the Sabines' settling in Rome.

Dividing the people into nobles, called patricians, and commoners, called plebeians, Romulus organized a senate of one hundred *patres,* fathers, from among the wisest patricians and an assembly composed according to the thirty *curiae,* or wards, into which he divided the city. For many years he ruled wisely. When he disappeared during a thunderstorm, it was believed that he had been taken to dwell with the gods; in fact later Romans said that the god Quirinus was really Romulus.

NUMA
POMPILIUS

After an interregnum of a year, during which Rome was ruled by senators chosen for five-day periods, the wise Sabine, Numa Pompilius, was elected as the second king. Advised by the Greek Pythagoras (who lived nearly two centuries later) and by the Muse Egeria, he established the civil and religious law. He divided the land among the citizens and consecrated the boundary stones; he established associations of artisans, drew up a calendar of festivals, forbade the making of images of the gods, ordained simple bloodless sacrifices of cakes and milk, assigned priests to the great gods, inaugurated the Vestal Virgins to guard the sacred fire, and appointed augurs to learn and explain the will of the gods. Numa built the temple of Janus, whose door was to be shut only during time of peace but always open when the Roman army was off at war. During his own reign the door remained closed.

TULLUS
HOSTILIUS

After Numa's death, the Romans chose for king a warlike man, Tullus Hostilius. During his reign occurred the war with Alba Longa, which was decided in favor of the Romans by the quick victory of three Roman champions, the brothers Horatius, over the Alban fighters, the brothers Curiatius. Alba was razed and its citizens were transferred to Rome. Tullus proved to be a wicked king and Jupiter destroyed him with lightning.

ANCUS MARTIUS

Ancus Martius, grandson of Numa, was then chosen to be the fourth king of Rome. He was a wise man and a peaceful one, but when the enemies of Rome forced him into war, he was victorious, adding many conquered peoples to the inhabitants of Rome. He built a wooden bridge across the Tiber, fortified the Janiculum Hill, and founded Ostia at the mouth of the Tiber, the better to work the salt mines.

TARQUINIUS
PRISCUS

During the reign of Ancus there came to Rome from Tarquinii a certain Lucumo, son of Demaratus, the Corinthian, with his Etruscan wife, Tanaquil. Under the name Lucius Tarquinius he became chief adviser to the king and guardian of the king's sons. When Ancus died, Tarquinius contrived his own election. Known to history as Tarquinius Priscus, that is Tarquin the Elder, he was a great warrior who conquered the Latins and defeated the Sabines. He subdued the Etruscans also and received from them the insignia of power, the crown and scepter, the ivory chair (*sella curulis*), the purple toga, and the *fasces,* axes bound in bundles of rods. He constructed the great sewer which drained the marsh between the hills and there laid out the public square, the Forum; he also began the construction of the temple of Jupiter on Capitoline Hill. Assassins hired by the sons of Ancus murdered him. Tanaquil, Tarquin's wife, by a trick then secured the election of Servius Tullius, concerning whose birth and childhood miraculous stories were told.

SERVIUS
TULLIUS

This good king established peace and alliance with the Latins in token whereof festivals were held at a temple built to Diana on Aventine Hill. He built a strong wall around the hills of Rome. To secure justice for the common people and to provide a more effective army for Rome, he reorganized the state and divided the land into thirty wards or tribes. Taking a census of the people, he enrolled them in five classes according to their wealth. In accordance with these classes men were summoned to the army, voted in the assembly, and paid their taxes. Some say that Servius planned to abrogate his power in favor of a republic. But wickedness triumphed. His daughter Tullia and her paramour, the son of Tarquin, contrived his death. This younger Tarquin then seized the power as a tyrant, in contravention of the laws and without the consent of the senate and the people.

TARQUINIUS
SUPERBUS

Tarquin, surnamed the Proud, though a great ruler, was destined to be the last king of Rome. He finished the construction of the great sewer, the buildings of the market place, and his father's temple to Jupiter. He established Roman power over Latium and warred with the Volscians in the hills to the south. In 509 B.C. his son violated the noble Lucretia, wife of Collatinus, whereupon the army, led by Brutus, expelled the Tarquins and established the republic as Servius had planned it.

CRITICISM
OF THE
TRADITIONS

This body of tradition contains some probable elements of truth, many possibilities, many myths, and many stories invented to explain later names and customs. The Aeneas story, a good example of Greek mythmaking, pleased the Romans because it brought them within the circle of Greek civilization. Romulus himself is clearly an eponymous creation, the very steps of which can be traced, and the stories of his reign are attempts to explain the origin of later institutions and customs.

There is a possibility that the remaining kings are historical; in any event Numa, Tullius and Ancus are very ancient names. Such a reform as the arrangement of the calendar, attributed to Numa, would almost certainly bear the name of the king who carried it out. Sicilian historians might well have known and recorded the names of the Tarquins, the last family of kings. The name of Servius Tullius is so definitely associated with constitutional reforms and with the early wall that he seems to be historical. Furthermore, all of the traditions of wars are so definitely localized in Latium and fit in so perfectly with what is known of later history that they can hardly be considered creations of later writers. On the other hand, there are many chronological impossibilities such as the story of Numa's relations with Pythagoras. The younger Tarquin must have been seventy years old when he murdered Servius, over ninety when he was expelled, and well past one hundred when he died.

THE GROWTH
OF ROME

Something of the story of the foundation and growth of Rome may be learned from archaeological evidence and topographical considerations. In the twelfth or eleventh century B.C. a village of herdsmen and farmers was erected on Palatine Hill, which was fortified with a moat and an earthen wall. An increase in numbers led to settlements on neighboring hills and to the formation of a league called the *Septimontium*. Sabine words in Latin, and interment in the cemeteries instead of cremation prove that Sabine peoples had a share in this expansion. Then, almost surely under sixth-century Etruscan rulers, the valley of the Forum was drained by the great sewer, the city was enlarged into "Four Regions" and fortified, with the Capitoline as the citadel and the residence of the chief god. Probably at this time Rome first received its name, which means "the river city." At the same time Etruscan rituals and symbols of power were introduced. The traditional story and the presence of a temple of the Latin Diana on the Aventine combine to indicate that Rome gained control over the Latin League. It acquired sufficient economic importance so that Carthage made a commercial treaty with it in 508 B.C.[1]

It is impossible in the present state of our knowledge to equate the traditional and the topographical accounts of the city's growth and to admit or deny absolutely the truth of the legends.

SOCIAL
ORGANIZATION

The traditions and the presence in later times of earlier institutions and customs make it possible to trace the social, political, and religious organization of Rome in the regal period. The earliest unit of social organization among the Romans seems to have been a kinship group called the *gens,* and every Roman had a gentile name, *nomen,* before which he placed his personal name, *praenomen*. When the *gentes* grew and became divided into families, a third name, the *cognomen* or family name, was added[2] (e.g., Marcus, praenomen; Tullius, nomen; Cicero, cognomen). When a man was adopted he assumed the name of his foster father and added his own gentile name in adjectival form. Thus when Octavius was adopted by Caesar his name became Gaius Julius Caesar Octavianus. The family, which became all-important as the social unit, was a patriarchal group under the absolute rule of the father, the *pater*

---

[1] Many scholars prefer a fourth-century date for this treaty.

[2] The cognomen was a relatively late development and did not become usual or significant until the last century of the republic.

familias. Only the wealthier and more powerful families could afford to fulfill the religious and social obligations of the *gens,* so that gentile organization came to be the characteristic of the aristocracy. The leaders of the *gentes* became therewith very powerful men and were called *patres,* fathers; from among them, the king selected his senate.

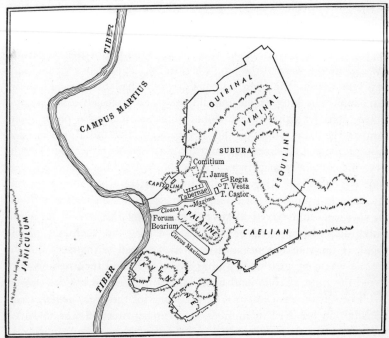

EARLY ROME

From the word *patres,* the nobility which had thus developed derived the name *patrician.* The rest of the people were called *plebs* or *plebeians,* which seems to mean the filling or the mass.

The patricians were great landowners. Many of the plebeians owned small farms, and some had shops in the city and belonged to the associations of artisans. Those who had neither land nor trade attached themselves to patrician patrons as clients. The patron looked after the legal interests of the client and probably secured him means of support. The client in turn attended and served his patron. The relationship also had religious significance and was hereditary. The great families owed much of their power to large numbers of such retainers. There were few slaves.

GOVERNMENT   Governmental organization comprised king, senate, and assembly. The king had two fundamental powers; *imperium*, the right of issuing commands which had to be obeyed under penalty of death, and *auspicium*, the right of consulting the gods to learn their will. Rome's location at the crossing of the Tiber was vulnerable from a military standpoint. In case of sudden menace, therefore, Rome needed the strength of leadership which the military character of the imperium afforded. Too, by virtue of the imperium, law and justice were in the king's hands. It is significant that for military reasons also the king and not a priest had the second power, auspicium. The king might and did use priestly officials called *augurs* to interpret the signs, but he alone might see them. No priest could hamper the free action of the government. Because Rome needed strong leaders at all times, the kingship was elective rather than hereditary, and a definite machinery was established for the election. It was said that when the king died the imperium returned to the people, the auspicium to the senate. The senate elected an *interrex* who "took the auspices" and served for five days. During that period he nominated, with the approval of the senate, a king on whom the people voted. If the vote was negative, that man served as interrex, and the process was continued until a king was elected and the assembly conferred the right of command upon him by the *lex curiata de imperio*.

The senate was composed of the *patres* of the great *gentes*, traditionally one hundred in number. Its primary function was to advise the king by a *senatus consultum*, "advice of the senate." It gave its consent to measures and nominations submitted to the people by the *patrum auctoritas*, "authority of the fathers." It took the leading part, as we have seen, in the choice of a king.[3] Patricians and plebeians alike took part in the assembly. The plebeians were represented by the assembly, which was organized by wards, *curiae*, of which there were thirty. Each man voted within his own ward group; the majority vote controlled, whereupon the ward vote was cast in the assembly as a unit. The chief function of the assembly was the election of the king;

---

[3] These were the powers of the senate during the early republic. To what extent they were exercised under the monarchy is a matter of question. Some scholars are inclined to place the organization of three tribes (see next paragraph, *The Army*) likewise in the republican period.

it dealt also with such family matters as wills and adoptions, and gave its consent to the declaration of war.

THE ARMY   The Romans were divided into three tribes: the Ramnes, Tities, and Luceres, organizations of military rather than of political character. The nobility served in the cavalry, two companies from each tribe, while commoners were marshaled by tribes and curiae. The need for a phalanx of heavy-armed warriors to withstand the Greeks and Etruscans led to the Servian reforms, described above. Instead of the thirty tribes of the tradition, however, there were probably twenty—four in the city and sixteen in the country. The five classes ascribed to Servius seem to have been a later development. The people were divided at this time into two military classes, the *classis* or "summoning" and the *infra classem* or "below the summoning." The *classis,* which consisted of those able to buy arms, were organized into centuries.

ECONOMIC   The early Romans were pastoral people, and their CONDITIONS   wars were fought with their neighbors for the right of way to hill country for summer pasturage. Agriculture first became important under the Etruscans. Industry was probably limited to the family in scope, and trade, until the time of the Etruscans, was almost nonexistent except for fairs. The organization of associations of artisans by Numa seems clearly impossible, and there were no gods of industry or trade in the early Roman lists. While exploitation of the salt mines ascribed to Ancus seems probable in the early history of Rome, the development of industry and commerce began only with the Etruscan conquest.

RELIGION   Religious beliefs and ceremonies centered around the family, the unit of Roman society, and the great gods guarded the state, itself a great family. Since pastoral pursuits were the Roman's chief occupation, his divinities were gods who watched over the crops and herds.

GODS OF THE   The Romans were not highly imaginative, and their FAMILY   religion, though deeply spiritual, had none of the beauty and color of Greek mythology. The Romans conceived of the gods as formless powers, *Numina,* inherent in objects and in the processes of life, and possessing names, but without human form and sometimes even without sex. The family was protected and perpetuated by the *Genius,* guardian spirit and reproductive power of its head, the *pater familias.* The *Lar* took care of the farm, and the

Penates were the spirits of the storeroom. *Janus* was the power resident in the door; and *Vesta,* in the fire. The dead lost personality and merged with the ancestors, whom the family worshiped as the *Di Manes,* divine shades of the underworld. During certain festivals of the year, these shades returned to earth to visit the living members of the family.

GODS OF THE STATE   In similar fashion a group of divinities protected the state. Of these the greatest was Jupiter, who gave it power and prosperity. Mars guarded it with his martial power. The doorway of the state was represented by the shrine of Janus, whose door stood open when the army was away at war. A number of powers looked after the crops and herds: Saturn was the spirit of sowing; Robigus kept away the mildew; Consus and Ops were deities of the harvest; Faunus and Pales guarded the sheep. The Roman calendar was full of simple festivals designed to secure the favor of the powers. The priesthood did not form an organized hierarchy. Individual gods and special festivals had priests assigned to them; the most powerful religious officials of the Romans were the pontiffs, whose peculiar domain was the care of the law.

NEW GODS   The absence of gods of commerce and industry from this list is particularly significant, since it implies lack of development in these fields. Greek merchants from the south brought with them and introduced into Rome those patrons of travelers, Heracles (the Romans called him Hercules) and the twins, Castor and Pollux. From a near-by town came Italian Minerva, patroness of craftsmen, and from the Latin League, Diana, goddess of Aricia. As Rome's conquests spread, the gods of conquered peoples were brought in to increase the city's protectors. New circumstances and new needs led to the creation of new divinities. It is quite typical of these early Romans that there should be a small shrine beside the great sewer in honor of the *dea cloacina,* goddess of the sewer.

ETRUSCAN INFLUENCES   To religion as well as to politics and military organization the Etruscans made their contributions. They established the triad, Jupiter, Juno, and Minerva (the greatest of which was Jupiter), and built for them a three-room temple. They introduced elaborate rituals into state procedure and possibly organized the great priesthoods. From them the Romans first learned to erect statues of their gods. The principles of architecture, including the use of the arch, city buildings, walls, and sewers were Etruscan gifts to Rome. Only after the Etruscan conquest did Rome become a true city, possessing agriculture, industry, and trade, and with them a desire for expansion and conquest.

Under the Tarquins, Rome became virtually an Etruscan city, equipped with a strong army, developing commerce and industry, and extending its power over neighboring communities until it probably controlled the Latin League. The revolution which drove the Tarquins out was due to the reaction of the landowning farmers under patrician leadership, and to the rising of the Latin element against the Etruscan. Rome emerged from the storms which followed as the strong center of Latin culture.

═ XVIII ═

THE EARLY REPUBLIC

THE CONQUEST
OF ITALY

The revolution which established the Roman Republic caused momentary confusion. Rome quickly recovered, however, and within a little more than two centuries made herself the center of a federation which controlled all Italy. Contemporary with the conquest, influencing it and affected by it in turn, went an internal class struggle and a constitutional development.

The validity of the tradition of the early republic to the time of the Gallic catastrophe (p. 346) has, like that of the monarchy, been seriously questioned. The truth of many of the stories has been denied, and to others later dates have been assigned by scholars. Institutional history has been reconstructed from chance allusions by classical writers or from inferences derived from later practices. Answers to the questions of historicity depend in large measure on the solution of the problem of how great was the destruction of records by the Gauls, itself a matter of controversy. The nearer we approach to the age of written history in the third century B.C., the more credibility can be granted to the story. Lacking definite agreements on all these disputed points, we shall follow the traditional story with reservations.

THE
REVOLUTION

The events of the revolution are completely lost in the mist of legend. The stories of Lucretia, of Brutus, of Scaevola in the camp of Lars Porsenna, and of Horatius at the bridge belong to literature rather than to history. But later hatred of the title of king in Rome attests to the fact of revolution, and certain it is that the last kings of Rome were driven out. Apparently there was then an alliance of Etruscans and Latins against Rome not to restore the Etruscan kings but to weaken the power of the city. Though Porsenna took the city and forbade the use of iron weapons, the Romans freed themselves and prosecuted the war with vigor. Tradition records the Roman victory in the battle of Lake Regillus in

493 B.C., followed by the treaty of Spurius Cassius with the Latins. This famous document, which survived into historic times, provided for an offensive and defensive alliance between Rome and the Latin League, with provisions for alternation in command of the army, for rights of trade and of intermarriage, and for prompt settlement of suits of law. The principles which it embodied formed the cornerstone of Rome's foreign policy for over two centuries.

REPUBLICAN ORGANIZATION
Two generals of the army, called *consuls* ("colleagues") and elected annually by the people from among the nobility, succeeded the king as magistrates. They possessed his imperium and auspicium, but their power was checked by the principle of collegiality, that is, the division of powers between two men and the right of one to veto the action of the other. To secure unity of command in times of crisis, the consuls, with the consent of the senate, nominated a dictator, who possessed absolute power for six months, the normal period of a campaign. Control over the law passed into the hands of the aristocratic pontiffs. The senate, increased to three hundred patricians named by the consuls, soon assumed a dominant position in the government. A new assembly, composed of wealthier citizens who fought in the army, took over the function of electing the consuls and voting on measures submitted to it by the consuls, subject to approval by the senate. Whether it continued for a time the older curiate organization or assumed a new form based on the centuries of the army is not certain.

THE FIRST CONQUESTS
Thus organized at home under an aristocratic rule, the Romans proceeded to conquest. For a hundred years they were beset by a ring of enemies: the Volscians in the hills to the south, the Aequians and the Sabines to the west and north, and the Etruscan cities, particularly Veii, on the other side of the Tiber. During the first half of the fifth century B.C., Rome's enemies took advantage of internal disorders in the city to raid its territories for plunder. When these local troubles were temporarily composed, Rome gained the upper hand; the hill people were defeated, and colonies of Romans and Latins were placed in their territory to act as permanent garrisons. In 396 B.C. the famous dictator Camillus captured Veii, after which he confiscated and divided among the Romans a large area of Etruscan land. The celebrated story of Cincinnatus bears repeating here. In the crisis which arose when the Aequians had trapped a Roman consul and his army, Cincinnatus was

named dictator. He received the message while he was plowing, left his plow, organized an army, defeated the enemy, celebrated a great triumph, resigned his post, and returned to his farm—all in sixteen days.

THE GAULS The end of the first century of wars thus found Rome victorious over her neighboring enemies. Scarcely had this been achieved when a devastating blow was struck. In 390 or 387 B.C. a horde of Gauls, barbarian warriors who had invaded the Po Valley and expelled the Etruscans during the fifth century B.C., crossed the Apennines and besieged Etruscan Clusium. Angered by Roman intervention, they marched against Rome, defeated the Roman army in the battle of the Allia River, and took and sacked the city. The citadel alone held out against them.

There are many celebrated stories of this sack; the most famous follows. The Romans agreed to ransom the city for a thousand pounds of gold. When a dispute arose about the weights, Brennus, the Gallic leader, threw his sword on the scales, exclaiming, *"Vae victis"* ("Woe to the conquered"). According to Roman tradition, however, Camillus drove the Gauls out without paying the ransom. At all events, the barbarians retired to the Po Valley, where they remained a perpetual threat against the peace of Italy. The stories tell of later invasions which were repelled.

THE LATINS After the retreat of the Gauls, Rome appeared to be stricken. Her old enemies quickly endeavored to take advantage of the situation, but they soon learned that they were mistaken, for Rome had lost little but prestige. The citizens promptly rebuilt their houses, and the army constructed a fine stone wall to enclose the city, making it one of the most strongly fortified cities in the West. The annexation of the Etruscan territory had led to the formation of two new tribes and the addition of at least ten thousand men to the army. Order was quickly restored on the borders of Latium, but the Latins themselves had become disaffected. In 358 B.C. the old treaty between them and Rome was patched up and renewed. But, when in 340 B.C. the Latins' demands for citizenship and seats in the Roman senate were refused, war broke out afresh. Roman success was sure and swift. In 338 B.C. the Latin League was dissolved, and in place of it Rome substituted treaties with each individual state.

THE SAMNITES The conquest of the hill country to the south had brought Rome into contact with the fertile lands of Campania, and Capua was brought into alliance. From it grain was purchased in years of shortage, and the earliest Roman silver coins were struck in the Capuan mints. Such an expansion of Roman power seemed intolerable to the Samnites, a powerful mountain tribe who themselves coveted the Campanian land. There are traditions of a treaty of alliance in 354 B.C. between Romans and Samnites, and of a short war for the control of Capua (343-341 B.C.) in which the Romans were victorious. The great Samnite Wars (327-290 B.C.) were caused by Roman interference in Naples, which had a large Samnite element in its population. The Romans, although disgracefully defeated at the Caudine Pass in 321 B.C., eventually won. After a peace made in 304 B.C. had provided a breathing spell, a great alliance of Samnites, Umbrians, Etruscans, and Gauls attacked Rome in 300 B.C. The Roman general Decius Mus led his forces to a decisive victory at Sentinum in 295 B.C. By 293 B.C. Samnium was conquered and annexed, and Etruria was annexed in 283 B.C. After arresting a raid of Gauls called Boii at Lake Vadimon in 283 B.C., the Roman army crossed the Apennines and took possession of Picenum with the northern boundary at the Rubicon River. Apart from the expansion of Roman territory, the most important results of the war were the building of the Appian Way and the transformation of the Roman army from the phalanx to the manipular legion, a reform which will be described later (p. 359).

THE GREEKS Only the southern end of Italy remained outside of Roman power. After the Samnite wars the cities of Magna Graecia had fallen on evil days. They had been materially weakened by the conquests of Dionysius (p. 270) and had suffered much from the raids of the Italic tribes in the interior, until only Tarentum retained any vestige of its former power. With this city the Romans had made a treaty in which they promised to send no ships into the Gulf of Tarentum. Nevertheless, when Thurii appealed to Rome for help against the Lucanians in 282 B.C., the Romans, in violation of the treaty, sent an army and some ships. Tarentum at once declared war, and called upon Pyrrhus, king of Epirus, for aid. This warrior, with a vision of a great western empire for himself, brought over an army trained to the Macedonian phalanx. He defeated the Romans at Heraclea and at Asculum, but lost so many men that a victory whose cost is too great has ever since been called a "Pyrrhic victory." After unsuccessfully trying to make terms of peace, Pyrrhus attempted the conquest of Sicily in a war with the Carthaginians and failed again. He returned to Italy, was defeated in the battle of Beneventum in 275 B.C., and left for home. The Greek cities, surrendering in 272 B.C., were added to the Roman federation, and Rome was master of all Italy south of the Po.

The Roman advance to power had been evolutionary rather than planned. In theory, at least, all of the wars had been defensive. The conquest of one territory established a new frontier, and this caused new difficulties and led to new conquests until the natural boundaries of Italy had been attained. Land hunger on the part of the Roman populace and the desire of the leaders for military glory lay in the background as effective causes for all the wars. It was but a short time before similar causes involved Rome in wars outside the peninsula.

ORGANIZATION OF ITALY — During the years of conquest, the senate had developed a system of organization which appears in its completeness at the end of the Greek War. In many communities land was confiscated and given to land-hungry Romans until the number of tribes had been increased to thirty-five and Roman citizens had been scattered over all of Italy. All of the cities within annexed territories were drawn within the Roman state and organized. Certain seacoast towns, twenty-two in number, were garrisoned with three hundred Roman veterans and their families and were called Roman colonies. The veterans retained full rights as citizens of Rome. Other towns received charters from the senate and were known as *municipia*, municipalities. Of these, some, *municipia optimo jure,* had full Roman rights: the people were Roman citizens, could vote and hold office in Rome, paid taxes, and served in the legions. Since they were subject to the Roman magistrates, their local organization was simple and provided merely for local needs. The greater number were *municipia sine suffragio*—municipalities without vote. They had full local autonomy under a government prescribed by the senate and modeled on that of Rome. Their citizens paid taxes and served in the army, could trade and intermarry with Romans, but could not vote or hold office in Rome. In the Roman colonies, it should be noted, the original inhabitants occupied this position also. This type of organization, which had been instituted as a punishment for a revolted ally, Gabii, so that its citizens might carry the burdens but not enjoy the privileges of citizenship, proved a most successful method for the Romanization and absorption of conquered peoples.

The allies were divided into two classes, Latin and Italian. Many of the old Latin cities had been annexed; others were allowed their freedom and given a privileged status of equal alliance with Rome, all of the rights of the *municipia sine suffragio* without the burden of taxation. Of the same status as the Latin cities were the Latin colonies. In conquered territories the Romans settled garrisons of Roman and Latin veterans, giving them grants of land for their support. The Romans in such a community gave up their Roman citizenship, and all acquired Latin rights. The colonies were legally Latin allies.

The Italian communities were united to Rome each by a separate treaty. They paid no taxes, retained complete local autonomy, even to the right of issuing coins, worshiped their own gods, but gave all control over foreign affairs to Rome.

All of the allies, both Latin and Italian, furnished contingents to the Roman army commanded by their own officers. The federation, with a population of about three million, could muster, after 272 B.C., a fighting force of about seven hundred and fifty thousand men. Italy under Roman control has been likened to a telephone exchange with Rome in charge at the switchboard.

INTERNAL CONFLICTS AND CONSTITUTIONAL DEVELOPMENTS

CAUSES OF THE CONFLICTS
The patrician aristocrats, having been the leaders of the revolution, garnered to themselves its fruits. The basis of their claim to power was their right to consult the gods through the auspicium. Since this was the necessary counterpart of the consular imperium, it followed that patricians alone could hold office, establish, know, and apply law. It followed further that patrician blood could not be contaminated by intermarriage with lower classes, lest the gods be angered. After the admission of the Sabine, Attius Clausus (Appius Claudius), who moved to Rome in 504 B.C. with a great throng of retainers, the patricians became a closed caste. They endeavored and eventually succeeded in making a rule forbidding intermarriage between the classes, which later was made law in the Twelve Tables.

The plebeians, as a result, found themselves in a difficult position.

The wealthier of them felt keenly the stigma of political and social inequality. They desired the share in government to which they felt their political and military abilities entitled them and they resented the prohibition of intermarriage between the classes. The small farmers suffered from raids of the enemy as well as from the constant war tax and the annual military levy of men which took them away from their fields.

The collapse of industry and trade which followed in the train of the revolution wrought great hardships on the city population. The situation was aggravated by the fact that in years of scarcity the patrician leaders sold at famine prices grain which they had imported from Campania and from Sicily. The severe law of debt was strictly applied by the patrician magistrate-judges, so that many plebeians were sold into slavery for debt. The rigid requirements of procedure in Roman legal custom, the control of the law by the aristocratic pontiffs, and the absence of written law made it exceedingly difficult for the commoners to secure justice in the courts.

Yet in the ensuing struggle for political and legal equality, success rested inevitably with the plebeians. They were needed for the army, and their economic well-being was essential to the welfare of the state. As soon as they had learned to act in unison and had acquired leaders, they were sure to win, though indeed the wealthier plebeians gathered the major fruits of the victory (p. 353). The striking character of the struggle is that plebeian success partook of the nature of a gradual evolution, of a series of timely surrenders and intelligent compromises on the part of the patricians. Though there were riots and secession, there were no bloody civil wars, tyrannies, or exiles, nor any of those wild excesses which mar the history of most of the Greek states. Roman sense of discipline and Roman obedience to tradition kept the ship of state on a fairly even keel.

TRIUMPH OF THE PLEBEIANS The story of the plebeian triumph is confused by contradictory sources, by historical problems arising from later traditions, and by knotty constitutional and legal problems. The first plebeian achievement was certainly that of organization. Their natural rendezvous was the temple of Ceres, the Earth Mother, patron divinity of farmers. Under the presidency of the caretakers of the temple, the *aediles,* whom they elected, they met together on the basis of the old curiate assembly. Tradition tells of a strike or secession, which supposedly took place in 493 B.C., when the plebeians withdrew in a body to the Sacred Mount to found a new city. They were brought back to Rome by the patricians' offer to allow them to elect two protectors, called *tribunes,* who should have the right to veto any oppressive act of a magistrate. This story is generally rejected by scholars as unhistorical.

Instead, scholars generally agree that the tribunate, with its right of intercession or veto, was first established in 471 B.C. with four tribunes, one for each of the city wards, and that in that year the plebeians gained the legal right to an organization based on the tribes, or wards. Since only landowners were listed in the tribes, the landless clients of the patricians were thus excluded from the plebeian deliberations.

This plebeian assembly elected the tribunes and under their presidency passed measures called *plebiscita* ("decisions of the plebs") which were binding on its members. The tribunes, in response to personal appeals, could stop any magistrate in his actions, and the sacred character which they claimed for themselves protected them from violence. At once they began agitation for the writing down of the laws, their method of procedure being to veto the annual levy. After several years of confusion and of military disaster the patricians yielded. The result of this victory for the tribunes was the Twelve Tables of the Roman law, the great achievement of the board of ten men, *decemvirs,* which ruled Rome in 451-449 B.C. Difficulties with the second board of decemvirs led to a second plebeian secession and to the Valerio-Horatian laws. By these, the plebeian assembly probably became the *Comitia Tributa* ("tribal assembly"), the number of tribunes was increased to ten, and their sacred character legally recognized. Citizens were given the right of appeal to the people from a death sentence imposed by the consul within the city.

From that time forward plebeian advance was rapid, concessions being made by the patricians in all phases of the struggle. The social stigma, felt most keenly by the wealthier plebeians, was removed by the Canuleian Law of 445 B.C. which repealed the prohibition of marriage between the classes. Possibly to satisfy the demand of the plebeians for higher office and more certainly to meet the exigencies of wars, provision was made for the election in certain years of military tribunes with consular power to serve in the place of consuls; among these might be plebeians.

At the same time (443 B.C.) the power of these officials was lessened and the duties of the consuls were made less onerous by the establishment of the censorship, consisting of two *censors,* patricians, elected every five years and usually holding office for eighteen months. The censors took the census of the people, assigned each man to his tribe and class, let and supervised public contracts. Later they acquired the right to draw up the list of senators, which made them an important political factor in the state.

It was probably at this time also that the *infra classem* of the earlier period were divided into four classes according to their wealth, making five classes in all, so that every man might be called upon to serve the state as his means allowed and might also have a share in the assembly.

During the following generation the debt problem was met by prohibiting slavery for debt, and also on several occasions by lessening or remitting debts. The economic pressure on the poorer plebeians was eased by introducing pay for soldiers, possibly to prevent them from serving as mercenaries in the armies of the Sicilian cities, and by providing land for the landless in the conquered territories.

During the conquest, considerable portions of enemy territories were confiscated and made public land. Some of this land was used for the establishment of colonies and some was divided into small farms and given to Roman citizens. This was the case after the conquest of Veii, for example, when four new tribes were created from the Veientine land. Tracts which were not allotted to small farmers were leased to wealthy landowners who, in return for small rents, were allowed to pasture their cattle and sheep on lands unfit for cultivation.

Agitation, arising annually when it was found that the senate regularly fought any proposal for the election of military tribunes and that the ruling class was still occupying the greater part of the public land, resulted in the Licinian-Sextian Laws of 367 B.C. These laws contained provisions which limited the amount of public land any one man might occupy and the number of cattle he might keep on the public pastures; they decreed that henceforth one consul should be a plebeian; but they also created a new patrician office, the *praetorship.*

The praetor had the right of military command, subject to the superior power of the consul, but his chief duty was to relieve the consul of all his judicial duties. By the praetorship the ruling class met the growing needs of government, weakened the consular office by further separation of its powers, and reserved for the patricians control over the law.

Nevertheless, the patrician cause was lost. In the years that followed, one office after another was opened to the plebeians until in 300 B.C. the Ogulnian Law made them eligible for the priesthoods. Political and economic controversies arising chiefly from the condition of the debtor group led to a great plebeian secession in 287 B.C. and thus to the passing of the Hortensian Law. This measure settled the debt controversy and also gave the tribal assembly authority to pass laws binding on the entire population. Exactly how the debt problem was solved by this law is not known, but in any event no more is heard of it for one hundred and fifty years.

Apparently the plebeians had won a complete victory. The burden of debt had been lifted from them; they had been assured a part in the public lands; their votes put men into office and into the senate; furthermore, the offices were now open to all men; and they had the right to pass laws under the presidency of their tribunes, whose power of intercession protected them in all their rights.

As a matter of actual practice, however, the facts were far different. Since no office carried any pay, only the well to do could afford an official career. Consequently, in place of the patrician aristocracy there developed an officeholding nobility (men who were "known") composed of about one hundred wealthy families, both patrician and plebeian, who, through their prestige and their power over the timocratic centuriate assembly, were able to control the elections. Tribunes who looked for advancement found it wiser to follow the policies of these leaders than to serve the people. In addition, since the enforcement of the land provisions of the Licinian-Sextian Laws was in the hands of these wealthy landowning officials, naturally the limitations on public land were disregarded and the law became a dead letter. Although ostensibly in the hands of the people, in actuality the government of Rome was controlled by the wealthy officeholders—the large landowners—who composed the senatorial group.

ROMAN INSTITUTIONS   A century later, the Greek Polybius declared that Rome's rise to power was based on her institutions, which, he said, combined the best features of monarchy, aristocracy, and democracy, each checking the others. A survey of these institutions as they appeared at the end of the Italic Wars (272 B.C.) will explain his conception.

THE
MAGISTRACIES

The magisterial system, comprising the consuls, praetors, censors, aediles, and quaestors, provided the monarchical element in the Roman constitution. The higher magistrates possessed such power of command that they were literally masters, as the word *magistrate* implies. They wore a robe with purple border; on official occasions they sat on an ivory chair; and they were. attended by lictors bearing the *fasces,* bundles of rods, symbolizing magisterial power to compel obedience. When displayed outside of the city, the fasces contained an ax, indicative of the power of life and death.

The most important limitations on the power of the magistrates were the board form of the office and the shortness of the term. All regular officials were elected in groups, and for one year, the sole exception to this practice of annual election being the office of censor. To these restrictions should be added the powerful right of veto of the tribunes on the actions of any magistrate except the dictator.

SEQUENCE
OF OFFICES

Tradition required that an aspirant for high office in Rome should pass through a regular succession of positions from the lowest to the highest. In the later period of the republic this succession, called the *cursus honorum,* "sequence of offices," was definitely established by law, with required intervals between offices; holding two offices at the same time and reelection to the same office within ten years were prohibited. A young Roman headed for an official career began by serving in at least ten campaigns as a junior officer in the army. He would then post his name with the proper official, consul or tribune, as a candidate. If he were a plebeian, he would run for the office of tribune. The tribunes, ten in number, had steadily increased in power. They could come to the aid of any individual citizen when called upon; they could veto any proposal of a magistrate before an assembly or any action of the senate. For a period they sat outside the senate door to listen; later they were allowed to enter the senate, and finally even to convoke that body and present measures to it. They presided over the tribal assembly, presented measures (*plebiscita*) to it, and called magistrates before it for criminal trial in cases of malfeasance in office. Thus they were the cornerstone of democracy in checking the ruling classes.

AEDILES

The next step in the political career of the plebeian was the office of aedile. (The patrician, however, began his official service as a quaestor.) In early days the two plebeian aediles had been assistants of the tribunes. Gradually they developed a set of separate duties of such importance that the parallel patrician aedileship, which often followed the quaestorship in the *cursus,* was established. The aediles were charged with the care of public buildings, the supervision of the grain market, and the task of providing the games for the people. In later days the games gave them an opportunity to curry popular favor by lavish expenditures from their own means beyond the money provided by the state.

QUAESTORS   The highest of the minor officials were the *quaestors.* There were two originally, and their number was increased to four in 421 B.C. and to eight in 267 B.C. They were at first assistants of the king, and then of the consuls, in criminal cases. To that duty the care of the treasury and the management of funds on campaigns came to be added. They also presented appeals of citizens before the assembly. In the early period they were appointed by the consuls; later they were elected by the tribal assembly.

PRAETORS   The praetorship, established in 367 B.C. to relieve the consuls, was the lowest of the offices which carried with them the imperium. Though the praetor often exercised military command, his activities normally were confined to the city, where as *praetor urbanus* he dealt with civil and criminal cases arising under the law. In 242 B.C., a second, the *praetor peregrinus,* was added to take cognizance of cases involving non-Romans. At the beginning of his term the praetor issued an edict in which he stated the principles of law and the rules of procedure he would apply.

CONSULS   The consuls were chief executives and commanders of the army. Their power was in theory autocratic, for they were masters (*magistri*) of the state. In actual practice limitations on their power developed. First there was the limitation of collegiality: in case of dispute between the two consuls, the negative vote prevailed; that is, if one said "go," and the other said "stay," they stayed. Though not legally bound to follow the advice of the senate, custom decreed that they should consult that body and abide by its decisions. In fact, the control which the senate exercised over the raising and allotment of money made such action necessary. Furthermore, the consul knew that he would be consul for but one year, and senator for the rest of his life; consequently he was not likely to jeopardize his future career by actions which would weaken the power of the senate. Within the city there were definite restrictions which regulated the consul's imperium: his actions might be vetoed by a tribune; appeals from his decisions in capital cases might be taken to the people; and he might be brought before the tribal assembly for an account at the end of his office. But in the field on a military campaign, his power (*imperium militiae*) was supreme and brooked no interference.

DICTATOR
In times of great emergency, the consuls, usually after consultation with the senate, named a dictator, whose power was truly monarchical: all guarantees of appeal, intercession, or veto were suspended. His term of office was limited to six months, but many dictators prided themselves on completing their task and surrendering their power in less time. The record belongs to Cincinnatus (p. 345). It is a noteworthy evidence of the strength of Roman tradition that no dictator ever used his power to make himself king or tyrant in Rome.

PROCONSULS
The chief disadvantage which accrued to Rome from this magisterial system arose from the fact that the command of the army changed hands annually. This problem was solved and needed additional commanders were provided during the Samnite Wars (327-290 B.C.) by the practice of prorogation. The senate, with consent granted by the tribal assembly, might prolong the imperium of a consul or reappoint an ex-consul for purposes of military command. The official so designated served *pro consule,* in place of the consul, and was later called *proconsul*. His imperium was limited, however, to a specific task and was subject to the superior command of the consuls.

The crowning honor of an official career was election to the censorship, the duties of which office have already been described.

SENATE
The senate became the chief administrative body under the Roman constitution. It was made up of three hundred senators, appointed at first by the consuls and later, after the Ovinian Law (ca. 300 B.C.), by the censors. In early times its membership was patrician, but when the public offices were opened to the plebeians, seats in the senate were yielded to them also. The senate had no responsibility to the people and so was aristocratic in character. Since it was understood that senatorships should preferably be given to ex-magistrates of the grade of quaestor or above, the senate was composed of a body of experienced men. Experience was emphasized by the fact that in its deliberations the presiding official called on the *consulares,* ex-consuls, to express their opinions first.

The senate's powers, never clearly stated, developed gradually through custom, often more potent among the Romans than law. The senate advised the consuls and gave its consent to legislation. Its approval was necessary for the validation of contracts let by the censors. It provided for the levy of armies, the raising of taxes and the allocation of funds; it appointed proconsuls and it assigned commands. It controlled and directed foreign affairs, received embassies, and regulated the affairs of the Italian federation. In times of emergency it could suspend constitutional guarantees of personal liberty by the *Senatus consultum ultimum* ("final decree"), a declaration of martial law. It has been maintained that no finer body of men has ever directed the course of any state with greater success than did the senate during Rome's rise to power.

THE COMITIA CENTURIATA — The powers of election and legislation belonged to the people. The older curiate assembly continued, but its powers dwindled to mere formalities usually attended to by thirty *lictors* (attendants of the magistrates who carried the fasces). It ratified wills and adoptions and conferred the imperium on magistrates, after their election, by the famous *lex curiata de imperio*. Throughout the period of the Italic Wars, the centuriate assembly was the dominant voice of the people. It was composed of 193 centuries arranged by classes.

ORGANIZATION OF THE COMITIA CENTURIATA

	JUNIORS (17-46 years) (in centuries)	SENIORS (above 46 years) (in centuries)
I. Class	40	40
II. Class	10	10
III. Class	10	10
IV. Class	10	10
V. Class	14	14
	84	84

Total	168

Cavalry	18
Substitutes for the killed and wounded	2
Musicians and workmen	4
Landless	1
	25

Total	193 [1]

[1] Botsford, *History of the Ancient World*, p. 341.

The cavalry, which was always composed of the wealthiest men, voted first and were followed by the classes in their order. Since the cavalry and the first class together had a majority, ninety-eight votes, this assembly was timocratic in character, that is, it was controlled by the well to do. It elected the magistrates, voted on laws submitted to it, declared war, ratified treaties of peace, and heard appeals from capital decisions of the consuls. It had no rights of nomination or of the initiation of legislation, since no one could invoke it or address it save a magistrate. Candidates for office presented their names to the consuls; if acceptable to them, officeseekers then campaigned in a white toga, *toga candida,* to solicit votes. The presiding consul presented the candidates' names to the centuries for their votes. Legislation was proposed by the magistrates, after discussion and consent by the senate. If popular debate was deemed necessary, a less formal meeting called a *contio* was summoned, which private citizens might address with the consent of the presiding magistrate. The action of the centuriate assembly could be controlled by religious devices, for if the direction of affairs displeased the magistrate he could conveniently observe an unfavorable omen and terminate the deliberations. If a man were stricken with a fit of epilepsy, all action was suspended. So frequently was epilepsy feigned that it was called "comitial sickness."

THE COMITIA
TRIBUTA

The more democratic *comitia tributa* elected tribunes under the presidency of a tribune, and quaestors under the presidency of a consul. It dealt with judicial cases brought before it by tribunes or aediles. It voted on laws presented to it by tribunes (*plebiscita*) or by consuls (*leges*) with the previous consent of the senate. This senatorial restriction was reduced to a formality in 339 B.C. and was removed by the Hortensian Law of 287 B.C. In 312 B.C. the censor Appius Claudius enrolled the landless in the tribes; however, after 304 B.C. they were confined to the four city tribes. The major constitutional measures of the period were passed by the centuriate assembly; but many laws and plebiscites, particularly those which dealt with debts, emerged from the tribes. The tribal assembly ratified the senate's recommendations for the appointment of promagistrates for particular tasks, and eventually took over the right of the declaration of war. The great days of the legislative activity of this body came in the later years of the republic.

THE ARMY   The Roman army of the early republic was a phalanx composed of those able to furnish arms, assisted by the rich as cavalry, and the poor as light-armed troops. The introduction of pay for service enabled all to buy armor and thus broke down the military distinction between the classes. The Second Samnite War brought an end to the phalanx (p. 347). The Romans adopted their enemy's formation and also their arms: the dart, *pilum,* and the oblong shield, *scutum*. Henceforth, instead of being massed into a single body, the Roman troops were organized into maniples, mobile companies of one hundred and twenty men each. There were thirty such companies to a legion, deployed, checkerboard fashion, in three lines.

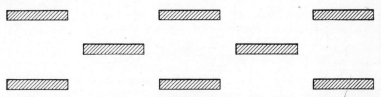

The men fought in open order, about eight feet apart. The first line was composed of recruits, the second of experienced men, the third, or reserve, of veterans. Each man wore heavy body armor, carried two darts and a short sword. As the line advanced, the men threw their darts and then closed in with their swords. At this close fighting the Romans were supreme. The open order of the legion proved in the end superior to the Macedonian phalanx of Pyrrhus. Four legions made up the normal annual levy, to which would be added troops from the allies. Training was rigid and exacting, discipline absolute. Perhaps the most famous of the Roman rules of war was that which required the army to build a carefully planned camp complete with moat and mound, wherever it stopped for the night.

THE ROADS   The most renowned of Roman accomplishments, excepting, of course, Roman law, was their system of road building, which, begun in the early republic, was extended with conquest throughout Italy and eventually became widespread in the Roman Empire. While it is possible that salt was being transported over the *Via Salaria,* "Salt Way," from the marshes beside the lower Tiber northeast into the Sabine country, and that the *Via Latina* climbed over the hills to Capua both as early as the fourth century B.C., still the famous Appian Way, built in 312 B.C. by the censor, Ap-

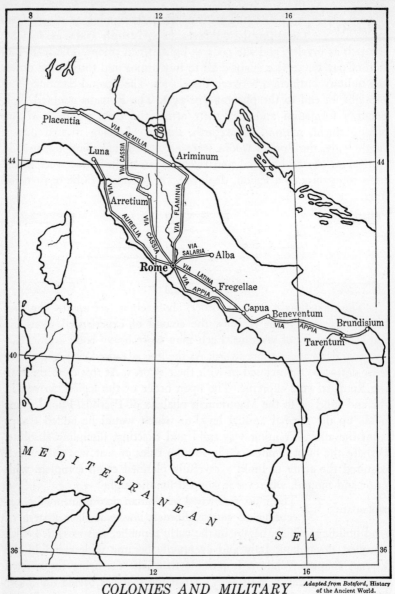

COLONIES AND MILITARY
ROADS OF ITALY

BRONZE CALDRON

BRONZE FIGURES
ETRUSCAN ART
The National Museum of the Villa Giulia, Rome

SALE OF BELTS AND PILLOWS

EXHIBITION OF A SAMPLE OF CLOTH

SHIPBUILDING　　　　　　BLACKSMITH

ROMAN LIFE

pius Claudius, established the method and the precedent for Roman road building of later generations. The Appian Way crossed the Pontine Marshes on solid foundations and then ran straight as an arrow to Capua. Later it was extended to Beneventum, to Tarentum, and to Brundisium. It was famed not only for its directness but also for its durability. The roads built in later periods clearly show the Roman method of road building. Gravel was laid on hardpan or on a solid foundations over that lime was poured to form a sort of concrete; upon this base were laid huge paving blocks with convex surface to provide drainage. The roads were built for military purposes, but naturally they were used by travelers and merchants as well. By thus providing means of communication and trade routes, the roads helped greatly to bind Italy, and in later times the Mediterranean world, together.

THE FAMILY   The basic Roman institution for the development of character was the family. The Roman *familia* consisted of the father and mother, sons and sons' wives, unmarried daughters, grandsons, and so on, and all clients and slaves. Over the *familia* presided the *pater familias,* father of the family. His *patria potestas* gave him power to inflict punishment for disobedience, even to the penalty of death; the latter was usually imposed only after a trial before a family court.

The father had full charge of the family estate, and it was his pride to hand on to his sons at his death an estate larger than it was when he had received it. The sons were educated by their father in reading, writing, and arithmetic, in the family traditions, which inculcated the stern Roman virtues, in the law, and in the management of affairs. Only at the father's death, or after he had gone through the fiction of selling them into slavery three times, were the sons free of his control and independent. At his death they divided the property [2] and became *patres* in their own right.

Daughters learned household affairs from their mothers. Women and their possessions were always under the control (*in manu*) of their father, brothers, or husband.

Family life was very simple. The house was characterized by the *atrium,* a large central room with a roof which sloped inward and

---

[2] There are some indications that in early times indivisible family ownership prevailed.

down to convey rain water into a cistern in the center, and in the rear of which stood the bed of the father and mother. Around the atrium were built smaller rooms for various household uses. Food consisted of vegetables, milk, bread, pork, and perhaps a little beef. Women wore a long garment, the *stola,* which reached their feet, and for out-of-doors added the *palla,* a large rectangular woolen garment which they draped around them. Men wore the tunic which reached just below the knees and the characteristic Roman woolen cloak, the *toga.*

THE CITY The city of Rome must have been very unprepossessing. Its best feature was the fine wall built after the Gallic disaster. The houses had been hastily rebuilt after that occurrence; streets were crooked and dirty; the temples of local volcanic stone could not have been very attractive. The fine buildings of the later Forum had not yet been erected. The lower ground, where lived the poor, was frequently flooded and the buildings there destroyed. Marshes and cisterns were constant sources of fever, and epidemics were frequent. The city was served by two aqueducts, the Aqua Appia built by Appius Claudius in 312 B.C., which brought fine water from the hills and distributed it in fountains, and the Anio Vetus, whose water from the Anio River was not potable.

ECONOMIC LIFE Economic conditions were slowly improving. The necessities of an important and expanding city led to the development of those industries essential to its life, pottery manufacture, leather working and metallurgy, particularly the manufacture of weapons and armor. Contact with the Italic tribes and with the Greek cities contributed to the development of trade. The period of conquest witnessed the first appearance of Roman coins, the copper *as,* weighing twelve ounces. After a brief period during which silver coins were minted in Capua, Rome established in 269 B.C. a silver coinage with the standard a *denarius,* a silver coin equivalent to the Athenian drachma; a smaller coin, one-fourth its size, was called the *sestertius;* an *as,* made of two ounces of bronze, was one-tenth of a *denarius.*

In spite of these developments, trade and industry were of relatively small importance in the Roman economy; the Romans were pre-eminently farmers. Lands acquired from the conquered tribes were distributed among the poorer Romans for the creation of new tribes; others were given in allotments to the Roman and Latin colonists; and much more came into the possession of the ruling class in leasehold in spite of the restrictions of the Licinian-Sextian Laws. Agrarian rather than commercial interests controlled Roman policies and motivated the program of expansion.

Conquest and the acquisition of land led to a very rapid increase in the citizen body. Accurate figures are lacking for the early period, but the first reliable census, dating from the year 318 B.C., gives the number of two hundred and fifty thousand men of military age which indicates a total population of approximately a million citizens scattered throughout Italy. Estimates of the city population are little more than guesses.

MORES
MAJORUM

Controlling all Roman activities were the *mores majorum,* the customs of the ancestors. Tradition prevailed in the constitution, in law, in religion, in education, and in daily life. Discipline and conservatism were the keynotes of these customs. Yet Roman conservatism was not blind. It made constitutional progress slow, but it did not block necessary improvements. It did not prevent the Romans from taking bodily the Samnite military system when it proved better than their own. The lessons which tradition taught the people are evident from the large number of Latin words representing qualities: *constantia, diligentia, continentia, fides,* and preeminently *virtus, gravitas,* and *pietas. Virtus* is valor, illustrated by the story that on the battlefields of Heraclea all of the Roman dead received their wounds in front, and by the ancient legends of Scaevola and Horatius. *Gravitas* is seriousness of outlook, characteristic of the Romans in all their dealings, as contrasted with the lightheartedness and changeability of the Greeks. *Pietas* is loyalty, the culmination of all virtue, the performance of all duties and obligations due to the family and its gods, to the state and the great gods who made Rome great.

APPIUS
CLAUDIUS

Appius Claudius (censor in 312 B.C.), surnamed Caecus, the Blind, whose vivid personality made an impression on his own and succeeding generations, stands out among the many famous heroes of the period as the symbol and epitome of the period, as does Pericles for his Age in Athens. Three times military tribune, quaestor, aedile, three times praetor, thrice interrex, twice consul, dictator, and censor, serving with distinction in the Samnite Wars, he had had a long and honorable career. During his censorship he caused something of an uproar by enrolling the landless in the tribes and by putting even freedmen in the senate.

He had his own freedman publish the pontifical rules of procedure of the law. His greatest achievement was the building of the Aqua Appia and the Via Appia, the latter immortalizing his name. To him was ascribed the authorship of many an ancient maxim such as "Each man is the blacksmith of his own fortune." He was the first great Roman orator whose orations were preserved in later times. When the senate was about to accept the offers of peace from Pyrrhus after Asculum (279 B.C.) (p. 347), Appius Claudius, by that time over ninety and so blind that he had to be led by a boy, entered the senate house and thundered, "Rome never makes terms of peace with a victorious enemy on Italian soil."

During the first centuries of the republic the fundamental principles of the Roman government had been developed and the once discordant peoples of Italy had been welded together into a most potent federation. The same evolutionary process which led to these accomplishments next drew Rome into the vortex of Mediterranean affairs and raised therewith a whole new series of problems—imperial, constitutional, and economic.

THE ROMAN CONQUEST OF THE MEDITERRANEAN
(264-133 B.C.)

The Roman conquest of the Mediterranean is one of the most astounding stories in all history. In 272 B.C. Rome completed her conquest of the Italian peninsula. Eight years later, the first war with Carthage began, and within less than a century and a half Rome possessed or controlled nearly every country within the periphery of the Mediterranean. This extraordinary achievement had profound and lasting effects upon the Roman constitution, upon Roman society and culture, and upon the conquered lands as well—effects which still influence the world today.

THE FIRST PUNIC WAR

CAUSES OF THE WAR — In 264 B.C. the Mamertines, mercenaries in Messana, were attacked by Syracuse and appealed to both Carthage and Rome for aid. Carthage responded, but in Rome the senate hesitated. Affirmative action would violate agreements with Carthage to leave Sicily alone and would be certain to

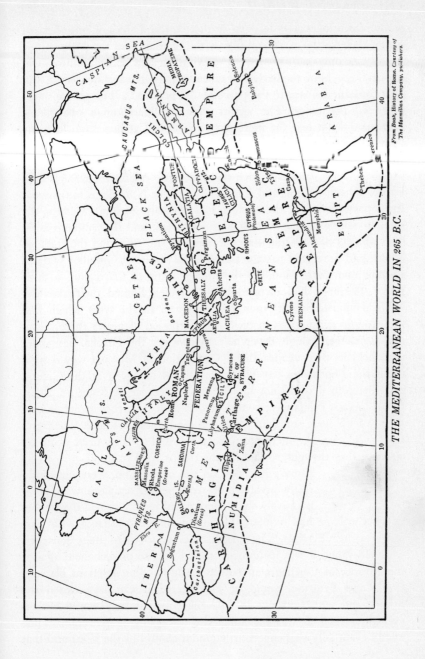

THE MEDITERRANEAN WORLD IN 265 B.C.

From Boak, History of Rome. Courtesy of
The Macmillan Company, publishers.

arouse resentment and lead to war with the Carthaginians. Refusal meant that Carthage, in coming to the assistance of the Mamertines, would not only gain possession of Messana and secure control over the Straits, a blow to the Greek cities in Italy, Rome's new allies, but be a constant menace to the peace of the peninsula. The people, however, did not delay. The victors over the Macedonian phalanx of Pyrrhus did not fear the mercenary armies of Carthage, and in Sicily there was rich booty to be had. The centuriate assembly voted to send aid, and so began the long duel with Carthage.

CARTHAGE Carthage, rich and powerful, ruled over what is now Tunis and was allied with the Numidians to the west. In its possession were the western half of Sicily, Sardinia, Corsica, the smaller islands of the western Mediterranean, and the southern coast of Spain. Its fleet, dominating the western sea, restricted the trade of others, and prevented passage through the Straits of Gibraltar without Carthaginian permission. To the smaller states of the region, such as Rome, Carthage had dictated treaties which limited their activities while demonstrating its own pre-eminence. In the wars which had been fought at intervals in Sicily over a period of nearly three centuries, Carthage, though never able to conquer the Greeks, had more than held its own against them. Occupation of Messana would have given the Phoenician city an important advantage over the Greeks, and therefore it could not brook the interference of Rome in Sicily. Its aristocratic rulers were confident that their fleet, their generals, and their wealth were sufficient to stop the advance of Rome. Carthage's chief weakness, the mercenary character of the army, need cause no concern, they thought, so long as the troops were paid.

THE ROMAN Rome's interests, on the other hand, were not so directly involved. Its commercial activities were comparatively slight, and it had readily signed the treaties which Carthage had requested, even entering into alliance with Carthage against Pyrrhus. The Greek cities of southern Italy, however, were allies, and it was incumbent upon Rome to protect them against the advance of Carthaginian power. Long-standing relations between Rome and Syracuse would be endangered if Carthage closed the Straits, and with Carthage in Messana peace in Italy would be forever threatened. It was inevitable that the growing power of Rome would eventually challenge Carthaginian control of the West and that

Carthage would meet the challenge. In resources Rome seemed pitifully weak. Without fleet, money, or tribute from the allies, its wealth
was solely in the produce of its land and its strength in the citizen-
soldiers of the legions and the levies of the Italian allies.

THE WAR   Rome met with immediate success on land. The
                   Carthaginian and Syracusan forces were driven from
Messana and the city was occupied. Hiero II of Syracuse, who had
joined with Carthage at first, immediately changed sides and remained
Rome's faithful ally until his death in 215 B.C. The Romans then, in
262 B.C., besieged and conquered Agrigentum (the Greek Acragas),
which had become the center of Carthaginian power in Sicily.

Their experiences in this siege demonstrated to them their need of
a naval force, and they at once proceeded to build a fleet. There is a
famous story of questionable authenticity which relates how Roman
carpenters, using a wrecked Carthaginian quinquereme as a model,
built the ships, while oarsmen were being drilled on benches on the
shore. Each battleship was equipped with grappling devices and provided with a boarding party of one hundred and twenty soldiers—an
innovation in naval warfare. With this fleet of one hundred and
twenty ships Duilius in 260 B.C. won a great battle off Mylae on the
north of Sicily.

The Romans then determined upon the invasion of Africa, and
in 256 B.C., after a second naval battle off Ecnomus had cleared the
way, they despatched an expeditionary force under Regulus. The fate
of this invasion revealed the weakness of the Roman military system.
Though the consul won a victory, he failed to take Carthage or to secure a treaty of peace. Then in the fall, according to Roman custom,
the greater portion of his army went back to Rome, while he remained
in Africa with a small force awaiting the consul who would take his
place and bring fresh troops. During the winter, a wandering Spartan,
Xanthippus, coming to Carthage, reorganized and drilled the Punic
army. In the spring he tempted Regulus to battle before reinforcements
came, and succeeded in destroying the Roman forces, taking its commander prisoner. The fleet which was sent to the rescue was wrecked
off Sicily.

After the failure of the African expedition the war dragged on
interminably in Sicily. At sea two Roman fleets were wrecked by
storms and one was defeated in the harbor of Drepana. On land the
Carthaginian force commanded by Hamilcar Barca waged guerilla

warfare and kept the Romans in continual difficulty. Meanwhile Carthage, its trade at a standstill, was forced to borrow money from Egypt. In Rome the treasury was empty and the currency depreciated. Polybius compared the contestants to two gamecocks who have fought to exhaustion. Rome, however, was the first to recover.

THE END OF THE WAR
In 242 B.C. a group of wealthy Romans built and equipped a fleet of two hundred vessels. Catulus, the commander, trapped a Carthaginian transport fleet on its way to Sicily and destroyed it off the Aegates Islands. Thereupon Carthage yielded, and in 241 B.C. a treaty of peace was signed by which Carthage surrendered its possessions in Sicily to the Romans and agreed to pay a large indemnity. Immediately after the war, Carthage, unable to pay its mercenaries, found itself involved in a fearful struggle with these warriors, a struggle which required all of Hamilcar Barca's genius to suppress. Rome took advantage of the situation to occupy Sardinia and Corsica, and, when Carthage attempted to regain these possessions, declared war and forced the cession of the islands and the payment of an additional indemnity. The story is told that Hamilcar Barca thereafter caused his son Hannibal, before the altar of Moloch, god of Carthage, to swear eternal and undying enmity toward Rome, and then took him off to Spain to gather men and money for a war of revenge.

THE SECOND PUNIC WAR

ROME BETWEEN THE WARS
The victory over Carthage did not end the advance of Roman power. Rome fought two wars in Illyria to check piracy in the Adriatic and to protect the trade of her Greek allies. These conflicts brought about friendly relations with the Greek leagues and hostility with Macedon. A fresh invasion of Italy by Gauls in 225 B.C., after terrifying Rome, was barely stopped in a fierce battle at Telamon. The Romans promptly retaliated by conquering the Boii and Insubres in the Po Valley and pushing the Roman frontier to the Alps. A new agrarian policy developed by a popular leader, Flaminius, was adopted, and Latin colonies, with large allotments to the colonists, were established at Placentia and Cremona after which, to strengthen the Roman hold on this region, the Flaminian Way was built. Scarcely had the Romans entered upon the

exploitation of these rich lands when war with Carthage began for the second time. The occasion was the Carthaginian advance in Spain, whither Hamilcar Barca had gone to secure the rich mineral wealth and the assistance of its able fighters.

HANNIBAL   The Roman occupation of Sicily, Sardinia, and Corsica deprived Carthage of markets for the sale of its articles of export and import as well as of the sources of its mercenary troops. To compensate for these losses Hamilcar Barca developed Carthaginian control over southern Spain, a land rich in metals and inhabited by warlike tribes whose men proved a valuable addition to the forces of Carthage. Through the resources so obtained the Carthaginian hoped to crush Rome and re-establish the greatness of his city. After his death in 229 B.C. his son-in-law, Hasdrubal, founded Cartagena and sent wealth back home from the silver mines. He readily agreed to a treaty with Rome requested by the Massaliots and limiting Carthaginian power to the Ebro River on the north. In 221 B.C., at the death of Hasdrubal, Hannibal, at the age of twenty-six, succeeded to his brother-in-law's power in Spain. The history of the next twenty years is largely the biography of this remarkable man, in some respects the greatest of all military tacticians. A born leader of men, he understood the psychology of his own troops and of his enemy's as well. He knew how to use the terrain of a battlefield to the fullest advantage, and he was a master in the disposition of his troops on the field of battle. Ever since his time great generals, from his opponent Scipio to von Hindenburg, have studied his campaigns. His abilities were first manifested in 219 B.C. when he besieged and took Saguntum, a Spanish city allied to Rome. Angered by this presumption, Rome forthwith declared war in 218 B.C.

THE INVASION OF ITALY   The Roman plans were quickly made. One consul, Sempronius, was to gather an army in Sicily and invade Africa, which could easily be done since Rome controlled the sea; the other, Publius Cornelius Scipio, was to proceed with two legions to Spain and deal with Hannibal directly. But Hannibal's actions upset both plans. With great precision he crossed the Pyrenees and the Rhone, while Scipio was dallying a few days at Marseilles, and entered the passes of the Alps. What pass he crossed by is not known; it was possibly the Little St. Bernard in Mont Cenis. After a difficult time owing to the hostility of the mountaineers, the lack of proper roads, and the September snows, during which most of

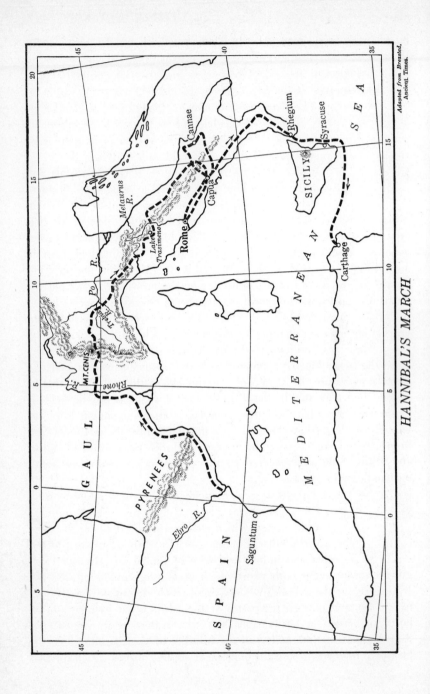

HANNIBAL'S MARCH

Adapted from Breasted,
Ancient Times.

his elephants were lost, he entered the valley of the Po with twenty thousand infantry and six thousand of the best cavalry in the world. His route brought him into the territory of the newly conquered Boii and Insubres, still hostile to Rome. He planned to rouse the Gauls, to break the Italian federation by promises of liberation from Rome, and to accomplish thereafter the destruction of the city itself. To attain his ends he needed resounding victories that would offer to Gauls and Italians hopes of success.

THE TREBIA RIVER

Scipio, after sending his army into Spain under his brother's command and returning to Italy to raise fresh troops, was defeated on the Ticinus River. Sempronius, recalled from Sicily, sent his army north in small detachments, reassembled it two months later at Ariminum, and joined Scipio at Placentia. Hannibal defeated the combined armies on the Trebia River in December, 218 B.C. By a clever ruse he engaged the Roman troops before breakfast and then drew them through an icy mountain stream into an ambush from which but few escaped.

LAKE TRASIMENE

For the following year the Romans elected to the consulate their popular hero, Flaminius. He took his stand at Arretium. Hannibal crossed the Apennines at Bologna, led his army for three sleepless days and nights through the marshes of Etruria, and placed himself between Flaminius and Rome. By well-designed atrocities, such as the burning of farmhouses, he brought the Romans down upon him, only to lead them into the hills around Lake Trasimene, where he trapped them by placing his troops upon the mist-covered slopes and by blocking the road before and behind them. The Roman army was annihilated. Italian prisoners were sent home with promises of freedom, but the Italians, nevertheless, were not yet ready to exchange Roman leadership for Carthaginian promises.

FABIUS, THE DELAYER

Amid great consternation at Rome Fabius Maximus was chosen dictator. His policy of delay and refusal to attack, while continually harassing the enemy, has given the name Fabian to policies of slow advance. Hannibal fell into a trap laid by Fabius in the Campanian hills and again showed his resourcefulness in his clever escape. He tied lighted faggots to the horns of cattle and drove them up the slopes at night. When the Roman guards rushed to stop this seemingly rash move, Hannibal and his men marched out by the pass. Minucius, master of the horse, elected co-dictator by the impatient Roman people, was soundly defeated but was rescued by Fabius.

CANNAE,
216 B.C.

Hannibal spent the winter in Apulia and in the spring met the Romans on the banks of the Aufidus River near Cannae. Rome put her greatest army into the field—traditionally eighty thousand men, but certainly not so large —led by Aemilius Paullus, conservative, and Terentius Varro, popular leader. They expected to sweep Hannibal off the field with their overwhelming numbers. But Hannibal allowed his weakened center to fall back, swung his wings of heavy-armed Africans around the Roman flanks, and sent his heavy cavalry against the Roman rear. Only ten thousand Romans escaped. The plan of Hindenburg's great victory over Russia in 1914 at the Mazurian Lakes was based on Hannibal's tactics at Cannae.

Hannibal made no attempt to attack Rome, which doubtless he could not have taken, but his original purpose seemed nearly achieved. Philip V of Macedon made an alliance with him; Syracuse, with Hiero dead, came over to him; Capua joined him, and he was later able to secure Tarentum save for its citadel. One more such victory and he might win! But that victory he never achieved.

Though he remained in Italy until 203 B.C. and fought many skirmishes, he never again met the Romans in pitched battle. Instead, Rome, standing like a rock, sent troops to watch and harass him, while it dealt singly with his allies. By timely assistance to the Greeks they kept Philip V busy at home. Marcellus, overcoming both the bravery of the Syracusans and the genius of Archimedes, took Syracuse and carried its treasures to Rome. Carthage, either from inability or unwillingness to act, failed to support its great commander or his ally in Sicily. Even so, when the Romans besieged Capua, Hannibal made a sudden raid on Rome. But the army stood firm around Capua, and, though mothers might frighten their children into good behavior with the cry, "Hannibal is at the gates," Rome remained unharmed behind its walls, while Capua fell and was destroyed.

THE METAURUS
RIVER

The last great threat of the Carthaginians came, like the first, from Spain. Hasdrubal, Hannibal's brother, after gaining successes over the Roman forces in Spain, eluded the Roman army and sped to Italy to join Hannibal, in the hope that the union of their forces might strike the deathblow at the war-weary Romans. His messenger to Hannibal was caught, however, and the Roman armies, hastening north, defeated and killed Hasdrubal on the banks of the Metaurus River in 207 B.C. Hannibal withdrew into the hills of Bruttium, where he stayed until 203 B.C.

THE RISE
OF SCIPIO
The genius of a young man, Publius Cornelius Scipio, son of the Roman commander at the battle at the Trebia River, finally brought victory to Rome. In 211 B.C. the youthful Scipio, though too young to be eligible for high command, was given proconsular power by special act and sent to Spain to replace his father and uncle, who had been killed in battle the preceding year. Though he let Hasdrubal slip through his fingers with almost fatal consequences, he seized Cartagena, the Carthaginian stronghold, expelled the Punic forces from Spain, and entered into friendly relations with the Numidians, who had theretofore supplied Carthage with its fine cavalry. Returning to Rome a hero to the populace, he was elected consul. Straightway he proposed an invasion of Africa. With Hannibal in Italy, the senate hesitated; but when Scipio threatened an appeal to the people, it yielded, and Scipio crossed over in 204 B.C. The Carthaginians sought for peace; and during the armistice which followed, Hannibal returned home in 203 B.C.

ZAMA
For fifteen years Hannibal had lived in an enemy country, had won great victories, and had held Roman forces at bay. His return to Africa brought fresh hopes to the Carthaginians, who at once renewed the war. In 202 B.C. he met Scipio on the battlefield of Zama. The Roman commander used Hannibal's favorite weapon, the Numidian cavalry, against him, and won a victory which brought the war to an end. By the terms of peace dictated by Scipio and agreed upon by Hannibal in 201 B.C., Carthage surrendered its possessions in Spain and its alliance with Numidia, disbanded its army, destroyed its fleet, promised to wage no war without Rome's consent, and agreed to pay an enormous indemnity. Scipio was rewarded by the title Africanus, and Rome was mistress of the western Mediterranean.

CONSEQUENCES
OF THE WAR
From the long struggle with Carthage Rome emerged victorious but indelibly scarred by the conflict. The loss of men had been appalling. The ravages of Hannibal's army and the demands of the long years of constant military service had led to the abandonment of many small farms and therewith to the further development of the great estates of the senatorial class. The services of supply for the armies and the fleet, the tasks of

management of the finances of newly acquired territories, and the appearance at Rome of a large supply of mobile capital gained from booty and the indemnities led to the appearance in Rome of a new class of capitalists and men of business, who were ready at the end of the war for new fields of exploitation, and whose interests eventually clashed, as we shall see, with those of the ruling group of senators.

In the meantime senatorial power had consistently advanced. During the period between the wars the popular leader, Flaminius, had challenged it successfully. He had secured the passage of laws reorganizing the centuriate assembly on a more democratic basis and restricting the activities of individual senators in trade. Democratic interest in the land program was evidenced by the provision of farms larger than customary for colonists in the Po Valley. But the need for consistent direction of military affairs, the wretched failure of Flaminius and his follower, Varro, in the struggle with Hannibal, and the firm strength which the senate displayed—all combined to crush this nascent democratic movement and to leave the senate in control of the state. The powers of the senate, however, depended not upon legal sanctions but on its prestige and that of its members and upon Roman adherence to custom and precedent.

The victory over Carthage made the Romans rulers of the western Mediterranean and almost inevitably involved them in the troubled waters of the Hellenistic East. When the opportunity offered, the senatorial leaders, jealous and fearful of their newly acquired position, but avid for wealth and military glory and abetted by the business leaders, who looked for new outlets for their capital and recently discovered abilities, were ready to seize it and to draw the war-weary but still rapacious populace with them. The declaration of war upon Macedon in 200 B.C. launched them upon a series of wars which made Rome mistress of the Hellenistic world.

THE EASTERN WARS The reason or excuse for the first entrance of Rome into Hellenistic affairs is hard to find. Until Pyrrhus came to Italy the Romans had had little if any relations with the Aegean. The Illyrian Wars, fought during the interval of the Punic Wars for the protection of Adriatic commerce, led to favorable relations with the Greek leagues and hostile feelings upon the part of Macedon. But neither this nor Philip V's abortive alliance with Hannibal in what is called the "First Macedonian War" gave the Romans any real interest in the East.

Yet Rome's position as the first power of the western Mediterranean in control of Sicily and the western waters made it almost inevitable that it would be drawn into the maelstrom of Eastern politics. The occasion was a crisis in Eastern affairs, which arose in 203 B.C. When Ptolemy IV died in that year, leaving his throne to an infant son controlled by a corrupt and weak regency, Antiochus III of Asia (p. 300), flushed by the success of his eastern campaigns, immediately advanced upon southern Syria, while Philip V in agreement with him set to work to capture the Ptolemaic possessions in the Aegean area. Egypt, thus beset, appealed to Rome for aid. True, there was no reason why Rome should go to the rescue of Egypt, since thus far the only relations between these states had been the sale of Egyptian grain to the Romans at exorbitant prices during the Hannibalic War. When, however, to the appeal of the Egyptians was added the request of Attalus of Pergamum, of Rhodes, and especially of the Aetolians, who had been Rome's allies during the First Macedonian War, all alarmed by the advance of Macedon, the Romans ordered Philip to cease harassing the Greeks and Ptolemy V and to arbitrate his differences with Pergamum and Rhodes. Philip's refusal was followed by a declaration of war.

The senate persuaded the assembly to change a negative to a positive vote by presenting the danger, indeed remote, of a Macedonian invasion of Italy. Many modern authorities believe that Attalus aroused Roman fears by pointing to the growing might of Antiochus and exaggerating the danger presented to the whole Mediterranean by the alliance between Macedon and Asia and its threatened conquest of Egypt. It is sometimes argued, but without sufficient evidence, that the real basis of the senate's action was the sentimental desire on the part of some Roman senators to be recognized as civilized people by the cultured Greeks. Rome apparently desired, by establishing protectorates over the Greeks and Egypt, to preserve a balance of power in the East, to check the advances of Macedon and Asia, and yet to avoid the problems and perils of territorial aggrandizement.

THE SECOND
MACEDONIAN
WAR

The Second Macedonian War (200-197 B.C.), after lagging for a period, was brought to a victorious conclusion when in 197 B.C. Titus Flamininus, a young philhellene serving as proconsul, secured the aid of the Achaean League and forced and won a battle at Cynoscephalae in Thessaly. Philip at once agreed to evacuate Greece, the Aegean, and

Illyricum and to ally himself with Rome. When at the Isthmian games in 196 B.C. Flamininus announced the freedom of the Greeks, he was nearly overwhelmed by the enthusiastic people. Flamininus restored order, settled disputes between cities, arranged boundaries, and recalled his troops. The Greeks quickly learned, however, that they were bound by his decisions and that Rome intended quietly but firmly to interfere with their foreign relations. In short, the Greeks had merely exchanged masters. The irritation which inevitably resulted helped to bring on the later wars.

The Aetolians, greatly aggrieved because they had secured neither the spoils nor the power which they felt was their due from the wars with Philip, and resenting the postbellum interference of the Romans, invited Antiochus III to come to their assistance. Although Hannibal, banished from Carthage in 196 B.C. on the order of Rome, was at his court, the king did not avail himself of the great general's services and experience. A small Seleucid force was defeated in 191 B.C. at Thermopylae, and in 190 B.C. a Roman army commanded by Lucius Scipio and his brother, the great Africanus, won a decisive victory at Magnesia in Asia Minor. Antiochus III was forced by the treaty to surrender all Asia Minor.

Continued irritation against Rome resulted in 171 B.C. in the formation of an anti-Roman alliance of Macedonians and Greeks, led by Perseus, son of Philip V. After the Romans had suffered a number of defeats due to incapable leaders, Aemilius Paullus won a great victory at Pydna in 168 B.C. Macedon was thereupon divided into four tribute-paying republics; its treasure, the royal domains and mines became the property of Rome. The Achaean League suffered for its attitude in the war when one thousand of its leading citizens were taken to Rome as hostages; at the same time, for an unfortunate offer to arbitrate, Rhodes was punished by the loss of its Anatolian possessions and by the ruin of its trade when Rome opened Delos (p. 300) as a free port. Though Rome had not annexed a single foot of territory, its will was supreme throughout the East. The order of a single Roman envoy was strong enough to compel Antiochus IV to retire from Egypt.

The Roman program of control without annexation was, however, a failure. Revolts led in 146 B.C. to the formation of a province of Macedonia. When in the same year the Achaean League refused to obey orders, Mummius, the Roman commander, sacked the city of

Corinth; the Achaean League was dissolved, and the Greek cities were thereupon placed under the supervision of the governor of Macedonia. This first period of Roman expansion in the East reached its climax and end when in 133 B.C. Attalus III died. Having accepted the inevitable, in his will he left Pergamum to the Roman people. From it the rich province of Asia was formed.

THE WEST
Meanwhile, the Roman legions had been engaged in consolidating Roman control over the West. Cisalpine Gaul was recovered after the Hannibalic War, and more roads were built and new colonies founded. In spite of the heroic resistance of the native tribes, particularly under the first Spanish hero, Viriathus (147-139 B.C.), Roman power steadily advanced in Spain, until in 133 B.C. the capture by Scipio Aemilianus of the city of Numantia, which had defied and defeated the Romans, brought the struggle to an end. In the following years Roman fleets secured control of the Balearic Islands, and in 121 B.C. southern Gaul was annexed to protect the land route to Spain.

THIRD PUNIC
WAR (149-
146 B.C.)
For two generations Carthage remained the traditional foe of Rome and the constant object of Roman suspicion. When Hannibal, after Zama, reorganized the state and restored its prosperity, the Romans in alarm ordered his banishment. Their enmity followed him to the court of Antiochus and to Bithynia, whither he fled after the battle of Magnesia and where he took poison rather than be led a captive to Rome. Still Carthaginian prosperity aroused the fears of conservative Romans, possibly also the jealousy of Roman landowners, who resented the competition of Carthaginian olive oil, and almost certainly it aroused the land hunger of the agrarian interests at Rome. Cato, farmer and leader of the senate, is said to have ended all his speeches with the words, "Carthage must be destroyed."

At length pretexts were found for war, which began in 149 B.C. After two years of failure in the field, the Romans again elected a young Scipio as proconsul. This youth, son of Aemilius Paullus, victor of Pydna, and adopted by the son of Scipio Africanus, is known to history as Scipio Aemilianus (p. 338), and as Africanus Minor, the latter adjective to distinguish him from the first Africanus. Carthage fell before him in 146 B.C., was utterly destroyed, and its very site accursed. Its territory was organized into the province of Africa; much of its land was confiscated and handed over to Roman settlers, and the great estates of its aristocrats passed into the hands of Roman land-lords.

In the same year Corinth also fell. The forces of Carthage and the East, dependent upon mercenaries, disunited and weak, had proved no match for the vigorous action of the Roman legionaries, guided wisely in the main by the senate and led in their victorious campaigns by a series of brilliant commanders. Of the Hellenistic powers only Asia and Egypt were left; Egypt was a protected ally, however, and Asia was crushed and humiliated. The entire Mediterranean world lay at the feet of Rome.

THE EFFECTS OF ROMAN IMPERIALISM

Within the space of one hundred and thirty-one years the entire structure of the Mediterranean area had been completely transformed by the meteoric rise of Rome. Political, economic, social, and cultural changes, accompanying and reacting upon each other, appeared every-where and affected life in the conquered lands, in Italy, and, most vitally, in Rome itself.

THE PROVIN-
CIAL SYSTEM
The Roman provincial system was an emergency product. At the end of the First Punic War Rome found itself with Sicily, and soon thereafter with Sardinia and Corsica, on its hands. Since to include them in the Italian federation was impossible, the senate decided to treat them as subjects, literally as *praedia populi Romani* ("estates of the Roman people") and to exact tribute from them. Two new praetors were elected to take these territories as their *provincia,* or sphere of duty. When Spain was organized into two provinces in 197 B.C., two more praetorships were established. As the number of provinces increased, proconsuls and propraetors were regularly assigned to them by the senate.

Each province was an aggregate of local communities whose status was carefully defined in the *lex provinciae.* This important document was drawn up at the time of annexation by the conquering general and a committee of ten senators subject to approval or amendment by the senate. A few ancient cities of great honor such as Athens, Rhodes, and Marseilles were recognized as allies of Rome and were theoreti-cally free from interference and from all burdens. To some others the senate granted, in return for services rendered, immunity from taxa-tion. The great majority were tax-paying communities which governed themselves according to their ancestral customs. But their foreign relations were strictly under Roman control, and they paid to Rome either 10 per cent of their annual produce, as in Sicily, or a fixed annual sum, as in Asia.

The provincial governor's duty was to protect the frontier, to keep order, to see that taxes were paid, and to judge cases involving Roman citizens. His imperium, or right of command, was limited by the borders of the province. He was assisted by three *legati*, lieutenants, appointed by the senate, and by a number of *comites*, young men who went out with him at their own expense to gain experience. Royal monopolies, mines, and domains, and all confiscated properties were worked under lease or contract by Roman businessmen usually acting in partnerships. The system of itself was not burdensome. The taxes were no more than most of the cities had already been paying. Peace and order, uniform systems of law and coinage should have brought great prosperity; yet, in point of fact, the situation was quite different. The Romans regarded the provinces as so much booty. Not only did commanders and soldiers plunder freely at the time of conquest, but the tax collectors rapaciously seized more than was their due. Roman businessmen exploited the provincial resources mercilessly and loaned money to cities at exorbitant rates of interest. Many of the governors corruptly levied exactions and extortions to enrich themselves. As a result many of the provincials were impoverished and men of intelligence either were drawn to Rome or became so discouraged by Roman interference that progress in the Hellenistic world slackened materially.

ITALY   The effects of Roman imperialism on the Italians were no less disastrous. Though the Italians had taken part in the wars, they did not share in the profits. Furthermore the Romans, swollen with pride and no longer dependent upon the Italians for military assistance, began to treat them also as subjects, to interfere in their local affairs, and to make demands upon them. Italian merchants were ruined by the overwhelming power of the business class in Rome, and Italian farmers suffered in the general transformation of agriculture. When as a matter of self-protection they demanded that they be accorded Roman citizenship, they were promptly rebuffed.

ROME

The conquest made itself felt in every phase of Roman life. An agricultural revolution vitally affected the lives and property of the senatorial and the popular classes, while the demands of imperial finance gave added impetus to the development of a new class of businessmen. Significant constitutional changes took place as the government of a city-state endeavored to adapt itself to the needs of imperial control. The wealth of empire created new standards in social life, and contact with the Greeks led to the absorption of Hellenistic culture, to the growth of Roman literature, and to the appearance at Rome of Hellenistic religions and philosophic systems. Rome of the early period had been a community of farmers ruled by an agricultural aristocracy, with only such trade or industry as local demand required. The city of the late republic was imperial and populous, active with the affairs of the world, replete with wealth and all of wealth's embellishments and refinements.

AGRICULTURE The agricultural revolution was marked by the decline of the number of small farms and the growth of great estates devoted to cattle raising or to the production of the olive and the grape. There were several reasons for these changes. Many of the soldiers who had fought for years in Sicily, Africa, Spain, or the East had no desire to return to the humdrum life of the ancestral farm. Some who did desire to return found it difficult if not impossible to do so because of the condition of their farms. Large areas of southern Italy had been so thoroughly devastated by the forces of Hannibal that they never recovered; others had declined or had suffered soil erosion as the result of neglect; on still others the soil had been exhausted by generations of intensive cultivation. The competition of foreign, particularly Sicilian grain, though not serious except in Rome itself, made grain farming less lucrative than previously. On the other hand, the more profitable raising of cattle or growing of olive orchards and vineyards required larger areas and greater outlays of capital than were possible for the small farmer. There was constant pressure to sell land to the aristocracy who, forbidden by law to engage directly in commercial activities, were compelled to invest their wealth in land. Finally, some small farmers were doubtless forced off their lands illegally by rapacious senators. Nevertheless, there were still many men who continued to work their small domains or to find occupation as laborers on the great estates.

The growth of *latifundia* ("great estates"), beginning with the conquest of Italy, continued unchecked, since the restrictions of the Licinian-Sextian Laws were not enforced. Large tracts of abandoned or confiscated land were turned over to great landowners after the Hannibalic War, and the process of growth continued throughout the second century B.C.

Much of our information about these estates comes from Cato, who in his *de Agricultura* gave instructions in estate management. To Cato the most profitable type of farming was cattle raising, and throughout northern and eastern Italy, the large cattle or sheep ranch tended by gangs of slaves became the dominant type. The careful attention which Cato paid to the handling of olive orchards and vineyards is indicative of the great importance of the growth of these phases of agricultural activity in Italy, particularly in the southern area. In the raising of grain and vegetables Cato laid emphasis upon specialization to suit the soil or the market and advised fertilization and the rotation of crops. The management of the estate, according to Cato, should be strictly regulated in all its details; at the head should be a slave bailiff and his wife; free laborers were to be hired for special tasks and at harvest time; the rest of the force, mostly slaves, should be worked until old or worn out, when they should be turned out like cattle to die; household and farm equipment and food should be simple and doled out only as required. Cato made a careful list of everything that should be needed and allowed. Cato's book, drawn in part from Italian tradition and in part from Greek and Phoenician sources, and the translation into Latin of the agricultural manuals of Mago of Carthage are evidences of the interest of wealthy landowners in the development of scientific and income-producing farming on their estates.

SLAVERY   Slavery first became an important factor in Roman life in the period of conquest. The demand for labor on the great estates together with the presence of large numbers of prisoners of war combined to accelerate the development of slavery as an institution. Too, piracy in the Hellenistic world contributed to the number of slaves. Thracians and Illyrians were in great demand as herdsmen on the cattle ranches, and Greeks and Syrians, experienced in the culture of the olive and the vine, were eagerly sought for by owners of southern estates. Many highly skilled slaves served as clerks, secretaries, or artisans in the city; others were employed in ever-growing numbers in the households of men of wealth. Slaves were by no means so numerous, however, as entirely to dispossess free labor, some of which was still used on the estates or employed in the city. Manumission, except on the great ranches, was easy and frequent, and the freedmen secured citizenship along with release from servile status.

The menace which the great extension of slavery presented to the Roman state was evidenced by a great outbreak in Sicily in 134-132 B.C. The slaves on the Roman and Greek estates of that island, terribly oppressed by their owners, found leaders in a Syrian named Eunus, "Well-wisher," and in a Cilician named Cleon who headed a revolt which rapidly spread over the whole island. After killing their owners and being joined by peasant farmers who rejoiced in the destruction of great estates, they successfully met detachments of the Roman army. The rebellious slaves endeavored to establish an independent kingdom of their own in Sicily with Eunus as "King Antiochus" and Cleon as his chief general. Vigorous action by Roman consuls in person was required to suppress the revolt. After fearful engagements and wholesale executions of captives, the slave forces were subdued, order was restored, and the working of the great estates resumed. No effort was made to redress the grievances which had led to the outbreak, and the slave question remained a pressing and unsolved problem for the Roman senate.

THE OPTIMATES The senatorial group, *Optimates,* "best men," as they came to be called, thus emerged from the war period as a group of aristocrats who derived their wealth from great estates which they managed for profit. Their chief occupation was with the offices and affairs of government, which they monopolized. The wars gave them opportunities for military glory and booty, and the provincial governorships provided openings for recouping or increasing their wealth at the expense of the provincials. Though the law forbade them to engage in business or to own a ship larger than a small yacht, many individuals who desired increased incomes circumvented the law by investments or loans through agents.

The glory and prestige which accrued to the *Optimates* made them more conscious than even before of their position as a class, so that they drew the lines more closely about themselves. Through control of the election machinery they made it impossible for any but men of extraordinary ability and tenacity like Cato to break into their class. At the same time, affected more than any other group in Rome by Greek culture, they began, despite the opposition of some conservatives, to ignore the traditions of their ancestors, to depart from ancient ideals and standards of simplicity, to live in luxury, and to seek intellectual attainments. Devotion to their own interests as individuals and as a class took the place of loyalty to the best interests of the state and they failed, as we shall see, to manage successfully the affairs of Rome and the empire.

THE EQUITES   Commerce and industry remained relatively undeveloped in Rome, partly because of the aversion, both traditional and sanctioned by law, of the ruling classes for those forms of occupation, and partly because of the competition of the highly developed eastern centers. Not until the last century of the republic did Roman merchants appear as active participants in Mediterranean affairs. The requirements of war and of imperial management, however, led to the rapid expansion of a class of businessmen as contractors for the construction of roads, bridges, and public buildings, for the transportation of troops and supplies, and as managers of mines and state properties in the provinces. These men had a share in the collection of taxes, though their most celebrated activities in this sphere and in the exploitation of the provinces belongs to the succeeding period of the Roman revolution. The influx of mobile wealth which poured into Rome as booty or as tribute resulted in the appearance of bankers who invested it and who also loaned money to needy senators or to provincial cities. For larger undertakings the businessmen formed "societies," partnerships comparable to joint-stock companies, in which senators secretly invested and even poorer men sometimes had shares. Those who engaged in the public or private phases of these business affairs were called *publicani* or *negotiatores,* respectively, although, since men of wealth doubtless acted in both capacities, these groups overlapped. The class as a whole was called *equites,* knights, or horsemen, because they had sufficient wealth to qualify for the cavalry, though their actual occupations prevented them from taking any part in this military service. Since they did not hold office and had no social standing with the aristocracy, their only measure of success was money. Consequently they were distinctly imperialistic and increasingly inclined to be grasping and corrupt. The rival activities of the *Optimates* and the *Équites* in the province led eventually to controversies of vital importance to the Roman state.

THE POPULARES While some of the expropriated peasant farmers remained in the country as hired laborers, many of them drifted into the city where, with returning veterans, they formed a landless and poverty-stricken proletariat. They were supported by such employment as they might find, assisted by the charity or the bribes of the wealthy, who expected applause and votes in return. Since landownership was still a prerequisite for military service, the census lists of eligible soldiers steadily declined as the restless and turbulent mob of the city increased to the detriment of civic and political life. This group, the *Populares,* which found its leaders in the liberal group in the senate, presented to the ruling class of the state problems —military, economic, and moral—which were, as we shall see, the starting point of the revolutionary movement.

POLITICAL CHANGES The senate reached the acme of its powers in the strain and stress of conflict. The obvious need of wise and consistent direction in war and in the management of conquered lands led to silent acquiescence in a senatorial control which far transcended its legal powers. The senate assumed full control of military affairs, of the assignment of commanders and provincial governors, of dealings with foreign and allied states, and of finance. At home it kept a watchful eye on manners and morals, and developed its right to establish extraordinary judicial commissions and, at times of crisis, to suspend constitutional guarantees of appeal by the *Senatus consultum ultimum,* equivalent to a decree of martial law. The senate showed itself to best advantage in the Hannibalic War, when the courage and tenacity of the ruling class saved Rome from collapse. In the following century, jealous of its prerogatives, torn by factions, and with its members greedy for money, far too frequently it displayed weaknesses in the management of the wars, even though success crowned its efforts in the end. Not only did it fail lamentably and completely in the control and direction of the provinces and even more disastrously in the handling of the complex problems presented by the Italian allies, by the city mob, and by the political corruption of Rome itself, but by its treatment of these questions it aggravated the existing evils.

At the same time that the power of the magistrates declined, the system of choosing them proved utterly inadequate. Admirably adapted to produce men trained in the traditions of command and rule and competent to deal with ordinary affairs, the system had no means of providing an extraordinary man for a crisis without striking a danger ous, even disastrous blow at the constitutional machinery. Regularly elected consuls like Flaminius, Varro, and Paullus failed completely against Hannibal. The time-honored institution of the dictatorship [3] was abandoned after the command of Fabius because it did not meet the needs of the situation. The use of experienced men in continued command as proconsuls, although helping to solve the immediate diffi culties, proved to be the opening wedge which eventually destroyed the old governmental machine.

The first open step toward Caesarism was taken when Scipio, who had been given proconsular power in Spain before he was quaestor, was able to force from the senate permission to go to Africa. Under the pressure of circumstance the great man had become more power ful than the constitution. The senate realized its danger and fought vigorously to retain its strength. Charges of mismanagement of finances were brought against Scipio when he returned with his brother from the Asiatic War, and, though the great man disdainfully tore up the accounts, he passed into eclipse. The events of the Greek Wars further revealed the weaknesses of the machine. Offices which promised to be lucrative from spoils became the prize of political struggles between factions within the senate, with the result that in competent men were often chosen. Consuls, elected in ordinary course, failed wretchedly against Philip V and against Perseus, while the bril liant proconsuls Flamininus and Aemilius Paullus succeeded. In the Third Punic War, likewise, the regular magistrates were incompetent, and Scipio Aemilianus, though only a candidate for the aedileship, was sent as proconsul against Carthage.

In response to this pressing need for better machinery to choose able men without unconstitutional action, the senate merely attempted to strengthen the constitutional tradition against the rise of individuals stronger than the state. The succession of offices (*cursus honorum*)— quaestorship, praetorship, and consulship with fixed age limits (twenty-eight for the quaestorship) and a two-year interval between successive magistracies—was established by law in 180 B.C. Yet in the election of Scipio Aemilianus in 146 B.C. this law was completely ignored.

[3] The later dictatorships of Sulla and of Caesar were of different character.

Another problem which the senate failed to solve was the control of provincial governors. The promagistrates in the provinces held the imperium and though the senate made the assignments and might punish the governors on their return, they were virtually independent during their term of office. The consuls, eventually finding their power restricted to Italy, were likewise unable to check the overseas officials. Appointments were made on principles of favoritism or for political motives without regard to ability or to honesty. As a result, the mismanagement, graft, and corruption, which followed from the attempts of the governors to pay off the expenses of their political career at Rome and to gain great wealth at the expense of the provincials, became an open scandal. An attempt to correct the evil by the *Lex Calpurnia de repetundis* of 149 B.C., which provided a jury of fifty senators presided over by a praetor to try cases of extortion, was almost a complete failure. The expenses of prosecution at Rome were so great as to discourage provincial action, and convictions were hard to secure from a jury of men who had been or hoped to be governors in their turn. Furthermore, provincial graft had an unfortunate effect on Rome since the opportunities thus afforded for the attainment of great wealth increased the competition for offices and induced bribery and lavish expenditures on games to curry favor with the populace. Finally, the unrestricted power of promagistrates in command of great armies in the provinces proved, in the next period, to be a force greater than the constitution and eventually brought the republic to its end.

The grievances of the Latin and Italian allies were intensified when the senate cut in half their share of the booty after victory and gave conquered lands only to citizens, and also when individual magistrates demanded entertainment from Italian towns through which they passed. More and more the Italians approached the status of subjects. Efforts to deal with the problem of the proletariat by putting them back on the land were blocked to protect the vested interests of the ruling class. Senatorial power likewise prevented any attempt to secure reform by action of the assemblies. The popular movement led by Flaminius and Varro during the interval of the Punic Wars attained a small success in the settling of citizens on lands in the Po Valley. It was their program also which secured the restrictions against senatorial entrance into business. To break down the influence of wealth in the centuriate assembly, they passed a law redividing the centuries among the tribes and providing for the choice by lot of a century to cast the first vote. Their movement collapsed, however, with the death of its leaders in the war, and for almost a century no strong leader of the popular element appeared. Tribunes who looked forward to a political career found it necessary to obey the wishes of the senatorial machine, and vetoes of colleagues were always available to stop any who might prove recalcitrant. Small attendance, bribery, and influence rendered worthless the reform of the centuriate assembly. As the farmers ceased to come to the city to vote, the tribal assembly degenerated even more than the centuriate into a venal city mob easily controlled by skilled politicians. Laws were passed to prevent bribery, and secret balloting was established, but to no avail. In spite of the presence of many honorable men who still clung to the ancient standards, Roman politics were unmistakably corrupt.

ROMAN CULTURE

The wealth derived from conquest began, during the period of the wars, to affect the city, the living standards of its inhabitants, and their intellectual, artistic, and religious interests. In the earlier period the Romans had possessed the foundations of a Roman culture. In literature they had begun the development of legal writings, of maxims, and of oratory. Rude verses of loose construction and ribald content were composed in the so-called Saturnian meter, and for drama they had the native Italian puppet show, the *fabula Atellana*. Unlovely death masks of great men took the place of portrait sculptures. Under Etruscan and, to a lesser extent, Greek influences they had erected temples and statues on Etruscan models. For example, the Scipio family at the time of the Samnite Wars possessed a tomb with an inscribed and decorated sarcophagus of Etruscan style for the hero Barbatus. Roads and aqueducts, practical arts, were the great Roman contributions to architecture. But these modest beginnings were completely surpassed when Rome, conquering the Hellenistic world, fell under the spell of Greek culture.

THE HELLENIZATION OF ROME

Graecia capta ferum victorem cepit. "Captive Greece took her barbarian conqueror captive." So wrote the poet Horace. The long years in Sicily during the First Punic War and the continued campaigns in the East during the second century acquainted Roman officers and soldiers with the beauties of Greek art and literature, the amusements of the Greek theater, the intricacies of Greek philosophies, and the consolations of Hellenistic religions. Prisoners of war, bought as slaves, became secretaries to wealthy Romans or tutors to their sons. Greek doctors began to practice in the city, and rhetoricians and philosophers found it profitable to set themselves up as teachers. The ambassadors from the Greek cities were frequently learned men, and one of them, Carneades, the Skeptic, gave lectures while waiting for the senate to hear his cause. Among the thousand Achaean hostages (p. 376) were many scholars who became attached to noble families and planted the seeds of culture in Roman soil. The greatest of these was Polybius, the historian, friend and teacher of the younger Scipio.

ART AND ARCHITECTURE Empowered by wealth and enlightened by these experiences and teachings, the Romans began to refurbish their physical and intellectual surroundings. Though temples were still erected of tufa or of concrete covered with stucco and adorned with terra-cotta ornaments and though most houses were still simple *atria,* at the same time basilicas, spacious halls modeled after the Greek porches, were erected in the Forum while a few nobles had pictures painted on the walls and added peristyles to their dwellings. A fine new aqueduct was built on arches to bring water to the city. Statues, brought from Greek cities, especially from Syracuse by Marcellus and from Corinth by Mummius, were placed in temples and Roman gentlemen liked to possess galleries of Greek objects of art. Of creative work in this field by Romans there was little. Tapestries, rugs, silverware, fine gowns and jewelry were new luxuries and signs of Hellenistic influence. Laws were passed to outlaw luxury and forbid extravagance, and Cato as censor in 186 B.C. vainly endeavored to check these vices by vigorous action. From the old city a new and beautiful Rome was slowly rising.

LITERATURE Roman literature passed rapidly under Greek influence from its crude beginnings to the time of its flowering. After the First Punic War, Livius Andronicus (fl. 220 B.C.), a Greek freedman, translated the *Odyssey* into Saturnian verse and wrote and produced in Latin plays taken from the Greek. At about the same time Naevius, possibly a Campanian, made translations, wrote plays on Roman subjects, and composed an epic poem on the First Punic War. Plautus (ca. 254-184 B.C.) wrote comedies based on

Menander's works but with a broad Roman flavor. Terence (ca. 195-159 B.C.), his follower, adhered more closely to the Greek originals. That the Roman populace had little understanding or interest in the Greek theater is well illustrated by the story of how an audience once made a chorus engage in mimic battle on the stage. Ennius (239-169 B.C.), the greatest of the poets of the time and friend of Scipio Africanus, composed a great epic, the *Annals of Rome,* and translated into Latin works of philosophy as well as plays.

History appeared when the Romans found it necessary to explain themselves to the Greeks, and, during the Second Punic War, a number of annalists, notably Fabius Pictor, wrote histories of Rome in Greek. Cato, in addition to his treatise on farming (p. 381), composed the first Latin history of Rome, the *Origines,* for his son. These writings made the Romans conscious of their own past and served in a later period as sources for the great historian, Livy. The loss of all except a few fragments of these early historical works has made the task of reconstructing early Roman history much more difficult for modern historians.

PHILOSOPHY   Philosophy, as well as literature, made its appeal to the Roman mind. But what the Greek teachers who brought the enlightened thought of the Hellenistic world to Rome chiefly accomplished was the undermining of the simple and narrow, though virile, Roman tradition. Ancestral customs and ideas no longer satisfied the men of the new age, introduced as they were suddenly to wealth, luxury, and freedom of thought. One group endeavored to draw from Greek culture the best there was in it: this was the famous Scipionic circle led by Scipio Aemilianus and his friend Laelius and advised by Polybius. They studied and discussed history and philosophy, invited Panaetius, the Stoic, to Rome, and through their influence made Stoicism the dominant Roman philosophy, aided, of course, by the fact that its principles best coincided with the Roman traditions of valor and endurance. But many of the younger generation misinterpreted the teachings of the philosophers and with pseudointellectual nonchalance claimed freedom from the restraint of ancient sanctions on the authority of intellectualism.

A vigorous faction in the senate, however, fought against the Greek influences as well as against the forces of corruption and the new luxury. Cato, its leader, affected to despise all things Greek and wrote in Latin for his son, though he made use of Greek sources in his *de Agricultura.* In 173 B.C. two Epicureans were expelled, and in 161 B.C. all Greek rhetoricians were despatched from Rome. When Carneades in his lectures (p. 388) proved that justice was relative and not absolute, Cato urged the senate to finish his business and send him back to Athens. But the tide was irresistible, and soon all educated Romans were learning Greek. Even Cato did so, for business reasons.

RELIGION The effect of Greek influence on Roman religion was distinctly bad. Down to the end of the Italic Wars, Roman religion, in spite of accretions, had retained much of its simple spirituality. Thereafter Roman and Greek gods were identified with each other—Jupiter with Zeus and Juno with Hera, for example—and the whole gorgeous imagery of mythology was handed over to the literal-minded Romans. But instead of making the gods more human and appealing, these changes tended to destroy them. The Romans, failing to penetrate through the story to the experience behind it, lost confidence in gods who possessed human weaknesses. Greek philosophy removed the faith of the educated classes in the ancestral gods, and the Punic Wars also wrought untold havoc in the old Roman religion when, in the crisis of the second war, it seemed as if the gods themselves had deserted the Romans. The people turned to such barbaric practices as human sacrifice, and finally on the advice of the Sibylline books, invited the Great Mother of Pessinus to Rome. The conservative senate, shocked by the orgies of her religion, forbade any Roman to become her priest; nevertheless many people found solace in her emotional worship. In southern Italy, in Sicily, and in the East, Roman soldiers became aware of other emotional cults. Among the western Greeks the secret bands of Orphist worshipers of Dionysus had always been strong. The Romans called the god Bacchus, his festivals, Bacchanalia. So strong did this hidden and emotional cult become that the senate ordered an investigation in 186 B.C. and suppressed the society, though individuals who felt themselves bound by religious scruples to worship the god were, with special permission, allowed to do so. It proved as impossible, however, to stop the coming of Eastern religions to Rome as it was to halt the advance of Greek education. Rome was becoming a cosmopolitan city.

GAMES The wealth acquired by conquest and the changes in the character of religion revealed themselves in the amusements of the people. Many festivals and games provided the city populace with relaxation from the toils of life. Originally, there had been frequent festivals connected with the religious life of early Rome, but with the growth of the city many of these were abandoned. The most beloved, however, was kept, the feast of Saturnalia on December 17, when all the people, freeman and slave, exchanged gifts and made merry together. Games, *ludi,* took the place of those festivals which had lost their meaning. At these functions, which were public and therefore free to the populace, processions were held, followed by chariot races in the Circus, and by exhibitions and hunts of wild animals. The aediles were in charge of the games, and those who hoped for political preferment spent much more money on them than the state granted; in fact in the later republic young men went heavily into debt to please the people. Gladiatorial combats were introduced from Etruria in 264 B.C. The gladiators were usually slaves, trained in special schools and offered for hire. For a long period they were exhibited at funeral games held in honor of great men and at the expense of the family. Until the close of the republic they were exhibited almost exclusively by private persons, but in the imperial period the combats became great public spectacles. In addition to the games of this sort there were many dramatic presentations which, apparently, were never very popular with the mob (p. 389).

CONCLUSION   Rome had gained an empire; but the institutions and character by which, as Polybius said, she had risen to power, failed to meet the tests imposed by the victory. Senatorial failure to produce and to control competent leaders in times of crisis and to develop an intelligent, well-directed system of provincial administration made possible, even essential, the rise of great men with power superior to the constitution. The acquisition of great wealth by the senators and the growth of a capitalistic class of businessmen resulted in the decline of the Roman traditions of simplicity and even of honesty. Hellenistic ideas, poorly comprehended, destroyed the spiritual and social bases upon which the traditions rested. The populace was slowly degenerating from a class of independent farmers into a city proletariat, poverty-stricken and, at least in part, venal in politics.

The failure of Rome's leaders in the senate to rise to the occasion, remodel the government, and correct the social and economic evils, resulted in a century of revolution which ended with the fall of the senate and the rise of one-man power, Caesarism. As Scipio Aemilianus stood on the hill overlooking burning Carthage, he turned to his friend and recited the words of Hector: "The day shall come when this our sacred Troy shall fall, and Ilium, and Priam's towering citadel." Troy had fallen; Carthage was falling; the symptoms of decay which he had observed convinced him that Rome also would fall in the cycle of time; and as censor he prayed to the gods to preserve rather than to increase the state.

XIX

THE ROMAN REVOLUTION
(133-31 B.C.)

THE DEMOCRATIC REFORMERS
(133-88 B.C.)

THE Roman Revolution was that epoch-making series of events which transformed the Roman Republic into an empire ruled by the autocratic Caesars. It was caused by the failure of the ruling class to solve the economic and social problems which had developed with the conquest and to adapt or expand the constitutional machinery of the city-state to meet the needs of empire.

The problems which Rome faced at the end of the period of expansion were varied and difficult enough to daunt the most intelligent and sincere leaders of the state. The equestrian order of businessmen, growing rapidly in numbers and in wealth, was already causing difficulties for the senatorial governors in the provinces. Jealous of the political and social prerogatives of the aristocracy in Rome, this class was eager to share in directing the destinies of empire to its own profit. The debts which youthful aspirants for political power owed in increasing amounts to the moneylenders contributed to the friction. This rivalry between the classes runs as a continuous thread throughout the century of revolution. The decline in the number of small farmers threatened not only the economic health of Italy, but also the recruiting strength of the Roman army. The growth of an urban proletariat for whom gainful occupation was not available also presented great political and social questions pressing for an answer. To these was added during the period the difficult task of absorbing into peaceful pursuits the veterans returning from the wars. The spasmodic slave revolts indicated new dangers resulting from the growth of great estates, and presented new problems to the leaders of Rome. The Italian allies were demanding a fuller share of the benefits of empire which their arms had helped to win, and their insistent requests for citizenship could not long be resisted without disaster.

Imperial control, repression of piracy, which had flourished after the fall of Rhodes, proper regulation of provincial governors, the suppression of graft and plundering in the provinces, and the need for a good method of selecting able men to meet difficult situations without recourse to unconstitutional procedure were all essential for the political and economic well-being of the empire and of Rome itself.

The revolution began with the attempt of a young reformer to secure agrarian reform against the opposition of the vested interests. It witnessed bitter struggles for control between the classes, a series of economic crises, rioting in the city streets and threatened revolts, the formation of professional armies ready to follow their leaders even against the state, and the rise of great personalities who proved stronger than the constitution. In the end it became a contest not to determine whether the senate or the great man should rule, but to decide which of the leaders should succeed. Since the personalities and programs of individuals were the decisive factors in the events, even though problems of economic and imperial significance were the fundamental circumstances which made their activities possible, the political history of the period is essentially biographical.

TIBERIUS GRACCHUS
Tiberius Sempronius Gracchus, a young man of illustrious family, was elected tribune for 133 B.C. The safe future of a Roman aristocrat lay before him; his father had gained renown as consul and proconsul; his mother was Cornelia, daughter of the great Scipio; his wife was the daughter of Appius Claudius. He had been brought up in the Scipionic circle, educated by the best Greek teachers of the day, and had served creditably as quaestor in Spain. With youthful confidence he undertook to carry through a vital reform.

THE PUBLIC LAND
The solution which Gracchus proposed for the economic problems of Rome was a distribution of state lands to the city proletariat. For this he had ample precedent in Greek experience and in Roman tradition. The program of Agis and Cleomenes in Sparta was doubtless well known to him through his Stoic teachers. The Roman tradition of homestead-distribution dated back to the conquest of Italy, when, as we have seen (p. 348), considerable portions of confiscated lands were distributed to Roman farmers. The Licinian-Sextian Laws of 367 B.C., it will

be recalled, were an attempt to regulate this distribution and to prevent the ruling class from securing too large a share. Since the enforcement of these laws depended upon the plutocratic officials who benefited by their violation, they speedily became dead letters and the greater portion of the state-owned lands in Italy became the virtual possessions of the senatorial class.

Flaminius, as tribune in 232 B.C., revived the older policy and distributed lands in the Po Valley among the citizens, but after his death at Lake Trasimene his program was abandoned. The alarming decline in the number of small farmers revealed by the census lists of the second century B.C. caused much discussion because of its military significance, and the Scipionic circle agreed among themselves that the proper remedy for this decline was renewed distribution of land. Laelius, in 145 B.C., went so far as to draft a bill to that end, but withdrew it because of opposition.

THE GRACCHAN
LAND LAW

Tiberius Gracchus returned to the program of Laelius. He drew up a bill which provided for the reenactment of the Licinian Law limiting the holding of the public land of any individual to five hundred *jugera,* with two hundred and fifty more for each of two sons, for the repossession by the state of such lands as were held in violation thereof, and for the distribution of these lands to needy citizens in small lots, inalienable and subject to a quitrent. Three commissioners were to carry out the examination of land titles and the distribution of the land. The bill aroused a storm of opposition. Title deeds had been lost; lands had changed hands; and determination of ownership was exceedingly difficult. Senators who saw their cherished estates threatened claimed that the bill would rob them. Accordingly they persuaded the tribune Octavius to veto the bill. Tiberius, however, was convinced that his proposed reform was vital to the well-being of Rome, and he therefore persuaded the tribal assembly to take the unprecedented step of removing Octavius from office as a betrayer of the popular will. The bill was then passed.

The commission, composed of Tiberius, his brother Gaius, and his father-in-law, Appius Claudius, went directly to work. Tiberius challenged senatorial control over public finance when he proposed to use the money from the recently acquired treasury of Attalus III of Pergamum to equip the restored farms. In order to carry this measure through the assembly and to protect himself and his cherished reforms from senatorial enemies, he determined to make a further break with custom by offering himself for re-election. When the consul refused to take action to stop him, a group of senators attended by armed slaves and clients descended upon the Forum. In the ensuing riot Tiberius and some three hundred of his followers were killed. Others of his supporters were punished by a senatorial investigating commission.

THE YEARS OF REACTION The following years were filled with strife between the senate and the popular party, which now had a program and a martyred leader. The land law remained in force for a brief period; the committee proceeded to work, reclaimed much land and made many allotments, as is shown by the decided increase in the census lists. To senatorial opposition, however, were added the complaints of wealthy Italians whose lands had been taken by the commissioners. Scipio Aemilianus, returning from Numantia, espoused the conservative side and secured the passage of a law depriving the three commissioners of their judicial powers, thus putting an end to their activities. The popular party, on the other hand, secured recognition of the right of re-election to the tribunate.

GAIUS GRACCHUS In 123 B.C. Gaius Gracchus, younger brother of Tiberius, a polished and forceful orator, entered upon the tribunate. He was re-elected for the following year. In these two years he presented a carefully thought-out program by means of which, he hoped, the political and economic ills of Rome would be corrected. He proposed: (1) to center the civil administration in the tribunate, somewhat in the manner in which that of Athens had been centralized in the office of general in the days of Pericles; (2) to break the political power of the senatorial machine, at the same time punishing the murderers of his brother; (3) to put in its place an effective combination of business and popular interests strengthened by admission of the Italians to citizenship; and (4) to provide economic opportunities for the poor of the city.

As tribune Gracchus presented a series of measures to the tribal assembly and took upon himself direction of their administration. These prohibited extraordinary courts, the putting of Roman citizens to death without trial, and denial of the right of appeal. The senate was ordered to assign provinces to the consuls before their election, thus losing its most effective means of control over those magistrates. Political power was given to the business leaders by a law providing that juries were henceforth to be drawn from those businessmen of wealth who were listed as *Equites*, or knights. This move not only gave political recognition to this new group, but also provided an effective means of checking senatorial aggrandizement. The knights were further pleased by an act which changed the taxes of Asia from a fixed sum to a percentage basis and which, by allowing the contract for collection to be paid in a lump sum at Rome, gave them a monopoly of this lucrative business. Gracchus provided that grain received in payment of taxes should be sold to the poor at a very low price. This was in accord with Greek precedent and had the further merits of binding the city proletariat firmly to himself and of relieving the poor from that economic dependence upon the rich which was in part the basis of senatorial control. He worked steadfastly, however, to remove the necessity for this dole. A public-works and road-building program was inaugurated; Tiberius' land law was re-enacted, and many of the poor were placed on farms. In addition Gracchus proposed to locate commercial colonies at Tarentum and near Croton, in Italy, and on the site of Carthage in Africa.

Finally, the Latins were to be given full citizenship and the Italian allies, Latin rights. The last two measures, indispensable for the success of his program, cost Gracchus his hold on the city mob, who did not wish to share with the Italians their cherished rights as Romans. While Gracchus was in Africa superintending the planting of the colony Junonia, at Carthage, the senate, having induced another tribune, Drusus, to bid against him by proposing twelve colonies of the older type, gained control over the populace; the businessmen, alarmed by the prospective competition of commercial colonies deserted Gracchus; and in the elections for 121 B.C. he failed to be re-elected. When attacks against the Gracchan laws increased, Gaius endeavored to defend them. The senate however decreed martial law; a riot ensued; and Gracchus in despair committed suicide.

RESULTS OF
GRACCHUS'
PROGRAM
Estimates of the value of the Gracchi and their program have varied ever since their time, chiefly in accord with the political and economic sympathies of the observer. They have been lauded as heroes and martyrs who would have saved Rome; they have been condemned as revolutionaries, destroyers of the Roman constitution, who debauched the people by a dole. Tiberius certainly broke with Roman tradition when he deposed Octavius and ran for re-election. On the other hand,

the will of the people was law and technically, therefore, his acts were not unconstitutional. In this connection it might be noted that in the case of the death of each brother the conservatives violated the law by provoking violence.

No answer can be given to the question of whether the agrarian program was feasible or advisable. It was not given a fair chance. Within ten years after the death of Gaius, division had ceased, the lots had been declared private property, and the land was reverting to the possession of the wealthy. That the knights, following senatorial precedents, abused their power in the courts and in Asia to enrich themselves was not a fault of the law. It is significant that the rest of the Gracchan program was carried out substantially, most of it by Caesar and Augustus, both of whom used the tribunician power as the basis of their civil administration. For the moment, however, the reform movement was stopped by the death of Gaius. But the knights had tasted political power and were more than ever a force to be reckoned with. The popular party also had a program and two martyrs to venerate. The senate, though seemingly victorious, was both weakened and alarmed. The revolution advanced, as a three-cornered struggle broke out between the senators, the knights, and the followers of the Gracchi.

THE WAR WITH JUGURTHA

The coalition between the senatorial and equestrian classes which had finally wrought the downfall of Gaius Gracchus lasted but ten years. It was broken by the failure of the senate to regulate the affairs of Africa.

The throne of Numidia had come by intrigue and assassination into the hands of an able but unscrupulous prince, Jugurtha. The destruction of the town of Cirta, an incident in the rise of Jugurtha, led to the death of many Roman and Italian merchants. Senatorial incompetence and corruption were responsible for the disaster. Second-rate men sent to deal with Jugurtha were defeated or bribed, and when the senate in 109 B.C. finally sent to Africa an able and honorable commander, Metellus, it had already lost the confidence and support of the business element.

This class found a leader in a new man on whom they and the popular party united, Gaius Marius, a lieutenant in Metellus' army. Marius, a native of Arpinum, belonged to a plebeian family of equestrian rank. He had demonstrated his ability in warfare and in finance and had risen to the rank of praetor. His marriage with Julia of the family of the Caesars had gained for him a measure of recognition among the aristocrats. Nevertheless he was regarded by the aristocrats with disdain as a "new man"; and his request for support for the consulship was abruptly refused by his patron and commander, Metellus, with whom he was serving as lieutenant in Numidia.

Marius therefore broke with Metellus and with the support of the knights and the democrats was elected consul for 107 B.C. Furthermore, by action of the tribal assembly and in defiance of the senate he was appointed to supersede Metellus. He was successful in bringing the African war to a brilliant end. His lieutenant, Sulla, captured Jugurtha through treachery, and in 104 B.C. Marius returned in triumph to Rome.

THE GERMANS   While Marius had been gaining victory and glory in Africa, another crisis in the affairs of empire had arisen with which the senatorial leaders had proved incompetent to cope. Southern Gaul had been made into a Roman province in 121 B.C.; a Roman colony was established at Narbo in 118 B.C., and a military road was constructed from Italy to Spain. Hardly had this been accomplished when the Gallic province was seriously threatened by the appearance of Germanic tribes—the Cimbri, Teutones, and related groups—on the Roman frontier. After a series of minor defeats the Roman army suffered a great catastrophe at Arausio (Orange) in 105 B.C. The way to Italy lay open, and Rome, with visions of a second sack, was in a panic. Marius, the hero of the hour, was at hand, and in defiance of all precedent he was elected consul successively for 104, 103, 102, and 101 B.C. Fortunately for him and for Rome the Germans turned aside to plunder Gaul and Spain.

THE ARMY   These years under the consulship of Marius reveal
OF MARIUS   not only a marked step toward Caesarism in the reliance of the state upon a military hero, but also the creation of the machine by which future leaders were to rise to power. Marius established a professional army by enrolling volunteers for a term of sixteen years without regard to property qualification, drawing many from the proletariat of the city. He put his recruits through a rigorous regime of military training, thus securing an efficiency impossible with the annual levies of citizen soldiers of former years. The former distinction between the three lines of the army, based on military experience, was thereby destroyed, thus enabling Marius to replace the maniple as the unit of tactical maneuver by a larger body,

the cohort, which corresponded in size and use to the battalion of the modern American army.

The legion contained six thousand men divided into ten cohorts. *Esprit de corps* was secured by giving each legion a silver eagle as its standard. This became the idol of the soldiers and the center of legionary tradition. The political danger of this professional soldiery arose from the fact that the loyalty of the men was given not to the state but to their commander, to whom they looked for rewards in fighting and for lands and pensions at the end of their term of service. Marius had three years in which to organize, equip, and drill his army. In 102 B.C. he defeated the Teutones at Aquae Sextiae in Gaul, and in 101 B.C. he annihilated the Cimbri at Vercellae in northern Italy. Again he returned to Rome in triumph to be hailed as the saviour of the city and the third founder of Rome.[1]

While Marius had been winning victories, the state had been involved in a second slave revolt in Sicily (105-101 B.C.) and in piratical raids in the Mediterranean. After a number of small outbreaks of slaves in southern Italy had served to remind the senate of the dangers of plantation slavery, the slaves in Sicily again rose against their masters. As before, a slave, Sabius, was chosen king with the name Tryphon, and efforts were made to conquer and organize the land. Again, also, vigorous efforts and ruthless executions were necessary to restore peace and order. The eastern pirates, too, were suppressed, but only for the moment. Neither of these affairs brought glory to the senate or renown to any leader who might rival Marius.

MARIUS THE REFORMER

The popular hero now felt called upon to become a great democratic leader and to solve the political problems of Rome as he had dealt with its imperial difficulties. He formed an alliance with the leaders of the popular party, Saturninus and Glaucia, and, as a democratic reformer, he was elected consul for the sixth time for the year 100 B.C. The program upon which he and his allies embarked was based upon that of Gaius Gracchus. But as a politician, Marius proved a complete failure. He lost the support of his equestrian followers, and when disorder arose out of the elections for the year 99 B.C. he turned upon Saturninus and Glaucia. In the ensuing difficulties the popular leaders were killed, and Marius, disappointed and discredited, went out of office.

[1] Romulus was the first and Camillus the second.

RUTILIUS RUFUS For another brief period after Marius' defeat the senatorial and equestrian combination dominated Roman politics. But the equestrian control of the juries made this an unnatural alliance, and a scandalous episode of 93 B.C. was to shake it. A Roman noble, Rutilius Rufus, a Stoic renowned for his probity and honor, had served as lieutenant of Scaevola, proconsul in Asia for the year 98 B.C. There he had sternly repressed the illegal exactions of Roman businessmen. Accordingly they attacked him in Rome; in 93 B.C. he was brought to trial on the charge of extortions, and, in defiance of all the evidence, an equestrian jury convicted him. He retired into exile, spending the rest of his life in the province he was said to have despoiled. The scandal of his conviction made clear to thoughtful men the dangers of the situation in Rome.

LIVIUS DRUSUS From the ranks of the senators arose a new reformer to correct conditions. Livius Drusus, probably the son of the opponent of Gaius Gracchus, elected tribune for the year 91 B.C., set forth a program which had the support of a portion of the senate. Three hundred leading knights were to be enrolled in the senate, and from this enlarged body the juries were to be chosen. To please the people he added a grain dole and colonial settlements to his program. When an opportunity arose, he submitted a proposition for the enfranchisement of the Italians, which he had apparently promised to accomplish. At this the opposition became vehement. Drusus, accused of being involved in an Italian secret society in defiance of the law, lost support on every hand and was finally murdered by an unknown assassin. With Drusus' death perished the last attempt which had any real hope of succeeding in the reformation of the Roman constitution by legal and peaceful means. Future reforms were destined to come from military leaders supported by armed force.

THE SOCIAL WAR (90-88 B.C.) The Social War followed immediately on the death of Drusus. A large group of the Italian allies (*socii*), disappointed in their hope of enfranchisement, determined upon a struggle for independence. They revolted and formed a new state, Italia, with two consuls, twelve praetors and a senate of five hundred. Their armies, composed of veterans of Roman wars, were generally successful in a bloody war against Rome. The senate, yielding to superior force and impelled by a critical situation in the East, gave citizenship by the *Lex Julia* of 90 B.C. to all Italians who had not revolted, and by the *Lex Plautia Papiria* of the following year conferred it on all who would register with a Roman praetor within sixty days. Their end achieved, the Italians yielded. To their great chagrin, however, instead of being distributed among the thirty-five tribes where their numbers would make their influence strong, they were enrolled together in eight new tribes with little resultant political power.

SULLA

THE RISE
OF SULLA

The year 88 B.C. saw the senate in full control with Sulla as consul. He had shown his ability as lieutenant of Marius and as commander in the Social War, and his loyalty to the senate was unquestioned. Senatorial leadership, however, did not remain long unchallenged. A crisis appeared in the East when Mithradates, king of Pontus, invaded Asia, secured control of the Aegean Sea and of Athens, and then ordered the massacre of all Romans resident in Asia. The senate quickly assigned Sulla to deal with the eastern king.

The loss of men, property, and revenues produced a panic on the Roman market; interest rates rose and many senators found themselves in difficulties; to protect them, a praetor revived an obsolete law against usury. He was thereupon murdered, but the proposal completed the breach between the senators and capitalists, which had begun with the trial of Rufus. The knights now thoroughly aroused, turned for a leader to their hero of former days, Marius, who, at his own request, was to be chosen to displace Sulla in the Mithradatic command.

The popular leaders at the same time were disappointed by the citizenship provisions made for the Italians, which broke down their hopes of new voting power for their party. The tribune, Sulpicius, combined the two interests (popular and equestrian) by proposing to distribute the Italians among the thirty-five older tribes, and to supersede Sulla with Marius as general in the war. When word came to Sulla of his deposition after he had already started from Rome, he wheeled his army about and marched upon the city to deal with his opponents. Marius escaped, but Sulpicius and many of the leading knights were killed. After introducing a few measures designed to replace the senate in full control, Sulla left for the East. Military power had been used for the first time to settle political problems in Rome by a leader of the conservative forces.

FIRST MITHRA-
DATIC WAR
(89-85 B.C.)
Sulla invaded Greece in the spring of 87 B.C. After a bitter siege he took Athens in 86 B.C. and defeated the forces of Mithradates in two battles at Chaeronea and at Orchomenus. After his quaestor, Lucullus, had cleared the seas, Sulla invaded Asia where in the meantime another Roman army had won victories in northern Anatolia. Sulla, anxious to return to Rome, failed to follow his victories to their logical conclusion and made peace with Mithradates. The king surrendered his conquests, paid a small indemnity, and retired to his kingdom. The cities of Asia which had aided him suffered the penalty of an enormous indemnity, which brought great profit to Roman capitalists who loaned them the money with which to pay it. Greece, devastated and despoiled, suffered long from the effects of the war.

THE FIRST
CIVIL WAR
Meanwhile the democratic forces had regained control of Rome. Cinna, a popular leader, was elected consul for 87 B.C. and met opposition by calling upon Marius for aid. The aged general raised an army, seized the city, put his leading enemies to death, and was elected consul for the seventh time. Hardly had he assumed that office in 86 B.C. when he died. The following years were consumed with useless bickering between Cinna, Carbo, and the younger Marius. The only real achievement of these leaders was the completion of the political unification of Italy by the final enrollment of the Italians in the thirty-five tribes. Plans to deal with Sulla in the East failed, and the senatorial champion returned in 83 B.C. to begin the First Civil War. He won a series of victories in Italy, culminating in a fierce battle at the Colline Gate in Rome. His victory was followed by a terrible proscription. Lists of names were posted to indicate that their bearers might be killed without judicial action and their property confiscated. Not only were equestrian and popular leaders marked out for murder but many names were added to please Sulla's friends. Nearly five thousand persons were murdered; their property was confiscated and sold at public auction and their descendants were disenfranchised. Those Italians who had sided with Cinna and Marius saw their lands taken from them and given as rewards to Sulla's veterans, who were thus provided for by a return to the land.

Sulla, victorious and all-powerful, turned to problems of state. He secured his own election for an unlimited time as *dictator legibus scribundis et rei publicae constituendae* (dictator for the writing of

the laws and establishing the republic) with full power over the constitution. This office found its precedent in the powers of the decemvirs
of 451-449 B.C. rather than in the ancient military dictatorship. Sulla's
constitutional reforms were calculated to establish full control for the
senate. The consul's power was limited to Italy; the praetors were
increased to eight and given charge of a number of permanent courts
to deal with extortion, bribery, treason, murder, and similar offenses,
with juries composed entirely of senators; the number of quaestors
was increased to twenty. Definite age limits were established for each
grade in the *cursus honorum* (the succession of offices) and re-election
was forbidden within a ten-year period. The tribunate was rendered
negligible by forbidding those who had been tribunes to run for any
other office and by re-establishing the senatorial veto over legislation.
The proconsuls and propraetors received their provinces from the
senate with power strictly limited to the province. If they crossed its
bounds without consent of the senate, they lost their power of military
command and might be declared public enemies. The senate, increased
to six hundred, was in full control of imperial administration. Sulla,
then possibly realizing that the time was not yet ripe for a permanent
dictatorship, resigned his office in 79 B.C. and retired to Campania, where
he died the following year. The senate was thus given its last chance
at control; but its own weaknesses and the forces of history were
against it. The succeeding years were filled with struggles, upon the
issue of which depended not the power of the senate but the choice of
the leader who should succeed Sulla as the dictator of Rome.

THE RISE OF POMPEY

A new set of leaders arose after Sulla's time to fill the pages of
Roman history. The center of the stage was occupied by men like
Pompey, Crassus, Cicero, Cato, Caesar, and Catiline. The most pre-
eminent of these men, the "first man" in Rome, from the death of
Sulla to the battle of Pharsalus, was Pompey. Yet beneath the surface
the struggle of the classes continued. The problems of debt and poverty, of the agrarian situation, the urban proletariat, the retired veterans,
the mistreated slaves, and provincial control still remained unsolved.

POMPEY Pompey had already made his appearance as an able
lieutenant of Sulla. Though vain and pompous, he
was a military leader of great ability and a gentleman of honor and
had won the youthful admiration of Cicero and Caesar. History has

dealt harshly with him because he failed. Pompey as a youth had entered the Civil War as a supporter of Sulla with an army of his own which he had raised. Though he had not held public office, he was sent as propraetor to Sicily and Africa, where he crushed remnants of the Marian party. For this success he demanded a triumph and the title Magnus, the "Great," both of which were accorded him by Sulla.

SERTORIUS　　　　　Shortly after the death of Sulla, Pompey was sent to Spain, this time as proconsul, though he was not yet old enough to be consul according to the law. Sertorius, Marian governor of Spain, had established himself as ruler there. Regarding himself as a true Roman, acting in the best interests of his country and the equestrian order against the power of the senate and the Sullan faction, he gathered around him the followers of Marius, organized a senate, and ruled the Spaniards so tactfully and well that they followed him willingly. He seems to have intended the formation of a state in Spain independent of the senate from which he might return to Rome to establish a democratic rule over an empire in which Romans and provincials should share in a common rule and a common culture. He defeated Roman armies sent against him and withstood the forces of Pompey for several years (78-71 B.C.). At length his Spanish allies weakened and many of his Roman supporters, by their mistreatment of the Spaniards, proved a detriment rather than an aid. Finally he was assassinated by one of his lieutenants, and Pompey victoriously regained Spain for Rome.

SPARTACUS　　　　　Meanwhile a slave revolt in Italy had given Crassus, the financier, an opportunity to appear as a rival to the pre-eminence of Pompey. The rebellion revealed a new danger in Italy in the presence of slaves trained to fight as gladiators in addition to the permanent menace of the servile groups on the great estates. In 73 B.C. Spartacus, a Thracian gladiator, led a band of his fellows in a search for freedom. When they had fortified themselves on the slopes of Vesuvius, large bands of runaway slaves joined them. Spartacus had planned to lead his followers beyond the Alps with the hope that they might return to their original homes in freedom. They preferred, however, the plunder of Italy and refused to follow him. After two consular armies were defeated by Spartacus in 72 B.C., Crassus, as praetor, given the task of defeating the rebel leaders, succeeded in defeating and killing Spartacus the following year. Though Crassus was the victor, Pompey, returning from Spain, reached Italy in time to kill five thousand slaves and to claim a share in the success.

CRASSUS

By his handling of the Spartacan trouble Crassus proved his real ability. Like Pompey, he had been a lieutenant of Sulla. He had reaped his reward during the proscription, when he had bought up large quantities of confiscated property for very low prices and had thus accumulated a huge fortune. Plutarch recounts other tales which show Crassus' reputation for financial greediness. There was no public force to fight fires in Rome, and when they broke out Crassus was able to buy the burning and surrounding properties at ridiculously low prices, whereupon a private fire department of slaves owned and trained by him speedily extinguished the conflagrations. One cannot help wondering how many fires were started by his agents.

POMPEY AND
CRASSUS AS
CONSULS

Rivals under Sulla, the two leaders found themselves face to face in 71 B.C. Both demanded triumphs for their campaigns as well as consulships for 70 B.C., for which office neither was legally eligible. The senate rejected both. Thereupon they united, overawed the opposition with the threat of military force, and secured the election. As consuls they restored the tribunician power and reorganized the juries, which were henceforth to be drawn one-third from the senate, one-third from the knights, and one-third from a lower class of businessmen, known as *tribuni aerarii*.

CICERO AND
VERRES

The year 70 B.C. saw the rise of the third of the new leaders, Cicero. Cicero, son of a knight of Arpinum, educated in Rome and in Athens, had already shown courage and ability in the defense of Roscius during the Sullan regime. He had been honest and successful as quaestor in Sicily in 75 B.C., and to him the Sicilians brought his great opportunity when they engaged him to prosecute Verres, propraetor of the island in 73-71 B.C., who had been shamelessly corrupt in his handling of Sicilian affairs. Verres was a member of the inner circle and with the leading Roman orator, Hortensius, to speak for him, he had no doubt of the outcome. Cicero, however, gathered evidence with unusual speed and then instead of making a speech, presented that evidence. It was so overwhelming that Verres retired into exile before he was condemned. Cicero afterwards published his undelivered *Orations against Gaius Verres,* a complete exposé of the methods and materials of provincial corruption. His success brought him prominence in Rome and he was elected praetor for the year 66 B.C.

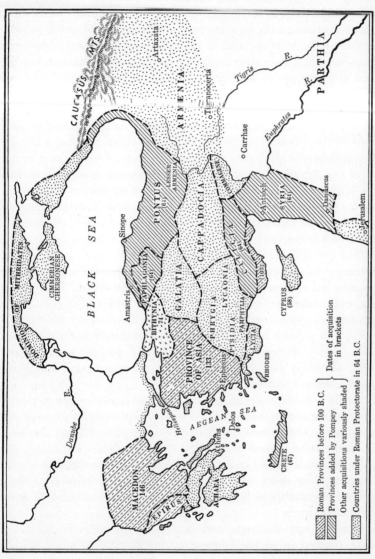

ROME IN THE EAST

CAESAR

Caesar, who had made himself notorious as an exquisite in dress and a roué in conduct, made his entrance on the political stage in 69 B.C. at the funeral of his aunt, Julia, widow of Marius, with an address in which he proclaimed his championship of the Marian cause, of the disenfranchised, and of the popular party. There are earlier stories of his defiance of Sulla and of his defeat of the pirates in the East; but in 69 B.C. he gave no evidence of his ability, no foreshadowing of the power which was subsequently his.

THE PIRATES

The inability of the Sullan political machine to deal with emergencies, which had been made apparent by the appointments of Crassus and Pompey, showed itself again in the case of the pirates. For centuries the naval powers in the Aegean had kept piracy under control. With the collapse of Rhodes this protection for sea-borne merchandise had ceased. The Romans failed to comprehend the necessity for permanent policing, and so allowed the fleets which had served in the Punic and Greek Wars to decay.

The piratical residents of Cilicia and Crete were quick to take advantage of their opportunity. Temporarily suppressed in 104-102 B.C., they returned as soon as the Roman fleet was withdrawn. They raided Italy, even entering the mouth of the Tiber and stopping the grain fleets which carried supplies to Rome. When the regular officials failed to deal with them, it became apparent that an extraordinary command was necessary. Pompey was clearly indicated for the task, but the senate, ostensibly out of respect for the constitution but jealous of Pompey, refused to act.

Again a combination of *Equites* and *Populares* took the initiative, depriving the senate therewith of its traditional right to imperial administration. The tribune Gabinius in 67 B.C. proposed and carried a law in the tribal assembly to create an extraordinary command, the holder of which should control the entire Mediterranean and a strip of territory fifty miles wide around it in Roman provinces for three years, with authority to appoint his lieutenants and to enlist an army and a naval force.

Pompey was the man, and his appointment, forced upon the senate, resulted in an immediate drop in the price of grain. Within three months he had accomplished the task with brilliant success. The pirates were completely crushed, and many of them were settled as farmers on abandoned lands in the provinces.

SECOND MITHRA-
DATIC WAR
(74-63 B.C.)

A second need for Pompey's services immediately arose in the East. Mithradates had renewed the war with Rome when Nicomedes III of Bithynia had willed his kingdom to Rome in 75 B.C. In this war Rome was well served by the proconsul, Lucullus, a member of the senatorial group. He defeated Mithradates, drove the king out of his realm, invaded Armenia, and took its capital, Tigranocerta. Lucullus, however, offended the business element by interfering with their exorbitant interest charges and offended his army by preventing excesses of plunder. While his soldiers mutinied in Armenia and he was forced to retire, his enemies attacked him bitterly in Rome. At this crisis Manilius, tribune in 66 B.C., proposed to add to Pompey's power the command of Bithynia and Cilicia and of the war against Mithradates. The senate opposed it. Cicero, praetor for that year, needing powerful support for the consulship and motivated by an unbounded admiration for Pompey, supported the bill with a panegyric on Pompey, *On the Power of Gnaeus Pompey*. The bill was passed, and the great general again showed his ability: he reduced Pontus to a province in 64 B.C. and made Armenia a client kingdom; turning south he entered Syria, brought the dynasty of the Seleucids to an end, and made Syria a province to which he added Judaea after the capture of Jerusalem (63 B.C.). After setting the affairs of the East in order in regal fashion, he prepared to return to Rome in 62 B.C., a conquering hero, the most powerful citizen of the state—at least in his own estimation. A rude awakening was prepared for him.

CICERO'S
CONSULSHIP

Throughout the years of Pompey's wars in the East, the political pot of Rome had been kept boiling by the attempts of leaders to place themselves in impregnable positions before Pompey's return. Caesar, serving as aedile in 65 B.C., and backed financially by Crassus, made an extravagant display in the games and brought forth for public view the trophies and statues of Marius in an effort to curry favor with the mob and to make his own position clear. He and Crassus found a ready tool in a ruined aristocrat, Catiline, whom they backed for the consulship for 63 B.C. against Antonius and Cicero. This backing forced the senate to throw its support to the despised "new man," and Cicero was elected with Antonius as his colleague.

Thus defeated, Caesar and Crassus turned to other measures. A will, possibly forged, had given Egypt to Rome. The senate had refused to recognize it and had allowed Ptolemy Auletes, the "Flute-Player," to assume the throne. Crassus, as censor in 65 B.C., had suggested the annexation of Egypt but had been blocked. In 63 B.C. a tribune, Rullus, proposed an agrarian bill to give extraordinary power —military, legal, and financial—to a commission of ten to confiscate or purchase lands for distribution among the people, the funds for the project to be secured by a sale of public property throughout the empire. This bill would have made possible the conquest of Egypt as a state possession, and Caesar and Crassus, if appointed commissioners, would have been strongly entrenched as rivals to Pompey. Cicero, however, attacked the bill so vigorously that it was never brought to a vote. Caesar, a realist, then turned his back on grandiose schemes and although, like many of his contemporaries, utterly without religious beliefs or scruples, secured his own election as *Pontifex Maximus,* head of the Roman religion.

CATILINE   Catiline, deserted by his influential backers, determined upon a daring revolutionary program of cancellation of debts and the establishment of a democratic regime. He found supporters among those aristocrats who, like himself, were heavily in debt, among poverty-ridden members of the populace, and among the Sullan veterans who, unsuccessful as farmers on the lands assigned to them, had become aggrieved and turbulent. Defeated again as consular candidate for 62 B.C., he organized a conspiracy and planned a *coup d'état,* the murder of the consuls and the seizure of the government. His movement is an indication of the critical economic conditions in Rome. Cicero, becoming aware of the plot and of its program through the mistress of one of the conspirators, was ready for it. He secured from the senate a decree of martial law and with a brilliant and famous speech (the first oration against Catiline, November 8) so confounded Catiline that he left the city. In a second speech the following day Cicero exposed the plot and described the conspirators to the people.

Catiline and his followers continued their work, but their final plans for action were betrayed by a group of Gallic Allobroges to whom the conspirators in Rome gave letters for Catiline. The conspirators were called before the senate, where Cicero presented the evidence. That evening (December 3) he reported the events of the session to the people in the third Catilinarian oration. When in a later session (December 5) the question of punishment was discussed,

Caesar argued for a sentence of imprisonment, but Cicero, backed by Cato, that Stoic philosopher and rigid conservative, who now appeared as a senatorial spokesman, called for the sentence of death, which was enforced.

By this action Cicero, though he gained considerable renown, put himself definitely on the side of the *Optimates,* who despised him. Henceforth, he worked for a program of the "harmony of the orders," the union of senators and leading knights—"the best men of Rome"— to run the state. He was inordinately proud of his victory over Catiline and even wrote a poem on his consulship.

THE FIRST
TRIUMVIRATE

Pompey returned to Rome in the fall of 62 B.C. He failed to capitalize upon his position and to become dictator when, in obedience to the law and relying upon his prestige, he disbanded his army. The senate refused to recognize Pompey's acts in the East without examination in detail, and pushed him aside. At the same time the senate, on the advice of Cato, declined to release the business group led by Crassus from an unfortunate contract for the taxes in Asia, where harvests had been poor. Once more therefore Pompey and Crassus were forced to combine. Caesar, returning from a successful propraetorship in Spain and needing their support for the consulship, engineered the combination. There was thus formed a political alliance, the first triumvirate, which has been described as a "union of genius, position, and capital against the law." No real community of interests beyond jealousy of senatorial power held them together. Rather, the achievements of each man had created a balance of power among the three, and in the jockeying for position they found that through union they could best attain their immediate ends—prestige and recognition of his acts for Pompey, financial protection and political backing for Crassus, advancement for Caesar.

THE PERIOD OF THE TRIUMVIRATE

CAESAR'S
CONSULSHIP

The triumvirate at once began to pay returns to its members. Caesar, with the powerful backing of Pompey and Crassus and through his own vote-getting ability, secured election as consul for the year 59 B.C. with Bibulus, a conservative, as colleague. Caesar forced legislation through the assembly over the opposition of Bibulus and with an utter disregard of the constitutional checks which Bibulus invoked. Pompey's acts in the East were ratified, and his veterans were settled on lands in Campania. Crassus and his associates were granted a rebate of one-third on their contract. The throne of Egypt was conferred on the "Flute-Player," for a large price. Caesar himself was granted a provincial command for five years in Illyricum and the two Gauls, where trouble threatened from the Helvetians and the Germans. Before he left Rome he consolidated his position by arranging a marriage between his daughter Julia and Pompey and by removing Cato and Cicero, his two most dangerous opponents from Rome.

THE BANISH-
MENT OF CICERO
Cato was easily dealt with by giving him the task of reorganizing Cyprus, which he felt he could not honorably refuse and which took him three years to accomplish. Caesar offered Cicero an opportunity to join with the triumvirate through a lieutenancy in Gaul. When this offer was refused, Clodius, a brilliant product of the fast younger set and the able leader of Caesar's political clubs, was given a free hand against him. Clodius had earlier committed sacrilege, and at the time of his trial, in 61 b.c., Cicero's testimony had destroyed his alibi. To secure acquittal Clodius was forced to resort to wholesale bribery, and he therefore had his own score to settle with Cicero. In 59 b.c. he secured a transfer for himself to plebeian status, was elected tribune for 58 b.c., and carried a measure to banish all who had put Roman citizens to death without trial, as Cicero had done with the followers of Catiline. Cicero at once went into exile in Macedon, and his property was confiscated.

CAESAR
IN GAUL
Caesar's success in Gaul, recounted in his own *Commentaries,* revealed him as a military genius. He defeated the Helvetians and the Germans, conquered northern and western Gaul, invaded Germany, after building a famous bridge, and crossed into Britain. The first revolts against his conquest were put down with ease. In 52 b.c., however, a revolt led by an able youth, Vercingetorix, caused Caesar much trouble. Finally, however, he besieged the Gallic leader in Alesia near modern Dijon, drove off a relieving host, and secured his submission. By 50 b.c. Gaul had been thoroughly pacified, and Caesar, now very wealthy, was ready to return to Rome, where he had won prestige with the people as a result of his victories, and popularity with the business element, who had reaped riches from the spoils of his conquest. More important, he had with him a loyal army of veterans who had shared in his campaigns.

ROME
(58-56 B.C.)

In Rome, however, all had not gone well. The triumvirate was substantially an unnatural alliance of three potential rivals. With Caesar present it had worked well; with Caesar away it verged toward collapse. Clodius, Caesar's agent, was a vigorous leader of the mob, opposed to all that Pompey and Crassus represented. From the poorer section of the populace, who still hoped for improvement in their economic and political status, he organized armed groups with which he dominated the assemblies, where he passed laws to suit himself, and created such confusion in the streets that Pompey himself did not dare leave his house.

Pompey, to regain power, secured the election of Milo as tribune for 57 B.C. Milo armed groups of his own and contended with Clodius in riots to secure political control over the Roman government. To strengthen himself further, Pompey obtained the recall of Cicero, who received a tremendous ovation on his joyous return. Cicero immediately paid his debt to Pompey by persuading the senate to grant him the control of the grain supply of Rome for five years together with proconsular imperium in the Mediterranean. Pompey with his usual efficiency dealt well with this problem. The senate, however, not yet willing to recognize his pre-eminence in the state and rejecting proposals which would have made him in effect the first emperor, thus drove him once more into the arms of Caesar.

THE CONFER-
ENCE AT LUCCA

Cicero, in the hope of splitting the triumvirate, began an assault on Caesar's agrarian laws. Caesar, with troublesome problems in Gaul on his hands, did not welcome the open breach threatened by Cicero's attack, and accordingly he invited Pompey and Crassus to meet him in April, 56 B.C., at Lucca in Cisalpine Gaul. There they journeyed, attended by some two hundred senators, and there the affairs of empire were settled and the spoils divided. Pompey and Crassus were to be consuls for 55 B.C. and were to be given five-year provincial commands the following year; Crassus was to receive Syria and the command of a war against the Parthians, who were disturbing that province; Pompey was to be governor of the two Spains, but he was to manage his provinces through *legati,* while he remained in Italy and kept watch; Caesar's command in Gaul was to be renewed for another five-year period. Clodius was ordered to behave himself, and Cicero was forced to acquiesce in the plans of the ring. To appease Cicero, his brother was made one of Caesar's lieutenants in Gaul, where he speedily won distinction. In return the orator delivered a brilliant speech in favor of the provincial commands.

THE PRINCIPATE OF POMPEY

These well-laid plans soon went astray. Crassus left for the East in 54 B.C. with highest hopes of returning with a military glory equal to that of his colleagues. In 53 B.C., however, he was drawn into the desert, defeated, and slain at Carrhae. The influence of Pompey was not sufficient to keep order in Rome, and Caesar was too busy with revolts in Gaul to interfere. Clodius and Milo fought in the assembly and in the streets; elections could not be held; the authorities were powerless. In 52 B.C. Clodius was slain by Milo's group on the Appian Way, and in the riot which followed the senate house was burned. In despair the senate turned to Pompey and caused his election as "sole consul." Since at the same time Pompey still had charge of the grain supply and ruled the Mediterranean and the provinces of Spain through his lieutenants, he at last had attained the long-desired position as the indispensable man, *princeps,* first citizen of the state. In the meantime, Julia, through whom he had been held close to Caesar, had died (54 B.C.). In his new position he could not brook a rival; accordingly he severed relations with Caesar. The one man who might have prevented an open break, Cicero, was absent in 51 B.C. as governor of Cilicia, where he won a reputation for honesty and efficiency in provincial administration.

THE SECOND CIVIL WAR

The issue between Caesar and Pompey came to an open break over Caesar's position at the expiration of his provincial command. Caesar had no intention of returning to Rome as a private citizen and exposing himself to the attacks of his enemies, so he demanded the right to remain in Gaul until the end of 49 B.C., though his command terminated in the first of March of that year, and to run for the consulship for 48 B.C. *in absentia.* At first Pompey agreed but then withdrew his consent. Throughout December, 50 B.C., there was spirited debate in the senate, enlivened by compromise offers from Caesar and by vetoes imposed by Caesarian and Pompeian tribunes. Finally, Caesar offered to lay down his powers if Pompey would do the same. When Pompey refused, Caesar prepared for action. On January 7, 49 B.C., the senate passed a decree of martial law and declared Caesar a public enemy. Antony and Cassius, Caesarian tribunes, vetoed the law and were forced to flee for their lives. This enabled Caesar to act in defense of the sanctity of the tribunician office.

With the famous remark, "the die is cast," Caesar crossed the Rubicon River, boundary of his province on January 10, 49 B.C. *"Hoc voluerunt; tantis rebus gestis Gaius Caesar condemnatus essem nisi ab exercitu auxilium petissem."* "They wished it; after the great things that I had accomplished, I, Gaius Caesar, would have been condemned, had I not sought aid from my army." [2] The senate had sealed its own fate.

THE RIVALS — Caesar had a large following in Italy among the equestrian and popular parties, and a loyal army at his back. Pompey had the senate and the administration with its experience and prestige to add to his own record. He had one army in Spain, another in Epirus, which he had been gathering for the Parthian War and to which Caesar had sent two legions. He also controlled the sea. However, he had no troops in Italy, and he did not foresee the speed with which Caesar would advance. Hampered rather than helped by his senatorial advisers, he failed to act with his customary precision.

ITALY AND SPAIN — Caesar moved with such speed and such success, as the Italian communities went over to him, that Pompey was forced to abandon Italy for the East. There he planned to close in on Caesar from both sides. The latter, however, after failing to cut Pompey off from Brundisium, went at once to Rome. There he called together what was left of the senate, demanded funds, and, when they were not granted, seized the treasury. He satisfied the business element by announcing that there would be no proscription.

After eight days in the capital, he left for Spain. In a hazardous campaign around Ilerda he defeated Pompey's lieutenants and absorbed their armies; on the way home he received the surrender of Massilia, which had resisted until besieged. Back in Rome as dictator, he devoted eleven days to his own election as consul for 48 B.C., to the easing of the debt situation by a moratorium and by the application of interest payments to principal, and to the grant of citizenship to the Transpadane Gauls. Then at the end of October he left for the East.

[2] Suet. *Jul.* XXX, 4.

PHARSALUS

Though Bibulus controlled the Adriatic with his fleet, Caesar managed to slip part of his army across to Epirus. Bibulus died during the winter, and Antony had little difficulty in crossing with the rest of the army in March. After a failure to besiege Pompey in Dyrrhachium, Caesar led his army into Thessaly in search of supplies, and there Pompey's senatorial officers, anxious to return to Rome, forced him into battle with Caesar at Pharsalus. Caesar's veterans, though outnumbered two to one, defeated the Pompeian forces with ease. Pompey fled to Egypt, where he was murdered by agents of the young Ptolemy.

EGYPT

Caesar, following Pompey to Egypt, found himself quickly involved in the tangled affairs of that kingdom, where the two children of the "Flute-Player," Ptolemy and Cleopatra, were contending for the rule. Won by the youth and charm of the famous Cleopatra, Caesar placed her on the throne. He suppressed riots in Alexandria, and with aid from Syria defeated an Egyptian force in a battle on the Nile. Then, while there was rioting in Rome and the Pompeian forces were gathering in Africa, Caesar dallied with Cleopatra in Alexandria until June.

ZELA, THAPSUS, AND MUNDA

Once on his way he acted with dispatch. Pharnaces of Pontus was defeated at Zela with such speed that Caesar sent his famous message: *"Veni, vidi, vici."* In April, 47 B.C., he was back in Rome. There he again dealt with the debt problem, put down a mutiny of his veterans, and engineered his own election as consul for 46 B.C. In April of that year, he defeated the Pompeians and their ally, Juba, king of Numidia, at Thapsus in Africa. Cato, unwilling to surrender, and unable, as he thought, to live longer with honor, committed suicide at Utica, a manner of death which made him a hero to later ages. Numidia was made a province with Sallust, the historian, proconsul. A final concentration of Pompeians in Spain was defeated at Munda in March, 45 B.C. After Thapsus, Caesar, elected dictator for ten years, held a great fourfold triumph over Gaul, Egypt, Pontus, and Africa. Statues symbolic of the Rhone, the Rhine, the Ocean, and the Nile were carried in the procession. Games were celebrated and presents distributed to the people. The following year a three-day festival glorified the final victory at Munda.

CAESAR, EMPEROR

CAESAR'S
POWERS
From the crossing of the Rubicon in January, 49 B.C., to his death on the Ides of March, 44 B.C., Caesar was in Rome but sixteen months in all. During this time he carried out a series of reforms calculated to change the aspect of the Roman world. He gathered into his own hands the major power of the Roman constitution. He was elected dictator (of the Sullan type) for brief periods in 49 B.C. and in 47 B.C., for ten years after Thapsus, and for life after Munda; he was consul continuously from 48 B.C.; he held the tribunician power (by special grant) with its right of presidency over the assemblies and its sacrosanctity; he had proconsular power with full command over all the armies of the state. He had the right to nominate magistrates and appoint all provincial governors. As *praefectus morum* he had not only supervision of public morals but full censorial control over citizen and senatorial lists. The office of Pontifex Maximus gave him control over the machinery of religion and the religious law. In addition, by vote of the senate, he bore the title *Imperator,* signifying a victorious general, and was hailed by the senate as *pater patriae.* He wore the laurel wreath of triumph continually and showed his superiority to the senate by receiving it while seated. In addition to these titles and powers which belonged to the Roman tradition, he was granted a series of honors which placed him in the succession of Hellenistic monarchs. *Venus genetrix* was established as a goddess by edict to indicate his divine ancestry and was given a temple. His statue was placed in the temples, his portrait on the coins. The month, *Quintilis,* was renamed July in his honor. His liaison with Cleopatra, who came to Rome in 46 B.C. and remained in his house and gardens across the Tiber until his death, gave color to the rumor, probably false, that he intended to marry her and to establish an eastern monarchy with its capital at Alexandria or on the ancient site of Troy.

The significance of Caesar's titles and powers was revealed in the autocratic character of his policies in the administration. He, Caesar, was above parties and was, indeed, not merely a magistrate of Rome but ruler of the world.

CAESAR'S
REFORMS

In an all-embracing program of reform, Caesar endeavored to cure the ills which had beset the Roman body politic. He ended the long struggle between the senators and the knights by using the latter widely in the administration and enrolling great numbers of them in the senate, thus awarding them the palm of victory over the senators. He added provincials to the senate as well, increasing its numbers to nine hundred in an attempt, his opponents said, to degrade it, but actually to break down the republican tradition of the rule of Rome and of the senatorial class and to make the body representative of the empire. He abolished the political clubs through which he himself had risen to power.

Through his supreme command of the military forces and his right to nominate and appoint his assistants, Caesar was able to control the magistrates and the provincial governors and thus to end the confusion and corruption of the preceding century. By this act and by conferring citizenship on many Spaniards and Gauls he began a program intended to destroy the distinction between Italians and provincials and so level off the Mediterranean world in fulfillment of the hopes of Sertorius. For the same purpose Caesar proposed but did not carry out a census of the entire empire. A uniform charter was provided for the Italian communities by the *Lex Julia Municipalis,* probably drawn by Caesar but made law after his death by Antony. Carthage and Corinth were re-established as Roman cities.

In Rome he improved the administration by increasing the number of magistrates and reforming the law courts; he also planned a codification of the Roman law. The influx of wealth from Gaul and the moratoria and reductions of debts during the Civil War had brought relief to the overburdened debtors. For the proletariat and the veterans he returned to the program of Gaius Gracchus, and settled many, not only on Italian lands, but throughout many colonies in the empire as well. Laws compelling the use of free labor on the great estates provided employment for many poor in Italy and lessened a little the dangers of slave revolts. At the same time, the list of the recipients of the public grain was investigated and reduced to 150,000. He had many plans in mind for the imperial city, such as the enlargement and beautification of the city, the gathering of a great library, the regulation of the bed of the Tiber, and the development of Ostia as a port for Rome.

Caesar's entire program was calculated to establish unified and orderly imperial control under himself as autocrat; provincial misrule and the threat of civil war were to be removed; local government was to be put in order and local prosperity secured in Italy and throughout the empire; the economic ills of Rome were to be healed; and Rome was to be made a city worthy of being the capital of an empire. Even time, as represented by the calendar, was to be made correct in Caesar's world. In the most lasting of his reforms, Caesar, with the assistance of a Greek astronomer, brought the official year into accord with the sun and established a year of 365 days with every fourth year a leap year. The Julian calendar, with certain minor changes made by Pope Gregory XIII in 1582, is the one we still use.

THE CONSPIRACY

For the year 44 B.C. Caesar and Antony were consuls, and Brutus and Cassius praetors. The latter pair were to be governors of Macedon and Syria the following year. Officials were also designated for 43 B.C. and 42 B.C., and Caesar prepared to leave for the Parthian War. The Sibylline Books declared that only a *rex* could conquer Parthia, and in accordance with this Antony, at the feast of the Lupercalia, offered Caesar the crown. But popular opposition showed itself, and Caesar refused.

On the Ides of March he went, unattended by a bodyguard as was his custom, to address the senate. At the foot of Pompey's statue, as everyone knows, he was surrounded by a band of conspirators and murdered. The conspiracy responsible for Caesar's murder was compounded of Pompeians, disappointed Caesarians like Cassius, and republican doctrinaires who objected to his tyrannical powers and the evident trend toward monarchy. The leader of the last group was Brutus, traditionally descended from that Brutus who had expelled the Tarquins. The self-styled Liberators planned to address the senate and declare the restoration of the republic; but when the senate fled in alarm and confusion reigned in the streets of Rome, the Liberators retired to the Capitol where they barricaded themselves.

JULIUS CAESAR

Caesar has left an indelible imprint on the pages of history. Schoolboys still read his commentaries; scholars have followed his career and scrutinized his every act; generals have studied his campaigns and sought to learn the secrets of his victories; kings have envied his power and sought to equal it. His very name has come to mean emperor and has been borne proudly by the Roman Caesars and modern czars and kaisers.

He was without doubt a man of extraordinary potentialities,

whose abilities and character developed with his opportunities. The young Caesar, first known for his irreverence and his escapades, matured into the scheming but skillful politician who knew both how to charm men by the force of his personality so that they did his will, and at the same time how to organize and get out the vote. His powers of organization and leadership were best revealed when, though over forty years of age, he won his first military campaign and became one of the world's great generals. He knew the value of speed and surprise, and was the first general in antiquity to make proper use of trenches and siege engines. His calculated daring in warfare was based on a full knowledge of the capabilities of his own men and on an understanding of the psychology and weaknesses of his opponents. Ultimate success made him the mighty Caesar, organizer and ruler of empire, who did indeed "bestride the narrow world like a Colossus." His deeds and his ideas survived him, and later Caesars carried his plans to completion.

THE LAST STAGE OF THE REVOLUTION

ANTONY The conspirators had failed lamentably to arrange plans for dealing with Caesar's lieutenants—Lepidus, master of the horse, and Antony, consul. Lepidus at once occupied the Forum with troops, while Antony secured possession of Caesar's papers and money. The stalemate which resulted was temporarily solved by a meeting of the senate at which a general amnesty, engineered by Cicero, was proclaimed. Again a mistake was made when Antony was given permission to make an address at Caesar's funeral. With a skillful speech Antony inflamed the mob so that they burned Caesar's body in the Forum. Rome became unsafe for the conspirators, and Brutus and Cassius soon left for the East, where they hoped to secure men and money for the struggle with Antony which they saw was soon to come.

OCTAVIAN Antony's advance to power received a rude check, however, when the young Octavius came to Rome. Caesar's will had revealed that in addition to royal gifts to the Roman people he had adopted his grand-nephew, Octavius, who had been waiting in Epirus to join him for the Parthian War. On learning of the murder, the eighteen-year-old boy, with his friend Agrippa, left at once for the capital city. When Antony rebuffed him, he raised enough money to pay Caesar's bequests and in 43 B.C. he secured the formalities which made him Julius Caesar Octavianus. Cicero supported Octavian, rallied the republican forces with letters and speeches, and in his famous Philippics opened a savage attack on Antony which drove the former Caesarian to his province of Cisalpine Gaul.

In the war with senatorial troops which followed, Antony was defeated, but both the consuls commanding the troops were killed. Octavian, as he should be called after the adoption ceremonies, thereupon demanded the consulship for himself. When this was refused, he seized Rome with an army of Caesar's veterans which he had raised, and forced his election. He left at once to deal with Antony, but instead of fighting he came to terms.

THE SECOND TRIUMVIRATE

Antony, joined by Lepidus, met Octavian near Bononia, and the three laid plans for the future. In accordance with these plans they seized Rome and secured legal election as triumvirs with dictatorial powers for five years. Thus the second triumvirate was established as a legal office. The triumvirs divided the western provinces among them and prepared for the war with Brutus and Cassius. Because they desired vengeance and needed money, they declared a proscription. Many tales of horror and heroism have survived from this butchery, and among the victims was Cicero, whose death Antony desired. In the summer of 42 B.C., Antony and Octavian defeated Brutus and Cassius in two battles at Philippi. Cassius committed suicide after the first, Brutus after the second. Antony then remained in the East, while Octavian returned to restore order in Rome and to deal with the piratical Sextus Pompey, son of the Great, who had seized Sicily and was interfering with Rome's grain supply. Lepidus, to whom had been given the office of Pontifex Maximus and the province of Africa, became and remained a negligible factor.

In spite of their apparent agreement, the future portended a struggle between Octavian and Antony for the rule of Rome. The hopes of the Liberators and of Cicero could no longer be realized. One-man rule supported by the army and relying upon control of the provinces was too firmly entrenched, and the republican forces were entirely too weak to make possible any restoration of the ancient constitution. The care with which the triumvirs took over the provinces and divided them among themselves indicates their realization of the powers, dangers, and potentialities of the situation.

OCTAVIAN
IN THE WEST

Octavian faced the more difficult tasks of providing for the veterans, of restoring order and prosperity to Italy, which had been ravaged by the late war, of dealing with Sextus Pompey, and of handling the remaining republican leaders and the populace in Rome. His path to success in these matters was rendered difficult by the watchful jealousy and constant interference of Antony and his adherents. When, to provide farms for the veterans, Octavian confiscated much land in Italy, Lucius and Fulvia, the brother and the wife of Antony took advantage of the unpopularity of this act to lead a revolt, known as the Perusian War, against him. After Lucius had been besieged in Perusia and starved into submission, Octavian with undue severity destroyed the ancient Etruscan town.

Antony returned, but when the veteran armies refused to fight against each other, peace was made at Brundisium. By formal agreement Octavian received the West and Antony the East, the agreement being sealed by a marriage between Antony, Fulvia having died, and Octavia, sister of Octavian. Another quarrel which broke out over the war with Sextus was patched up by Octavian at Tarentum in 37 B.C., and the triumvirate was renewed for five years.

In the face of these difficulties Octavian met with great success. After several difficult campaigns his lieutenant, Agrippa, defeated Sextus Pompey in Sicily. In Italy Octavian laid aside his former ferocity and showed himself a wise statesman. He put an end to confiscations of land, restored order by wiping out brigandage, fostered agriculture, and brought prosperity back to Italy. With a careful regard for republican tradition and a skillful use of propaganda in his own favor and against Antony he secured the support of the Roman people and became the hero of the day in Rome.

ANTONY AND
CLEOPATRA

The story of Antony in the East was far different. On his first trip to the East after Philippi he showed he had inherited Caesarian ideas when he allowed the cities to give him divine honors as the New Dionysus. Requiring money of Egypt, he summoned Cleopatra to meet him at Tarsus. To the charms of the lovely Egyptian he succumbed so completely that he retired to Alexandria with her, where they both reveled in luxury while his lieutenants struggled with the Parthians. Recalled to Italy by the Perusian War, Antony, apparently putting aside Cleopatra, married Octavia and spent three years in Athens with her, a model

Roman husband and governor. When he finally set out for the Parthian War in 36 B.C., however, he sent Octavia back to Rome and
renewed his alliance with Cleopatra. The Parthian expedition was a
complete failure and only a skillful retreat saved Antony and part of
his army. In 36 B.C. Antony openly married Cleopatra and in 34 B.C.
he bestowed the Oriental provinces as kingdoms on the children whom
she had had by Caesar and himself.

These affronts to Rome enabled Octavian to arouse the city
against his ancient enemy. Many of Antony's Roman followers deserted him when he refused to abandon the queen. Open war broke
out and in the spring of 31 B.C. Agrippa succeeded in blocking Antony's fleet in the harbor at Actium and in cutting his army off from
supplies. To break the blockade the battle of Actium was fought. A
part of the fleet, led by Cleopatra and bearing the treasure, succeeded
in getting through and left for Egypt, whereupon Antony, seeing certain defeat, followed her, abandoning the rest of his fleet and his army
to their fate; but these, left with no choice, went over to the victor.

The following year, when Octavian advanced upon Egypt, Antony, unable to establish a strong defense, committed suicide and died
in Cleopatra's arms. The queen, after her pleas for clemency for her
children and herself had failed, took poison rather than grace Octavian's triumph in Rome. Plutarch has made the death scenes of the
"Inimitable Livers" immortal in literature and history.

Antony's ability had been frittered away by dissipation and by a
dream of a power for which, as Caesar's fate had shown, the world
was not ready, while the shrewd statesmanship and propaganda of
Octavian had triumphed. Cleopatra remains an enigma. Her charm
was great, though her portraits indicate that she was not particularly
beautiful. Caesar and Antony neglected their imperial duties for her,
and her Roman contemporaries, both hating and fearing her, could
not say too much evil against her. As administrator of Egypt she
showed ability, energy, and wisdom, and she certainly had great
dreams of a world empire in which she would be queen. Whether she
really loved Caesar and Antony, or whether she played a shrewd and
mercenary game with them are matters of opinion. Her whole story
is clouded with romance and "the truth no one knows" as Plutarch
said of her death.

The victory of Octavian ended the revolution. The democratic
reformers had not succeeded in establishing their program. The senate,

despite the bolstering power of Sulla's enactments, had failed to handle the problems of empire and had been cast down from its high estate. Caesar's attempt at dictatorship had resulted in conspiracy and assassination, and the attempt of the triumvirs to divide the world between them had ended in civil war. The triumph of Octavian at Actium brought to an end the Rome ruled by the "senate and the Roman people" and marked the beginning of the Roman Empire under the Caesars.

XX

ROMAN LIFE DURING THE REVOLUTION

THE SENATO-
RIAL CLASS
Enormous increases of wealth and its attendant luxuries and the continued absorption of Hellenistic culture mark the life of the upper classes of Rome during
the revolutionary period. Senators brought home large sums acquired
from booty or extortion in the provinces. With these they built fine
houses in Rome and villas in the country, which they adorned with the
finest products of eastern craftsmanship. They held elaborate banquets
and made great displays of wealth. By making loans or investments
through freedmen secretaries or agents who regularly managed their
estates, they evaded the law which forbade them to engage in industry
and trade. Thus Brutus, through a representative, loaned money to
Salamis on Cyprus, at the exorbitant interest rate of 48 per cent and
protested bitterly when Cicero, as governor of Cilicia, interfered.

In contrast to this picture of wealth was the problem of debt. The
way to office was expensive; standards of living were high; and moneylenders considered senatorial youths good risks. Caesar is said to have
owed as much as two million dollars before he became consul. Those
who failed thus to rise found themselves overwhelmed, and many were
ruined. It was such a situation that gave rise to Catiline's conspiracy.
In fact it was the debt problem that caused many of the difficulties
which arose between the *Optimates* and the equestrian moneylenders.

Problems of the possession and inheritance of wealth, coupled with
newer ideas, led to the decline of the old-fashioned Roman family.
Heiresses, unwilling to be under the control of any man, secured
freedom from the ancient restrictions of the law. Marriages were arranged for financial or political reasons, and divorce became easy and
frequent.

The spread of Stoic and Epicurean philosophies destroyed the
belief of educated Romans in the ancestral religion; ancient standards
were therefore laid aside. A younger group, led in the latter period

by Clodius and his sister Clodia, used their wealth and skepticism as excuses to engage in fast living and in every kind of vice. On the other hand, there were some, like the Metelli and Cato, who in spite of all followed the old tradition. The stories of the proscription of 42 B.C. are filled with evidence of family devotion and honorable behavior. Similarly, not all provincial governors were as corrupt as Verres.

The senatorial group failed, not because of their vices, but because they blindly clung to the traditional constitutional forms and refused to establish an effective system of imperial administration. Their policy of futile resistance to change played directly into the hands of Pompey and of Caesar. The proscriptions of Sulla and of the triumvirate weakened them by depriving them of many of their bravest and most intelligent leaders and by cowing the remainder.

THE EQUITES   The business element as a whole prospered, in spite of proscriptions and disasters, as their leaders came into political power and they obtained a large share in the profits of the wars in the East and in Gaul. The contract system of tax collection for which "societies," joint-stock companies, were formed brought them great wealth, whereupon they began to play a leading part in Mediterranean commerce and to invest their means in industrial establishments. They acquired real estate in Rome, Italy, and the provinces, bought or leased from the state the mines and former royal monopolies of the East, and owned great numbers of slaves, whom they employed or leased for multifarious activities. The capitalists served as money-changers and as bankers to receive deposits, issue letters of credit, and make loans, especially to senators and provincial cities. Their major interest in politics was the protection and extension of their financial transactions.

THE COMMON   Information is lacking about the commoners of the
PEOPLE   city except for the stories of the riots in the streets. They lived in huge tenements, called *insulae,* where rents were low. Though faced by slave competition, many must have found employment as laborers. Others engaged in the ancient crafts, particularly in the manufacture of arms, for which there was great demand, and some kept small stores, bakeries, and wineshops to supply the needs of the city. The state assisted them with cheap grain and amused them with free shows, and they could always count on gifts from office seekers who desired their votes. Their poverty made them

fair spoil for politicians like Catiline, Clodius, and Milo, and they were easily induced to join the political clubs and to riot in the streets.

SLAVES The slave population of Rome and Italy increased enormously with wealth and conquest. Skilled slaves from the East were in demand for the olive and grape plantations, and rougher barbarians for the cattle ranches. In the city there were slave architects, builders, copyists, readers, and craftsmen. Some were employed in their owner's establishments; others were rented out; many had shops of their own under the patronage of their masters. Work in the wealthy households was directed by slave stewards and performed by menials of servile status. Other slaves did the clerical work of the officials and of the business houses. Some were secretaries who, like Cicero's Tiro, a freedman, looked after the correspondence and managed the estates of their masters or served as tutors for the children of the family. Manumission was easy and frequent; indeed, Sulla is said to have freed ten thousand slaves in one block for political and military purposes. As the result of such occurrences the grant of citizenship, which in earlier times had accompanied freedom, was restricted toward the end of the period to the traditional Latin rights which precluded voting or the holding of office.

ROME Rome itself was still far from being a worthy capital of a great empire. The houses of the nobility were fine structures, but the *insulae* of the poor were hastily constructed and liable to collapse or catch fire. Though new basilicas and temples were built and covered with marble veneer, many of the older buildings were in a sad state of disrepair, and the streets were narrow, dirty, and crooked. The administration of the city was in utter confusion, without any effective police or fire department, and the government proved itself incapable of handling the street disorders of the period without recourse to military aid.

ITALY The political situation of Italy was thrown into confusion by the wholesale grant of Roman citizenship which followed the Social War. Until Octavian restored order, there was much brigandage, as runaway slaves, dispossessed farmers, and dissatisfied veterans plundered unwary or unattended travelers. The economic condition of the peninsula is more difficult to assess. The great estates of wealthy Romans and Italians continued to grow in size and in the number of the slaves they employed, though there are evidences that the great landowner was beginning to find it more profitable to let his land out to tenants than to work it with slaves. The small farming class was badly upset by the series of confiscations and resettlements, but the eagerness of veterans for a piece of Italian land indicates, however, that farming on a small scale was still profitable and prevalent. The industries which are found in Campania in imperial times—the manufacture of pottery and of wares of copper and iron—had already made their appearance. Puteoli prospered as the chief port of Rome.

THE PROVINCES   The provinces suffered most during the revolution. Sicily was terribly impoverished by the slave wars and by the plundering of its governors, and Africa was just beginning to recover from the ravages of the Third Punic War. The continuous wars kept Spain in a turmoil, while Gaul was ravaged by Caesar's conquests. The East, plundered in turn by its governors, by pirates, by Mithridates, by Sulla, Cassius, Antony, and Octavian, also paid heavy tribute to the Roman businessmen in the form of interest payments on the debts which the monetary exactions created. At the same time the demand in Rome for eastern manufactures brought much of the wealth back. Also the increase of maritime business and of commercial banking, which, in spite of the appearance of Roman merchants and bankers, naturally fell for the most part into the hands of skilled Greeks, brought new opportunities and wealth to many individuals. The provinces poured extraordinary sums in tribute into Rome which were spent on public works, on the pleasures of the Roman mob, the army, and on imperial administration. Since the treasury was in the hands of quaestors, most of them without much experience in administration, much of the tribute was squandered, and the provinces failed to get in return the efficient management and protection which was their due. Real prosperity came to the empire only under the well-organized system of the Caesars.

ROMAN LAW   Roman civil law, Rome's greatest and most enduring contribution to the civilization of the world, was developed during the republican period into an instrument readily adapted by the Caesars for the ordering of an empire. Later it was to dominate the law of the Middle Ages and to be the model for the European and Latin-American civil codes of today.

Roman law had its beginnings in the regal period under the authority of the king and in the hands of the pontiffs who probably acted as his advisers in legal matters. It was at that time primarily *fas*, religious law or custom, which the state controlled to preserve the favor of the gods. Certainly in very early times, however, the king served as arbitrator or judge in private disputes, and so there developed methods of procedure and principles of private law for citizens, the *jus civile,* or civil law, which, like *fas,* was held under the guardianship of the pontiffs. The difficulty of access to these patrician priests and, as a consequence, the difficulty of securing justice in the courts were among the chief grievances of the plebeians (p. 350), whose agitation resulted, as we have seen, in the composition of the Twelve Tables. This famous document, with its rules, maxims, definitions, and remedies, was in the language of the Roman jurists, the basis of the *jus civile*. It stated the fundamental rules of procedure, giving the plaintiff the right to summon the defendant into court and compel his attendance by force if necessary, and likewise to force him to obey the decision of the court. If the debtor failed to make his payments after proper judicial procedure, he became the property of his creditors and might be sold or killed. The famous provision "Let him be cut into pieces; if anyone cut too much or too little it will not be a crime," was characteristic of the rigid logic of the code rather than a statement of actual practice. The creditors fared better if they sold the debtor and divided the proceeds.

The section of the Tables which dealt with family law established the power of the *pater familias* over his wife, children, clients, and slaves. It recognized marriage by religious rites, by a ceremony of purchase, and by cohabitation, and it provided for the inheritance of the property, together with the religious duties which belonged to the family, by the direct heir or close relations, or in default of legal heirs it permitted a man to adopt or designate an heir so that the continuity of family life might not be lost.

In its definitions of property law the law distinguished between that kind of property which required legal forms of transfer in the presence of witnesses, such as land, slaves, and cattle, and less valuable things which might readily be bought and sold without technicalities. For the former it provided the procedure of conveyance and by establishing contractual rules it created forms of bond and mortgage.

In respect to injuries the code rested on the ancient principle of retaliation, modified, as were the earlier Oriental codes, by provisions for restitution or payment. A famous article, still the rule, ran, "If a thief breaking in and stealing at night be killed, let him be killed rightly." The rigidity of the law as applied to transactions and to procedure is illustrated by the phrase "As the tongue hath pronounced, so shall the law be."

Those articles of the Tables which dealt with public law, in part derived from Greek codes, forbade illegal assemblies at night, provided the death penalty for murder, arson, libel, false witness, and similar offenses, prohibited the burning or burying of a man within the city, and the burial of gold with a dead man save that which was in his teeth.

The Twelve Tables were the product of a people, literal-minded and narrow, but with a great sense of justice. The code represented a community in the economic stage of agriculture and herding. The landless man (*proletarius*) had to have a landowner as security in court. To adapt it to the needs of economic and intellectual growth it needed interpretation, procedural reform, and expansion; and all these in time it received.

For a period the power of interpretation of the code and the knowledge of procedure under it remained in the possession of the pontiffs. Litigants and judges alike turned to them for information and opinions (*responsa*) about the law. Roman procedure (*legis actiones*), including the summons, the charge, and the execution of the judgment, were all carefully regulated. The plaintiff, as we have seen, haled or hauled the defendant into court, where his case appeared *in jure*. He recited a formal charge, the wording of which had to be exact, for if he used the wrong formula or word in his statement, his case was lost and he could never bring it again. After this formal proceeding the magistrate turned the case over to a private judge, *judex,* who, *in judicio,* examined the facts and applied the law as he received it from the Tables or, in case of doubt, from the pontiffs. The victor in the suit then executed the judgment himself. The rigidity of this procedure and the necessity of securing the wording from the pontiffs prevented many from securing justice, and the limited number of *actiones* (there were only five types), due to the early period of their formulation, blocked the development of the law to meet new needs.

The first break in this system came in 304 B.C. when Flavius, freedman of Appius Claudius (p. 364), published the *legis actiones.* Tiberius Coruncanius, the first plebeian pontiff (ca. 250 B.C.), by public lectures made known to all the science of interpreting the law, and in 204 B.C. Aelius composed a treatise containing the Twelve Tables, the interpretations, and the *legis actiones*. As the result, knowledge of the law became general property, and there developed a number of lay jurists, *prudentes,* who made knowledge of the law their specialty and their pride and who gave *responsa* freely to all.

After the creation of the office of *praetor peregrinus,* the methods of procedure were reformed under its influence in order to deal with cases involving foreigners. Since foreigners could not be expected to know or to use the exact Latin wording of the actions, this praetor adopted the practice of calling litigants before him and, after a discussion of the case, of drawing up in writing a formula which stated its nature, and which he turned over to the *judex*. This simplified procedure was so advantageous that it was made available for citizens by the *Lex Aebutia* (ca. 150 B.C.), which allowed action *per formulam* as an alternative to *per legis actionem*. The *legis actiones* rapidly declined and were brought to a final end by Augustus.

Expansion of the law to meet new conditions was the work of the magistrates, primarily the praetors, and particularly after the passage of the Aebutian Law. The praetor had a good deal of power over the law. If it worked injustice, he might set it aside in effect, though not directly; or if new cases developed, he might evolve through the formulary process new rules of law. The aediles, who possessed judicial authority in minor cases, followed the praetor's example, and the law which developed through this process of legislation by magistrates was called *jus honorarium*. Since the largest part of it was created by the praetors, however, it is often spoken of as *jus praetorium*. The *jus honorarium* received formal statement and sanction in the edicts. Upon entrance into office each magistrate issued an edict in which he stated the principles by which he would be guided in carrying out the duties of his office. In the case of the praetor this consisted of a statement of the *formulae,* upon which he would accept action at law. Normally he simply took over the edict of the preceding year with such additions or changes as his own knowledge, or the experience of his predecessor, made him feel were desirable. Thus through the praetor's edicts the *jus civile* was kept up to date and developed to fit changing needs, while through the habitual continuity of the edicts and the recognized, though not legal, authority of the *responsa prudentium* it held to its traditional character of a law founded on custom and inherited from the fathers.

The *praetor peregrinus* made a further contribution to Roman jurisprudence in the development of the concept of the *jus gentium* "law of all nations," fundamentally a new idea. In antiquity, law was commonly regarded as the peculiar possession of the citizens of a state, and foreigners had no part in it. Thus Greek cities had agents to represent their citizens in the courts of other states (p. 139), and metics in Athens had patrons to aid them in legal cases (p. 225). Rome, respecting this concept, allowed local codes to remain in force in conquered territory. Nevertheless there developed in the Hellenistic period (p. 309) certain recognized principles of commercial relations between citizens of different states, generally understood and enforced throughout the Mediterranean. The foreign praetors discovered these principles in their discussion of cases involving aliens, and called them *jus gentium*. The principles of equity were developed in their courts in Rome, and the experience of the Roman governors in the provinces enlarged them. Technically, however, the *jus gentium* was never more than a body of principles, since its provisions received the force of law only when recognized by the praetor or by the provincial governor and embodied in the edicts which these magistrates issued. When so stated, they became *jus honorarium*. Thus, however, they had their part in laying the broad foundations of the Roman law on which the world continues to build.

LITERATURE IN THE CICERONIAN AGE

In the momentous last years of the Roman Republic, Latin literature began to attain the full heights of its greatness. Catullus and Lucretius, poets, Caesar and Sallust, historians, Nepos, biographer, Varro, antiquarian, and Cicero, orator, essayist, and letter writer, were the chief ornaments of a literary period which has been called after its greatest writer, the Ciceronian period.

CATULLUS
(CA. 84-54 B.C.)

The influence of the Alexandrian poets on Roman literature was most clearly revealed in the works of Catullus. He was a master of verse, skilled in the lore of the Greeks and able to adapt their varied meters to Latin, particularly the lively eleven-syllable verse. He composed many lyrics, a little epic, and an elaborate wedding hymn. But his fame rests on a group of short poems which reveal him as one of the sweetest of love poets. Madly in love with Clodia, he addressed her as Lesbia in impassioned verse.

> Let's live, my Lesbia, and love.
> Let's value not a whit above
> A penny all that dotards grey
> In tones of condemnation say.
> The sun can set, the sun can rise;
> Once let the brief light quit our eyes,
> And we through endless night must keep
> The couch of one unbroken sleep.
> Give me a thousand kisses—more!
> A hundred yet: add to the score
> A second thousand kisses: then
> Another hundred, and again
> A thousand more, a hundred still.
> So many thousands we fulfil,
> We must take care to mix the count—
> Bad luck to know the right amount—
> Lest evil eye impose its spell
> When it can all our kisses tell.[1]

When she proved unfaithful he poured out his heart in reproaches and endeavored to steel himself to renunciation:

> I hate yet love: you ask how this may be,
> Who knows? I feel its truth and agony.[2]

Equal depth in feeling and beauty in words are revealed by his poetic greeting to his home on Lake Garda and his address to his dead brother ending with the famous line

> *Atque in perpetuum, frater, ave atque vale.*
> "And so forever, brother, hail and farewell."

LUCRETIUS
(CA. 99-55 B.C.)

Though equally under Greek influence, Lucretius was an exact opposite of the passionate Catullus. In the first successfully written Latin hexameter he endeavored to bring to the Romans the Epicurean message of quietude. In the *De Rerum Natura,* "On the Nature of Things," he appealed to men with evangelistic fervor to lay aside their troubles and worries and find rest in Epicureanism.

> Naught sweeter than to hold the tranquil realms
> On high, well fortified by sages' lore,

[1] Duff, *Literary History of Rome,* p. 319.
[2] *Ibid.,* p. 315.

> Whence to look down on others wide astray—
> Lost wanderers questing for the way of life—
> See strife of genius, rivalry of rank,
> See night and day men strain with wondrous toil
> To rise to utmost power and grasp the world.[3]

Praising the Greek as the man who first liberated men from the weight of superstition, he explained the atomic and mechanistic universe which Epicurus had portrayed. He described the evolutionary growth of the world and of man and endeavored to explain the processes of nature. With a deep religious feeling he endeavored to free the Romans from those fears which were even then driving them to the emotional religions of the East, and especially from the fear of death. In the third book he discusses the problem of the soul and marshals his arguments against immortality.

> "Soon shall thy home greet thee in joy no more,
> Nor faithful wife nor darling children run
> To snatch first kiss, and stir within thy heart
> Sweet thoughts too deep for words. Thou canst no more
> Win wealth by working or defend thine own.
> The pity of it! One fell hour," they say,
> "Hath robbed thee of thine every prize in life."

But he does not let pathos daunt him; his comment is that of the philosopher:

> Hereat they add not this: "And now thou art
> Beset with yearning for such things no more." [4]

His work was great poetry and extraordinary in its value to science. From it the modern world of scholarship has derived most of its knowledge of the philosophy of Epicurus.

THE HISTORIANS   In prose which is terse and clear, with words and phrases handled like cohorts on the field of battle, Caesar recounted his deeds in Gaul and in the civil wars. Though his *Commentaries* were campaign documents, written to explain and defend his own actions, they were composed with such apparent detachment and impersonality that it is rarely possible to separate propaganda from fact and to prove that Caesar distorted history for his own justification. Nothing has survived of his orations, essays, or poems.

---

[3] Duff, *op. cit.*, pp. 279-80.
[4] *Ibid.*, p. 286.

Sallust (86-35 B.C.), quaestor, proconsul of Numidia, and follower of Caesar, devoted the closing years of his life to the composition of historical writings. In two brilliant monographs—one on the Jugurthine War, which was a glorification of Marius; the other on the Catilinarian conspiracy, a virulent excoriation of Catiline—both of which have survived, and in the *Histories* which covered the decade after Sulla's death, now lost except for fragments, he abandoned the annalistic method of composition and composed readable, if inaccurate works of history.

NEPOS (CA. 100-CA. 25 B.C.)   A Gaul from the Po Valley, Nepos became a learned member of Cicero's circle and contributed a long series of biographies of which only a few, mostly of famous Greeks, have survived. Though not scientifically composed, they are lively, popular, and clear, and hence are often read by modern schoolboy students of Latin.

VARRO (116-27 B.C.)   Varro, "the most learned of the Romans," wrote encyclopedic works covering a wide range of activities. Modern scholars estimate that he produced seventy-four different works consisting of six hundred and twenty single volumes. Of these the most famous were his *Antiquities,* his books on farming and on the Latin language. Though he was studied and quoted throughout the imperial period and often referred to by the early medieval scholars, only fragments of his works have survived.

CICERO (106-43 B.C.)   Statesman, orator, and philosopher, Cicero looms large in the political history of the period and in the history of the humane studies. He was a master of Latin prose and of rhetorical form. His orations disclose the crosscurrents of Roman politics and society. The characters of Verres, Catiline, and Antony have never recovered from the fierceness of his invective. His tribute to the liberal arts in the defense of Archias is one of the noblest expressions in any language. Though not a profound thinker, he carried the message of the Greek philosophers to his own generation through his essays, and at the same time contributed much to modern knowledge of ancient thought. He created a vocabulary for philosophy in Latin which has descended through the medieval schools to our own time. He was an inveterate letter writer and his freedman-secretary, Tiro, and his friend, Atticus, preserved and published his correspondence. The letters reveal the man—vain, at times hesitating, even weak, but ever sincere, honest, and patriotic. The noble character of the statesman shines through his defects. His hopes for the preservation of the Roman Republic failed before the onslaught of Caesarism, but, like Demosthenes in Athens, he stands in the historic Hall of Fame ennobled by the courage of his failure. Augustus' comment on him was a fitting epitaph, "A great orator, and one who loved his country well."

EARTH MOTHER

Florence. From Strong, Roman Sculpture from Augustus to Constantine. *Courtesy of Duckworth and Co., publishers.*

Louvre

SCENE OF SACRIFICE

THE ALTAR OF THE AUGUSTAN PEACE

Copenhagen. *From Rostovtzeff*, History of
the Ancient World, *II.*

POMPEY

Rome. *From Rostovtzeff*, History of
the Ancient World, *II.*

CICERO

Naples

CAESAR

Boston. *From Boak*, History of Rome. *Courtesy of
The Macmillan Company, publishers.*

AUGUSTUS

FOUR GREAT ROMANS

≡ XXI ≡

THE AGE OF AUGUSTUS
(31 B.C.-14 A.D.)

HE triumph of Augustus Caesar (the name by which Octavian has ever since been known) brought to a close the century of revolution and civil war and ushered in an era of peace and prosperity for the Mediterranean world which lasted for two centuries and which was due in large measure to the wisdom and statesmanship of the victorious Caesar. During his reign, he reorganized the imperial government, secured the political and economic rehabilitation of Rome, Italy, and the provinces, regulated the frontiers, and undertook a broad program of moral and religious reform and artistic and literary advance. Because of his achievements his generation has been called the Age of Augustus.

THE IMPERIAL SYSTEM

When Augustus returned to Rome after the battle of Actium he was faced with the difficult tasks of fitting a system of one-man rule into the republican constitution without doing outrage to Roman sensibilities. He also had to secure for himself a body of loyal and efficient supporters for the rule of the provinces, the command of the army, and the administration of the empire. He had no intention of giving up his own power, which rested basically on his control of the military forces, but his pride in the Roman tradition and his comprehension of the needs of the situation made him cling to established forms and avoid those autocratic ideas and actions of Julius Caesar which had resulted in conspiracy and assassination. He desired rather to perpetuate the idea of a Rome which should rule the world and in which he should be the "first citizen." The system which he established therefore followed the programs of Gaius Gracchus and of Pompey,

437

rather than those of Sulla or of Caesar. The dictatorship had been abolished, and Augustus made no attempt to revive it. In its place he assumed a position which assured him command of the army and control over the civil administration. He was careful, however, to refuse all offices inconsonant with republican custom. In addition to these formal powers he received a number of titles indicative of his influence, and he surrounded himself with an aura of sacrosanctity which bound the people of the empire to his person.

POWERS AND
TITLES

For some years after the legal expiration of the triumvirate in 32 B.C., Augustus continued to rule by virtue of the consular office and by common consent. In January of 27 B.C., however, he announced to the senate the end of his extraordinary powers and the restoration of the republic. Thereupon the senate conferred upon him that series of offices and titles which made him in effect the ruler of Rome. He was annually elected consul (with a colleague). At the same time he was given not only proconsular power over certain of the provinces where an army was required, being allowed to remain in Rome and govern these provinces through lieutenants, but also the tribunician power [1] with its important privileges of intercession, of calling and presiding over the senate and the assemblies, and of making nominations.

When the consular office proved to be too much of a burden because of its ceremonial obligations, and his tenure prevented the rise of many senators to the coveted honor, he surrendered the position in 23 B.C. As proconsul, however, he was allowed a seat between the consuls, and by an extension of the tribunician power he was given primacy over them in the deliberative bodies. The emphasis which he laid upon this position is indicated by the fact that from that time he and later emperors dated the years of their rule by the annually renewed *tribunicia potestas.* Though he refused to accept a sort of perpetual censorship because of its unrepublican character, he did take charge of the grain supply and of the administration of the city of Rome, in which he established police and fire departments. By virtue of his tribunician power he reformed the senate and endeavored by a series of laws to secure moral reform. When Lepidus died in 17 B.C. Augustus was elected Pontifex Maximus, head of the Roman religion.

In addition to these powers he bore a group of titles which expressed his prestige and influence in Roman affairs. As *princeps,* he

[1] Since he was a patrician he could not be tribune.

was consulted first on all nominations and on all questions of policy or of legislation and he was thus able to dominate the activities of the state. His military prestige was expressed by the word *imperator*, "victorious general," which he had inherited from Julius Caesar as a personal name. *Augustus,* a name conferred upon him by the senate, signified "consecrated," and carried with it the implication of divinity or of divine protection. It is significant that this name had never before been conferred upon any living person. His lofty position and his great services to the world in the restoration of peace and order made him the natural recipient of those divine honors which the Hellenistic East had learned to confer on its rulers. In that region therefore he allowed himself to be worshiped as a god in temples dedicated to *Roma et Augustus.* This imperial cult throughout the provinces proved a great unifying center of patriotic devotion to the person of the ruler. In Italy, however, not Augustus but the *Genius Augusti* associated with the *Lares,* received worship. Augustus himself laid great stress on the divinity of Julius Caesar and associated the great deities, particularly Apollo and Vesta, with his household. By ceremonies and by reliefs on monuments throughout the empire he fostered the conception that his rule had brought a new age of peace and plenty to a troubled world. Opposition to such a man, or even criticism of him, verged upon sacrilege and became an injury to the majesty of the Roman people whom he represented and was punishable with death. The veneration with which he was held received further expression when, in 2 B.C., the senate hailed him as *pater patriae,* "father of his country." After his death he was formally deified and listed among the gods of the Roman state.

In theory, the senate and the Roman people ruled the world under his leadership. Perhaps it was the desire and intention of Augustus that this be so. But in actuality, his military command, his control of the civil administration, his extraordinary wealth (for he was by far the richest man in the world) and the prestige of his personality made him an autocrat—the first of the long line of Roman emperors.

PROBLEM OF
THE SUCCESSION

The greatest failure of Augustus, his failure to provide a proper means of choosing his successor, was due to the anomaly of his own position. The ideal of his system called for the selection of the ablest man by the duly constituted authorities of the state. In actual fact the power was certain to descend to that man who inherited the Augustan wealth and who received the support of the army. Roman ideas of inheritance combined with the natural wishes of Augustus to keep the position in the possession of his family. Though he seems to have expressed a certain unwillingness to found a dynasty, his own actions and the attitude of the people indicated a belief that the person whom he designated as his personal heir would inherit the position of princeps as well. When his nephew Marcellus was married to Julia, only child of Augustus, and was advanced to high office in early manhood, the world assumed that these actions were equivalent to designation for succession. After the death of Marcellus in 22 B.C., Agrippa, chief assistant of Augustus in his rise to power and recipient of the latter's signet ring during his illness of 23 B.C., was married to Julia and received proconsular and tribunician powers almost equal to those of Augustus.

It is evident that Augustus planned to bridge the gap between his own reign and that of his successor by conferring these powers with the concurrence of the senate. Fatality, however, dogged the footsteps of Augustus. When Agrippa died in 12 B.C. the princeps turned to his stepsons, Tiberius and Drusus, children of his third wife, Livia, and designated them as guardians for his grandsons, Gaius and Lucius, who had been born to Agrippa and Julia. After Drusus died in 9 B.C., Tiberius, compelled to divorce his wife and marry Julia, received the proconsular and tribunician powers by grant of the senate. The marriage was not a happy one, and when Augustus began to advance Gaius and Lucius, Tiberius retired in pique to Rhodes. Julia, equally unhappy, engaged in a series of love affairs which resulted in her banishment. When, however, Lucius died in 2 A.D. and Gaius in 4 A.D., of all the heirs of Augustus only Tiberius was left. Recalled from Rhodes, he received the tribunician and proconsular authorities again, was the actual ruler during the last ten years of Augustus' life, and succeeded to power when the great princeps died in 14 A.D. The problem of succession remained undetermined and returned to vex later generations.

THE SENATE   The great deliberative body of the republic was theoretically still the guiding force from which Augustus received his powers and to which he rendered account. In reality it became one of the agencies which the autocrat used to execute his will. A great deal of trouble during succeeding reigns was caused by Augustus' failure to define clearly the relations between the princeps and the senate. This omission was due, perhaps, to his understanding of the conflict between theory and reality and his unwillingness to offend senatorial feelings. He offered various suggestions to make the senate clear its membership of the provincials and other undesirables who had secured enrollment during the Civil Wars, but after these methods failed he assumed a personal control over the senatorial list which made him master of that body. He organized a council composed of certain of the magistrates and fifteen (later twenty) senators to assist him in administrative matters and to prepare measures for senatorial discussion and action. Through this he was able to sense the feelings of the senate, avoid opposition, and at the same time make his own wishes known in a tactful but effective manner. Though he showed great deference to that body and referred important problems to it for legislation, it is doubtful if he would have allowed really inde-pendent action. In any case the members, except for a few outspoken malcontent republicans, were so overawed by his power and cowed by their revolutionary experiences that they hesitated to act or to speak freely and instead merely ratified his wishes. As a result the famous Senatus consulta in actuality came to be legislation by Augustus which was merely consented to by the senate. Though some measures were still carried to the assemblies for legislation, the power and activities of these bodies rapidly declined. Imperial control of nominations made even their elective function formal and in the reign of Tiberius both legislation and elections were transferred *in toto* to the senate. Control over foreign affairs, the reception of embassies, and the negotiation of treaties passed naturally into the hands of Augustus. However the senate during his reign assumed as a body the functions of a high court of justice, taking cognizance of cases involving its members under charges of corruption or malfeasance in office, or offenses against the majesty of the emperor or the state.

OFFICIALS OF THE EMPIRE

In accordance with his stated adherence to republican tradition Augustus continued to use members of the senatorial order in military and political positions as officers of the legions, governors of the provinces, and magistrates in Rome. The old senatorial career continued therefore with some addi-tions. The aspirants to office served in minor military commands and judicial positions (the latter a new feature), held the magistracies in Rome in proper order, and then served as governors of provinces or lieutenants of Augustus. The holding of the quaestorship carried with it membership in the senate. To these duties Augustus added administrative positions by creating senatorial curatorships, permanent boards to look after such functions as the care of roads, public buildings, aqueducts, and the bed and banks of the Tiber.

The republican magistrates, however, gradually declined in power. Imperial appointees overshadowed the quaestors in the provinces, while in Rome care of the treasury was given to two senators of consular rank. Though the praetors retained their judicial functions in the courts, their powers became circumscribed and gradually declined until later in the empire they were merely city magistrates. The consuls likewise lost most of their administrative duties as Augustus assumed charge of the direction of the city and entrusted its care to prefects of equestrian rank.

The senators retained withal their lofty social position, and public opinion demanded of them high standards of wealth, morals, and manners. Accordingly Augustus revised the senatorial list to weed out undesirables and to rebuild the order. Proscriptions and small families had brought to an end many of the great houses of early times, and the old patrician class, still needed for certain priesthoods, had almost disappeared. Moreover, many of the senators had lost the financial means of maintaining their position; manners and morals had grown distressingly lax; skepticism had broken down religion; the old glory of service to Rome had been lost; and those senators who still clung to the ancient ideals were openly critical of Augustus and the new regime. Reorganization of the senate and reawakening of its old religious and patriotic loyalties were imperative. To meet these needs Augustus established a high property qualification for the office, provided pensions for worthy but impoverished senators, elevated many to the patriciate, and took measures, which we shall study later, to revive religion and morals and to secure support for himself. By these means he built up a senatorial class which, in spite of the dissensions and troubles of following reigns, served the Roman Empire well and loyally.

For the higher posts in the civil service and for efficient management of imperial finance, Augustus turned to the equestrian class, which thus reaped the fruits of its long struggle with the senatorial order and of its loyalty to Caesar and to Augustus. The class of *Equites* was definitely established to include all Roman citizens of means, excluding senators, but with a property qualification much lower than that required of the senatorial order. The knights bore special marks of distinction and passed through a definite series of offices. After service in the army with the auxiliary forces, they entered upon secretarial and financial positions, becoming procurators in the various bureaus of government and governors of such minor provinces as Judaea. (Pontius Pilate was such a procurator.) The summit of their career was the holding of a great prefecture by which the rule of Egypt, the command of the watch and of the imperial bodyguard, the care of the grain supply, or the administration of the city of Rome was entrusted to them. In these capacities they gradually assumed the functions of the republican magistrates, as we have seen, and became powerful officials in the empire. The knights could be depended upon for loyalty to the system which brought them prosperity and recognition.

For the lower posts in the financial and secretarial service, skilled freedmen were widely used. They entered upon these tasks as secretaries of great men or as clerks performing duties which the Romans regarded as beneath their dignity. Of their ability and their loyalty to the new regime there was no doubt. Their opportunities in the imperial service and in business were unrestricted, and many acquired important posts and great wealth. The municipalities in which they served conferred high distinction upon some of these freedmen when they were chosen as *Augustales,* priests for the worship of Augustus.

THE ARMY   The army, the real foundation of Augustus' power, was the object of his greatest solicitude. Great numbers of the revolutionary troops were dismissed and given land as pensions. A permanent army of three hundred thousand men was established. Twenty-five legions of six thousand citizens each formed the main body, to which were added an equal number of provincials who were enrolled as auxiliaries. In addition to their numbers and standards, the legion and the auxiliary cohorts received names expressive of their achievements or of their place of enlistment. Thus Legion III Gallica was organized in Gaul, and XX Valeria Victrix received its name from its general Valerius Messalinus and its victory under his command in the Pannonian revolt of 6 A.D. Similarly Cohort I Gallica was raised among the provincials in Gaul. A select body of nine thousand troops drawn from Italy was stationed in the vicinity of Rome under two prefects as the praetorian cohort or bodyguard of the princeps. Soldiers, enlisted for fixed terms of years, were entitled to bonuses or lands at the end of their service. Auxiliaries received the grant of Roman citizenship. When the cost of the army proved too great for the treasury Augustus established the *aerarium militare*, "military treasury," a special fund supported by a 5 per cent inheritance and a 1 per cent sales tax. A permanent fleet with head-quarters at Ravenna and Misenum was organized to keep down piracy.

ITALY   The Augustan peace brought political order and eco-nomic restoration to Italy and the provinces. The problems of Italy had been solved during the time of the triumvirate when, after the period of confiscations and resettlement, Augustus had entered upon a definite program for the encouragement of Italian agriculture. In this he made use of the erudition of Varro, who com-posed his *De Re Rustica,* a textbook on farming, and of the poetic skill of Vergil, whose *Georgics,* written at imperial behest, form both a textbook on farming in poetic form and a glorious tribute to the beauties and richness of the Italian land.

THE EMPIRE   Augustus divided the provinces between himself and the senate. He took all the newer and the frontier provinces where an army was required for the imperial provinces to be governed by his lieutenants. Those provinces which were thoroughly pacified were retained by the senate and governed as before by promagistrates.

The senatorial provinces were Asia, Bithynia, Cyprus, Crete with Cyrene, Macedonia, and Achaea in the East; Sicily, Africa, Hispania Baetica, and Gallia Narbonensis in the West. Edicts recently found at Cyrene prove that Augustus possessed the power of interfering in the affairs of the senatorial provinces, "until the senate comes to a de-cision on the subject or I find a better plan." The control which he exercised over the appointment of governors to the imperial provinces and this practice of supervision in the others enabled him to check the malpractice of republican years and to repress any tendency toward revolutionary action. The establishment of a paid secretariat to collect certain taxes and supervise finances removed at the same time the worst burdens of corruption under which the provincials had suffered at the hands of the *Equites.* He clung to the republican idea of Roman rule in the hands of men of senatorial rank, and departed from the precedents and ideas of Caesar, who had extended citizenship to pro-vincials and allowed provincial representation in the senate.

Augustus spent the years 27-24 B.C. in the West and 22-19 B.C. in the East setting provincial affairs in order. While the older province of Gaul, modern Provence, was left as Gallia Narbonensis under senatorial control, Caesar's conquests were organized into three imperial provinces with a common center at Lyons. Out of Spain, whose conquest was finally ended by the subjugation of the mountain tribes in 16 B.C. after two centuries of almost continual warfare, three provinces were created. Two were imperial, the third, in the south, was senatorial. The Romanization of both Gaul and Spain proceeded apace as both regions became prosperous. In later generations many men of letters and even some of the emperors were of Spanish or Gallic descent. Africa, a senatorial province with one legion under its proconsul to guard the frontier, speedily became wealthy once more. Though Carthage was a Roman colony—the remains of cities, temples, and aqueducts prove that it was well Romanized—the older Phoenician elements in the population remained strong, and the Phoenician language continued to be spoken down to Christian times. Herod the Great (p. 477) was permitted to remain as king of Judaea, but shortly after his death the kingdom became a province (6 A.D.) under a procurator of equestrian rank subject to the supervision of the governor of Syria. Egypt was unique among the provinces. Since Augustus feared to entrust its wealth and its control over Rome's grain supply to an ordinary governor, and since its own system of government did not fit into the Roman scheme, Augustus kept it as a personal possession. For actual administration he appointed a prefect of equestrian rank; he even went so far as to forbid senators to visit Egypt without permission. The Egyptians recognized him as Pharaoh; his statues were set up and his name was written in hieroglyphs in the temples.

THE FRONTIER   The Augustan frontier policy was one of completion and pacification. The southern frontier of Egypt was made secure by a war with the Ethiopians, and, although an expedition in southern Arabia failed, the Romans secured control of the Red Sea trade. In Asia Minor Galatia was annexed; Armenia became a client kingdom under a native ruler nominated by Rome; and peace was made with the Parthians who surrendered the standards and the captives of the earlier wars. The northern frontier was extended to the Danube by a series of expeditions in the Balkans and in the Alps. Britain was definitely abandoned, but Augustus planned to shorten the Rhine-Danube frontier by extending the boundaries to the Elbe. A series of brilliant campaigns led by Drusus and Tiberius, the stepsons of Augustus, brought the region partially under Roman control. But by a sudden revolt in 9 A.D. under a Roman-trained chieftain named Arminius, the Germans succeeded in defeating and destroying a Roman army of three legions under Varus in the Teutoberg Forest. The loss of men was serious, and Augustus gave up the idea of reconquest.

FINANCES   The state treasury received its income from the tribute of the senatorial provinces, collected as of old, although Augustus corrected the worst evils of the tax-farming system by proper supervision. The expenses of the government were too great for this income, however, and Augustus was constrained on several occasions to come to the rescue with substantial contributions from his own wealth. The management of the personal property of Augustus and of the finances of the imperial provinces was in the hands of procurators—secretaries who were knights or freedmen. No fixed rule was laid down for the collection of taxes: many were still sold to tax farmers, others were handled directly by imperial agents. Out of the tribute from these provinces the expenses of the army were met, and when it proved insufficient to provide pensions as well, the military treasury, as we have seen, was established. To facilitate imperial collections, Augustus decreed a census of the entire empire. An echo of this order is to be found in the story of the birth of Christ.[2]

ECONOMIC   The restoration of peace and order was accompanied
REHABILITATION by general economic rehabilitation. With security of property assured, farmers throughout the Mediterranean world were able to work their lands and reap the fruits of their toil. With piracy suppressed, with the road system repaired, extended and policed, and with the world at peace, merchants and goods could pass freely by sea and land from one corner of the empire to the other. In these phases of life private enterprise was free to act and develop without fear of governmental interference, and, indeed, with the assurance of imperial support. The relations with Parthia and the campaign in Arabia were both based primarily on a desire to secure the benefits of trade. Consequently, large-scale concerns appeared, particularly in the pottery, metal, glass, and paper industries, though many small shops continued to prosper in filling local needs and in manufacturing goods for profit.

[2] The date of this census, probably 9-8 B.C., and the date of the death of Herod in 4 B.C. indicate that the medieval chroniclers made a mistake in their dating of the birth of Christ, which is variously placed by modern scholars as between 8 and 4 B.C.

Italian pottery (the famous Arretine ware) and metal goods were exported along with wine and oil into other sections of the empire. The papyrus, glassware, and linens of Egypt, the silk, wine, and fruits of Syria, the textiles of Phoenicia and Anatolia, the grain, meats, fruits, and vegetables of Sicily, Africa, and Gaul, and the metals of Spain traveled far from their places of origin.

Roman capitalists invested in provincial concerns, and Roman merchants vied with Greeks and Syrians for a share in the trade. Partnerships were established, centers for the exchange of market information were developed, and banking kept pace with the needs of commerce. Many in the world had, indeed, reason to be grateful to the princeps for the restoration of peace and for the latitude which he allowed to individual action in the economic field.

Yet slavery was widely used in industry and agriculture, save in those regions like Egypt, where free labor was cheap. The low scale of wages did little to relieve the condition of the poverty-burdened lower classes of the empire. In Rome though a free man could usually secure some occupation, Augustus found it necessary to aid the populace by giving free grain and occasional sums of money, and to provide games and shows to keep the people contented.

MORAL AND
RELIGIOUS
REFORM

To restore the older standards and at the same time to secure support for himself, Augustus tried many devices. Clubs composed of the youth of the aristocracies in the cities of Italy and of the upper classes in Rome provided the new generation with military and athletic exercises along with patriotic training. Laws in 19 and 18 B.C. and again in 9 A.D. laid heavy penalties on adultery and on celibacy, encouraged marriage and the bearing of children, and forbade marriage between the senatorial and freedmen classes. Men and women with three children were given special preference in all positions of honor or power. The older senators opposed these laws as contrary to the republican tradition. The legislation, however, proved generally ineffective. Not even the imperial family respected the laws, for Augustus had to banish his own daughter and granddaughter for violations of the law concerning adultery.

At the same time he tried to bring about a religious revival by rebuilding old temples and reviving obsolete priesthoods. At his behest Ovid wrote the *Fasti,* a poetic account of the Roman festivals; Livy's *Roman History* and Vergil's *Aeneid* were literary attempts to acquaint the Romans with their great past and to arouse their dormant patriotism; and many of Horace's *Odes* praising simple ways and civic loyalties were written in the same service. In 17 B.C. the secular games were held, a jubilee festival to celebrate the revival of Roman power under Augustus. For this occasion Horace composed a hymn to be sung by a chorus.

But to what extent the whole Augustan program met with success it is difficult to say. While Augustus and his successors were well served in the administration of the empire, in Rome jealousy and discontent remained to vex and harass both princeps and senators.

CULTURE OF THE AUGUSTAN AGE

ARCHITECTURE Meanwhile the city of Rome was being rebuilt to make it a worthy capital of an empire. Augustus boasted, "I found Rome a city of brick, I left it marble." Eighty-two temples were repaired; the Capitoline Temple of Jupiter and the Senate House were rebuilt. Near the spot where Caesar's body had been burned, a temple to the "Deified Julius" was erected. The Forum of Julius Caesar was completed and the new Forum of Augustus constructed. In the latter, as the Hall of Fame for imperial Rome, was the temple of Mars Ultor, guardian of the Augustan Peace. On the Palatine near the home of Augustus were erected temples to Apollo, with libraries attached, to the Great Mother, and to Vesta. Older theaters and basilicas were repaired, and the new theater of Marcellus was added. In the Campus Martius Agrippa built the Pantheon, dedicated to the Stoic "All-divine." Most beautiful of the monuments and symbolic of the new order was the Altar of the Augustan Peace, ornamented with pictures symbolizing peace, prosperity, and plenty, and with a processional relief containing portraits of the imperial family and the leading men of Rome.

Latin literature reached its climax, its Golden Age, under Augustus. Its great historian, Livy, and its poets, Vergil, Horace, and Ovid, masters of language and form, produced works filled with the richness and peace of the Augustan era.

LIVY
(59 B.C.-17 A.D.) A native of Padua, Livy composed a magnificent history of Rome, *From the Founding of the City*. He wrote this prose epic of the greatness of Rome with the avowed purpose of calling the Romans back from the vices of the

day to ancient virtues by a recital of the glorious deeds through which Roman power was obtained and increased. Though a literary artist interested primarily in the telling of a great story, and without Polybius' stern conception of history as a textbook for generals and statesmen, Livy nevertheless showed ability as an historian. He was intelligent in the handling and criticism of his sources. He recognized the lack of accurate information for the earlier period and the weaknesses of the family traditions on which the annalists from whom he drew had depended and which he himself was forced to use. When he found varying opinions, he chose that which seemed best founded. With a clear and vivid historical imagination, he wove so well the strands of information collected by his predecessors or his erudite contemporaries that no ancient historian ever again attempted the task which he had accomplished. In fact, those who wrote later of republican Rome leaned heavily upon him. His style was vigorous, at times poetic and dramatic; Tacitus proclaimed him renowned for eloquence and truthfulness, "and it must be remembered that his very art attains a truth of its own. He possessed gifts of real historical worth—the gift of reverence for the majesty of Rome; the gift of enthusiasm for olden times, olden heroes, olden virtues; the gift of imagination through sympathy which feels, even if imperfectly, the spirit of the past." [3] The modern student may still feel the thrill which comes from reading Livy's account of Rome's rise to power and of the men whose virtues made Rome great. His work remains our chief source, at times our only source, for the early history of Rome. The disappearance of all but thirty-five books of his history, save for a late epitome, is an irreparable loss.

VERGIL
(70 B.C.-19 B.C.)

Vergil was an epic poet of the first rank. Born in Mantua of a peasant father, he went to Rome to secure an education. There, by his group of pastoral poems called *Eclogues,* written after the style of Theocritus, he attracted the attention of Maecenas, friend of Augustus and patron of letters. The fourth of these, containing a prediction of the return of the Golden Age to the world, has been called the "Messianic Eclogue," and because of its supposed reference to the birth of Christ it gave Vergil an important place in Christian history.

> On thee, child, everywhere shall earth, untilled,
> Show'r, her first baby-offerings, vagrant stems

---

[3] Duff, *Literary History of Rome,* p. 650.

Of ivy, foxglove, and gay briar, and bean;
Unbid the goats shall come big-uddered home,
Nor monstrous lions scare the herded kine.
Thy cradle shall be full of pretty flowers:
Die must the serpent, treacherous poison-plants
Must die; and Syria's roses spring like weeds. . . .

The pilot's self shall range the seas no more;
Nor, each land teeming with the wealth of all,
The floating pines exchange their merchandise.
Vines shall not need the pruning-hook, nor earth
The harrow: ploughmen shall unyoke their steers.
Nor then need wool be taught to counterfeit
This hue and that. At will the meadow ram
Shall change to saffron, or the gorgeous tints
Of Tyre, his fair fleece; and the grazing lamb
At will put crimson on. . . .[4]

Maecenas, securing for Vergil means of support, encouraged him to compose the *Georgics,* a poetic treatise on farming. Inspired by the Augustan Age and prompted by Augustus himself, the poet wrote the *Aeneid.* While this great poem dealt with the story of the trials of Aeneas as he journeyed from Troy to Italy, it was really the epic of Rome itself. It consecrated that *pietas,* "devotion to duty," which had made Rome great, and it declared the mission of Rome to conquer and organize the world. In it poetic skill was blended with the poet's deep feeling for humanity to produce many memorable pictures and unforgettable lines. "In no other poetry are the chords of human sympathy so delicately touched, its tones so subtly interfused. In none is there so deep a sense of the beauty and sorrow of life, of keen remembrance and shadowy hope, and, enfolding all, of infinite pity."[5]

Let others better mould the running mass
Of metals, and inform the breathing brass,
And soften into flesh a marble face;
Plead better at the bar; describe the skies,
And when the stars ascend, and when they rise.
But Rome! 'tis thine alone, with awful sway,
To rule mankind, and make the world obey.
Disposing peace and war thy own majestic way;

[4] Howe and Harrer, *Roman Literature in Translation,* pp. 342-343.
[5] Mackail, *Virgil and His Meaning,* p. 110.

To tame the proud, the fetter'd slave to free;
These are imperial arts, and worthy thee.[6]

HORACE
(65-8 B.C.)

Horace, the friend of Vergil, was also of humble birth (his father was a freedman) and also owed his means of living to the patronage of Maecenas. He became a skilled writer of lyrics and an urbane interpreter of his own age and of the art of living. In matchless verse he portrayed the pleasures of the simple life, wished with mild affairs of the heart, glorified the civic virtues, and sang the praises of Augustus. He has been studied, translated, and paraphrased by other poets down to our own times, and many of his poems ring as true today as they did when they were written. In a famous ode, the eleventh of the first book, he expressed his attitude toward life.

Strive not, Leuconoe, to know what end
The gods above to me or thee will send:
Nor with astrologers consult at all,
That thou mayst better know what can befall;
Whether thou liv'st more winters, or thy last
Be this, which Tyrrhen waves 'gainst rocks do cast.
Be wise! Drink free, and in so short a space
Do not protracted hopes of life embrace:
Whilst we are talking, envious time doth slide;
This day's thine own; the next may be denied.[7]

In another poem he offered the poet's prayer to Apollo:

Health to enjoy the blessings sent
From heaven; a mind unclouded, strong;
A cheerful heart; a wise content;
An honored age; and song.[8]

THE ELEGIAC
POETS

Among a number of youths of wealth who amused themselves and delighted their friends by producing polite love songs written in the elegiac meter were Tibullus, Propertius, and Ovid. Of these the most brilliant and versatile was Ovid (43 B.C.-18 A.D.). Belonging to the younger set who rejected the strict standards of Augustus, he composed a series of verses on love affairs and on the art and remedy of love itself. He wrote the

[6] Howe and Harrer, *op. cit.*, p. 318.
[7] *Ibid.*, p. 389.
[8] Showerman, *Horace and His Influence*, p. 33.

Fasti, an account of Roman festivals, to please Augustus, and in his celebrated poem, the *Metamorphoses,* he presented the greatest myths of the ancient Greeks. Involved in the scandal of the younger Julia, he was banished to an island in the Black Sea, where he portrayed and lamented his sad fate in the *Tristia.*

THE
MONUMENTUM
ANCYRANUM

Augustus himself composed a résumé of his own achievements and of his services to Rome, which was inscribed on a bronze tablet in front of his tomb in Rome. A copy of it in Latin and Greek was found in Angora, ancient Ancyra, and recently fragments have been discovered in other eastern cities. Called the *Monumentum Ancyranum,* it is one of our most precious sources for the history of the period.

EPILOGUE

Estimates of the character and the services of Augustus have varied ever since his own time. Admirers of the great Julius have regarded Augustus as a crafty politician, a time-server who gave Rome not a republic but a monarchy, disguised under republican forms like a sugar-coated pill. Others have seen him as a great statesman, sincere in his protestations of loyalty to the republic, the restorer of order to a troubled world, the "architect of the Roman Empire." It is almost impossible to arrive at any sound judgment of him. In his early years he was indeed crafty and not too honest, as evidenced in his dealings with Cicero. The sanction which he gave to the proscription and the destruction of Perusia proved him cruel and ruthless. Accession to power transformed him into a wise, farseeing statesman. He bowed to the sentiment of the times, proclaimed the restoration of the republic and, for the most part, observed republican traditions. Yet he guarded his own position carefully. He retained command of the army, allowed himself to be worshiped as a Hellenistic god-king, and planned the hereditary succession to his power. At the same time with carefully considered policies he brought tranquillity and wealth to the Mediterranean world. The system which he established endured through the vicissitudes of two centuries, and when it was finally overthrown, Rome began her decline. Augustus, therefore, must always occupy a place in the front rank of the statesmen of the world.

XXII

THE GREAT AGE OF THE ROMAN EMPIRE
(14-180 A.D.)

DURING the years which elapsed between the accession of Tiberius in 14 A.D. and the death of Marcus Aurelius in 180 A.D. the Roman Empire flourished and expanded under the guidance of the successors of Augustus. The age is readily divided into three periods: from 14-68 A.D. the Julian-Claudian house held the office of princeps; after a year of revolution the Flavian family, Vespasian and his two sons, ruled from 69-96 A.D.; the third division is the Age of the Antonines, 96-180 A.D.

The successive emperors were concerned with the varied problems of empire—the direction of provincial affairs, the control of the army, the defense of the frontiers, the building of roads, bridges, aqueducts, and triumphal arches throughout the empire—with the management and adornment of the imperial capital, with the difficult relations between the ruler and the senate, with the social life of the court, and with the problem of succession.

SOURCES   Two types of sources, literary and archaeological, contribute information of varying sorts about the period. The surviving fragments of Roman literature furnish accounts of the lives and the wars of the emperors, and pictures of the imperial court, with its intrigues, scandals, and murders, and of the busy and exciting life of the capital city. To the second group belong the inscriptions, papyri, coins, and remains of buildings, monuments, and public works which provide revelations of economic conditions and of governmental activities, both imperial and local. They disclose also the occupations, thoughts, and religions of the inhabitants of the empire.

THE JULIAN-CLAUDIAN EMPERORS
(14-68 A.D.)

TIBERIUS
(14-37 A.D.)

Fifty-six years of age when he succeeded to power, Tiberius was, by virtue of his character and his experience, an excellent administrator. Under his guidance order was maintained in Rome, and the governors of the provinces were held sternly in check. The northern frontier was definitely established on the Rhine. Though Germanicus, his nephew and recognized heir, avenged the defeat of Varus with three victorious campaigns in Germany, Tiberius refused to allow him to complete the conquest to the Elbe River because of the difficulty and the expense. On the eastern frontier friendly relations were maintained with Armenia and Parthia, and two small client kingdoms were changed into provinces to protect communications with these states.

As we look back, the most important event in world history which took place in the empire under Tiberius was the trial and execution in Jerusalem of Jesus of Nazareth. But its significance was so little understood at the time that it passed unnoticed by imperial chroniclers until the rise of Christianity brought it to their attention.

In his personal relations with the senatorial class, Tiberius was unfortunate. The bitterness and suspicion engendered by the disappointments of his earlier years had not softened a character naturally reserved and austere. His difficulties were intensified when, after the death of Germanicus in the East in 19 A.D., Agrippina, widow of Germanicus, accused the princeps of removing his nephew from Germany because of jealousy, and of complicity in a supposed plot to poison him. Disgusted with the quarrels and recriminations which followed, Tiberius retired to Capri in 26 A.D., leaving his praetorian prefect, Sejanus, in charge of the city. Sejanus, an able man but deluded with dreams of grandeur, set out to secure the succession for himself. He poisoned Tiberius' son, Drusus, and obtained the exile of Agrippina and two of her sons on charges of treason. Tiberius, learning of Sejanus' plans, removed him from office and had him and his followers put to death. In the last years of his reign, the princeps struck savagely at the rebellious senators. The law of treason, *lex majestatis,* with its penalty of death, was extended to include any expression critical of the emperor, and paid "informers" watched for violations. The horrors of the reign of terror which followed are vividly described by the historian Tacitus. When the death of Tiberius in 37 A.D. brought an end to the persecution, the senate conferred his powers upon Gaius, sole surviving son of Germanicus and Agrippina.

GAIUS CALIGULA (37-41 A.D.)   Gaius, born in camp, was known to the army affectionately as Caligula, "Little Boot." His reign started auspiciously with promises of peace in Rome and renewal of imperial expansion into Britain. Soon after the succession, however, he became deranged. Regarding himself as a god, he built a bridge from his house on the Palatine to Jupiter's temple on the Capitoline and ordered his statue to be set up in the temple of Jerusalem. In 41 A.D., assassination by an officer of the pratorian guard brought his mad career to an end.

CLAUDIUS (41-54 A.D.)   A soldier of the guard looting in the palace discovered Claudius, brother of Germanicus and uncle of Gaius, hiding behind a curtain. Recognizing him as a member of the imperial family, the guardsman hailed him as emperor. The whole cohort took up the cry and forced the senate to consent to the accession of Claudius. Crippled in youth, and reputed to be a half-wit because of his foolish and ungainly appearance, Claudius had lived quietly and safely in the troubled times of Tiberius and Gaius and had pursued undisturbed his studies in the antiquities of Rome. But Claudius proved to be no fool. During his reign the empire was well and shrewdly managed. His most important administrative achievement was the creation of a permanent bureaucracy for the civil administration. Pallas, his freedman-secretary in charge of finance, concentrated the funds of the imperial provinces and estates into a single treasury, the *fiscus;* other freedmen took charge of correspondence, of petitions, and of information. Together they exercised a powerful influence on the mind and activities of the princeps.

Claudius constructed two new aqueducts at Rome, the *Claudia* and the *Anio Novus,* to bring more water to the city, and endeavored by the construction of breakwaters and docks at the mouth of the Tiber to make Ostia a suitable port for Rome. Returning to the policy of Julius Caesar, he conferred Roman citizenship and Latin rights on many Gauls and made some Aeduan nobles members of the senate. During his reign, also, southern Britain was conquered and Thrace was added to the list of Roman provinces.

Claudius married Messalina, by whom he had a son, Britannicus, and a daughter, Octavia. Messalina's reputation was shockingly bad, and when in 48 A.D. the freedman Narcissus claimed to have discovered her in a plot to overthrow the princeps, Claudius ordered her execution. The following year he married his niece Agrippina, daughter of Germanicus and the elder Agrippina. This ambitious woman, gaining complete dominance over the aging emperor, substituted her son by a former marriage for Claudius' own son as successor. When Claudius died in 54 A.D. all Rome believed that Agrippina had murdered him.

NERO
(54-68 A.D.)

The son of Agrippina and husband of Octavia, Nero succeeded to power without opposition. He promised a return to the Augustan principles of senatorial rule and a wise administration. Under the guidance of his tutors and advisers, the philosopher Seneca and the praetorian prefect Burrus, the promise was kept for eight years. An intelligent reform of the coinage was effected; measures were taken to assist Italian agriculture; able governors were selected to manage provincial affairs; and in Britain the dangerous revolt of Boadicea was put down.

Nero's private life, on the other hand, was filled with scandalous behavior. Nightly revels in the streets and taverns of Rome led him into all kinds of excesses, and Agrippina, who tried to restrain him and to keep the power she had enjoyed under Claudius, was sent away from the court and was murdered in 59 A.D. After first divorcing, then banishing, and finally executing Octavia, Nero married Poppaea Sabina, the most celebrated beauty of her day. When Burrus died in 62 A.D. and Seneca lost all control of his pupil, Nero turned to fresh dissipations with the assistance of the new prefect, Tigellinus. Preferring music and the drama to gladiatorial shows, in curious opposition to Roman tastes, and regarding himself as a great artist, he began to appear in public in his own compositions.

A great conflagration in Rome in 64 A.D., which began in the shops at the east end of the Circus and burned ten of the fourteen wards of the city, involved Nero in serious trouble. Though he hastened to take proper relief measures, it was said that during the fire he sat in his palace on the Palatine, played his lyre and recited verses from his own tragedy on the fall of Troy. The city was rebuilt with wider streets and better materials, but when he reserved a large area between the Palatine and the Esquiline for a park and an imperial palace, the Golden House, beautifully designed and decorated, Nero was accused of starting the fire. Though it was an idle accusation, he looked for a scapegoat and found it in an obscure sect called Christians. These unfortunates, convicted of arson, were put to death in most horrible fashions to satisfy public clamor. Tradition records that St. Peter and St. Paul met their deaths in this first of the Christian persecutions.

The years that followed were filled with terror. To obtain money to pay for rebuilding the city and to provide for his own extravagances, Nero revived the law of treason, struck down many wealthy senators or trumped up charges against them in order to confiscate their estates. A plot against him in 65 A.D. was discovered and ruthlessly suppressed; among the victims were Seneca and his nephew, the poet Lucan. In 66 A.D. Nero left for Greece to appear as a contestant in the national games where, in a burst of enthusiasm, he declared the freedom of the Greek cities. While in Greece, he sent Vespasian to suppress a serious revolt in Judaea. When he returned to Italy he heard graver news of an uprising in Gaul, not against Rome but against himself. Hated by the senate and deserted by the praetorians, he fled from Rome, was declared a public enemy, and was killed by a faithful servant at his own command. His name has ever since been a symbol of excesses of all kinds and an object of execration to Christian writers. With the death of Nero the house of Caesar became extinct. As his successor, the senate recognized Galba, the able, experienced, but aged governor of Spain, who was already on the march to Rome.

During the year 68 A.D., Nero, Galba, Otho, and Vitellius wore the imperial purple and in the following year Vespasian succeeded to the throne.

The events which followed the death of Nero revealed at once the consequences of Augustus' failure to provide for an orderly succession, the weakness of the senate, and the fundamental military basis of the principate. Galba was the candidate of the praetorian guards, who had already revealed their power in the selection of Claudius. When he proved unfit for the imperial task after a rule of seven months, the guards overthrew him and placed Otho in power. After a reign of eighty-eight days Otho fell on his sword when the Rhine legions took Rome and established their commander Vitellius as princeps. Vitellius was even less capable than his two immediate predecessors, and while he indulged in banquets of extraordinary cost, Italy was being plundered by his army. He was easily overthrown in 69 A.D. by the armies of the East, who hailed Vespasian as emperor. Not the votes of the senate but the civil war between the military forces of the empire settled the question of who was to rule Rome.

THE FLAVIAN DYNASTY
(69-96 A.D.)

VESPASIAN
(69-79 A.D.)
The eastern armies, jealous of the army of the Rhine, chose as their candidate Vespasian, commander in the war against the Jews. After the army of the Danube had killed Vitellius and had sacked Rome, the senate yielded, and in one act, the famous *lex de imperio Vespasiani,* conferred upon Vespasian all the powers which had been held by his predecessors. An able ruler, he proceeded at once to restore order to the empire, and by strict economy and new taxes carefully collected to rebuild the shattered finances of the state. The senate received a needed infusion of new blood by the admission of provincials from Gaul and Spain. The ravages of the sack of the city were removed; the Capitoline Temple was rebuilt; a Forum and Temple of Peace were erected; and on the walls of the new Temple of the Sacred City was placed a marble map of Rome. Nero's Golden House was partly demolished and in its park Vespasian began to build the famous amphitheater, the Colosseum. To establish a high intellectual level for his court, he patronized men of letters and founded professorships of Greek and Latin rhetoric. The chief event of Vespasian's reign in the provinces was the Jewish War, which he had begun and which his son Titus brought to a victorious conclusion by the destruction of Jerusalem in 70 A.D. (p. 479).

TITUS
(79-81 A.D.)
Titus, who had been associated in power with Vespasian, became princeps at his father's death. He was a man of great charm, ability, and universal popularity, and was well trained in administration. After confirming his father's acts and gifts, he erected baths and completed the Colosseum, which he dedicated with a hundred days of games. His reign is best known for a famous catastrophe, the eruption of Vesuvius which buried Pompeii and Herculaneum. He died of a fever in 81 A.D. and was succeeded by his brother, Domitian.

DOMITIAN
(81-96 A.D.)
Excluded from a share in the administration by his father, Domitian spent his youth in a study of history, particularly of the memoirs of Tiberius. The sound conception which he thus secured of the resources and the dangers of the empire was reflected in his policies as emperor. In

Rome he followed a policy of adherence to tradition. As perpetual censor, he endeavored to revive old practices in morals and religion. Scandalous actions and writings were suppressed, and a vestal who had broken her vows was buried alive according to the ancient law. Attempts to restore the old religion brought the Christians to his attention and there were sporadic persecutions. He continued the imperial attempts to improve the condition of Italian agriculture by encouraging the growing of grain and by restricting vineyards.

The northern frontier occupied much of his attention. Agricola, a competent general whose renown is due to Tacitus' biography of him, finished the conquest of Britain but was recalled when he planned a costly expedition to Ireland. To improve the frontier defenses on the Rhine, where the restlessness of German tribes were a presage of coming events, Domitian built the *limes,* a line of forts across the base of the triangle formed by the Rhine and the Danube. Trouble with the Dacians north of the Danube was settled by a compromise. Decebalus, the Dacian king, recognized the sovereignty of Rome and was promised a subsidy to assist him in his struggles with the wilder tribes to the east.

Domitian's rule marked a long step forward to the monarchical principle, with a demand for a clear recognition of the supremacy of the emperor over the senate. A thoroughgoing autocrat, he assumed control over the appointment of senators through the perpetual censorship and insisted that he be addressed as *"dominus et deus,"* "lord and god." The dynastic principle by which he had attained the purple and which he emphasized by building a temple to the deified Vespasian offended the senators and was regarded with hostility by the Stoic philosophers, who wanted the rule of the "wisest man." Criticism was intolerable to Domitian, and the friction which inevitably resulted between himself and the senators from his policy of suppression produced a reign of terror toward the end of his reign that recalled the last years of Tiberius. After the discovery of a plot against Domitian, philosophers were banished and senators were put to death, while literary men who had been encouraged to write in the early years of his reign no longer dared to express themselves. Finally a plot, in which his wife had a share, was successful, and Domitian was assassinated in 96 A.D. By order of the senate his name was erased from his monuments and his memory forever cursed. The historians, Tacitus and Dio Cassius, record the terror of these years of oppression. The senate chose Nerva, a senator over sixty years of age, to succeed him.

During the Flavian period, the monarchical principle of the Roman Empire made a great advance. The military foundation of the ruling family, the principle of dynastic inheritance, and the policies of Vespasian and more particularly of Domitian made clearly evident the real mastery of the emperor in the Roman state.

THE AGE OF THE ANTONINES
(96-180 A.D.)

The accession of Nerva ushered in the Age of the Antonines, sometimes called the Age of the Good Emperors. The superior power of the princeps, immensely strengthened by the Flavian dynasty, was definitely recognized by the senate, and dreams of republican liberty were forgotten. The rulers left individual senators alone and received in return wholehearted co-operation in the administration of the empire and in the various commissions and offices which were created. Tacitus declared that Nerva combined the principate and liberty, two elements once considered opposites. The care taken by the emperors to secure the best man available to succeed them pleased the philosophers. Under the five emperors from Nero to Marcus Aurelius the empire was well governed and prosperous.

NERVA
(96-98 A.D.)

Nerva appointed senatorial commissions to reorganize the finances and to further the cause of Italian agriculture. The latter aim was combined with a measure to increase population, by which money was distributed to municipalities to be loaned to farmers at low rates of interest. The income therefrom was applied to helping the children of the poor. Nerva adopted as his successor the ablest of his generals, M. Ulpius Trajanus, governor of upper Germany.

TRAJAN
(98-117 A.D.)

Trajan was born to a Roman family long resident in Spain and hence was the first non-Italian emperor. He was by character and training a soldier—sharp, precise, and practical. The letters which passed between him and his governor, Pliny, display these characteristics and at the same time indicate his interest in the smallest details of provincial and municipal government.

His reign was distinguished by extraordinary building activities and by frontier wars which carried the Roman Empire to its furthest bounds.

In Rome he constructed a magnificent forum with colonnades, apses, basilica, libraries, and a temple. In one of the courts still stands the great column (dedicated after his death) on which his Dacian Wars were recorded in spiral relief. Throughout the empire he built many roads, including a great military highway from Gaul along the Danube to the Black Sea. A bridge which bears his name is still in use in Spain.

He completed the northern frontier by the conquest of Dacia, where Domitian's program of subsidization had become a source of irritation. In two wars during which Trajan built a bridge across the Danube, the Dacians were conquered and destroyed, and the land was so thoroughly settled with Romanized provincials that it bears today the name Roumania. Trajan endeavored to extend the empire on the eastern frontier as well. One of his generals added to the empire Arabia Petraea, important for its control over the caravan routes from Southern Arabia to the Mediterranean, and famous today for the ruins of the rose-red city of Petra. When trouble arose with Parthia, Trajan himself conquered and annexed Armenia, created a province of Assyria, and captured the great cities of Babylonia. Before the war could be brought to a victorious conclusion, however, he was recalled by a great revolt in Syria. On his way back to deal with this problem he died in Cilicia in 117.

HADRIAN
(117-138)
Hadrian, a cousin of Trajan, and probably adopted by him as he lay dying, was recognized by the army and the senate as his successor. Four generals who quarreled with this decision were put to death by order of the senate. The new emperor was far different in character and ideals from his predecessor, for Hadrian was a scholar and administrator rather than a conqueror. He spent fourteen out of his twenty-one years of rule in the provinces or on the frontier, and his reign is of great importance in the history of Roman imperial organization.

His general policy on the frontiers was one of consolidation and defense. The Roman wall was built across the northern end of Britain; the defenses (limes) of the Rhine-Danube line were extended, and forts were built to protect Dacia, which was organized into two provinces. The tribes without the border received native rulers educated at Rome and named by Hadrian. A number of kingdoms in the Black Sea region submitted to Roman power when Arrian, famous scholar and assistant to the emperor, led the Roman fleet around the Black

Sea. In the East, Armenia was re-established as a client kingdom, Assyria was abandoned, but Arabia was kept, and peace was maintained with Parthia. Hadrian suppressed a Jewish revolt, built a temple on Mt. Zion, and forbade the Jews entrance to the temple area.

The army was extensively reorganized. Hadrian placed cohorts in permanent camps along the frontier and allowed recruiting in the region around them. At the same time he completed the organization of the detachments of engineers and of the hospital service. He introduced a solid formation, a modification of the older phalanx system, to secure the steadiness necessary for meeting the wild charges of the barbarians. Hard drills and three long marches each month kept the soldiers in condition.

The central administration was put on a sound basis. Since the days of Claudius, the secretariat had been filled with freedmen or with knights at the choice of the individual princes. Hadrian established a permanent equestrian bureaucracy opening to the knights a definite civil career (p. 468). The civil service thus established developed traditions of its own apart from the military, and served the empire well during the confusion of the third century. Hadrian's legal reforms, the codification of the praetor's edicts and the formation of a council of jurists, belong to the history of Roman law, where we shall later study them.

Hadrian, like Trajan, was a great builder. In Athens, where he spent much time discussing philosophy, he completed the Peisistratean temple of Olympian Zeus. In Rome he built a great temple to Venus and Rome, and also his own tomb, which, after many transformations during the Middle Ages, was renamed the Castello Sant' Angelo and is now used as a military museum. At Tibur, in the Sabine Hills, he erected a splendid villa in which he endeavored to duplicate parts of the great buildings he had seen in the provinces. After his first heir died, Hadrian adopted Titus Aurelius Antoninus, who succeeded him in 138.

ANTONINUS
(138-161)

Antoninus, surnamed Pius because of his character and his devotion to the memory of Hadrian, was of Gallic descent. Under his rule the empire reached its acme of peace and prosperity. A few difficulties on the frontiers, the necessity of building a second more advanced wall in Britain, and the killing of a handful of Christians as the result of local uprisings, were but minor episodes. The law was humanized. Aid, heretofore given only to boys, was extended to poor girls. Antoninus had adopted two sons, Marcus Aurelius and Lucius Verus, and, when he died in 161 the former succeeded him.

MARCUS
AURELIUS
(161-180)

The last of the Good Emperors, Marcus Aurelius remains one of the great names of ancient times. From his boyhood he had been a student of philosophy and he looked at the problems of empire from the viewpoint of a Stoic. On the whole he grappled with them successfully. It was his misfortune that two great catastrophes descended upon the empire under his rule. After a successful war with the Parthians, the returning army in 166 brought with it a terrible plague which lasted twenty years, destroyed a large part of the population of the empire, and had incalculable effects on the courage of the remainder. In the midst of it a group of Germanic tribes, led by the Marcomanni, pushed across the Danube in 167 and even invaded Italy itself. Marcus Aurelius met the challenge heroically and spent most of the remainder of his life on the frontier. He defeated the invaders, settled some on abandoned lands within the empire, re-established the frontier, and was on the verge of the conquest of Bohemia when he died in 180.

Throughout his life even in camp it was his custom to record his thoughts of life and its meaning. These Meditations, a most precious human document, have been preserved and have offered as much comfort to many in succeeding ages as they did to the emperor who wrote them. With his death the great age of the Roman Empire came to an end. Succeeding generations witnessed its transformation from a principate into an undisguised military autocracy and the gradual decline of ancient civilization. During the great age, however, Roman political institutions, Roman law, economic and social life, and culture had developed under the rule of the successive emperors and had been carried north and west to establish the foundations on which Western civilization still rests.

XXIII

THE INSTITUTIONS OF THE EARLY EMPIRE

ROMA AETERNA

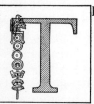THREE cultural streams of the ancient world—Oriental, Greek, and Roman—met and mingled in the Roman Empire. Rome, having created an empire by conquest, gave to it an admirable set of institutions and laws. From the Greeks came not only science and art, but a philosophic theory of the unity of the world which affected even the masses and gave organic vitality to the Roman creation. The Orient, contributing religious beliefs and attitudes rooted in its distant past, was destined to play a major role in the transition from the ancient to the medieval world.

The city of Rome, the capital of a great empire, was adorned with splendid palaces and public buildings. Its populace was feasted and entertained with the tribute of the provinces. Rome was the center of arts and letters, the goal of every ambitious man's dreams. Its power centered in the Mediterranean Sea, extended from the Arabian Desert on the east to the Atlantic Ocean on the west, from the Sahara Desert on the south to the Rhine, the Danube and the Carpathian Mountains on the north, and even reached across the channel to include England. Within its frontiers were Syrians, Jews, Phoenicians, Egyptians, Greeks, Iberians, Celts, Germans, and numerous other tribes of peoples.

To the people of the empire Rome was more than a city. Its name stood for the civilized world, membership in which was gained by the magic phrase used so proudly by St. Paul, "I am a Roman citizen." The many and varied peoples of the empire were united into one organic structure by a common citizenship and a common allegiance. The Stoic concept of a universal state, ruled according to the divine law of nature by the wisest citizen, seemed to have found fulfillment in the Roman Empire. So strong was the idea of unity, thus made fact, that it persisted after the collapse of Roman power. The Greeks of the early Byzantine period called themselves Romans, and the peoples of Western Europe in the Middle Ages clung to a belief in a world church and in a world state long after actual unity had disappeared.

The center and focus of the Roman world was the princeps, the source of all law, the fountain of all wisdom and power, united with divinity as living ruler, and god, indeed, after death. The imperial cult was the symbol of imperial unity. When the provincial offered sacrifice to or for the emperor, or cast a handful of incense on the altar before his statue, he was but asserting himself as a partaker in Roman universality and proclaiming his loyalty to the world in which he lived.

Augustus had apparently endeavored to establish himself as the first citizen in a Rome which ruled the world, but Julius Caesar's idea of an emperor superior to Rome and the provinces prevailed. Men of provincial origin succeeded to the throne during the Antonine period and, though holding Rome as their capital, considered themselves as supreme rulers over the empire. Though the senate was, as has been said, "an imaginative symbol of the glory of Roman power" and though it became in a measure representative of the empire as provincials were drawn into it, it had lost its effectiveness and had been made an advisory and assisting rather than a ruling body.

THE EMPEROR   The emperors bore the names *imperator* and *Caesar* and the title *princeps,* emblematic of their power. They became imperator by acclamation of the army upon their accession and received the formal grant of power which made them Caesar and princeps by acts of the senate. As holders of the imperium they were commanders-in-chief of the army and navy, and supreme judges in all matters of law. The tribunician power gave them direction of civil affairs of state and, by the ancient right of intercession, made them the center of all appeals. The office of *Pontifex Maximus* gave them control over religious practices and laws. The title *pater patriae* conferred on them the added prestige of Roman tradition. They controlled all nominations for offices in Rome, appointed the prefects, curators, procurators, legati in the imperial provinces and in the army, and lesser officials of the state. Their commands, speeches, letters, and decisions had the full force of law. Pliny described Trajan as "he who may at his will dispose of all that others possess."

The wide extent of imperial power as it developed from the Augustan establishment during the Julian-Claudian period is displayed by the famous *lex de imperio Vespasiani,* a part of which has been recovered from an inscription.

Let it be permitted him to make treaties with whom he wished, as was permitted to the divine Augustus, to Tiberius Julius Augustus, and to Tiberius Claudius Caesar Augustus Germanicus. Let it be permitted him to hold the Senate, bring matters before it, to dismiss it, and to make decrees of the Senate through the presentation and decision as was permitted to the divine Augustus, Tiberius Julius Augustus and to Tiberius Claudius Caesar Augustus Germanicus. When the Senate shall meet in accordance with his wish, authority, order, or command, or in his presence, let him have and preserve the right of all things therein as if the Senate had been proclaimed and called by law.

To whomsoever of those seeking a magistracy, power, command or care of anything whom he shall commend to the Senate and the Roman people and to whom he shall have given or promised his suffrage, let extraordinary consideration be given in the comitia.

Let it be permitted him to move the boundaries of the provinces when he shall be censor as was permitted to Tiberius Claudius Caesar Augustus Germanicus.

Let him have the right and power to do whatever he may deem best to serve the interest of the state and the majesty of all things divine and human, public and private, as had the divine Augustus, Tiberius Julius Augustus, and Tiberius Claudius Caesar Augustus Germanicus.

By whatever laws or plebiscites it was written that the divine Augustus, Tiberius Julius Augustus, and Tiberius Claudius Caesar Augustus Germanicus should not be bound, let the imperator Caesar Vespasianus Augustus be freed from these laws and plebiscites. Whatever it was permitted by any law or rogation to the divine Augustus, Tiberius Julius Augustus, and Tiberius Claudius Caesar Augustus Germanicus to do, all those things let it be permitted to imperator Caesar Vespasianus Augustus to do.

Those things which have been performed, done, decreed or ordered by the imperator Caesar Vespasianus Augustus or by any one at his command or order, these things are henceforth right and ratified as if they had been done by order of the people or the plebs.[1]

The legislative and administrative powers of the emperor become apparent from this decree. It is evident that the princeps is not thought to be above the law but to be exempted or given power to act in special cases which have the authority of precedent.

The overwhelming power of the princeps cast a shadow over the

[1] Dessau, *Inscriptiones Latinae Selectae,* I, p. 170.

aspirations and activities of men throughout the empire. No freedom of political action was possible for the individual. Provincials of independent mind were sternly checked by the ever-watchful agents of the emperor, and those men of ability who would bow the knee were drawn into the imperial circle. Renown in government or in war could only be attained in the service of the emperor and at his order, and leaders like Germanicus and Agricola who sought to transgress the limits laid down for them were speedily recalled. The only avenue of success for the ambitious general, as the events of the years 68-69 A.D. showed, was the attainment of the imperial purple, and many who tried to achieve this were ruthlessly suppressed. In the sphere of economic pursuits, the attainment of great wealth made Romans and provincials alike objects of suspicion and envy. In fact, in times of hardship the mere possession of wealth often led to the death of its owner and to the confiscation of his property. Freedom of thought was as dangerous. Emperor-worship made loyalty to the emperors and obedience to their will a matter of religious duty, and even criticism became a crime against their majesty. Many of the emperors, using this as a weapon against their enemies, had wielded despotic power, throttled all free expression of opinion, and, at times, instituted reigns of terror.

THE
MAGISTRATES

The chief assistants of the emperor were drawn from the senatorial and equestrian orders, according to the nature of their duties. Military and political positions were still held by senators who, in accordance with the tradition, passed through the republican offices from quaestor to consul. With the exception of the praetorship, which involved judicial duties, these were but honorary posts, steppingstones to the imperial service. Under Trajan six pairs of consuls holding office two months each were elected every year. Members of the senatorial class served as officers in the army, as judges in the lower courts, as proconsuls in the senatorial provinces, and as curators. In addition to the Augustan curatorships of the grain supply, of the roads, public works, aqueducts, and care of the bed and the banks of the Tiber, the Antonines had established senatorial commissions to regulate finance and to supervise the management of the relief program for the poor of Italy. In spite of occasional difficulties in Rome, the senators proved to be faithful and competent servants in the work of the empire. The senatorial class was recognized as superior and its members received the distinguishing title *clarissimus*, "most noble sir."

The civil administration of the empire was in the hands of the secretariat organized under Claudius by his freedmen, and transformed into a civil service of equestrian rank by Hadrian. The five great secretariats were *a rationibus*, finance; *ab epistulis*, correspondence, with separate secretaries for Greek and Latin; *a libellis*, petitions; *a cognitionibus*, investigations; and *a studiis*, intelligence and records. The minor posts in the central offices were held by knights, freedmen, and slaves. Under the secretaries were the procurators, who had charge of tax collections or the management of imperial lands or other properties, subprocurators, and the *advocati fisci*, prosecutors for the treasury. These procuratorships were grouped in four salary classes by Hadrian, and a fairly definite equestrian career was established. The business of government in the empire was well centralized and efficiently managed by this system. In recognition of their position and services, members of the equestrian class were hailed with the title *splendidus eques Romanus*, "glorious Roman knight."

The great prizes of the equestrian career were the prefectures, the most powerful official positions in the Roman Empire. The praetorian prefect, commander of the bodyguard, became the emperor's personal representative and acquired by custom great judicial authority. The prefect of the city was in general charge of the urban government of Rome. He was assisted by the prefect of the watch, who kept order; and the prefect of the grain supply, who kept Rome's granaries full and distributed the free grain to the populace. The prefect of Egypt, always a knight, was the Roman Pharaoh's viceroy. Though the freedmen were demoted from the chief offices by Hadrian, they still held posts within the secretariat. Their great glory, however, was in the order of *Augustales*. In this capacity leading freedmen served in Italy and in the provincial towns as priests for the celebration of the festivals of the imperial cult.

SYSTEM OF IMPERIAL FINANCE   At the accession of Tiberius there were two treasuries, the republican treasury, *aerarium Saturni*, and the military fund, *aerarium militare*. The accounts for the imperial provinces belonged to the former. Pallas, secretary of Claudius, however, established the *fiscus* as a central treasury for the public finance of the princeps and refused to render an accounting to the senate. The republican treasury continued to exist as the depository of funds from the senatorial provinces but steadily declined in importance. The fiscus absorbed the military fund.

Revenues were derived from port duties and tolls, income and rents from state lands, mines, and quarries. A 5 per cent inheritance tax was collected from Roman citizens; there were also a tax on auction sales (the per cent varied), a 4 per cent tax on the sale of slaves and a 5 per cent tax on their manumission. These taxes, at first levied in Italy, were later extended to the provinces. The provincials paid the land tax, usually a tithe, the poll tax on all noncitizens, and a tax on the income of artisans and small tradesmen. For the purpose of levying these taxes a census was taken every five years (after Hadrian, every fifteen years) in which all persons and properties were recorded. The collection was in the hands of procurators who at some times and in some places collected directly. Elsewhere the taxes were farmed locally. In many cases the municipalities were made responsible, and the collection was carried out by local officials, who often had to advance the revenue themselves before collection. The taxes were not burdensome in themselves, and the imperial system corrected the abuses of republican times and prevented or checked extortion. Most of the money was spent in the provinces on roads, on public works, on supplies for the army, and on the defense of the frontier. The price of the Roman imperial service in the flourishing days of the empire was not exorbitant.

Another branch of the treasury of great importance was the "patrimony of Caesar." Augustus had become the richest man in the world. By legacies and confiscations the property of the princeps had grown to extraordinary size by the time of Nero's death. Vespasian assumed it as "crown property" and established a special procurator to control it. Family property of the Flavians was kept separate. Eventually the fiscus absorbed the patrimony, and the personal wealth of the emperor was set up in a distinct department known as the *res privata*.

THE LAW   The greatest and most enduring achievement of the empire was the law, both administrative and civil. After the reign of Tiberius, the assemblies ceased to meet, except for the formal recognition of the princeps's imperium, as in the case of the *lex de imperio Vespasiani,* and administrative legislation passed into the hands of the princeps and the senate. Until the time of Hadrian, the senate continued to meet and pass Senatus consulta. But since, to an ever-increasing degree, all the senate did was to discuss, sometimes formulate, and ratify the wishes of the emperor as expressed in his *oratio,* the emperor's words came to have the force of law by themselves. After the time of Hadrian the senate became little more than an urban council for the city of Rome, and the *orationes* became fully recognized as law. To these were added the *constitutiones principum,* consisting of *edicta* ("proclamations"), *decreta* ("decisions in particular cases"), *rescripta* ("answers to questions from officials or private citizens"), and *mandata* ("orders to imperial officials"). The rescripts dealt often with particular cases and did not acquire the force of general law or become important until after Hadrian's reign.

Civil law came under the control of the emperor. The *jus honorarium* (p. 431), developed by the republican magistrates through their edicts, was fully recognized by imperial officials, and throughout the early empire the praetors continued to issue edicts, doubtless controlled and supplemented by the edicts and decisions of the emperor. The Cyrenaic edicts of Augustus (p. 444), which dealt with the rights of noncitizens in the province, are a case in point.

One of the sources of contention between the senate and the earlier emperors had been the interference of the princeps in the courts. Claudius, particularly, had liked to preside over the hearing of cases and render decisions. By Hadrian's time it had been definitely established that the princeps, usually represented by the praetorian prefect, was the highest court of appeal. Since the power of legislation inherent in the praetor's edict was inconsonant with the principle of autocracy, Hadrian removed the power and with the assistance of Salvius Julianus codified the edictal law and issued the Perpetual Edict. Thereafter changes were made through the imperial constitutions. For the same reason it became essential for the emperors to control the work of the *juris prudentes,* the jurists who through their advice influenced the interpretation of the law. Augustus permitted only qualified men, whom he licensed, to give opinions with the force of law, and Hadrian formed a council of these jurists to advise judges and to assist the imperial court in the decision of its cases.

The writings of the jurists were carefully preserved and selections from them appear as definitive law in the Digest of Justinian's Code. Of these and of the many legal commentaries composed during the empire, only the *Institutiones* ("Principles of the Civil Law") of Gaius, written in the reign of Antoninus Pius, and fragments of the writings of Paul and Ulpian, who lived in a later period, have survived apart from the Digest.

An important development in the character of the law took place in the imperial period, since the concept of Rome as a world state led inevitably to discussions of the Stoic idea of a world-law emanating from the divine principle and based on universal reason. This, called by the Romans *jus naturale,* natural law, was never recognized as formal, but its philosophic ideas inevitably reacted on the interpretations of the *jus gentium* and on the principles of the civil law itself. The power of the father of the family was weakened; the harsh rules regarding slaves were softened; women gained control over their property; and the principle that an accused was innocent until proved guilty was firmly established. An interesting growth was the appearance of distinctions between the privileges and obligations of the *honestior* ("noble") and the *humilior* ("commoner"). Caracalla's edict in a later generation extending citizenship to all provincials made Roman law the rule of the civilized world.

Between the years 529 and 535 Justinian issued the famous *Corpus Juris Civilis* containing an elementary treatise on the principles of the law, a digest (actually a series of selections) of the written opinions of the great jurists, and a code made up from the *constitutions* of the earlier emperors. In the course of his reign a fourth book, called *Novellae,* was added, containing new rulings that were found necessary. This great collection of documents provided the cornerstone for the structure of medieval, and much of modern, law.

THE ARMY   While the law went with Roman citizenship and Roman governors into every corner of the empire, the most evident symbol of empire was the army. It was a far different organization from the citizen body of republican or even of Augustan times. Since recruits from Italy barely filled the ranks of the imperial guards of the city, provincials were drawn in under a system of voluntary enlistment. Those so enlisted were usually citizens of the towns; they were at least partially Latinized and either were Roman citizens or received citizenship upon enlistment. A rigorous course of training made them competent professional soldiers. The Latin language used in the legions and their distinctly Roman tradition speedily completed the process of Romanization. While they were not allowed to marry until their discharge, illicit unions were permitted. They served enlistments of twenty years, keeping order in the provinces, executing many public works, and defending the frontier. At the end of that time they were entitled to retirement with a grant of land or a pension. Other provincials were enlisted in the auxiliary forces organized in cohorts. They served for twenty-five years and received citizenship and a bonus upon retirement. Each legion had its number, its name, and its eagles. During the early empire it was customary to transfer legions and cohorts from the area in which they had been recruited to other frontiers. Hadrian changed that to a principle of territorial defense, recruiting and employing troops in the same district.

The frontier was defended by a long series of walls of stone or earth, the limes, on the north, and elsewhere by forts and watch towers strategically placed with connecting roads and permanent legionary camps at convenient points. The most famous section of the northern line was the Roman wall in Britain, built by Hadrian and improved by later emperors. Moats protected the advances to the wall on either side; towers were placed four to the mile with guardhouses at the mile posts and seventeen garrison stations at regular intervals behind the seventy miles of wall. Around the great camps clustered the *canabae* or huts of camp followers, traders, and women who accompanied the army. Many of the camps developed into permanent communities, some of which, surviving to the present, have preserved their names, such as Chester in England. Cologne, Coblenz, Mainz, and Vienna were famous centers along the Rhine-Danube frontier.

The camps served as Romanizing influences over the surrounding territory and with the purchase of supplies, particularly grain and meat, did much to disseminate prosperity among the provincials. In times of peace the army was employed in constructing roads, bridges, aqueducts, and many other public works which likewise made their contributions to the civilization and prosperity of the empire.

The navy was a permanent establishment in imperial times under the command of prefects, with stations at Ravenna and Misenum and with fleets of small boats on the Rhine and the Danube. The personnel, drawn chiefly from the eastern provinces, consisted of free men who received citizenship after a service of twenty-six years. It was effective in its control of piracy.

THE PROVINCES Of the forty-five provinces in the time of Hadrian, eleven were recognized as senatorial and were governed by promagistrates, who held office for a year. Asia and Africa normally received ex-consuls, the other provinces ex-praetors, but all

senatorial governors had the title of *proconsul*. They received assignments from the senate according to lots, and each was assisted by
three legati and a quaestor. The right of imperial interference, indicated by the often-cited Cyrenaic decrees, and the presence of imperial
procurators of equestrian rank, who took care of imperial property
and supervised the collection of taxes, made senatorial control illusory.

The remaining provinces were imperial, and their governors, senators of praetorian or consular rank, called *legati Caesaris propraetore*
("propraetorian lieutenants of Caesar"), were chosen with great care
by the emperor and held office at his will. The normal term of office
was five years, but there was no fixed rule. The governor was assisted
by the commanders of the legions and by the equestrian procurators
who, directly responsible to the emperor, served, as in the senatorial
provinces, as a check on the governor. Smaller provinces were governed
by procurators, who in that case performed military and judicial as
well as financial duties.

Though provincial conditions were far better than under the late
republic, there were still occasional venal governors and grasping
procurators who proved as rapacious as the equestrian tax collectors of
earlier periods. At times discontent led to provincial uprisings. Too,
in many regions local feelings persisted or racial antagonisms led to
clashes between discordant elements in the populace.

In most of, if not all, the provinces, there existed local councils,
representative of the communities. These organizations, whose purpose
was religious, met once a year to hold festivals in connection with
the imperial cult. Nevertheless they acquired some political importance.
Matters pertaining to the whole province were discussed; representations may have been made to the governor; and embassies were certainly sent to Rome to praise or to accuse the imperial agents.

THE
MUNICIPALITIES

The preferred unit of local government in Italy and
in the provinces was the municipality. The East was
already a land of cities, and all that was necessary for
Rome to do was to recognize the existing order. The Greek cities continued therefore to be ruled by their magistrates, councils, and assemblies, as in earlier times. The franchise, however, was restricted to men
of property. The West had been for the most part a region of tribal
or rural communities. Such cities as existed were drawn into the
Roman system and, though the Romans utilized the pre-existing cantonal forms of government under aristocratic rule, as in Gaul, efforts

were made to develop urban organizations in country districts. Market places and court houses were erected at cross roads, and the people in the surrounding territory were listed and encouraged to settle around them. The *canabae* around the great camps received a city form of government, and colonies of Roman veterans were settled in the provinces.

The excitements of city life, with its elections, shows, games in the arena, schools, and libraries, proved so attractive that the West rapidly became transformed into an aggregation of cities. To those cities which were sufficiently Latinized was granted a charter which prescribed the form of government and gave Latin or Roman rights. These grants freed the citizens from the poll tax. The land tax, however, was removed only by the grant of the *jus Italicum,* rarely given except to Roman colonies.

The charters regulated citizenship, which was based on birth. Citizenship so acquired was never transferred except by gift of the city or of the princeps. St. Paul was to the end of his life a "citizen of Tarsus, which is no mean city." Voting depended upon the possession of property. In the East the Greek custom of voting by head was followed, while voters in the West were organized into groups on the Roman model. Chief magistrates were the *duoviri,* patterned after the consuls, assisted by aediles and quaestors, all drawn from the upper class. The charters also established age limits and financial qualifications. The expenses of officeholding were great, for the magistrate was expected to make a gift on taking office, to hold games, and to undertake other expenditures of similar nature. The rewards of a magistrate were membership in the local curia or senate and full Roman citizenship. Every fifth year the magistrates took a census of the people and drew up the list of the curia, usually to the number of one hundred. Ex-magistrates were entitled to membership, and other citizens of wealth and good repute might be enrolled to fill out the number. The council assumed general direction of the affairs of the city and was usually held responsible for the collection of imperial taxes. Members were very proud of their titles and position. The towns frequently hired doctors and schoolteachers to serve their people, and they sometimes possessed hospitals and libraries.

Throughout the first century of the empire, political life flourished in the cities. Echoes of a vigorous political campaign have survived in the notices on the house walls of Pompeii. Offices were eagerly sought for, and gifts were generously made by officeholders and citizens of wealth. The status of municipal finance, however, was never satisfactory. The income of the town depended chiefly upon its property, local tolls and fines, and the contributions of the officeholders. Accounts were poorly kept; public property was often mismanaged; debts once incurred proved difficult to meet; and the increasing burdens caused men of wealth to avoid officeholding. Accordingly, later charters contained provisions for the drafting of candidates. As a result of inefficient management and financial confusion, correctors or curators, Roman citizens, were appointed in many cities during the second century to direct or advise the municipal officials. Such interference aggravated the decline of political vitality in the cities of the empire.

THE JEWS IN THE EMPIRE   The Jewish question is worthy of special study because of its part in the history of the Roman Empire and its significance in the development of Christianity. The Jewish question in this period was the product of developments in Jewish history after the return from exile in Babylon (p. 111).

When the Persians allowed the re-establishment of Jerusalem with the return of those exiles who cared to go, Judaea became a small, theocratic state governed by its priests. The temple was reconstructed, the walls were rebuilt by Nehemiah, and, most important, the Law, center of Judaism, brought from Babylon by Ezra, was codified and sworn to by all of the people in a great covenant with Jahweh. Probably in the same period the history of the kingdom was rewritten by the Chronicler and the sacred literature was gathered into a collection. Since it was all-important that the people should know the law, synagogues, "houses of the law," were established in the cities and villages, the law and the prophets were read, and liturgies of prayer and praise were developed for the Sabbath gatherings. Scribes, sometimes priests but often laymen, learned the law and began to interpret it in the schools which they established in the synagogues, and to apply it to specific cases, a service similar to that rendered by the Roman jurisprudents. The most famous of these masters or rabbis, as they came to be called, were Hillel and Shammai, who lived during the reign of Herod the Great. From the teachings of the scribes there grew a body of traditional unwritten law developing out of, but distinguished from, the Torah or Law of the Pentateuch. Though later disputes arose over the validity of their teaching, they served to keep alive and growing the religion which the Jews had inherited from Moses and from the Prophets.

Though Jewish teaching was narrow in its emphasis upon its own people and its insistence on their strict adherence to the law, yet it was deeply penetrated and enlivened by the prophetic assurance that their God was a universal deity whose name would become great among the Gentiles and who would raise His chosen people to dominion with Him. Filled with longing for the great days of David and Solomon, the Jews dreamed of a Messiah of Jahweh who would re-establish their independence, make Jerusalem the spiritual capital of the world, and therewith bring about a Golden Age. Writers who saw visions of the coming of this Kingdom of God, hence called Apocalyptic, "revealing," took the place of the prophets of old among the people.

The events of the second century B.C. promised fulfillments of their hopes. After the conquest by Alexander in 331 B.C. and the long rule of the Ptolemies, as the spoils of war in 199 B.C. the Jews passed into the possession of Antiochus III of Asia. Under this monarch and his successor the question of Hellenization became acute. Many of the wealthy and cultured Jews had come under the seductive influence of the Greek manner of life. They learned Greek in order to read its literature, they admired its art and its architecture, and the athletically inclined youth among them delighted in the Greek games. When Antiochus III allowed the establishment of a palaestra in Jerusalem, many young Jews scandalized their elders by attending it and by even assuming the broad-brimmed hats, characteristic of Greek youth but contrary to the Jewish custom.

The work of the scribes, however, had been well done. There was a vigorous reaction against Hellenization, and when Antiochus IV made war upon Egypt, Jewish sympathies were openly with the Ptolemies. The king, understanding well the source of hostility, determined to wipe out the Jewish religion and secure the unification of his realm by the spread of Greek culture. But when he set up a statue of Zeus in the temple at Jerusalem and ordered celebration of Greek festivals, the Jews revolted under the leadership of a priest, Mattathias, and his four sons. The oldest son, Judas, surnamed Maccabaeus, "The Hammer," was the hero of the war and gave the name of Maccabee to the family. After twenty-five years of struggle, during which Rome aided them, an independent kingdom was established in 143 B.C. But the Messianic hope was not fulfilled; the Maccabean kings, allied to

Rome, ruled over their little state amid constant dynastic confusion while dreamers wrote new revelations of the "Day of Jahweh" when the Messiah, a godlike figure coeval with God, should establish not a political restoration but a spiritual kingdom on earth.

The religious crisis, however, resulted in the appearance of the two famous sects, the Pharisees and the Sadducees. The latter were chiefly members of the upper class associated with the priests in the temple, and were believers in ritual and in a strict adherence to the Mosaic Law. They denied the validity of the scribal tradition and of the growing belief in immortality. Their influence ceased when the city fell and the temple was destroyed by the Romans. The Pharisees, on the other hand, were followed by the great mass of the people and supported the scribes. With the greatest scholars in Judaism among their number, they were progressive and liberal in their interpretations of the Law to meet the changing needs of the time. In contradistinction to the Sadducees, they believed in a future life. The work which they accomplished survived to be the foundation of later Judaism.

When Pompey appeared in the East, there were two factions in the kingdom, headed by the brothers Hyrcanus and Aristobulus. The latter had the backing of the Sadducees, while the former enjoyed the support of the Pharisees and the advice of the Idumaean Antipater. Pompey, intervening in the quarrel, took Jerusalem in 63 B.C. and made Hyrcanus high priest. During the following years Antipater was the actual ruler of the land, and Caesar made him procurator of Judaea. His son Herod, who succeeded him in 43 B.C., killed the last of the Maccabees and received the title "King of the Jews" from the Roman senate on the advice of the triumvirs. He supported Antony and Cleopatra until their overthrow, and then by a frank statement of his past and a promise of future loyalty he won confirmation of his power from Augustus.

Herod's achievements as king gave him the surname "the Great." Though he offended the Jews by his nonobservance of the Jewish law and by the celebration of Greek rites and games, he pleased them by refortifying Jerusalem and rebuilding the temple on a magnificent scale. Of his marital difficulties and of the splendor and corruption of his court many tales are told. After Herod's death in 4 B.C., his kingdom was divided into four parts and, as the result of disorders which followed, Judaea was made a procuratorial province in 6 A.D. Claudius restored it to his friend Agrippa, grandson of Herod, but shortly after Agrippa's death it became again a province.

Meanwhile there had taken place the great *diaspora,* the scattering of the Jews throughout the civilized world. There were many in Babylonia, descendants of exiles who had not returned to the homeland, and during the Hellenistic period great numbers moved into the cities of Syria, Asia Minor, and Greece. Egypt, a haven of refuge for many at the time of the Babylonian exile, received great additions during the Ptolemaic period. Under the aegis of Rome they moved west into Africa, Spain, and Gaul, and a large colony gathered in Rome on the Janiculum side of the Tiber. In many cities they lived in special quarters and in some, certainly in Alexandria, were governed by their own officials.

Wherever they went they carried with them their religion, their sacred writings, and the synagogue. Though it became necessary to translate the law and the scriptures into Greek for the use of Jews in Egypt,[2] they resisted Hellenization or Romanization. The Jews presented a difficult problem to the Roman government not only because of their religious peculiarities but because of the quarrels which arose between them and the other peoples of the provinces. Caesar and Augustus confirmed the status which the Hellenistic rulers had conferred upon them and tolerated their presence in Rome. Their ancestral pride and exclusiveness, their devotion to their own God, their refusal to conform to the religious and social customs of their neighbors made the populace regard them with suspicion and derision. At the same time they were jealous of the special privileges the Jews enjoyed. Amid constant disorders and occasional persecutions the Jews managed to cling tenaciously to their religion and customs and to their faith in the coming of the Kingdom. They even proselyted among the Gentiles, and those they gathered into their fold were called "God-fearers."

The Jews were freed from obeisance to the imperial cult and from attendance upon the public festivals on the ground of religious scruple and were permitted to substitute prayers for the well-being of the emperor. They were even allowed to collect a small temple tax and send it to Jerusalem. But the authorities frowned on proselyting, and when a flagrant case, combined with sharp practice, appeared in Rome in

---

[2] This was traditionally done in the reign of Ptolemy II by seventy-two scholars, hence called *Septuagint* ("Seventy"). Philo of Alexandria in the first century A.D. tried to explain Judaism by allegory in the light of Platonism.

29 A.D., Tiberius expelled the entire Jewish population of the city—but they soon returned. Caligula caused an uproar by ordering them to worship his statue. Only his timely death saved them. Claudius, influenced by Herod Agrippa, confirmed their privileges of self-government in Alexandria in edicts mentioned by the Jewish historian, Josephus, as well as in a letter of the emperor recently found among the papyri. He even extended these rights to other Greek cities.

In Judaea, however, where Roman rule bore hard upon them, the Jews were discontented, and radical sects kept the people in constant ferment as one leader after another claimed to be the Messiah. Finally in 66 A.D. war broke out against the Roman governor, Florus, as the result of a quarrel over the desecration of a synagogue in Caesarea by a Greek. The Judaeans expelled the Roman garrison and put the land into a state of defense. Vespasian, sent against them by Nero, started methodically to reduce their strongholds. At Jotapata he captured a young priest, Joseph, who became his client, was henceforth called Flavius Josephus, and later wrote a history of the war and a book on Jewish antiquities. Titus assumed command when his father became emperor, and completed the conquest. After a fearful siege, Jerusalem fell in 70 A.D. The city and the temple were destroyed, and thousands were sold into slavery. The ornaments of the Holy of Holies were carried to Rome, where they are still represented in the relief on the Arch of Titus.

Troubles between Jews and Greeks and general hatred of the Romans involved the Jews in revolt against Trajan (115-117). When Hadrian settled Romans in Jerusalem, called it Aelia Capitolina and built a temple to Jupiter on the site of the temple, a great uprising took place led by a priest, Eleazar, and a popular hero, Simon, called Bar Kochba. Hadrian pitilessly suppressed the revolt and forbade the Jews entrance into the temple area. From that time Judaism, though preserving memories of past glories, and never giving up the hope of a restoration of Israel to its home land, centered its devotions in the law and its interpretations. The legal teachings of the scribes, codified into the Mishna, and the expositions and tales of later authorities were gathered together into the collections known as the Talmud, the source not only of the law but also of the strength of medieval and modern Judaism. Christianity, likewise freed from attachment to its place of origin by the destruction of Jerusalem, was the more easily adapted into a religion for the Gentiles.

ECONOMIC LIFE

"Regions, once desert solitudes, are thickly dotted with flourishing cities. . . . The world has laid the sword aside and keeps universal festival, with all pomp and gladness. All other feuds and rivalries are gone, and cities now vie with one another only in their splendor and their pleasures. Every space is crowded with porticoes, gymnasia, temple fronts, with studios and schools. Sandy wastes, trackless mountains, and broad rivers present no barriers to the traveler, who finds his home and country everywhere. The earth has become a vast pleasure garden." [3] Such was the description of the Roman world by Aristides, a rhetorician of the Age of the Antonines. The *Pax Romana* made the civilized world one. A common code of laws and a uniform system of weights, measures, and coins made trade between distant areas easy. Greek remained the language of the East, but the spread of Latin in the West established for the empire a two-language system far easier for the merchant of the period than the polyglot character of the same area today. Military roads facilitated commercial travel by land, and policing of the seas protected the transport of goods by water.

TRAVEL   Throughout the empire Rome followed its republican policy of good roads, built with a substantial and elastic substructure, and paved with smooth blocks of native stone. The roads radiated from Rome to the seaports and borders of Italy, and from central points in the provinces to the frontiers. Every mile was marked by a milestone, usually carrying upon it the name of the emperor under whom it was erected, the number of miles from the provincial center, and sometimes the number from the Golden Milestone, center of the world, in Rome. More than thirteen thousand miles of roads are said to have been constructed in Gaul alone. The road from the Atlantic to the Black Sea was over a thousand miles long. In the East the older roads of the Persians and the Greeks were kept in use and new ones were added. Important roads were maintained at imperial expense; others were placed as burdens upon the local communities.

The roads followed natural routes, as straight as possible without regard for grades. The average speed of travel for horse-borne traffic was probably about five miles an hour, though we hear of a journey

[3] Dill, *Roman Society from Nero to Marcus Aurelius,* pp. 199-200, paraphrased from Arist. XIV.

of eight hundred miles in eight days and of one extraordinary trip of three hundred and thirty-two miles in thirty-six hours. Travelers were provided with maps and roadbooks. Inns, which seem to have had a reputation for uncleanliness and dishonesty, sprang up at convenient points. Some innkeepers were thieves, and there were occasional highwaymen. Unwary travelers were sometimes kidnaped and sold as slaves, though the penalties for such crimes were severe. The roads were policed, and there was probably less brigandage than in the same area in the eighteenth century.

THE POST The imperial post, provided with relays of horses and riders, carried public dispatches from Rome to every corner of the empire. At first the expense was borne by the provincials, but Hadrian placed the burden on the imperial fiscus. Businessmen maintained corps of secretaries who carried their documents. Private letters had to depend on chance travelers who might be willing to carry them.

Travel by sea had not changed particularly in its methods since Hellenistic times; indeed the sea captains of the imperial period were still mostly Greeks and Orientals. Piracy, which had caused so much trouble in the last century of the republic, was repressed by the vigilance of the fleet, and navigation had only natural perils to face. Ships sailed the Mediterranean with reasonable safety in the summer. Spring and fall were dangerous, however (St. Paul's voyage is a good example of the danger of a late fall sailing), and in the winter navigation ceased save in cases of dire necessity. Speed depended entirely upon the winds. The ordinary voyage from Puteoli to Alexandria took eighteen or nineteen days; the return trip, against the wind, an average of fifty, and often many more. The usual size of merchantmen may be estimated from the ship on which St. Paul sailed for Rome, which carried a load of grain, 276 passengers, and its crew. The ships for ordinary trade and local voyages must have been much smaller. Puteoli was the port of Rome until the second century when Trajan finished the rebuilding of Ostia. Corinth again became an important port of call and transshipment between East and West. Ephesus was the greatest port in Anatolia, Antioch in Syria, and Alexandria in Egypt.

COMMERCE By land and by sea men traveled on errands of trade from one corner of the empire to another with a universal law to protect them, no tariff barriers to hinder them, and only regional collection of small tolls to bother them. Italians appeared in the East, and Greeks and Syrians carried their goods to Gaul and even to distant Britain. The striking feature of imperial development in commerce was its universality, which bore in its train decentralization and extreme individualism and freedom of enterprise. Alexandria, Antioch, Ephesus, Carthage, centers of earlier times, and Lyons, as the distributing center for wealthy Gaul, became rivals of Rome itself in wealth and size; Corinth flourished again; and many other lesser provincial cities prospered.

Most business activities were carried on by single individuals. Partnerships might be formed for single enterprises, but there is no evidence of any large-scale corporations engaged in trade. The merchants' associations were social and religious clubs, employed by the government for such regulations as it deemed necessary. Apart from the exchange of information and the erection of common buildings like that at Ostia, they served no economic purposes. Most of the great fortunes were founded on commerce and moneylending. Within the empire, trade handled chiefly foodstuffs and products of industry— metal wares, lumber and its products, textiles, and pottery. For Rome proper the most important trade was that which brought the grain of Egypt and Africa to the city. The emperors kept careful watch over it, offered bounties to the grain merchants, and in time of shortage gave special rewards to those who would sail in winter. The great grain warehouses still standing in the ruins of Ostia are sufficient evidence that it was primarily for the purpose of this trade that the port of Rome was developed.

Banking expanded its services to meet the needs of commerce. The royal banks of Ptolemaic Egypt were turned over to private enterprise and participated in the active life of that province. There and throughout the empire men of wealth engaged in money changing (for some Greek coins persisted), in the receipt of deposits, in the making of loans, and in the transfer of credit from one section of the empire to another.

Commerce was not limited to the confines of the empire. Ships sailed the Atlantic coasts of Africa and Europe; traders penetrated Germany as far as the Baltic Sea; others sought the markets of Turkestan to buy Chinese goods. The canal from the Nile to the Red Sea was kept open; a Red Sea fleet protected merchants in those waters; and ships sailed to and from India with the monsoons which Hippalus had discovered in the last century b.c. Goods from India which were landed in southern Arabia were carried by the Nabataeans through Petra to Mediterranean ports. Chinese records show that a Roman embassy reached the court of the Chinese emperor in the reign of Marcus Aurelius. The silks and spices which came from the East were paid for with coins, great quantities of which have been found in India. Roman merchants had a fine reputation for honesty among the Eastern peoples with whom they did business.

INDUSTRY   Industry, like commerce, profited from the prosperity of the provinces and became decentralized. Save for the mines, which in large measure became the property of the imperial patrimony, the monopolies in industry and trade, once assiduously maintained by the Ptolemies and Attalids, were surrendered by the Roman emperors. The advanced industrialization of the Hellenistic East gave that region a continuing pre-eminence in the practical arts, particularly in the production of textiles, glassware, and metal goods. For a period the West was primarily a source of raw materials, especially of metals, which came from the Spanish mines. Gradually, however, the West advanced in importance as a manufacturing region. In the Augustan Age, the great pottery works in Campania, north of Naples, producing a red ware, captured the imperial markets from the Greek potters, but during the first century similar vases from southern Gaul displaced the Italian. Furnaces and warehouses excavated in the Auvergne indicate that from twenty-five to thirty thousand people were employed in this industry. At the same time the cost and difficulty of transportation made profitable the development of local industries. Gallic clothing and Spanish metal and leather goods appeared, and many skilled Greeks and Syrians moved to the West to establish shops for the production of such objects as glassware and silks. In spite of the appearance of some large centers of production, manned by slaves, industry remained characteristically a small shop business employing both free and slave labor in proportions which varied with local conditions of supply. In competition with the city shops industrial establishments also appeared on some of the great estates to serve the needs of the people there.

As in the case of commerce, the associations of artisans, with a few exceptions like the silversmiths of Asia Minor, were not trade unions but were social and religious in character and paid no attention to hours, wages, or conditions of labor. Slavery, a plentiful supply of cheap labor, and the absence of industrial organizations combined to strip the laboring class of industrial weapons and to hold it to very low levels of subsistence.

The chief purchasers of goods were the urban population and the peasants on the great estates. Though the wealthy demanded fine goods, most of the sales were made to the very poor. In satisfaction of their needs for low-priced products, technique and ornamentation declined and standardization was introduced in the interest of cheapness.

The decentralization of commerce and industry contributed to the urbanization of the West and to the decline of Italy, which, always more a purchaser than a seller of goods, lost to local centers its market in the empire. The process of urbanization was accompanied by the formation of a class of wealthy merchants, shopowners, and landholders, who had invested their wealth in farms for income. They presided over a large group of pauperized laborers—free, slave, or freed—who, like the populace at Rome, looked to the upper stratum for gifts and shows to help them to live and to keep them amused and contented. At the same time a great body of tenant peasants were appearing on the farms.

AGRICULTURE   In spite of the growth of trade, industry, and towns throughout the empire, agriculture remained the basic source of wealth and the chief occupation and interest of the greater portion of the population. Its products were essential to life. Men of wealth invested their means in it; soldiers returned to it after their period of service; and poor men sought in it a relief from the uncertainties of labor in the cities.

Throughout the period agriculture was generally in a prosperous condition. While the greater portion of the grain supply of the city of Rome came from Africa and Egypt, the cost of transportation made it possible for Italian farmers to compete with their produce in the markets of Rome and of the smaller Italian cities, and the same element of price protected provincial farmers from world competition. The growth of urban communities provided local markets, and the agriculturalists behind the frontier prospered from sales to the army commissariat. This was particularly true of northern Gaul and of the Danubian region. Around Rome, and presumably near the other cities of the empire, were many small farmers who did a flourishing business in vegetables and flowers. In Greece, however, where population was decreasing amid a general decline, there were many abandoned farms.

No estimate is possible of the number or proportion of small independent landowners. The various measures taken by the emperors to protect them and the alimentation program of the Antonines (p. 460) are proofs of their presence in Italy. The practice of giving lands to veterans must have augmented their numbers in the provinces. The pressure of the wealthy, who wished to secure or expand great estates, and the attractiveness of city life, on the other hand, operated against them. The Hellenistic and republican tendency to the formation of great estates continued with increasing force under the empire, as senators and businessmen invested their surplus wealth in land. The greatest landowner was the emperor. Large tracts came into the possession of Augustus by legacy and confiscation, and the amount increased under succeeding emperors. In Africa, for example, Nero, finding six men owning more than one-half of the province, condemned them and confiscated their possessions.

The great estates, however, changed in the character of their operation. During the late republic and the early empire most of the estates in Italy were worked by slaves herded in gangs and often imprisoned in fearful underground dungeons called *ergastula.* The wasteful character of this type of farming, the imperial ban on *ergastula,* and the increasing cost of slaves, as conquests diminished, caused the system to decline. Owners found it more profitable to settle their slaves on a piece of land, sometimes giving them freedom, to be paid for with produce. The literary sources for our knowledge of agricultural conditions cease to deal with the handling of slaves and treat instead of the problems of tenant farming.

In Egypt and the Eastern world tenant farming had a history which went back to the early millennia. The systems of management which had developed in early times, modified somewhat by the Ptolemies and Seleucids, continued into the Roman period. The tenants on the royal estates or the temple possessions of the earlier periods simply transferred their allegiance to the Roman masters. Eastern methods of control, somewhat changed to meet new conditions, were adapted by the emperors for their western estates into a system of tenancy under procuratorial control. The land in each province was divided into tracts, the tracts into regions, and each region into estates. The lessee of an estate was called a *conductor,* his tenants, *coloni.* Each *colonus* rented a lot, usually 200 *jugera,* on a five-year lease and paid a quota of his produce and a small sum per head for cattle on the common pasture. In addition he was compelled to work a fixed number of days for the conductor at plowing, seeding, and harvesting, and occasionally also on buildings and fortifications. The *coloni* lived in the *vicus,* village, around the villa of the conductor. There stood the bakery, mill, barns, pleasure grounds and shrines. Leases were normally renewed after the five-year period, both tenant and conductor being protected by law in their respective rights, which could be transmitted by inheritance. Wastelands could be occupied and worked for a period of five or ten years without payment. This system developed by the emperors spread to the private estates, where freemen and slaves alike became *coloni.* In the second century the peasant population sank everywhere from the rank of small farmers into tenantry, but it was not until the following century that the tenants were reduced to serfdom.

The first notable result of imperial agriculture for profit was the wide extension of those familiar sources of income, the olive tree and the vine, until Gaul and Spain produced their native brands and competed successfully in the world market with the Italian oil and wines. In regions adapted for grazing, especially those close to the army camps, cattle and sheep were raised for their meat and their hides.

The decentralization of industry, which had resulted in urbanization, particularly in the West, along with the formation of great military centers created great local demand for the growing of cereals, and for this tenant farming was best adapted. Attention to scientific farming, the rotation of crops, and the fertilization of the soil, declined, however, as the tasks of labor passed into the hands of ignorant, poor, and unambitious peasants.

All economic activities bore their share of the tax burden. Commerce contributed to the tolls, for which the empire was divided into districts; industry paid special license fees levied on trades and occupations; landowners paid the land tax according to its produce. All transactions were subject to the sales tax; and the estates of citizens were subject to the 5 per cent inheritance tax. Provincials who were not citizens or landowners paid the poll tax, which fell heaviest upon the urban proletariat and upon the impoverished tenant farmers. Moreover, the provincials were obliged to supply goods and services upon requisition, for which they were paid but which, nonetheless, proved serious economic burdens. The imperial service, agriculture, industry, and commerce brought prosperity and its attendant comforts to the upper and middle classes of the empire; but below them were the great multitude of the proletariat in the cities and the tenant farmers in the country, miserably paid, wretchedly housed, overtaxed, continually exploited, often dependent, at least in part, on charity, unhappy and hopeless in the midst of plenty.

SOCIAL LIFE

THE IMPERIAL CITY

Rome was the focal center of all men's eyes, the goal of every ambitious provincial, the hub of all activities. Its population, composed of elements from every corner of the empire, had spread far beyond the republican wall.[4]

On the Palatine stood the splendid imperial palaces. At the foot of the hill was the republican Forum and beyond it, the fora of the emperors. The Circus Maximus lay between the Palatine and the Aventine, the Colosseum, on the other side, at the foot of the Esquiline. Temples, theaters, and baths dotted the city. The fine houses of the men of wealth were erected on the hills, while the huge *insulae* where the poor lived stood on the lower ground. Aqueducts supplied the city with water, which overflowed in the many fountains which still add charm to modern Rome. Water was carried into private houses by lead pipes, bearing the emperor's stamp to show payment.[5] The paved streets, wider after the fire of Nero's reign, were filled all day with throngs, and at night the noise of the carters conveying the city's supplies kept the restless or the visitor awake. The poems of Juvenal and Martial resound with the bustle and the excitement of imperial Rome.

THE ARISTOCRACY

On the income from their landed estates the aristocrats lived in magnificent style. The *atria* of their houses were constructed with marble pilasters and columns. The walls of the rooms were adorned with paintings; the floors were covered with beautiful mosaics; the gardens in the peristyle contained many plants and flowers; Greek statuary or copies of the great masters gave an atmosphere of refinement; and draperies and

---

[4] Estimates of the population based on known numbers of houses and tenements, though made by competent scholars, vary all the way from two hundred and sixty thousand to eight hundred thousand. The smaller number is probably more nearly correct. There were between fifty and sixty million people in the empire.

[5] Pipes occasionally found without the stamp are indications of illegal connections.

tapestries added color. The decorative furniture was elegant and costly. For convenience they had water, piped in from the aqueducts to faucets and fountains, and heat, supplied by flues built into the walls.

After an early morning breakfast of a roll and a cup of sour wine, the great man received his morning callers and then went about his

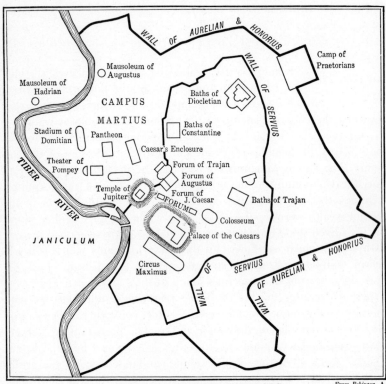

ROME UNDER THE EMPERORS

From Robinson, A History of Rome.

business. Lunch at eleven was followed by a siesta, and the afternoon was devoted to exercise and the bath. In the luxurious *thermae* ("baths") the Roman met his friends, discussed the topics of the day, and enjoyed the pleasures of libraries, hot rooms, hot and cold water baths, and massage. The chief social event of the day was the dinner, which frequently lasted three or four hours and was made noteworthy by a wide variety of food brought from all corners of the empire. Fish and oysters were considered such delicacies that many men kept private fish ponds; grouse, thrush, peacocks, and cranes pleased the taste of the epicure; melons and fruits, pastry and nuts were served as desserts. Mosaics which represent bones, shells, and vegetables scattered on the floor are indications of a rather low standard of table manners. The entertainment which followed the food depended upon the taste of the diners. Frequently the time was passed in gambling with dice. For the frivolous there were music-girls and shows, while the reading of poems, essays, or orations and the discussion of ancient authors or of the standards of rhetoric and the meaning of words occupied the erudite.

Women in high society enjoyed greater freedom than in earlier periods. The strict laws which placed women under male control had been relaxed and customs had changed. The new woman participated freely in the social and intellectual life of the time. In spite of imperial discouragement, divorce was easy, and in a society where marriages were arranged there was much moral laxity.

The moralists inveighed against the luxury and corruption of Roman society. Stories of orgies, of expensive feasts and luxurious appointments were ever popular. There is ample evidence, however, that these were the exception rather than the rule, that many of the customs against which Juvenal thundered were simply advances in the standard of living. Many of the aristocrats had no part in the wickedness of Nero's court. The group which surrounded Vespasian and the circle of the younger Pliny were simple in their tastes, reserved, and intellectual. Inscriptions show that family affection and loyalty were abiding qualities of Romans of the better class. Conservative traditions, still living and enforced by maternal wisdom, prevented Agricola from pursuing the study of philosophy further than "was fitting for a Roman and a senator." The very fact that the Roman aristocracy served the emperor so well in the armies and provinces of the empire and in the administration of Rome is ample evidence of the stability of the class and of the continuing strength of the old Roman tradition of devotion to the state.

THE BUSINESS CLASS   The men of business, *Equites,* and the freedmen found great opportunities for amassing wealth in commerce and industry and in the offices in the civil administration. Their social activities, imitations of senatorial society, were often marked by the vulgarity and ostentation with which they displayed their wealth. These qualities are brilliantly portrayed in the

Satyricon of Petronius, a gentleman of Nero's period, a humorous novel which describes the life of a successful freedman. Venality was the chief fault of this group, arising from the fact that money alone could gain them social distinction. Yet in the work which they did and in the offices they occupied, they too proved themselves able and loyal servants of the empire.

THE CITY
POPULACE

Juvenal portrayed the Roman populace as a mob in which all the elements of the Roman Empire were mingled and which sought only "bread and shows." Rome was an imperial city to which came people from all corners of the empire, but the city populace was far from being an idle and pampered mob. Two hundred thousand people received from the state a grant of grain, which assisted them to live but did not provide entire sustenance. Some received gifts of money or of food from men of wealth. But for the most part they occupied themselves in the industries, the small shops, the tasks of transport, and all of the varied activities of a busy metropolis. They lived in huge tenements sometimes five stories in height and always subject to fire or collapse. For amusement the state provided regular festivals, with chariot races, wild-beast shows, gladiatorial combats, and even naval contests in the Colosseum and the Circus. Plays were produced in the theaters and puppet shows were frequently presented on the street corners.

THE COLLEGIA

The common man in Rome and in the provincial municipalities found companionship, a sense of security, and a small opportunity for distinction in the *collegia,* or clubs. Some of these were artisan and trade organizations which dated back to the early days of Rome; others were newly organized societies of similar sort; still others were social or sporting clubs or religious associations. All probably had religious features, and all had to have legal charters with the permission of the senate. Secret meetings and all unlicensed associations were strictly forbidden. Trajan frowned on all new organizations as likely to be centers of sedition or disturbance, but other emperors fostered them, and Marcus Aurelius gave them the right to receive bequests.

The *collegia* differed from medieval guilds or modern trade unions in the objects of their organization. They made no attempts to regulate methods or conditions of work or to raise wages. But they secured for those in the lower walks of life companionship and a measure of recognition from their fellow men, and gave dignity and meaning to their life. Their organization was the Roman state in miniature; some had clubhouses; many secured patrons of wealth in whose house they met and to whom they paid great deference. Most of them provided burial places for their members. The dead were cremated and the cinerary urns placed in niches in the great underground passages, known as the catacombs, along the Appian Way. Members often left small sums so that the brothers could celebrate their memory with feasts on the anniversary of death.

SLAVES AND
FREEDMEN

Slavery continued as a legally recognized and widely prevalent institution under the empire but under changing conditions. Wars within the Mediterranean area, once the great source of Roman slaves, had almost ceased. However, rebellious provincials were still sold, and Titus threw thousands of Jews on the market after the fall of Jerusalem. Piracy and brigandage, though checked by the government, continued to feed the supply, though any person who could prove he had been so enslaved was instantly freed. Exposed children were still raised by dealers, and some poor people sold their children and themselves into slavery. But in general these ancient sources were drying up, and most of the slaves were born into slavery to slave mothers whose status they acquired. As a result, the prices of slaves rose appreciably.

Slaves were used widely in all sorts of activities. In the household they were, as always, menials, tutors, and secretaries, many of the latter acquiring a knowledge of shorthand. Imperial and municipal clerks and the laborers on public buildings were slaves belonging to the state. Many worked in the industrial or retail shops of the cities, at times managing them for the profit of their owners and even owning slaves of their own. Barbarians from the frontier were apt to be recalcitrant and only suited for the rougher work of the cattle ranches or the mines. Agricultural slavery, however, was declining, since landowners were finding that, instead of purchasing slaves, it was more profitable to turn the slave into a permanent tenant or to find free tenants.

The treatment of slaves varied, of course, with the character of the master; but in general slaves born in the household were kindly treated, and sometimes held in real affection. In any case the law protected them against cruelty. Slaves who were guilty of crimes or who revolted, however, were punished severely, often being sent to the mines. Many belonged to clubs restricted to freedmen and slaves and enjoyed a social life of their own. They had a right to their *peculium,* a sum of money derived from tips or gifts or sometimes from a share of their wages, and could either spend it for their own pleasure or save it to purchase their freedom. Manumission was easy and frequent. Sometimes it was bought, but often it came by gift of the owner, the result of gratitude, or of a desire to have a large following of clients, or for economic reasons, or to save the expense of maintenance, or because of sentiments of universal brotherhood induced by a study of Stoic philosophy. The grant of freedom by will was especially popular.

Freedmen no longer received full citizenship, except by grant of the emperor. They were given a Latin status, and were, as always, attached to their former owner who acted as patron. This relationship involved legal protection on the part of the owner, and loyalty on the part of the freedman, including attendance upon the patron, the protection of his interests and often services rendered to him in accordance with the provisions of the grant of freedom. Ungrateful freedmen who did not perform these duties might be sold into slavery again. Though their freedom was thus restricted and they could no longer attain high office in the empire after Hadrian's reforms, the world of business and the lower branches of the imperial service lay open before them, and many of them achieved great wealth and power, and some, even renown as scholars and philosophers.

PROVINCIAL LIFE

Superficially the provincial communities presented small-scale replicas of life in the capital. Fora, temples, and administrative buildings were erected; aqueducts supplied water, and sewers provided drainage. The wealthy lived in fine houses, elegantly adorned and furnished, and enjoyed the pleasures of sumptuous bath houses, while the poor lived in hovels or were concentrated in tenements. Schools, libraries, medical service and hospitals, and frequent or regular donations of grain were provided for the people through the civic funds or by the gifts of public-spirited men of wealth.

On the great estates the landowners built handsome villas elaborate in plan, ornamented with mosaics and wall paintings, and luxurious in their appointments. Temples, pleasure parks, and exercise grounds provided centers of social life for the tenants whose villages surrounded the great houses.

Yet amid this seemingly prosperous and happy life there was much discontent and misery, and under the surface appearance of uniformity was a wide diversity. The ever-watchful imperial agents, as we have seen, hindered freedom of thought or expression and independence of action. Fear of confiscation, the load of taxation, and the expenses of public careers limited the acquisition of wealth by the middle class, while to the poor the burden of living was almost more than they could bear.

Political diversity was in large part the product of the Roman system of provincial administration. In the first place the Romans willingly recognized and perpetuated local forms of government: the nomes and villages of Egypt; the peculiarities of rule of the Jewish groups; the popular assemblies and boards of archons or generals among the Greeks; the rule of chieftains or princes, as clients of the empire, over tribes and states along the frontier; and the cantonal form of rural government in Gaul, Spain, and Africa. The variations among the charters to the colonies and municipalities produced still further divergency. These concessions to traditional practices tended to foster rural pride and patriotism and to produce a healthy balance between centralization and local control. Local pride, however, was thus accentuated, and the resultant jealousy among neighboring communities became the cause of frequent wranglings and, at times, of disturbances. The beginning of imperial interference in the reign of Trajan presaged the later end of local independence and the triumph of centralization.

Historic differences—arising from local characteristics of race, language, and religion and varying with the extent and character of the impact of Roman culture—persisted between regions of the empire, between provinces, and even between sections of the provinces. The most striking and fateful of these was the division between the Eastern and Western halves of the empire. Though the West was Romanized, the East remained Hellenistic. There Greek was the language of daily life and of literature; architecture and art preserved their Hellenic character; classical plays were produced in the theater; the great games and the historic festivals of classical time were still celebrated, while the gladiatorial contests and the circuses of the Roman arena received scant applause. Indeed the first and second centuries witnessed a distinct revival of Greek culture, and Athens continued to be the center of philosophic studies.

Though the Greek motherland, while remaining the Mecca of students and tourists, declined in population and wealth, the cities of Anatolia thrived as wealth accrued from the products of the rich lands, from industry, and from the trade which still flowed overland from

Asia. Antioch in Syria, cosmopolitan in its population, was one of the great cities of the empire, and the remains of many cities in the interior of Syria bespeak the prosperity of that region. The Roman government fostered the Hellenization of the mixture of peoples who lived in Asia Minor and of the native Semites of Syria. Yet particularistic elements were strong; native languages persisted; and contemporary religious tendencies brought the Eastern religions into prominence and strengthened therewith the Oriental aspects of civilization. The Jews were a constant source of trouble, and the revolt which recalled Trajan from his victorious campaign in Mesopotamia was caused by a wave of Oriental fanaticism.

In Egypt the institutions and social conditions which had developed under the Ptolemies continued almost unchanged under Roman domination. The administration and the management of commerce and industry were almost entirely in Greek hands. Indeed, though Romans were at the head of the government, though Roman tourists visited the temples and the pyramids, and though Roman businessmen had investments in Egypt, senators, following the order of Augustus, were carefully excluded from the land. All pieces of property were carefully registered and the status of every individual inhabitant was recorded. The natives, bound to the soil, overworked and heavily taxed, still clung to their ancient practices and beliefs; the Egyptian language, writing, methods of work, and religion persisted. Roman emperors repaired the temples on whose walls their pictures and hieroglyphic titles appeared after the manner of Pharaonic times. The cults of the gods, though deprived of much of the land which they had once possessed, even of that which the Ptolemies had left to them, continued, and Isis-worship spread throughout the Roman world.

The same story of local variations amid general uniformity is to be told of the West. Though Sicily remained predominantly Greek, elsewhere the Latin language and Roman culture spread. Roman senators bought land, and Roman colonists settled in Africa, Spain, Gaul, and Britain. Agriculture, industry, and trade were developed. Cities were built or enlarged; aqueducts, roads, and bridges were constructed. Seneca, Lucan, Quintilian and Martial were the leaders of a Spanish school of Latin literature, and in later centuries literary works of note were produced in Gaul. Spain provided Trajan and Hadrian as rulers of the empire, and Antoninus and Marcus Aurelius were of Gallic descent.

PONT DU GARD

Nîmes

THE COLOSSEUM

Rome. From *Rostovtzeff*, History of
the Ancient World, *II*.

BATH

Pompeii

ROMAN CONSTRUCTION

ROME RECONSTRUCTED

Wide World Photos

Yet in these regions local traditions were also strong. The native tribes of Sicily, Sardinia, Africa and Spain continued in the use of their native dialects; Phoenician was still spoken in Africa and local gods, though generally identified with Roman deities, preserved much of their pristine strength.

Of all the western lands Gaul was most thoroughly Romanized. Its Celtic elements were almost completely submerged; the Druids were suppressed, and Celtic religion assumed a Roman aspect. The Roman policy of urbanization was especially effective, and the presence of army cantonments on the northern frontier with their incessant demands for the products of the fields and the workshops of Gaul brought prosperity to the people.

Along the Rhine and the Danube and in Dacia, camps and colonies provided centers from which Roman influence spread among the provincials to the rear and to the Germanic peoples beyond. Newly conquered and often troublesome, these regions created many problems for the imperial administrators, and the restless barbarian tribes proved a constant menace which became a positive danger in the reign of Marcus Aurelius. Of local conditions along the frontier, little is known. Yet it is certain that when at last the flood could no longer be stemmed, the Germanic invaders had secured a veneer of Roman culture and an appreciation of the institutions and customs of the Romans.

Such, in brief survey, was the empire which the might of Roman arms had secured and which Rome through its military force, its emperor-worship, its bureaucracy, its roads, and its work of civilization, not only taxed and exploited but also endeavored to hold together, to administer, and to protect.

THE CULTURE OF THE ROMAN EMPIRE

Throughout the territory of the empire still stand the symbols of its prosperity and greatness. The ruins of Ostia, Herculaneum, and Pompeii, in Italy; of Carthage and Timgad (Temesa) in Africa; the temples and arenas and aqueducts at Nîmes, Arles, and Orange in southern Gaul; the remains of towns and villas and the great wall in Britain; traces of the limes across the northern frontier; the buildings of Roman times in Athens, Eleusis, and Corinth, in Asia Minor and at Baalbek in Syria; hieroglyphs of the Roman emperors in the temples of Egypt; and everywhere remains of roads and bridges and thousands of inscriptions—all convey to the modern student the message of the imperial majesty of Rome.

ARCHITECTURE The achievements of Rome in architecture are amply represented in the many structures which have survived and in the traditions which influenced the architects of the Middle Ages. The Romans learned the basic elements—the column, the arch, the vault, and the dome—from their Oriental, Greek, and Etruscan predecessors, and with a shrewd sense of the practical and the effective they developed and combined them in the great works of the empire.

The column, derived from the Greek, was used profusely, not only for structural needs but also for ornamental purposes in the façades of great buildings and in the piers of triumphal arches. The Romans liked the ornate Corinthian style and endeavored to make it even more luxuriant. They delighted in colored marbles and often omitted the fluting. By combining elements of the Greek orders, they produced the so-called Composite or Roman order.

The arch, which came to them from the Etruscans, was used for the construction of bridges and thence for the erection of aqueducts like the Claudian at Rome and the celebrated Pont du Gard near Nîmes in southern Gaul. The great memorial arches of imperial triumphs were a Roman creation. As a structural element the arch was used in the lower courses of massive structures and in the exteriors of the Colosseum and other amphitheaters.

The barrel vault for the covering of passageways and even of rooms was essentially a Roman contribution. The intersection of two barrel vaults at right angles produced the groined or cross vault which was employed to great effect in the ceilings of the great halls of the baths and the basilicas. The use of the dome as a roofing device, though known to the Orientals, was first developed on a magnificent scale by the Romans. The greatest domed structure in the world was a round building, the Pantheon. But the architects learned to erect on arches triangular segments called *pendentives,* and so to place the circular dome over a square space. The semicircular apse, covered with a half dome on the side or at the end of temples and public buildings, became a favorite device of the designers. These achievements in the use of the dome and the vault made possible the development of the Byzantine and Romanesque styles of the Middle Ages.

For basic materials the Romans used bricks and concrete. The surfaces, however, were covered with a veneer of tiles or, in the finer buildings, with slabs of granite or marble. Thus were achieved buildings with great vaults or lofty domes massive in size and magnificent in appearance.

The temple, the theater, the stadium, and the stoa were the structural productions of the Greek architects. To these the Romans added the triumphal arch, the basilica, the bath, the amphitheater, and the great *insula* or apartment house.

The triumphal arch, with its massive piers often adorned with columns, its arched openings, and its superstructures which bore inscriptions, medallions, and bands of relief, was characteristically Roman.

The basilica was a development of the Greek stoa into a colonnaded building with a large central nave often covered with barrel or groined vaulting, side aisles, and often an apse at one end. Arches, resting on piers beside the nave, raised the central roof above the sides to admit light, thus creating a clerestory. This structure was the ancestor of later church architecture.

The distinctive feature of the bath and, it should be added, of the imperial palaces, was complexity of plan. A variety of rooms for different purposes were disposed to produce an effective, useful, and harmonious whole. The *thermae* contained dressing rooms, hot rooms to induce perspiration, a hot bath, and a cold plunge. In addition there were frequently exercise rooms, lounging places, and even lecture halls and libraries. Heat was carried from the furnace by flues set into the floors and walls.

The amphitheaters, oval in form, contained tiers of seats resting upon rows of arches; ramps, stairways, and vaulted passages gave access to the spectators. Underneath the central arena were extensive substructures containing the dens of the wild animals and rooms for the storage of scenic materials. The Colosseum, most celebrated of the amphitheaters, was 57 meters high and 527 in circumference. Four great stories resting on piers, arches, and vaults, supported the seats. Spacious stairways and eighty arcades made rapid ingress and exit possible, and each of the seats bore a number or the name of its occupant. Great awnings, drawn by ropes and supported by huge beams, protected the spectators from rain and sun. The building held about 45,000 spectators.

> While stands the Colosseum, Rome shall stand;
> When falls the Colosseum, Rome shall fall;
> And when Rome falls, the world.[6]

The *insulae,* chief feature of city architecture, were huge apartment houses of many stories. The first floor contained shops or business offices. In front of these, arches supported the façade of the upper stories and provided a sheltering arcade. The higher levels contained apartments of varied size and elegance. In early days the inner supports were of wood or cheap stone which resulted in many fires and collapses. After the great fire, however, the law required brick or better materials in the lower courses, and though many were still poorly constructed, the general improvement was marked. These arcaded buildings are still characteristic of Italian cities.

SCULPTURE   Though in sculpture, as in architecture, the Romans learned their basic lessons of technique from the Greeks, they infused it with their own spirit. In reliefs they portrayed historic scenes and processions and added elaborate floral ornaments for decorative purposes. Of this character are the carvings on the Altar of the Augustan Peace representing members of the imperial family and their attendants, and the sacrifice with symbolic figures, wreaths, and flowers. The procession on the Arch of Titus and the reliefs of Trajan on balustrades in the Forum are famous examples of reliefs of historical significance. The memorial column covered with bands of relief in spiral, like those of Trajan and of Marcus Aurelius, was a Roman creation. Portrait sculpture was distinctively Roman in its realistic faithfulness to life in contrast with Greek idealization. It had its origin in the wax death masks of great men, which were carefully kept by the leading families as evidence of their nobility. From these masks sculpture acquired a sense of naturalness and an adherence to the details of appearance, even to the furrowed lines of the face. As a result, the portraits have made familiar to the modern world the appearance of the emperors and the women of their families.

LITERATURE IN THE SILVER AGE

Post-Augustan Latin literature belongs to the so-called Silver Age, the chief characteristic of which was the development of rhetoric. As

[6] A maxim attributed to the Venerable Bede. Cf. Gibbon, *Decline and Fall of the Roman Empire* (ed., J. B. Bury), VII, p. 317.

patronage, on the one hand, and fear of the tyrannic power of the princeps and his informers, on the other, discouraged free expression of opinion, the writers in general paid greater attention to the words and the forms which they employed than to the substance of what they wrote. Nevertheless, they produced great works of literary value and erudition. Significant of the spread of Roman culture is the fact that many of the ablest writers came from the provinces, notably from Spain

Of the voluminous writings of histories, memoirs, treatises, essays, poems, and plays not much has survived. The loss of the memoirs of Tiberius and of Agrippina, mother of Nero, is particularly to be deplored. Seneca, Spanish tutor of Nero, composed literary tragedies and philosophic essays of lasting value. Petronius, *arbiter elegantiarum* of Nero's court, in his *Satyricon* (p. 490) created the Latin novel. Seneca's nephew, Lucan, wrote an historical epic of the Civil War, the *Pharsalia,* famous for its portrayal of the great leaders and for its striking and poignant lines.

> "Heaven favored the winning side, Cato, the lost."

> "For those who are to live the gods conceal
> The bliss of death; so they endure their life." [7]

Vespasian's friend and helper, the elder Pliny, was the author of a history of the German Wars, no longer extant, and of an encyclopedia of miscellaneous information called the *Natural History.* Many tales are told of the energy and erudition of this distinguished man. He read continuously even while being carried about the city in his litter, dictating to a writer of shorthand as he read. Lest he lose a moment of time he had someone read to him during his bath. Scientific curiosity, incidentally, was the cause of his death at the eruption of Vesuvius.

The tyranny of Domitian brought about a temporary silence, but in the period of the Antonines a new group of literary men appeared, led by Pliny the Younger, the historians, Tacitus and Suetonius, and Martial and Juvenal, poets. Pliny, nephew of the naturalist, servant and loyal supporter of Trajan, regarded himself as a second Cicero and composed orations, most of them now lost, and letters, which have been preserved. Pliny's correspondence is of great value for its pictures of Roman life, for the description of the eruption of Vesuvius,

---

[7] Duff, *Literary History of Rome in the Silver Ages,* p. 327.

and for the very important book of letters between himself and Trajan which deal with provincial and municipal problems and policies.

TACITUS
(CA. 55-120 A.D.)

Tacitus is one of the great figures in the history of history. In matchless style and with an extraordinary gift for epigrammatic terseness, he wrote the *Annals,* a history of Rome from the death of Augustus to the death of Nero, the *Histories,* on the events from Galba to Domitian, a treatise on Germany, a biography of his father-in-law, Agricola, and an essay on oratory. A large part of the *Annals,* the first books of the *Histories,* and the shorter works have survived. His pages reflect bitter indignation at the tyranny of the rulers and the luxury and vices of the aristocracy. His characterizations of Tiberius, Claudius, Nero, and Domitian, though prejudiced, are indelibly fixed on the pages of history.

History, in the opinion of Tacitus, had a moral purpose. "This, I regard as history's highest function, to rescue merit from oblivion and to hold out the reprobation of posterity as a terror to evil words and deeds." [8] To this end he devoted some of his most brilliant epigrams with which he characterized the deeds of the Romans. "They make a solitude and call it peace," was a description of conquest. "This among the ignorant is called civilization, when it is really the badge of slavery," portrayed the Romanization of Britain. "The persecution of genius fosters its influence," was his comment on the tyranny of Tiberius.

SUETONIUS
(CA. 75-150 A.D.)

Suetonius was a biographer rather than an historian. Of the many works which he composed, only the *Lives of the Twelve Caesars* from Julius to Domitian have survived, except for scattered fragments. As Latin secretary to Hadrian he had access to the imperial archives and might have written biographies of outstanding merit. He preferred, however, to write character studies filled with gossip and episodic materials paying little attention to chronology or to the great affairs of state. Nevertheless, his manner of writing became the pattern for later Roman and medieval biographers, and his work remains a valuable, if irritating, source for the history of the first century of the empire.

The *Golden Ass* of Apuleius is a book of magical adventure written in the Antonine period by a native of Africa. It deals with the experiences of a youth traveling in Greece who, through misadventure, is

[8] *Annals,* III, 65.

turned into an ass and passes through a series of mishaps until he is finally rescued through the intervention of Isis. The romantic character of the narrative, the tales of magic, and the religious devotion to Isis distinguish it from other classical works. From this viewpoint Apuleius might be called the first medievalist.

MARTIAL
(CA. 40-102 A.D.)

Born in Bilbilis in northeastern Spain, Martial went to Rome as a young man, made his mark there as a man of letters, and returned in his old age to his native town. The Greeks had developed the epigram; Martial established it as a Latin form and gave to it the content of pungent Roman satire. In a series of brilliant verses, sometimes noble, sometimes biting, he described the life of Rome in his day in both its finer and shadier aspects. One of his loveliest epigrams follows:

> Your birthday, April first, is here,
> A day I love, yes, Quintus dear,
> Love much as my own natal day—
> The first of March—and well I may.
> Red letter days are both for me,
> Both days I welcome gratefully.
> One gave me life, dear Quintus,—true;
> But one gave more, it gave me you.[9]

JUVENAL
(CA. 55-130 A.D.)

A younger friend of Martial, Juvenal employed the satire for the same purpose that Tacitus used history, and Martial the epigram. The noise and confusion of the city streets, the crime, the self-seeking, the graft, the favoritism and corruption of the imperial city were the themes of his poems.

> For since their votes have been no longer bought,
> All public care has vanished from their thought,
> And those who once, with unresisted sway,
> Gave armies, empire, everything, away,
> For two poor claims have long renounced the whole,
> And only ask—the Circus and the Dole.[10]

In the famous tenth satire on "The Vanity of Human Wishes" he mocked the desire of men for power, eloquence, beauty, wealth, and

[9] Nixon, *Martial*, p. 46.
[10] Howe and Harrer, *op. cit.*, p. 582.

fame. The standard which he proclaimed—*mens sana in corpore sano*—has become the ideal of modern education.

In addition to these works of literature there has survived a number of specialized treatises by other writers: Columella on agriculture, Frontinus on aqueducts, Celsus on medicine, Gaius on law, and Quintilian on oratory. Quintilian, professor of Latin Rhetoric under Vespasian, gave to the world the ancient literary canon and at the same time composed a textbook of educational principles which are still valid. He laid emphasis on the choice of the best teachers, on the beginning of education in infancy, on proper training of the memory, and upon the value of cultural subjects. The purpose of the training of an orator, he held, was not only to produce a competent public speaker, but to make him the best man in culture, in ethics, and in devotion to the state.

GREEK LITERATURE Greek literature continued under the impulse of the Hellenistic Age and in the forms and patterns of that period it is represented by many famous men. The *Library of History,* an annalistic collection of excerpts and comments, was composed by Diodorus, the Sicilian, during the revolutionary period. In the Augustan Age Dionysius of Halicarnassus wrote on rhetoric and composed a book on the antiquities of Rome which is one of our chief sources for the early period of Roman history. His contemporary, Strabo, provided a mine of information in a descriptive geography of the Mediterranean world. For the tourists who thronged to Greece to enjoy the ancient glories, Pausanias under Hadrian composed a guidebook which today remains the chief aid to archaeologists. Ptolemy's *Geography* and Galen's treatise on medicine, both composed in the period of the Antonines, were the texts of the Middle Ages. Hadrian's reign is noteworthy, in addition, for Appian, a civil servant, who composed histories of Rome's foreign and civil wars, and for Arrian, likewise an official of the emperor, who wrote a life of Alexander the Great and an account of a voyage around the Black Sea.

PLUTARCH In the list of names of Greek men of letters in the Roman period two are pre-eminent—Plutarch and Lucian—and of these the most familiar to the modern world is Plutarch. Born about 50 A.D. in Chaeronea, he was prouder of holding in his native city a local office which Epaminondas had once held than of any position or title which Rome could confer upon him. In quiet, refined leisure he discussed historical and moral problems and composed a number of essays on them. To discover the secret of greatness he studied and wrote biographies of illustrious Greeks and Romans, arranging them in pairs and making comparisons for purposes of elucidation. His *Lives* are not only historical sources of immeasurable value; they form also one of the greatest pieces of the world's literature. Believing in the old gods, the old ways, and the ancient city, he remained a classic Greek in a changing world.

LUCIAN   Lucian, a Syrian born about 125 in Samosata, was more a product of his own generation. Rhetoric, he said, "made a Greek of him," and he used the dialogue form as a means of expression. His dialogues are one-act plays in which gods and men discuss every sort of problem, natural and supernatural, and in which the religious and philosophic thought of the age is reviewed and dissected with keen and brilliant sarcasm. Lucian's ultimate conclusions are that human life and ambition are alike worthless and that virtue must be its own reward.

MORALS AND RELIGION

It is at once apparent that morality is the absorbing interest of most of the Latin and Greek men of letters in this imperial age. The arbitrary and uncertain power of despotism, the restraint on intellectual discussions about questions of public policy, and the lack of any real political activity or opportunity for social service as outlets for the energies of the leisure class made men introspective. Luxury and wickedness in high society and abject poverty and the degradation of slavery at the base aroused in thoughtful minds considerations of the problems of humanity. In the midst of prosperity the wealthy became afflicted with an abnormal consciousness of sin, a *taedium vitae,* "weariness with life"; while the poor and enslaved, with little hope of economic betterment, sought every means of mental and emotional escape from the hard facts of life. In answer to the cries from all strata of society, moralists, philosophers, and missionaries of a multitude of religions went from one end of the empire to the other and found audiences ever-ready to listen to their messages. In all history there has hardly been an age in which there has been more discussion of the nature and the problem of human life than in that of the most flourishing epoch of the Roman Empire.

To meet the needs of men, the moralists and teachers cast aside the scientific elements of the Greek philosophic systems and turned philosophy into ethics. Great moral preachers like Dio Chrysostom went about teaching temperance and justice, the reality of virtue, and the freedom of the individual who, released from the tyranny of illicit desires, gives himself over to simple pleasures in a confident reliance upon the fatherhood of God. Epicureans endeavored to bring contentment and freedom from superstition by means of the messages of Epicurus and Lucretius, which taught release from vain desires and superstitious fears through the acceptance of a materialistic universe. But hated and feared by the populace as atheists and almost as subject to persecution as the Christians, they made little headway except among the intellectuals. On the other hand, pairs of Cynic philosophers, though often obscene and corrupt, carried to the poor the lesson of the wise man who searches for the life according to nature after he has renounced vain desire and has liberated himself from evil. Neo-Pythagoreans, talking of virtue and knowledge of hidden words and signs and the recurrence of life, promised to their converts rest in the underworld and eventual release. In a later period Philostratus wrote the life of the great leader of this sect, Apollonius of Tyana, who according to his credulous biographer visited the Brahmans in India, conversed with Egyptian sages, slept in temples, wrought miracles, and preached sermons of virtue with revivalist force.

The dominant philosophy of the empire, however, was a Roman version of Stoicism, which, laying aside interest in the nature of the world and all thought that had no bearing on conduct, turned its attention fully to the position and duties of man and the power and character of that "Pantheon," all-divine world god, the all-in-all. The great spokesmen of Roman Stoicism were Seneca, Epictetus, and Marcus Aurelius. To the jaded aristocrats of Nero's court, Seneca preached the Stoic doctrines of self-control, of moral self-discipline, of obedience to a "rational law of conduct," and of social obligations. "No one outside the pale of Christianity has ever insisted so powerfully on the obligation to live for others, on the duty of love and forgiveness as Seneca has done." [11]

In the next generation lived Epictetus, a poor, lame Phrygian freedman, whose Golden Sayings drew crowds to Epirus to listen to him. Recorded by Arrian, they are still a source of comfort and delight to many. He taught personal cleanliness, decent behavior, freedom

[11] Dill, *Roman Society from Nero to Marcus Aurelius*, p. 326.

Restored

TEMPLE OF ISIS

Restored

HOUSE OF CORNELIUS RUFUS

FORUM

HOUSE OF CORNELIUS RUFUS

POMPEII

PROCESSION IN HONOR OF ISIS

EXAMPLES OF RELIGIOUS ART

from worry, and reliance upon the will of a wise creator. The thoughts of Seneca and of Epictetus recur in the *Meditations* of the philosopher-emperor, Marcus Aurelius, wherein he describes himself as a citizen of the world ruled by a divine Providence. He was confident that though life was but a play whose lines were written and whose limit was set, the inner will was free. He felt that no man could do him injury save himself alone, and that to live fully as befitted a man he must serve his fellow men as far as his abilities and resources permitted.

RELIGION   Though many of the philosophers had drawn religious dependence upon the gods or upon a Divine Being into their systems, their message was still the intellectual demand that men should save themselves by the power of thought. Someone has pointed out that Stoicism, despite all its force and values, had no message for children. As in the Hellenistic Age, men, weary of philosophic thought, turned to religion, where emotion ruled and where salvation might be found by faith. The great gods of old were no longer vital forces, for they had been slain by the skepticism of the philosophers, by the failure of the civic institutions they had once served, and by their very elevation to supremacy over a world empire. Emperor-worship was more real and gave a deeper sense of hope and satisfaction than did the festivals of Jupiter himself. The provincial prayed to the god-emperor for economic betterment, and participation in that worship carried with it a sense of patriotism, of community in a civilized world.

Amid the decay of classic religion, both Greek and Roman, superstition was everywhere rife, from the highest to the lowest ranks of society. Men and women sought charms to secure good luck or to avoid evil; they thronged the wonder-working shrines of Asclepius in search of health; they crowded the oracles and poured money into the hands of fortunetellers. A widespread belief in miracles made them the victims of many clever fakers and even the emperors consulted astrologers, believed in horoscopes, and feared unhappy omens. Only when philosophy would compromise itself by alliance with magic did it become acceptable to the people. By so doing, however, it lost all dignity and value as philosophy.

Though many turned for contentment to the little gods of early times, the Lares and Penates of the Romans and the deities of springs or trees or countryside of the Hellenic or Italian world, most of the people of the world sought salvation in the mystery religions. These, with their initiatory ceremonies, their ecstatic rituals, their calls to service, and their promises of immortality, spread throughout the empire. Traders, soldiers, travelers, and missionaries spread their doctrines from the eastern frontier to the wall in Britain. Pre-eminent among them were two religions: the worship of Isis (p. 322), whose maternal loveliness captured the hearts of men and women, and the soldier religion of Mithras. Mithraism was an adaptation of the Zoroastrian worship of Ahura Mazda. Mithras was the chief agent of that great god of light, general of his forces. His initiates, passing through a series of seven degrees, were soldiers in the battle of life fighting for Light and Truth under their heroic leader. The chapels of their lodges are found in Rome (one can still be seen in the baths of Caracalla) and in the ruins of the camps of the Roman legions. In the third century Mithraism became the chief rival of Christianity.

CHRISTIANITY   In scattered places in the empire, particularly in the East, there began to appear groups of people called Christians. They attributed the foundation of their religion to Jesus of Nazareth, who was crucified during the reign of Tiberius. His message and the belief in the divinity of the Risen Christ was spread and firmly planted in the Roman world by St. Paul and the Apostles.

In the struggle with the pagan cults, Christianity had certain advantages. In place of the nature myths on which most of them were based, it had as its background the fine creation story of Genesis and the grand theological concepts of the Hebrew prophets. Its code of morals, with its greater emphasis on behavior than on ritual, was of a higher order than any possessed by its rivals. It claimed fulfillment of the Jewish Messianic hope and gave definite promises of immortality in a glorious Paradise. Above all, in place of a mythical founder, it looked back to a Personality who had fixed himself on the minds and hearts of the Apostles and who remained vivid and living. Freed from the burden of Jewish law by the efforts of Paul and by the destruction of Jerusalem, it made a universal appeal. The poor and oppressed flocked to it, and even members of the imperial family of the Flavians became converts. For a period the Roman government paid no attention to it. The Christians in Rome in Nero's persecution were punished as incendiaries, not as Christians. Domitian's religiosity led him to punish a Christian member of his own family on the charge of "leading a Jewish life."

However the Christians were in constant trouble in the provinces. They took no part in festivities; they failed to worship the gods; and they refused to sacrifice to the emperor. Such persons were regarded as certainly guilty of the *odium generis humani,* "hatred of the human race," which Tacitus imputed to them. In addition, in the regions where they were strong, the sale of sacrificial animals and votive offerings of silver declined and business suffered. Accordingly, there were sporadic outbreaks and some executions. Charges against them were brought before Pliny who wrote to Trajan for a ruling. Trajan's reply was direct and clear. If accusations were properly made (no anonymous charges were to be heard), the governor should investigate and punish in accordance with the offense. A rescript of Hadrian confirmed this ruling. All Christians violated the law by belonging to associations for an unlicensed religion, by holding secret meetings, and by offending the majesty of the emperor, and for these offenses they were punished when brought to trial. There was, however, little interest in them in the imperial administration, and no concerted effort was made to destroy them.

Of the early organization of the Christian church little is known. The Christians were organized into groups under bishops (i.e., overseers) and elders, or presbyters. Finances and the care of the poor and sick were in the hands of deacons. The Christians at Rome buried their dead, as did other societies, in the underground catacombs, and they probably held meetings in the chambers where lay the bones of their martyrs. Early Christian art produced pictures of Biblical scenes, of the Good Shepherd, and of a fish, symbol of Christ. The initial letters of the Greek words for Jesus Christ, of God, the Son, Savior, formed the word *Ichthus,* a fish. The period of trial and triumph for Christianity was the third century.

⸻ XXIV ⸻

THE LAST CENTURY OF THE ROMAN EMPIRE
(180-305 A.D.)

THE successors of Marcus Aurelius witnessed the end of the dream of universal peace and prosperity of the Antonine Age and the triumph of those forces of disruption which had always been present though latent in the imperial structure. As the martial basis of the principate came into greater prominence, the empire passed into the hands of military rulers; the armies, localized on the frontiers, rose to claim the imperial purple for their commanders and to secure for themselves the rewards of booty; civil wars wracked the empire; and for the greater part of the third century the throne was the prize of victorious generals. With the armies thus engaged, the barbarians broke through the frontier and laid waste the border provinces. Political disorder, civil war, the advance of economic decentralization, an increase in the number of self-sufficient estates, and the overwhelming burdens of taxation and of exactions by generals and their armies were accompanied by the decline of towns and general economic decay. Intellectual life became sterile, and religious controversies and persecutions brought confusion and dismay. It was a dark period in the history of the Mediterranean world.

Unfortunately, good sources for this period are almost entirely lacking. A series of biographies, known as the *Historia Augusta* and probably composed in the next century as a continuation of Suetonius' works, was so poorly written and so filled with superstition as to be almost worthless. Papyri furnish information about Egypt, however, and inscriptions and coins carry scattered bits of information from the provinces. Some knowledge may be gleaned from the writings of religious controversialists. But our ignorance of the period has made exceedingly difficult any clear and certain explanation of the decline of ancient civilization during this century.

THE EMPERORS

The worthless Commodus succeeded to his father's power in 180. He made terms of peace with the Germanic tribes with whom Marcus Aurelius had been fighting and returned to Rome to enjoy his favorites and to appear in public as a gladiator. Murdered in 192, he was succeeded by Pertinax. He in turn was killed by the praetorians, who then sold the throne to the highest bidder, Didius Julianus. Once more the armies asserted their authority, and the army of the Danube, led by Septimius Severus, was victorious over the forces of the East and of Gaul. Local feeling which animated these military activities was indicative of the increasing decentralization of the empire and portended the scissions which came later. With the triumph of Septimius Severus, the military side of the principate emerged triumphant, and the title *imperator,* with which armies hailed victorious generals, became dominant over that of *princeps*.

SEPTIMIUS SEVERUS (193-211)

It was Septimius, an African of equestrian family, who, having risen to power on the basis of his military ability, openly made the government of the empire a military institution. With an utter disregard for the traditional position of the senate and the privileged status of the Italians, he put members of the equestrian order with the title "prefect of the legion" into high command in the army and reconstructed the imperial bodyguard, hitherto drawn from Italy, into a military reserve picked from the elite of the entire army. To secure the support of the soldiers, he increased their pay and allowed them to contract legal marriages. The latter reform enhanced a tendency toward an hereditary military caste and made the armies more than ever peasant in composition and local in character.

Of much more enduring significance than these military reforms was the work of Papinian, the praetorian prefect. The great jurist made this office the center of the judicial structure of the empire. His decisions, along with those of his pupils and successors, Paul and Ulpian, were a major contribution to the final development of Roman law.

The cultural interests of Rome were left in the capable hands of the emperor's wife, Julia Domna, daughter of the priest of the sun at Syrian Emesa. At her court and under her patronage lived Philostratus, biographer of Apollonius of Tyana; Diogenes Laertius, who wrote the *Lives of the Philosophers;* Athenaeus, an anthologist of poetry; and Dio Cassius, whose history of Rome from the beginning to his own time has survived in fragments and epitomes.

CARACALLA
(211-217)

The process which reduced Rome and Italy to the level of the provinces was begun by Julius Caesar. Extended by the acts of many emperors, particularly Claudius and Hadrian, and accelerated by the military reforms of Septimius, it was completed by the son of Septimius, M. Aurelius Antoninus, better known as Caracalla. In 212 he issued a proclamation conferring Roman citizenship on all freemen in the empire. This act had the merit and probably the purpose of unifying the administration and equalizing taxation. To secure funds with which to meet the increased needs of the military establishment, he issued coins seriously debased in value. The economic crisis which resulted in part from this inflation continued without surcease throughout the century. Apart from these measures Caracalla is known chiefly for the magnificent baths which he built at Rome, the ruins of which are still standing.

Caracalla was murdered in 217 by the order of Macrinus, praetorian prefect, who succeeded him. After Macrinus had ruled a year he was overthrown, and the Syrian army put on the throne the priest, Elagabalus, grandnephew of Julia Domna. Under this degenerate the imperial office sounded the depths of degradation. When he was murdered in 222, his cousin, Alexander Severus, became emperor.

ALEXANDER
SEVERUS
(222-235)

In the reign of Alexander Severus the senate made its last appearance as a ruling force in the empire when a council of senators was appointed to assist the emperor's mother, Julia Mamaea, and the prefect Ulpian during the youth of Alexander. At this time the imperial government regularly sought the advice of the senate. After a brief period, however, the senate lost its favored position and as a body it remained henceforth little more than a municipal council in Rome. Septimius had taken from the senatorial order its pre-eminence in the administration, and during the following period the time-honored division of the empire into senatorial and imperial provinces was completely ignored. The title of senator during the later centuries was conferred on certain men because of their wealth or for services rendered the emperor. For the most part the senators lived not in Rome but on their estates scattered throughout the empire.

...in an attempt to remedy the economic conditions in Rome resulting from the financial disorder, Alexander commanded the wine merchants, greengrocers, and shoemakers of the city to form associations through which their activities might be regulated.

His reign was also marked by the appearance of enemies on the frontiers, who in succeeding generations threatened the life of Rome. In the East appeared the second Persian Empire. After long centuries of Parthian rule the Persians reasserted themselves and under the leadership of a family called Sassanids established their second empire in 227. The kings, claiming to be descendants of Darius, planned the restoration of ancient imperial glory. Zoroastrianism was made the official religion and the writing of the Avesta (p. 113) was completed. Again in the name of Ahura Mazda the Persian emperors beautified their capital, Ctesiphon, with palaces and temples and went forth to do battle in an effort to regain the territory and greatness of the fifth century B.C. In a continuing series of wars with Rome and later with the Eastern emperors, though they failed in their aim of conquest, the Persians acquitted themselves creditably until they were finally overthrown by the followers of Mohammed. Over them Alexander won a victory sufficient to protect the Roman frontier. At the same time the German Alemanni threatened to cross the Rhine. The emperor held them back by negotiation and purchase, but a mutiny of the army, which was indignant at his seeming lack of energy against the enemy, resulted in his death in 235.

THE ANARCHY   Fifty years of anarchy followed the period of the Severi. The military program of these emperors had resulted in the formation of armies drawn from the peasantry in the provinces in which they served and animated therefore by strong local feeling. The soldiers also had learned of their power over the imperial throne and of the booty and high position to which they might attain. Accordingly claimants to the purple were established in the provinces by armies who hailed their commanders as *imperatores*. Emperors in Rome followed each other with great rapidity, the nadir being reached at the succession of Gallienus (260-268) when there were as many as nineteen candidates for the throne.

This disintegration of the political and military structure of the empire resulted in calamities on the frontier. During these years the Franks and the Alemanni crossed the Rhine and devastated Gaul and Spain; the Saxons began to raid Britain; the Goths from Russia occupied Dacia and, in 251, defeated and killed the emperor Decius (249-251). On the eastern frontier the Persians under Sapor seized Armenia and invaded Syria, defeating and taking prisoner the emperor Valerian (253-260). The West, forced to defend itself against the Germans, set up an empire in Gaul. In the East, Odaenathus, ruler of Palmyra, defeated the Persians and established himself as an independent monarch. In the midst of these troubles pestilence again decimated the populace; succeeding rulers debased the coinage until it became utterly worthless; commerce almost ceased. The Roman world was threatened with collapse.

The great vitality which two centuries of peace and power had given to the empire made possible a rebirth of imperial strength under the able men who followed Gallienus. Claudius Gothicus (268-270) defeated the Goths. Aurelian (270-275) overcame Tetricus, ruler of the Gallic empire, and repulsed the Germanic tribes on the Rhine frontier. Abandoning Dacia to the Goths, he succeeded in protecting the line of the Danube, and finally, conquering Zenobia, widow of Odaenathus, he re-established the unity of the Roman world and the defense of the frontier. Still, cognizant of the perils of barbarian invasion which threatened even the imperial city, he built a wall around Rome. Though he endeavored to strengthen his own position by proclaiming himself to the superstitious soldiery as the earthly incarnation of the sun god, whose worship he established as the official religion of Rome, he was murdered in 275. Four emperors followed Aurelian in quick succession until in 285 Diocletian was elevated to the throne by the eastern army and entered upon a program of reform which gave new life to the Roman Empire.

THE REFORMS OF DIOCLETIAN

The period of the anarchy had revealed many weaknesses in the imperial system and had presented many economic problems which demanded settlement. In a well-ordered state the position of the ruler could not be allowed to depend on the whim of an army which could elevate its commander to power by acclamation and the force of arms, and with equal readiness overthrow him by mutiny and assassination. If the empire was to continue as a unit, the attempts of the provincial armies to establish local kingdoms like those of Tetricus and Odaenathus had to be rendered impossible. At the same time the increasing of taxes so that the administration and the army might function effectively.

Diocletian (285-305), a Dalmatian soldier who had risen by sheer ability from the lowest ranks to the imperial purple, determined to carry out a reorganization of the imperial structure which would correct these political and economic evils, prevent civil wars, and secure adequate protection for the frontiers.[1]

His first reforms were the logical conclusions to the militarization of the empire by the Severi and its orientalization by Aurelian. Though recognizing the army as the basis of his power and providing, as we shall see, a coherent structure for the military rule of the empire, he endeavored to break down the control which the soldiers had exercised over the imperial office by expanding Aurelian's policy and setting up an Oriental court with himself as a divine ruler surrounded by a host of palace officials. In the interests of more efficient direction of military affairs, and with the realization that one man could not hope to defend the entire frontier, he associated with himself Maximian, to whom he gave the title Augustus. Without any formal division of the empire and steadfastly maintaining his own pre-eminence, he entrusted the West to his colleague, while he himself resided in and looked after the East. To secure further assistance and to prevent wars of succession he appointed two assistant emperors, called Caesars, Constantius Chlorus in the West and Galerius in the East, with a further provision that after a period of years the Augusti should retire, the Caesars become Augusti, and new Caesars be selected.

Along the frontier Diocletian established small bodies of border troops, called *limitanei,* in permanent stations with lands for their support and a system of local recruiting which, completing the process of the preceding century, made the troops definitely peasant in composition and virtually hereditary. To assist the frontier guards in resisting sudden onslaughts of barbarian tribes, each of the rulers was

[1] The reorganization was begun by Diocletian and finished by his successors. We will survey it in the completed form.

provided with a large mobile force of *comitatenses* placed at strategic points within the empire to be available for emergencies. In place of the praetorian cohort, the emperor and his assistants maintained imperial guards of young men drawn chiefly from the upper class and trained to be future officers. The frontier forces were thus no longer of sufficient size to continue the third-century practice of elevating their commanders to the purple or of establishing local kingdoms. The commanders of the larger armies were placed in such a secure line of succession that, it was hoped, their rivalries and ambitions could be satisfied without recourse to war. In addition, the division of the command was planned to provide efficient direction of the long line of the frontier.

The administration of the empire was rebuilt on a civil basis entirely distinct from the military. The provincial system was completely revamped. The division between senatorial and imperial provinces had disappeared during the preceding century, and Diocletian proceeded to wipe out the older provinces themselves. The empire was redivided into more than a hundred small provinces controlled by civil administrators. These were grouped into thirteen dioceses, ruled by *vicarii,* and these in turn into four prefectures, each under a praetorian prefect. The duties of these magistrates were judicial and administrative, including general supervision of finance and, in the case of the provincial governors, control over municipal affairs, but without any military authority. Thus Diocletian hoped to secure efficient administration and to remove the menace of the revolt of provincial commanders. The bureaus of the central administration were reorganized to accord with this new system, and many agents and spies were assigned to the divisions or traveled about keeping check on local administrators and on each other. At the head of the civil services was a group of palace officials: the Master of Offices, who had general supervision over the bureaus, superintended military factories and arsenals, and commanded the imperial bodyguard; the Quaestor or Chancellor, chief judge and legal adviser of the emperor; the Count of the Sacred Bounty, director of imperial finance; the Count of the Private Estate, who managed the imperial domains; and the Great Chamberlain, who had charge of the imperial palace. From the highest group of officials and nobles was drawn the consistory, a body of twenty men who formed the supreme council of advisers to the emperor.

The city of Rome was governed by the city prefect with the assistance of the senate, which continued to meet as the local governing body of Rome. The senatorial order, however, was spread over the entire empire as great landowners and higher officials received the title *clarissimi,* which entitled them to membership in the order. The powers of local government within the provinces were both municipal and rural. The cities still maintained their local *curiae,* senates, and their magistrates, but actual government was in the hands of imperially appointed curators, who had supervision of public finance. In the country districts the senators had secured immunity from municipal control and were allowed to act as magistrates and tax collectors on their own estates.

A large and steady income was needed to support this tremendous system of officials. Taxes in money were levied upon tradesmen, municipal aristocrats and senators. But their value varied so greatly because of the debasement of the coinage and the wide fluctuation of prices that Diocletian collected payments in kind from the landowning class. Land, capital, labor, and livestock were assessed by units arranged according to value. The amount to be raised, announced annually in a proclamation called the *indictio,* was apportioned over the empire according to the units in each region. In addition, communities were compelled to render services in the support of the imperial post and of the army, and merchants were forced to transport without payment the taxes in kind.

These taxes worked to the advantage of the bureaucracy and the army, which were thus assured of a steady income of fixed value. Although they conferred considerable power on the great senatorial landowners, they constituted a heavy burden on this class, whose produce was essential to imperial well-being. At the same time, of course, they wrought even greater hardships upon the smaller landowners and upon the municipal councilors, the *curiales.* Many of the small farmers surrendered their farms to near-by senators to evade the exactions. The *curiales,* however, compelled to pay taxes on their own property, to render governmental services, and to be responsible for the collection of taxes in their own communities, were allowed no relief. When they endeavored to escape by resigning or by moving to another city, the government interfered and by the law of *origo* (origin) compelled them to stay in their native city and to hold office as long as they possessed sufficient property. On the same principle of *origo,* which involved the performance of service to the community, merchants and artisans were forced to remain members of their associations (*collegia*), pay the taxes, and render the required labors.

To such burdens was added the further expense caused by graft and corruption. This continued everywhere in spite of spies and of spies on spies. When a later emperor (Valentinian I) appointed a *defensor plebis* to protect the people from illegal exactions, he merely added one more official to be paid or to be bribed.

In an era of confusion when coinage was debased and the state was again resorting to collections and payments in kind, prices varied greatly between regions and fluctuated widely within them. In 301, to secure stabilization and to prevent undue excess, Diocletian issued the celebrated "Edict of Prices" which fixed the maximum cost of goods and labor under penalty of death but which proved impossible to enforce.

Possibly to restore imperial unity and to magnify his own claim to divinity, Diocletian, on the persuasion of Galerius, opened warfare upon the Christians. During the preceding century the Roman government had taken definite steps against the Christian menace to imperial worship. Decius and Valerian, in particular, had ordered all persons to offer sacrifices to the emperor or to suffer death. Many Christians lapsed and secured certifications (*libelli*) of sacrifice, while others suffered martyrdom. But the enforcement of the decrees varied between provinces and periods according to the interests of local administrators and the demands of the populace. In 302 Diocletian ordered the confiscation of all church property and the enforcement of imperial worship. In the East Galerius was particularly vigorous in enforcing the edict, while in Gaul Constantius, whose wife was a Christian, paid no attention to it. When the persecution came to an end with the Edict of Toleration of Galerius in 311 and Constantine's Edict of Milan in 313, which placed Christianity on a level with the other religions, the church, of course, was immeasurably strengthened.

Diocletian succeeded in restoring order throughout the empire, in re-establishing the northern frontier in Britain, on the Rhine and the Danube, and in defeating the Persians. In 305 he retired, forcing Maximian to resign at the same time. His system of succession thereupon proved a failure. Rivalries arose over the appointment of the new Caesars, and wars broke out afresh. From these, Constantine (306-337), son of Constantius, emerged triumphant. The recognition of Christianity and the establishment of an eastern capital, Constantinople, both of which took place under his reign, make it the beginning of a new era. The renewed life which Diocletian's reforms had given the Roman Empire enabled it to continue as a powerful force in succeeding centuries. It was, however, an empire in a world very different from that of Augustus' day. Not only the imperial structure but all phases of government, economic life, culture, and religious outlook had been transformed during the dark years of the third century.

ECONOMIC AND POLITICAL LIFE

The collapse of the Roman imperial system, beginning under the Severi and continuing with cumulative effect to the end of the ancient period, was the product of a number of forces so inextricably interwoven that they can scarcely be separated or followed. Agriculture on the small farm or on the great estate, industry and trade in the town and commerce along the great roads or on the highways of the seas, the political and economic status of landowners and peasants, financiers, shopkeepers and merchants, the political life of the municipalities and the provinces, the efficiency of the central administration, the composition and the attitude of the army, the defense of the frontier, the fortunes, fates, and wars of emperors and of aspirants to the imperial purple, and the mental outlook of the inhabitants of the empire—all were interrelated and affected one another. A survey of each of these phases of life as they appeared during the third century will suggest an explanation of the historical phenomenon called the decline of ancient civilization.

AGRICULTURE   The process of the formation of great estates, which had been prevalent in the Orient from the time of the Sumerians and the early Egyptians, reached its climax in the Western world during the third and fourth centuries A.D. Land had always been the major form of investment in ancient times, and its stability as a source of income made it particularly attractive to men of wealth during the confusion and fluctuations of the later period. In addition the control which its possession enabled them to exercise over the essential supplies of food for the army placed them in a position of power, particularly after the introduction of taxes and payments in kind. During the centuries of decline the great landlords throughout the empire became Roman senators and a potent group in the state.

The same forces which contributed to the power of the great land-owner wrought the destruction of the free farmer, who fell under the burdens of increased taxation, the plundering of officials, the collapse of municipal markets, and the constant pressure of greedy senators. Many a farmer gave up the struggle and surrendered his farm to the nearest landlord, receiving it back as a leasehold. Others, compelled by the officials to remain on their farms, became virtual serfs of the state. The landless men, however, found opportunity for themselves by receiving grants of land and becoming tenants. On the imperial estates, likewise, in response to governmental demands for grain, the peasants were compelled to remain on their leaseholds and transmit them to their sons. The practice of settling Germans, called *inquilini,* on imperial lands with the hereditary obligation of military service added another class of tenants. The peasant farmer class all over the empire was becoming a serf class. To be sure, free farmers never entirely disappeared. But the result of the growth of tenancy was a general decline in agricultural technique.

The first aim of management, no longer the capitalistic desire for income of a city-dwelling absentee landlord, was self-sufficiency. In its interest the senators built mills and ovens and fostered the development of industry to serve the needs of their tenants. Likewise, in order to advance their own power, they secured rights of local government and immunity from municipal control. Many became so powerful through the size of their estates and the number of their tenants that they were able to resist with armed force the imperial tax collectors. The decline of urban markets and the prevalent desire for self-support led generally to a decline in the culture of the olive and the vine, except for local needs, and to an increased production of cereals, vegetables, and cattle, any surplus of which was in great demand for the army. This was particularly true in Italy, where agricultural prosperity suffered an almost complete collapse.

COMMERCE AND INDUSTRY
Commerce, industry, and town life suffered together. Though the presence of Constantinople and the renewed vitality of Greek life, which displayed itself in the later Byzantine Empire, preserved the Eastern urban centers for several centuries, industrial and commercial activities in the West suffered a marked decline. The civil wars of the third century made

travel unsafe and dislocated the course of commerce, while the localization of industry tended to prevent its renewal. Governmental compulsion, in an effort to revive trade and to keep in operation the necessary service of supplies for the city of Rome and for the army, laid heavy burdens on the merchants' associations and resulted in their ruin. Industrial establishments, losing their distant markets with the collapse of trade, and their rural sales with the growth of industry on the great estates, decreased in size and in technique. Heavy taxation also contributed to their woes. Again the government interfered through the *collegia* in an endeavor to keep them at work. The system of trade associations was extended for purposes of governmental control, and the members were compelled to carry on their crafts and to teach them to their sons.

THE TOWNS   Commerce, industry, and agriculture had been the life of the towns, and the decline of the first two and the transformation of the last brought fearful hardships to their population. Political stagnation had already become their lot. In the first years of the empire men had sought eagerly for office, and the people had taken an active part in the elections. Gradually but surely this vitality had diminished. Later charters contained provision for the drafting of officials. The populace had lost interest in voting and then, as elections were transferred to the councils, the right to vote. The paternalism of the Antonines which expressed itself in interference in the rectification of finance and the appointment of *curators,* broke down local independence and pride. The troubles of the third century aggravated the situation, and the reforms of Diocletian almost destroyed the political activities of the local units of the empire. Public spirit vanished; the common people were indifferent save as they clamored for the gifts and shows of more prosperous times; and the curial class, oppressed by the central administration and no longer proud of their position or of their communities, sought to avoid rather than to gain office.

At a time when the income of individuals was decreasing, the demands of the government upon the local aristocrats were becoming greater. The loss of old endowments for public service, due to economic decline and monetary confusion, increased the cost of local government. The burden of taxation, the third-century exactions of generals, and the depredations of booty-hungry peasant soldiers, whose desire for pelf was sharpened by a hatred of the superior aristocrats of the cities, made the condition of the upper class almost unbearable. On the aristocrats fell the heavy burden of local expense; they were subject to heavy taxes in money on their own account; the ten richest among them had to advance the amount of the imperial taxes, and when the burden became too great for ten to bear, it was laid on the shoulders of the entire group.

From this intolerable situation the *curiales* had but two avenues of escape. The first was to rise in the imperial service or to gain additional wealth and to become a senator, a road open only to a few; the other was to become bankrupt and to lose membership in the group. The government endeavored to block the first avenue of escape, refused to allow them to resign and, by enforcing the law of *origo,* which obliged them to remain in their native cities and render the required services, it prevented their removal to another municipality. As the *curiales,* faced with this outlook, became tyrannical in their handling of the lower classes and corrupt in their dealings with the imperial officials, bribery and misdealing became the order of the day. The inevitable end of the system was the ruin of the middle class of the empire.

MONETARY COLLAPSE

Debasement of the coinage accentuated this economic crisis. In the first century Nero had reduced the quantity of gold in the *aureus* and of silver in the *denarius,* adding copper alloy. His reform, which was intended to make the coins harder, was beneficial in its effects but set a bad precedent for future emperors. Trajan and Marcus Aurelius increased the quantity of copper without materially affecting the value of the money, but Caracalla caused a financial panic when he issued silver coins which were half copper. The supply of precious metals in the Mediterranean was decreasing because of the exhaustion of known sources, the export of quantities of coins to India in payment for luxury goods, and, in very large measure, because of hoarding. When the needs of government and the army led Caracalla to debase the coinage, hoarding increased and matters became worse. The emperors of the period of the anarchy, requiring funds for their wars and unable to secure the regular collection of taxes, followed Caracalla's example. The value of the coins declined still further until in the time of Gallienus they were little more than copper dipped in acid to resemble silver. The double denarius contained two per cent silver, and the smaller coins were almost worthless. Under such conditions prices fluctuated, chiefly upward; it became impossible to conduct business affairs successfully, and taxes became so hard to collect that the government, as we have seen, was forced to requisition services and to accept payments in kind. Creditors and investors suffered tremendous losses; municipal and charitable foundations dependent upon investments for their income were completely destroyed. Aurelian, Diocletian, and Constantine endeavored with some success to restore coinage to a sound basis of value. Monetary economy was partially restored but the former prosperity was never regained.

THE CASTE SYSTEM

The efforts of the government were directed to the collection of taxes and the preservation of needed services. Taxes, as we have seen, were laid upon everything. Every man, woman, slave, every head of cattle, every unit of land was taxed; fees and forced labors were levied upon merchants and artisans; the *curiales* were forced to pay "crown-gold" to the emperor, and the senators to make "free-will" gifts. The cost of the enormous bureaucracy erected by Diocletian and the system for the collection and handling of taxes in kind increased the amount to be raised. As a result, the burden of taxation destroyed the purchasing power of the people and, by making impossible an adequate revival of trade and industry, played an important part in economic decline.

The general enforcement of the law of *origo* created a caste system in the empire. Trade, the crafts, the soldiery, and even the municipal aristocracy became fixed and hereditary. Free enterprise and intelligent workmanship, like the proper cultivation of land, became impossible and unprofitable under such a system of regimentation. The empire degenerated into a class of wealthy senatorial landowners and a great mass of peasant serfs with only a small struggling caste-ridden middle class and a hopeless proletariat still demanding "bread and shows" left in its cities. The city-state, pride of the Hellenes, characteristic unit of classical polity, and source of inspiration for so many great achievements, was gone. Wretched towns and huge rural units, worked by an ignorant peasantry and governed by an arbitrary bureaucracy, had taken its place.

In generalizing it is very easy to exaggerate the picture of decline. Some areas undoubtedly suffered greater economic hardships than others. Conditions were worse in the older regions such as Greece, Italy, and Sicily, where intensive cultivation for centuries had exhausted the soil. Gaul, on the other hand, was fairly prosperous. In

Africa, Bishop Cyprian in the middle of the third century devoted a large part of his sermons to inveighing against the luxury and self-seeking of wealthy Christians. Egypt, likewise, was still a rich land, eternally renewed by the inundations of the Nile, and the industrial cities of the East showed a remarkable power of recuperation. Many of the Western senators were men of culture and ability who made contributions of lasting merit to civilization. In fact the bureaucracy had a vitality of its own.

THE
BUREAUCRACY
The civil administration, well established by Hadrian, carried on much of its work even during the disorder of the third century. Diocletian's reorganization infused it with new life. In the East it continued to function for centuries; in the West much of it was taken over and perpetuated by the Germanic kings. In spite of its oppressive character it provided order and a fair amount of justice for the people. Able men were attracted to it by its freedom from military burdens in a period of confusion, and they found in it power and a career worthy of their talents.

THE ARMY
The army had fallen from its once high estate. In the early republic it had been the body of citizens in arms. Marius had made it a professional force without, however, destroying its citizen character. During the early empire the traditions of the Roman legions were transmitted to urban provincials under the command of Roman senators. Intelligent, highly trained, and well disciplined, the legionaries with unbroken ranks withstood the wild charges of the barbarians and overawed them by their efficiency, speed, and engineering achievements.

Changes in personnel during the third century destroyed much of this effectiveness and were in a large measure responsible for the military disorders of the period. Marcus Aurelius, to fill the gaps left by the plague, settled Germans on lands within the empire on the condition that they should furnish men to serve in the Roman army. Succeeding emperors followed his example. Septimius Severus drew his soldiers from the peasantry or, by allowing them to marry and to acquire lands along the frontier, made peasants of them. The resultant army, composed of Germans and peasants, was without the intelligence and the culture of the municipal classes, which it hated, envied, and was ever ready to plunder. It possessed local attachments and a feeling of personal loyalty to its commander which, replacing patriotic allegiance to the empire, made the army corps ready for rebellions. The soldiery seized the opportunity to establish provincial kingdoms like that of Tetricus or to make their general emperor of Rome.

Discipline suffered along with intelligence in leadership and soldiery. The new personnel did not yield readily to the iron rule which had made the Roman army great, and when the soldiers discovered that they had the power to make their generals into emperors, they were less ready than ever to subject themselves to regulation. Those commanders who endeavored to restore the *disciplina Augusti* were speedily overthrown and killed. This process of decline continued as the border forces of Diocletian and the armies of his successors were increasingly filled with Germans. At the same time constant fighting against the Romans taught lessons in warfare to the Germans, and when the two opposing forces became equal in the qualities of discipline and intelligence, the superior numbers of the invaders prevailed, and the Western Empire was overwhelmed. The Eastern, being better served and less open to invasion, survived.

CULTURE

Cultural productions of lasting merit were almost entirely lacking during the troubled times of the third century. The emperors were provincials, many of them peasants, with no knowledge of, or interest in, literature and art. The confused political conditions and the economic situation were not conducive to intellectual or artistic work. The literary productions that appeared were works of erudition and book learning, rather than of creative thought. The group of writers which surrounded Julia Domna, wife of Septimius Severus, including Dio Cassius, Philostratus, Diogenes Laertius, and Athenaeus, was distinctly second-rate. Anthologies of poetry, collections of maxims and quotations, and *scholia,* which were commentaries on the writings of classical authors, were characteristic of the age. There was some provincial literature. In the Gallic empire of Tetricus oratory of a bombastic style was developed, and in the court of Zenobia, queen of Palmyra, the sophist Longinus wrote a famous essay, "On the Sublime." Christian literature, vigorous in character, appeared in the polemical diatribes of Tertullian and in the letters of Cyprian, bishop of Carthage.

Amid the general decay, however, juristic writing advanced. The opinions and treatises of the great jurists—Papinian, Ulpian, and Paulus—marked, as we have seen, a great advance in the law and became the foundation of the later code of Justinian. One of the contributions which they made to law, however, was the principle of autocratic control, the product of the period in which they lived, but used by lawyers as a justification for the despotic power of the European kings of the later Middle Ages.

Architecture and art suffered from the same conditions which affected literature. The Severi, though lacking in taste, were active builders. Septimius did much work of restoration in Rome, added to the imperial palaces on the Palatine Hill, and erected an arch in the Forum. The baths of Caracalla, overwhelming in their size and magnificence, and the temple of Jupiter at Baalbek in Syria remain today as among the great monuments of Roman architectural skill. The succeeding reigns, however, were almost barren of worth-while achievements. Diocletian built a huge palace at Salona in Dalmatia and a set of baths still standing on the Viminal Hill in Rome. Maxentius added a basilica in the Forum, and Constantine, an arch near the Colosseum. These structures are ponderous and without great artistic value. The best reliefs on the arch of Constantine were taken from works of an earlier period. In comparison with them the contemporary carvings were clumsy and crude. Cultural, like political and economic, vitality seemed to have passed.

PHILOSOPHY AND RELIGION

The psychological aspects of the decline appear most clearly in the trends of philosophy and religion. The Antonine period had revealed a weariness with life, a conviction that the world was growing old and tired, and a willingness to turn to philosophy or religion for escape. The insecurity of life during the next century augmented this feeling. The pestilence which ravaged the empire at intervals throughout the third century; the depopulation of Greece, of Sicily, and of some sections of Italy, due to economic decay, disease, and race suicide; the triumph of the uncultured peasant armies and their rude generals— all contributed to the depressing conviction that the world was a place of darkness, that mankind was evil and life a burden.

NEOPLATONISM   The stern philosophies of the classic age were not an adequate defense against these convictions. To meet them Plotinus and his student, Porphyry, in Alexandria during the third century evolved the philosophic system known as Neoplatonism. Adopting the mystical aspects of Plato's teaching, these philosophers taught the baseness of matter and the reality of the spiritual world of "ideas." By the successive stages of reason, intuition, and ecstasy, and with the assistance of gods and spirits (*daemones*) individuals might escape from the world and commune with the sublime and perfect supernatural realm. Greek philosophy, which had begun in Ionia with a denial of the gods, had at last surrendered completely to them.

THE PAGAN RELIGIONS   Religion witnessed a great revival. The worship of the old gods, great and small, from Jupiter to the Lares and Penates of the Romans and the local divinities of the provinces was actively renewed. The Oriental mystery cults gained ever more adherents. Isis and the Great Mother had their devotees. Mithraism (p. 506), coalescing with the worship of the Syrian sun god, became the official worship of the military emperors. A Babylonian priest, Mani, who lived in the third century, developed from Babylonian and Persian doctrines a religious dualism of good and evil, symbolized by light and darkness. His cult, called Manichaeism, attracted many, and even St. Augustine turned to it in his youth. It is characteristic of the cosmopolitanism of the period in its search for gods that Alexander Severus, according to report, suggested the erection of statues to Abraham and Christ along with the gods of Rome. Religiosity was accompanied by a belief in all kinds of superstitions; prodigies and signs were multiplied; and all possible devices were used to appease angry gods. Yet with all this multiplication of divinities there came a syncretism, a growing feeling that all of the gods and daemons were but manifestations or perhaps assistants of the one divine ruler of the universe.

The conviction which both religion and philosophy held and taught, that the world was evil, drove many to lives of asceticism and celibacy. Some went into the desert to live as hermits or into retirement as members of pre-Christian monastic sects.

Meanwhile Christianity firmly held its ground and advanced amid the fires of persecution with a dogged intolerance of its pagan rivals that gave it much of its strength. Throughout the third century the Christian religion spread into all sections of the empire and attracted a growing number of adherents in all classes of the population, especially among the poorer people. It produced intellectual leaders of great acumen like Irenaeus of Lyons, Tertullian and Cyprian of Carthage, Clement and Origen of Alexandria. Amid discussions arising from many concepts considered heretical, it evolved its body of doctrine, its ceremonies and ritual. Its organization also developed as the clergy became distinguished as a separate group from the laity and as the supremacy of the bishops, now heads of great churches, was recognized.

Perhaps the most striking and important feature of Christian history was the growth of the power of the Church at Rome. In addition to the prestige natural to an establishment in the capital of the empire, the Roman Church possessed the advantage of a tradition that it was founded by St. Peter and St. Paul. During a period when the Eastern churches were torn by heresies which seem to have been indigenous to their region, the Roman Church held steadfastly to what it considered the basic doctrine. By the time of Constantine, the bishop of Rome was on the way to being recognized as the leader of the Western Church. Throughout the empire the Church set itself steadfastly against any compromise with the pagan religions or with the demands of the imperial government. Many of its members suffered martyrdom rather than yield. No estimate can be made of the number of Christians at the time of Constantine. The Church, however, was powerful, well organized, and militant, ready to assume its position of leadership in the new era.

THE DECLINE OF ANCIENT CIVILIZATION

The process of continuous change to which all living things are subject during the centuries ultimately brought about a gradual transformation in the character of the ancient world. This change, which involved virtually every phase of life, has been called "the decline of ancient civilization." Although nearly every philosopher of history has endeavored to explain it and although almost every possible reason for it has been suggested, the decisive solution of the problem remains elusive. The changes can be described and their influences noted; but the causes generally assigned are perhaps as much symptoms or evidence of change as they are explanations. Emphasis on a few of the broader phases of the movement, however, will serve to focus attention on the fundamental differences between the ancient world and that which was soon to emerge.

The first stages in the process may be noted as far back as the fourth century B.C. in the decline of the Greek city-state. The city-state was the basic unit of the Greek life, and devotion to it was the vital element in works of art and literature and in all the great achievements of the classic period. The weaknesses which it developed struck a blow at the source of inspiration. Yet the peace and unity imposed first by the leagues and kingdoms of the Hellenistic Age and later by the Roman Empire carried with them advantages. Economic prosperity followed, and the widespread flow of trade made possible industrial specialization and improvement in techniques. The feeling of cosmopolitanism, and its concomitant emphasis upon the individual, provided new inspirations. Science, knowledge of the world and of man, made marked progress. Artists and writers perfected their skills under the patronage of kings, of cities, of men of wealth, and finally of emperors. Although the Romans during the period of conquest and revolution lost their simplicity of character and their republican institutions, nevertheless they emerged in the empire as a ruling people, conscious and proud of their mission as the conquerors and civilizers of the world.

The life of the city-state continued in modified form in the Roman Empire. The municipality remained—albeit in a subordinate position —the characteristic organization and the basis of political, economic, and cultural life. But during the second century A.D., imperial interference began the destruction of municipal political life, culminating in the time of Diocletian in the almost complete substitution of imperial bureaucracy for local control. Imperial exactions, the depredations of the peasant armies, the debasement of coinage, the collapse of trade, the decentralization of industry, the loss of invested funds, and the rising caste system, all combined to place ruinous burdens on the shoulders of the middle class. The towns declined in population and in wealth until at last the great estates of the emperor and the senators, worked by servile tenants and self-sufficient in status, took the place of the classic city-state as the unit of political and economic organization in the Western world. Urban institutions were beginning to give way to the agrarian life and economy which were to become characteristic of the early Middle Ages.

Imperial unity was likewise destroyed. Economic decentralization

weakened it; the civil wars of the third century shattered it; the fundamental differences between the Hellenistic East and the Latin West
were a constant obstacle to its continuance. Diocletian's division of the
empire was a tacit recognition of the difficulty of its preservation, even
though it was reunited and held together for a time by Constantine.
Theodosius made permanent the administrative separation between
the East and West in 395. The western half, suffering vital blows from
the barbarian invaders, surrendered its power in 476 and fell apart into
Germanic kingdoms. The East, escaping the worst of the barbarian
ravages, stronger politically and economically, and inspired by the continuing flow of Hellenic thought, preserved its unity for centuries and
persisted in its existence as the Byzantine Empire with its capital at
Constantinople until the triumph of the Turks in 1453.

These political and economic mutations were accompanied by a
change in mental attitude as the Hellenic glorification of the individual yielded to an attitude of apathy. The men of the early Orient
had produced great empires and brilliant cultures. Yet in the end they
had come to the conviction that man was as clay in the hands of the
potter, as a flower of the field, here today and gone tomorrow. To that
idea the Greeks had triumphantly opposed the doctrine of the freedom
of the individual in life and in thought. On that principle they had
performed great deeds and produced glorious works. The Romans
introduced law and order, discipline, and a sense of power. The classical man was eager to fight and to rule, ready to plunge into the mysterious depths of the universe and to explore the ranges of human
thought. But after the fall of the city-states in the Hellenistic Age, a
sense of failure, of futility, and of weariness, a desire for escape from
reality began to appear. It was present in the flourishing times of the
Roman Empire, became distinctly evident in the period of Antonines,
and gained acceleration as the imperial structure crumbled.

Although revolutions, proscription, wars, and imperial despotism
had cost the ancient world many of its ablest minds, and although race
suicide affected the educated classes to a certain extent, there were men
of ability and intelligence in these later days who might have found
solutions for the political and economic problems which beset mankind. But their thoughts were turned in other directions. They despised
the material world and all its works, and sought in philosophy or religion an avenue of escape. Classical religion had made men at home in
the world; Neoplatonism and the mystery religions offered them a

refuge from it in a realm of emotions and dreams. In the end the Oriental concept of man triumphed over that of the Greeks. The victory of Christianity introduced a new age which was not more religious than the old but which had as the center of its thought the doctrine of the salvation of man in eternal life.

Ancient civilization did not fall or disappear. It continued with great vitality for a thousand years in the Byzantine Empire; it gripped the Germanic invaders and taught them the ways of the civilized life; it profoundly influenced the Roman Church; and it provided the inspiration for works of art, architecture, and literature for succeeding generations. It thus played an important part in the creation of the civilization which is called medieval, and it remains today the substructure upon which our own culture rests.

CHRONOLOGICAL TABLES

Many dates in ancient history are doubtful or in dispute; some can merely be approximated. The three tables on the following pages therefore are of value chiefly in showing the order and time relationship of events.

TABLE I

The Orient to 500 B.C.

TABLE II

The Graeco-Roman World to 133 B.C.

TABLE III

Rome 133 B.C.-305 A.D.

Era	Egypt	Babylonia
5000-4000	Predynastic period Development of hieroglyphs 4241 Calendar	Painted Pottery Folk Entrance of Sumerians 4500 Flood Calendar Development of cuneiform
4000-3000	Two kingdoms 3400 Union of Egypt First and second dynasties	Entrance of Semites 3400 First dynasty of Ur 3050 Eannatum of Lagash
3000-2000	2980-2900 Third dynasty 2900-2750 Fourth dynasty Pyramids 2750-2625 Fifth dynasty 2625-2475 Sixth dynasty Period of darkness	2700 Urukagina of Lagash 2650 Sargon of Akkad 2450 Gudea of Lagash 2298-2180 Third dynasty of Ur 2180 Raid of Elamites
2000-1000	2000-1788 Middle Kingdom Twelfth dynasty 1700 Hyksos invasion	1947-1905 Hammurabi 1900 Entrance of Kassites 1850 First Assyrian bid for power 1750 Hittite raid 1746-1180 Kassite rule in Babylon

Old Kingdom 3400-2475

Empire 1580-1150

1580-1557 Ahmose
Eighteenth dynasty

1501-1447 Hatshepsut and Thutmose III
1411-1375 Amenhotep III

1375-1358 Ikhnaton
Nineteenth dynasty
1313-1292 Seti I
1292-1225 Ramses II
1225-1215 Merneptah
Twentieth dynasty
1198-1167 Ramses III
Twentieth dynasty
Twenty-first dynasty

Syria	*Asia Minor*	*Aegean*
Prehistoric period	Prehistoric period	Neolithic Age
Entrance of Canaanites		
		Early Minoan and Helladic periods
Entrance of Phoenicians		
	Entrance of Hittites	2100 Middle Minoan period
		Middle Minoan Entrance of Greeks Middle Helladic —Troy II 1600 Late Minoan and Helladic
		1450-1400 Great Age of Cnossus
1500 Entrance of Aramaeans, etc.		
Egyptian conquest	1400 Hittite Empire	1400 Sack of palace
Development of alphabet		1400-1100 Mycenaean Age
Hittite conquest		—Troy VI
1288 Battle of Kadesh	1288 Hattusil	
1200 Exodus		
		1184 Fall of Troy 1100 Dorian invasion
	Entrance of Phrygians	1100 Settlement of Asia Minor by Greeks

Era	Egypt	Babylonia
1000-500	945-670 Twenty-second to twenty-fifth dynasties	

		885-860 Assurnasirpal
		746-727 Tiglath Pileser III
		727-722 Shalmaneser
		722-705 Sargon II
		705-681 Sennacherib
	670 Assyrian conquest	681-669 Esarhaddon
	663-525 Twenty-sixth dynasty	669-626 Assurbanipal
		612 Fall of Nineveh
	663-609 Psamtik I	676-539 Chaldaean dynasty in Babylon
	609-593 Necho	604-561 Nebuchadrezzar
	593-588 Psamtik II	633-550 Median Kings
	569-525 Amasis	550-529 Cyrus
		539 Fall of Babylon
	525 Persian conquest	529-523 Cambyses
		521-485 Darius

Assyrian Supremacy 885-612

Syria	*Asia Minor*	*Aegean*
1000-967 Hiram of Tyre	Phrygian kingdom	
1010-970 David		
970-935 Solomon		900-500 Rise of Greek states
933 Division of the kingdom		(see next table)
876-853 Ahab		
841-815 Jehu		
	800-546 Lydian kingdom	
750 Amos and Hosea		
732 Fall of Damascus		
722 Fall of Samaria		
722 698 Hezekiah		
Isaiah		
637-609 Josiah		
Jeremiah		
597 Capture of Jerusalem		
586 Destruction of Jerusalem	585 Battle with Medes	
Babylonian Exile	560-546 Croesus	
	546 Persian conquest	
539 Return to Jerusalem		
450 Ezra and Nehemiah		

TABLE II

THE GRAECO-ROMAN WORLD TO 133 B.C.

Era	The East	The Greeks	The West
3000-1000		Aegean civilization 1100 Dorian invasion 1100- Greek settlement	Neolithic peoples 2000 Entrance of Terremare folk Minoans in Sicily and Southern Italy Formation of Italic tribes
1000-500	1000-500 Phrygian Kingdom 885-612 Assyrian Empire 800-546 Lydian kingdom	900 of Asia Minor 850 Homer 800-600 Colonial expansion 776 First Olympiad 750 Hesiod 725 First Messenian War 682 Athenian archon list begins 670 Archilochus 650 Second Messenian War Tyrtaeus and Alcman 627 Periander tyrant of Corinth 621 Draco's code 610-595 Alcaeus and Sappho 594 Solon's reforms 585 Thales 566 Glaucus of Chios Anaximander	1000 Iron Age of Villanova 1000-800 Entrance of Etruscans 825 Carthage founded 800-600 Greeks in Southern Italy and Sicily 753 Founding of Rome 753-509 Regal period of Rome 664 Zaleucus of Locri 600-509 Etruscan domination of Rome
	560-546 Croesus 546 Cyrus conquers Lydia 550-529 Cyrus 529-523 Cambyses 521-485 Darius	560-527 Peisistratus tyrant of Athens 540 Anaximenes 535 Pythagoras Xenophanes Anacreon Theodorus of Samos Thespis Theognis of Megara 527-512 Hippias tyrant of Athens 514 Murder of Hipparchus by Harmodius and Aristogeiton 508 Cleisthenes' reforms	510 Sybaris destroyed by Croton 509 Roman Republic established 508 Treaty between Carthage and Rome 505 Battle of Aricia 504 Attius Clausus
500-400		500 Hecataeus 500-494 Ionian Revolt 494 Destruction of Miletus 493-492 Themistocles archon	497 Battle of Lake Regillus 493 Treaty of Spurius Cassius First Secession of the Plebs

Era	The East	The Greeks	The West
		492 First Persian expedition	492 Gelon tyrant of Gela
		490 Marathon	490-400 Wars between
		487 Archons chosen by lot	Rome and the hill tribes
	485-464 Xerxes		485 Gelon conquers Syracuse
		483 Ostracism of Aristides	
		480 Battles of Thermopylae and Salamis	480 Battle of Himera
		479 Battles of Plataea and Mycale	478 Hieron tyrant of Syracuse
		477 Confederacy of Delos	474 Death of Tarquin
		468 Revolt of Naxos	471 Tribunate established
		468 Battle of Eurymedon	
		464 Revolt of helots	
		462 Ostracism of Cimon	

464-424 Artaxerxes I

Generation of Marathon 490-461

- Pindar 520-441
- Aeschylus 525-456
- Simonides
- Calamis
- Myron
- Polygnotus
- Panaenus
- Micon
- Parmenides
- Zeno
- Heraclitus
- Temple of Zeus at Olympia
- Temple of Aphaia on Aegina

462-454 Egyptian revolt

Age of Pericles 461-431

	The Greeks	The West
	459 Settlement of Naupactus	
	457 Battle of Tanagra	
	456 Completion of Long Walls	
	454 Defeat in Egypt	
	451 Law of citizenship in Athens	451-449 Decemviri
	449 Cimon's victory in Cyprus	449 Twelve Tables Valerio-Horatian Laws
	448 Peace with Persia	
	447 Battle of Coronea	
	445 Thirty Years' Peace	445 Canuleian Law
	440 Revolt of Samos	443 Censorship established
	438 Parthenon completed	
	437 Propylaea begun	
	435 Alliance of Athens with Corcyra	
	432 Megarian Decrees	

- Sophocles 496-406
- Herodotus 484-425
- Meton
- Anaxagoras 500-428
- Empedocles 495-435
- Leucippus
- Phidias

Era	The East	The Greeks	The West
500-400	424-404 Darius II	430 Plague at Athens	

	The East	Peloponnesian War 431-404	The Greeks	The West

Era *The East* *The Greeks* *The West*

500-400   424-404 Darius II

                                 ┌ 430 Plague at Athens

                                 │ 429 Death of Pericles

(Peloponnesian War 431-404)

- 430 Plague at Athens
- 429 Death of Pericles
- 428-427 Revolt of Lesbos
- 425 Capture of Pylos
- 421 Peace of Nicias
- 416 Capture of Melos
- 415-413 Syracusan expedition
- 411 Four Hundred in Athens
- 410 Battle of Cyzicus
- 407 Erechtheum constructed
- 406 Battle of Arginusae
- 405 Battle of Aegospotami
- 404 Fall of Athens
- Rule of Thirty Tyrants
- 403 Restoration of the Democracy
- Ionic alphabet
- Code of Laws

Thucydides 460-395
Euripides 480-406
Aristophanes 450-385
Socrates 469-399
Democritus
Protagoras 490-415
Gorgias 480-395
Hippocrates
Polyclitus
Zeuxis

415-413 Syracuse attacked by Athenians

404-359 Artaxerxes II
401 Expedition of Cyrus
Battle of Cunaxa

401 Expedition of 10,000 (Anabasis) Cunaxa

400-339

400-394 War in Asia Minor
395-387 Corinthian War
393 Long Walls rebuilt
387 King's Peace
382 Sparta seizes Thebes
379 Olynthian League destroyed
378-377 Second Athenian Confederacy formed
378-371 War with Sparta
371 Peace Conference
Battle of Leuctra
371-362 Hegemony of Thebes
362 Battle of Mantinea

359-338 Artaxerxes III

359-336 Philip II of Macedon
356-346 Second Sacred War
357-346 War between Athens and Philip
346 Peace of Philocrates

405-367 Dionysius of Syracuse
390 (387) Battle of Allia R. Gauls sack Rome

367 Licinian-Sextian Laws

358 Treaty with Latin League
354 Treaty with Samnites

Era	The East	The Greeks	The West
		340 Philip attacks Byzantium	343-341 First Samnite War
		339 Third Sacred War	339 Publilian Laws
		338 Battle of Chaeronea	338 Latin League dissolved
			344-338 Timoleon at Syracuse
		Xenophon 430-350	
		Lysias 440-380	
		Isaeus	
		Isocrates 436-338	
		Demosthenes 381-322	
		Plato 428-347	
		Aristotle 384-322	
		Scopas	
		Praxiteles	
		Lysippus	
		Parrhasius	
		Apelles	
338-301	338-330 Darius II	338-337 Hellenic League formed at Corinth	
	Alexander's conquest	335 Destruction of Thebes	
		334 Battle of Granicus	
		333 Battle of Issus	
		332 Siege of Tyre	
		332 Conquest of Egypt, Cleomenes, administrator	
		331 Battle of Arbela	
		330-327 Invasion of the East	327-290 Samnite Wars
		327 Defeat of Porus	
		323 Death of Alexander	
		323-322 Lamian War	
		323 Ptolemy satrap of Egypt	
		323-276 Wars of Succession	321 Battle of Caudine Pass
		317-307 Demetrius of Phalerum in Athens	312 Censorship of Appius Claudius
		305 Siege of Rhodes	304 Landless enrolled in city tribes at Rome
		301 Battle of Ipsus	300 Ogulnian Law
300-133	323, 305-283 Ptolemy I	Aetolian League organized	317-289 Agathocles of Syracuse
	305-281 Seleucus I		
	281 Battle of Corupedium	281 Lysimachus, ruler of Thrace, killed at Corupedium	295 Battle of Sentinum
			293 Annexation of Samnium
			287 Hortensian Law
	283-247 Ptolemy II	280 Revival of Achaean League	283 Annexation of Etruria
			283 Battle of Lake Vadimon
		279 Raid of Gauls	282-275 War with Pyrrhus
	Founding of Pergamum	277-239 Antigonus Gonatas of Macedon	279 Battle of Asculum
	281-261 Antiochus I		275 Battle of Beneventum
	263-241 Eumenes of Pergamum		269 First Roman coinage
	261-247 Antiochus II	266-262 Chremonidean War	269-215 Hiero II of Syracuse
		258 Macedonian victory at Cos	264 First gladiatorial games
			264-241 First Punic War

(margin note beside the 338-301 Greek entries: *Alexander 336-323*)

Era	The East	The Greeks	The West
		251 Rise of Aratus of Sicyon	262 Siege of Agrigentum
	247-221 Ptolemy III		260 Battle of Mylae
			256 Battle of Ecnomus
			Expedition of Regulus
	241-197 Attalus I of Pergamum	244 Agis IV of Sparta	249 Battle of Drepana
			242 Battle of Aegates Islands
			242 *Praetor peregrinus* established
		239-229 Demetrius II of Macedon	241 Treaty with Carthage
	221-203 Ptolemy IV	229-221 Antigonus Doson of Macedon	232 Flaminius tribune
	217 Battle of Raphia	226 Reform of Cleomenes in Sparta	230-228 Illyrian Wars
	222-187 Antiochus III	222 Battle of Sellasia	229 Death of Hamilcar Barca
			225 Battle of Telamon
		221-179 Philip V of Macedon	219 Siege of Saguntum
	197-159 Eumenes II of Pergamum		218-201 Second Punic War
			218 Battle of Trebia River
		215-205 First Macedonian War with Rome	217 Battle of Trasimene Lake
			Fabius dictator
			216 Battle of Cannae
			215-205 First Macedonian War
			214-212 Revolt of Syracuse
		207 Nabis tyrant of Sparta	207 Battle of Metaurus River
			202 Battle of Zama
	191-189 War of Antiochus III with Rome	200-197 Second Macedonian War with Rome	200-197 Second Macedonian War
			197 Battle of Cynoscephalae
		191-189 Aetolian League joins Antiochus III against Rome	191-189 War with Antiochus III
	175-163 Antiochus IV		186 Bacchanalia episode
	166-132 Maccabean wars		186 Cato censor
	159-138 Attalus II of Pergamum		
		179-168 Perseus of Macedon	173 Epicureans expelled
		171-168 Achaean League joins Perseus against Rome	171-168 Third Macedonian War
		168 Delos a free port	168 Battle of Pydna
			150 *Lex Aebutia*
			149 *Lex Calpurnia de repetundis*
			149-146 Third Punic War
			146 Destruction of Carthage
		146 Roman destruction of Corinth	146 Annexation of Macedon
			Destruction of Corinth

Era	The East	The Greeks	The West
			147-139 War with Viriathus in Spain
	138-133 Attalus III	Nearchus	143-133 Numantine War in Spain
		Megasthenes	
		Theophrastus	134-132 Slave revolt in Sicily
		Herophilus of Chalcedon	
	133 Pergamum united to Rome	Menander	133 Annexation of Pergamum
		Euclid	
		Diogenes	
		Epicurus in Athens 306	Plautus 254-184
		Zeno in Athens 308	Titius Apolloniis fl. 200
		Aristarchus 310-230	Naevius fl. 200
		Eratosthenes 275-200	Ennius 239-169
		Archimedes 287-212	Terence 195-159
		Aratus of Soli	
		Timaeus d. 264	
		Callimachus	
		Theocritus	
		Apollonius of Perge	
		Apollonius of Rhodes	
		Polybius 198-117	
		Poseidonius of Rhodes 135-51	
		Carneades	
		Hero	

TABLE III

133-131	Roman Revolution	56	Conference of Lucca
121	Province of Gaul organized	55	Consulship of Pompey and Crassus
111-105	War with Jugurtha		sus
105	Disaster at Arausio (Cimbri and Teutons)	53	Battle of Carrhae
		52	Death of Clodius; Pompey sole consul
104-101	Consulship of Marius; army reform	51	Cicero governor of Cilicia
102	Battle of Aquae Sextiae	49-44	Second Civil War
101	Battle of Vercellae	48	Battle of Pharsalus
105-101	Slave revolt in Sicily	46	Battle of Thapsus
104-102	War with Pirates	45	Battle of Munda
100	Sixth consulship of Marius	44	Assassination of Caesar
99	Saturninus and Glaucia	44-43	War of Mutina
93	Trial of Rutilius Rufus	43	Formation of Second Triumvirate
91	Drusus the reformer		Death of Cicero
90-88	Social War	42	Battle of Philippi
89	*Lex Plautia Papiria*	40	Perusian War
89-85	First Mithradatic War		Treaty of Brundisium
88	Sulla consul; Sulpicius tribune	40-36	War with Sextus Pompey
87	Consulship of Cinna	37	Treaty of Tarentum
86	Seventh consulship of Marius	36	Parthian War
86	Siege of Athens	31	Actium
83-82	First Civil War		
82-79	Dictatorship of Sulla		Cicero 106-43
78-71	War with Sertorius		Varro 116-27
75	Cicero quaestor		Nepus 100-25
74-67	War with Pirates		Lucretius 99-55
74-63	Second Mithradatic War		Catullus 84-54
73-71	Revolt of Spartacus		Augustus 27 B.C.-14 A.D.
70	Consulship of Pompey and Crassus	27	"Restoration of Republic"; establishment of Principate
	Trial of Verres		
69	Caesar at the funeral of Julia	27-24	Augustus in Spain and Gaul
67	Gabinian Law	23	Revision of government (Augustus receives proconsular imperium)
66	Manilian Law		
	Cicero praetor		
65	Crassus censor	22-19	Augustus in the East
63	Pompey in Judaea	17	Augustus Pontifex Maximus
63	Cicero consul: Conspiracy of Catiline		Secular games
		15-9	War in Germany
62	Return of Pompey	9	Death of Drusus
60	Formation of the First Triumvirate	8 or 4	Birth of Christ
		6 B.C.-4 A.D.	Tiberius at Rhodes
59	Caesar consul	4	Death of Gaius (Augustus' last heir); recall of Tiberius
58-51	Conquest of Gaul by Caesar		
58	Clodius tribune; Cicero banished	6	Creation of *aerarium militare*
57	Milo tribune		Judaea a province

	Livy 59 B.C.-17 A.D.	167-180	Germanic Wars
	Vergil 70 B.C.-19 B.C.		
	Horace 65 B.C.- 8 B.C.		Tacitus 55-120
	Ovid 43 B.C.-18 A.D.		Suetonius 75-150
14-37	Tiberius		Martial 40-102
19	Death of Germanicus		Juvenal 55-130
26	Tiberius retires to Capri		Plutarch 50-125
31	Conspiracy of Sejanus		Lucian 125-192
37-41	Gaius Caligula		Epictetus 50-120
41-54	Claudius		Arrian
43	Conquest of Britain		Dio Chrysostom 40-115
48	Death of Messalina		Appian
54-68	Nero		
59	Death of Agrippina	180-192	Commodus
64	Burning of Rome; first Christian	193-211	Septimius Severus
	persecution	211-217	Caracalla
65	Conspiracy of Piso	212	Edict of Citizenship
66-70	Jewish War	218-222	Elagabalus
68	Galba, Otho, Vitellius	222-235	Alexander Severus
69-79	Vespasian	227	Sassanid Empire established in Persia
70	Destruction of Jerusalem		
78-85	Agricola in Britain	233	Invasion of Alemanni
79-81	Titus	249-251	Decius
79	Eruption of Vesuvius; destruction	250	Plague; persecution of Christians
	of Pompeii and Herculaneum	251	Invasion of Goths
80	Dedication of Colosseum	253-260	Valerian
81-96	Domitian	257	Persecution of Christians
85	Recall of Agricola	260	Valerian captured by Sahor of Persia
86-89	Dacian War		
		260-268	Gallienus
	Petronius	268-270	Claudius Gothicus
	Seneca 4-65	270-275	Aurelian
	Lucan 39-65	271	Wall of Rome built
	Pliny the Elder 23-79	272	Zenobia captured
	Quintilian 35-95	285-305	Diocletian
		301	Edict of Prices
96-98	Nerva	303	Persecution of Christians
98-117	Trajan	306-337	Constantine
105-106	Second Dacian War	311	Edict of Toleration of Galerius
111	Pliny governor of Bithynia	313	Edict of Milan
113-116	Wars in East		
115-117	Revolt in the East		Diogenes
117-138	Hadrian		Philostratus
122	Wall in Britain		Athenaeus
125	Perpetual Edict		Dio Cassius 155-240
132-135	Revolt of Bar Kochba		Papinian d. 212
138-161	Antoninus Pius		Ulpian d. 228
161-180	Marcus Aurelius		Paulus
162-166	Parthian War		Plotinus 204-270
165-166	Plague throughout the Empire		Porphyry 233-304

BIBLIOGRAPHY

In this bibliography an attempt has been made to select those books which will best meet the needs of the elementary student. Books in foreign languages are included only where no adequate work exists in English; the only exceptions are a few classics which should be known at least by name to every student of ancient history. The reader will also note the omission of many of the older books which have lost their value. More general works have been listed under general categories and have not been repeated in the special chapter bibliographies.

At the end of each section the more useful articles in the *Encyclopaedia of the Social Sciences* are assembled under the abbreviation *EnSS*. The student will find excellent detailed bibliographies in the *Encyclopaedia*.

INTRODUCTION

Barnes, H. E., *The New History and the Social Studies,* Appleton-Century, 1925

Becker, C. L., *Everyman His Own Historian,* Crofts, 1935

Crump, C. G., *History and Historical Research,* Routledge, 1928

Johnson, Allen, *The Historian and Historical Evidence,* Scribner's, 1926

Langlois, C. V., and Seignobos, C. L. V., *Introduction to the Study of History,* Holt, 1925

Shotwell, J. T., *An Introduction to the History of History,* Columbia, 1923

Teggart, F. J., *Theory of History,* Yale, 1925

Vincent, J. M., *Historical Research,* P. Smith, 1929

EnSS: "History" (Berr & Febvre); "Records, Historical" (Evans)

GENERAL BOOKS ON ANCIENT HISTORY

Breasted, J. H., *Ancient Times,* Ginn, 2nd ed., 1935

Burns, A. R., *Money and Monetary Policy in Early Times,* Knopf, 1927

Cambridge Ancient History, edited by J. B. Bury and Others, Macmillan, 1923– , Vols. I–XI

Casson, S., *Progress of Archaeology,* McGraw-Hill, 1935

De Burgh, W. G., *The Legacy of the Ancient World,* Macmillan, 1926

Glover, T. R., *Democracy in the Ancient World,* Macmillan, 1927

Gsell, S., *Histoire ancienne de l'Afrique du Nord*, Hachette (Paris), 1913–28, 8 vols.

Hammerton, J. A., *Universal History of the World*, Amalgamated Press, 1928–29, 8 vols.

———, *Wonders of the Past*, Putnam's, 1923–26, 4 vols.

Laistner, M. L. W., *A Survey of Ancient History to the Death of Constantine*, Heath, 1929

Meyer, Eduard, *Geschichte des Altertums*, Cotta (Stuttgart), 3rd to 5th ed., ॥॥॥ ॥॥॥ ॥॥॥॥

Moore, G. F., *History of Religions*, Scribner's, 2nd ed., 1922, 2 vols.

Nairn, J. A., and Blackwell, B. H., *A Hand-List of Books Relating to the Classics and Classical Antiquity*, Blackwell, 1931

Paulys Real-Encyclopädie der classischen Altertumswissenschaft, edited by G. Wissowa and W. Kroll, Kohlhammer (Stuttgart), 1894–

Perkins, C., *Ancient History*, Harper, 1936

Pöhlmann, R. von, *Geschichte der sozialen Frage und des Sozialismus in der antiken Welt*, Beck (München), 3rd ed., 1925, 2 vols.

Poland, F., and Others, *The Culture of Ancient Greece and Rome*, Little Brown, 1926

Reinach, S., *Orpheus: A History of Religions*, Liveright, 1930

Rostovtzeff, M., *A History of the Ancient World*, Oxford, 1926–27, 2 vols.

Sarton, G., *Introduction to the History of Science*, Williams & Wilkins, 1927, Vol. I

Toutain, J., *The Economic Life of the Ancient World*, Knopf, 1930

Tozer, H. F., *A History of Ancient Geography*, Cambridge, 2nd ed., 1935

Trever, A. A., *History of Ancient Civilization*, Harcourt, Brace, 1936–37, 2 vols.

EnSS: "Calendar" (Nilsson); "Empire" (Breyssig); "Guilds: Antiquity" (San Nicolò); "Historiography: Antiquity" (Glover); "Land Tenure: Ancient World" (Heichelheim); "Law: General View of Ancient" (Wenger); "Slavery, Ancient" (Westermann); "Tribute" (Heichelheim)

CHAPTER I: PRELITERARY HISTORY

Boas, Franz, *The Mind of Primitive Man*, Macmillan, 1924

———, *Primitive Art*, Harvard, 1927

Burkitt, M. C., *The Old Stone Age*, Macmillan, 1933

Capitan, L., *La préhistoire*, Payot (Paris), rev. ed., 1931

Childe, V. G., *The Bronze Age*, Macmillan, 1930

———, *The Dawn of European Civilization*, Knopf, 1925

Goldenweiser, A. A., *Early Civilization*, Knopf, 1926

———, *History, Psychology and Culture*, Knopf, 1933

Hooton, E. A., *Up from the Ape*, Macmillan, 1932

Keith, A., *The Antiquity of Man*, Lippincott, rev. ed., 1931, 2 vols.

———, *New Discoveries Relating to the Antiquity of Man*, Norton, 1931

Kroeber, A. L., *Anthropology*, Harcourt, Brace, ed. with suppl., 1933

Linton, R., *The Study of Man*, Appleton-Century, 1936

Lowie, R. H., *An Introduction to Cultural Anthropology*, Farrar & Rinehart, 1934

———, *The Origin of the State*, Harcourt, Brace, 1927

———, *Primitive Religion*, Liveright, 1924

Luquet, G. H., *The Art and Religion of Fossil Man*, Oxford, 1930

Macalister, R. A. S., *A Textbook of European Archaeology*, Macmillan, 1922; Vol. I only

MacCurdy, G. G., *Human Origins*, Appleton-Century, 1926, 2 vols.

Osborn, H. F., *Men of the Old Stone Age*, Scribner's, 3rd ed., 1934

Peake, H., and Fleure, H. J., *The Corridors of Time*, Yale, 1927–36, 9 vols.

Perrier, E., *The Earth before History*, Knopf, 1925

Renard, G., *Life and Work in Prehistoric Times*, Knopf, 1929

Sapir, E., *Language*, Harcourt, Brace, 1921

Sayce, R. U., *Primitive Arts and Crafts*, Macmillan, 1933

Thurnwald, R., *Economics in Primitive Communities*, Oxford, 1932

Tyler, J. M., *The New Stone Age in Northern Europe*, Scribner's, 1922

Tylor, E. B., *Primitive Culture*, Brentano, 7th ed., 1924, 2 vols.

Vendryes, J., *Language*, Knopf, 1925

EnSS: "Anthropology" (Boas); "Archaeology" (Kroeber); "Culture" (Malinowski); "Diffusionism" (Kroeber); "Family, Primitive" (Mead); "Folklore" (Benedict); "Folkways" (Davis); "Kinship" (Lowie); "Land Tenure: Primitive Societies" (Lowie); "Law, Primitive" (Radcliffe-Brown); "Magic" (Benedict); "Man" (Hooton); "Pottery, Primitive" (Stern); "Prehistory" (Childe); "Priesthood" (Bertholet); "Race" (Boas); "Slavery, Primitive" (Stern); "Totemism" (Goldenweiser)

GENERAL BOOKS ON THE ANCIENT ORIENT

Ariens Kappers, C. U., *An Introduction to the Anthropology of the Near East in Ancient and Modern Times*, Noord-Hollandsche (Amsterdam), 1934

Childe, V. G., *New Light on the Most Ancient East*, Appleton-Century, 1934

Delaporte, L., *Mesopotamia*, Knopf, 1925

Hall, H. R. H., *The Ancient History of the Near East*, Methuen, 8th ed., 1932

Harper, R. F., *Assyrian and Babylonian Literature*, Appleton-Century, 1901

Hertzler, J. O., *The Social Thought of the Ancient Civilizations*, McGraw-Hill, 1936

Jastrow, M., *The Civilization of Babylonia and Assyria*, Lippincott, 1915

Johns, C. H. W., *Babylonian and Assyrian Laws, Contracts and Letters*, Scribner's, 1904

Luckenbill, D. D., *Ancient Records of Assyria and Babylonia*, University of Chicago, 1926–27, 2 vols.

Meissner, Bruno, *Babylonien und Assyrien*, Winter (Heidelberg), 1920–25, 2 vols.

EnSS: "Law: Cuneiform" (Koschaker)

CHAPTER II: THE EARLY ORIENT

Barton, G. A., *The Royal Inscriptions of Sumer and Akkad*, Yale, 1929

Gadd, C. J., *History and Monuments of Ur*, Chatto (London) 1929

Harper, R. F., *The Code of Hammurabi*, Chicago, 1904

King, L. W., *A History of Babylon*, Stokes, 1915

———, *A History of Sumer and Akkad*, Stokes, 1923

Maspero, G. C., *The Dawn of Civilization*, Appleton-Century, 4th ed., 1901

Mendelsohn, I., *Legal Aspects of Slavery in Babylonia, Assyria and Palestine*, privately printed (Williamsport, Pa.), 1932

Moret, A., and Davy, G., *From Tribe to Empire*, Knopf, 1926

Speiser, E. A., *Mesopotamian Origins*, University of Pennsylvania, 1930

Woolley, C. L., *The Sumerians*, Oxford, 1929

———, *Ur of the Chaldees*, Benn, 1930

CHAPTER III: EGYPT UNDER THE OLD AND MIDDLE KINGDOMS

Breasted, J. H., *Ancient Records of Egypt*, Chicago, 1906–07, 5 vols.

———, *Development of Religion and Thought in Ancient Egypt*, Scribner's, 1912

———, *A History of Egypt*, Scribner's, 2nd ed., 1912

Capart, Jean, *Egyptian Art*, Allen & Unwin, 1923

———, *Lectures on Egyptian Art*, University of North Carolina, 1928

Erman, A., *A Handbook of Egyptian Religion*, Dutton, 1907

———, *Life in Ancient Egypt*, Macmillan, 1894

———, *The Literature of the Ancient Egyptians*, Methuen, 1927

Glanville, S. R. K., *Daily Life in Ancient Egypt*, Routledge, 1930

Maspero, G. C., *The Dawn of Civilization*, Appleton-Century, 4th ed., 1901

Moret, A., *The Nile and Egyptian Civilization*, Knopf, 1927

———, and Davy, G., *From Tribe to Empire*, Knopf, 1926

Petrie, W. M. F., *The Arts and Crafts of Ancient Egypt*, Foulis (London), 1923

——, *Social Life in Ancient Egypt*, Houghton Mifflin, 1924

EnSS: "Law: Egyptian" (Seidl)

CHAPTER IV: THE ORIENT IN THE SECOND MILLENNIUM

Syria:

Lods, A., *Israel*, Knopf, 1932

Olmstead, A. T., *History of Palestine and Syria to the Macedonian Conquest*, Scribner's, 1934

Hittites:

Childe, V. G., *The Aryans: A Study in Indo-European Origins*, Knopf, 1926

Cowley, A. E., *The Hittites*, Oxford, 1926

Delaporte, L., *Les Hittites*, Renaissance du Livre (Paris), 1936

Aegean Civilization:

Baikie, J., *The Sea Kings of Crete*, Black, 4th ed., 1926

Bell, E., *Prehellenic Architecture in the Aegean*, Bell, 1926

Burn, A. R., *Minoans, Philistines and Greeks*, Knopf, 1930

Burrows, R. M., *The Discoveries in Crete*, Dutton, 1907

Childe, V. G., *The Dawn of European Civilization*, Knopf, 1925

Evans, A. J., *The Palace of Minos*, Macmillan, 1921–35, 4 vols.

Glotz, G., *The Aegean Civilization*, Knopf, 1927

Hall, H. R. H., *The Civilization of Greece in the Bronze Age*, Methuen, 1928

Hawes, C. H. and H. B., *Crete: The Forerunner of Greece*, Harper, 4th ed., 1922

Nilsson, M. P., *Homer and Mycenae*, Methuen, 1933

——, *The Minoan-Mycenaean Religion and Its Survival in Greek Religion*, Gleerup (Lund), 1927

Ridgeway, W., *The Early Age of Greece*, Macmillan, 1901–31, 2 vols.

CHAPTER V: CONFLICT OF EMPIRES

Egypt (see also under Chap. III):

Capart, J., *Thebes*, Allen, 1926

Maspero, G. C., *The Struggle of the Nations*, Appleton-Century, 1897

Pendlebury, J. D. S., *Tell-el Amarna*, Dickson & Thompson (London), 1935

Syria:

Albright, W. F., *The Archaeology of Palestine and the Bible* Revell, 3rd ed., 1935

Barton, G. A., *Archaeology and the Bible,* American Sunday School Union, 6th ed., 1933

Bevan, E. R., and Singer, C., *The Legacy of Israel,* Oxford, 1928

Bewer, J. A., *The Literature of the Old Testament in Its Historical Development,* Columbia, rev. ed., 1933

Contenau, G., *La civilisation phénicienne,* Payot (Paris), 1926

Foakes-Jackson, F. J., *Biblical History of the Hebrews to the Christian Era,* Heffer (Cambridge), 1921

Graham, W. G., *The Prophets and Israel's Culture,* Chicago, 1934

Jack, J. W., *The Ras Shamra Tablets; Their Bearing on the Old Testament,* Clark (Edinburgh), 1935

Kent, C. F., *A History of the Hebrew People,* Scribner's, 1922–23, 2 vols.

Kittel, R., *The Religion of the People of Israel,* Macmillan, 1925

Lods, A., *Israel,* Knopf, 1932

———, *The Prophets and the Rise of Judaism,* Kegan Paul, 1937

Macalister, R. A. S., *The Philistines,* Milford, 1914

Meek, T. J., *Hebrew Origins,* Harper, 1936

Moore, G. F., *The Literature of the Old Testament,* Holt, 1913

Olmstead, A. T., *History of Palestine and Syria,* Scribner's, 1931

Smith, John M. P., *The Origin and History of the Hebrew Law,* Chicago, 1931

Smith, W. Robertson, *Lectures on the Religion of the Semites,* Macmillan, 3rd ed., 1927

Sprengling, M., *The Alphabet: Its Rise and Development from the Sinai Inscriptions,* Chicago, 1931

Ullman, B. L., *Ancient Writing and Its Influence,* Longmans, Green, 1932

EnSS: "Law: Jewish" (Gulak)

Assyria (see also under Chap. II):

Driver, G. R., and Miles, J. C., *The Assyrian Laws,* Oxford, 1935

Johns, C. H. W., *Assyrian Deeds and Documents,* Cambridge, 1898–1923, 4 vols.

Mallowan, M. E. L., and Rose, J. C., *Prehistoric Assyria,* Oxford, 1935

Maspero, G. C., *The Passing of the Empires,* Appleton-Century, 1900

Mendelsohn, I., *Legal Aspects of Slavery in Babylonia, Assyria and Palestine,* privately printed (Williamsport, Pa.), 1932

Olmstead, A. T., *History of Assyria,* Scribner's, 1923

Smith, Sidney, *Early History of Assyria,* Dutton, 1928

Waterman, L., *Royal Correspondence of the Assyrian Empire,* University of Michigan, 1930–36, 4 vols.

The New Orient:

Cameron, G. G., *History of Early Iran,* Chicago, 1936
Herzfeld, E., *Archaeological History of Iran,* Milford, 1935
Hogarth, D. G., *Ionia and the East,* Oxford, 1909
Huart, C., *Ancient Persia and Iranian Civilization,* Knopf, 1927
Jackson, A. V. W., *Zoroaster, the Prophet of Ancient Iran,* Macmillan, 1899
Rogers, R. W., *A History of Ancient Persia,* Scribner's, 1929
Ross, E. D., *The Persians,* Oxford, 1931
Sykes, P. M., *A History of Persia,* Macmillan, 3rd ed., 1930, 2 vols.

GENERAL WORKS ON GREEK HISTORY

Beloch, K. J., *Griechische Geschichte,* Trübner (Strassburg), 2nd ed., 1912–27, 4 vols.
Botsford, G. W., *Hellenic History,* Macmillan, 1923
Bury, J. B., *A History of Greece to the Death of Alexander the Great,* Macmillan, 2nd ed., 1913
Glotz, G., *Histoire grecque,* Les Presses Universitaires (Paris), 1925–36, 3 vols.
Grote, G., *A History of Greece,* Dutton, 1906, 12 vols.
Jardé, A., *The Formation of the Greek People,* Knopf, 1926
Laistner, M. L. W., *Greek History,* Heath, 1932
Robinson, C. E., *A History of Greece,* Crowell, 1929
Whibley, L., *A Companion to Greek Studies,* Macmillan, 4th ed., 1931
EnSS: "Greek Culture and Thought" (Westermann)

SOURCE COLLECTIONS

Bakewell, C. M., *Source Book in Ancient Philosophy,* Scribner's, 1907
Botsford, G. W., and Sihler, E. G., *Hellenic Civilization,* Columbia, 1915
Brock, A. J., *Greek Medicine,* Dutton, 1929
Cary, Max, *Documentary Sources of Greek History,* Blackwell, 1927
Cornford, F. M., *Greek Religious Thought from Homer to the Age of Alexander,* Dutton, 1923
Howe, G., and Harrer, G. A., *Greek Literature in Translation,* Harper, 1924
Laistner, M. L. W., *Greek Economics,* Dutton, 1923
Livingstone, R. W., *The Pageant of Greece,* Oxford, 1923
————, *The Mission of Greece,* Oxford, 1928
Toynbee, A. J., *Greek Civilisation and Character,* Dutton, 1924
————, *Greek Historical Thought from Homer to the Age of Heraclitus,* Dutton, 1924
Warmington, E. H., *Greek Geography,* Dutton, 1934

POLITICAL AND ECONOMIC LIFE

Andreades, A. M., *A History of Greek Public Finance,* Harvard, 1933, Vol. I only

Bonner, R. J., and Smith, G. V., *The Administration of Justice from Homer to Aristotle,* Chicago, 1930

Calhoun, G. M., *The Ancient Greeks and the Evolution of Standards in Business,* Houghton Mifflin, 1926
  ——, *The Growth of Criminal Law in Ancient Greece,* University of California, 1927

Fowler, W. W., *The City-State of the Greeks and Romans,* Macmillan, 1893

Fustel de Coulanges, N. D., *The Ancient City,* Lothrop, 12th ed., 1901

Glotz, G., *Ancient Greece at Work,* Knopf, 1926
  ——, *The Greek City and Its Institutions,* Knopf, 1930

Greenidge, A. H. J., *A Handbook of Greek Constitutional History,* Macmillan, 1902

Halliday, W. R., *The Growth of the City-State,* Small, Maynard, 1923

Hasebroek, J., *Trade and Politics in Ancient Greece,* Bell, 1933

Headlam, J. W., *Election by Lot at Athens,* Cambridge, 2nd ed., 1933

Heitland, W. E., *Agricola,* Cambridge, 1921

Knorringa, H., *Emporos: Data on Trade and Trader in Greek Literature from Homer to Aristotle,* H. J. Paris (Amsterdam), 1926

Ormerod, H. A., *Piracy in the Ancient World,* University of Liverpool, 1924

Phillipson, C., *The International Law and Custom of Ancient Greece and Rome,* Macmillan, 1911, 2 vols.

Seltman, C., *Greek Coins,* Methuen, 1933

Tod, M. N., *International Arbitration among the Greeks,* Oxford, 1913
  ——, *Sidelights on Greek History,* Blackwell, 1932

Trever, A. A., *A History of Greek Economic Thought,* University of Chicago, 1916

Vinogradoff, P., *Outlines of Historical Jurisprudence,* Vol. II, *The Greek City,* Oxford, 1922

Zimmern, A. E., *The Greek Commonwealth,* Oxford, 5th ed., 1931

EnSS: "City-State" (Piganiol); "Law: Greek" (Weiss); "Public Domain, General" (Heichelheim)

CULTURE

Anderson, W. J., Spiers, R. P., and Dinsmoor, W. B., *The Architecture of Ancient Greece,* Scribner's, 1927

Beazley, J. D., and Ashmole, B., *Greek Sculpture and Painting,* Macmillan, 1932

Blumner, H., *The Home Life of the Ancient Greeks,* Cassell, 3rd ed., 1910

Bowra, C. M., *Greek Literature,* Holt, 1933

Burnet, J., *Early Greek Philosophy,* Black, 4th ed., 1930

———, *Greek Philosophy, Thales to Plato,* Macmillan, 1914, Vol. I only

Bury, J. B., *The Ancient Greek Historians,* Macmillan, 1909

Buschor, E., *Greek Vase-Painting,* Dutton, 1922

Cook, A. B., *Zeus,* Cambridge, 1914–25, 2 vols.

Cornford, F. M., *The Origin of Attic Comedy,* Arnold, 1914

Croiset, A. and M., *An Abridged History of Greek Literature,* Macmillan, 1904

Croiset, M., *Hellenic Civilization,* Knopf, 1925

Fairbanks, A., *A Handbook of Greek Religion,* American, 1910

Farnell, L. R., *The Cults of the Greek States,* Oxford, 1896–1909, 5 vols.

———, *Outline-History of Greek Religion,* Duckworth, rev. ed., 1921

Flickinger, R. C., *The Greek Theater and Its Drama,* Chicago, 4th ed., 1936

Fowler, H. N., and Wheeler, J. R., *A Handbook of Greek Archaeology,* American, 1909

Freeman, K. J., *The Schools of Hellas,* Macmillan, 3rd ed., 1922

Gardiner, E. N., *Athletics of the Ancient World,* Oxford, 1930

Gardner, E. A., *A Handbook of Greek Sculpture,* Macmillan, 2nd ed., 1915

Gardner, Percy, *The Principles of Greek Art,* Macmillan, 1914

Gomperz, T., *The Greek Thinkers: A History of Ancient Philosophy,* Scribner's, 1901–12, 4 vols.

Gulick, C. B., *The Life of the Ancient Greeks,* Appleton-Century, 1902

Harrison, J. E., *Mythology,* Longmans, Green, 1924

———, *Prolegomena to the Study of Greek Religion,* Cambridge, 3rd ed., 1922

Livingstone, R. W., *The Legacy of Greece,* Oxford, 1921

Mackail, J. W., *Lectures on Greek Poetry,* Longmans, Green, new ed., 1926

Mahaffy, J. P., *Social Life in Greece from Homer to Menander,* Macmillan, 7th ed., 1890

Moore, C. H., *The Religious Thought of the Greeks from Homer to the Triumph of Christianity,* Harvard, 2nd ed., 1925

Murray, G., *Five Stages of Greek Religion,* Oxford, 1925

———, *A History of Ancient Greek Literature,* Appleton-Century, 1897

Nilsson, M. P., *A History of Greek Religion,* Oxford, 1925

Norwood, G., *Greek Comedy,* Luce, 1932

———, *Greek Tragedy,* Methuen, 2nd ed., 1928

Richter, G. M. A., *The Craft of Athenian Pottery,* Yale, 1923

———, *The Sculpture and Sculptors of the Greeks,* Yale, 2nd ed., 1930

Ridder, A. H. P., and Deonna, W., *Art in Greece,* Knopf, 1927

Robin, L., *Greek Thought and the Origins of the Scientific Spirit*, Knopf, 1928

Robinson, C. E., *Everyday Life in Ancient Greece*, Oxford, 1933

Rohde, E., *Psyche*, Harcourt, Brace, 1925

Rose, H. J., *A Handbook of Greek Literature from Homer to the Age of Lucian*, Methuen, 1934

————, *A Handbook of Greek Mythology*, Dutton, 1928

Sheppard, J. T., *Greek Tragedy*, Cambridge, 1911

Singer, C. J., *Greek Biology and Greek Medicine*, Oxford, 1922

Swindler, M. H., *Ancient Painting*, Yale, 1929

Van Hook, L., *Greek Life and Thought*, Columbia, 2nd ed., 1930

Ward, C. O., *The Ancient Lowly*, Kerr, 5th ed., 1910, 2 vols.

Zeller, E., *Outlines of the History of Greek Philosophy*, Harcourt, Brace, 1931

Zielinski, T., *The Religion of Ancient Greece*, Oxford, 1926

BOOKS OF INTERPRETATION

Burns, C. D., *Greek Ideals*, Bell, 2nd ed., 1919

Cooper, L., *The Greek Genius and Its Influence*, Yale, 1917

Dickinson, G. L., *The Greek View of Life*, Doubleday, Doran, 7th ed., 1925

Earp, F. R., *The Way of the Greeks*, Oxford, 1929

Greene, W. C., *The Achievement of Greece*, Harvard, 1923

Hamilton, Edith, *The Greek Way*, Norton, 1930

Livingstone, R. W., *The Greek Genius and Its Meaning to Us*, Oxford, 2nd ed., 1915

Stobart, J. C., *The Glory That Was Greece*, Sidgwick & Jackson, 3rd ed., 1933

CHAPTER VI: RISE OF THE HELLENES

(See also under Chaps. IV and V)

Sources: Homer, *Iliad, Odyssey*
            Homeric Hymns

Allen, T. W., *Homer: The Origins and the Transmission*, Oxford, 1924

Chadwick, H. M., *The Heroic Age*, Cambridge, 1912

Lang, A., *The World of Homer*, Longmans, Green, 1910

Leaf, W., *Homer and History*, Macmillan, 1915

————, *Troy: A Study in Homeric Geography*, Macmillan, 1912

Murray, G., *The Rise of the Greek Epic*, Oxford, 3rd ed., 1924

Myres, J. L., *Who Were the Greeks?* University of California, 1930

Rose, H. J., *Primitive Culture in Greece*, Doubleday, Doran, 1925

Scott, J. A., *Homer and His Influence*, Longmans, Green, 1925

Scott, J. A., *The Unity of Homer,* University of California, 1921
Seymour, T. D., *Life in the Homeric Age,* Macmillan, 1907
Thomson, J. A. K., *Greeks and Barbarians,* Macmillan, 1921

CHAPTERS VII–X: THE CITY-STATES

Sources: Aeschylus, *Persians*
    Aristotle, *The Constitution of the Athenians*
    Herodotus (especially Books V–IX)
    Hesiod, *Works and Days, Theogony*
    Plutarch, *Lives of Aristides, Lycurgus, Solon, Themistocles,* and
       Theseus
    Xenophon, *The Constitution of the Lacedaemonians*

    Edmonds, J. M. (ed.), *Lyra Graeca* (in Loeb Classical Library),
       Harvard, 1922–27, 3 vols.; 2nd ed. of Vol. I, 1928

Bowra, C. M., *Greek Lyric Poetry from Alcman to Simonides,* Oxford,
    1935
Burn, A. R., *The World of Hesiod,* Kegan Paul, 1936
Carpenter, R., *The Greeks in Spain,* Longmans, Green, 1925
Freeman, E. A., *The History of Sicily from the Earliest Times,* Oxford,
    1891–94, 4 vols.
Freeman, K., *The Work and Life of Solon,* with a Translation of His
    Poems, Milford, 1926
Grundy, G. B., *The Great Persian War and Its Preliminaries,* Murray, 1901
Linforth, I. M., *Solon, the Athenian,* University of California, 1919
Minns, E. H., *Scythians and Greeks,* Cambridge, 1913
Randall-MacIver, D., *Greek Cities in Italy and Sicily,* Oxford, 1931
Rostovtzeff, M. I., *Iranians and Greeks in South Russia,* Oxford, 1922
Seltman, C. T., *Athens: Its History and Coinage before the Persian Inva-
    sion,* Macmillan, 1924
Ure, P. N., *The Greek Renaissance,* Methuen, 1921
————, *The Origin of Tyranny,* Macmillan, 1922
Whibley, L., *Greek Oligarchies, Their Character and Organisation,* Put-
    nam's, 1896
EnSS: "Solon" (Glotz)

CHAPTERS XI–XIII: ATHENS IN THE DAYS OF HER GLORY

Sources: Aristotle, *The Constitution of the Athenians*
    Plato, *Apology, Crito*
    Plutarch, *Lives of Alcibiades, Cimon, Lysander, Nicias,* and
       Pericles

Sources: Thucydides

Xenophon, *Memorabilia*

Plays of Aeschylus, Sophocles, Euripides, and Aristophanes

Botsford and Sihler, *Hellenic Civilization,* Chaps. VI–XI

Barker, E., *Greek Political Theory: Plato and His Predecessors,* Methuen, 1918

Bonner, R. J., *Aspects of Athenian Democracy,* University of California, 1911

———, *Lawyers and Litigants in Ancient Athens,* Chicago, 1927

Calhoun, G. M., *The Business Life of Ancient Athens,* Chicago, 1926

Cochrane, C. N., *Thucydides and the Science of History,* Oxford, 1929

Croiset, M., *Aristophanes and the Political Parties at Athens,* Macmillan, 1909

Davis, W. S., *A Day in Old Athens,* Allyn & Bacon, 1914

Decharme, P., *Euripides and the Spirit of His Dramas,* Macmillan, 1906

D'Ooge, M. L., *The Acropolis at Athens,* Macmillan, 1908

Glover, T. R., *Herodotus,* University of California, 1924

Gomme, A. W., *The Population of Athens in the Fifth and Fourth Centuries B.C.,* Blackwell, 1933

Grundy, G. B., *Thucydides and the History of His Age,* Murray, 1911

Henderson, B. W., *The Great War between Athens and Sparta,* Macmillan, 1927

Laistner, M. L. W., *A History of the Greek World from 479 to 323 B.C.,* Methuen, 1936

Lucas, F. L., *Euripides and His Influence,* Longmans, Green, 1923

Murray, G., *Aristophanes,* Oxford, 1933

———, *Euripides and His Age,* Holt, 1913

Taylor, A. E., *Socrates,* Appleton-Century, 1933

Tucker, T. G., *Life in Ancient Athens,* Macmillan, 1907

Weller, C. H., *Athens and Its Monuments,* Macmillan, 1913

EnSS: "Ostracism" (Mishnun); "Sophists" (Fuller)

CHAPTER XIV: THE FOURTH CENTURY B.C.

(See also under Chaps. XI–XIII)

Sources: Aristotle, *Nichomachean Ethics, Politics, Rhetoric*

Plato, *Laws, Republic*

Plutarch, *Lives of Agesilaus, Demosthenes, Lysander,* and *Pelopidas*

Xenophon, *Agesilaus, Anabasis, Cyropaedia, Hellenica, Ways and Means*

Orations of Aeschines, Andocides, Demosthenes, Isaeus, Isocrates, Lycurgus and Lysias

Barker, E., *The Political Thought of Plato and Aristotle,* Putnam's, 1906
Casson, S., *Macedonia, Thrace and Illyria,* Oxford, 1926
Cornford, F. M., *Before and after Socrates,* Macmillan, 1932
Dobson, J. F., *The Greek Orators,* Dutton, 1919
Field, G. C., *Plato and His Contemporaries,* Methuen, 1930
Glover, T. R., *From Pericles to Philip,* Methuen, 3rd ed., 1919
Grube, G. M. A., *Plato's Thought,* Methuen, 1935
Jaeger, W. W., *Aristotle,* Oxford, 1934
Jebb, R. C., *The Attic Orators from Antiphon to Isaeos,* Macmillan, 2nd ed., 1893, 2 vols.
Marshall, F. H., *The Second Athenian Confederacy,* Cambridge, 1905
Parke, H. W., *Greek Mercenary Soldiers from the Earliest Times to the Battle of Ipsus,* Oxford, 1933
Pickard-Cambridge, A. W., *Demosthenes and the Last Days of Greek Freedom,* Putnam, 1914
Ross, W. D., *Aristotle,* Methuen, 2nd ed., 1930
Shorey, P., *What Plato Said,* Chicago, 1933
Taylor, A. E., *Plato: The Man and His Work,* Dial, 3rd ed., 1929
EnSS: "Cynics" (Eisler); "Cyrenaics" (Eisler)

CHAPTERS XV–XVI: THE HELLENISTIC AGE

Sources: Arrian, *The Anabasis of Alexander*
        Menander
        Plutarch, *Lives of Agis, Alexander, Aratus, Cleomenes, Demetrius, Eumenes,* and *Philopoemon*

        Botsford and Sihler, *Hellenic Civilization,* Chaps. XVI–XIX
        Hunt, A. S., and Edgar, C. C., *Select Papyri* (Loeb Classical Library), Harvard, 1932–34, 4 vols.

Bevan, E. R., *A History of Egypt under the Ptolemaic Dynasty,* Methuen, 1927
———, *The House of Seleucus,* Arnold, 1902, 2 vols.
———, *Stoics and Sceptics,* Oxford, 1913
Bouché-Leclerq, A., *Histoire des Lagides,* Leroux (Paris), 1903–7, 4 vols.
Bury, J. B., and Others, *The Hellenistic Age,* Macmillan, 1923
Cary, M., *The Legacy of Alexander: A History of the Greek World from 323 to 146 B.C.,* Methuen, 1932
———, and Warmington, E. H., *The Ancient Explorers,* Dodd, Mead, 1929
Dickins, G., *Hellenistic Sculpture,* Oxford, 1920
Ferguson, W. S., *Greek Imperialism,* Houghton Mifflin, 1913
———, *Hellenistic Athens,* Macmillan, 1911

Freeman, E. A., *History of the Federal Government in Greece and Italy,* Macmillan, 2nd ed., 1893

Fyfe, T., *Hellenistic Architecture,* Macmillan, 1936

Griffith, G. F., *The Mercenaries of the Hellenistic World,* Macmillan, 1935

Haverfield, F. J., *Ancient Town-Planning,* Oxford, 1913

Heath, T. L., *Archimedes,* Macmillan, 1920

——, *Aristarchus of Samos, the Ancient Copernicus,* Oxford, 1913

——, *A History of Greek Mathematics,* Oxford, 1921, 2 vols.

Hicks, R. D., *Stoic and Epicurean,* Scribner's, 1910

Jouguet, P., *Macedonian Imperialism and the Hellenization of the East,* Knopf, 1928

Körte, A., *Hellenistic Poetry,* Columbia, 1929

Laidlaw, W. A., *A History of Delos,* Blackwell, 1933

Le Grand, P. E., *The New Greek Comedy,* Putnam's, 1917

McEwan, C. W., *The Oriental Origin of Hellenistic Kingship,* Chicago, 1934

Macurdy, G. H., *Hellenistic Queens,* Johns Hopkins, 1932

Mahaffy, J. P., *Greek Life and Thought from the Death of Alexander to the Roman Conquest,* Macmillan, 2nd ed., 1896

Powell, J. U., and Barber, E. A., *New Chapters in the History of Greek Literature,* Oxford, 1921-33, 3 vols.

Rostovtzeff, M. I., *A Large Estate in Egypt in the Third Century B.C.,* University of Wisconsin, 1922

Tarn, W. W., *Antigonos Gonatas,* Oxford, 1913

——, *Hellenistic Civilisation,* Arnold, 2nd ed., 1930

——, *Hellenistic Military and Naval Developments,* Cambridge, 1930

Taylor, H. O., *Greek Biology and Medicine,* Longmans, Green, 1922

Winter, J. G., *Life and Letters in the Papyri,* University of Michigan, 1933

Wilcken, U., *Alexander the Great,* Dial, 1932

——, and Mitteis, L., *Grundzüge und Chrestomathie der Papyruskunde,* Teubner (Leipzig), 1912, 4 vols.

EnSS: "Epicureanism" (Mondolfo); "Euhemeros" (Oertel); "Law: Hellenistic and Graeco-Egyptian" (Schiller); "Stoicism" (Barker)

GENERAL BOOKS ON ROMAN HISTORY

Abbott, F. F., *The Common People of Ancient Rome,* Scribner's, 1911

Bloch, G., and Others, *Histoire romaine,* Les Presses Universitaires (Paris), 1926-36, 3 vols.

Boak, A. E. R., *A History of Rome to 565 A.D.,* Macmillan, rev. ed., 1929

Cary, M., *History of Rome down to the Reign of Constantine,* Macmillan, 1935

Ferrero, G., and Barbagallo, C., *A Short History of Rome,* Putnam's, 1918–19, 2 vols.

Frank, T., *A History of Rome,* Holt, 1923

Jones, H. S., *Companion to Roman History,* Oxford, 1912

Moore, F. G., *The Roman's World,* Columbia, 1936

Robinson, C. E., *A History of Rome from 753 B.C. to A.D. 410,* Crowell, 1935

Sandys, J. E., *A Companion to Latin Studies,* Cambridge, 3rd ed., 1925

Showerman, G., *Rome and the Romans,* Macmillan, 1931

EnSS: "The Roman World" (Frank)

SOURCE COLLECTIONS

Bailey, C., *The Mind of Rome,* Oxford, 1926

Bakewell, C. M., *Source Book in Ancient Philosophy,* Scribner's, 1907

Botsford, G. W., *The Story of Rome as Greeks and Romans Tell It,* Macmillan, 1903

Howe, G., and Harrer, G. A., *Roman Literature in Translation,* Harper, 1924

Munro, D. C., *A Source Book of Roman History,* Heath, 1904

POLITICAL AND ECONOMIC LIFE

Abbott, F. F., *A History and Description of Roman Political Institutions,* Ginn, 3rd ed., 1911

——, *Roman Politics,* Longmans, Green, 1923

Buckland, W. W., *The Roman Law of Slavery,* Cambridge, 1908

Fowler, W. W., *The City-State of the Greeks and Romans,* Macmillan, 1893

Frank, T., *An Economic History of Rome,* Johns Hopkins, 2nd ed., 1927

Greenidge, A. H. J., *Roman Public Life,* Macmillan, 1901

Heitland, W. E., *Agricola,* Cambridge, 1921

Homo, L., *Roman Political Institutions from City to State,* Knopf, 1929

Jolowicz, H. F., *Historical Introduction to the Study of Roman Law,* Cambridge, 1932

Louis, P., *Ancient Rome at Work,* Knopf, 1927

Mommsen, T., *Römisches Staatsrecht,* Hirzel (Leipzig), 3rd ed., 1887–88, 3 vols.

Ormerod, H. A., *Piracy in the Ancient World,* University of Liverpool, 1924

Phillipson, C., *The International Law and Custom of Ancient Greece and Rome,* Macmillan, 1911, 2 vols.

Radin, M., *Handbook of Roman Law*, West, 1927
Salvioli, G., *Il capitalismo antico*, Laterza (Bari), 2nd ed., 1929
Schultz, Fritz, *Principles of Roman Law*, Oxford, 1936
Sohm, R., *The Institutes: A Textbook of the History and System of Roman Private Law*, Oxford, 3rd ed., 1907
EnSS: "City-State" (Piganiol); "Jus Gentium" (Radin); "Latifundia" (Piganiol); "Legal Profession, Ancient" (Hazeltine); "Public Domain, General" (Heichelheim); "Roman Law" (Schiller)

CULTURE

Abbott, F. F., *Society and Politics in Ancient Rome*, Scribner's, 1909
Bailey, C., *The Legacy of Rome*, Oxford, 1923
Duff, J. W., *A Literary History of Rome, from the Origins to the Close of the Golden Age*, Unwin, 2nd ed., 1920
Fowler, W. W., *The Religious Experiences of the Roman People*, Macmillan, 1911
Huelsen, C., *The Forum and the Palatine*, Bruderhausen, 1928
Johnston, H. W., *The Private Life of the Romans*, Scott, Foresman, 2nd ed., 1932
Mackail, J. W., *Latin Literature*, Scribner's, 1895
Platner, S. B., and Ashby, T., *A Topographical Dictionary of Ancient Rome*, Oxford, 1929
Strong, E. S., *Art in Ancient Rome*, Scribner's, 1928, 2 vols.
Swindler, M. H., *Ancient Painting*, Yale, 1929
Walters, H. B., *The Art of the Romans*, Methuen, 2nd ed., 1928

BOOKS OF INTERPRETATION

Conway, R. S., *New Studies of a Great Inheritance*, Murray, 2nd ed., 1930
Greene, W. C., *The Achievement of Rome*, Harvard, 1933
Grenier, A., *The Roman Spirit in Religion, Thought, and Art*, Knopf, 1926
Hamilton, E., *The Roman Way*, Norton, 1932
Showerman, G., *Eternal Rome*, Yale, 1924
Stobart, J. C., *The Grandeur That Was Rome*, Sidgwick & Jackson, 2nd ed., 1920

CHAPTER XVII: THE RISE OF ROME

Sources: Livy, Book I
Plutarch, *Lives of Numa* and *Romulus*

Fell, R. A. L., *Etruria and Rome,* Cambridge, 1924
Homo, L., *Primitive Italy and the Beginnings of Roman Imperialism,* Knopf, 1927
Pais, E., *Ancient Italy,* Chicago, 1908
———, *Ancient Legends of Roman History,* Dodd, Mead, 1905
Peet, T. E., *The Stone and Bronze Ages in Italy and Sicily,* Oxford, 1909
Randall-MacIver, D., *The Etruscans,* Oxford, 1927
———, *Italy before the Romans,* Oxford, 1928
Rose, H. J., *Primitive Culture in Italy,* Methuen, 1926
Whatmough, J., *The Foundations of Roman Italy,* Methuen, 1936

CHAPTERS XVIII–XX: THE ROMAN REPUBLIC

Sources: Appian, *Roman History*
    Caesar, *Civil War, Gallic War*
    Cato and Varro on farm management
    Cicero, *Letters, Orations*
    Livy, *History of Rome*
    Plutarch, *Lives of Caesar, Camillus, Cicero, Coriolanus, Crassus, Tiberius and Gaius Gracchus, Lucullus, Marius, Pompey, Poplicola,* and *Sulla*
    Polybius, *History*
    Sallust, *Conspiracy of Catiline, Jugurthine War*

Bailey, C., *Phases in the Religion of Ancient Rome,* University of California, 1932
Beesly, A. H., *The Gracchi, Marius, and Sulla,* Scribner's, 1888
Boissier, G., *Cicero and His Friends,* Putnam's, 1925
Botsford, G. W., *The Roman Assemblies from Their Origin to the End of the Republic,* Macmillan, 1909
Ferrero, G., *The Greatness and Decline of Rome,* Putnam's, 1907–9, 5 vols.
———, *The Life of Caesar,* Putnam's, 1933
Fowler, W. W., *Social Life at Rome in the Age of Cicero,* Macmillan, 1909
Frank, T., *An Economic Survey of Ancient Rome,* Johns Hopkins, 1933, Vol. I
———, *Life and Literature in the Roman Republic,* University of California, 1930
———, *Roman Imperialism,* Macmillan, 1914
Hadzits, G. D., *Lucretius and His Influence,* Longmans, Green, 1935
Hardy, E. G., *The Catilinarian Conspiracy in Its Context,* Blackwell, 1924
Harrington, K. P., *Catullus and His Influence,* Longmans, Green, 1927
Heitland, W. E., *The Roman Republic,* Cambridge, 1909, 3 vols.
———, *A Short History of the Roman Republic,* Cambridge, 1911

Holmes, T. R., *Caesar's Conquest of Gaul*, Oxford, 2nd ed., 1911
———, *The Roman Republic and the Founder of the Empire*, Oxford, 1923, 3 vols.
Homo, L., *Primitive Italy and the Beginnings of Roman Imperialism*, Knopf, 1927
Marsh, F. B., *The Founding of the Roman Empire*, Oxford, 2nd ed., 1927
———, *A History of the Roman World from 146 to 30 B.C.*, Methuen, 1935
Mommsen, T., *The History of Rome*, Scribner's, new ed., 1903–5, 5 vols.
Morris, W. O'C., *Hannibal*, Putnam's, 1897
Oliver, E. H., *Roman Economic Conditions to the Close of the Republic*, University of Toronto, 1907
Park, M. E., *The Plebs in Cicero's Day*, privately printed (Cambridge, Mass.), 1921
Petersson, T., *Cicero*, University of California, 1920
Santayana, G., *Three Philosophical Poets: Lucretius, Dante, and Goethe*, Harvard, 1910
Scullard, H. H., *A History of the Roman World from 753 to 146 B.C.*, Methuen, 1935
Sihler, E. G., *Cicero of Arpinum*, Stechert, 2nd ed., 1933
Sikes, E. E., *Lucretius, Poet and Philosopher*, Cambridge, 1936
Strachan-Davidson, J. L., *Cicero and the Fall of the Roman Republic*, Putnam's, 1898

CHAPTER XXI: THE AGE OF AUGUSTUS

(See also under Chaps. XVIII–XX)

Sources: Appian, *Roman History*
            Augustus, *Res gestae*
            Dio Cassius, *History*
            Horace, *Epodes, Odes, Satires*
            Ovid, *Metamorphoses*
            Virgil, *Aeneid, Eclogues, Georgics*

Conway, R. S., *Harvard Lectures on the Vergilian Age*, Harvard, 1928
Hadas, M., *Sextus Pompey*, Columbia, 1930
Holmes, T. R., *The Architect of the Roman Empire*, Oxford, 1928–31, 2 vols.
Mackail, J. W., *Virgil and His Meaning to the World of Today*, Longmans, Green, 1927
Reinhold, M., *Marcus Agrippa*, privately printed (Geneva, N. Y.), 1933
Sellar, W. Y., *The Roman Poets of the Augustan Age*, Oxford, 2nd and 3rd ed., 1897–99, 2 vols.

Winspear, A. D., and Geweke, L. K., *Augustus and the Reconstruction of Roman Government and Society,* University of Wisconsin, 1935

CHAPTERS XXII–XXIII: HISTORY AND INSTITUTIONS OF THE EARLY EMPIRE

Sources: Dio Cassius, *History*
Josephus, *The Jewish Wars*
Pliny the Younger, *Letters*
Seneca, *Apocolocyntosis*
Scriptores Historiae Augustae
Suetonius, *Lives of the Twelve Caesars*
Tacitus, *Agricola, Annals, Germany, Histories*

Abbott, F. F., and Johnson, A. C., *Municipal Administration in the Roman Empire,* Princeton University, 1926
Arnold, W. T., *The Roman System of Provincial Administration to the Accession of Constantine the Great,* Blackwell, 3rd ed., 1914
Balsdon, J. P. V. D., *The Emperor Gaius,* Oxford, 1934
Barrow, R. H., *Slavery in the Roman Empire,* Methuen, 1928
Bouchier, E. S., *Spain under the Roman Empire,* Blackwell, 1914
———, *Syria as a Roman Province,* Blackwell, 1916
Brewster, E. H., *Roman Craftsmen and Tradesmen of the Early Empire,* privately printed (Menasha, Wis.), 1917
Buckland, W. W., *A Text-Book of Roman Law from Augustus to Justinian,* Macmillan, 2nd ed., 1931
Chapot, V., *The Roman World,* Knopf, 1928
Charlesworth, M. P., *Trade-Routes and Commerce of the Roman Empire,* Cambridge, 2nd ed., 1926
Collingwood, R. G., *Roman Britain,* Oxford, 2nd ed., 1932
Duff, A. M., *Freedmen in the Early Roman Empire,* Oxford, 1928
Fustel de Coulanges, N. D., *Histoire des institutions politiques de l'ancienne France,* Vol. I, *La Gaule romaine,* Hachette (Paris), 5th ed., 1922
Hammond, M., *The Augustan Principate in Theory and Practice during the Julio-Claudian Period,* Harvard, 1933
Haverfield, F. J., *The Romanization of Roman Britain,* Oxford, 4th ed., 1923
Henderson, B. W., *Civil War and Rebellion in the Roman Empire, A.D. 69–70,* Macmillan, 1908
———, *Five Roman Emperors: Vespasian, Titus, Domitian, Nerva, Trajan, A.D. 69–117,* Cambridge, 1927
———, *The Life and Principate of the Emperor Hadrian, A.D. 76–138,* Methuen, 1923
Johnson, A. C., *An Economic Survey of Ancient Rome,* Vol. II, *Roman Egypt,* Johns Hopkins, 1936

Juster, J., *Les juifs dans l'empire romain*, Geuthner (Paris), 1914, 2 vols.

Marsh, F. B., *The Reign of Tiberius*, Oxford, 1931

Mattingly, H., *The Imperial Civil Service of Rome*, Cambridge, 1910

———, *Roman Coins from the Earliest Times to the Fall of the Western Empire*, Methuen, 1928

———, and Sydenham, E. A., *The Roman Imperial Coinage*, Spink, 1923– , vols. I–III, IV^1, V^1

Momigliano, A., *Claudius: The Emperor and His Achievement*, Oxford, 1934

Mommsen, T., *The Provinces of the Roman Empire from Caesar to Diocletian*, Scribner's, new ed., 1909, 2 vols.

Nilsson, M. P., *Imperial Rome*, Harcourt, Brace, 1926

Parker, H. M. D., *A History of the Roman World from A.D. 138 to 337*, Methuen, 1935

———, *The Roman Legions*, Oxford, 1928

Reid, J. S., *The Municipalities of the Roman Empire*, Cambridge, 1913

Rostovtzeff, M. I., *Caravan Cities*, Oxford, 1932

———, *The Social and Economic History of the Roman Empire*, Oxford, 1926

Schürer, E., *A History of the Jewish People in the Time of Jesus Christ*, Scribner's, 2nd ed., 1890–91, 5 vols.

Sedgwick, H. D., *Marcus Aurelius*, Yale, 1921

Stevenson, G. H., *The Roman Empire*, Nelson, 1930

Warmington, E. H., *The Commerce between the Roman Empire and India*, Cambridge, 1928

CHAPTERS XXII–XXIII (*continued*): CULTURE OF THE EARLY EMPIRE

Sources: Dio Chrysostom, *Orations*
Josephus, *Antiquities of the Jews*
Juvenal, *Satires*
Lucian, *Dialogues*
Marcus Aurelius, *Meditations*
Petronius, *Satyricon*
Seneca, *Essays, Letters*

Allbutt, T. C., *Greek Medicine in Rome*, Macmillan, 1921

Anderson, W. J., and Spiers, R. P., *The Architecture of Ancient Rome*, Scribner's, rev. ed., 1927

Angus, S., *The Mystery-Religions and Christianity*, Scribner's, 1925

Ayer, J. C., *A Source Book for Ancient Church History*, Scribner's, 1913

Bevan, E. R., *Jerusalem under the High Priests*, Arnold, 1930

Bouchier, E. S., *Life and Letters in Roman Africa*, Blackwell, 1913

Cadoux, C. J., *The Early Church and the World*, Clark, 1925

Carrington, R. C., *Pompeii*, Oxford, 1936

Carlyle, R. W. and A. J., *A History of Mediaeval Political Theory in the West*, Putnam's, 1903, Vol. I

Charlesworth, M. P., *Five Men: Character Studies from the Roman Empire*, Harvard, 1936

Cumont, F., *The Mysteries of Mithra*, Open Court, 2nd ed., 1910

——, *The Oriental Religions in Roman Paganism*, Open Court, 1911

Davis, W. S., *The Influence of Wealth in Imperial Rome*, Macmillan, 1910

Dill, S., *Roman Society from Nero to Marcus Aurelius*, Macmillan, 2nd ed., 1905

Duchesne, L. M. O., *Early History of the Christian Church*, Longmans, Green, 1922–26, 3 vols.

Dudden, H., *The Life and Times of St. Ambrose*, Oxford, 1935, 2 vols.

Duff, J. W., *A Literary History of Rome in the Silver Age*, Scribner's, 1927

——, *Roman Satire: Its Outlook on Social Life*, University of California, 1936

Eisler, R., *The Messiah Jesus and John the Baptist*, Macveagh, 1931

Friedländer, L., *Roman Life and Manners under the Early Empire*, Dutton, 1908–13, 4 vols.

Glover, T. R., *The Conflict of Religions in the Early Roman Empire*, Methuen, 9th ed., 1920

Gummere, R. M., *Seneca the Philosopher and His Modern Message*, Longmans, Green, 1922

Gwynn, A. O., *Roman Education from Cicero to Quintilian*, Oxford, 1926

Halliday, W. R., *The Pagan Background of Early Christianity*, University of Liverpool, 1925

Hardy, E. G., *Christianity and the Roman Government*, Longmans, Green, 1894

Harnack, A., *The Expansion of Christianity in the First Three Centuries*, Putnam's, 1904–5, 2 vols.

Hatch, E., *The Influences of Greek Ideas and Usages upon the Christian Church*, Williams and Norgate, 8th ed., 1901

——, *The Organization of the Early Christian Churches*, Longmans, Green, 1918

Kidd, B. J., *A History of the Church to A.D. 461*, Oxford, 1922, 3 vols.

——, *The Roman Primacy to A.D. 461*, Macmillan, 1936

Lanciani, R., *The Ruins and Excavations of Ancient Rome*, Houghton Mifflin, 1897

Lowrie, W., *Monuments of the Early Church*, Macmillan, 1923

Mahaffy, J. P., *The Silver Age of the Greek World*, Chicago, 1906

Mau, A., *Pompeii, Its Life and Art*, Macmillan, new ed., 1902

Nock, A. D., *Conversion: The Old and the New in Religion from Alexander the Great to Augustine of Hippo,* Oxford, 1933

Ramsay, W. M., *The Church in the Roman Empire before A.D. 170,* Putnam's, 3rd ed., 1894

Streeter, B. H., *The Primitive Church,* Macmillan, 1929

Strong, E. S., *Roman Sculpture from Augustus to Constantine,* Scribner's, 1907

Taylor, L. R., *The Divinity of the Roman Emperor,* [American Philological Association; Philological Monographs, no. 1, 1931]

Thackeray, H. St. J., *Josephus: The Man and the Historian,* Jewish Institute of Religion (New York), 1929

Thorndike, L., *A History of Magic and Experimental Science,* Macmillan, 1923, Vol. I

Troeltsch, E., *The Social Teaching of the Christian Churches,* Macmillan, 1931, Vol. I

Tucker, T. G., *Life in the Roman World of Nero and St. Paul,* Macmillan, 1910

Whittaker, T., *The Neo-Platonists,* Cambridge, 2nd ed., 1918

EnSS: "Epictetus" (Eisler); "Messianism" (Kohn); "Mysteries" (Nock)

CHAPTER XXIV: THE LAST CENTURY OF THE ROMAN EMPIRE

(See also under Chaps. XXII–XXIII)

Arragon, R. F., *The Transition from the Ancient to the Medieval World,* Holt, 1936

Bury, J. B., *The Invasion of Europe by the Barbarians,* Macmillan, 1928

Cambridge Medieval History, edited by M. Gwatkin and Others, Macmillan, 1911, Vol. I

Dill, S., *Roman Society in the Last Century of the Western Empire,* Macmillan, 2nd ed., 1905

Ferrero, G., *The Ruin of Ancient Civilization and the Triumph of Christianity,* Putnam's, 1921

Gibbon, E., *The History of the Decline and Fall of the Roman Empire,* ed. by J. B. Bury, Macmillan, 1900–2, 7 vols.

Heitland, W. E., *The Roman Fate,* Cambridge, 1922

Hodgkin, T., *Italy and Her Invaders,* Oxford, new ed., 1916, 8 vols.

Lot, F., *The End of the Ancient World,* Knopf, 1931

Mickwitz, G., *Geld und wirtschaft im Römischen reich des vierten jahrhunderts, n. Chr.,* Centraltryckeri (Helsingfors), 1932

Moss, H. St. L. B., *The Birth of the Middle Ages, 395–814,* Oxford, 1935

Seeck, O., *Geschichte des Untergangs der antiken Welt,* Metzler (Stuttgart), 1897–1921, 6 vols.

INDEX

References to complete discussions are italicized

Abdera, 181, 257
Abdkhiba, 87
Abraham, 33, 98, 525
Abu Simbel, 94, 108
Abydos, in Egypt, 94; in Asia Minor, 134
Abyssinia, 39
Academus, Grove of, 282
Academy, 241, *283, 318*
Acarnania, 118
Achaea, 118, 120, 132; province of, 444
Achaean League, *297, 302*, 305, 310, 315, 375-377
Achaeans, 78, 81, 89, 120, 158, 200
Acheulean, 4, 6-8, 42
Achilles, 121, 123, 255
Acragas, 132, 192 f., 256, 367
Acropolis, 124; Athenian, 156, 163, 239 f., 244
Actium, 423 f., 437
Adonis, 322; Feast of, 313
Advocati fisci, 468
Aediles, 350, 354
Aeduan, 455
Aegates Islands, 368
Aegean civilization, 68-81: discovery of, 68; chronology, 69; race, 69; New Stone Age, 69; history, 70; culture, 71-77; Mycenaean period, 77-81
Aegean Sea, geography of, 115
Aegina, 132, 139 f., 160, 187, 189, 200, 244
Aeginetan standard, 139
Aegospotami, 209, 211
Aelia Capitolina, 479
Aelius, 430
Aemilius Paullus, 372; son of, 376 f., 385
Aeneas, 334, 337
Aeneid, 447, 450
Aeolians, 78
Aeolis, 120, 127
Aequians, 333, 345
Aerarium militare, 444, 468

Aerarium Saturni, 468
Aeschines, 281, 295
Aeschylus, 193, 195, 246, 248 f.
Aesculapius, 505
Aethiopians, 89
Aetna, 325
Aetolia, 118, 262
Aetolian League, 305, 375
Agamemnon, 68, 248
Agariste of Sicyon, 144, 163, 212, 237, 259
Agariste of Athens, 259
Agathocles, 304
Age of Pericles, 199-204
Agesilaus, 264 f., 274
Agis IV, 296 f., 310, 394
Agora, 229
Agricola, 459, 467, 489, 500
Agriculture: discovery of, 14; Sumerian, 27; Babylonian, 33; Egyptian, 52, 92; Greek, 126, 129, 160, 222, 277; Roman, 327, 380, 444, 484, 517
Agrigentum, 367
Agrippa, 420, 423, 440, 448
Agrippa, Herod, 478, 479
Agrippina, elder, 454-456; younger, 456, 499
Aha, 45
Ahab, 101
Ahmose, 83, 90
Ahriman, 113
Ahura Mazda, 113, 506, 511
Akhetaton, 86, 88
Akkad, 29, 31
Alba Longa, 334-336
Alcaeus, 141, 146, 180, 289, 313
Alcibiades, 144, 207, 258
Alcmaeonidae, 144, 160, 162, 164, 185 f., 188
Alcman, 181
Alemanni, 511
Alesia, 412
Alexander, 290 f., 271, 273 f., 283, 286,

288, 294, 296, 300, 302 f., 309, 311, 319, 476
Alexander Severus, 510, 525
Alexandria, 85, 185, 283, 290 f., 293, *304*, 302-318 *passim;* 416, 422, 478 f., 481 f., 526
Allia River, 346
Allobroges, 410
Alphabet, Phoenician, 24, 75, 97, 179; Greek, 179, 332; Ionic, 179, 275
Alpheus River, 131
Alpine race, 17, 64
Altamira, 11
Altar of Augustan Peace, 448, 498
Amasis, 108, 135, 147
Amazons, 243, 245
Amenemhet, 57
Amenhotep III, 84, 91
Amenhotep IV, 85
Ammianus Marcellinus, 324
Amon, 52, 59, 86, 90, 93 f., 182, 290; Amon-Re, 59, 93, 291, 303
Amorites, 30 f., 64, 67
Amos, 102
Amphictyonic Council, 272
Amphictyony of Delos, Ionian, 144, 300
Amphictyony of Delphi, 145
Amphipolis, 206
Amphissa, 273
Amphitheaters, 497
Amraphel, 62
Amyclae, 149
Anabasis, 263, 279, 288
Anacreon, 147, 163, 181
Anatolia, 110, 146, 290, 298, 322, 403, 447, 493
Anaxagoras, 237, 256
Anaxilaus, 191
Anaximander, 182, 184
Anaximenes, 182 f.
Ancus Martius, 336 f.
Andromache, 123
Androtion, 281
Animals, domestication of, 14
Anio River, 362
Anio Vetus, aqueduct of, 362
Anthesteria, 235
Anthropomorphism, 170
Antigone, 248 f.
Antigonus, 286, 294, 297, 299, 300, 302
Antigonus Gonatas, 298
Antigonus Doson, 296

Antioch, 301-310 *passim,* 481 f., 494
Antiochus III, 300, 302, 375 f., 476
Antiochus IV, 302, 376 f., 476
Antipater, 295
Antipater, the Idumaean, 477
Antiphon, 208
Antisthenes, 319
Antonines, Age of, 460-463
Antoninus Pius, 462, 470, 494
Antonius, 409
Antonius, Lucius, 411
Antony, Mark, 415-428 *passim,* 477
Anu, 35
Anubis, 322
Apamea, 301
Apaturia, 229, 235
Apella, 155
Apelles, 285 f.
Ape man of Java, 6 f.
Apennines, 191, 325
Aphaia, 244
Aphrodite, 143, 168, 232, 285, 322
Aphrodite of Melos, 285, 311 f.
Apis, 322
Apocalyptic, 476
Apoikia, 130
Apology of Socrates, 282
Apollo, 117 f., 130, 143-145, 147, 148, 160, 168 f., 171 f., 175, 181, 188, 198, 202, 248, 258, 300 f., 311, 439, 448
Apollo Belvedere, 312
Apollonius of Perge, 317
Apollonius of Rhodes, 313
Apollonius of Tyana, 504, 510
Apostles, 506
Apoxyomenos, 285
Appian, 502
Appian Way, 347, 359, 361, 414, 491
Appius Claudius, 349, 359, 361-364, 394 f., 430
Apuleius, 500
Apulia, 372
Aqua Anio Novus, 455
Aqua Appia, 362, 364
Aqua Claudia, 455
Aquae Sextiae, 400
Arabia, 22 f., 28, 98, 308, 445 f., 483
Arabia Petraea, 461
Arai, 240
Aramaeans, 62, 97
Aramaic, 97
Aratus, 296 f.

Aratus of Soli, 313
Arausio, 399
Arbela, 291
Arcadia, 118, 131, 262, 274, 279
Arcadians, 262, 268
Arch of Constantine, 524
Arch of Titus, 498
Archelaus, 271
Archias, 132
Archidamian War, 206
Archidamus, 206
Archilochus, 180
Archimedes, 317 f., 372
Architecture: Sumerian, 27; Egyptian, 54,
    58, 94; Hittite, 66; Minoan, 71; My-
    cenaean, 79; Assyrian, 107; Persian,
    112; Greek, 174, 239, 285, 311; Etrus-
    can, 331; Roman, 448, 496, 524
Architrave, 177
Archon, 159, 216
Arctic Ocean, 316
Areopagus, Council of, 159, 162, 166, 186,
    197-199, 216, 248, 295
Areopagus, hill of, 240
Ares, 168, 240
Arethusa, 131
Arginusae, 208, 225
Argolis, 118, 120
Argonauts, 81, 134, 313
Argos, 118, 126, 148, 155, 173, 200
Ariadne, 71
Aricia, 332, 342
Ariminum, 371
Arion, 143
Aristagoras, 185
Aristarchus, 316
Aristides, 186, 189, 190, 195, 197 f., 249
Aristides (rhetorician), 480
Aristobulus, 477
Aristodemus of Messene, 150
Aristodemus of Cumae, 332
Aristogeiton, 163, 244
Aristophanes, 222, 231, 251, 257, 278, 313
Aristotle, 217, 246, 248, 256, 275, 282,
    283 f., 290, 316, 318
Arles, 495
Armenia, 22 f., 65, 409, 445, 454, 461 f.,
    512
Arminius, 446
Army: Sumerian, 28; Babylonian, 32;
    Egyptian, 47, 57, 90, 93; Minoan, 75;
    Assyrian, 105; Persian, 112; Greek, 121,

141, 153, 219, 262, 272; Roman, 359,
    399, 443, 471, 522
Arno, 327
Arpinum, 398, 406
Arretine ware, 447
Arretium, 371
Arrian, 288, 461, 502
Arsinoe, 302
Art: palaeolithic, 11; Sumerian, 27; Baby-
    lonian, 34; Egyptian, 54, 58, 86, 109;
    Minoan, 75; Assyrian, 107; Greek, 178,
    285, 311; Roman, 388, 448, 498, 524
Artaphernes, 186
Artaxerxes I, 201
Artaxerxes II, 263
Artemis, 124, 146, 168 f., 286
Artemis Brauronia, 235
Artemis of the Ephesians, 169
Artemis Orthia, 150, 152
Artemisia, 285
Artemisium, 189
Aryans, 65
As, 362
Asclepius, 240, 254 f., 505
Asculum, 347, 364
Ashtoreth, 63
Asia, 204, 494
Asia, Seleucid, 294, 298, 300-302, 307,
    375, 378
Asia, province of, 377, 401 f., 444, 472
Asia Minor: New Stone Age in, 18, 23 f.;
    Hittites in, 65; Phrygians in, 65, 89;
    Persian conquest of, 111; Greeks in,
    120; war in, 264; Alexander's conquest
    of, 290; Pergamum in, 298; cities of,
    129, 146-148, 185, 264, 290; Roman
    province in, 377
Asiatic War, 376, 385
Asoka, 301
Aspasia, 232, 251
Asshur, 104, 107
Assurbanipal, 105, 108
Assurnasirpal II, 104
Assyria, 67, 104-107
Assyrians, 37, 67, 89, 102, 138
Astarte, 35
Astrology, 34, 108, 321
Astronomy, 316
Astyages, 110
Athena, 79, 124, 139, 163, 168, 188, 197,
    202, 235-237, 241
Athena of the Brazen House, 150

Athena Ergane, 169
Athena Hygeia, 168
Athena Nike, 242
Athena Parthenos, 168, 243, 245
Athena Polias, 168, 236, 243
Athena Promachos, 242
Athenaeus, 510, 523
Athenian empire, 198, 202
Athens: Mycenaean, 79; early history of,
    155-166; in Persian Wars, 186-190;
    greatness and fall of, 194-218; govern-
    ment of, 211-222; economic life in, 222-
    229; private life in, 229-234; religion
    in, 235-238; culture in, 239-260; in
    fourth century, 275-287; Hellenistic,
    294, 295; in Roman Empire, 493
Athos, Mt., 186, 188
Atlantic, 96
Aton, 86
Atrium, 331, 361
Attalus I, 298, 312
Attalus III, 377, 395
Atthides, 281
Atthis, 314
Attica, 118, 120, 125, 156, 160, 164, 166,
    186, 190, 195, 201, 206, 209, 216, 220,
    225, 241
Atticus, 435
Attis, 322
Attius Clausus, 349
Aufidus, 372
Augustales, 443, 468
Augustine, St., 525
Augustus, 398, 470, 477, 494; Age of,
    437-452
Aurelian, 512 f., 521
Aureus, 520
Aurignacian, 5 f., 9, 10
Auspicium, 340
Auxiliaries, 443
Avaris, 82
Aventine Hill, 336, 338, 487
Avesta, 113, 511
Azilian, 6, 17
Azores Islands, 96

Ba, 53
Baalbek, 495, 524
Baalim, 63, 101 f.
Babylon, 30 f., 35, 63-68 passim, 84, 92,
    96 f., 103 f., 107-111 passim, 130, 146,
    174, 252, 255, 262, 291, 316, 321, 330

Babylonia: sources, 21; geography of, 21;
    early civilizations, 21; Sumerians in, 24;
    Semites in, 28; Amorites in, 31; Hittite
    raid on, 37, 67; Kassites in, 37, 67;
    influence of, on Syria, 62; Assyrians in,
    67; Phoenicians in, 97; Chaldeans in,
    107; Persian conquest of, 110; influence
    of, on Greeks, 146, 174; Alexander's
    conquest of, 291; Seleucids in, 300; in-
    fluence of, on Etruscans, 332; Trajan in,
    461
Bacchae, 250
Bacchanalia, 390
Bacchiads, 141, 143
Bacchus, 390
Bacchylides, 193, 289
Bactria, 293, 308
Badarians, 42
Baetica, 444
Bagdad, 20, 22
Baltic Sea, 482
Banking, 482: Babylonian, 36; Greek, 229,
    277, 309, 426
Bar Kochba, 479
Basilica, 388, 497
Bath, Roman, 497
Bathsheba, 100
Beehive tombs, 77, 80, 158
Behistun Rock, 26
Beirut, 92
Bellerophon, 81
Belshazzar, 108
Beneventum, 304, 348, 361
Ben Hadad, 102
Benjamin, 99
Berossus, 21
Bible, 21, 35, 38, 98, 100
Bibulus, 411, 416
Bilbilis, 501
Birds, 251 f.
Bishop of Rome, 526
Bithynia, 300, 377, 409, 444
Blegen, 68 n.
Boadicea, 456
Boeotia, 81, 118 f., 125, 127, 155, 190,
    200 f., 267 f.
Boeotian League, 200, 265, 267 f.
Boeotians, 228
Boghaz Keui, 65
Bohemia, 463
Boii, 347, 368, 371
Bologna, 331

Book of the Dead, 59, 94
Bosporus, 66, 200, 273, 299
Boucher de Perthes, 4
Boule. *See* Council of Four Hundred
Brahmans, 504
Brasidas, 206
Brennus, 346
Britain, 316, 412, 445, 455, 459, 462, 472, 482, 494, 500, 511, 516
Britannicus, 455
Brittany, 18
Brundisium, 361, 415, 422
Bruttium, 373
Brutus (early republic), 337, 344, 419
Brutus (Caesarian period), 419-421, 425
Bug River, 134
Burrus, 456
Butadae, 236
Byblos, 60, 62 f., 87, 92, 97
Byzantium, 130, 134, 196, 200, 269, 272 f., 299

Caesar, 324, 338, 398, 404, 408, 410, *411-420*, 426, 434, 437 f., 455, 465, 477, 510
Caesarea, 479
Caesarism, 385, 399
Calamis, 244
Calendar, Sumerian, 26; Egyptian, 44; Roman, 335, 337; Julian, 419
Caligula, 455, 479
Callias, 201
Callicrates, 242
Callimachus of Athens, 187
Callimachus of Alexandria, 313
Cambyses, 111, 192
Camillus, 345 f.
Campania, 327, 331, 333, 347, 350, 428, 483
Camps, Roman, 359, 472
Campus Martius, 448
Canaan, 62, 98, 99, 101
Canaanites, 62 f., 99-101
Canabae, 472, 474
Canal, Nile to Red Sea, 57, 112, 307, 482
Canals: Babylonian, 22; Egyptian, 41
Cannae, 372
Canopic Way, 304
Canuleian Law, 351
Caphtor, 98
Capitoline Hill, 335 f., 448, 455
Capitoline Temple, 336, 458

Cappadocia, 300
Capri, 454
Capua, 331, 347, 359, 361, 372
Caracalla, 471, 506, *510,* 520, 524
Carbo, 403
Carchemish, 89
Cardia, 314
Caria, 98, 269, 285
Carian, 188
Carmel, Mt., 60
Carneades, 319, 388, 390
Carrhae, 414
Cartagena, 369, 373
Carthage: founding of, 96; government of, 192; wars of, with Greeks, 192 f., 270, 304; wars of, with Rome, 191, 196, 291, 307, 330, 332, 338, 348, *364-377,* 381, 385, 392, 397, 418, 445, 482, 495, 523, 526
Caryatids, 244
Caspian Sea, 291
Cassiterides, 96
Cassius, 415, 419 f., 428
Castello Sant' Angelo, 462
Castor, 342
Catacombs, 491
Catana, 132
Catiline, 404, 409 f., 427, 435
Cato, the Elder, 377, 381, 383, 388-390
Cato, the Younger, 404, 411, 416, 426
Catullus, 432
Catulus, 368
Caucasus, 134
Caudine Pass, 347
Cecrops, 188
Celsus, 502
Celts, 64, 327, 330, 333. *See* Gauls
Censors, 352, 356
Centaurs, 243
Cephalus, 280
Ceramicus, 240, 241
Ceres, 350
Chaeronea, *273,* 280 f., 286, 288, 290, 294, 403, 502
Chalcedon, 134, 150, 316
Chalcidae, 137
Chalcidice, 134, 143, 266, 272
Chalcis, 118, 129, 132, 136, 156, 160 f., 166, 187, 201, 283
Chaldaeans, 105, 107 f.
Chamberlain, Great, 514
Champollion, 44

Chancellor, 514
Chandragupta, 301, 316
Charioteer of Delphi, 244
Charybdis, 119
Chellean, 4, 6, 7 f., 42
Chersonese, 187, 200
China, 20, 34, 112, 204, 483
China man, 6
Chios, 118, 129, 137, 202, 269, 281
Choregos, 247
Choros, 71
Chremonidean War, 295, 302
Christian church, organization of, 507
Christianity, 479, 506, 517, 525
Christians, 457, 462, 516
Chronicler, 475
Chronology: prehistoric, 3; table of, 6; neolithic, 14; Babylonian, 28; Egyptian, 38; Aegean, 69; Israelite, 99
Chrysippus, 320
Church of Rome, 526
Cicero, 324, 404, 406, 409, 411, 414, 420 f., 425, 427, 435 f., 452, 499
Cilicia, 290, 408 f., 414, 425, 461
Cimbri, 299, 400
Cimmerians, 110, 134, 147
Cimon, 195, 197-199, 201, 220, 231, 241, 248 f.
Cinadon, 275
Cincinnatus, 345, 356
Cinna, 403
Circus, 391
Circus Maximus, 487, 490
Cirta, 398
Cisalpine Gaul, 327, 377, 421
Cithaeron, 188
City-state: Sumerian, 26; Greek, 124
Civil War: First, 403; Second, 414
Clarissimus, 468, 515
Classis, 341
Claudius, 455, 462, 470, 477, 479, 510
Claudius Gothicus, 512
Clay tablets, 21
Clazomenae, 256, 265
Cleanthes, 320
Cleisthenes of Athens, 164-166, 186, 194, 196, 199, 212, 259
Cleisthenes of Sicyon, 144
Clement, 526
Cleomenes I, 164, 166
Cleomenes III, 296, 297, 302, 310, 394
Cleon, 206, 224, 251, 253, 382

Cleopatra, 416, 422, 423, 477
Cleopatra (sister of Alexander), 294
Cleophon, 224
Cleruchies, 202, 224
Clients, 339
Clodia, 426, 432
Clodius, 412-414, 426 f.
Clusium, 346
Clytemnaestra, 248
Cnidian Aphrodite, 285
Cnidus, 264
Cnossus, 68, 70-72, 77, 81, 92
Code: Hammurabic, 31 f.; Hittite, 66; Israelite, 101, 103; of Zaleucus, 191; Draconian, 160; Athenian, 275; Roman, 429; Justinian, 324, 429
Cognomen, 338
Cohorts, 400, 443, 472
Coinage: Assyrian, 107; Lydian, 107, 110, 138; Persian, 112; Greek, 107, 138; Aeginetan, 139; Spartan, 153; Athenian, 161; Roman, 362, 520
Colacretai, 158
Collatinus, 337
Collegia, 490, 516, 519
Colline Gate, 403
Coloni, 485, 486
Colonial expansion, Greek: causes of, 130; methods of, 130; new states founded by, 131; of cities, 132; areas of, 132, 134; results of, 135
Colonus, deme of, 213
Colosseum, 458, 487, 490, 496 f., 524
Colossus of Rhodes, 299
Colossi of Memnon, 85
Columella, 502
Comedy: Athenian, 251, 278 f.; Hellenistic, 313
Comitatenses, 514
Comites, 379
Comitia centuriata, 357
Comitia tributa, 351, 358
Committee of Public Safety, 208
Commodus, 509
Companions, 272
Composite order, 496
Conductor, 485
Confederacy of Delos, 198, 200-202, 266, 300
Confederacy, Second Athenian, 266, 268 f., 280
Congress of Corinth, 280

Conon, 209, 264, 276
Conquest of the Mediterranean, Roman, 364-378
Constantine, 516, 521, 524, 526
Constantinople, 517
Constantius Chlorus, 513, 516
Constitutiones principum, 470
Consuls, 345, 355, 467
Consulares, 356
Consus, 342
Contio, 358
Coptic, 44
Coptos, 307
Corcyra, 119, 131 f., 141, 143, 205
Corinna, 156
Corinth, 118, 120, 126, 129, 130-132, 134, 139, 140, 142 f., 155-161, 172, 175, 189, 200, 205, 261 f., 270 f., 297, 305, 306, 377 f., 388, 418, 481 f., 495
Corinth, Gulf of, 118-120
Corinthian order, 175, 311
Corinthian War, 264
Cornelia, 394
Cornice, 177
Coronea, 201
Corpus Juris Civilis, 471
Corsica, 134, 332, 368 f., 378
Corupedium, 298
Cos, 118, 255
Council of Four Hundred, 162, 165
Council of Five Hundred, 199, 214
Councils, provincial, 473
Count of the Sacred Bounty, 514
Count of the Private Estate, 514
Couriers, Persian, 111
Covenant Code, 101
Crannon, 295
Crassus, 404 f., 410 f., 413
Cremona, 331, 368
Crete, 51, 57, 68, 70, 83, 98, 119-121, 150, 330, 408, 444
Crimea, 134, 204
Crissa, 144
Critias, 210, 223, 258, 275
Croesus, 110 f., 147, 252
Cro-Magnon, 6
Croton, 132, 183, 185, 191, 255, 397
Ctesiphon, 511
Cumae, 132, 193, 281, 332 f.
Cunaxa, 263
Cuneiform writing, 24; used in Syria, 62
Curator, 467, 519

Curatorships, 442
Curia, imperial, 474, 515
Curiae (Roman), 340
Curiales, 515, 520 f.
Curiatius, 336
Cursus honorum, 354, 385, 404
Curtius Rufus, 288
Cyaxares, 110
Cybele, 322
Cyclades, 118, 300
Cycladic culture, 69
Cynics, 319, 504
Cynosarges, 319
Cynoscephalae, 375
Cynuria, 155
Cyprian, 522 f., 526
Cyprus, 70, 75, 81, 120, 196, 201, 265, 308, 320, 412, 444
Cypselus, 143
Cyrenaics, 319
Cyrene, 134, 302, 313, 316, 444
Cyrus the Great, 110, 147, 185
Cyrus, Prince, 209, 263 f., 279
Cythera, 119, 149, 151, 155
Cyzicus, 134, 139, 208

Dacia, 461, 495, 512
Dacians, 459
Dacian Wars, 461
Daedalus, 69, 71
Daemon, 258
Daemones, 525
Dalmatia, 524
Damascus, 62, 92, 97, 104
Damon, 270
Daniel, 108
Danubian culture, 18, 78
Danubians, 64
Daphnae, 135
Darius I, 111-113, 185 f., 188, 255, 511
Darius II, 263
Darius III, 291
Datis, 186
David, 98, 100, 476
Dawn stones, 5
Dea cloacina, 342
Deborah, 99
Decarchies, 264 f.
Decebalus, 459
Decelea, 208
Decelean War, 208, 223, 262
Decemvirs, 351, 404

Decius, 512, 516
Decius Mus, 347
Decline of ancient civilization, 526-529:
    Sumerian, 30; Babylonian, 37; Minoan,
    77; Mycenaean, 81; Egyptian, 95; As-
    syrian, 107; Oriental, 109
Decretum ultimum, 357
Dedi, 50
Defensor plebis, 516
Deified Julius, 448
Delos, 118, 144 f., 186, 198, 200, 203,
    300, 305 f., 309, 376
Delphi, 118, 130, 144, 147, 155, 160, 164,
    169, 172, 182, 188, 190, 228, 258,
    268 f., 273, 297 f., 321
Delta, 41
Deluge Epic, 26
Demaratus, 185, 336
Demarch, 165
Demes, 164, 213
Demeter, 17, 145, 168, 172, 235 f., 321
Demetrius, 294, 298-300
Demetrius of Phalerum, 295
Demiurgoi, 159
Democedes, 148, 185, 255
Democracy, Athenian, 221
Democritus, 256
Demos, 222
Demosthenes (general), 207
Demosthenes (orator), 273, 277 f., *281,*
    295, 436
Demotic, 25, 44, 289
Denarius, 362, 520
Der el Bahri, 83
Deuteronomist, 102
Diadumenus, 245
Diana, 336, 338, 342
Diana of Aricia, 333
Diaspora, 478
Dicasteria, 217
Dicasts, 217
Dictator, 345, 356, 403
Didius Julianus, 509
Didyma, 311
Digest, 324, 470
Di Manes, 342
Dio Cassius, 324, 459, 510, 523
Dioceses, 514
Dio Chrysostom, 504
Diocletian, 512 f., 516, 521, 523 f.
Diodorus, 38, 288, 314, 324, 333, 502
Diogenes, 319

Diogenes Laertius, 510, 523
Dionysia, 216, 235, 246
Dionysiac, 306
Dionysius of Halicarnassus, 324, 333, 502
Dionysius of Syracuse, 270, 304, 347
Dionysus, 143, 163, 168, 171 f., 181, 222,
    231, 235, 240, 246, 285, 322, 390
Dionysus, the New, 422
Dipylon Age, 158
Dipylon gate, 158, 241
Discobolus, 245
Divination, 36, 107 f., 169, 332
Divine Youth, 76, 79
Dodona, 155, 169, 321
Domitian, 458-460, 499, 506
Dorian invasion, 81, 119, 121, 149, 155,
    158
Dorians, 120
Doric order, 174, 177
Dörpfeld, 68
Doryphorus, 245
Doura, 301
Drachma, 139
Draco, 140, 160
Drama: Athenian, 246-252; Hellenistic,
    312-313
Drepana, 367
Drusus: opponent of Gracchus, 397; re-
    former, 401; stepson of Augustus, 440,
    445; son of Tiberius, 454
Dungi, 30, 32
Duoviri, 474
Duilius, 367
Dur Sharrukin, 104
Dying Gaul, 311
Dynasties, Egyptian, 45
Dyrrhachium, 416

Ea, 35
Eagle, 400
Eannatum, 28
Earth Mother, 328, 350. *See* Mother god-
    dess
Eastern wars, Roman, 374-377
Ebro River, 369
Ecclesia, 162, 215
Ecclesiastes, 314
Ecclesiazusae, 231
Eclipse of 585 B.C., 110
Eclogues, 449
Ecnomus, 367
Edict of Milan, 516

Edict of Prices, 516
Edict of Toleration of Galerius, 516
Education: Babylonian, 34; Egyptian, 50; Athenian, 229 f.; Roman, 361
Egeria, 335
Egypt: sources, 38; geography, 39; predynastic period, 42; Old Kingdom, 45-56; Middle Kingdom, 56-59; Empire, 82-95; Saite period, 108 f.; Ptolemaic period, 302-304; Roman, 445
Eighteenth dynasty, Egyptian, 83-88
Eisphora, 219, 276
Elagabalus, 510
Elam, 23, 65, 105, 110
Elamites, 31
Elamite culture, 23
Elba, 327, 332
Elbe River, 454
Elea, 255
Eleatics, 256
Electron, 139
Eleusinian mysteries. *See* Mysteries
Eleusis, 156, 172, 236, 248, 253, 285, 321, 495
Elijah, 101 f.
Elis, 118, 120, 172 f.
Elisha, 102
Elissa, 192
Elymi, 330
Elysian Fields, 322
Emesa, 509
Emperor-worship, 505
Empire: Sumerian, 27 f.; Akkadian, 28; Amorite, 31; Egyptian, 82-95; Athenian, 202; Roman, 379 f., 464-479
England, 5, 7, 18
Enlil, 35
Ennius, 334, 389
Entasis, 175, 177
Enyalios, 180
Eoliths, 5
Eolithic Age, 4, 6
Epaminondas, 125, 261, 267-269, 271, 295, 502
Empedocles, 256
Ephebos, 230
Ephesus, 119, 129, 255, 286, 306, 481 f.
Ephialtes, 199
Ephors, 154
Ephorus, 281
Epictetus, 504
Epicureanism, 319

Epicureans, 390, 425, 504
Epicurus, 319, 434, 504
Epidamnus, 143
Epirus, 118, 155, 304, 347, 415
Epitaphia, 235
Equals, 151
Equites, 383, 397, 408, 426, 442, 444, 489
Eratosthenes, 316 f.
Erech, 26, 28, 35
Erechtheum, 243
Erechtheus, 236, 243, 244
Eretria, 118, 156, 186
Ergastula, 485
Eridanus, 241
Eridu, 26, 35
Eros, 181
Esarhaddon, 105
Esdraelon, 60, 62, 99
Esquiline, 456, 487
Etesian winds, 115, 119
Ethiopian rulers in Egypt, 89, 104
Ethiopians, 445
Ethnos, 124
Etruria, 136, 327, 332, 347, 371, 391
Etruscan influences on Rome, 342
Etruscans, 120, 134, 191, 193, 197, 270, *330-333,* 336, 345, 347, 496
Euboea, 118, 129, 132, 137, 156
Euboic standard, 139
Eubulus, 276, 277
Euclid, 317
Eumenides, 240
Eumenes, 298
Eumolpid, 236
Eunomia, 150
Eunus, 382
Eupatridae, 126, 158
Euphrates, 19 f., 22, 28, 64 f., 83, 98, 108, 301
Euripides, 248, 250
Eurotas, 118, 148
Eurymedon River, 198
Euxine Sea, 119, 263. *See* Black Sea
Evans, Sir Arthur, 68
Exile, Babylonian, 103, 478
Exodus, 98 f.
Ezekiel, 97, 103
Ezra, 475

Fabian tactics, 371
Fabius Maximus, 371

Fabius Pictor, 389
Fabula Atellana, 387
Family, Roman, 361
Fas, 428
Fasces, 336, 354
Fascias, 175, 177
Fasti, 447, 452
Far East, 308
Faunus, 342
Fayum, 39, 57
Federation, Italian, 348
Fertile Crescent, 22
Fifth dynasty, Egyptian, 46
Finances: Athenian, 218; Hellenistic, 309;
    Augustan, 446; imperial, 468
Fire, in Rome, 456
First dynasty, Egyptian, 45
Fiscus, 455, 468
Fist hatchets, 7, 8
Five-hundred-bushelmen, 213
Five Hundred, Council of, 199, 214
Flaminian Way, 368
Flamininus, 375 f., 385
Flaminius, 368, 371, 374, 385 f., 395
Flavius, 430
Flavius Josephus, 479
Fleet: Athenian, 220; Roman, 367, 444,
    472
Flint, mined, 15
Flint tools: palaeolithic, 7; neolithic, 15;
    Egyptian, 43
Flood, 26
Font-de-Gaume, 11
Formulae, 431
Fortune of Antioch, 311
Forum: 336, 338, 388, 396, 420, 487, 498,
    524
Forum, of Augustus, 448; of Julius Caesar,
    448; of Vespasian, 458
Four Hundred, 208, 223
Four Regions, 338
Fourth dynasty, Egyptian, 46
Franks, 511
Freedmen, 492
Frieze, 177
Frogs, 251 f.
Frontier policy, Augustan, 445
Frontinus, 502
Fulvia, 422
Furniture: Egyptian, 49; Athenian, 233;
    Roman, 488

Gabii, 348
Gabinian Law, 408
Gabinius, 408
Gades, 96, 317
Gaius (grandson of Augustus), 440
Gaius (Emperor), 455
Gaius (jurist), 470
Galatia, 445
Galba, 457
Galen, 502
Colonius, 313, 716
Gallia Narbonensis, 444
Galilee, 62
Gallic empire, 512
Gallienus, 511 f., 520
Games, Roman, 390
Garden, 319
Gaul, 132, 270, 312, 330, 399, 412, 414,
    416, 428, 447, 458, 461, 478, 482, 484,
    486, 493, 494 f., 511 f.; Cisalpine, 327,
    377, 421
Gauls, 297 f., 327, 344, 346 f., 368, 371
Gaza, 308
Gedrosian Desert, 291
Gela, 132, 192, 248
Gelon, 192 f., 270
Genē, 158
Generals, Athenian, 216
Genesis, 33, 98, 506
Genius, 341
Genius Augusti, 439
Genos, 234 n.
Gens, 338, 339
Geography: Babylonian, 21; Egyptian, 39;
    Syrian, 60; Greek, 115; Spartan, 148;
    Athenian, 156; Italian, 325; Ptolemaic,
    502
Geomoroi, 126
Georgics, 313, 444, 450
Georgoi, 159
Germanicus, 454 f., 467
Germans, 399, 495, 500, 509, 522 f.
Germany, 325, 412, 482
Gerusia, 154, 159
Gilboa, Mt., 99
Gilgamesh, 34
Gizeh, 55
Gla, 79
Glacial periods, 6
Gladiatorial games, 391
Gladstone, quoted, 219
Glaucia, 400

Glaucus, 137
Golden Ass, 500
Golden House, 456, 458
Golden Milestone, 480
God-kings, 307, 465
Gorgias, 257
Goths, 511 f.
Gournia, 74
Government: Sumerian, 27; Babylonian, 31; Egyptian, 46, 57, 90; Hittite, 60; Minoan, 71; Mycenaean, 79; Hebrew, 99; Assyrian, 105; Persian, 111; Homeric, 122; early Greek, 126, 140 f.; Spartan, 154; Athenian, 158 f., 162, 165, 213; Aetolian League, 296; Achaean League, 297; Seleucid, 300; Ptolemaic, 303; Roman, 340, 354, 384, 417, 438, 465, 513
Gracchus, Gaius, 395 f., 400, 418, 437
Gracchus, Tiberius, 394 f.
Grain trade: Athenian, 189, 229; Roman, 482
Granicus River, 290
Gravitas, 363
Great Mother, 301, 390, 448, 525. *See* Mother goddess
Grotefend, 26
Gudea, 29 f., 34
Guti, 29

Hades, 168, 172
Hadrian, 241, *461-462,* 470, 472, 479, 494, 500, 502, 507, 510, 522
Hagar, 33
Haldians, 104
Halicarnassus, 129, 252
Halys River, 65, 110
Hamilcar Barca, 367-369
Hammurabi, 31 f., 35, 37, 62, 64, 66 f., 98
Han dynasty, 308
Hanging Gardens, 108
Hannibal, 369, 371 f., 376 f., 380, 385
Harajel culture, 62
Harmhab, 88
Harmodious, 163, 244
Harmony of the orders, 411
Harmosts, 210
Harpalus, 295
Hasdrubal, 369
Hasdrubal (Hannibal's brother), 372
Hatshepsut, 83, 91 f., 94
Hattusas, 65

Hattusil, 66, 89
Hebrews, 62, 98
Hecataeus, 182, 184, 316
Hectemoroi, 160
Hedonism, 319
Heidelberg man, 6
Helen, 81, 149
Helepolis, 299
Heliaea, 162
Helicon, 117
Heliopolis, 86, 90
Helios, 299
Helladic culture, 69
Hellas, 114, 130, 138, 194 f., 197, 204, 209 f., 255, 259, 264, 267, 278
Hellenes, 114, 170, 172, 178, 209, 252, 261, 263
Hellenica, 265, 268 n., 279
Hellenic League of 481 B.C., 189, 195 f.; organized by Philip, 275, 296
Hellespont, 81, 119, 134, 160, 163, 187, 209
Helots, 150, 154, 196, 210, 296
Helvetians, 412
Hephaestus, 122, 168, 241
Hera, 124, 147, 168, 390
Heraclea, 347, 363
Heraclea in Pontus, 134
Heracleopolis, 56
Heracles, 78, 81, 271, 342
Heraclitus, 255
Herculaneum, 312, 458, 495
Hercules, 342
Hermae, 207, 223
Hermes, 207, 285
Hero, 318
Herod Agrippa, 478 f.
Herod the Great, 445, 475, 477 f.
Herodotus, 21, 33, 38 f., 55, 108, 110, 114, 147, 182, 188, 252 *f.,* 315 f., 330, 334
Heroes, 169
Herophilus, 316
Hesiod, 127, 138, 156, 170, 179, 182
Hetaerae, 232
Hezekiah, 102
Hieratic writing, 25, 44, 97
Hiero I, 193, 270, 332
Hiero II, 304, 367, 372
Hieroglyphics, 25, 44, 494 f.
Hieronymus, 314
Hill, the, 163-165

Hillel, 475
Himera, 192 f.
Hippalus, 482 f.
Hipparchus, 163; the scientist, 317
Hippeis, 159, 162, 213
Hippias, 163 f., 181, 185 f.
Hippo, 96
Hippobotae, 126
Hippocleides, 144
Hippocrates, 255
Hippodamus, 218
Hiram, 100
Hispania, 444
Hissarlik, 68, 70, 80
Historia Augusta, 324, 508
History: Athenian, 252 f., 279, 281; Hellenistic, 314; Roman, 434 f., 448, 499-501
Hittite treaty with Egypt, 89
Hittites: origin of, 65; language of, 65; empire of, 66; culture of, 67
Homer, 68, 71, 120, 129, 170, 178, 230, 248, 290
Homeric question, 120 f.
Homeric poems, 96
Homonoia, 306
Hoplite, 153, 220
Horace, 387, 448, 451
Horatius, 336, 344, 363
Hortensian Law, 353, 358
Hortensius, 406
Horus, 46, 53, 94
Hosea, 102
Household Zeus, 216
Houses: palaeolithic, 10; neolithic, 16; Babylonian, 21; Egyptian, 49, 52; Minoan, 74; Mycenaean, 78; Athenian, 232; Hellenistic, 311; early Italian, 329; Etruscan, 331; Roman, 361, 427, 487-490
Hrozny, 65
Hyakinthos, 168
Hyksos, 82, 90, 99
Hymettus, 117, 156
Hyperbolus, 206
Hypereides, 281
Hyrcanus, 477
Hypostyle hall, 94

Ictinus, 242
Ida, Mt., 77
Ides of March, 417, 419

Idumaeans, 477
Ikhnaton, 85 f., 94
Ilerda, 415
Iliad, 68, 120, 170
Ilissus River, 240
Illyria, 368
Illyrian Wars, 374
Illyrians, 271, 381
Illyricum, 412
Imbros, 265
Imbundu, 466, 90
Immortality, belief in: neolithic, 17; Babylonian, 36; Egyptian, 53, 94; Minoan, 77; Greek, 169; Hellenistic, 321; Roman, 342, 506, 525; Christian, 506, 529
Imperator, 417, 439, 465, 509
Imperial organization: Akkadian, 29; Babylonian, 32; Egyptian, 90; Assyrian, 105; Persian, 111; Athenian, 202; Alexandrian, 293; Roman, 378, 472; Augustan, 444
Imperium, 340, 349, 379
Imperium militiae, 356
India, 20, 34, 65, 112, 204, 290 f., 293, 304 f., 307 f., 316 f., 482 f., 504, 520
Indictio, 515
Indo-Europeans, 64, 78, 110, 168, 330
Indus, 112
Industry: neolithic, 16; Sumerian, 27; Babylonian, 33; Egyptian, 51, 58, 92; Minoan, 74; Phoenician, 63, 96; Homeric, 122; Greek, 135; Athenian, 163, 227; Hellenistic, 308; Roman, 341, 483, 518
Inferiors, 153, 275
Informers, 277
Infra classem, 341, 352
Inquilini, 518
Institutiones, 470
Insubres, 368, 371
Insulae, 426 f., 487, 497 f.
Intef, 57
Interrex, 340
Interstate relations: Greek, 123, 139, 144, 173; Hellenistic, 306
Ionia, 129, 143, 158, 178 f., 264
Ionians, 78, 120, 139, 146, 158, 160, 163, 183, 185, 188, 195, 197, 209
Ionic order, 175, 177
Ionian revolt, 185, 195
Ionian Sea, 328
Iphicrates, 276

Ipsus, 294, 300
Ipuwer, 57
Iran, 19, 23, 300
Iraq, 20
Ireland, 459
Irenaeus, 526
Iron, 66, 329
Iron Age, 329
Isaac, 98
Isaeus, 280
Isagoras, 164
Isaiah, 102, 103
Ishtar, 35, 63, 102, 107, 138, 301
Isis, 17, 53, 94, 322, 501, 506, 525
Isocrates, 265, 272, 274, 280 f.
Israel, 98, 104
Issus, 290
Isthmian games, 143, 172, 376
Isthmus of Corinth, 118,¯138
Ithaca, 119
Italic tribes, 64
Ithome, 149 f., 198
Iulus, 334

Jacob, 98
Jahweh, 99-102, 475
Janiculum Hill, 336, 478
Janus, 335, 342
Jason, 81
Javan, 129
Jehu, 102
Jeremiah, 102
Jericho, 99
Jeroboam, 100
Jerusalem, 87, 99 f., 103 f., 108, 409,
    454 f., 458, 475, 479, 491, 506
Jesus of Nazareth, 454, 506
Jewish War, 458
Jews, 108, 111, 302-304, 491, 494; in
    Roman Empire, 475-479
Jezebel, 101 f.
Job, 103
Joppa, 92
Jordan River, 60
Josiah, 102, 108
Joseph, 48, 98
Joshua, 99
Jotapata, 479
Juba, 416
Judaea, 409, 443, 445, 457, 475, 479
Judah, 102, 104, 108
Judaism, 103, 477, 479

Judas, 476
Judex, 430
Judges, Book of, 99
Jugurtha, 398 f.
Jugurthine War, 435
Julia (wife of Marius), 398, 408
Julia (daughter of Caesar), 412, 414
Julia (daughter of Augustus), 440
Julia Domna, 509 f., 523
Julia Mamaea, 510
Juno, 332, 342, 390
Junonia, 397
Jupiter, 332, 336, 342, 390, 448, 455, 479,
    505, 524
Jupiter Latiaris, 333
Juries: Athenian, 217 f.; Roman, 386, 397,
    406
Jus civile, 429
Jus gentium, 309, 432, 471
Jus honorarium, 431, 470
Jus Italicum, 474
Jus naturale, 471
Jus praetorium, 431
Justinian, 471
Jutland, 316
Juvenal, 487, 490, 499, 501

Ka, 53
Kadesh, 88, 93
Karnak, 83, 85, 93
Kassites, 37, 65, 67, 83
Khabiri, 87, 99
Khafre, 46, 55
Khufu, 46, 55
King archon, 216
King's Peace, 265 f.
Kish, 26, 28
Kitchen-Midden, 6, 17
Knights: Athenian, 159, 162, 213; Roman,
    383, 397, 468
Koine, 306
Korai, 163
Ku Bau, 28

Labyrinth: Egyptian, 57; Cretan, 69
Lacedaemon, 137, 148, 268
Laconia, 118, 120
Lade, 186
Laelius, 389, 395
Laertes, 122
Lagash, 26, 30
Lake dwellers, 18

Lamachus, 207
Lamia, 295
Lamian War, 295
Language: Sumerian, 24, 34; Semitic, 29; Egyptian, 43; Indo-European, 64; Hittite, 65; Greek, 78; Aramaic, 97; Etruscan, 331
Laocoön, 299, 311
Laodicea, 301
Lapiths, 243
Lar, 241
Lares, 505, 525
Lars Porsenna, 344
Latifundia, 381
Latins, 330, 346
Latin colonies, 349
Latin League, 338, 342, 345, 346
Latinus, 334
Latium, 327, 330, 333
Laudationes funebres, 334
Laurium, 156, 189, 218, 226
Lavinia, 334
Lavinium, 334
Law: Babylonian, 32; Egyptian, 47, 90; Hebraic, 101; Jewish, 103, 479; Athenian, 217; Hellenistic, 309; Roman, 428-432, 469-471
Lebanon Mts., 60
Legion, 347, 359, 400, 443, 471
Legis actiones, 430
Legati, 379
Legati Caesaris propraetore, 473
Lelantine War, 156
Leleges, 78
Lemnos, 265
Leonidas, 189 f.
Leontini, 132, 257
Leosthenes, 295
Lepidus, 420 f., 438
Lesbia, 432
Lesbos, 118, 129, 134, 160, 180, 202, 206
Leucippus, 256
Leuctra, 268, 274 f., 295
Lex Aebutia, 431
Lex Calpurnia de repetundis, 386
Lex curiata de imperio, 340, 357
Lex de imperio Vespasiani, 458, 466, 469
Lex Julia, 401
Lex Julia Municipalis, 418
Lex majestatis, 454
Lex Plautia Papiria, 401
Lex provinciae, 378

Lex talionis, 32
Libelli, 468, 516
Liberator, 271
Liberators, 419, 421
Libraries, Hellenistic, 312
Libyans, 41 f., 57, 88 f.
Licinian-Sextian Laws, 353, 363, 381, 394
Lictors, 354, 357
Ligurians, 330
Limes, 459
Limitanei, 513
Literature: Sumerian, 30; Babylonian, 34; Egyptian, 50, 58; Assyrian, 107; Greek, 178-182; Athenian, 246-254, 278-281; Hellenistic, 312-315; Roman, 388 f., 432-436, 448-452, 498-502; Greek, in the Roman period, 502 f.
Little St. Bernard Pass, 369
Liturgies, 219, 276
Livia, 440
Livius Andronicus, 388
Livy, 324, 334, 389, 447 f.
Locri, 191
Locris, 200 f.
Loess, 7
Logos, 255
Longinus, 523
Long Walls, 199, 205, 209, 241, 264
Lucan, 457, 494, 499
Lucanians, 347
Lucca, 413
Luceres, 341
Lucian, 503
Lucius, 440
Lucretia, 344
Lucretius, 433, 504
Lucullus, 403, 409
Lucumo, 336
Ludi, 391
Lugal, 31
Lugal Zaggisi, 28
Lupercalia, 419
Luxor, 94
Lycabettus, 241
Lyceum, 283, 318
Lycurgus: Spartan, 148, 162; Athenian, 281, 285
Lydia, 109-111, 129, 135, 143, 146 f., 185
Lydians, 110, 139, 330
Lyons, 445, 482, 526
Lysander, 209 f., 264, 266, 274, 293
Lysias, 280

Lysippus, 285, 311
Lysimachus, 298
Lysistrata, 251

Ma, 322
Maat, 47
Maccabaeus, 476
Maccabean, 302
Macedon, 118, 188, 261, 271, 283, 290, 294, 298, 304, 307, 368, 376, 419
Macedonia, province of, 376, 444
Macedonian War: First, 374; Second, 375; Third, 376
Macrinus, 510
Maeander, 119
Maecenas, 449-451
Magdalenian, 5 f., 9 f.
Magi, 113
Magic: prehistoric, 10; Egyptian, 94
Magna Graecia, 132, 328, 347
Magnesia, 376 f.
Mago, 381
Magistracies, Roman, 354
Malta, 18
Mamertines, 304, 364, 366
Manetho, 38, 56, 81 f.
Mani, 525
Manichaeism, 525
Manilian Law, 409
Manilius, 409
Mantinea, 155, 266, 269 f., 275, 295
Mantua, 449
Marathon, 156, 166, 186-188, 190, 194, 211, 220, 235, 237, 248
Marcellus, 372, 388
Marcellus (husband of Julia), 440
Marcomanni, 463
Marcus Aurelius, 453, 460, *463,* 483, 494 f., 498, 504, 520, 522
Mardonius, 186, 190
Marduk, 35, 107
Marius, 398-400, 402 f., 408, 435
Marius, the Younger, 403
Mars, 335, 342
Marseilles, 132, 316, 369, 378
Mars Ultor, 448
Martial, 487, 494, 499, 501
Massaliots, 369
Massilia, 132, 204, 415. *See* Marseilles
Mastaba, 53, 54
Master of Offices, 514

Mathematics: Babylonian, 34; Egyptian, 50, 91; Hellenistic, 317
Matrilineal society, 15
Mattathias, 476
Mausoleum, 285
Mausolus, 269, 285
Maxentius, 524
Maximian, 513, 516
Medea, 81, 250
Medes, 65, 105, 110
Medicine: Babylonian, 36; Egyptian, 51; Greek, 254; Hellenistic, 316
Medinet Habu, 94
Meditations, 463, 505
Mediterranean race, 17 f., 78, 328, 330
Medontidae, 159
Megacles, 144, 160, 163, 259
Megalithic folk, 18, 62
Megalopolis, 268, 314
Megara, 118, 120, 129, 132, 134, 155, 160 f., 163, 209, 251
Megarians, 228
Megaron, 79, 174, 181, 200 f.
Megasthenes, 316
Melkarth, 102
Melos, 70, 118, 224, 254
Memphis, 46 f., 56, 290
Menander, 289, *313,* 389
Menelaus, 149
Menes, 45
Menkure, 46
Mentuhotep, 57
Mercenaries, use of, 32, 89, 93, 107 f., 262 f., 269, 273
Merneptah, 89
Mesannipadda, 28
Mesogeia, 156
Mesopotamia, 20, 23, 28-30, 64 f., 97, 104, 263, 293, 301, 494
Messalina, 455 f.
•Messana, 149, 192, 304, 307 f., 364, 366 f.
Messana, Straits of, 119
Messene, 118, 125, 268, 279, 295
Messenia, 118, 120, 149, 269, 275
Messenian revolt, 150
Messenians, 192, 200
Messiah, 476, 479
Messianic Eclogue, 449
Metals, Age of, 6, 19
Metallurgy: Sumerian, 27; Babylonian, 35; Egyptian, 51; Hittite, 66; Minoan, 76; Greek, 136; Etruscan, 332

Metamorphoses, 452
Metellus, 398 f., 426
Metaurus River, 373
Metics, 212, 219, 225
Metoikoi, 225
Metopes, 174, 177
Micah, 102
Micon, 245
Midas, 109
Middle Kingdom, Egyptian, 56-59
Middle Age, Greek, 110-122
Miletus, 81, 119, 129 f., 132, 134, 140, 143, 147, 182, 184-186, 190 f., 194, 241, 311
Milo of Croton, 191
Milo, Roman tribune, 413 f., 427
Miltiades, 162 f., 187, 195
Mina, 34
Minerva, 332, 342
Minoans, 328
Minos, 68, 71, 75, 77
Minotaur, 69, 76
Minucius, 371
Minyans, 78
Misenum, 444, 472
Mishna, 479
Mitanni, 65, 67, 81 f., 84
Mithradates, 402 f., 409, 428
Mithradatic War: First, 403; Second, 409
Mithraism, 506, 525
Mithras, 506
Mohammed, 511
Moira, 169
Moloch, 368
Money. *See* Coinage
Monopolies, 483
Monumentum Ancyranum, 452
Mores majorum, 363
Moses, 98-101, 476
Mother goddess, 35, 63, 67, 76, 79, 169, 178, 301, 322, 328, 350, 390, 448, 525. *See* Earth Mother; Great Mother
Mousterian, 4, 6, 8
Mummification, 53
Mummius, 376, 388
Munda, 416
Municipalities, Roman, 348, 473
Munychia, 295
Muses, 117, 180
Mycale, 190
Mycenae, 68, 79 f., 92, 121, 129, 149, 155

Mycenaean Age: discovery of, 68; sources of, 79 f.; culture of, 81; decline of, 81
Mylae, 367
Myron, 245
Mystai, 172   [285
Mysteries, 163, 223, 231, 235, 236, 258,
Mystery religions, 321, 525
Mythology, Greek, 169
Mytilene, 61, 129, 143, 146, 160, 180, 224

Nabataeans, 208, 487
Nabis, 296, 310
Nabonidus, 108
Nabopolassar, 108
Naevius, 388
Nahum, 105
Nannar, 30, 35
Naples, 132, 327, 347, 483
Naples, Bay of, 132
Naram Sin, 29, 35
Narbo, 399
Narcissus, 456
Narmer, 45
Naucraries, 159
Naucratis, 130, 135, 141, 302
Naupactus, 200 f., 268
Nausicaa, 121, 123
Navy: Athenian, 220; Roman, 472
Naxos, 118, 132, 186, 198, 202
Neanderthal man, 6, 8, 62
Neapolis, 132
Nearchus, 316
Nebuchadrezzar, 103, 108
Necho, 105, 108
Nefert, 55
Negotiatores, 383
Negroes, 57
Nehemiah, 475
Nemean games, 172
Nemesis, 169
Neolithic Age: distinctive features of, 13-16; cultures of, 17-19
Neoplatonism, 525
Neo-Pythagoreans, 322
Nepos, 435
Nero, 456, 460, 479, 490, 499, 506
Nerva, 460
Nicaea, 317
Nicias, 207, 223 f.
Nicomedes III, 409
Niebuhr, 334

Nile, 19 f., 38, 52 f., 112, 115, 180, 290, 416, 522
Nile, Battle of the, 416
Nîmes, 495 f.
Nineteenth dynasty, Egyptian, 88 f.
Nineveh, 104 f., 110
Nippur, 26, 35
Noah, 26
Nobility, Roman, 353
Nofretete, 86
Nomads, 14, 16, 29, 64, 98
Nome, 45, 47, 58, 303
Nomen, 338
Nomoi, 215
Nomothetae, 215
Nordics, 17 f.
Northern Greece, divisions of, 155
Notium, 208
Nubanda, 32
Nubia, 42, 57, 83, 85, 92, 308
Numa, 337
Numa Pompilius, 335
Numantia, 377, 396
Numidia, 373, 398 f., 416, 435
Numidians, 373
Numina, 341

Obelisk, 54, 83
Oboi, 149
Obol, 139
Ocean, 416
Octavia, 422 f., 456
Octavian, 428, 437
Octavius, 338, 395, 397, 420-422
Octavianus, 338
Odeon, 240 f.
Odaenathus, 512
Odysseus, 81, 119, 121 f.
Odyssey, 120-122, 170, 388
Oedipus, 78, 81
Oedipus at Colonus, 248
Oedipus Tyrannus, 248
Ogulnian Law, 353
Olbia, 134
Old Kingdom, Egyptian, 45-56
Old Man of Cro-Magnon, 9
Old Testament, 97
Oligarchy, 140
Olympia, 131, 172 f., 228, 244, 280, 285
Olympiad, 172, 236
Olympian Zeus, 240
Olympias, 274, 290, 294

Olympic games, 118, 155, 172, 191
Olympus, Mt., 78, 117, 168, 188
Olynthian League, 266
Olynthus, 134, 266, 273
Oppression of Hebrews, 98
Ops, 342
Optimates, 411, 425
Oracles, 169
Orange, 495
Oratio, 470
Oratory, Athenian, 279
Orchomenus, 79, 403
Orestes, 248
Oriental religions. See Mystery religions
Origen, 526
Origo, 520 f.
Orontes, River, 88
Orpheus, 171
Orphists, 171, 182, 322, 390
Orthagoras, 144
Ortygia, 132
Oschophoria, 235
Osiris, 17, 52, 54, 59, 62, 94, 322
Ossa, 117
Ostia, 336, 418, 455, 481 f., 495
Ostracism, 165 f., 189
Otho, 457
Ovid, 447, 451
Ovinian Law, 356
Owls, 228

Padua, 448
Paeonians, 271
Paestum, 132
Paidagogoi, 225, 230
Painted Pottery Folk, 23
Painted Porch, 237, 245, 320
Painting: palaeolithic, 11; Egyptian, 56, 58; Minoan, 76; Mycenaean, 79; Athenian, 245 f., 285 f.; Hellenistic, 312
Palace: Minoan, 71 f.; Mycenaean, 73, 79 f.
Palaeolithic Age: stages of, 4; geography of, 5; Lower, 5; Middle, 8; Upper, 9; decline of, 13, 42, 328
Palaestra, 233, 476
Palatine Hill, 335, 448, 456, 487, 524
Pales, 342
Palla, 362
Pallas, 188, 455
Palmyra, 512, 523
Panaenus, 245
Panaetius, 320, 389

Panathenaea, 220
Panathenaic festival, 163, 231, 236
Panathenaic procession, 243
Panathenaicus, 280
Panegyricus, 280 f.
Pankration, 173
Panoply, 220
Pantheon, 448, 496
Papinian, 509, 524
Papyrus, 39, 42, 44, 51, 179 f., 228, 279, 305, 447
Papyri, 39, 44, 58, 90, 283, 289, 298, 325, 453
Parchment, 299
Parma, 331
Parmenides, 255
Parnassus, 117 f.
Parnon, 148
Paros, 118, 134, 180
Parrhasius, 285
Parthenon, 217, 236, 242 f., 249, 259; plan of the, 175
Parthia, 419, 446, 454, 461
Parthian War, 415, 420, 423
Parthians, 294, 300, 302, 413, 445
Pasion, 278
Pater familias, 339, 341, 361, 429
Pater patriae, 417, 439, 465
Paternal Apollo, 216, 232
Patesi, 27, 31
Patria potestas, 361
Patriarchal society, 16, 64
Patres, 339
Patrician, 339, 349
Patrimony of Caesar, 469
Patrum auctoritas, 340
Paul, 471, 509, 524
Paul, St., 457, 463, 481, 506, 526
Pausanias, 190, 196 f., 502
Pax Romana, 480
Peace, 251
Peace Conference of 371 B.C., 267
Peace of Nicias, 206, 251
Peasantry, Egyptian, 52
Peculium, 491
Pediment, 177
Peiraeus, 157, 187, 197, 199 f., 229, 241, 275
Peisander, 208
Peisistratus, 163 f., 199, 246
Pelasgi, 77
Peleset, 331

Pelion, 117
Pella, 271
Pelopidas, 267, 269
Peloponnesian League, 155, 164, 166, 189, 195, 200 f., 207, 275
Peloponnesian War, 194, 205, 239, 243, 251, 258 f., 261, 263, 275 f.
Peloponnesus, 8, 118, 132, 145, 196, 200, 206, 256, 265, 269, 279, 296 f.
Pelops, 78
Penates (see Lares), 421
Pendentives, 496
Penelope, 121, 123
Pentateuch, 475
Pentathlon, 173
Pentelicus, Mt., 156
Pepi, 46, 65
Peplos, 236
Perdiccas, 271
Pergamentum, 299
Pergamum, 283, 300, 308, 311, 375, 377, 395
Periander, 143, 160
Pericles, 144, 194, 199-204, 211, 216 f., 223 f., 232, 241, 251, 256, 259, 277 f., 363
Pericles, Age of, 199-204
Perioeci, 151, 154, 196
Peripatetics, 283
Peristyle, 174
Perpetual Edict, 470
Persephone, 17, 172, 236
Persepolis, 112, 291
Perseus (hero), 81
Perseus (king of Macedon), 376, 385
Persia: empire of, 110-113; invasion of Greece by, 185-190; in the Peloponnesian War, 208 f.; during the fourth century, 262-265; invasion of, by Alexander, 290 f.; Second Empire, 511; 184, 194-196, 198, 201, 204, 228, 262-264, 269
Persians, 24, 65, 105, 239, 248, 252, 300, 475, 511, 516
Persian Gulf, 22, 301, 307
Pertinax, 509
Perusia, 422, 452
Perusian War, 422
Pessinus, 390
Petra, 308, 461, 483
Peter, St., 457, 526
Petronius, 490, 499

Phaeacians, 121
Phaestos, 70
Phalanx: Sumerian, 28; Greek, 141; Spartan, 153; Athenian, 220; Macedonian, 272, 347, 366; Etruscan, 332; Roman, 341, 347, 359, 462
Phalerum, 156, 187, 235, 241
Pharaoh, 47, 291
Pharisees, 477
Pharnaces, 416
Pharos, 85
Pharsalia, 499
Pharsalus, 416
Pheidippides, 187
Pheidon, 155, 173
Phidias, 236, 242, 243, 245
Philebus, 282, 287
Philetaerus, 298
Philip II, 271-274, 278, 286, 290, 294
Philip V, 372, 375, 385
Philip Arrhidaeus, 294
Philippi, 421 f.
Philippics, 273, 281, 421
Philistines, 89, 98-100, 331
Philo, 478
Philopator, 303
Philosophy: Greek, 182-184, 255-259, 318-320, 389; Roman, 425, 433 f., 503-505, 524 f.
Philostratus, 504, 509, 523
Phocaea, 129, 132, 139
Phocaeans, 132, 332
Phocians, 272
Phocion, 295
Phocis, 118, 155, 200 f., 267, 272
Phoenicia, 447
Phoenicians, 62 f., 96 f., 121 f., 134 f., 138, 188, 191 f., 194, 208, 270, 495
Phoenicians' star, 138
Philochorus, 314
Phormio, 206
Phratry, 125, 158
Phrygia, 129, 146
Phrygians, 89, 109
Phrynichus, 186
Phyle, 125
Phylobasileis, 159
Piltdown man, 6, 8
Picenum, 347
Pietas, 363, 450
Pilum, 359
Pindar, 156, 188, 195, 230

Piracy and pirates, 122, 147, 204, 400, 408, 481
Pithecanthropus, 7
Pittacus, 146
Placentia, 331, 368, 371
Plain, the, 162, 164 f.
Plataea, 187, 190, 197, 201, 206
Pharos, 75
Plague: in Athens, 206; in the Roman Empire, 463, 524
Plato, 231, 257, 259, 277, 282 f., 306
Plautus, 313, 388
Plebeians, 339, 349
Plebiscita, 351, 354, 358
Plebs, 339
Pleistocene, 5
Pliny, the Elder, 286, 499
Pliny, the Younger, 460, 489, 499, 507
Pliocene, 5
Plotinus, 525
Plutarch, 115, 288, 324, 423, *502 f.*
Pnyx, 240
Po Valley, 325, 328, 330, 333, 346, 348, 368, 386, 395
Polemarch, 159, 165, 187
Polis, formation of, 124; nature of, 125
Politics, 284
Pollux, 342
Polybius, 289, *314-315,* 324, 353, 389, 449
Polyclitus, 285
Polycrates, 146 f., 181
Polygnotus, 242, 245 f., 285
Pompeii, 312, 331, 458, 474, 495
Pompey, 404 f., 409, 411, 413, 416, 426, 437; his *princeps,* 414
Pompey, Sextus, 421 f.
Pont du Gard, 496
Pontifex Maximus, 410, 417, 421, 438, 465
Pontiffs, 345, 350
Pontius Pilate, 443
Pontus, 300, 402, 409, 416
Poppaea Sabina, 456
Populace, Roman, 490
Popular Supreme Court, 162, 166, 199, 217
Populares, 384, 408, 426
Population: of Athens, 212; of Rome, 363, 487 n.
Porch of the Maidens, 244
Porphyry, 525
Porus, 291

Poseidon, 143, 168, 172, 243
Poseidonia, 132, 191
Poseidonius, 317
Post: Persian, 111; Roman, 481
Potidaea, 134, 143
Pottery: invention of, 14; as an historical source, 15; Mesopotamian, 23 f.; Egyptian, 43, 51; Minoan, 76; Trojan, 80; Greek, 136; Italian, 447, 483; Gallic, 483
Praefectus munimum, 443
Praenomen, 338
Praetor, 352, 355, 467
Praetor peregrinus, 355-431
Praetor urbanus, 355
Praxiteles, 285
Pre-Chellean, 6
Predynastic period, Egyptian, 42
Prefectures, 443, 468
Preliterary, ages, 4
Priam, 121
Priene, 129
Princeps, 414, 438, 465, 509
Proconsuls, 356, 438, 473
Procurator, 443, 468
Proletarius, 430
Prometheus Bound, 248
Propertius, 451
Prophets, 101, 476
Propontis, 119, 134, 204
Propylaea, 241 f., 245
Proscription, 403, 421, 426
Prostyle, 174
Protagoras, 257
Provinces, Roman, 428, 444 f., 472 f.
Provincia, 378
Provincial system, Roman, 378 f.
Proxenia, 123, 139
Prudentes, 431, 470
Prytaneis, 165, 214 f.
Prytany, 165, 214
Psamtik I, 105, 108
Psamtik II, 108, 135, 180
Psephismata, 215
Ptah, 52
Ptolemies, *302-304,* 307 f., 476, 485, 494
Ptolemy, 303
Ptolemy (brother of Cleopatra), 416
Ptolemy of Alexandria, *Geography* of, 502
Ptolemy Auletes, 410
Ptolemy I, 294, 302, 314, 322
Ptolemy II Philadelphus, 302, 313, 316

Ptolemy III Euergetes, 302
Ptolemy IV, 375
Publicani, 383
Punic Wars: 314, 364-378; First, 364-368; Second, 368-373; Third, 378, 387-389, 428
Punt, 46, 57, 83, 92, 100
Purple dye, 63, 115
Puteoli, 428, 481
Pydna, 376 f.
Pylos, 1111
Pyramids, 46, 55
Pyrenees, 369
Pyrrhic victory, 347
Pyrrhus, 304, 347 f., 359, 364, 366, 374
Pythagoras, 183, 191, 335
Pythagoreans, 132, 504
Pythian games, 172, 272
Pythias, 270, 316

Quaestor, 355, 467
Quinquereme, 367
Quintilian, 494, 502
Quintilis, 417
Quirinus, 335

Rahotep, 55
Ramnes, 341
Ramses I, 88
Ramses II, 66, 88 f., 93 f., 302
Ramses III, 89, 93, 98, 120, 331
Rape of the Sabine Women, 335
Raphia, 300, 303
Rawlinson, Sir Henry, 26
Ravenna, 444, 472
Re, 46, 52, 86, 93
Red Sea, 46, 57, 83, 92, 100, 112, 482
Reform, moral and religious, Augustan, 447
Regillus Lake, 344
Regulus, 367
Rehoboam, 100
Religion: palaeolithic, 9 f.; neolithic, 16 f.; Babylonian, 35 f.; Egyptian, 52-54, 59, 93-95; Indo-European, 64; Hittite, 67; Minoan, 76 f.; Mycenaean, 79; Canaanite, 63; Hebrew, 100-103; Persian, 112 f.; Homeric, 123; Greek, 167-173; Athenian, 234-237; Hellenistic, 321 f.; Etruscan, 332; Roman, 341 f., 390, 447, 505-507, 525 f.
Remus, 335

Rephaim, 100
Republic, 282
Responsa, 430 f.
Res privata, 469
Revolution, Roman: of 510 B.C., 344; of 133-31 B.C., 393
Rhea Sylvia, 335
Rhegium, 132, 191
Rhine, 416, 459, 472, 495, 512 f.
Rhodes, 118, 132, 269, 294, 299, 302, 306 f., 310, 317, 320, 375 f., 378, 408, 440
Rhoecus, 137
Rhone, 369, 416
Ribaddi, 87
Roads: Akkadian, 29; Assyrian, 105; Persian, 111; Seleucid, 301; Roman, 359, 480
Robigus, 342
Roma, 439
Roman colonies, 202, 348
Roman order, 496
Roman wall, 461, 472
Rome, 270, 294, 298, 305
Rome, City of, 335, 338, 362, 427, 487
Romulus, 335, 337
Roscius, 406
Rosetta Stone, 44
Roxana, 293, 294
Rubicon River, 347, 415, 417
Rullus, 410
Russia, 185, 204, 277, 511
Rutilius Rufus, 401

Sabellians, 330
Sabines, 333, 335 f., 345
Sabius, 400
Sacred Mount, 351
Sacred War: First, 144; Second, 272; Third, 273
Sacred Way, 241
Sadducees, 477
Saguntum, 369
Sahara, 117
Sais, 105, 108
Salamis, 160 f.; Battle of, 190, 193 f., 235, 249
Salamis on Cyprus, 425
Salisbury Plain, 18
Sallust, 324, 416, 435
Salona, 524
Salvius Julianus, 470
Samaria, 100-102, 104

Samnite Wars, 347, 356, 359, 363
Samos, 118, 129, 137, 146-150, 181, 208, 310, 316
Samosata, 503
Samuel, 99
Sanskrit, 65
Sappho, 110, 180, 313
Sapor, 512
Sarah, 33
Sardinia, 81, 368 f., 378, 495
Sardis, 110, 150, 186, 209, 263, 265, 291
Sargon of Akkad, 29, 62
Sargon II of Assyria, 104
Saronic Gulf, 118
Sassanids, 511
Satrap, 111
Saturn, 342
Saturnian meter, 387
Saturninus, 400
Satyr, 247, 285
Satyricon, 490, 499
Saul, 99
Saxons, 511
Scaevola, 344, 363, 401
Scandinavian culture, 18
Scarabs, 94
Schliemann, Heinrich, 68
Science: Babylonian, 34; Egyptian, 51; Assyrian, 107; Chaldaean, 108; Greek, 254 f., 315-318
Scipio Aemilianus, 377, 385, 389, 396
Scipio Africanus, 373, 376 f., 385, 389, 394
Scipio Barbatus, 387
Scipio, Lucius, 376
Scipio, Publius Cornelius, 369, 371
Scopas, 285
Scorpion King, 45
Scribes, Egyptian, 48, 91
Sculpture: palaeolithic, 11; Babylonian, 34 f.; Egyptian, 55 f., 58, 86; Hittite, 67; Minoan, 75; Assyrian, 107; Greek, 178, 244 f., 285; Hellenistic, 311 f.; Roman, 498
Scutum, 359
Scylla, 119
Scyros, 265
Scythians, 105, 185, 226
Seals, Babylonians, 35
Secession: first, 350; second, 351; third, 353
Secretariat, 468
Secular games, 448
Sejanus, 454

Seleucia, 300, 306
Seleucids, 409, 485
Seleucus, 294, 298
Sella curulis, 336
Sellasia, 296, 302
Semites, 24, 28, 42, 57, 62, 82, 108, 494
Sempronius, 369, 371
Senate, 340, 356 f., 384, 418, 440 f., 510, 515
Senatorial class, 353, 382 f., 425 f., 442, 467 f., 487-489, 515
Senatus consulta, 469
Senatus consultum, 340
Senatus consultum ultimum, 384
Seneca, 457, 494, 499, 504
Sennacherib, 102, 104
Sentinum, 347
Septimius Severus, 509, 522 f.
Septimontium, 338
Septuagint, 478
Serapis, 322
Sertorius, 405, 418
Servius Tullius, 336, 341
Sesostris III, 57
Sestertius, 362
Sestus, 134
Set, 53, 82
Seti I, 88, 94
Shammai, 475
Sharru, 31
Shawabtiu, 94
Shekel, 34
Shechem, 62
Sheik el Beled, 55
Shore, the, 162-165
Shubuliluma, 66, 88
Sibylline Books, 419
Sicans, 330
Sicels, 330
Sicily, 75, 81, 132, 134, 175, 192, 199, 250, 257, 268, 270, 304 f., 309, 313, 328, 332, 350, 364, 378, 380, 382, 400, 405, 444, 447, 494 f., 521
Sicyon, 142 f., 163, 212, 297
Sidon, 60, 63, 104
Sigeium, 160
Silphium, 134
Simon, 479
Simonides, 189, 193
Sinai, 46
Sinope, 134
Sinuhe, 58, 63
Sirius, 44

Sixth dynasty, Egyptian, 46
Siwah, 290
Skeptic, 319, 388
Slavery: Babylonian, 33; Greek, 137; Athenian, 225-227, 278; Hellenistic, 308 f., 381 f.; Roman, 427, 491 f.
Slave wars, 382, 400, 405
Smyrna, 119
Snefru, 46, 55
Sobk, 52
Social life: Babylonian, 33 f., Egyptian, 49 f., 91 f.; Minoan, 71, 74; Mycenaean, 80 f.; Athenian, 229-234; Hellenistic, 306 f.; Etruscan, 487; Roman, 361 f., 381-384, 425-427, 447, 487-492
Social organization: palaeolithic, 9 f.; neolithic, 15 f.; Sumerian, 27; Semitic, 29; Babylonian, 32 f.; Egyptian, 45, 48-52, 58, 91-93; Indo-European, 64; Hittite, 66; Minoan, 71; Mycenaean, 79; Assyrian, 105-107; Persian, 112; Homeric, 121 f.; early Greek, 126 f.; Spartan, 150-153; Athenian, 158 f., 222-227; Roman, 338 f., 361, 381-384, 425-427, 429 f., 487-492, 521
Social War: Athenian, 269; Roman, 401-402
Societies, Roman, 426
Socii, 349, 401
Socrates, 232, 234, 237, 239, 257-259, 275, 278 f., 318 f.
Solomon, 92, 100, 476
Solon, *161 f.,* 164, 181, 194, 199, 225, 230, 252
Solutrean, 5, 6, 9
Somaliland, 46
Sophists, 230, 256-258, 280
Sophocles, 246, 248
Sothic cycle, 45
Sources: prehistoric, 3; Babylonian, 21; Egyptian, 38 f.; Greek, 114 f.; Roman, 324 f., 333 f., 453, 509 f.
Spain, 81, 96, 100, 132, 192, 308, 368 f., 371, 377 f., 380, 399, 413-415, 428, 445, 447, 461, 478, 486, 493-495, 501, 511
Sparta: early history and government of, 148-155; in Persian Wars, 189 f.; leadership in, 196 f.; helot revolt in, 198 f.; wars of, with Athens, 200 f., 205-210; hegemony of, 261-268; in Hellenistic Age, 295 f.; 118, 123, 125, 142, 159, 164, 166, 173, 181, 186, 195, 269, 310

Spartacus, 405
Sphinx, 55
Splendidus eques Romanus, 468
Spurius Cassius, 345
Stagira, 283
State aid for the poor: Athenian, 275 f.;
    Hellenistic, 307, 310; Roman, 397, 426,
    490
Stele of the Vultures, 28, 35
Step Pyramid, 46
Stoa Poikile, 245, 320
Stoae, 311
Stoicism, 320, 389, 425, 504 f.
Stola, 362
Stonehenge, 18
Strabo, 502
Straits of Messana, 191
Stromboli, 325
Strategoi, 216 f.
Stylobate, 177
Sudan, 39
Suetonius, 324, 499 f.
Suffetes, 192
Sulla, 399, 402, 426-428, 438
Sulpicius, 402
Sumerians, 24-30: origin of, 24; writing
    of, 24; calendar of, 26; history of, 26-
    30; decline of, 30
Susa, 186, 269, 291
Sybaris, 132, 146, 191
Syene, 316
Symmories, 276
Symposium, 233; of Plato, 234
Synagogue, 475, 478
Synoecia, 235
Synoecism, 125, 149, 156
Syracuse, 130, 132, 141, 191-193, 254,
    269, 270 f., 304 f., 307, 313, 332, 364,
    366 f., 372, 388; expedition against, 207
Syria: geography of, 60; early history of,
    62; Phoenicians in, 63, 96; Canaanites
    in, 63, 98; Amorites in, 64; Aramaeans
    in, 97; Hebrews in, 87, 98; Hittites in,
    66, 88 f.; Egyptian conquest of, 83, 88;
    in Hellenistic Age, 300; Roman province
    of, 409; in Roman Empire, 494
Syrians, 381, 482, 483

Tacitus, 324, 449, 455, 459 f., 499, 500 f.,
    507
Talent, 34
Talmud, 479
Tanagra, 200

Tardenoisian, 6, 17
Tanaquil, 336
Tarentum, 132, 150, 191, 304, 327, 347,
    372, 397, 422
Tarquinii, 336
Tarquinius Priscus, 336
Tarquinius Superbus, 337
Tarquins, 419
Tarsus, 474
Tauromenium, 314
Taxes: Babylonian, 33; Egyptian, 48, 91;
    Minoan, 71; Athenian, 164, 219, 276;
    Hellenistic, 301, 303; Roman, 350,
    378 f., 469, 486, 515, 521
Taÿgetus, 118, 137, 148, 150
Tegea, 155
Telamon, 368
Telemachus, 123
Telesterion, 285
Tell el-Amarna, 86; letters, 84
Tellus, 252
Temesa, 495
Tempe, 189
Temple: of Karnak, 94; of Olympian Zeus,
    163, 462; of Peace, 458; of the Sacred
    City, 458; to Venus and Rome, 462
Temples: Babylonian, 35; Egyptian, 54;
    Greek, 174-176; Etruscan, 332; Roman,
    362, 449, 496
Ten Thousand, 274
Teos, 181
Terence, 313, 389
Terentius Varro, 372
Terpander, 150
Terremare, 329, 333
Tertullian, 523, 526
Teshub, 67
Tetricus, 512, 523
Teutones, 399 f.
Teutons, 64
Teutoberg Forest, 446
Thales, 182 f.
Thaletas, 150
Thapsus, 416
Thasos, 180, 202, 245
Theagenes, 160
Theater: of Dionysus, 240; of Marcellus,
    448
Thebes: Egyptian, 56 f., 82, 85, 92-94, 182;
    Greek, 117 f., 132, 156, 166, 187, 189,
    190, 200, 209, 261 f., 266 f.; period of
    hegemony, 268-269, 272, 290, 294

Themistocles, 186-188, 190, 195-199, 220, 240 f.
Theocritus, 313, 322, 449
Theodorus, 137
Theognis, 141, 181, 230
Theopompus, 281
Theophrastus, 316
Theoric fund, 276
Thera, 134
Thermae, 488, 497
Thermopylae, 117, 189, 196
Theron, 193
Thersites, 122
Theseum, 241
Theseus, 78, 81, 157, 235
Thesmophoria, 235
Thesmothetai, 159
Thespians, 189
Thespis, 163, 246
Thessaly, 78, 81, 118-120, 142, 155
Thetes, 159 f., 162, 212 f., 220
Thinis, 45
Third dynasty, Egyptian, 45
Third Punic War, 385
Thirty Tyrants, 210, 223, 261, 264, 275, 277
Thirty years' peace, 201
Thoth, 52, 54
Thrace, 65, 163, 181, 185 f., 188, 253, 257, 272, 294, 298, 455
Thracians, 381
Thrasybulus, 275, 277
Thucydides, 114, 197, 209, 252, *253 f.,* 278 f., 281, 314 f.
Thucydides (son of Melesias), 204, 223, 253
Thurii, 347
Thutmose I, 94
Thutmose III, 83, 93, 302
Tiber, 327, 330 f., 333, 336, 408, 418
Tiberius, 440, 445, 453 f., 479, 499 f.
Tiberius Coruncanius, 430
Tibullus, 451
Tibur, 462
Ticinus River, 371
Tigellinus, 456
Tiglath Pileser III, 104
Tigranocerta, 409
Tigris, 19 f., 22, 31, 67, 104, 110, 301
Timaeus, 314
Timgad, 495
Timocracy, 141
Timoleon, 271, 304

Timotheus, 276
Tiro, 427, 435
Tiryns, 73, 79
Tities, 341, 479, 491
Tiy, Queen, 85 f.
Toga, 362
Toga candida, 358
Tombs: Egyptian, 54 f., 95; Minoan, 77; Mycenaean, 80; Etruscan, 332
Torah, 475
Tiuu, Diiill II, 444
Trade: neolithic, 16; Sumerian, 27; Babylonian, 34; Egyptian, 51, 58, 92; Minoan, 74; Mycenaean, 81; Phoenician, 96; Assyrian, 105; Persian, 112; Homeric, 122; Greek, 129, 139, 163, 228 f.; Hellenistic, 307 f.; Roman, 362, 446, 481-483, 518 f.
Tragedy, Athenian, 247-250, 278, 312 f.
Trajan, 460 f., 479, 481, 494, 498 f., 507, 520
Trapezus, 134
Trasimene, Lake, 371, 395
Travel, Roman, 480
Trebia River, 371
Tribes: Athenian, 213; Roman, 341
Tribunes, 351, 354
Tribuni aerarii, 406
Tribunicia potestas, 438
Tristia, 452
Triumphal arch, 497
Triumvirate: first, 411; second, 421
Trierarchs, 221
Trierarchy, 223, 276
Triglyphs, 174, 177
Trireme, 137, 221
Trittyes, 165, 213
Troad, 68, 120
Troezen, 190
Trojans, 66
Trojan: War, 68, 81; women, 250
Troy, 21, 68, 70, 78, 80 f., 334, 392, 456
Tryphon, 400
Tullia, 337
Tullius, 337
Tullus Hostilius, 336
Turkestan, 19, 24, 65, 482
Tursha, 331
Tuscany, 327
Tutenkhamon, 88, 92
Twelfth dynasty, Egyptian, 57
Twelve Tables, 349, 351, 429
Twenty-sixth dynasty, Egyptian, 105, 108

Tyche, 321
Tyranny, Greek, 141-144
Tyre, 60, 63, 92, 96, 100 f., 104 f., 108, 192, 290, 308
Tyrrhenian Sea, 191, 328
Tyrseni, 330
Tyrtaeus, 150, 152, 161, 181

Ulpian, 471, 509 f., 524
Umbrians, 330, 347
Umbro-Sabellian group, 330, 333
Umma, 26, 28
Upper palaeolithic, 10
Ur: 26 f., 30 f., 35, 98; tombs of early kings of, 27; first dynasty of, 28; third dynasty of, 30
Ur of the Chaldees, 108
Urals, 204
Ur-Engur, 30
Urukagina, 28, 32
Ushebtiu, 94
Utica, 96, 416

Vadimon Lake, 347
Vae victis, 346
Valentinian I, 516
Valerian, 512, 516
Valerio-Horatian Laws, 351
Valley of the Kings, 95
Van, Lake, 104
Varro, 324, 374, 385 f., 435, 444
Varus, 446, 454
Veii, 345
Veneti, 330
Venus genetrix, 417
Vercellae, 400
Vercingetorix, 412
Verde, Cape, 96
Vergil, 313, 444, 447, 449 f.
Verona, 331
Verres, 406, 426
Verrius Flaccus, 324
Verus, Lucius, 463
Vespasian, 318, 457, 458, 460, 479, 489, 499, 502
Vesta, 342, 439, 448
Vestal Virgins, 335
Vesuvius, 325, 405, 458, 499
Via Appia, 359, 364
Via Flaminia, 368
Via Latina, 359
Via Salaria, 359

Vicarii, 514
Viceroy: Babylonian, 32; Egyptian, 47, 90
Victory, Temple of, 242
Victory of Samothrace, 312
Vicus, 486
Villanovan culture, 329
Viminal Hill, 524
Viriathus, 377
Virtus, 363
Vitellius, 457, 458
Volscians, 333, 337, 345
Volturnus, 327
Volute, 175

Warfare. *See* Army
Wasps, 251
Weaving, invention of, 15
Wen Amon, 96 n.
Women: neolithic, 15; Babylonian, 33; Egyptian, 48 f.; Minoan, 71 f.; Athenian, 231 f.; Hellenistic, 307; Etruscan, 332; Roman, 361, 429, 489
Writ of illegality, 215

Xanthippus, 259, 367
Xenophanes, 183, 193
Xenophon, 114, 257, 263, 265 n., 268 n., 279, 281
Xerxes, 112, 188, 190, 192, 200 f., 241, 248, 271

Yaru, 94

Zagros Mts., 29
Zaleucus, 140, 191
Zama, 373, 377
Zancle, 132, 149, 191
Zela, 416
Zeno, 255, 320
Zenobia, 512, 523
Zeugites, 159 f., 162, 189, 213, 217, 219, 222, 224
Zeus, 79, 123, 127, 154 f., 163, 168, 170, 172, 232, 235, 237, 243, 244, 245, 299, 322, 390
Zeus, Amon, 290
Zeus of the household, 216, 232
Zeuxis, 286
Zion, 462
Ziggurat, 27, 30, 35, 108
Zoroaster, 113
Zoroastrianism, 113, 506, 511
Zoser, 46, 54

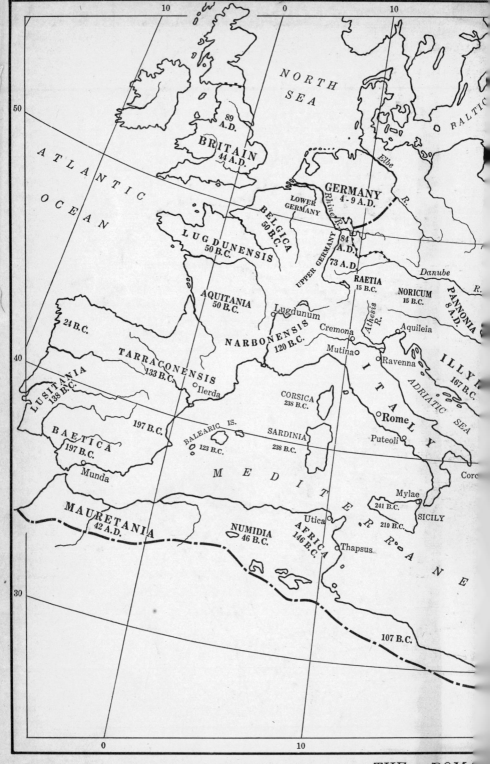

THE ROMA